HANDBOOK OF FINANCIAL ECONOMICS

HANDBOOKS
IN ECONOMICS

NORTH-HOLLAND PUBLISHING COMPANY
AMSTERDAM · NEW YORK · OXFORD

HANDBOOK OF
FINANCIAL ECONOMICS

Edited by
JAMES L. BICKSLER

NORTH-HOLLAND PUBLISHING COMPANY
AMSTERDAM · NEW YORK · OXFORD

Library of Congress Catalog Card Number 7915577

ISBN North-Holland for this volume 0 444 85344 8

First edition 1979
Second printing 1981

Publishers

NORTH-HOLLAND PUBLISHING COMPANY
AMSTERDAM · NEW YORK · OXFORD

Sole distributors for the U.S.A. and Canada

ELSEVIER NORTH-HOLLAND, INC.
52 VANDERBILT AVENUE
NEW YORK, N.Y. 10017

Library of Congress Cataloging in Publication Data

Main entry under title:

Handbook of financial economics.

    (North-Holland economics handbooks)
    Includes index.
    1. Finance--Addresses, essays, lectures.
2. Investments--Addresses, essays, lectures.
3. Corporations--Finance--Addresses, essays, lectures.
I. Bicksler, James L. II. Series.
HG175.H36   658.1'5   79-150
ISBN 0-444-85224-7

PRINTED IN THE NETHERLANDS

PREFACE

It is commonplace to recognize that microfinance has witnessed a veritable explosion in the past two decades. Recognition of this is usually acknowledged via reference to Markowitz and Tobin for portfolio theory, to Sharpe, Lintner, and Mossin for capital asset pricing, Miller, Scholes, Black, and Jensen for empirical tests of capital asset pricing, Fama and his former graduate students for tests of the efficient markets hypothesis, and Anow, Debreu and Hirschleifer for time-state preference theory. Furthermore, important and fundamental contributions to microfinance continue to abound and the rapidity of change within the profession remains high. Important examples in this regard are the option pricing theory of Black and Scholes, state preference contingent claims applications of Banz and Miller as well as the work of Merton, Hakanson, Roll, Friend, Blume, and Ross in such diverse areas as option pricing, superfunds, arbitrage theory, market risk premia, and financial market optimality.

For the individual unwilling or, perhaps, unable to devote a substantial portion of his professional career to keeping current with professional developments on the frontiers of finance knowledge, the significance and relevance of these developments remains largely undigested. With this in mind, North-Holland approached me to be the editor of this Handbook of Financial Economics, the first in a sequence of specialized Handbooks in Economics to be published by North-Holland. Thus, the genesis of this volume, which is intended to give exposure to an array of topics in modern finance. The volume is, however, not intended to be a complete encyclopedic treatment of issues comprising the complete set of issues in financial management, portfolio theory, and capital markets. Instead, a potpourri of topics are covered to give the reader a flavor of modern finance, its content, methodology, and implications. It is hoped that a cross section of finance professionals, including academics, financial economists, and capital market practitioners, will find the volume both useful and interesting.

I wish to thank each of the contributors to the Handbook. Specifically, I wish to thank:

Michael ADLER, Columbia University; Andrew H. CHEN, Ohio State University; Bernard DUMAS, E.S.S.E.C.; Edward ELTON, New York University; Irwin FRIEND, University of Pennsylvania; Michael GRANITO, University of Pennsylvania; Martin GRUBER, New York University; Patrick HESS, Ohio State University; Gailen HITE, Oklahoma State University and Ohio State

University; Michael C. JENSEN, University of Pennsylvania; M. PADBERG, New York University; Charles R. NELSON, University of Washington; George PHILIPPATOS, Pennsylvania State University; Marc R. REINGANUM, University of Southern California; Joshua RONEN, New York University; Robert SCHWARTZ, New York University; Clifford SMITH, University of Rochester; Charles UPTON, Rutgers University; Randolf WESTERFIELD, University of Pennsylvania; David WHITCOMB, New York University; Robert WINKLER, Indiana University.

I am grateful for the encouragement and support of Dean Horace J. De Podwin, Giles Mellon and George R. Morrison, Chairmen of the Finance and Economics areas. Also, I wish to acknowledge the capable typing of Lenore Rutz, Barbara Russell-Hicks and Judith Ross.

Finally, to my wife, Conchita, and to my parents, John and Katherine, a special note of appreciation in partial payment of debts unpaid.

J. L. Bicksler

CONTENTS

PART I

FOUNDATIONS OF CAPITAL MARKETS

Chapter 1

EFFICIENT CAPITAL MARKETS

PATRICK J. HESS and MARC R. REINGANUM
Ohio State University and University of Southern California

1. Introduction

The efficient market hypothesis links the concepts of information, prices, and economic profits in a specific way. In an efficient capital market, economic or supernormal profits cannot be earned, because equilibrium asset prices "fully reflect" all relevant and available information. Stated differently, the available information set cannot be exploited so as to yield abnormally high returns. This does not mean investors earn nothing. Rather, investors earn a rate of return commensurate with the equilibrium payoff structure of their portfolios.

While the general idea of market efficiency is that all relevant and available information is incorporated into asset prices, the hypothesis can be stated in rigorous and formal terms. This precise statement is presented in section 2. Section 3 summarizes and criticizes several empirical tests of the hypothesis, and section 4 contains a general discussion of information and market efficiency.

2. The efficient market hypothesis: a formal statement

The hypothesis that current asset prices "fully reflect" all relevant and available information can be formulated concisely in simple mathematical terms.[1] If the hypothesis is true, then

$$p_t^e = \psi(\phi_t) \quad \text{and} \quad p_t^e = \psi(\phi_t^m),\tag{1}$$

or

$$p_t^e = \psi(\phi_t) = \psi(\phi_t^m),\tag{2}$$

---

[1]Professor Fama deserves much credit for the development of efficient capital market theory. Our exposition follows some of his notation and logic. Cf. Fama (1970, 1976).

James L. Bicksler, Editor, Handbook of Financial Economics
© *North-Holland Publishing Company – 1979*

where

$p_t^e = N$-dimensional vector of equilibrium asset prices at time t;

ϕ_t = information set available to investors at time t;

ϕ_t^m = information set actually used by investors in the determination of asset prices at time t;

$\psi(\cdot) = \psi \colon A \to R^N$. That is, ψ maps A, the set of all potential information, into R^N, the asset price space. In terms of economics, ψ is the model of equilibrium that links a particular information set with equilibrium prices.

Eqs. (1) and (2) state that equilibrium prices derived from the information set investors actually use are identical to the equilibrium prices implied by the set of all available information. If the efficient market hypothesis were true in a world of certainty, no investor could ever earn supernormal profits by predicting prices from available information, because all relevant information would already be reflected in asset prices. If the efficient market hypothesis were true in an uncertain world, then no investor should expect to earn returns in excess of those normally associated with risky portfolios by predicting asset prices from the set of available information. Note that in contrast to a world of certainty, in an uncertain world excess returns are ruled out only in an ex ante sense. The difference arises because an investor may receive ex post an unexpectedly high or low return since asset prices are stochastic. The exposition of the efficient market hypothesis certainly does not make it so. Acceptance or rejection of the hypothesis must hinge on empirical tests of the proposition.

In an ideal setting, verification of the hypothesis would be a simple matter. One need only plug ϕ_t^m and ϕ_t into the specified $\psi(\cdot)$ function to check that the equilibrium prices implied by both information sets corresponded to the equilibrium prices actually observed, p_t^e. If

$$p_t^e = \psi(\phi_t^m) \quad \text{but} \quad p_t^e \neq \psi(\phi_t), \tag{3}$$

then the hypothesis would be rejected, because markets would be ignoring information. Unfortunately, such direct tests of the hypothesis are generally not possible. In practice the functional form of $\psi(\cdot)$ is not known a priori and must be estimated. Thus, one can only obtain an estimate of p_t^e from the estimated function $\psi^*(\cdot)$. The observable equilibrium prices can be decomposed into an estimated part plus an error term. That is,

$$p_t^e = \psi^*(\phi_t^m) + u_t, \tag{4}$$

where $\psi^*(\phi_t^m) \equiv$ the estimated equilibrium prices implied by the information set used by investors, and $u_t \equiv$ error term. Hence, all empirical tests of the efficient market hypothesis are actually tests of the joint hypothesis that: (a) asset prices "fully reflect" all available information and (b) the estimated function, or model of market equilibrium, is correctly specified (Fama (1976, p. 137)). Rejection can be due to a misspecified model, an inefficient market, or both.

3. Empirical tests

As discussed above, tests of the joint hypothesis require the investigator to specify a model of market equilibrium. The model of market equilibrium serves as the benchmark for determining whether supernormal profits can be earned by exploiting the available information. Different models of equilibrium naturally require different types of tests. Financial economists do not concur unanimously as to which model of equilibrium is the "best", although variants of the Sharpe–Lintner Capital Asset Pricing Model (CAPM) still enjoy widespread use. (See Sharpe (1964); Lintner (1965).) Predecessors to the CAPM were the market model and the random walk model. For each model, the researcher devised a test to assess whether a violation of the efficient market hypothesis as embodied in the model of equilibrium occurred.

In the early 1960s random walk researchers tested the joint hypothesis that the market is efficient and that the expected return on any asset is constant through time. If the joint hypothesis is true, then the equilibrium expected return equals the constant regardless of what other information is known. Mathematically, the joint hypothesis can be expressed as

$$E(\tilde{R}_{i,t+1}|\phi_t^m) = E(\tilde{R}_{i,t+1}|\phi_t) = \bar{R}_i. \tag{5}$$

An alternative joint hypothesis is that the expected return is linearly related to available information, I_t, and a constant. The alternative hypothesis can be written as

$$E(\tilde{R}_{i,t+1}|\phi_t^m, I_t) = E(\tilde{R}_{i,t+1}|\phi_t) = \bar{R}_i + I_t'\beta. \tag{6}$$

If (5) is correct, then one should discover in (6) that all the β values are equal to zero. If the coefficients are different from zero, the joint hypothesis in (5) must be rejected. One possible I_t vector is the vector of past returns. In an early study, Fama found that the β values associated with a security's past returns were not significantly different from zero (Fama (1965)). Thus, the evidence he examined is consistent with the model in (5).

Market efficiency was also tested within the context of a modified random walk model. This model restricted the drift parameter to be positive but not necessarily constant through time. In other words, the model only required the expected return on any asset to be positive. Hence, if the market were efficient, no trading strategy involving a single asset could expect to outperform buying and holding the single asset. The reason for this is simple: since the current equilibrium prices "fully reflect" all available information and since prices are set so as to make the expected returns positive, any investor who sold and took a short position in a single security would necessarily expect a negative return. If the returns from a trading strategy consistently exceeded the returns of a buy-and-hold rule, then the joint hypothesis would be rejected.

The number of potentially profitable trading strategies is perhaps unlimited. Buy-and-sell signals could be generated by changes in the Consumer Price Index, or recommendations of investment advisory services, or earning forecasts released by corporate officials, or by almost anything else. A popular source for signals is past price movements. Indeed, so-called "technical" analysis searches for patterns of price movements which can foretell future price behavior. One suggested trading scheme is based on a persistence filter. The basic idea is that the direction of the previous price change will be the direction of the next price change. If past prices were rising, one should be long in the security; but, if past prices declined, one should take a short position. Alexander (1961, 1964) compared the performances of the persistence filter based trading strategy and the buy-and-hold rule. He allegedly uncovered many cases where the trading rule was substantially more profitable than just buying and holding the single security. However, after correcting Alexander's methodological flaws and deducting transaction costs from the returns, Fama and Blume (1966) found that the excess profits of the trading strategy vanished. The Fama and Blume results do not preclude the possibility that some trading strategy may outperform the buy-and-hold rule. But their work offers evidence consistent with the efficient market hypothesis and the assumed form of market equilibrium.

A legitimate criticism of the tests described thus far is that the proposed models of market equilibrium are completely ad hoc. The reason why the equilibrium expected returns for each asset should be either positive or constant through time is absent. While the absence does not diminish the statistical findings, it does vitiate the academic significance of the tests.

In the late 1960s financial economists switched their attention to a model which "explained" the price movements of a security vis-à-vis the price movements of all other securities. The so-called "market model" posits that the expected return on security j, conditional on the market return, is linearly related to the market return. That is,

$$E(\tilde{R}_{j,t+1}|R_{M,t+1}) = \alpha_j + \beta_j R_{M,t+1}. \tag{7}$$

Of course, the actual return can be expressed as

$$\tilde{R}_{j,t+1} = E(\tilde{R}_{j,t+1}|R_{M,t+1}) + \tilde{\varepsilon}_{j,t+1}. \tag{8}$$

The "market model" itself is not an equilibrium model. Rather, the model is consistent (observationally equivalent) with many equilibria; for example, an equilibrium in which the returns of securities are jointly normal. So if (7) describes the return behavior of assets and if markets are efficient, then the expected value of $\tilde{\varepsilon}_{j,t+1}$ at time t is zero. If this expected value is not zero, then information available at time t could be used systematically to improve upon the prediction of $E(\tilde{R}_{j,t+1}|R_{M,t+1})$. Thus, tests of market efficiency within the framework of the market model focus on the term $E(\tilde{\varepsilon}_{j,t+1}|\phi_t)$. If $E(\tilde{\varepsilon}_{j,t+1}|\phi_t) \neq 0$, then either the market is inefficient or (7) is an incorrect specification of the asset return generating process or both.

In practice, investigators must obtain an estimate of $E(\tilde{\varepsilon}_{j,t+1}|\phi_t)$ and test whether it is different from zero. The statistical process often postulated is

$$\tilde{R}_{j,t+1} = \alpha_j + \beta_j \tilde{R}_{M,t+1} + \tilde{\varepsilon}_{j,t+1}, \tag{9}$$

where $\tilde{R}_{j,t+1}$ and $\tilde{R}_{M,t+1}$ are bivariate normally distributed, $\tilde{\varepsilon}_{j,t+1}$ is distributed normally with mean zero and variance σ_j^2, and $\tilde{\varepsilon}_{j,t+1}$ is distributed independently of $\tilde{R}_{M,t+1}$. With these assumptions, eq. (7) is seen to be the normal regression function. In order to estimate α_j and β_j, the above distributions must exhibit stationarity, i.e. the parameters of the distribution must remain the same during the period of estimation. The estimate of $\varepsilon_{j,t+1}$ is taken to be

$$\hat{\varepsilon}_{j,t+1} = R_{j,t+1} - \hat{\alpha}_j - \hat{\beta}_j R_{M,t+1}, \tag{10}$$

where $R_{j,t+1}$ and $R_{M,t+1}$ are the realized returns, and $\hat{\alpha}_j$ and $\hat{\beta}_j$ are estimates of α_j and β_j, respectively. If the joint hypothesis is correct, then predictions of $\hat{\varepsilon}_{j,t+1}$ based on information available at time t should not be systematically different from zero.

A study by Fama, Fisher, Jensen and Roll (FFJR) attempted to determine if stock splits convey any information not already incorporated into an asset's price at time t (Fama et al. (1969)). FFJR sampled 662 securities during the 1926–1960 period and examined 940 stock splits. They estimated α_j and β_j for the securities using monthly return data from 1926–1960. Unfortunately, their estimation procedure probably violates the crucial assumption of stationarity. Other investigators have found that the parameters of the return distributions can be treated as constant for perhaps five to seven years (Gonedes (1973)). The effect of nonstationarity is to make the computed residuals very poor estimators of $\varepsilon_{j,t+1}$. To see this, let $\hat{a}_j$ and $\hat{b}_j$ be the "estimates" when regression analysis is applied mechanically to the time-series data; let $\hat{u}_{j,t+1}$ be the subsequent residual. Hence,

$$\hat{u}_{j,t+1} = R_{j,t+1} - \hat{a}_j - \hat{b}_j R_{M,t+1}. \tag{11}$$

Furthermore, it is easily shown that

$$\hat{u}_{j,t+1} = (\alpha_j - \hat{a}_j) + (\beta_j - \hat{b}_j) R_{M,t+1} + \varepsilon_{j,t+1}. \tag{12}$$

Taking expectations in (12) yields

$$E(\hat{u}_{j,t+1}) = (\alpha_j - E(\hat{a}_j)) + (\beta_j - E(\hat{b}_j))R_{M,t+1} + \varepsilon_{j,t+1}. \tag{13}$$

Since $E(\hat{a}_j)$ and $E(\hat{b}_j)$ are not known, one cannot even assess whether $\hat{u}_{j,t+1}$ consistently overstates or understates $\varepsilon_{j,t+1}$. To treat $\hat{u}_{j,t+1}$ as if it were $\hat{\varepsilon}_{j,t+1}$, as FFJR did, is an inappropriate procedure for testing the joint hypothesis.

The above estimation difficulties severely limit the inferences that can be made from the FFJR analysis. But to give the reader a flavor of their analysis, it will be briefly sketched. FFJR examined the behavior of the average and cumulative average of computed residuals. The idea is that the average and cumulative average for stocks that split should not be different from zero after the stock split is publicly announced. FFJR report their findings in numerical and graphical form. By inspection, the average residuals appear to be nearly zero, and the cumulative average residuals do not change very much. But FFJR do not present statistical tests to establish the significance of their findings.

In their averaging process, FFJR time date the residuals relative to the split month. Thus, the residual of a stock that split in, say, October 1929 would be averaged with another stock that split in June 1953. However, there is no reason to suspect that the 940 residuals sampled from different securities and at different time periods are drawings from the same population. The implication is that the FFJR average residual is not an estimate of a mean residual drawn from the same population. Rather, the average residual itself is a new random variable. In particular, the underlying distribution of the average residual can be interpreted as a linear combination of 940 random variables. That is,

$$\widehat{AR}_s = \frac{\displaystyle\sum_{i=1}^{940} \tilde{\mu}_{i,s}}{940}, \tag{14}$$

where $\tilde{\mu}_{i,s}$ is the residual of security i s months from the split month. The average they compute is not a mean but rather one drawing from the newly defined random variable, $\widehat{AR}_s$. The problem is that one cannot reliably test any hypothesis on the basis of one drawing from a probability distribution.

A study by Ball and Brown (1968) followed procedures similar to those of FFJR and so naturally suffered from similar deficiencies. Ball and Brown wanted to test whether new earnings information was efficiently incorporated into a stock's price. They defined new information as the forecast error from a statistical model of a company's change in income. Ball and Brown expected to observe that the disturbances from the income model and the residuals from the market model would be positively correlated. Leaving aside possible criticisms of their income model, the disturbances from the market model are improperly estimated. Ball and Brown estimate the regression coefficients using monthly data from January 1946 through June 1966. But since the return distributions may be nonstationary, one cannot interpret the computed residuals as estimates of $\varepsilon_{j,t+1}$. Thus, while Ball and Brown report results consistent with their expectations, the statistical underpinnings of their results are very weak.

FFJR and Ball and Brown concluded that their studies were consistent with the efficient market hypothesis. However, it is questionable whether the studies actually tested the efficient market hypothesis within the context of the market model because of serious estimation difficulties. As noted, the difficulties arise from nonstationary return distributions and the aggregation of error distributions which differ across securities and over time.

Market efficiency has most recently been tested with variants of the Sharpe–Lintner Capital Asset Pricing Model (CAPM). A major virtue of the CAPM is that it is a financial model which explicitly formulates assumptions that lead to equilibrium pricing relationships based on the optimal behavior of individuals. The model is widely used in financial literature, and other sources should be consulted for details of the derivation (Jensen (1972), Fama (1976, pp. 257–319)). The equilibrium pricing relationships that result are:

$$E(\tilde{R}_{j,t+1}) = E(\tilde{R}_{0,t+1}) + \beta_{j,t+1}[E(\tilde{R}_{M,t+1}) - E(\tilde{R}_{0,t+1})], \tag{15}$$

where

$E(\tilde{R}_{0,t+1}) \equiv$ expected one-period rate of return on any asset or portfolio that is uncorrelated with the return of the market portfolio, $\tilde{R}_{M,t+1}$; and
$\beta_{j,t+1} \equiv \text{cov}(\tilde{R}_{j,t+1}, \tilde{R}_{M,t+1}) / \sigma^2(\tilde{R}_{M,t+1})$.

If the ex post returns are consistent with the ex ante expectations, then the statistical process can be expressed as

$$\tilde{R}_{j,t+1} = \gamma_{1,t+1} + \beta_{j,t+1}\gamma_{2,t+1} + \tilde{\varepsilon}_{j,t+1}. \tag{16}$$

$\gamma_{1,t+1}$ and $\gamma_{2,t+1}$, are market determined parameters. Using estimated coefficients, tests of market efficiency can be based on the computed residuals:

$$\hat{\varepsilon}_{j,t+1} = R_{j,t+1} - \hat{\gamma}_{1,t+1} - \hat{\beta}_{j,t+1}\hat{\gamma}_{2,t+1}. \tag{17}$$

The statistical estimation of the parameters is plagued with thorny problems including missing data, nonstationary return distributions, and errors-in-variables. The elucidation of these problems is beyond the scope of this essay and is available elsewhere (Fama and MacBeth (1973)). For present purposes, it will suffice to note that these problems may make the computed residuals unreliable estimates of $\varepsilon_{j,t+1}$. Thus, tests based on the computed residuals may be difficult to interpret.

An interesting study using the CAPM was conducted by Jaffe (1974). He sought to determine whether publicly released data about corporate insider trading could be used to earn abnormally high returns. A signal to buy or to sell the corporate security is generated by observing whether a month is classified as a month of net purchasing or a month of net selling. Jaffe concluded that a trading strategy based on this publicly available insider trading information could yield statistically significant abnormal returns of about 5 percent within eight months. The abnormal returns were positive even after deducting transaction costs.

If Jaffe's tests are correct, then one must reject the joint hypothesis. There are, however, potential problems with Jaffe's methodology. First, Jaffe studied insider trading because insiders presumably possessed some kind of special information. He eliminated small trades from his sample to emphasize this aspect, since small trades are less likely to be information trades. If large trades do contain special information, then the insider trades may reflect changes in the joint distribution of security returns. If this is the case, then Jaffe's estimation of the disturbances is wrong, because it is based on the assumption that the joint distribution is the same both before and after the insider trading event. This probable nonstationarity of return distributions is the most serious criticism of Jaffe's work. Another potential problem is that Jaffe's tests of statistical significance may not be applicable, since the tests require the disturbances to be drawn from independent and identically distributed random variables over time. But this point is minor in comparison to the nonstationarity problem.

In this section, no attempt was made to present an exhaustive survey of the empirical tests of the efficient market hypothesis. Rather, several important studies were used as examples to illustrate different types of market efficiency tests. The hypothesis has been tested within the framework of the random walk model, a modified random walk model, the market model, and the CAPM. Regardless of the model, the general testing procedures are the same. One identifies a signal contained in the information set; on the basis of the signal, one initiates the indicated trades. Lastly, one compares the returns from the trading strategy to the equilibrium returns predicted by the model. If the trading strategy returns are consistently greater than the model's predicted returns, then the joint hypothesis must be rejected. That efficient market studies usually fail to make definitive statements does not make them useless. Collectively, these studies lend support to the proposition that obvious arbitrage opportunities based on widely available information do not exist.

4. Information and market efficiency

Until now this essay has avoided one of the most important, yet often ignored, issues in efficient market research; namely, what is information? While equilibrium prices and supernormal profits are well defined, researchers bandy about the term "information set" as if its meaning were obvious. But the meaning is not obvious. The definition of "information set" is partially a philosophical matter, but it has important theoretical and empirical ramifications.

At first blush one might define the "information set" as the set of already present facts. After all, who would deny that past prices, stock splits or insider trades represent factual events? But what about a particular trading strategy: is it also a fact? Where is the dividing line between fact and analysis? Indeed, this last distinction is a crucial one for efficient market research, because one must distinguish between information and information production to accurately test the hypothesis. Perhaps this point can be illustrated by a nonfinancial example. Around 440 BC, Empedocles of Akragas asserted that there are four kinds of fundamental and eternal elements — earth, air, fire and water (Copleston (1962)). But does this mean that the periodic table of chemistry, which was constructed more than two millenia later, contains no new information because it only reorganizes the basic raw materials?

There is no reason why the same phenomenon should not be observed in financial markets. Reams of financial data are available daily for public inspection. What prevents an individual from reorganizing these data and analyzing them from a new point of view? Might not the reorganization and analysis be new information in itself? Indeed, one must admit that financial discoveries or inventions do occur, and these inventions are, in fact, a productive activity — the production of information. Under certain conditions, individuals may very well trade on their new information rather than sell it.[2] Thus, in tests of market efficiency suppose that a group of investors consistently earns what appears to be abnormally high returns. Does this mean that the market is inefficient? Even if the model of equilibrium is known a priori, the answer is not necessarily. The high returns may just reflect the compensation for information production activities. Unless the researcher could accurately model this compensation and disentangle it from an investor's overall return, the efficient market hypothesis per se may be empirically untestable.

5. Conclusions

Market efficiency occupies a center stage in financial theory and research. This essay only attempted to highlight the salient issues of the topic. In the first section, the efficient market hypothesis was presented in simple mathematical terms. As was noted, actual tests of market efficiency are embedded within

---

[2]Fama and Laffer (1971) state sufficient conditions under which new information will be sold and not used for trading.

particular equilibrium models. The following section outlined some basic tests of the joint hypothesis and presented some empirical results of these tests. While each test suffers from one or more problems, the tests collectively seem to indicate that arbitrage opportunities based on available information do not exist. The final section emphasized the distinction between raw information and the production of new information. Unless compensation for information production can be measured and subtracted from an investor's overall returns, one cannot conclude that abnormally high security returns indicate departures from market efficiency.

References

Alexander, S. S. (1961) "Price Movements in Speculative Markets: Trends or Random Walks", *Industrial Management Review* 2, May, 7–26.
Alexander, S. S. (1964) "Price Movements in Speculative Markets: Trends or Random Walks, no. 2", *Industrial Management Review* 5, Spring, 25–46.
Ball, R. and P. Brown (1968) "An Empirical Evaluation of Accounting Income Numbers", *Journal of Accounting Research* 6, Autumn, 159–178.
Copleston, F. S. J. (1962) *A History of Philosophy*. Vol. 1: *Greece and Rome*, Part 1 (Image Books, New York).
Fama, E. F. (1965) "The Behavior of Stock Market Prices", *Journal of Business* 38, January, 34–105.
Fama, E. F. (1970) "Efficient Capital Markets: A Review of Theory and Empirical Work", *Journal of Finance* 25, May, 383–417.
Fama, E. F. (1976) *Foundations of Finance* (Basic Books, New York) pp. 133–137.
Fama, E. F. and M. Blume (1966) "Filter Rules and Stock Market Trading Profits", *Journal of Business* 39, January, 226–241.
Fama, E. F. and A. B. Laffer (1971) "Information and Capital Markets", *Journal of Business* 44, July, 289–298.
Fama, E. F. and J. D. MacBeth (1973) "Risk, Return and Equilibrium: Empirical Tests", *Journal of Political Economy* 71, May/June, 607–636.
Fama, E. F. et al. (1969) "The Adjustment of Stock Prices to New Information", *International Economic Review* 10, February, 1–21.
Gonedes, N. (1973) "Evidence on the Information Content of Accounting Numbers: Accounting-Based and Market-Based Estimates of Systematic Risk", *Journal of Financial and Quantitative Analysis* 8, June, 407–444.
Jaffe, J. F. (1974) "Special Information and Insider Trading", *Journal of Business* 47, July, 410–428.
Jensen, M. (1972) "Capital Markets: Theory and Evidence", *Bell Journal of Economics and Management Science* 3, Autumn, 357–398.
Lintner, J. (1965) "The Valuation of Risk Assets and the Selection of Risky Investments in Stock Portfolios and Capital Budgets", *Review of Economics and Statistics* 47, February, 13–37.
Sharpe, W. F. (1964) "Capital Asset Prices: A Theory of Market Equilibrium under Conditions of Risk", *Journal of Finance* 19, September, 425–442.

Chapter 2

TESTS OF CAPITAL MARKET THEORY AND IMPLICATIONS OF THE EVIDENCE*

MICHAEL C. JENSEN**
University of Rochester

1. Introduction

My task here is to review the empirical evidence on the market model and the capital asset pricing model and discuss its implications for security analysis. To begin this discussion, let me point out that the Market Model (or what Sharpe (1963) originally called the diagonal model) and the Capital Asset Pricing Model are very distinct models. Neither one depends in any way on the other. Many people confuse these two models but they refer to quite different concepts and it is well to keep the distinction clearly in mind. I outline in section 2 the major characteristics of the market model, provide some illustrative examples and briefly summarize the evidence. In section 3 I outline the major characteristics of the asset pricing model and what I choose to call the combined market and asset pricing model and review the evidence on the model in some detail. Section 4 provides a discussion of the theoretical and empirical content of the two-factor model. Section 5 provides a discussion of the implications of the evidence for security analysis, portfolio policy and the problems associated with portfolio performance measurement. Section 6 contains some concluding remarks on the usefulness of financial analysis.

2. The market model

2.1. The assumptions and interpretation of the market model

The market model hypothesizes that we can represent the returns on an individual security (or portfolio) as a linear function of an index of market

---

*Presented at C.F.A. Seminar, 20 May, 1974, Houston, Texas.

**I have attempted to keep the explicit mathematics and notation to a minimum in this paper and to concentrate on providing an intuitive understanding of the major thrust of research in this area for practitioners and students. At times this means sacrificing rigor and increases the risk of introducing some ambiguities for the careful technical reader. Unfortunately, the two ends conflict. Some of the material dealt with here is also covered at a more technical level in Jensen (1972) for those that are interested.

James L. Bicksler, Editor, Handbook of Financial Economics
© *North-Holland Publishing Company – 1979*

returns. That is, if we let

R_{jt} = Returns on security j for period t including both dividends and capital gains expressed as a fraction of the beginning of period price, and

R_{Mt} = Returns on a market index for period t including both dividends and capital gains expressed as a fraction of the beginning of period price,

then the market model says that the relationship between the returns on security j and the market index is given by

$$R_{jt} = a_j + \beta_j R_{Mt} + e_{jt},\tag{1}$$

where a_j and β_j are constants specific to security j. e_{jt} is a random error term specific to the jth security for period t, and is assumed to be uncorrelated with the market returns and the error terms for all other securities. I emphasize the fact that there is no theory behind the market model given by (1). It is simply a statement about the empirical relationship between security and market returns and tells us nothing about what *causes* returns to be what they are in any period. It hypothesizes only that there is a systematic linear association between the returns on individual securities and the market index, and empirical tests confirm this characteristic of the model.

An example of the relationship between the monthly returns on Xerox and the market returns over the 107 month period from August 1961 to June 1970 is given in fig. 2.1. Each point denotes the return earned on Xerox for some month in this time interval and the corresponding return earned that month on the market index. The market index returns were calculated as the average return on all securities listed on the NYSE for each month during this period.[1] (Single data points are represented by an asterisk and multiple data points at the same location are plotted with a numeral representing the number of points at that location. M denotes the point of means.) The estimated regression or "characteristic" line given by eq. (1) with intercept, $a = 0.018$, and slope, $\beta = 0.97$, is drawn on the scatter diagram. (The standard errors of estimates of the coefficients and the correlation coefficient, which for Xerox is 0.488, are given in table 2.1 together with those for several other securities.)

The regression or characteristic line of the market model describes what return Xerox will earn on the average given any particular return on the market index. The slope coefficient β, the slope of the line drawn in fig. 2.1 (which for Xerox is 0.97) is often called the measure of "volatility" or "market sensitivity" or "systematic risk". In this case it tells us that when the market return for a given month is 1 percent above its mean, the returns on Xerox will on the average be 0.97 percent higher than its mean return and vice versa when the market return is 1 percent below its mean. Obviously, the return on Xerox is not

---

[1] The data were obtained from the Center for Research in Security Price (CRSP) monthly price relative file at the University of Rochester.

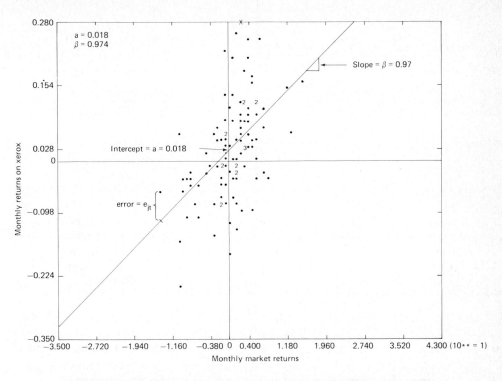

Figure 2.1. Market model for Xerox Corporation, August 1961 to June 1970.

Table 2.1. Illustrative regression estimates of the market model obtained from monthly data
$$R_{jt} = a_j + \beta_j R_{Mt} + e_{jt}$$
(Standard error of estimate in parentheses)

"Security"	Intercept a_j	Slope β_j	Correlation coefficient	Time period and sample size
Xerox	0.018 (0.008)	0.974 (0.170)	0.488	8/61–6/70 107
Consolidated Edison	−0.008 (0.007)	0.438 (0.140)	0.277	7/60–6/70 120
Homestake Mining	0.003 (0.008)	0.137 (0.163)	0.770	7/60–6/70 120
Teledyne	−0.015 (0.016)	1.789 (0.286)	0.675	6/66–6/70 49
17 Security Portfolio	−0.001 (0.018)	0.672 (0.037)	0.860	7/60–6/70 120

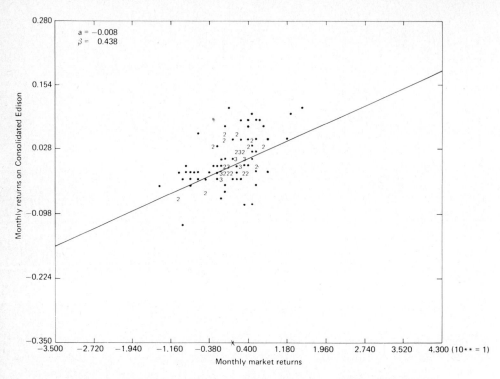

Figure 2.2. Market model for Consolidated Edison Co., July 1960 to July 1970.

always exactly 0.97 percent above its mean in such months, since if that were true all the points in the graph would lie exactly on the regression line. The vertical distance between each point and the regression line represents the error term, e_{jt}, in eq. (1)—also illustrated in fig. 2.1. The intercept, $a=0.018$, tells us that we expect Xerox to earn 1.8 percent per month on the average when the returns on the market are zero. These coefficients therefore have very simple and intuitive interpretations. Furthermore, we also know that the average intercept and slope coefficients for all securities are respectively zero and one given our definition of the market index.[2] Thus, securities with betas greater than one are

[2]To see this note that the returns on the market index, R_M, for month t are defined to be the average return for all securities (represented by N) for that month. Using this definition and substituting from (1) we have

$$R_{Mt} = \frac{1}{N} \sum_{j=1}^{N} R_{jt} = \sum_{j=1}^{N} \frac{1}{N} (a_j + \beta_j R_{Mt} + e_{jt}) = \bar{a} + \bar{\beta} R_{Mt} + \bar{e}_t,$$

where $\bar{a}$, $\bar{\beta}$, and $\bar{e}_t$ are respectively the average intercept and slope coefficients and average error term. Since R_{Mt} must equal itself we see from this equation that $\bar{a}$ must be 0, $\bar{\beta}$ must be 1.0 and $\bar{e}_t$ must be 0. (See Fama (1968) for a more detailed discussion of this point.)

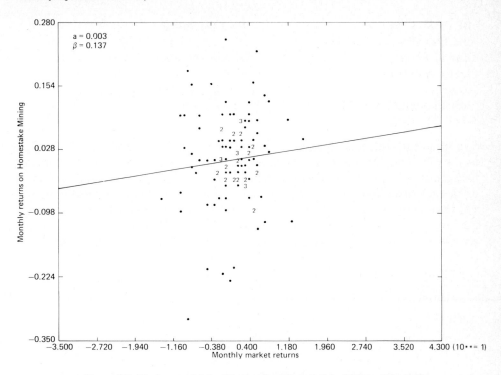

Figure 2.3. Market model for Homestake Mining, July 1960 to July 1970.

more volatile or more sensitive to general market conditions than the average and vice versa for securities with betas of less than one. The market model given by eq. (1) can be applied to bonds as well, and Sharpe (1973) shows that the beta for bonds over the period 1946–1971 was 0.252. He used quarterly returns on the Keystone B-2 bond fund and the Dow–Jones Industrial Average to obtain these estimates.

Several other examples of estimates of the market model for securities with widely different characteristics are given in figs. 2.2–2.4. The time periods used are July 1960–June 1970 or the period of listing on the NYSE, whichever is shorter. The securities and their regression statistics are also given in table 2.1. As the reader can see, the utility and gold stocks represented by Commonwealth Edison and Homestake Mining are far less sensitive to market movements (i.e. low betas) than Xerox, and Teledyne is far more sensitive (i.e. high beta).

In addition, fig. 2.5 portrays the market model for a portfolio made up of an equal dollar investment in the following 17 stocks, all of which are contained in the Dow–Jones Index:

US Steel   Eastman Kodak
General Electric   Union Carbide

International Paper	Allied Chemical
International Paper	Allied Chemical
American Brands	Sears, Roebuck
General Foods	General Motors
Procter & Gamble	Goodyear
Texaco	International Harvester
International Nickle	Owens–Illinois
Johns–Manville	

The intercept and beta for this portfolio are respectively 0.001 and 0.672. The major difference between the model as applied to the portfolio and the individual securities is the very noticeable reduction of the scatter around the regression or characteristic line. This is a direct reflection of the effects of diversification — the errors are on the average much smaller than for individual securities while the intercept and beta are just the average of the coefficients for the individual securities. This diversification effect is also reflected in the correlation coefficient of 0.86 which is much higher than the average of 0.53 that Blume (1971) finds for individual securities over approximately this period.

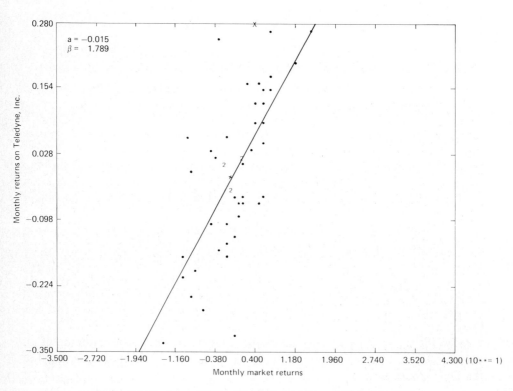

Figure 2.4. Market model for Teledyne, Inc., May 1966 to July 1970.

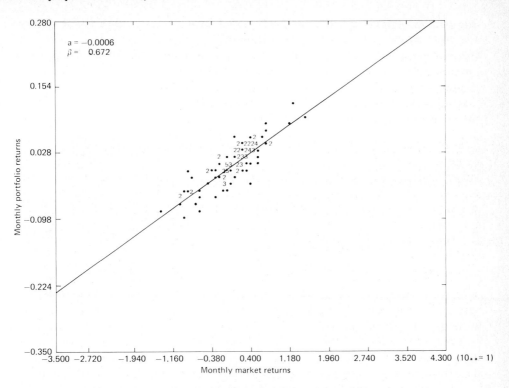

Figure 2.5. Market model for 17 Security Portfolio, July 1960 to June 1970.

2.2. *Empirical tests of the market model*

There has been considerable testing of the market model and the major conclusion of these tests is that the model is in general well specified. (See, for example, King (1966), Fama et al. (1969), and Blume (1970, 1971).) Empirical estimates of the intercept and beta coefficients do, of course, contain errors, but the evidence indicates that the beta coefficients are relatively stationary over time (especially for portfolios). This is an important result since these coefficients play an important role as the measure of systematic risk in the capital asset pricing model (as we shall see below). Blume (1970) demonstrates that the market model can be very useful in assessing the outcomes of security returns; especially forecasts of portfolio returns conditional on forecasts of future market conditions.

If the market is rising it would clearly be desirable to hold those securities with high betas and vice versa in periods in which the market is falling. In addition it would be desirable to find and use as investment vehicles those securities whose betas were high in bull markets and low in bear markets.

However, as the graphs indicate, there is no difference in the slope of the scatter between periods of positive and negative market returns. Systematic testing of this proposition indicates that there are apparently no securities which possess this desirable characteristic, i.e. the betas of securities appear to be unchanged in up and down markets.

In addition Blume (1971, 1974) has examined the question of the stationarity of the historically estimated beta coefficients over time in some detail. Table 2.2 gives the correlation coefficients between the estimated beta coefficients for portfolios of size $N = 1$, 2, 4, 7, 10, 20, 35, and 50 securities for pairs of seven-year time intervals in the period July 1926 through June 1968. He used data on all securities for which there was complete monthly data on the CRSP Price Relative File from 1926 to 1968. The number of securities ranged from 415 to 890 in his six subperiods. He constructed the portfolios by estimating the betas of individual securities, ranking them from high to low and then forming portfolios containing the first N securities, the second N securities, etc. The portfolio returns were then estimated in the first period and in the second period noted in the column headings of table 2.2. The portfolio returns in these periods were then regressed on a market index to obtain a portfolio beta for the first period (for example July 1926–June 1933) and similarly for the same portfolios in the second period (i.e. July 1933–June 1940). These beta coefficients for each portfolio of size N were then correlated with each other to obtain a measure of the accuracy of the historical beta as an estimator of the future beta. As can be seen from table 2.2, these correlations are quite high, ranging from 0.59 to 0.99 — especially for portfolios containing ten or more securities. Note that the squared correlation coefficient measures the percentage of variation in the future estimates of beta explained by the historical betas. Thus, roughly 36 percent of the variation in future individual security betas is explained by the historical betas and 96 percent of the variation in betas for portfolios of 50 securities is

Table 2.2. Correlation coefficients of betas for portfolios of N securities.[a]

Number of securities per portfolio N	7/26–6/33 and 7/33–6/40 P.M.	7/33–6/40 and 7/40–6/47 P.M.	7/40–6/47 and 7/47–6/54 P.M.	7/47–6/54 and 7/54–6/61 P.M.	7/54–6/61 and 7/61–6/68
1	0.63	0.62	0.59	0.65	0.60
2	0.71	0.76	0.72	0.76	0.73
4	0.80	0.85	0.81	0.84	0.84
7	0.86	0.91	0.88	0.87	0.88
10	0.89	0.94	0.90	0.92	0.92
20	0.93	0.97	0.95	0.95	0.97
35	0.96	0.98	0.95	0.97	0.97
50	0.98	0.99	0.98	0.98	0.98

[a]*Source*: Blume (1971).

explained by the historical betas. Thus, simple extrapolations of past betas appear to provide very good forecasts of future betas for large portfolios but somewhat poorer forecasts for individual securities and small portfolios.

Blume (1971, 1974) also provides evidence that the betas tend to regress towards the overall mean beta of 1.0. That is, securities with estimated betas greater than unity in one period have betas greater than unity in a future period but the future beta tends to be closer to unity and vice versa for low beta stocks. One can adjust for this regression tendency in making forecasts of β and fig. 2.6 provides a graphical illustration of the accuracy of the historical portfolio beta estimated from three years of past monthly data (for portfolios of 30 stocks) as a predictor of the beta over the subsequent year. Levitz (1974) studied the predictability of future portfolio betas for portfolios of 30 and 40 securities over the period February 1963–January 1971 for 800 stocks and fig. 2.6 characterizes the results he obtained from using past betas adjusted for the regression tendency for three different subperiods and two portfolio sizes. Levitz used an approximation to Blume's (1971) estimates of the regression tendency to obtain an adjusted beta. The equation used was[3]

$$\hat{\beta}_t = 0.30 + 0.75\beta_{t-1},$$

where β_{t-1} is the beta estimated from the previous three years of monthly portfolio returns and $\hat{\beta}_t$ is the adjusted forecast of the portfolio beta over the next year (obtained from weekly data). Figure 2.6 presents a plot of the actual beta for the period February 1971–January 1972 (estimated from weekly data), β_{71-72} versus $\hat{\beta}_{68-71}$, the adjusted beta estimated from monthly data in the period February 1968–January 1971. Perfect forecasts would, of course, lie on the 45° line and as can be seen, the forecasts were very good with a correlation of 0.97 with the future beta.

In addition to this evidence regarding the predictability of individual security betas and the betas of portfolios of constant composition, Jensen (1969) and Pogue and Conway (1972) have examined the predictability of the betas of managed portfolios such as mutual funds. Even if the betas of individual securities are stationary through time there is no a priori reason for the betas of managed funds to remain constant. The manager can change it easily by making systematic changes in the portfolio composition. However, the evidence indicates the systematic risk levels of portfolios are fairly constant over time indicating that managers tend to follow relatively constant risk policies. Fig. 2.7 is a plot of the beta coefficients estimated from annual data on 56 mutual funds

---

[3]While the adjustment equation used by Levitz seems to work fairly well it has the undesirable property that it will cause the adjusted β for estimates slightly less than 1.0 to be greater than 1.0, and will increase the β (and therefore move it away from the mean) for estimates in the range 1.0 to 1.2. This is inconsistent with the observed evidence that the betas tend to regress *towards* the mean over time. In order to be consistent with this observation the coefficients in the adjustment equation should sum to 1.0.

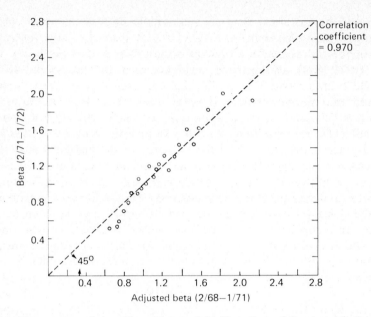

Figure 2.6. The accuracy of the adjusted betas of 24 30-stock portfolios in predicting their betas during subsequent year. (*Source*: Levitz (1974).)

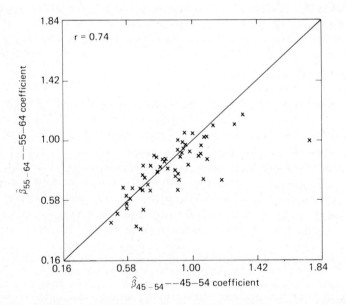

Figure 2.7. Scatter diagram of the estimated risk coefficients obtained for 56 mutual funds in two ten-year periods – 1945–1954 and 1955–1964. (*Source*: Jensen (1969).)

in the ten-year period 1955–1964 versus the betas for the same funds estimated in the period 1945–1954 presented by Jensen (1969). The correlation between the two samples was 0.74. Pogue and Conway (1972) performed similar tests on a sample of 90 mutual funds in the periods June 1970–October 1971 versus January 1969–May 1970. They estimated the betas over the two intervals on daily, weekly and monthly fund returns. The correlations between the betas were respectively 0.915, 0.895 and 0.703 for the daily, weekly and monthly betas. This is consistent with the Jensen results and also provides evidence of the benefits obtained by estimating the betas over shorter as opposed to longer differing intervals. As the frequency of observation of the returns increases (i.e. weekly as opposed to monthly) for a given total time interval, the number of return observations used in estimating beta increases. This decreases the measurement error in the estimates and thus increases the precision of the estimates.[4] Since some of the prediction error is due to this pure measurement error this increased precision will also increase the correlation of the estimates between present and future betas.

The major assumption of the market model which is not confirmed by the tests is the assumed independence of the error terms, e_{jt}, among all securities. King (1966) demonstrates that these errors are correlated across securities for a given time period and that these correlations can be related to industry effects. Friend and Blume (1970), Black et al. (1972), and Fama and MacBeth (1973) also present indirect evidence of the nonindependence of these errors and we shall deal with this evidence in more detail below since it is intimately related to the tests of the capital asset pricing model itself.

3. The capital asset pricing model

3.1. The assumptions and interpretation of the asset pricing model

The capital asset pricing model originally due to Sharpe (1964), Lintner (1965a, b), Treynor (1961), and Mossin (1966), provides us with an explicit expression for the equilibrium expected returns on all assets in terms of (1) the riskless rate of interest, (2) a market return per unit of risk and (3) the riskiness of each asset. The model as originally derived assumed (1) all investors choose portfolios on the basis of their single period mean and variance of return; (2) all investors can borrow or lend at a given riskless rate of interest and there are no restrictions on short sales of any asset; (3) all investors have identical subjective estimates of the joint probability distribution on the returns of all assets; (4) all

---

[4]Note, however, that the degree of precision of the estimated mean return for a portfolio or security depends on the total length of the time interval of observation and not on the frequency of the observations within the interval.

assets are perfectly liquid and divisible; (5) there are no taxes; and (6) the quantities of all assets are given and all investors are price takers. While these assumptions are quite restrictive, most are capable of being relaxed without changing the basic structure of the solution, although differences do arise in some extensions of the model. For a review and synthesis of the extensions of the model see Jensen (1972a, b). While I shall not review the derivation of the model here[5] its basic result is an expression for the equilibrium expected returns on all assets:

$$E(R_j) = R_F + [E(R_M) - R_F] \beta_j, \tag{2}$$

where

$E(R_j)$ = the expected returns on the jth security,
R_F = the riskless rate of interest,
$E(R_M) - R_F$ = the expected market return per unit of risk,
$E(R_M)$ = the expected return on a market portfolio which contains all assets in proportion to their total values, and
β_j = the systematic risk of the jth security.

The measure of risk, β_j, is defined as the covariance between the returns on security j and the returns on the market portfolio divided by the variance of the returns on the market portfolio,

$$\beta_j = \mathrm{cov}(R_j, R_M) / \sigma^2(R_M).$$

This is the exact definition of the market sensitivity or slope coefficient (or volatility parameter) β_j in the market model given by eq. (1) if we interpret the market index there to be a value weighted index (such as the NYSE).[6] This is true even though the assumptions upon which the derivation of the equilibrium relationship given by eq. (2) do not involve the market model assumptions at all. The market model, however, does, in this circumstance, provide an intuitive framework within which to interpret this risk measure. Assets which are highly sensitive (β greater than unity) to general business conditions (as represented by the market returns) are more risky in the sense that they fluctuate much more than the market returns and vice versa for β less than unity. Recognize also that as we saw in fig. 2-5 diversification through the effects of the statistical law of large numbers will tend to eliminate most of the risk due to the variability of the error terms e_{jt} in the portfolio (see Evans and Archer (1968)) (as long as there

---

[5]The reader may consult the original references cited in the text or for an excellent nontechnical intuitive discussion of the model I recommend Sharpe (1972).

[6]Although the theoretical definition of the market portfolio strictly includes all assets, not just those on the NYSE. Given the approximation involved in using only NYSE stocks which most researchers have used, the choice of which particular index of NYSE stocks to use does not seem to make a great deal of difference in the results as long as it is broad based and includes dividends.

are 15 or more securities in the portfolio). This means that the major source of uncertainty in the portfolio will be due to the variability of the market returns magnified (or reduced if $\beta < 1$) by the portfolio's β.[7]

Thus, given that investors are risk averse it seems intuitively sensible that high risk (high β) stocks should have higher expected returns than low risk (low β) stocks. In fact this is just what the asset pricing model given by eq. (2) implies. It says that in equilibrium a security with zero systematic risk ($\beta = 0$) will have expected return just equal to that on the riskless asset, R_F, and that the expected returns on all risky securities ($\beta > 0$) will be higher by a risk premium which is directly proportional to their risk as measured by β.

3.2. Empirical tests of the asset pricing model

Most tests of the asset pricing model have been performed by estimating the cross sectional relationship between the average return on assets and their betas over some time interval and comparing the estimated relationship to that predicted by eq. (2). Fig. 2.8 (from Black et al. (1972)) illustrates this relationship for all 1,952 common stocks listed on the NYSE for the 35-year period 1931–1965. The figure shows a plot of the average return versus beta for each of ten portfolios over this period. Every security on the exchange during each calendar year was allocated to one of these ten portfolios according to whether

---

[7]Assume, for simplicity, that the portfolio contains an equal dollar investment in N securities. The variance of the portfolio's returns,

$$R_P = \frac{1}{N} \sum_j R_j,$$

is then given by

$$\sigma^2(R_P) = \left(\sum_j \frac{1}{N} \beta_j \right)^2 \sigma^2(R_M) + \frac{1}{N^2} \sum_j \sigma^2(e_j)$$

$$= \bar{\beta}_P^2 \sigma^2(R_M) + \frac{1}{N^2} \sum_j \sigma^2(e_j),$$

as long as the e_j values are cross sectionally uncorrelated and uncorrelated with the market returns. As long as there is an upper bound to the variance of the error terms, $\sigma^2(e_j)$, the value of the last term on the right-hand side will grow in proportion to the number of securities, N, while the denominator grows according to N^2. Hence the contribution to portfolio variance from this source becomes small as the number of securities grows. If M is the upper bound to the $\sigma^2(e_j)$ (i.e. $\sigma^2(e_j) < M$ for all j) then by substitution we have

$$\sigma^2(R_P) < \bar{\beta}_P^2 \sigma^2(R_M) + \frac{1}{N^2} NM = \bar{\beta}_P^2 \sigma^2(R_M) + \frac{M}{N},$$

and as N gets larger the upper bound to the risk contribution from the nonsystematic or residual risk, M/N, goes to zero. However, as mentioned earlier, the e_j are not cross sectionally uncorrelated and therefore there is a limit to the extent that these diversification effects can reduce this source of risk.

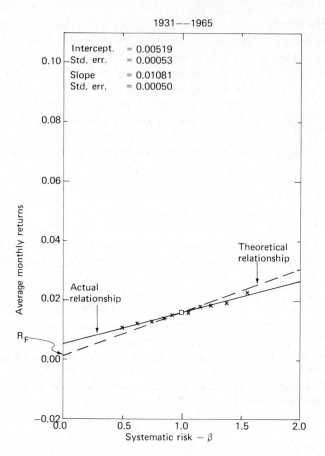

Figure 2.8. Average monthly returns versus systematic risk for the 35-year period 1931–1965 for the ten portfolios and the market portfolio. (*Source*: Black et al. (1972).)

the security beta fell in the top 10 percent of all securities for that year or the next lower 10 percent, etc.[8] The average return and beta for each of these ten portfolios was calculated and plotted in fig. 2.8. These procedures eliminate many potential statistical difficulties and also provide a simple summary of the crucial relationships for the massive amount of data involved. Each of the portfolios is represented in fig. 2.8 by an "X", and the symbol "□" denotes the average returns and risk (with $\beta_M = 1.0$) on the market portfolio.[9] The solid line

[8]In order to avoid introducing any bias into the results the exact portfolio grouping procedures were somewhat involved, and we will not discuss them in detail here. The interested reader may consult Black et al. (1972) for a detailed explanation.
[9]Estimated by the returns on an equal investment in all securities on the exchange

denotes the regression equation estimated from the empirical version of eq. (2)

$$\bar{R}_j = c + d\beta + u_j,\tag{3}$$

and therefore the estimate of c (the intercept in (2)) should be equal to R_F and d (the slope in (2)) should be equal to $(\bar{R}_M - R_F)$ if the asset pricing model is valid. That is, if the model were correct the points should plot along the dashed line with the slope equal to the actual market risk premium $(\bar{R}_M - R_F) = 0.0142$. While the empirical relationship is highly linear as the reader can see, the actual slope is only 0.0108 and the intercept is greater than the actual average one month riskless interest rate obtained from government bills (and commercial paper in the earlier periods). The correlation between return and beta for the estimated regression shown in fig. 2.8 was 0.996. On the average over this period, low risk (low beta) stocks earned higher returns than the asset pricing model implies, and high risk (high beta) stocks earned lower returns than the theory implies. These relationships are also plotted for four nonoverlapping 105-month subperiods in fig. 2.9. Here again we see that the estimated relationships do not conform to the theoretical relationship even though there does appear to be a linear relation between average return and beta. In the first subperiod the low beta stocks earned less than the model implies (and vice versa for high beta stocks) and in the other three periods the low beta stocks earned more than the model implies. In the last period there was a slightly *negative* relationship between risk and return. This negative relationship is inconsistent with the assumption that investors are averse to risk and that the results over the period April 1957 to December 1965 were consistent with investor's expectations. On the average high risk assets earned less than low risk assets, clearly contrary to what must have been the ex ante expected values of these variables.

The relationship between the market model and the capital asset pricing model. We emphasized earlier that the market and asset pricing models are independent entities neither depending upon the validity of the other. This does not mean, however, that they are unrelated to each other and it is useful at this point to investigate the implications of the two under the assumption that they are both valid since it will help us interpret the evidence.

We can rearrange the results of the asset pricing model given by (2) slightly to give

$$E(R_j) = R_F(1 - \beta_j) + \beta_j E(R_M).\tag{2a}$$

If we assume the market model is also valid we can obtain another expression of the expected return on security j by taking the expected value of eq. (1) which gives

$$E(R_j) = a_j + b_j E(R_M) + E(e_j)$$
$$= a_j + b_j E(R_M),\tag{4}$$

where the last equation results from the fact that $E(e_j)$ is zero by definition.

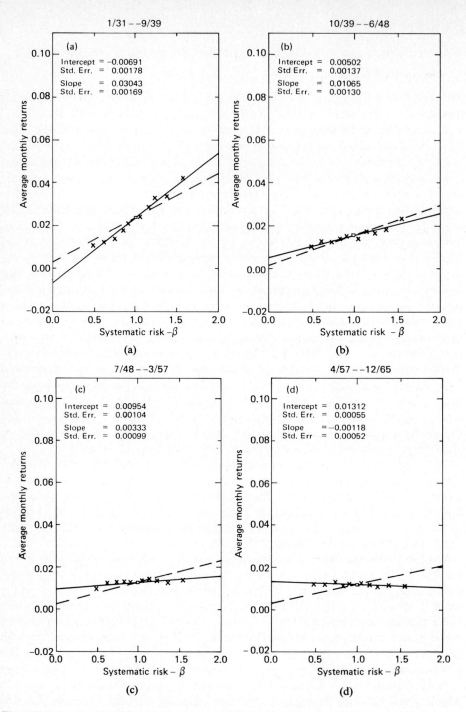

Figure 2.9. Average monthly return versus systematic risk for four 105-month subperiods in the interval January 1931–December 1965. (*Source*: Black et al. (1972).)

Recalling also from our earlier discussion that the definitions of β_j and b_j from the two models are identical,[10] we can rewrite (4) as

$$E(R_j) = a_j + \beta_j E(R_M) \tag{5}$$

and now comparing (2a) and (5) we see that

$$a_j = R_F(1 - \beta_j).$$

That is, if both models are valid, the intercept term, a_j, in the market model is equal to $R_F(1 - \beta_j)$.

One of the difficult problems we face in testing the asset pricing model (as in many other economic models) is the fact that it is a relationship between the ex ante expected returns on individual assets and the market portfolio. Such expected returns are of course not directly and objectively measurable. The usual procedure in such cases is to assume that the probability distributions generating the ex post outcomes is stationary over time and then to substitute the sample average returns for the ex ante expectations. If the time period is short, or if investors' expectations are not well approximated by the same averages, this is a highly inefficient test procedure. Often, however, it is all that is available.

The combination of the market model and the asset pricing model provides one of those relatively rare instances, however, in which we can formulate an exact test solely in terms of the ex post realizations of the model. To obtain this ex post model we simply use the fact that $b_j = \beta_j$ and the result obtained above that if both the asset pricing model and the market model are valid $a_j = R_F (1 - \beta_j)$. Substitute these into the market model given by eq. (5) for a_j and b_j to obtain

$$R_{jt} = R_{Ft}(1 - \beta_j) + \beta_j R_{Mt} + e_{jt}$$

$$= R_{Ft} + [R_{Mt} - R_{Ft}]\beta_j + e_{jt}. \tag{6}$$

We have subscripted the riskless rate R_F by t as well to allow for the fact that it may change through time.

Eq. (6) then gives us an expression for the ex post return on any asset j for any time period t in terms of the riskless rate of interest, the ex post returns on the market portfolio, the beta of the asset, and an independent random error term, e_{jt}, which has an expected value of zero. Thus, eq. (6) represents the process generating asset returns if the joint hypothesis obtained by assuming that both the market and asset pricing models are valid. If this joint hypothesis is valid then the returns on assets for any given time period (say a month) should scatter around a straight line in the return–beta plane. This is illustrated in fig. 2.10 which gives plots of R_j against β_j for a hypothetical set of assets for two

---

[10]See Black et al. (1972, fn. 1, p. 118), Beja (1972) and Fama (1973) for a discussion of this point.

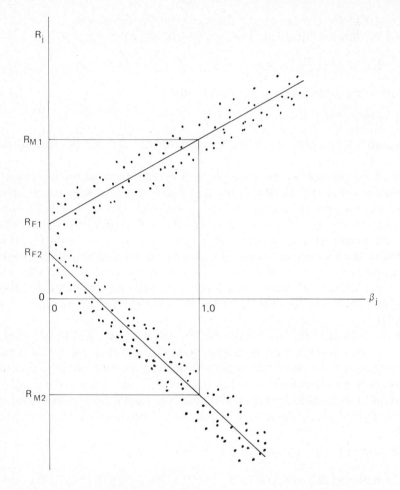

Figure 2.10. Ex post return–risk relation predicted by the joint market and asset pricing model for two time periods: (1) in which the market return, R_{M1}, is greater than the riskless rate, R_{F1}, and (2) in which the market return is negative.

different time periods having different riskless rates and different market re-turns. The top line represents the relationship implied by eq. (6) for some hypothetical time period labeled 1 in which the riskless rate of interest was given by R_{F1} and the ex post market return was R_{M1} (here assumed positive and greater than the riskless rate). The scatter about the line is caused by the residual terms, e_{j1}, for each security. The lower line represents another hypothetical period (denoted by the subscript 2) in which the riskless interest rate was R_{F2} and the ex post market return was R_{M2} (here assumed negative). In both cases the intercept and slope of the security market line (as this has been called) are given respectively by the riskless rate R_{Ft} and the difference between the market return and riskless rate, $R_{Mt} - R_{Ft}$ (see eq. (6)). Thus, this joint model implies that if R_{Mt} is greater than R_{Ft} the security market line should slope upward and vice versa if R_{Mt} is less than R_{Ft}. If, as sometimes happens, R_{Ft} should equal R_{Mt} the slope of the line should be zero, i.e. there should be no relationship between the returns on assets and their betas. These relationships should also hold if we take averages on both sides of eq. (6) and thus the plot of the actual security market line in fig. 2.8 provides a test of this model. As can be seen the plot is linear and close to but not exactly equal to that predicted by this joint hypothesis. The security market lines plotted in fig. 2.9 for the four subperiods show an even greater divergence from this combined model than that in fig. 2.8. Although a negatively sloped security market line is consistent with this more complicated model the negative relation shown for the period April 1957– December 1965 in fig. 2.9d is not consistent with the model since for that period the market returns were greater than the riskless rate. Therefore the joint hypothesis implies an upward sloping security market line in this period and it is not observed.

The results in fig. 2.9 suggest that the process describing the cross sectional relationship between average security returns and risk is not accurately described by the simple form of the asset pricing model as given in eq. (2) since the coefficients (c and d in eq. (3)) in the empirical relationship seem to be better described as random variables themselves. In addition, the results in these figures do not seem to be consistent with the joint market and asset pricing model given by eq. (6) either, since the intercept, c, and slope, d, do not correspond to R_{Ft} and $R_{Mt} - R_F$. Further evidence of this is presented in fig. 2.11 which presents plots of the average monthly returns versus systematic risk (β) for 17 nonoverlapping two-year periods from 1932 to 1965 (also from Black et al. (1972)). In these plots we again see a highly linear relationship between average returns and risk as measured by β, but the intercept and slope of this relationship is much more variable than that implied by eq. (6). Thus, while there is a strong relation between return and beta for any given subperiod, it is difficult to predict in advance what the coefficients in the relation will be in the future. Clearly, any analyst who could predict the intercept and slope of eq. (3) for a future period could earn substantial returns by appropriately switching between high and low risk securities.

Fama and MacBeth (1973) have replicated these results and have estimated the relations by running the cross sectional regressions given by (3) for each month over the interval 1935–1968. They also examined the time series behavior of the coefficients c_t and d_t and found that they behave as fair game variables (i.e. are serially uncorrelated) much like security returns themselves behave. Thus, it appears that the analyst cannot hope to increase his "timing" ability by using the time sequence of market lines (or more specifically the coefficients in

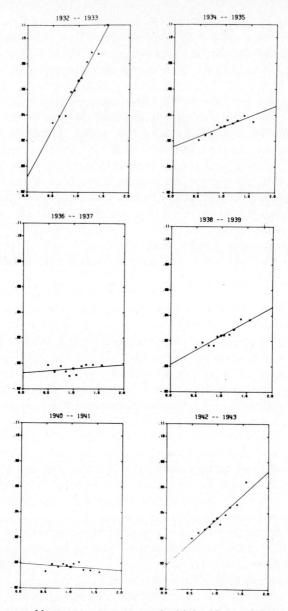

Figure 2.11. Average monthly returns versus systematic risk for 17 nonoverlapping two-year periods from 1932 to 1965. (*Source*: Black et al. (1972).)

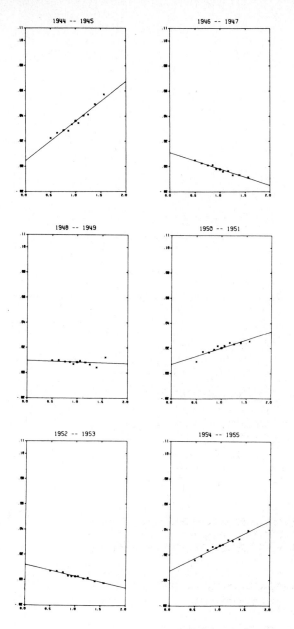

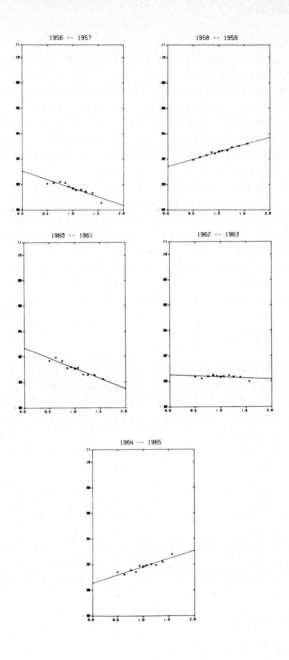

(3)) such as those given in fig. 2.11 to forecast the market line for a future period. In addition, no one to my knowledge has found any other way to forecast the future market line either.

Friend and Blume (1973) have also replicated the tests of Black et al. and in addition they, like Fama and MacBeth, tested explicitly for any nonlinearities in the relationship between return and beta. Plots of their results covering one four-year and two five-year periods from 1955 to 1968 are reproduced in fig. 2.12. They also used grouping techniques similar to those of Black et al. and the points in fig. 2.12 denoted by ∘ and ∘ represent the return–beta combinations of each of 12 portfolios containing approximately 80 securities over the periods indicated. The · denotes the portfolio returns calculated under the assumption of an initial equal dollar investment in each security and the · denotes the portfolio returns calculated under the assumption of an initial investment in each security in proportion to the total market value of the shares outstanding on 31 December 1954. The regression lines denoted by *LL* in fig. 2.12 were estimated from eq. (3) (as were those of Black et al.) and those denoted by *QQ* included a quadratic term in β to test explicitly for the existence of nonlinearities in the risk return relation. The estimated quadratic regression was

$$\overline{R}_j = c + d\beta_j + k\beta_j^2 + u_j. \tag{7}$$

Only one of the six regressions showed any (statistically) significant nonlinearity, i.e. k significantly different from zero; that for the period 1955–1959. Fama and MacBeth (1973) also tested explicitly for the existence of nonlinearities in the monthly cross sectional regressions of return versus risk. They conclude that although there are significant nonlinearities in the month-by-month results, this has no practical implications for investment decisions since the sign of k is random and, on the average, the relationship is linear (that is, the coefficient, k, in (4) is on the average zero over time). Furthermore, there appears to be no way for investors to forecast the sign or size of the nonlinearities for future periods.

Fama and MacBeth (1973) also provide careful tests of the hypothesis that the risk associated with the residual or error term, $\sigma^2(e_j)$, in (1) has no effect on the expected security returns. This risk is sometimes referred to as nonsystematic or diversifiable risk. They test this hypothesis by adding a term to (7) to represent the average nonsystematic risk of the securities in each of their 20 portfolios and estimate

$$R_j = c + d\beta_j + k\beta_j^2 + p\sigma_j^2(e) + u_j, \tag{8}$$

where $\sigma_j^2(e)$ is the average of the nonsystematic risks for each of the securities in each portfolio j. They found the coefficient p to be insignificantly different from zero, as the theory implies.

The conclusions of these empirical studies can be summarized as follows.

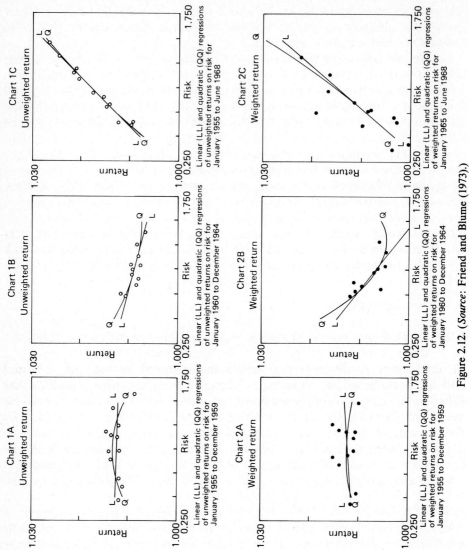

Figure 2.12. (*Source:* Friend and Blume (1973).)

(1) The average relationship between risk and return is positive. That is, on the average investors are compensated in the securities markets for bearing (systematic) risk.

(2) The average relationship between return and risk (as measured by systematic risk, β) is linear as predicted by the mean-variance Asset Pricing Model.

(3) There is some evidence of stochastic nonlinearities in the month-to-month risk–return relations, but these effects have very little impact on investment strategy since they are unpredictable with respect to sign and on average equal to zero.

(4) Nonsystematic risk, as measured by the residual or error variance from the market model, is not related to average security returns.

(5) The simple form of the asset pricing model (which predicts an average intercept in the risk–return relation equal to the riskless rate of interest) is not consistent with the data, nor is the joint market and asset pricing model.

(6) The major characteristics of the structure of the process generating asset returns seems to be well described by the two factor model suggested by Black et al. We discuss this model and some of its implications in more detail below.

4. The two-factor model

4.1. The foundations and interpretation of the two-factor model

In an attempt to describe the phenomena observed in figs. 2.8, 2.9, and 2.10–2.12, Black et al. suggested a two-factor model which specifies the equilibrium expected return on assets to be a function of (1) the market factor defined by the returns on the market portfolio, R_M, and (2) a beta factor defined by the returns on a zero beta portfolio — that is the minimum variance portfolio which is uncorrelated with the returns on the market portfolio. Defining the returns on the zero beta portfolio as R_Z, the two-factor model expresses the equilibrium expected returns on any individual asset or portfolio, j, as

$$E(R_j) = E(R_Z) + \left[E(R_M) - E(R_Z)\beta_j \right],\tag{9}$$

where the measure of systematic risk, β_j, is as defined earlier and the expected returns on the zero beta portfolio, $E(R_Z)$, play a role equivalent to that of the riskless rate of interest in the simple form of the Sharpe–Lintner–Treynor–Mossin asset pricing model given by eq. (2). Eq. (9) applies to any specific time period. To obtain a model which takes explicit account of the time series behavior of the cross sectional risk–return relationship we simply subscript the return variables in (9) by t to denote time, remove the expectations operators and add an error term, u_{jt}, to account for the individualistic variation in each security or portfolio:

$$R_{jt} = R_{Zt} + \left[R_{Mt} - R_{Zt} \right] \beta_j + u_{jt}.\tag{10}$$

Since all of the elements of (10) except for β_j are random variables this model is capable of capturing the fluctuating security market line phenomenon discussed earlier. In fact, as Fama and MacBeth argue, the estimated intercepts in the empirical risk–return relation portrayed in the previous figures are very good estimates of the returns on the zero beta portfolio over the time intervals dealt with.

While the two-factor model given by (10) seems capable of describing the major characteristics of the stochastic process generating asset returns I emphasize that at the current time it is no more than a formal representation of the empirical facts; in some sense an empirical law. We can speak about the "beta factor" or the returns on a zero beta portfolio or the intercept of the security market line with their explicit characterization as random variables. I have little doubt that this terminology is useful for facilitating communications among researchers and practitioners regarding these issues but we must be careful not to forget that we have simply given names to a well documented but as yet incompletely understood phenomena. The fact of the matter is that although we can write down a mathematical expression which seems to describe the empirically observed phenomena we do not really understand these phenomena in any fundamental sense. That is, we have no generally accepted theoretical understanding of the basic nature or causes of these phenomena. I hasten to add that we do have some models or theories which seem to be consistent with various aspects of the data, but we have not as yet put together any adequately tested and interpreted understanding of the phenomena. This is clearly one of the areas in finance where much work remains to be done (and, incidentally, where much work is currently being done). In the following sections I outline some potential theoretical justifications or interpretations of the two-factor model.

4.2. The all-risky asset model

Some theoretical justification for the two-factor model given by eq. (10) is provided by a number of authors. (See Black (1972), Brennan (1971), Vasicek (1971), and Lintner (1969).) In particular Black (1972) has demonstrated that one can obtain an equilibrium relationship between risk and return for all assets in a market in which no riskless asset or borrowing or lending opportunities exist (but there are no restrictions on short selling). He proves that in such a market the equilibrium portfolios of all investors consist of a linear combination of two basic portfolios.[11] While this point was recognized earlier (see Sharpe (1970,

[11]This separation property also holds for the mean-variance portfolio model, as was first pointed out by Tobin (1958). In this case, however, one of the two portfolios was the riskless asset. Cass and Stiglitz (1970) proved that the separation property also holds for two risky portfolios for certain classes of utility functions and general return distributions in the absence of a riskless asset. Lintner (1969) also investigates the nature of equilibrium in the absence of riskless borrowing or lending for the special case where all investors have preferences which exhibit constant absolute risk aversion and probability distributions are normal.

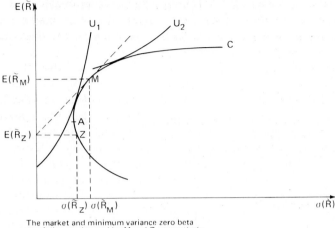

Figure 2.13. (*Source*: Jensen (1972b).)

Ch. 4)) Black lends empirical content to the proposition by demonstrating that the equilibrium conditions imply that one of these two portfolios can be taken to be the market portfolio, M, and the other a portfolio whose returns have zero covariance with the market portfolio. This separation property derives from the fact that given no constraints on short selling, the entire efficient set of portfolios can be generated by a linear combination of these two portfolios,[12] as is illustrated in fig. 2.13.[13] The points Z and M represent respectively the standard deviation and expected returns on the zero beta and market portfolios, and since the returns on these two portfolios are by definition uncorrelated, all points on the convex set given by $ZAMC$ can be obtained by various linear combinations of portfolios Z and M. If all funds are invested in portfolio Z, we obtain the risk–return combination given by Z, and as we reduce the fraction invested in Z and invest the remainder in M, we can obtain all points on the curve ZAM. At point M we have nothing invested in Z and hold only M. In order to move beyond M toward C we sell Z short and invest the proceeds in M. Note that all portfolios in the range AMC are efficient in the Markowitz sense, i.e. for a given level of variance each portfolio has maximum expected return and for a given level of expected return each portfolio has minimum variance. Each investor maximizes his utility by purchasing that combination of Z and M

---

[12]Merton (1972) also examines this point. In fact the entire frontier of the opportunity set can be generated by linear combinations of any two distinct frontier portfolios.

[13]As shown in fig. 2.13 the point $E(R_Z)$ must be the intercept of a line tangent to the frontier at point M. For a proof of this see Jensen (1972b).

at which his indifference curve between expected return and standard deviation is just tangent to the efficient set (as is true for indifference curves U_1 and U_2 for hypothetical investors 1 and 2). The equilibrium conditions imply that $E(R_Z)$ must be less than $(E(R_M)$ (see Vasicek (1971) and Black (1972)) and that the holdings of Z must net out to zero for all investors as a whole. Black demonstrates that in a market such as this the equilibrium expected returns on any asset will be given by

$$E(R_j) = E(R_Z) + \left[E(R_M) - E(R_Z) \right] \beta_j,$$

where $E(R_Z)$ is the expected return on the zero beta portfolio and this is exactly the expression for the equilibrium expected returns given by the two factor model specified in eqs. (9) or (10).

4.3. The model with riskless lending but no borrowing

While the above results are in many ways attractive, one might argue that the assumptions have been taken too far. The existence of government bonds which are virtually default-free gives investors the opportunity to lend, if not to borrow, at a rate which is for all practical purposes certain. This suggests investigation of equilibrium in a system with riskless lending opportunities but no riskless borrowing opportunities. Vasicek (1971) and Black (1972) have demonstrated that in such a world the equilibrium risk–return relation for individual *risky* securities corresponds exactly to that given by eq. (9). Their results also imply a piecewise linear relationship between expected return and β for *efficient* portfolios which has serious implications for the performance evaluation of portfolios containing both bonds and stocks. We shall return to this point below.

Given the existence of riskless lending but no riskless borrowing opportunities, the possible set of standard deviation and expected return combinations available to an investor is portrayed in fig. 2.14a. The efficient set *excluding* lending opportunities is given by the line segment $ATMC$. Point T denotes the tangency portfolio. It is defined as that portfolio on the efficient set which is located at the point where a straight line drawn from the riskless rate is just tangent to the efficient set. All portfolios which involve both lending at the riskless rate and investment in portfolio T lie on the straight line segment $R_F T$. Thus, the efficient set *including* optimal utilization of the lending opportunities is given by $R_F TMC$. Vasicek and Black prove that in equilibrium $R_F \leqslant E(R_Z) < E(R_M)$ that all investors will either hold combinations of portfolio T and the riskless asset (if they are on the segment $R_F T$) or combinations of portfolios Z and M (if they are on the segment TMC). Portfolios M and Z are defined exactly as before, i.e. the market portfolio and the zero beta portfolio, respectively, and T is a linear

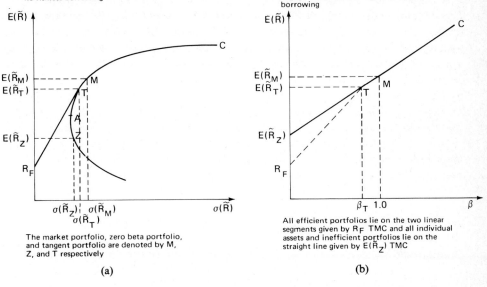

The locus of efficient portfolios, R_FTMC. When investors can engage in riskless lending but no riskless borrowing

The relationship between expected return and systematic risk β where investors can engage in riskless lending but no riskless borrowing

The market portfolio, zero beta portfolio, and tangent portfolio are denoted by M, Z, and T respectively

All efficient portfolios lie on the two linear segments given by R_F TMC and all individual assets and inefficient portfolios lie on the straight line given by $E(\tilde{R}_Z)$ TMC

(a)

(b)

Figure 2.14. (*Source*: Jensen (1972b).)

combination of these two portfolios. The expected return on every *individual risky asset or portfolio of risky assets* is still given by (9) and lies along the line $E(R_Z)TMC$ in fig. 2.14b.

However, unlike the situation for the other models, eq. (9) *does not now hold for all efficient portfolios*. In fact, the expected return–beta relationship for efficient portfolios is now given by the two straight-line segments making up R_FTMC in fig. 2.14b. All efficient portfolios which consist solely of risky assets lie along the portion *TMC* as in the previous models, *but all efficient portfolios made up of combinations of the riskless asset and portfolio T now lie along the segment R_FT*. This result becomes intuitively clear once one notes that if a fraction α is invested in portfolio T and $(1-\alpha)$ in the riskless asset, the β of the portfolio must equal $\alpha\beta_T$. In addition, the expected return on the portfolio will equal $\alpha E(R_T)+(1-\alpha)R_F$, the weighted average of the returns on portfolio T and the riskless asset. Hence, for all values of α in the range zero to one the portfolio must lie on the line R_FT in fig. 2.14b. However, all individual risky assets or imperfectly diversified portfolios must lie somewhere on the line $E(R_Z)TMC$, and hence those assets and inefficient portfolios with $\beta_j<\beta_T$ will appear to dominate the efficient portfolios lying on the segment R_FT in the mean–beta plane in fig. 2.14b. But of course they do not dominate these efficient portfolios in the mean–standard deviation plane, as illustrated in fig. 2.14a.

Since $E(R_Z)$ must be greater than or equal to R_F, the slope of the line $E(R_Z)TMC$ must be less than or equal to the slope of a hypothetical line drawn from R_F through M, which is the slope given by the simple asset pricing model (cf. eq. (2)). Recall the Black–Jensen–Scholes empirical results discussed earlier which were based on an examination of portfolios consisting *entirely of risky assets*. The present model predicts that the empirical slope of the cross-sectional return–beta relationship found in such a study should be less than that implied by eq. (2). If we can assume that for sufficiently long periods of time the sample averages $\bar{R}_M$ and $\bar{R}_Z$ are fairly good proxy measures of the ex ante expectations, the Black–Jensen–Scholes results are consistent with the predictions of this riskless lending but no riskless borrowing model. Over the period 1931–1965 the empirical slope was less than that predicted by eq. (2) (see fig. 2.8), and this also was true for three of the four 105-month subperiods examined.[14]

4.4. The model with differential riskless borrowing and lending rates

Brennan (1971) derives the market equilibrium conditions assuming that investors can borrow and lend but only at differential rates. He considers two cases: (1) all investors can borrow at a riskless rate R_B and lend at a riskless rate R_L and $R_B > R_L$, and (2) each investor, denoted by i, faces different riskless borrowing and lending rates and $R_{Bi} > R_{Li}$. In both cases, Brennan finds that the relation between an asset's expected return and risk (as measured by β_j) will be linear and identical to (9), the relation obtained by Black for the no riskless borrowing and lending case and by Vasicek for the riskless lending case. He demonstrates that the expected returns on the portfolio Z will be equal to a weighted average of (1) the borrowing rates of borrowers, (2) the lending rates of lenders, and (3) the equivalent riskless rates (marginal rates of substitution) of individuals who neither borrow nor lend. Thus, the Black–Vasicek results extend to the general case of differential borrowing and lending rates.

In conclusion, it appears that the relaxation of the assumptions regarding the nature of riskless borrowing and lending opportunities in the original model yields implications which appear to be consistent with some of the observed discrepancies between the empirical results and the simple model documented by Black, Jensen and Scholes, but do not explain the stochastic nonlinearities documented by Fama and MacBeth. There are a number of other theoretical extensions to the basic asset pricing model which show some potential to explain the empirical relation between risk and return, but little explicit empirical testing

---

[14]Interestingly enough, in the last subperiod shown in fig. 2.9, April 1957–December 1965, the empirical slope was slightly negative, which is inconsistent with this model. However, as mentioned earlier, this might be explained by the hypothesis that the observed $\bar{R}_M$ and $\bar{R}_Z$ did not adequately represent the ex ante expectations, $E(R_M)$ and $E(R_Z)$.

of most of these models has as yet been completed. These include the incorporation of the effects of nonmarketable assets such as human capital, differential
tax rates on dividends and capital gains, and the effects of interest rate changes
and uncertain inflation. For a review of most of these extensions see Jensen
(1972b) and for consideration of the effects of uncertain inflation see Long
(1974).

5. Implications of the evidence

5.1. Implications for security analysis and portfolio policy

The potential usefulness of the Market and Asset Pricing models for practical
investment and portfolio analysis has received increasing attention in the past
five years in the professional financial community. As we have seen above, our
current knowledge regarding all the factors determining the structure of asset
returns is far from perfect. We still have many unanswered questions. However,
there is no doubt that over the past ten years or so, our knowledge has increased
at an enormous rate. The common (and understandable) reaction of many
investors and professional money managers when exposed to this material is:
"How can I use it to make money?" My answer to that question is easily
summarized: "With difficulty and with care". Of one thing I am sure — it is
highly unlikely that anyone will find it easy to make large profits by any simple
mechanical application of these techniques to the selection of securities. On the
other hand, I do not believe they are useless either. But they do not in any way
represent the pot of gold at the end of the rainbow.

I believe the market model or the two-factor model can be of potential use to
the money manager by helping him to structure his organization and the efforts
of his analysts to increase the productivity of their efforts. He can do this by
recognizing that the market model can help him to break down the components
of an asset's return into two separable parts: (1) a market component represented by $\beta_j R_{Mt}$, and (2) an individualist component represented by $(a_j + e_{jt})$,
and he could then structure his organization to allow specialists to concentrate
on each of these components. That is, one group can concentrate on making
forecasts of the probability distribution of future market returns, R_{Mt}, and
perhaps also deal with the problems associated with obtaining predictions of
each asset's beta coefficient. This latter function, however, could also be considered part of the security analysts job. (There are, incidentally, a number of
commercial services which provide beta estimation services to aid in this effort.)

The major task of the security analyst could then be directed at providing
estimates of the firm specific components of the model $(a_j + e_{jt})$ — that is,
projections of the returns on a given asset which are unique to each firm and

independent of general market conditions. An important part of this task is to motivate the analysts to provide estimates of the uncertainty (i.e. standard deviation) of these forecasts.

The task of the portfolio manager would then lie in taking these estimates and constructing a portfolio which optimally incorporates them so as to maximize the expected portfolio returns subject to meeting the policy constraint with respect to the risk level of the portfolio. This risk policy can also be stated simply in terms of the permissible range of systematic (or beta) risk that the beneficiaries of the portfolio desire.

The first effort aimed at formally modeling the problems presented by the optimal use of analysts' forecasts on individual securities is the work of Treynor and Black (1973). Lloyd-Davies and Canes (1978) also addresses this problem in some detail. Jensen (1972c) considers the problem involving the optimal utilization of market forecasts in portfolio policy. All of these analyses involve the application of the concepts we have discussed above to some degree. A thorough review of this literature would be inappropriate here because of space constraints so I simply refer the interested reader to these works.

Before leaving this topic, however, I should point out that the Two-Factor Model could also prove useful for security analysis and portfolio construction in much the same way as the Market Model outlined above except that it admits one more level of complexity. This model implies the return on any asset can be broken down into three separate components (cf. eq. (10)):

(1) a market portfolio component given by $\beta_j R_{Mt}$,
(2) a beta factor component given by $(1 - \beta_j) R_{Zt}$, and
(3) an individualistic firm component given by e_{jt}.

Whether this model proves to be superior will depend on whether analysts or economists are able to derive models to aid in the prediction of R_{Zt} as well as R_{Mt} and e_{jt}. This will undoubtedly be a nontrivial task but the rewards to the successful will undoubtedly be high.

5.2. Implications for the evaluation of portfolio performance

Obviously, if the process generating asset returns is that described by eq. (10) the portfolio evaluation procedures suggested by Treynor (1965), Sharpe (1966), and Jensen (1969) which are based on the simple form of the asset pricing model will not correctly adjust for the risk–return tradeoff which actually occurs over any given time interval except by accident. An example of the problem is given in fig. 2.15, where we have assumed the actual risk – return tradeoff (such as that presented in figs. 2.8, 2.9, 2.11 and 2.12) is given by the solid line. The theoretical risk–return tradeoff given by the simple form of the asset pricing model is represented by the dashed line.

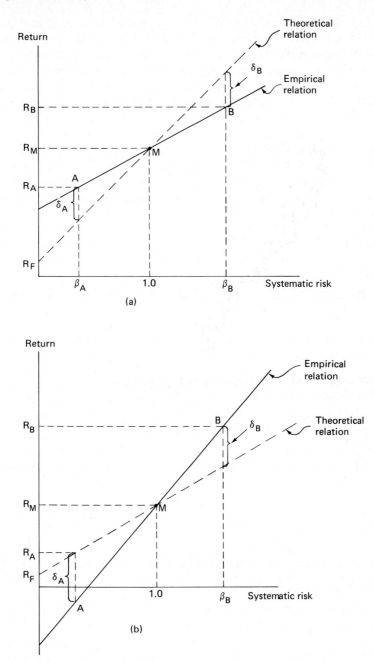

Figure 2.15. An illustration of the inadequacy of portfolio performance measures based on the combined Market and Asset Pricing Models as indicated by the empirical evidence on the risk – return relation.

The points labeled A and B in fig. 2.15a represent the risk–return combinations for two hypothetical funds which simply followed a buy and hold strategy of investing in perfectly diversified common stock portfolios with risk levels equal to β_A and β_B, respectively. Because of their policies they should earn no more and no less on the average than that earned by all stocks with their risk levels. Hence, they will on the average fall on the line denoting the empirical risk–return relationship, whatever it is for the particular period. However, consider taking as our measure of fund performance the difference between the fund returns and that which the combined market and asset pricing model says the fund ought to earn given its risk level and the actual market return; this latter return is given by the expected value of eq. (6) conditional upon the realized market return, and we write this conditional expected return as $E(R_j|R_M)$. It is given by

$$E(R_j|R_{Mt}) = R_{Ft} + (R_{Mt} - R_{Ft})\beta_j, \qquad (11)$$

and these returns can be read from the dashed lines in fig. 2.15. The difference between the fund return and that given by (11) is the measure of fund performance and is denoted by δ_A and δ_B in fig. 2.15. Since the performance measure δ for portfolio j for time period t is defined as

$$\delta_{jt} = R_{jt} - \left[R_{Ft} + (R_{Mt} - R_{Ft})\beta_j \right], \qquad (12)$$

we can see that δ_A is positive and δ_B negative for the particular empirical market line drawn in fig. 2.15a. Of course, by our assumptions the correct performance measure for both of these "buy and hold" funds should indicate neither superior nor inferior performance[15] for either fund (i.e. $\delta_A = \delta_B = 0$). It is this phenomena which Friend and Blume (1970) referred to in their criticism of "one parameter" or risk adjusted measures of portfolio performance.

The reader can easily see by reference to fig. 2.15b that when the market line has a negative intercept and the market returns are greater than the riskless rate δ_A will be negative and δ_B positive. Thus, in the first case (fig. 2.15a) the low risk

---

[15]By comparing eqs. (6) and (7) one can see that for a nonmanaged fund δ_{jt} is in fact identically equal to e_{jt}, the error term in the combined market and asset pricing model and since our portfolios A and B are by assumption perfectly diversified we know $e_A = e_B = 0$. For a portfolio whose management could forecast security prices, eq. (6) would not hold since the management's ability would cause the average returns on the fund to be higher than that given by the expected value of eq. (6). This is easily taken care of by rewriting eq. (6) as

$$R_{jt} = \alpha_j + R_{Ft} + (R_{Mt} - R_{Ft})\beta_j + u_{jt},$$

or alternatively in excess return form as

$$R_{jt} - R_{Ft} = \alpha_j + (R_{Mt} - R_{Ft})\beta_j + u_{jt}. \qquad (13)$$

The term α_j in (13) then measures the per period incremental portfolio returns due to the manager's security selection and timing ability. In this framework α_j can be estimated in two ways:

assets will have positive performance measures and high risk assets negative performance measures even though the actual returns for both funds are just equal to what all unmanaged assets at each risk level earn in the market as a whole in the period. Just the opposite is, of course, true for the situation portrayed in fig. 2.15b.

Thus, if one were to examine the relationship between the performance measure and risk for the period portrayed in fig. 2.15a, the relationship would be negatively sloped, and for the period portrayed in fig. 2.15b, the relationship would be positively sloped. Fig. 2.16 presents the scatter diagram of δ versus β for 200 randomly selected portfolios for the periods January 1960–March 1964 and April 1964–June 1968 calculated by Friend and Blume (1970). If the procedure correctly adjusts for risk there should be no relation between δ and β, and the reader can see that this is not true for these two periods. In fact, these two periods correspond almost exactly to the two illustrations in fig. 2.15. On the basis of this evidence Friend and Blume concluded that risk adjusted performance measures should not be used. I certainly agree that on the basis of the evidence which now exists one would be foolish to naively apply the simple form of the asset pricing model given by (2) or the combined market and asset pricing model given by (6) to calculate risk adjusted performance measures. But this does not mean that we cannot correctly calculate such risk adjusted measures.

The fact is that we now have at our disposal the techniques for obtaining quite accurate risk adjusted performance measures (at least for all stock portfolios — I shall return to the problem posed by balanced funds below). But I would be foolhardy to leave the impression that we now have all the answers to these issues. As I mentioned above we have been learning about the structure of security returns at a very rapid rate, and I expect that further developments will allow us to be even more precise than we now can be. However, at the current time we can obtain good risk adjusted portfolio performance measures by simply substituting into eq. (8) the appropriately calculated parameters of the actual market lines estimated from eq. (3) and portrayed in figs. 2.8, 2.9, 2.11,

---

(1) By running the time series regression of the portfolio excess returns on the market excess returns. α_j is then just the estimated intercept in this regression. Furthermore, the usual regression standard error of estimate of the intercept provides a direct measure of the uncertainty surrounding the estimated magnitude of the manager's return increasing abilities. A manager with no abilities who generates no expenses would have a performance measure, α_j, equal to zero (or insignificantly different from zero).

(2) By estimating δ_{jt} from eq. (12) for a particular time period t. In this case using the framework of eq. (13) we know that

$$\delta_{jt} = \alpha_j + u_{jt}, \tag{14}$$

and in order to get a measure of the significance of this measure one would have to obtain a time series of the measures δ_{jt} and then calculate the mean and standard deviation of these estimates. The mean $\bar{\delta}_j$ would then be identically equal to α_j calculated from (13) above. See Jensen (1968, 1969, 1972c) for a detailed derivation, discussion and application of these concepts.

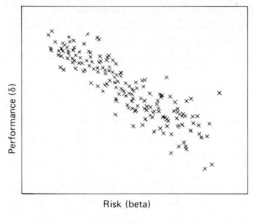

(a)

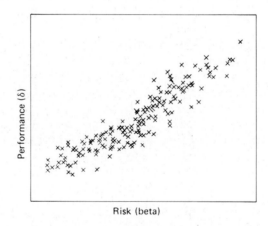

(b)

Figure 2.16. (a) Scatter diagram of Jensen's performance measure (using *log relatives*) on risk, January 1960–March 1964. (b) Scatter diagram of Jensen's performance measure (using *log relatives*) on risk, April 1964–June 1968. (*Source*: Friend and Blume (1970).)

and 2.12.[16] That is, we obtain estimates of the parameters c and d in eq. (3) for the time period under study and then calculate the risk adjusted excess return

[16]I would caution anyone who wishes to implement these procedures, however, to consult the Black et al. or Fama and MacBeth studies carefully regarding the econometric problems involved in obtaining unbiased estimates of these market lines since there are a number of severe pitfalls which must be avoided or the result will be seriously biased estimates of the true relation between risk and return. Friend and Blume (1970) fell victim to one such problem (ex post selection bias) in their study of risk adjusted performance measures.

for any portfolio j for any time period t as

$$\delta_{jt} = R_{jt} - [c_t + d_t \beta_j], \tag{15}$$

or rewriting this in terms of the parameters of the two-factor model we have

$$\delta_{jt} = R_{jt} - [R_{Zt} + (R_{Mt} - R_{Zt})\beta_j]$$
$$= \alpha_{jt} + u_{jt}. \tag{16}$$

δ_{jt} is our estimate of α_{jt} the per period incremental return on the portfolio due to the manager's security selection and timing ability and u_{jt} is the random error contained in our estimate (which has expected value equal to zero). Positive performance measures are obviously favorable and negative measures unfavorable. By the previous assumption that we were dealing with a perfectly diversified portfolio we could ignore in eq. (12) the additional complexity introduced by the error term u_{jt}. (See footnote 16 for the analogous derivation of (16) under the assumptions of the combined market and asset pricing model.)

Thus, realizing that the performance measure δ_{jt} is not an error free estimate of the manager's ability, α_j, it is important when performing such analyses to be very careful about drawing conclusions from only a small number of periods. We always have to worry about distinguishing between truly superior or inferior performance and mere random chance. To help avoid this it is desirable to have as many observations on performance calculated from different time periods as possible. Given this data we can then apply statistical tests of significance to the average performance measure (the usual t test on the mean) to test whether it is indeed significantly different from zero. A rough rule of thumb would be that at least three years (and preferably five years) of quarterly observations on performance are desirable in order to obtain any real degree of precision in these tests.

Problems with performance measures on balanced portfolios. While the ex post market line will serve quite well as a means of calculating risk adjusted performance measures on portfolios consisting entirely of common stocks there is reason to believe that this may not be satisfactory for measuring the performance of balanced funds, i.e. funds containing both equity and bond positions. Recall from fig. 2.14b that if we allow lending at the riskless rate R_F but do not allow borrowing, all individual stocks will lie along the line $E(R_Z)TMC$ given by the two-factor model in eq. (9) or its empirical counterpart, eq. (3). However, all those *efficient* portfolios which contain positive amounts of the riskless asset (bonds?) will lie along the line segment $R_F T$ in the risk return plane and this lies everywhere below the "market line" except at the intersection. Thus, if this model is an accurate description of reality, we must take care to avoid treating portfolios with bonds in them in a manner identical to all stock funds. The solution to this problem will obviously depend on the empirical relations, and studies of these issues are now in process.

6. Some remarks on the usefulness of financial analysis

In addition to surveying the evidence on the market model, the capital asset pricing model, and their implications for security analysis, portfolio management and portfolio evaluation, I have also been asked to address the question: "Is financial analysis useless?" My answer to that is bold and forthright — *it depends*. Now let me expand on that slightly.

The answer depends on how one defines useless, but let me be a little more positive and rephrase the question in several alternative ways. Suppose we mean:

Q. Does financial analysis enable the *average* portfolio manager or investor to increase the returns on the portfolio he manages?

A. The answer to this question is a resounding no! The evidence produced by study after study for mutual funds, bank managed pension funds and university endowment funds indicates that on the average these managed funds do not earn higher returns than a naive, equivalent risk, buy and hold policy. Indeed, there is some evidence that by generating large expenses for analysis and commissions, some funds do systematically worse than such naive policies.

Q. Does this evidence mean that *no one* can increase the returns on his investments by engaging in financial analysis?

A. Certainly not! In fact, the widespread attempts by many people to earn profits by engaging in analysis is undoubtedly one of the major reasons the security markets are so remarkably efficient (in the sense that prices appear to reflect in an unbiased way all currently available information).[17] But what may be true for a few‑is by no means true for the average (see previous answer).

Q. Does this argument mean that financial analysts serve a socially useful purpose?

A. Yes.

Q. Does this then mean that we would be worse off if there were fewer analysts?

A. Not necessarily. It is conceivable that at the margin losing a few analysts would leave us better off (as long as the benefits they generate are less than their costs). Furthermore, let me go on to outline two major reasons for why we have (in some sense) "too much" security analysis. These involve (1) the noncompetitive aspects of the New York Stock Exchange's fixed commission schedule (which is now in the process of being considerably weakened) and (2) what I refer to as my "religious theory" of the demand for security

---

[17]See Fama (1970) for a survey of this "efficient market" literature.

analysis. But before I do this, let me step back and ask another question regarding the usefulness or uselessness of financial analysis.

Q. Does financial analysis help increase the profits of various institutions such as brokerage firms, investment advisory services, bank trust departments and mutual funds.

A. Yes! (But note that the question says *profits* not portfolio returns.) Otherwise, I have serious doubts that these financial analysis services would continue to be provided by institutions solely because the managers believe that it is a "nice" thing to do. These services are undoubtedly provided because there is a widespread demand for them on the part of people who are able and willing to pay for them just as we pay for groceries.

Q. Why then are people willing to pay for advice which at the margin is worth less (in terms of increased portfolio returns) than its cost?

A. That is the $64 question. My own hypothesis (and that is all it is since I have no hard evidence to support it) is that this demand for analysis (advice?) derives from two major sources: (1) the cartel pricing policies of the NYSE which in the past have prohibited member brokers from charging customers anything less than the fees specified by the NYSE minimum fee schedule, and (2) a basic trait in human behavior — the trait I refer to is an intolerance for ambiguity or the unknown. That is why I refer to this as my "religious theory" of the demand for security analysis. Let me expand on these issues somewhat.

The elimination of price competition among NYSE member brokers for customers' business cannot and does not eliminate the strong incentives for the member firms to compete vigorously for customers.[18] One way to lower the effective price to a prospective customer is to provide him other services which he values (such as research) at no additional cost. Given that the customer cannot realize the savings in commissions directly he will then take these other services into account (given that he values them in *any* positive amount) in deciding on the allocation of his transaction business even though he might value the services at far less than their production cost to the broker. This problem is no different than the nonprice competition we observe in the airline industry where airlines have an incentive to provide "free" meals, liquor,

---

[18]Prior to their prohibition the widespread practice of "give-up" commissions on large volume transactions which ranged from 40 to 60 percent of the total commission provided a lower bound estimate on the amount by which the minimum fee schedule on these transactions exceeded the competitive rate which would have existed if brokers could have simply lowered their commission prices. The "give-up" commission denoted a practice in which the executing broker made available to the customer (usually institutions such as mutual funds, insurance companies, etc.) some fraction (usually 40–60 percent) of the total commission dollars generated by their large transactions for payment to other member firms who provided other services such as research, portfolio valuations, or sales (in the case of some mutual funds).

in-flight movies, etc. because the Civil Aeronautics Board has fixed a schedule of airline passenger fares which in the past has apparently been considerably higher than the equilibrium competitive rates that would prevail in the absence of their regulation. It is easy to see how this factor would tend to cause an overinvestment in the production of financial analysis as long as the consumers of the marginal service value the services at less than the cost to the brokers (and society) of their production. I doubt, however, that this hypothesis will explain all of the analysis which is produced (and consumed) whose value is less than its cost. The apparently large amount of financial analysis and investment advice which is worth less (in terms of its value in increasing investment returns) than its cost which is produced and *sold* directly to investors cannot be explained by the above cartel argument and this brings me to my "religious theory".

Casual reading and observation indicates that for as long as man has existed he has, when confronted with phenomena with no apparent explanation (or reason) reacted by attempting to devise an explanation for the phenomena. If it is not possible for him to understand or explain the unknown according to scientific principles which provide consistent and lasting explanations, he dreams up an explanation, and these fall generally under the rubric of what I call religion. They take the form of "God willed it that way" or the "stars destined it that way" or "the devil did it" (that one has become more popular recently) or "it is a matter of faith".

My point is that people want to believe that they understand the unknown and that they are willing to pay palm readers, mystics, clairvoyants, gurus, witch doctors, priests, scientists, etc. to tell them the answer; and I now add security analysts to that list. When they find that the "answer" provided by one source seems to fail systematically they simply change sources of explanation.

I had several students not too long ago (one of whom was a principal in a brokerage firm) do a thorough analysis of the forecasting ability of two well known research houses servicing the brokerage community. After extensive analysis they both became convinced that neither of these advisory services was able to forecast better than some simple, naive strategies. When discussing the results with them I asked the broker what changes this evidence would induce in his firm's policies, and he told me that he thought they would probably quit investing the principals' money on the basis of the research houses' advice but that the firm would continue to subscribe to the service. In response to my obvious question of, Why?, he said that his salesmen needed to have something to tell the firm's customers when they called to inquire about the state of affairs in the market, and these services provided a set of answers and stories to tell them at a cost which was probably lower than that at which the firm could supply the answers and stories themselves. I suspect that he may well have been correct and therefore perfectly rational in the decision to continue to subscribe to the services. It was profitable.

Now, lest you misinterpret me, I am not saying that people should not ask for such advice and explanations — neither would I argue that people should not patronize palm readers, gamble, etc. If these are their tastes and they are spending their resources, who am I to dictate what they should or should not do? They obviously must judge that they are better off for having obtained such services (perhaps only because of some additional comfort or peace of mind that it provides — not financial reward) or they would not have sacrificed the alternative uses of the resources spent on the services.

If I am correct and people do have such tastes for advice and financial analysis, this of course indicates that at the margin, the productivity of the analysis (as measured by the increment in monetary returns) will be much smaller than its cost, and the difference simply can be thought of as the cost of providing consumption services. Therefore, this latter hypothesis is consistent with the apparent lack of any substantial measurable monetary benefits at the margin to the consumer from financial analysis and yet consistent with the maximization of social welfare. I reiterate, however, that the "overproduction" which apparently results from the price fixing behavior of the NYSE represents a social loss.

References

Beja, A. (1972) "On Systematic and Unsystematic Components of Financial Risk", *Journal of Finance*, March, 37–45.

Black, F. (1972) "Capital Market Equilibrium with Restricted Borrowing", *Journal of Business*, July, 444–455.

Black, F., M. C. Jensen and M. Scholes (1972) "The Capital Asset Pricing Model: Some Empirical Tests", in: M. C. Jensen, ed., *Studies in the Theory of Capital Markets* (Praeger Publishers, New York).

Blume, M. (1970) "Portfolio Theory: A Step Towards Its Practical Application", *Journal of Business*, April, 152–173.

Blume, M. (1971) "On the Assessment of Risk", *Journal of Finance*, March, 1–10.

Blume, M. (1974) "The Behavior of Risk and Return: An Econometric Study", Rodney White Working Paper, unpublished.

Brennan, M. J. (1971) "Capital Market Equilibrium with Divergent Borrowing and Lending Rates", *Journal of Financial and Quantitative Analysis* 6 (4), 1197–1205.

Cass, D. and J. E. Stiglitz (1970) "The Structure of Investor Preference and Asset Returns, and Separability in Portfolio Allocation: A Contribution to the Pure Theory of Mutual Funds", *Journal of Economic Theory* 2 (2), 122–160.

Evans, J. L. and S. Archer (1968) "Diversification and the Reduction of Dispersion: An Empirical Analysis", *Journal of Finance*, December.

Fama, E. F. (1968) "Risk, Return and Equilibrium: Some Clarifying Comments", *Journal of Finance* 23 (1), 29–40.

Fama, E. F. (1970) "Efficient Capital Markets: A Review of Theory and Empirical Work", *Journal of Finance* 25, 383–423.

Fama, E. F. (1973) "A Note on the Market Model and the Two Parameter Model", *Journal of Finance*, December, 1181, 1186.

Fama, E. F. and J. MacBeth (1973) "Risk, Return and Equilibrium: Empirical Tests", *Journal of Political Economy*, May–June, 607–636.

Friend, I. and M. Blume (1970) "Measurement of Portfolio Performance Under Uncertainty", *American Economic Review*, September, 561–575.

Jensen, M. C. (1968) "The Performance of Mutual Funds in the Period 1945–1964", *Journal of Finance*, May 389–416.

Jensen, M. C. (1969) "Risk, the Pricing of Capital Assets, and the Evaluation of Investment Portfolios", *Journal of Business* 42 (2), 167–247.

Jensen, M. C. (1972a) "The Foundations and Current State of Capital Market Theory", in: M. C. Jensen, ed., *Studies in the Theory of Capital Markets* (Praeger Publishers, New York).

Jensen, M. C. (1972b) "Capital Markets: Theory and Evidence", *The Bell Journal of Economics and Management Science* 3 (2), 357–398.

Jensen, M. C. (1972c) "Optimal Utilization of Market Forecasts and the Evaluation of Investment Performance", in: G. P. Szego and K. Shell, eds., *Mathematical Methods in Investment and Finance* (North-Holland, Amsterdam), 310–335.

King, B. F. (1966) "Market and Industry Factors in Stock Price Behavior", *Journal of Business*, 39, Part II, 139–190.

Levitz, G. D. (1974) "Market Risk and the Management of Institutional Equity Portfolios", *Financial Analysts Journal*, January–February, 53ff.

Lintner, J. (1965a) "Security Prices, Risk, and Maximal Gains from Diversification", *Journal of Finance* 20 (5), 587–616.

Lintner, J. (1965b) "The Valuation of Risk Assets and the Selection of Risky Investments in Stock Portfolios and Capital Budgets", *The Review of Economics and Statistics* 47 (1), 13–37.

Lintner, J. (1969) "The Aggregation of Investors' Diverse Judgment and Preferences in Purely Competitive Securities Markets", *Journal of Financial and Quantitative Analysis*, 4 (4), 347–400.

Lloyd-Davies, P. and M. Canes (1978) "Stock Prices and the Publication of Second-Hand Information", *The Journal of Business* 51 (1) 43–56.

Long, J. B. (1974) "Stock Prices, Inflation and the Term Structure of Interest Rates", *Journal of Financial Economics*, July.

Merton, R. C. (1972) "An Analytic Derivation of the Efficient Portfolio Frontier", *Journal of Financial and Quantitative Analysis*, September.

Merton, R. C. (1973) "An Intertemporal Capital Asset Pricing Model", *Econometrica*, September, 867–888.

Mossin, J. (1966) "Equilibrium in a Capital Asset Market", *Econometrica* 34 (4), 768–783.

Pogue, G. and W. Conway (1972) "On the Stability of Mutual Fund Beta Values", Working paper, Massachusetts Institute of Technology, Sloan School of Management, unpublished.

Sharpe, W. F. (1963) "A Simplified Model for Portfolio Analysis", *Management Science*, January, 277–293.

Sharpe, W. F. (1964) "Capital Asset Prices: A Theory of Market Equilibrium Under Conditions of Risk", *Journal of Finance* 19 (4), 425–442.

Sharpe, W. F. (1966) "Mutual Fund Performance", *Journal of Business* 39 (1), Part 2, 119–138.

Sharpe, W. F. (1970) *Portfolio Theory and Capital Markets* (McGraw-Hill Book Company, New York).

Sharpe, W. F. (1972) "Efficient Capital Markets with Risk", Stanford University, Graduate School of Business, Research Paper 71.

Sharpe, W. F. (1973) "Bonds Versus Stocks: Some Lessons from Capital Market Theory", *Financial Analysts Journal*, November–December, 74–80.

Tobin, J. (1958) "Liquidity Preference as Behavior Towards Risk", *Review of Economic Studies* 25, 65–85.

Treynor, J. L. (1961) "Toward a Theory of Market Value of Risky Assets", unpublished.

Treynor, J. L. (1965) "How to Rate Management of Investment Funds", *Harvard Business Review* 43 (1), 63–75.

Treynor, J. L. and F. Black (1973) "How to Use Security Analysis to Improve Portfolio Selection", *Journal of Business*, January, 66–86.

Vasicek, O. A. (1971) "Capital Asset Pricing Model with No Riskless Borrowing", Wells Fargo Bank, unpublished.

Chapter 3

NEW EVIDENCE ON THE CAPITAL ASSET PRICING MODEL

IRWIN FRIEND, RANDOLPH WESTERFIELD and MICHAEL GRANITO*
University of Pennsylvania

1. Introduction

The original Sharpe–Lintner capital asset pricing model advanced to explain the variations in risk differentials on different risky assets has now been widely questioned on the basis of the empirical evidence, and a large number of modified theories have been proposed to explain the discrepancies between theory and observation. The evidence points to a reasonably linear relationship on the average between return and nondiversifiable risk of outstanding common stock, or at least those listed on the New York and American Stock Exchanges. However, this same return–risk linear relationship does not seem to imply a riskless market rate of return consistent with any reasonable measure of the actual risk-free rates of return. (See Friend and Blume (1970); Black et al. (1972); Blume and Friend (1973); Fama and MacBeth (1973); and Pettit and Westerfield (1974).)

Moreover, while over the long-run the observed linear relationship between return and risk on individual stocks yields the expected positive sign of the risk coefficient more often than not, the shorter-term relationship has been erratic and has not been explained satisfactorily by the observed difference between the market rate of return of stocks as a whole and the risk-free rate. As a result of these findings, questions have been raised about the nature of the relationship between expected and actual rates of return, i.e. about the return generating model, as well as about the theory relating expected return to risk.

A number of theoretical and empirical attempts have been made either to explain the apparent deficiencies in the original model on measurement and other statistical grounds or to modify that model to bring theory in closer

*The helpful comments of Marshall E. Blume and the statistical assistance of Sang Koo Nam are gratefully acknowledged. The contents of this paper are solely the responsibility of the authors.

James L. Bicksler, Editor, Handbook of Financial Economics
© *North-Holland Publishing Company – 1979*

conformance with reality. In our view, none of these attempts has been successful in bridging the gap between theory and measurement.[1] However, four recent
studies bearing on the plausability of the original or modified capital asset
pricing models and on the relevance of past tests of these models merit brief
mention prior to the introduction of the new tests presented in this paper.

The first of these studies, based on an analysis of the stock portfolios as well
as the major classes of assets and liabilities held by different individuals (Blume
and Friend (1975)), found that a surprisingly large proportion of portfolios and
assets were highly undiversified. It was concluded from an examination of the
other alternatives that the two most plausible explanations of this finding are
either, first, that investors hold heterogeneous expectations as to expected return
and risk and the short sales mechanism is imperfect or, secondly, that they do
not properly aggregate risks of individual assets to measure the risk of an entire
portfolio. Both of these explanations conflict with important assumptions typically made in capital asset theory, but the second is obviously basic since it
raises questions about the justification for sole reliance on beta or covariance
with the market return rather than on variance (or standard deviation) of the
asset's own returns as a measure of the market's appraisal of asset risk.

The second study, based on a survey of over 1,000 individual stockholders in
the fall of 1975, found that when the 82 percent of stockholding families which
customarily evaluated the degree of risk involved in purchasing stock were asked
what measures of risk they used, 45 percent stated they used earnings volatility,
30 percent price volatility and 17 percent betas (Blume and Friend (1978)).[2] The
answers to other questions also suggested that the preponderance of investors
including those who were rich had very little conception of the relationship of an
asset's covariance with the market to its contribution to the riskiness of a
portfolio. Thus, this second study like the first raises questions about at least one
of the basic assumptions made in current capital asset pricing theory.

Of course, even if the basic assumptions of the theory appear to be grossly
inconsistent with the facts, the theory might still be useful if it can explain the
observed phenomena in which we are interested, i.e. risky asset returns. (Con-
ceivably, it might also be of interest for normative reasons.) In the absence of
direct evidence that beta is the only or at least the predominant measure of
market risk for purposes of explaining asset returns, we might be satisfied with
strong indirect empirical evidence if we could adequately explain the discrepancies between the original or modified capital asset pricing theories and the
observed facts. Thus, it is of some interest to note that a third recent study finds
that a measure of co-skewness can be used as a supplement to the customary
beta or covariance measure of risk to explain the otherwise observed discrepan-

---

[1] These attempts are summarized in Friend (1977).
[2] Weighting the replies by the value of a family's stock portfolio does not change these results
substantially.

cies between theory and fact in relating the returns on individual NYSE stocks to the return on the NYSE stocks as a whole (Kraus and Litzenberger (1976)). In other words, this study finds that capital asset pricing theory now modified to make the plausible assumption that investors prefer positive skewness in their portfolios (and therefore positive co-skewness in individual assets) is apparently able to explain observed returns in the stock market without the substitution of a zero-beta construct for the risk-free rate.

The fourth recent study to which we want to refer is one which neither attempts to confirm or disprove the two-parameter capital asset pricing model but instead argues that it is defective as a scientific hypothesis, no valid test of this model has ever been carried out, and it is doubtful that a valid test can be made (Roll (1977)). The main thrust of this argument is that all testable implications of the theory follow from the ex ante efficiency of the market portfolio and thus the theory is not testable unless the true market portfolio is known and used in the test since even a small departure from the true market portfolio may vitiate the tests. To support this position, it is shown that it is possible to construct a market proxy that supports the Sharpe–Lintner model perfectly even though it has a 0.895 correlation with the market proxy used in one well-known test which resulted in a rejection of that model.

It would appear that this recent study has rediscovered the fact that the testing of a theory is a joint test of the validity of theory and the reasonableness of the empirical constructs used in testing it. If the study had been able to construct a market portfolio which had a priori reasonableness and supported the Sharpe–Lintner model, this would constitute scientific evidence in favor of that model. However, to our knowledge, no one has yet been able to do this even though various plausible combinations of marketable assets (mainly stocks and bonds) have been tried. To demonstrate that a "curve-fitting" process can provide a portfolio which is called the "market" because it supports the Sharpe–Lintner model has no obvious relevance to scientific testing.[3] It is mentioned here mainly because it has received widespread attention and because it has some relevance to the new tests in this paper.

These new tests are of two types. The first set substitutes ex ante (expected) for ex post (realized) measures of return in testing capital asset pricing theory. These ex ante data were obtained for a sample of common stocks from a sample of financial institutions for each of four periods in 1972, 1974, 1976 and 1977. Such data not previously available permit a more direct test of theory explaining the relationship between expected or required rates of returns and risk than is

---

[3]The computed tangent portfolio used by Roll, representing some unknown combination of assets, is presumably a much less satisfactory proxy for the market portfolio than the value-weighted total of stocks used in the studies he is criticizing. It may be worth adding that all proxies for the market portfolio selected ex ante (rather than ex post) have led to the same qualitative result Roll questions.

possible when only actual rates of return are available since it is no longer necessary to predicate the nature of the relationship between expected and actual rate of returns. They also permit the estimation of a direct measure of the heterogeneity of expectations for individual stocks and of the relationship between both expected and actual rates of return and the measure of heterogeneity.

The second set of new tests uses data on bond indexes and a large sample of individual bonds both to obtain improved measures of the rate of return on the portfolio of marketable risky assets[4] and to incorporate, for the first time to our knowledge, returns on individual bonds as well as on individual stocks in the return–risk relationships used to test capital asset pricing theory. The improved estimates of return on the market portfolio permit a more satisfactory test of the thesis that the discrepancies between Sharpe–Lintner theory and the observed facts are attributable to deficiencies in measurement of return on the market portfolio. The data on bond returns should provide an especially promising source of information to test the importance of co-skewness in explaining returns on risky assets since bonds would be expected to be quite different from stocks in their co-skewness properties. Moreover, it is difficult to understand why heretofore no systematic attempt has been made to determine whether the only major class of risky marketable assets other than stocks for which returns can readily be estimated appears to conform to the return–risk relationship observed for stocks.

2. Tests of the CAPM based on expected returns

As a by-product of another study, expected annual rates of return were collected on 41 common stocks from seven financial institutions in June 1972; the corresponding numbers were 66 and 21 in August 1974, 49 and 33 in March 1976, and 56 and 29 in February 1977. The institutions covered, including commercial banks, insurance companies and investment counseling firms were those with the largest equity portfolios and the response rates averaged over 80 percent.[5] The stocks covered, all listed on the NYSE and over $100 million in size, were as a whole of lower than average risk, with unadjusted beta coefficients and residual standard deviations (based on 60 monthly rates of return) varying in the 1974 survey from 0.57 to 1.16 and 0.035 to 0.080,

---

[4]That the introduction of the main nonmarketable risky asset, i.e. human capital, does not significantly alter the results of the tests of the capital asset pricing model which make no allowance for non-marketable assets is suggested by Fama and Schwert (1977).

[5]A number of the responses could not be used because the institutions did not have available the information required (in particular, five year or longer expected growth rates).

respectively, and with a comparable range for other years.[6] The annual rate of return in a particular stock expected by a specific institution was obtained for each of these years by adding a spot dividend yield (adjusted for the expected growth rate)[7] to the annual growth rate in per share earnings expected over a five year (or, if the data were available, longer) time period and used by these institutions to estimate expected returns for purposes of their investment decisions.

In the analysis of these data the 1972 results were omitted because of the much smaller size of the institutional sample than in the subsequent years. In each of the other years, mean expected returns were computed for every stock for which at least five institutions regularly estimated the long-run, i.e. five years or longer, expected growth rate.[8] In computing the mean expected return for each stock, equal weight was given to the estimate of each institution.

The mean expected return relatives for each stock, $\overline{E(R_i)}$, was regressed first on its beta coefficient (β_i) and then on β_i and the residual standard deviation (σ_{ri}),[9] both with and without the standard deviation of the returns for that stock expected by the different institutions (h_i). The latter variable, h_i, is basically a measure of the heterogeneity of expectations, although it also might be considered to be an ex ante measure of the market's risk assessment. These cross section regressions (where individual stocks are the units of observation) were computed for each year covered by the available data. For comparative purposes, similar regressions were also computed substituting the mean realized or ex post rates of return for the mean expected or ex ante rates. The β_i and σ_{ri} measures used in the regressions presented are based on monthly rates of return for the preceding five years, but other rates (quarterly, simiannual and annual) were also tested. In computing β_i and σ_{ri}, the market rate of return in this analysis was assumed to be the return on the Standard and Poors Index of 500 New York Stock Exchange stocks.

Table 3.1 presents the regressions of $\overline{E(R_i)}$ relatives on β_i, on β_i and σ_{ri}, and on β_i, σ_{ri} and h_i for 1974, 1976, and 1977, where the units of observation are data for individual stocks. The constant terms in the (β_i) regressions are uniformly much higher than the risk-free rate, and higher also than the risk-free rates implied by the constant terms in the cross section regressions of the mean

[6]These data were computed using the Standard and Poor 500 Composite Index and return relatives taken from a Rodney L. White Center data tape containing monthly returns on all NYSE firms.

[7]The adjustment used was to multiply the spot yield by one plus one-half the expected growth rate.

[8]There were 46 such stocks in 1974, 34 in 1976 and 48 in 1977. The long-run expected growth rates reported for these stocks almost invariably referred to five year periods.

[9]Regressions substituting residual variance and, separately, variance of returns for residual standard deviation were also estimated but the results were quite similar. A recent paper by Levy (1977), suggests that total variance is the appropriate variable to use together with β_i.

Table 3.1. Expected return–risk regressions for individual stocks for three periods: August 1974, March 1976, and February 1977.[a]

Period	Reg. no.	Estimates of regression coefficients				$\bar{R}^2$
		γ_0	γ_1	γ_2	γ_3	
August 1974	1	1.171 (0.018)	−0.028 (0.021)			0.02
	2	1.121 (0.022)	−0.027 (0.018)	0.918 (0.273)		0.21
	3	1.105 (0.023)	−0.019 (0.019)	0.926 (0.267)	0.506 (0.297)	0.24
March 1976	4	1.132 (0.010)	−0.002 (0.014)			0
	5	1.144 (0.012)	0.004 (0.014)	−0.282 (0.170)		0.02
	6	1.142 (0.014)	0.005 (0.014)	−0.283 (0.173)	−0.051 (0.285)	0
February 1977	7	1.210 (0.031)	−0.071 (0.037)			0.06
	8	1.179 (0.038)	−0.097 (0.041)	0.875 (0.604)		0.08
	9	1.179 (0.034)	−0.079 (0.037)	0.222 (0.586)	0.669 (0.208)	0.24

[a]These are cross section regressions of the general form $\overline{E(R_i)} = \gamma_0 + \gamma_1 \beta_i + \gamma_2 \sigma_{ri} + \gamma_3 h_i$. $\bar{R}^2$ is the coefficient of determination adjusted for degrees of freedom. The standard error of a regression coefficient is indicated by ( ). The number of observations is 46 for 1974, 34 for 1976 and 48 for 1977.

realized rate of return on these stocks $(\bar{R}_i)$ on β_i. Contrary to theoretical expectations, the coefficient of β_i in these $\overline{E(R_i)}$ regressions is uniformly negative though approaching statistical significance (at the customary 0.05 level) only in one year.

The coefficient of σ_{ri} in the (β_i, σ_{ri}) regressions is statistically significant and positive only for 1974, while again the coefficient of β_i is significant only in one year when it has the wrong sign. The σ_{ri} coefficient has the theoretically expected positive sign in two of the three years and the β_i coefficient in only one year. These results are not changed when h_i is added to these regressions, but the coefficient of h_i is significant in 1977, approaches significance in 1974 and is positive in all three years.[10] In contrast to the apparent slight superiority of σ_{ri} (and σ_{ri}^2 or σ_i^2 which were tested separately) over β_i in explaining the average ex ante return relatives, $\overline{E(R_i)}$, over the three years, the results for β_i and σ_{ri} are

---

[10]If the returns are generated by an asymmetric distribution, a significant relationship might reflect the fact that sample means and variances can be spuriously associated if skewness exists.

indistinguishable in the regressions relating the mean realized or ex post return relatives[11] to σ_{ri} and β_i for the same years. It should be noted that in those regressions relating realized returns to h_i as well as to β_i and σ_{ri}, h_i again seems a more useful explanatory variable than either of the other two. The explanatory power of the ex post regressions, it should be noted, is even lower than that for the ex ante regressions.

These findings while not at all strong support the view that the residual standard deviation of return and related variance measures play fully as significant a role in the pricing of risky assets as the beta coefficient. Virtually identical results are obtained when the logs of return relatives are substituted for the returns themselves to take cognizance of the difference in investment horizons reflected is the ex ante return and ex post beta measures used. However, the sample of observations is limited and the explanatory power of the regression is hardly impressive. Moreover, while the use of ex ante in lieu of ex post returns avoids some of the problems associated with such analyses, one basic problem remains — the substantial measurement errors in estimating β_i and σ_{ri} from observations on individual stocks.

To minimize this problem of measurement error, it is desirable to re-estimate the return–risk relationships from grouped data. Unfortunately the limited number of observations on mean expected returns for individual stocks does not permit a satisfactory grouping of individual stocks simultaneously by past values of β_i and σ_{ri} — a procedure followed in the next section of this paper for which much more data are available. It should be noted, however, that tests of capital asset pricing theory that rely only on grouped data, to the exclusion of tests based on individual assets, are not completely satisfactory, since it is the returns on individual assets which the theory is trying to explain and individual asset deviations from linearity may cancel out in the formation of portfolios (see Levy (1977) and Roll (1977)).

3. Tests of the CAPM based on bond returns

The first set of tests of the CAPM based on bond returns makes use of a data tape compiled by the Rodney L. White Center for Financial Research containing quarterly rates of return from the fourth quarter of 1968 through the third quarter of 1973 for every corporate bond listed on the New York Stock Exchange (NYSE) for which satisfactory price and interest data were available. After the removal of a small number of bonds for which data were not available for as many as ten quarters, a total of 891 individual bonds were used for testing

---

[11]The ex post return used for each stock in each of the three periods covered was the monthly average for the 60-month period preceding the month of the year for which the ex ante return was estimated.

the return–risk relationship implied by the CAPM. The same data tape was used to obtain for this period an equally-weighted quarterly index of market return on bonds (the RLW index) based on all issues covered by this tape. To compare the risk–return relationships for bonds with those for stocks, the quarterly rates of return for the same period were obtained for 867 NYSE common stocks from a second Center tape.[12]

To construct an overall market return index more satisfactory for testing the CAPM than the usual stock index, it was necessary to obtain appropriate market indexes for the major classes of marketable assets and then to apply the relevant market weights.[13] We used the NYSE Composite index to cover all common stocks, the RLW index to cover all bonds other than US Governments, and a US Government bond index developed by John Bildersee to cover long-term marketable US Government issues (Bildersee (1975)). The weights applied in estimating the overall market return (R_m) for 1973 from the three constituent returns were 60 percent for coporate equities (with a return of R_s), 30 percent for bonds other than US Governments (R_b), and 10 percent for long-term marketable US Government issues (R_g). These weights which varied from year to year were obtained from the annual Federal Reserve Board *Flow of Funds* data on the market value of stocks and bonds held by US individuals and financial institutions. A potential limitation of the R_m index as an estimate of return on all stocks and bonds is that in the absence of a satisfactory index for returns on municipal bonds, which account for about 10 percent of the value of all stocks and bonds held by individuals and institutions, they have been assumed to move in the same manner as the returns on corporate bonds.

Table 3.2 presents separately for stocks, for bonds, and for stocks and bonds combined, four risk–return cross section relationships in which average quarterly returns for individual issues over the period from the fourth quarter of 1968 through the third quarter of 1973 $(\bar{R}_i)$ are regressed on combinations of three variables, β_i (the beta coefficient), β_i^2 and σ_{ri}.[14] Unlike the β_i and σ_{ri} variables which can be given a strong a priori justification, β_i^2 is introduced to permit a simple test of the basic linearity assumption of the capital asset pricing model (either with a risk-free or zero-beta asset). The R_m estimates used for

[12]The common stocks were required to have 19 quarters of return data in each period from the first quarter 1964 to the second quarter 1968 and from the third quarter of 1968 to the second quarter of 1973. This requirement can introduce a potentially significant ex post selection bias. However, when the 1968–1973 regressions for the 867 individual assets having 38 quarters of continuous data are compared to those where 1,087 individual assets with 19 quarters of continuous data are included the qualitative results are the same.

[13]Correct weights on various classes of securities are difficult to determine because of problems associated with the treatment of government debt, financial intermediation and nonmarketable assets. As a result several different sets of weights were tested.

[14]The residual standard deviation for individual assets, σ_{ri}, is taken from estimates of the "market model", $R_{it} = \alpha_i + \beta_i R_{mt} + \varepsilon_{it}$, where R_{it} and R_{mt} are, respectively, returns on individual asset i and the composite market portfolio.

Table 3.2. Return–risk regressions for individual assets adjusted for order bias, fourth quarter 1968–third quarter 1973.[a]

Type of asset	Reg. no.	Estimates of regression coefficients				$\bar{R}^2$
		γ_0	γ_1	γ_2	γ_3	
Stocks	1	1.025 (0.0032)	−0.018 (0.0020)			0.087
	2	1.042 (0.0083)	−0.041 (0.0107)	0.007 (0.0032)		0.091
	3	1.044 (0.0083)	−0.035 (0.0108)	0.006 (0.0032)	−0.074 (0.0245)	0.099
	4	1.030 (0.0035)	−0.015 (0.0022)		−0.078 (0.0245)	0.097
Corporate bonds	5	1.016 (0.0009)	0.001 (0.0022)			−0.001
	6	1.018 (0.0014)	−0.010 (0.0070)	0.014 (0.0085)		0.001
	7	1.019 (0.0015)	−0.010 (0.0070)	0.014 (0.0085)	−0.037 (0.0101)	0.014
	8	1.017 (0.0009)	0.001 (0.0022)		−0.037 (0.0102)	0.013
Stocks and corporate bonds	9	1.022 (0.0009)	−0.016 (0.0008)			0.209
	10	1.021 (0.0014)	−0.014 (0.0030)	−0.001 (0.0012)		0.208
	11	1.022 (0.0014)	−0.008 (0.0032)	−0.002 (0.0012)	−0.064 (0.0143)	0.217
	12	1.023 (0.0009)	−0.012 (0.0011)		−0.060 (0.0141)	0.216

[a]The regressions are of the general form $\bar{R}_i = \gamma_0 + \gamma_1 \beta_1 + \gamma_2 \beta_i^2 + \gamma_3 \sigma_{ri}$. The number of observations is 867 for stocks, 891 for corporate bonds, and 1,758 for stocks and corporate bonds combined.

deriving the β_i and σ_{ri} measures in these cross section relationships are the quarterly time series of weighted stock and bond returns described above rather than the customary stock market index. The β_i measures have been adjusted for order bias using procedures suggested by Vasicek (1973).[15]

The intercepts in the three regressions which assume the validity of the Sharpe–Lintner version of the CAPM (Regs. 1, 5 and 9) point to a mean annualized risk-free rate of 10.0, 6.4 and 8.8 percent, respectively, on the basis of the stock, bond and combined regressions. All of these values are significantly

[15]See also Blume (1975). The exact procedure is found on pp. 790–91 of Blume, except that sample means replace the population means and the error in measuring beta for each asset is not assumed to be the same.

higher than the annualized mean three-month Treasury bill rate of 5.3 percent.[16] This result is qualitatively identical with those obtained in many earlier studies which regressed mean returns of individual stocks against a beta coefficient derived from a stock market index rather than from the combined stock and bond indexes used here. Nor was this result changed when different corporate bond indexes were used (such as S&P's Composite AAA Bond Price Index or Salomon Bros. Total Performance Bond Index), when bonds were reduced in weight to 20 percent (versus 80 percent for equities) or increased to 50 percent (versus 50 percent for equities), or when the logarithms of return relatives were substituted for the returns themselves.[17] Thus, these findings are inconsistent with Sharpe–Lintner theory if it is appropriate to use for empirical testing the customary return-generating function relating actual to expected return.[18] Moreover, it should be noted that if tax-adjusted rates of return instead of market rates of return are the appropriate variables for testing Sharpe–Lintner theory, the regression intercepts obtained through the use of market rates of return would be expected to be smaller than the risk-free rate,[19] so that our findings (and most earlier empirical results) would be even more inconsistent with Sharpe–Lintner theory.

Several other interesting findings emerge from these regressions. Residual standard deviation as well as the beta coefficient seems to affect asset return significantly, with both negatively related to asset return in this period (when $\bar{R}_m$ is less than the risk-free rate). While β^2 as well as β seems to affect the returns of both stocks and to a lesser extent bonds, this is no longer true when stocks and bonds are combined.

The differences between the stock and bond return–risk relationships are of particular interest. The Sharpe–Lintner models (Regs. 1, 5 and 9) as well as the

[16]Qualitatively similar results are obtained when β_i is not adjusted for order bias. We rely on the *t*-statistic in developing conclusions concerning statistical significance of regression coefficients. However, we report only standard errors.

[17]These results do not appear to be strongly dependent on the exact composition of our proxy for the true market portfolio. When the NYSE composite index R_s, is used in place of the composite Market index R_m, the following results are obtained for Regs. 1 and 4 in Table 3.2:

	γ_0	γ_1	γ_3	$\bar{R}^2$
(1′)	1.025	−0.023		0.087
	(0.0032)	(0.0025)		
(4′)	1.029	−0.019	−0.077	0.096
	(0.0035)	(0.0028)	(0.0250)	

Similar results are obtained for the other equations in the 1968–1973 period. However, comparisons have not been made for the 1964–1968 period.

[18]I.e. $R_i = E(R_i) + \beta_i \pi + \varepsilon_i$, where π is the market factor and ε_i is an independently distributed error term.

[19]If the average marginal rates of taxes paid by individuals and taxable institutions are 0.35 on risk-free assets and 0.20 on risky assets (including stocks, taxable and nontaxable bonds) and if tax-free institutions hold one-third of both types of assets, the intercept would be expected to be 0.89 R_f.

other regressions point to significantly different relationships for stocks and bonds, with the return–risk relationships for bonds implying a lower zero-beta or risk-free rate of return than the corresponding relationships for stocks.[20]

However, in view of the potentially substantial measurement errors in estimating the beta coefficient and the residual sigma from observations on individual stocks (even when adjusted for order bias), and the potential sensitivity of the regression coefficients in the return–risk relationships to such errors, it is desirable to re-estimate these relationships from grouped data so as to minimize this problem. Table 3.3 presents the same types of regressions as in table 3.2 except that the observations are now 50 groups of stocks, 50 groups of bonds, and 100 groups of stocks and bonds combined.[21] For stocks the procedure followed was to rank them first by beta decile on the basis of monthly data for the preceding 60-month period and then within each decile by residual standard deviation into five subgroups, resulting in a total of 50 groups.[22] Each equation was then estimated using subsequent betas and standard deviation estimates for each group. For bonds where the required data for the preceding 60-month period were not readily available for most issues, the ranking by beta decile and then by residual standard deviation decile within each beta decile was based on the expected values of β_i and σ_{ri} estimated from regressions of these measures of risk on the bond's Standard and Poors quality rating, its maturity and its coupon.[23]

---

[20]The mean return and mean beta for stocks and bonds, respectively (in return relatives) are

0.997,	1.569	and	1.016,	0.062.
(0.031)	(0.519)		(0.009)	(0.139)

The standard deviations are in parentheses. Not surprisingly, we can reject the hypothesis that the mean returns for bonds and stocks are from the same population. Furthermore, if the mean beta of bonds is substituted into Reg. 1 in table 3.2, the conditional expected return for bonds (from the stock return–beta equation) is equal to 1.0187 with standard deviation 0.0298. This value is significantly different from the actual mean return of bonds (the t value is 2.282), indicating that the return–beta relationship for stocks cannot explain the return–beta relationship for bonds. It should be noted that there is very little overlap in the distribution of means and betas between the population of bonds and stocks, making direct comparisons impossible.

[21]The values of β, β^2 and σ_{ri} in the grouped regressions represent group means. They are equally weighted averages of the values for the individual assets in the group.

[22]This procedure is similar to (but not identical with) that employed by Black and Scholes (1974).

[23]These regressions were

$$\beta_i = 0.28Q_1 + 0.23Q_2 + 0.23Q_3 + 0.19Q_4 + 0.30Q_5 + 0.23Q_6 + 0.47Q_7 - 0.06C + 0.01M; \qquad \bar{R}^2 = 0.13,$$
$$\quad (11.1) \quad (10.5) \quad (10.6) \quad (6.4) \quad (7.1) \quad (4.8) \quad (11.8) \quad (-.38) \quad (7.6)$$

where the parentheses represent the t-statistics of the regression coefficients and $\bar{R}^2$ is the coefficient of determination adjusted for degrees of freedom; and

$$\sigma_{ri} = 0.03Q_1 + 0.03Q_2 + 0.03Q_3 + 0.05Q_4 + 0.06Q_5 + 0.09Q_6 + 0.08Q_7 - 0.12C - 0.0004M; \qquad \bar{R}^2 = 0.33,$$
$$\quad (11.1) \quad (13.5) \quad (14.3) \quad (15.3) \quad (12.6) \quad (17.2) \quad (19.4) \quad (-7.2) \quad (5.4)$$

where Q_1 is the highest and Q_7 the lowest S&P quality rating, C is the coupon rate and M the years to maturity.

Table 3.3. Return–risk regressions for assets grouped to minimize measurement errors, fourth quarter 1968–third quarter 1973.[a]

Type of asset	Reg. no.	Estimates of regression coefficients				$\bar{R}^2$
		γ_0	γ_1	γ_2	γ_3	
Stocks	1	1.032 (0.0046)	−0.022 (0.0027)			0.556
	2	1.009 (0.0170)	0.009 (0.0216)	−0.010 (0.0066)		0.565
	3	1.005 (0.0148)	0.041 (0.0202)	−0.013 (0.0058)	−0.311 (0.0761)	0.674
	4	1.037 (0.0044)	−0.004 (0.0054)		−0.284 (0.0784)	0.645
Corporate bonds	5	1.016 (0.0018)	0.001 (0.0048)			−0.020
	6	1.029 (0.0033)	−0.070 (0.0161)	0.087 (0.0191)		0.276
	7	1.032 (0.0036)	−0.079 (0.0164)	0.106 (0.0209)	−0.060 (0.0302)	0.318
	8	1.016 (0.0018)	−0.001 (0.0058)		0.011 (0.0331)	−0.039
Stocks and corporate bonds	9	1.022 (0.0013)	−0.016 (0.0011)			0.693
	10	1.018 (0.0022)	−0.004 (0.0049)	−0.005 (0.0020)		0.709
	11	1.019 (0.0021)	0.0086 (0.0061)	−0.007 (0.0020)	−0.136 (0.0422)	0.734
	12	1.024 (0.001)	−0.010 (0.0029)		−0.099 (0.0428)	0.706

[a]The regression forms are identical to those described in table 3.2. Observations in this table are based upon the means for groups of individual assets (50 groups for each of stocks and corporate bonds and 100 groups for stocks and corporate bonds combined).

The results of the analysis of grouped data in table 3.3 are, with minor exceptions, consistent with those for the ungrouped data. The stock and combined regressions, but not the bond regressions, once more seem to imply risk-free rates or more precisely zero-beta rates of return significantly higher than the three-month Treasury bill rates. Residual sigma is not only still significant for stocks, for bonds and for stocks and bonds combined but in all three instances is more significant than the beta coefficient. Again the return–risk relationships for stock are quite different from those for bonds. Moreover, in the Sharpe–Lintner regressions the grouped like the ungrouped results point to a zero-beta return for bonds significantly lower than that for stocks.

The grouped results which point to a significant role for σ_{r_i} in the determination of $\bar{R}_i$ for all groups of assets tested might be expected to be biased against

σ_{ri} since the method of grouping permitted greater variation in β_i than in σ_{ri}. To check that possibility, a grouping method which ranks issues independently by β_i and σ_{ri} into two sets of deciles was also used.[24] This method, which yields 100 portfolios for stocks and another 100 for bonds, in which each stock or bond would enter into two different portfolios, is not biased in favor of β_i as is the procedure used in table 3.3 but suffers from the deficiency that the grouped observations are not independent so that measures of significance are over-stated. In any event, the results utilizing this grouping technique are quite close to those in table 3.3 except that if this technique were taken at face value, the intercept value in the bond regression (corresponding to Reg. 5 in table 3.3) would also appear to be significantly higher than the Treasury bill rate.

On the basis of this analysis of returns on individual stocks and bonds, and a broader measure of the overall market rate of return, it would appear that the Sharpe–Lintner model is unable to explain the observed data in the period covered, residual standard deviation seems to be at least as important as the beta coefficient in explaining these data, and the return–risk relationship appears to differ as between stocks and bonds.

Miller and Scholes (1972) also found that residual standard deviation (they used residual variance) was significant in determining returns using yearly data for individual common stocks. They examined several explanations for this result and concluded that skewness in the return generating process probably caused the association observed. In contrast Fama and MacBeth (1973) using monthly data for groups of common stocks found residual standard deviation was not cross-sectionally significant. Roll (1977) has argued the most important explanation for the difference between the Miller and Scholes and the Fama–MacBeth results stems from the grouping technique used by Fama–MacBeth — grouping has the effect of reducing the skewness in the return distributions. Our regressions detect a significant influence of residual standard deviation for both the individual asset and group tests and thus imply that return skewness is not an adequate explanation.

However, there are several differences in our estimations and those of Fama–MacBeth that could explain differences in our results. First, the standard errors of the residual standard deviation in the Fama–MacBeth model will be greater than those estimated in our regressions. Fama–MacBeth used an estimation procedure that allows for random variations in the true values of the coefficients as well as the measurement error. Secondly, our market proxy is different. Thirdly, and more importantly, Fama–MacBeth formed groups based upon beta estimates in previous periods. They did not group upon previous estimates of residual standard deviation. Thus, the Fama–MacBeth grouping procedures would tend to understate the influence of residual standard deviation when compared with the influence of beta.

[24]A similar procedure was followed by Kraus and Litzenberger (1976).

Table 3.4.   Regression estimates.

Equation	γ_0	γ_1	γ_2
(A)	1.034 (0.0184)	−0.009 (0.017)	−0.185 (0.1745)
(B)	1.037 (0.0182)	−0.004 (0.0168)	−0.284 (0.1582)
(C)	0.989 (0.0143)	0.004 (0.0134)	0.456 (0.1348)

To more closely examine the different results that can arise from grouping, we have re-estimated Reg. 2 in table 3.4 using grouping procedures designed to properly account for the real nonstationarities in the true values of the parameter coefficients (γ_0, γ_1 and γ_2) and to compare the Fama–MacBeth procedures with the ones used in this paper. The general method is to form portfolios on the basis of beta deciles for individual securities in 1964–1968 and then re-estimate group mean betas and group mean residual standard deviations in the subsequent period, 1968–1973. Next, for *each* quarter the cross section or individual common stock returns are regressed on the estimated betas and residual standard deviations. This procedure results in a time series of observations in the estimates (γ_0, γ_1 and γ_2) and averaging these 19 cross-sectional estimates provides an estimate of the risk–return trade-off. Standard errors of these averages are taken from the time series of $\hat{\gamma}_0, \hat{\gamma}_1$ and $\hat{\gamma}_2$, thus incorporating the variability of the risk–return trade-off. Eq. (A) reports statistics for 50 groups of common stocks formed from beta estimates (similar to the procedure adopted by Fama–MacBeth). Eq. (B) reports statistics for 50 groups formed from beta deciles and residual standard deviation subgroups (as explained previously). Eq. (C) uses the latter procedure (except that there are 144 groups) but reports values for the 1964–1968 time period. The values in parentheses are standard errors.

Note that σ_{ri} (γ_2) is statistically significant when the groups are formed from both previously estimated betas and residual standard deviations (eqs. (B) and (C)) but not when the groups are formed solely from previously estimated betas. It should be recalled that all these equations allow for nonstationarities in the same manner.

In sum, we feel our results are likely to be correct because of our more powerful grouping technique, because of our use of a more appropriate market proxy, and because the sign on the coefficient of residual standard deviation in both periods tested is as predicted by the hypothesis that individual asset standard deviation is an appropriate additional measure of risk.

However, we have yet to test the recent Kraus–Litzenberger thesis that through the modification of Sharpe–Lintner theory by adding co-skewness with the market portfolio to the usual beta coefficient, it is possible to explain the discrepancy between the risk-free rate and the observed intercepts in the

Table 3.5. Return–risk regressions for individual assets incorporating co-skewness measures, fourth quarter 1968–third quarter 1973.[a]

Type of asset	Reg. no.	Estimates of regression coefficients				$\bar{R}^2$
		γ_0	γ_1	γ_2	γ_3	
Stocks	1	0.033 (0.2465)	−1.119 (0.1351)	0.143 (0.0368)		0.093
Corporate bonds	2	0.089 (0.0554)	0.601 (0.1261)	−0.042 (0.0282)		0.023
Stocks and corporate bonds	3	0.596 (0.0820)	−1.327 (0.0641)	0.101 (0.0249)		0.196
Stocks	4	0.672 (0.3025)	−0.876 (0.1503)	0.147 (0.0366)	−8.651 (2.4075)	0.105
Corproate bonds	5	0.272 (0.0706)	0.571 (0.12519)	0.008 (0.0304)	−4.564 (1.1034)	0.041
Stocks and corporate bonds	6	0.919 (0.912)	−0.866 (0.0874)	0.134 (0.0248)	−10.051 (1.3228)	0.221

[a]The regressions are of the general form $\bar{r}_i = \gamma_0 + \gamma_1 \beta_i + \gamma_2 \delta_i + \gamma_3 \sigma_{ri}$, where δ_i, the measure of co-skewness, is equal to $\Sigma_t (R_{mt} - \bar{R}_m)^2 (R_{it} - \bar{R}_i) / \Sigma_t (R_{mt} - \bar{R}_m)^3$ and $\bar{r}_i$ is equal to $(\bar{R}_i - R_F)/R_F$. The number of observations is 867 for stocks, 891 for bonds, and 1,758 for the combined regression.

return–risk cross section regressions. They assume that just as investors are averse to variance in their portfolios, and therefore beta in individual assets, they prefer positive skewness in their portfolios. Thus, since they also assume that all investors hold the market portfolio, if that portfolio is characterized by positive skewness which seems likely (if there is any significant market skewness at all), investors other things equal would be willing to pay a premium for assets which possess positive co-skewness with the market. (If the market had negative skewness, investors would be averse to positive co-skewness with the market.)[25]

Table 3.5 indicates that with the introduction of co-skewness (δ_i) as an additional explanatory variable in the regressions of stock returns on beta, the intercept in the individual asset regression is not significantly different from zero, which means that the expected return on the zero-beta portfolio is not significantly different from the risk-free rate, even though a different period and more importantly a broader market index are used in this analysis than in the Kraus–Litzenberger paper.[26] However, for bonds this difference between the implied zero-beta return and the risk-free rate is marginally significant, and for stocks and bonds combined it is highly significant. Co-skewness is significantly and positively related to returns on stocks and on stocks and bonds combined, but insignificantly related to returns on bonds. The beta coefficient has a

[25]The Kraus–Litzenberger theory also holds if the market portfolio is symmetric in the returns distribution and individual assets exhibit co-skewness with the market.

[26]The form of the return variable $(\bar{R}_i / R_f - 1)100$ and therefore the interpretation of the intercept, which differ from those used in the earlier regressions, follow the Kraus–Litzenberger analysis.

Table 3.6. Return–risk regressions for asset groups incorporating co-skewness measures, fourth quarter 1968–third quarter 1973.[a]

Type of asset	Reg. no.	Estimates of regression coefficients			$\bar{R}^2$
		γ_0	γ_1	γ_2	
Stocks	1	0.976 (0.5518)	−1.770 (0.3349)	0.232 (0.1634)	0.349
Corporate bonds	2	0.478 (0.2120)	−0.683 (0.5877)	0.373 (0.1418)	0.022
Stocks and corporate bonds	3	0.903 (0.1116)	−1.689 (0.1190)	0.174 (0.0918)	0.732

[a]The regression forms are identical to table 3.5. The only difference is that observations in this table are groups of assets (50 for each of stocks and bonds and 100 for stocks and bonds combined) instead of individual assets.

significant positive relationship with bond return unlike the negative relationship for stocks and stocks and bonds combined.[27] When σ_{ri} is added as an explanatory variable in table 3.5, it has a consistently significant negative relationship with return for all three groups of assets. Both stock and bond returns appear to be affected in a similar manner by σ_{ri} but this does not seem to be true for β_i and δ_i.

When groups of assets are substituted for individual assets in these regressions (table 3.6), using the grouping techniques previously discussed, the differences between the implied zero-beta return and the risk-free rate are more marked and are significant even for stocks alone. Co-skewness is now significantly and positively related to returns on bonds and on stocks and bonds combined but not quite significant for stocks alone. The beta coefficient for bonds is now a negative factor but is not significant. (The extension of table 3.6 to include σ_{ri}, which requires a three-way grouping of assets by β_i, δ_i and σ_{ri}, has not yet been completed.)

Thus, while the introduction of co-skewness does appear to be useful in explaining asset returns in this period, it does not explain the differences between the implicit zero-beta return and the risk-free rate. It might also be noted that the sums of the beta and co-skewness coefficients in each of the stock and bond regressions, which might both be expected to be equal to $[E(R_m) - R_f)]/R_f$, are different from each other.

The evidence against the descriptive ability of the alternative versions of the CAPM tested would appear to be rather strong once bond returns and a broader market index are introduced into the empirical analysis. Nor are we aware of any versions of this theory in conjunction with plausible return-generating

[27]The return distribution of the composite market portfolio, R_m, had negative skewness in this period and also there was a negative realized risk premium (i.e. $R_m < R_f$).

functions likely to pass the tests in view of the relative importance of residual sigma (or variance) in explaining returns. However, we have been able to test the CAPM against comprehensive new bond data and the broader market index only for the period from the fourth quarter of 1968 through the third quarter of 1973. To obtain some additional insights for at least one other period, quarterly rates of return from the first quarter of 1964 through the third quarter of 1968 were computed for a random sample of 86 corporate bonds included in our group of 891 bonds covered in the subsequent period, except that not more than one bond was included from a single corporation. The S&P Composite AAA Bond Price Index was used to obtain for this period a quarterly index of market return on bonds. Again, to compare the risk–return relationships for bonds with those for stocks, the quarterly rates of return over this period were obtained for 802 NYSE stocks having continuous return data from the second quarter of 1959 to the third quarter of 1968 from a Rodney L. White Center data tape. The appropriate overall market return index was then constructed following the same procedures as for the 1968–1973 period.

Tables 3.7 and 3.8 present the individual and grouped asset risk–return relationships for the 1964–1968 period corresponding to those for the 1968–1973 period shown in tables 3.2 and 3.3. The results for stock and bonds separately are probably more meaningful than for both combined in view of the relatively low representation of bonds in the total number of assets used in the combined regression.[28]

The results for individual assets over the 1964–1968 period indicate a significantly lower intercept for the stock and bond return regressions on beta (but not for stocks and bonds combined where it is higher) than the annualized mean three-month bill rate of 4.2 percent.[29] Again residual sigma is significantly related to bond and stock returns, indicating a strong positive relationship in this period for both types of securities, with sigma apparently much more important than beta. The usual return–beta risk relationships (Regs. 1, 5 and 9) for stocks and bonds separately, unlike the results for the subsequent period, do not appear to be significantly different.

Moreover, for 1964–1968 unlike 1968–1973, the relationships between returns and both the beta and sigma measures of risk are quite close for stocks and bonds suggesting that at least in this period an identical return–risk relationship

---

[28]The understatement of the risk-free rate in this period by the Sharpe–Lintner model is also found in more traditional tests based on a market portfolio consisting only of stock (e.g. see Blume and Friend (1975)). On the other hand, it should be noted that this is one of the few periods for which this is true.

[29]The grouping procedure is identical to that described for the 1968–1973 period, except that only five individual assets are included in each group. The grouping for stocks was based upon beta estimates in the 19 quarters preceeding the first quarter of 1964. The grouping for bonds was based upon the instrumental variable equations described previously, estimated for the 86 bonds covered in this period.

Table 3.7. Return–risk regressions for individual assets adjusted for order bias, first quarter 1964–third quarter 1968.[a]

Type of asset	Reg. no.	Estimates of regression coefficients				R^2
		γ_0	γ_1	γ_2	γ_3	
Stocks	1	1.004 (0.0035)	0.029 (0.0022)			0.185
	2	0.994 (0.0077)	0.043 (0.0102)	−0.004 (0.0032)		0.186
	3	0.992 (0.0062)	0.002 (0.0083)	0.003 (0.0026)	0.392 (0.0184)	0.481
	4	0.986 (0.0039)	0.011 (0.0019)		0.389 (0.0182)	0.481
Corporate bonds	5	1.001 (0.0025)	0.024 (0.0069)			0.114
	6	1.003 (0.0037)	0.009 (0.0204)	0.018 (0.0229)		0.109
	7	0.990 (0.0025)	0.015 (0.0129)	−0.017 (0.0148)	0.397 (0.0351)	0.648
	8	0.992 (0.0017)	0.001 (0.0048)		0.385 (0.0344)	0.647
Stocks and corporate bonds	9	1.0144 (0.0025)	0.031 (0.0016)			0.281
	10	0.997 (0.0039)	0.040 (0.0059)	−0.003 (0.0021)		0.282
	11	0.992 (0.0031)	0.002 (0.0050)	0.003 (0.0017)	0.392 (0.0173)	0.546
	12	0.988 (0.0021)	0.010 (0.0016)		0.387 (0.0170)	0.545

[a]The regression forms are identical to table 3.2. The number of observations is 802 for stocks, 86 for bonds, and 888 for stocks and bonds combined.

(though not the Sharpe–Lintner model) is able to explain returns in both markets. It should be noted that the explanatory power ($\bar{R}^2$) of these return–risk relationships is quite high in this period, and very much higher than for 1968–1973, perhaps reflecting a closer coincidence between ex ante and ex post returns (and the inadequacies of the return generating functions implied by the regressions fitted). Obviously, an examination of other periods will be required before a more definitive conclusion can be drawn on this point.

When the assets are grouped following the procedures described earlier, the intercepts of the return regressions on beta for stocks and bonds separately remain significantly lower than the three-month bill rate (using a t-statistic at the usual 2σ level). Again, when sigma is introduced into those regressions it

Table 3.8. Return–risk regressions for assets grouped to minimize measurement error, first quarter 1964–third quarter 1968.[a]

Type of asset	Reg. no.	Estimates of regression coefficients				$\bar{R}^2$
		γ_0	γ_1	γ_2	γ_3	
Stocks	1	1.006 (0.0050)	0.027 (0.0030)			0.360
	2	1.002 (0.0133)	0.033 (0.0158)	−0.002 (0.0045)		0.361
	3	0.999 (0.0080)	−0.010 (0.0099)	0.004 (0.0028)	0.461 (0.0292)	0.768
	4	0.989 (0.0032)	0.004 (0.0023)		0.456 (0.0291)	0.767
Corporate bonds	5	0.999 (0.0021)	0.026 (0.0055)			0.583
	6	1.007 (0.0036)	−0.024 (0.0193)	0.056 (0.0212)		0.708
	7	1.004 (0.0065)	−0.018 (0.0220)	0.045 (0.0292)	0.075 (0.1272)	0.693
	8	0.995 (0.0027)	0.014 (0.0077)		0.204 (0.0996)	0.661
Stocks and bonds	9	1.016 (0.0034)	0.029 (0.0021)			0.549
	10	0.997 (0.0053)	0.038 (0.0073)	−0.003 (0.0025)		0.550
	11	0.991 (0.0032)	0.000 (0.005)	0.001 (0.0015)	0.457 (0.0279)	0.834
	12	0.989 (0.0022)	0.004 (0.0020)		0.453 (0.0275)	0.834

[a]The regression forms are identical to those described in table 3.7. Observations in this table are based upon the means of groups of individual assets (144 groups for stocks, 16 groups for corporate bonds and 160 groups for both stocks and corporate bonds combined).

dominates the results and an identical return–risk relationship is able to explain returns in both markets.

The results of the introduction of co-skewness into the return–risk relationships for the 1964–1968 period (tables 3.9 and 3.10) are not much more consistent with the Kraus–Litzenberger version of Sharpe–Lintner theory than for 1968–1973. The intercepts in two of the six stock, bond and combined regressions for individual and grouped assets (not including those with the residual standard deviation) imply strongly significantly different risk-free rates from the annualized three-month bill rate, two imply marginally significant differences between the implied and actual risk-free rates, and two are consistent

Table 3.9. Return–risk regression for individual assets incorporating co-skewness measures, first quarter 1964–third quarter 1968.[a]

Type of asset	Reg. no.	Estimates of regression coefficients				$\bar{R}^2$
		γ_0	γ_1	γ_2	γ_3	
Stocks	1	0.696 (0.2367)	1.935 (0.1339)	−0.027 (0.0056)		0.206
Corporate bonds	2	−0.920 (0.1478)	1.843 (0.2767)	−0.017 (0.0159)		0.364
Stocks and corporate bonds	3	0.177 (0.1943)	2.180 (0.1150)	−0.028 (0.0054)		0.287
Stocks	4	−1.938 (0.2280)	0.818 (0.1200)	−0.013 (0.0045)	37.729 (1.8002)	0.487
Corporate bonds	5	−1.793 (0.1433)	0.681 (0.2359)	0.007 (0.0117)	33.398 (3.7110)	0.676
Stocks and corporate bonds	6	−1.954 (0.1802)	0.820 (0.1089)	−0.013 (0.0043)	37.745 (1.6521)	0.551

[a]The regression forms are identical to table 3.5. The number of observations is 802 for stocks, 86 for bonds, and 888 for stocks and bonds combined.

Table 3.10. Return–risk regressions for asset groups incorporating co-skewness measures, first quarter 1964–third quarter 1968.[a]

Type of asset	Reg. no.	Estimates of regression coefficients			$\bar{R}^2$
		γ_0	γ_1	γ_2	
Stocks	1	0.445 (0.4820)	2.105 (0.2951)	−0.042 (0.0143)	0.261
Corporate bonds	2	−0.713 (0.3994)	0.904 (1.0886)	−0.075 (0.0635)	0.023
Stocks and corporate bonds	3	−0.564 (0.3203)	2.691 (0.2067)	−0.046 (0.0139)	0.513

[a]The regression forms are identical to tables 3.5 and 3.9. The number of observations is 144 for stocks, 16 for bonds and 160 for stocks and bonds combined.

with the Kraus–Litzenberger version of Sharpe–Lintner theory. The intercepts in the stock and bond regressions are now significantly different from each other, unlike the results obtained without co-skewness. It should be noted that the addition of the residual sigma to beta to explain returns on individual assets yields much better fits than the addition of co-skewness to beta ($\bar{R}^2$ of 0.49 versus 0.21 for stocks, 0.68 versus 0.36 for bonds, and 0.55 versus 0.29 for stocks and bonds combined).[30] When residual sigma, beta and co-skewness are all used

---

[30]In the 1968–1973 period, the differences in fit provided by the addition of residual sigma versus co-skewness were quite small.

to explain returns on individual assets, sigma not only is uniformly of correct sign and statistically significant but dominates beta and co-skewness in importance in all six of the relationships tested for this period.[31]

4. Risk–return relations for bonds versus stocks

The preceding analysis has indicated that there may be significant differences in the risk–return relations for bonds as compared with those for stocks, suggesting at least some degree of segmentation in the factors affecting the two markets. Such segmentation to the extent it exists might reflect a clientele effect dependent upon such institutional factors as the tax status of different classes of investors (e.g. individuals versus tax-exempt institutions). Or it might reflect very substantial differences in holding periods for the two types of assets or the hedging potential inherent in bond investment.

While we plan to pursue the nature and degree of any market segmentation in another paper, we present in table 3.11 for the 1968–1973 and 1964–1968 periods a test of a specific two-factor model which permits a further test of the segmentation hypothesis as well as of Sharpe–Lintner theory. That model relates mean return of the ith bond to the usual beta factor (β_{1i}) which measures covariance of the bond's returns with the general market for stocks and bonds combined, and to a second factor (β_{2i}) which measures covariance of the bond's return with that part of return in the bond market which is independent of return in the general market.[32] In an integrated market, the B_{2i} coefficient should be insignificantly different from zero, since it measures the effect of a special type of diversifiable risk. Its influence on the risk of an individual bond should be zero if the market for stocks and bonds is integrated.

Both the ungrouped and grouped regressions in table 3.11, which are based on the same bond data, market index, and grouping procedures as those used earlier, point to significant segmentation as indicated by the apparent influence of an independent bond factor in the 1968–1973 period, but only the grouped regression implies significant segmentation in the 1964–1968 period.[33] When

---

[31]Again, the regressions for asset groups relating returns to σ_{ri} as well as to β_i and δ_i have not been completed.

[32]Three regressions are estimated sequentially in the development of this model:

(1) $R_{bt} = \alpha_0 + \alpha_1 R_{mt} + \phi_t$ for bonds as a whole from time-series data, where R_{bt} is the return on a bond market portfolio;

(2) $R_{it} = \beta_0 + \beta_{1i} R_{mt} + \beta_{2i} \phi_t$ for individual bonds from time-series data; and

(3) $\bar{R}_i = \gamma_0 + \gamma_1 \beta_{1i} + \gamma_2 \beta_{2i}$ for individual bonds from cross section data. If there is no segmentation, the expected value of $\gamma_2 = 0$ but the expected value of $\gamma_1 = \bar{R}_m - R_f$ and $\gamma_0 = R_f$.

[33]The grouping procedure used in the 1964–1968 period is based upon beta and residual standard deviation estimates from the instrumental variable estimation equation described earlier. The grouping procedure in the 1968–1973 period is based upon beta and gamma estimates. Thus, they are not completely comparable.

Table 3.11. Market segmentation test for bonds and stocks based upon individual assets and groups of assets

Reg. no.	Estimates of regression coefficients				$\bar{R}^2$
	γ_0	γ_1	γ_2	γ_3	
	I. Fourth quarter 1968–third quarter 1973				
	Individual bonds				
1	1.019	0.006	−0.006		0.055
	(0.0009)	(0.0021)	(0.0008)		
2	1.020	0.006	−0.006	−0.026	0.061
	(0.0007)	(0.0012)	(0.0008)	(0.0100)	
	Groups of bonds				
3	1.021	0.0097	−0.010		0.422
	(0.0020)	(0.0047)	(0.0020)		
	II. First quarter 1964–third quarter 1968				
	Individual bonds				
1	1.001	0.022	0.000		0.093
	(0.0043)	(0.0067)	(0.0041)		
2	0.997	0.000	−0.006	0.405	0.66
	(0.0026)	(0.0045)	(0.0025)	(0.0342)	
	Groups of bonds				
3	1.001	0.032	−0.005		0.924
	(0.0022)	(0.0024)	(0.0022)		

[a]From the regression $\bar{R}_i = \gamma_0 + \gamma_1 \beta_{1i} + \gamma_2 \beta_{2i} + \gamma_3 \sigma_{ri}$ where $\beta_{1i} = \text{cov}(R_{it}, R_{mt})/\text{var}(R_{mt})$ and $\beta_{2i} = \text{cov}(R_{it}, \delta_t)/\text{var}(\delta_t)$ (see footnote 30). R_{bt} and R_{it} represent, respectively, the rates of return for bonds as a whole (a market portfolio of bonds) and individual bonds. R_{mt} is the corporate market index described previously. $\bar{R}_i$ represents the average annual rate of return for individual bonds, with the relevant regression estimates of γ_0, γ_1 and γ_2 from cross section data relating $\bar{R}_i$ to β_{1i} and β_{2i}.

residual standard deviation is added to the ungrouped regressions, its effect on return is again significant in both periods, and the bond market seems to evidence an independent influence on returns even in the ungrouped regression for 1964–1968.[34]

References

Bildersee, J. S. (1975) "Some New Bond Indexes", *Journal of Business*, October.
Black, F. and M. Scholes (1974) "The Effect of Dividend Yield and Dividend Policy on Common Stock Prices and Returns", *Journal of Financial Economics*, May.
Black, F., M. Jensen and M. Scholes (1972) "The Capital Asset Pricing Model: Some Empirical Tests", in: M. Jensen, ed., *Studies in the Theory of Capital Markets* (Praeger, New York).

[34]The corresponding grouped regressions have not been completed.

Blume, M. (1975) "Betas and their Regression Tendencies", *Journal of Finance*, June.

Blume, M. and I. Friend (1973) "A New Look at the Capital Asset Pricing Model", *The Journal of Finance*, March.

Blume, M. and I. Friend (1975) "The Asset Structure of Individual Portfolios and Some Implications for Utility Functions", *The Journal of Finance*, May.

Blume, M. and I. Friend (1978) *The Changing Role of the Individual Investor* (The Twentieth Century Fund).

Fama, E. and J. D. MacBeth (1973) "Risk, Return and Equilibrium: Empirical Tests", *Journal of Political Economy*, May.

Fama, E. and G. Schwert (1977) "Human Capital and Capital Market Equilibrium", *Journal of Financial Economics*, January.

Friend, I. (1977) "Recent Developments in Finance", *Journal of Banking and Finance*, October.

Friend, I. and M. Blume (1970) "Measurement of Portfolio Performance Under Uncertainty", *American Economic Review*, September.

Kraus, A. and R. H. Litzenberger (1976) "Skewness Preference and the Valuation of Risk Assets", *The Journal of Finance*, September.

Levy, H. (1977) "Equilibrium in an Imperfect Market: A Constraint on the Number of Securities in the Portfolio", Hebrew University.

Miller, M. H. and M. Scholes (1972) "Rates of Return in Relation to Risk: A Re-Examination of Recent Findings", in: M. Jensen, ed., *Studies in the Theory of Capital Markets* (Praeger, New York).

Pettit, R. and R. Westerfield (1974) "Using the Market Model and Capital Asset Pricing Model to Predict Security Returns", *Journal of Financial and Quantitative Analysis*, December.

Roll, R. (1977) "A Critique of the Asset Pricing Theory's Tests", *Journal of Financial Economics*, March.

Vasicek, O. A. (1973) "A Note on Using Cross-Sectional Information in Bayesian Estimation of Security Betas", *Journal of Finance*, December.

Chapter 4

APPLICATIONS OF OPTION PRICING ANALYSIS

CLIFFORD W. SMITH, JR.
The University of Rochester

1. Introduction

Since the publication of the Black–Scholes (1973) paper in which the pricing models for simple put and call options were originally derived, there has been much work employing the continuous time, option pricing analysis which they developed. In this paper these developments, representing a fundamental advancement in the theory of finance, are summarized and presented so that a unified picture of the state of the art in this area can be more easily acquired.

The rest of the paper is divided into three sections. Section 2 analyzes the simplest contingent claims — European puts and calls. Section 3 examines the pricing of corporate liabilities — the equity and debt of a levered firm, plus more unusual instruments like common stock purchase warrants, subordinated debt, and convertible debt. Finally, section 4 describes the pricing of other contingent claims, such as underwriting contracts, collateralized loans, insurance contracts, and leases.[1]

2. The pricing of European put and call options

2.1 European call option pricing

A European call is an option to buy a share of stock at the maturity date of the contract for a stated amount, the exercise price. Since these assets are contracts between two agents external to the firm, two propositions follow. First, the aggregate quantity of the contracts is always zero; the long positions in this asset

---

[1]This paper is especially written to augment the discussion of option pricing in Smith (1976). The major thrust of that paper is in the investments area. This paper concentrates more on the corporate finance applications of the option pricing model.

James L. Bicksler, Editor, Handbook of Financial Economics
© *North-Holland Publishing Company – 1979*

are exactly equal to the short positions. Secondly, the behavior of the underlying stock price is unaffected by the existence of the option market.[2]

Black and Scholes (1973) demonstrate that a riskless hedge can be created using the proper proportions of call options and shares of underlying stock. Since the hedge is instantaneously riskless, if perfect substitutes yield the same rate of return, then the rate of return to the hedge will equal the riskless rate. From this equilibrium condition the call price can be obtained.

To derive the call price, make the following assumptions: (1) there are no penalties for short sales; (2) transactions costs and taxes are zero; (3) the market operates continuously; (4) the riskless rate is known and constant; (5) the stock price follows a continuous Itô process; (6) the stock pays no dividends; and (7) the option can only be exercised at the terminal date of the contract.

In general, the value of the hedge, V_H, can be expressed as

$$V_H = Q_s S + Q_c c, \tag{1}$$

where V_H is the value of the hedge portfolio, S is the price of a share of the stock, c is the price of a call option to purchase one share of the stock, Q_s is the quantity of stock in the hedge, and Q_c is the quantity of call options in the hedge.

The change in the value of the hedge, dV_H, is the derivative of (1):

$$dV_H = Q_s dS + Q_c dc. \tag{2}$$

(Since at a point in time the quantities of options and stock are given, the change in the value of the hedge results from the change in the prices of the assets.)

Since the stock price is assumed to follow a continuous Itô process and the call price is assumed to be a function of the stock price and time, Itô's lemma can be employed to express the change in the call price. Itô's lemma provides an expression for the differential of functions of variables which follow Itô processes.[3] The change in the call price, dc, can be expressed as

$$dc = \frac{\partial c}{\partial S} dS + \left(\frac{\partial c}{\partial t} + \frac{1}{2} \frac{\partial^2 c}{\partial S^2} \sigma^2 S^2 \right) dt, \tag{3}$$

where $c = c(S,t)$, t is time, and σ^2 is the instantaneous variance rate on the stock price. Note that the only stochastic term on the right-hand side of (3) is the first,

---

[2]This statement is perhaps too strong. If the agents who write option contracts are very different from those people who buy options then there may be "second order of magnitude" effects associated with wealth transfers between these two groups. (Preliminary results of a study of the individuals who transact on the American Options Exchange finds no significant demographic heterogeneity.) Additionally, effects may arise from increased "market completeness and lowered transactions costs" — however, these social benefits are likely to be too small to measure empirically.

[3]A discussion of Itô processes and a derivation of Itô's lemma is provided in the Appendix to this paper.

$(\partial c/\partial S)\,\mathrm{d}S$; the rest are deterministic. Substituting (3) into (2) yields

$$\mathrm{d}V_H = Q_s\,\mathrm{d}S + Q_c\left[\frac{\partial c}{\partial S}\,\mathrm{d}S + \left(\frac{\partial c}{\partial t} + \frac{1}{2}\frac{\partial^2 c}{\partial S^2}\sigma^2 S^2\right)\mathrm{d}t\right]. \tag{4}$$

For arbitrary quantities of stock and options, the change in the value of the hedge, $\mathrm{d}V_H$, is stochastic; however, if the quantities of stock and call are chosen so that Q_s/Q_c equals $-(\partial c/\partial S)$ then the first two terms on the right-hand side of (4) sum to zero. Since these are the only stochastic terms, the change in the value of the hedge becomes riskless. With the appropriate long position in the stock and short position in the call, then an increase in the price of the stock will be offset by the decrease in the value of the short position in the call, and vice versa. Note that the above restriction is placed on the ratio Q_s/Q_c; it makes no difference which asset is short. If the quantities of the stock and option in the hedge portfolio are continuously adjusted in the appropriate manner as asset prices change over time, then the return to the portfolio becomes riskless.

Setting $Q_c = -1$ and $Q_s = (\partial c/\partial S)$ in (4) yields   *[should be Q_s?]*

$$\mathrm{d}V_H = -\left(\frac{\partial c}{\partial t} + \frac{1}{2}\frac{\partial^2 c}{\partial S^2}S^2\sigma^2\right)\mathrm{d}t. \tag{5}$$

If in equilibrium two perfect substitutes earn the same rate of return, then since this hedge is riskless, its return must equal the riskless rate:[4]

$$\frac{\mathrm{d}V_H}{V_H} \overset{e}{=} r\,\mathrm{d}t. \tag{6}$$

Substituting (1) and (5) into (6) defines a differential equation for the value of the option:

$$\frac{\partial c}{\partial t} = rc - rS\frac{\partial c}{\partial S} - \frac{1}{2}\frac{\partial^2 c}{\partial S^2}S^2\sigma^2. \tag{7}$$

The required boundary condition for the solution of this differential equation is that at the terminal date of the option contract, t^*, the option price must equal the maximum of either the difference between the stock price and the exercise price, $S^* - X$, or zero:[5]

$$c^* = \max\left[S^* - X, 0\right]. \tag{8}$$

---

[4] The equality sign $\overset{e}{=}$ should be read "equal in equilibrium". This notation is employed to highlight the economic interpretation of this equation which is very different from that of functional relations, $=$, or definitions, $\equiv$.

[5] In general, for the solution of a partial differential equation (a differential equation which is a function of more than one variable) one boundary equation is required for each dimension. Eq. (8) is the boundary condition in the time dimension. In the stock price dimension, the boundary condition is that the call price is zero if the stock price is zero. However, because it is explicitly assumed that the call price is log normally distributed, the stock price cannot be zero, the boundary condition will never be binding, and therefore can be ignored.

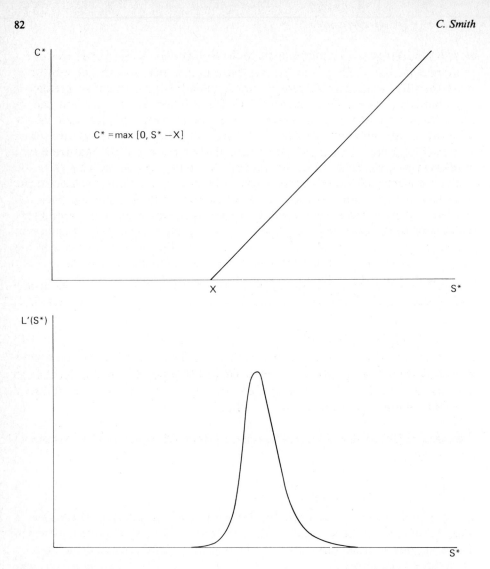

Figure 4.1. Dollar payoff to call as a function of stock price, $C^* = \max[0, S^* - X]$, and log normal density function of stock prices at $t^*, L'(S^*)$.

Before deriving the solution to (7) subject to (8), notice that whatever the form of the solution, it must be a function only of the stock price, S, the exercise price, X, the variance rate, σ^2, time, t^* and t, and the riskless rate, r, because these are the only variables in the problem.

The solution to the differential equation can be found by transforming (7) into the heat exchange equation from physics, for which the solution is known. A more intuitive solution technique[6] relies on the fact that, in describing the

[6]See Friedman (1975, esp. p. 148), for a mathematical proof of the solution technique.

equilibrium return to the hedge, the sole assumption involving preferences of the economic agents in the market is that two assets which are perfect substitutes must earn the same rate of return: no assumptions involving risk preference have been employed. This suggests that if a solution to the problem can be found assuming a particular preference structure, then it must also be the solution to the differential equation for any other preference structure which permits a solution. Therefore, in solving the equation choose the preference structure which simplifies the mathematics.

The simplest preference structure would be one in which all agents are risk neutral. In a risk neutral world the rate of return on all assets would be equal. Therefore, the current call price would be the expected terminal call price $E[c*]$, discounted to the present:

$$c = e^{-rT} E[c*], \tag{9}$$

where T is $t* - t$. The assumption that the distribution of stock prices at any future date will be distributed log normally implies that (9) can be expressed as

$$c = e^{-rT} \int_X^\infty (S* - X) L'(S*) \, dS*, \tag{10}$$

where $L'(S*)$ is the log normal density function. The payoff function for the call and the density function for the stock are represented in fig. 4.1. A useful theorem for solving this and similar problems is

Theorem.[7]   If $L'(S*)$ is a log normal density function with

$$Q = \begin{cases} 0, & \text{if } S* > \phi X, \\ \lambda S* - \gamma X, & \text{if } \phi X \geqslant S* > \psi X, \\ 0, & \text{if } S* < \psi X. \end{cases}$$

Then

$$E[Q] \equiv \int_{\psi X}^{\phi X} (\lambda S* - \gamma X) L(S*) \, dS*$$

$$= e^{\rho T} \lambda S \left[N \left\{ \frac{\ln(S/\psi X) + (\rho + \sigma^2/2)T}{\sigma \sqrt{T}} \right\} - N \left\{ \frac{\ln(S/\phi X) + (\rho + \sigma^2/2)T}{\sigma \sqrt{T}} \right\} \right]$$

$$- \gamma X \left[N \left\{ \frac{\ln(S/\psi X) + (\rho - \sigma^2/2)T}{\sigma \sqrt{T}} \right\} - N \left\{ \frac{\ln(S/\phi X) + (\rho - \sigma^2/2)T}{\sigma \sqrt{T}} \right\} \right],$$

where ψ, ϕ, λ, and γ are arbitrary parameters and ρ is the average expected rate of growth in S ($E[S*/S] = e^{\rho T}$) and $N\{\cdot\}$ is the cumulative standard normal.

[7]The proof of this theorem follows the proof of a less general result in Sprenkle (1964).

Now (10) can be solved by applying theorem 1 with $\lambda = \gamma = e^{-rT}$, $\psi = 1$, $\phi = \infty$ and noting that for a risk neutral world, $\rho \stackrel{e}{=} r$. Therefore, the solution to the European call pricing problem is

$$c = SN\left\{ \frac{\ln(S/X) + (r + \sigma^2/2)T}{\sigma\sqrt{T}} \right\} - e^{-rT}XN\left\{ \frac{\ln(S/X) + (r - \sigma^2/2)T}{\sigma\sqrt{T}} \right\}.$$

(11)

Fig. 4.2 illustrates the relationship between the call price and the stock price, given the exercise price, the time to maturity, and the riskless rate.

The solution can be written in general form as

$$c = c(S, X, T, \sigma^2, r),$$

(12)

where

$$\frac{\partial c}{\partial S} > 0; \qquad \frac{\partial c}{\partial \sigma^2} > 0; \qquad \frac{\partial c}{\partial X} < 0; \qquad \frac{\partial c}{\partial r} > 0; \qquad \frac{\partial c}{\partial T} > 0.$$

These partial effects have intuitive interpretations: as the stock price increases, the expected payoff of the option increases. With a higher exercise price, the expected payoff decreases. With a longer time to maturity or with a higher interest rate, the present value of the exercise payment is lower, thus increasing the value of the option. Finally, with a longer time to maturity or with a larger variance rate on the underlying stock price, the probability of a large price change in the security during the life of the option is greater. Since the call price

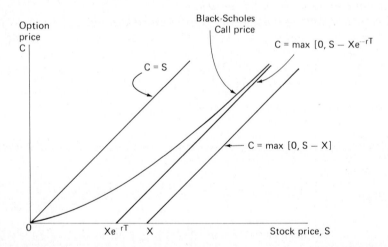

Figure 4.2. Diagram of Black–Scholes call option price for different stock prices, with a given interest rate, variance rate, and time to maturity. The Black–Scholes call option price lies below the maximum possible value, $C = S$ (except where $S = 0$), and above the minimum value, $C = \max[0, S - X\exp(-rT)]$. Note that the curve relating the Black–Scholes call price with the stock price asymptotically approaches $C = \max[0, S - X\exp(-rT)]$ line.

cannot be negative, a larger range of possible stock prices increases the maximum value of the option without lowering the minimum value.

Quite restrictive assumptions have been employed in this section; however, there has been much work by Merton (1973, 1976), Ingersoll (1976), and Cox and Ross (1976) on the effect of the relaxation of the assumptions. The model seems quite robust with respect to relaxing the basic assumptions. For a survey of this literature see Smith (1976).

2.2. European put option pricing

A European put is an option to sell a share of stock at the maturity date of the contract for a stated amount, the exercise price. Therefore, at the expiration date of the option it will be worth either the difference between the exercise price and the stock price or zero, whichever is greater. Merton (1973) has demonstrated that when borrowing and lending rates are equal, then the price of a European put, $p(S, T; X)$ is equal to the value of a portfolio of a European call with the same terms as the put, $c(S, T; X)$, riskless bonds with a face value equal to the exercise price of the options, $XB(T)$, and a short position in the stock, S.

To demonstrate this equivalence, consider two portfolios where Portfolio I contains one European call, one share of stock sold short, and X pure discount bonds maturing at the expiration date of the options with a current value of $B(T)$ and a face value of one dollar; and Portfolio II contains one European put with the same terms as the call (see table 4.1).

With no restriction on short sales, with borrowing and lending rates equal, and with no transaction costs, this position can be reversed. Therefore, if the prices of the put and call do not stand in this relationship, one to another, arbitrage opportunities exist. Thus, the European put option must be priced so that

$$p(S, T; X) = c(S, T; X) - S + XB(T). \tag{13}$$

Table 4.1. Demonstration that a portfolio containing a European call, one share of stock sold short, and discount bonds with a face value of X will yield the same terminal values as a European put.*

Portfolio	Current value	Stock price at $T=0$	
		$S^* \leqslant X$	$X < S^*$
I	$c(S, T; X) - S + XB(T)$	$0 - S^* + X$	$S^* - X - S^* + X$
II	$p(S, T; X)$	$X - S^*$	0
Relationship between the terminal values of portfolios I and II		$V_I^* = V_{II}^*$	$V_I^* = V_{II}^*$

*Terminal values of portfolios I and II for different relationships between the stock price and exercise price at the expiration date ($T=0$) of the options.

Black and Scholes (1973) employ (13) with their solution to the European call pricing problem (11) to derive the European put pricing solution:[8]

$$p = SN\left\{\frac{\ln(S/X) + (r + \sigma^2/2)T}{\sigma\sqrt{T}}\right\}$$

$$- Xe^{-rT}N\left\{\frac{\ln(S/X) + (r - \sigma^2/2)T}{\sigma\sqrt{T}}\right\} - S + Xe^{-rT}, \tag{14}$$

$$= -SN\left\{\frac{-\ln(S/X) - (r + \sigma^2/2)T}{\sigma\sqrt{T}}\right\}$$

$$+ Xe^{-rT}N\left\{\frac{-\ln(S/X) - (r - \sigma^2/2)T}{\sigma\sqrt{T}}\right\}. \tag{15}$$

This solution can be written in general form as

$$p = p(S, X, T, \sigma^2, r), \tag{16}$$

where

$$\frac{\partial p}{\partial S} = \frac{\partial c}{\partial S} - 1 < 0,$$

$$\frac{\partial p}{\partial X} = \frac{\partial c}{\partial X} + e^{-rT} > 0,$$

$$\frac{\partial p}{\partial T} = \frac{\partial c}{\partial T} - rXe^{-rT} \gtreqless 0,$$

$$\frac{\partial p}{\partial \sigma^2} = \frac{\partial c}{\partial \sigma^2} > 0,$$

$$\frac{\partial p}{\partial r} = \frac{\partial c}{\partial r} - TXe^{-rT} < 0.$$

These partial effects also have intuitive interpretations. An increase in the stock price increases the probability that the stock price will be above the exercise price, and therefore worthless. An increase in the exercise price increases the likelihood that the stock price will be below the exercise price and therefore valuable. There are two effects, either capable of dominating, from a change in the time to maturity. A longer time to maturity delays the receipt of the proceeds from the expiration of the option; this effect dominates where the ratio of stock price to exercise price is low. A longer time to maturity increases the

---

[8]With the Black–Scholes assumptions, $B(T) = e^{-rT}$. Note that this solution can also be derived using the above technique where:

$$P = \exp(-rT) \int_0^X (X - S^*)L'(S^*)\,dS^*.$$

Applying the above theorem yields (15).

dispersion of the distribution of stock prices at the expiration date, this effect dominates where the ratio of stock price to exercise price is high. An increase in the variance rate also increases the dispersion of the distribution of stock prices at the expiration date increasing the probability that the stock price will be significantly below the exercise price. Of course, the probability that the stock price will be significantly above the exercise price also increases but the put price cannot be below zero. Finally, an increase in the interest rate reduces the present value of the proceeds of the exercise of the option.

3. The pricing of corporate liabilities

3.1. Pricing the debt and equity of a firm

Black and Scholes suggest that the option pricing model can be used to price the debt and equity of a levered firm. Assume that: (1) The firm issues pure discount bonds which prohibit any dividend payments until after the bonds are paid off. The bonds mature at t^*, T time periods from now, at which time the bondholders are paid (if possible), and the residual is paid to the stockholders. (2) The total value of the firm is unaffected by capital structure.[9] (3) There are homogeneous expectations about the dynamic behavior of the value of the firm's assets; the distribution at the end of any finite time interval is lognormal with a constant variance rate of return. (4) There is a known constant riskless rate, r. Then the Black–Scholes call pricing model provides the correct valuation of the equity.

In essence, issuing bonds is equivalent to the stockholders selling the assets of the firm to the bondholders for the proceeds of the issue plus a call option to repurchase the assets of the firm from the bondholders with an exercise price equal to the face value of the bonds. Fig. 4.3 illustrates the payoff function to the equity and the debt. Thus, under the above assumptions, the equity of the firm is like a call option. Applying the Black–Scholes call option solution yields

$$E = V \left\{ \frac{\ln(V/X) + (r + \sigma^2/2)T}{\sigma\sqrt{T}} \right\} - e^{-rT}XN \left\{ \frac{\ln(V/X) + (r - \sigma^2/2)T}{\sigma\sqrt{T}} \right\},$$

(17)

[9]Long (1974) emphasizes the point that to apply stochastic calculus it must be assumed that the process describing the total value of the firm can be fully specified without reference to the value of the contingent claims. Thus, this analysis applies to a Modigliani–Miller (1958) world with no taxes or transactions costs of bankruptcy. Jensen and Meckling (1976) suggest that the existence of any agency cost (costs borne by one class of owners of the firm which are imposed by managers or another class of owners — e.g. costs of restrictive covenants within bond contracts, auditing costs, and costs of monitoring managers' activities) would cause the total value of the firm to be a function of the debt equity ratio, and thus would invalidate the specific conclusions of the analysis. However, there is no suggestion that the general form solutions would change.

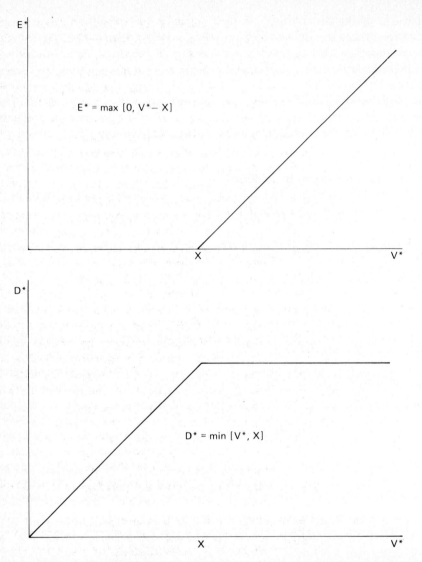

Figure 4.3. Dollar payoff to debt with a face value of X as a function of the value of the firm's assets at the maturity of the debt, $D^* = \min[V^*, X]$; and dollar payoffs to equity as a function of the value of the assets of the firm, $E^* = \max[0, V^* - X]$.

where E is the value of the equity of the firm, V is the value of the assets of the firm, X is the face value of the debt of the firm, σ^2 is the variance rate on V, and T is the maturity date of the debt. The value of the debt, D, is then

$$D = V - E$$

$$= VN\left\{\frac{-\ln(V/X)-(r+\sigma^2/2)T}{\sigma\sqrt{T}}\right\} + e^{-rT}XN\left\{\frac{\ln(V/X)+(r-\sigma^2/2)T}{\sigma\sqrt{T}}\right\}.$$

$$(18)$$

In general form, the value of the debt can be expressed as:

$$D = D(V, X, T, \sigma^2, r),$$

$$(19)$$

where $\partial D/\partial V$, $\partial D/\partial X > 0$ and $\partial D/\partial T$, $\partial D/\partial\sigma^2$, $\partial D/\partial r < 0$. These partial effects indicated are in the expected direction and have intuitive interpretations: an increase in the value of the firm directly increases the value of the equity and increases the coverage on the debt, thereby lowering the probability of default and increasing the value of the debt. An increase in the promised repayment amount increases the bondholders' claim on the firm's assets thus increasing the value of the debt and, since the stockholders are residual claimants, reduces the current value of the equity. An increase in the time to repayment of the debt or in the riskless rate lowers the present value of the debt and increases the market value of the equity, and finally, an increase in the time to maturity or in the variance rate increases the dispersion of possible values of the value of the firm at the maturity date of the bonds. Since the bondholders have a maximum payment which they can receive, X, an increase in the dispersion of possible outcomes increases the probability that the value of the firm's assets will be below the promised repayment, thereby increasing the probability of default, lowering the value of the debt, increasing the value of the equity.

3.1.1. The option pricing model and the capital asset pricing model

The pricing of the equity (and debt) is consistent with the continuous time capital asset pricing model, which implies that the equilibrium rate of return to an asset at every point in time is

$$\bar{r}_j \overset{\text{e}}{=} r + \beta_j(\bar{r}_m - r),$$

$$(20)$$

where $\bar{r}_j$ is the instantaneous expected return to asset j, $\bar{r}_m$ is the instantaneous expected return to the market portfolio, and $\beta_j[\equiv \text{cov}(\tilde{r}_j, \tilde{r}_m)/\sigma^2(\tilde{r}_m)]$ measures the systematic risk of security j.

If the systematic risk of the firm, β_v, is constant over time, the instantaneous risk of the equity, β_E, will not be stable. By Itô's lemma, the change in the value of the equity, E, is given by

$$dE = \frac{\partial E}{\partial V} dV + \left(\frac{\partial E}{\partial t} + \frac{1}{2}\frac{\partial^2 E}{\partial V^2}\sigma^2 V^2\right) dt, \tag{21}$$

and the instantaneous return to the stockholders can be expressed as

$$r_E \equiv \frac{dE}{E} = \frac{\partial E}{\partial V}\frac{V}{E}\frac{dV}{V} + \left(\frac{\partial E}{\partial t} + \frac{1}{2}\frac{\partial^2 E}{\partial V^2}\sigma^2 V^2\right)\frac{dt}{E}$$

$$\equiv \frac{\partial E}{\partial V}\frac{V}{E}r_v + \left(\frac{\partial E}{\partial t} + \frac{1}{2}\frac{\partial^2 E}{\partial V^2}\sigma^2 V^2\right)\frac{dt}{E}. \tag{22}$$

Substituting into the definition of the systematic risk of the equity, β_E, yields

$$\beta_E \equiv \frac{\mathrm{cov}(\tilde{r}_E, \tilde{r}_m)}{\sigma^2(r_m)} \equiv \frac{\partial E}{\partial V}\frac{V}{E}\frac{\mathrm{cov}(\tilde{r}_v, \tilde{r}_m)}{\sigma^2(r_m)} \equiv \frac{\partial E}{\partial V}\frac{V}{E}\beta_v. \tag{23}$$

Thus, the beta of the equity can be expressed as the elasticity of the value of the equity with respect to the value of the firm, $\varepsilon(E, V)$, times the beta of the firm, β_v:

$$\beta_E \equiv \varepsilon(E, V)\beta_v, \tag{24}$$

where

$$\varepsilon(E, V) \equiv \frac{\partial E}{\partial V}\frac{V}{E}.$$

Since the elasticity of the value of the stock with respect to the value of the firm is greater than one,[10] the absolute value of the systematic risk of the stock is greater than the absolute value of the systematic risk of the firm; and the algebraic sign will be the same.

3.1.2. Bond covenants

Black and Scholes (1973), Jensen and Meckling (1976), Black and Cox (1976), Myers (1977), and Smith and Warner (1978) analyze the nature of the restrictive

---

10

$$\varepsilon(E, V) = \frac{\partial E}{\partial V}\frac{V}{E} = N\left\{\frac{\ln(V/X)+(r+\sigma^2/2)T}{\sigma\sqrt{T}}\right\}\frac{V}{E}$$

$$= \frac{VN\left\{\frac{\ln(V/X)+(r+\sigma^2/2)T}{\sigma\sqrt{T}}\right\}}{VN\left\{\frac{\ln(V/X)+(r+\sigma^2/2)T}{\sigma\sqrt{T}}\right\} - Xe^{-rT}N\left\{\frac{\ln(V/X)+(r-\sigma^2/2)T}{\sigma\sqrt{T}}\right\}} > 1.$$

Since the denominator differs from the numerator by the subtraction of a positive magnitude, the elasticity is greater than 1.

covenants which arise in corporate bonds. Since increases in dividend payments lower the ex-dividend value of the firm, reducing the bondholders' claim, bond contracts typically restrict the dividend payments which the firm can make.

If the firm obtains very risky projects (the variance rate is increased) the value of the equity rises, the value of the debt falls. There are three ways for the bondholders to protect themselves. (1) The caveat emptor solution would involve the bondholders' offering a price for the bonds low enough (insisting on a promised interest rate high enough) to compensate the bondholder for the risk associated with the most unfavorable action by the stockholders. If the stockholders do not acquire assets at least as risky as those presumed by the bondholders, then the bondholders will be overcompensated for the risk which they bear. Thus, if this solution is employed, low risk assets will not be acquired by firms with bonds in their capital structure. (2) The stockholders can write a restrictive covenant into the bond issue restricting the kinds of risky assets the firm can acquire. (3) The stockholders can collateralize the bonds (issue secured debt). This minimizes the uncertainty about the nature of the risk of that portion of the firm's assets, since these assets cannot be disposed without the permission of the bondholders.

It should be noted that in the Modigliani–Miller world employed in this option pricing analysis, the firm's owners have neither an incentive nor a disincentive to offer debt instruments which contain covenants. It is true that if the firm can issue claims which contain protective covenants, it will realize a higher price for those claims than it would for unprotected claims (which might sell for a zero price). However, the other claims which the firm issues will sell for a correspondingly lower price — any gain which a covenant provides to the protected claimholders will be a "loss" to other claimholders. Thus, for a given set of production investment decisions it is still the case that no particular set of financial contracts can alter the value of the firm. In this sense, covenants are "irrelevant". For the irrelevance propositions to be violated this analysis must be extended beyond the perfect markets assumptions. See Jensen–Meckling and Smith–Warner for analyses which include costly negotiation and enforcement of contracts.

The analysis has general applicability for a number of important issues in corporate finance and managerial economics. (1) Changes in capital structure and payout policy have implications for the value of the stockholders' and bondholders' claims. (2) The discount due to default risk in corporate bonds can be measured by subtracting the value of the bonds given by (18) from the value of a riskless bond with the same maturity and face value. (3) Coupon bonds are like compound options, or options on options. (4) Since unanticipated changes in the arguments in (17) and (18) affect the market values of the stockholders' and bondholders' claims, this analytical apparatus is useful in analyzing changes in corporate policy. Several papers have explicitly examined these issues.

3.1.3. Risk structure of interest rates

Merton (1974) suggests that since discussions of bond pricing frequently employ yields rather than bond prices, it is convenient to transform (18) into an excess return. Let the yield to maturity of a risky corporate bond with T periods to maturity (provided it does not default), $\hat{r}(T)$, be defined as

$$e^{-\hat{r}(T)T} \equiv D/X. \tag{25}$$

Then the risk premium on risky corporate debt can be measured by

$$\hat{r}(T) - r \equiv (-\ln(D/X)/T) - r. \tag{26}$$

This implicitly defines a risk structure of interest rates. Because of the relationship between the value of the debt and the other variables in the model (i.e. eq. (19)) the risk structure can also be expressed as a function of these variables:

$$\hat{r} = \hat{r}(V, X, T, \sigma^2, r) \tag{27}$$

where

$$\frac{\partial \hat{r}}{\partial V} < 0; \qquad \frac{\partial \hat{r}}{\partial X}; \qquad \frac{\partial \hat{r}}{\partial \sigma^2}; \qquad \frac{\partial \hat{r}}{\partial r} > 0 \quad \text{and} \quad \frac{\partial \hat{r}}{\partial T} \gtrless 0.$$

The interpretation of the effect on the promised interest rate of the value of the assets, the variance rate, and the riskless rate are straightforward; those values which increase the value of the bonds reduce the promised interest rate. There is a less than proportional increase in the value of the bonds from an increase in the promised repayment because of the increased probability of default; thus, the promised interest rate rises. There are two effects on the promised interest rate of an increase in the time to maturity, either of which can dominate: (1) given the current value of the debt and promised repayment, an increase in the life of the loan lowers the promised interest rate; or (2) an increase in the time to repayment reduces the value of the debt, increasing the promised interest rate.

3.1.4. Coupon bonds

Thus far, only the simplest bond contracts have been considered, contracts which call for only one payment of principal plus interest at the maturity date of the contract. With required interest payments the stockholders' equity is like an option on an option on...an option on the assets of the firm. By paying the last coupon, the stockholders buy the option to purchase the firm by paying the face value of the debt. At the time of the next to last interest payment, the stockholders have an option on an option on an option. Although complicated (see Geske (1977)) the closed form solution to this case involves the same arguments as (17) and (18). Furthermore, it should be clear that a bond with a sinking fund provision will be strictly more valuable than one which is not.

Galai and Masulis (1976) employ comparative static analysis to examine the effect on changes in corporate investment policy. Given their assumptions they show that: (1) acquisitions which increase the variance rate of the firm will increase the value of the equity and decrease the value of the debt; (2) conglomerate mergers which reduce σ^2 increase the value of the debt and decrease the value of the equity; (3) only increases in the scale of the firm which are financed by proportional increases in the debt and equity cause no redistribution of ownership; and (4) spinoffs where assets are distributed only to stockholders reduce the value of the debt.

3.2. Convertible bond pricing

Ingersoll (1977) and Mikkelson (1978) analyze the pricing of a convertible discount bond, B. In addition to the standard assumptions, they assume that the convertible bond and the stock are the only liabilities issued by the company. The convertible bond contract specifies that at the bondholders' option, at the maturity date the bondholders can either receive the face value of the bonds, X, or new shares equal to α, fraction of the firm. Thus, the value of the convertible bonds at the maturity date, B^*, will be

$$B^* = \min\left[V^*, \max\left[X, \alpha V^* \right] \right]. \tag{28}$$

Fig. 4.4 illustrates the payoff function to equity and convertible bonds.

With the above assumptions, Merton has shown that any contingent claim must satisfy the following equation:

$$\frac{\partial f}{\partial t} = \frac{1}{2} \frac{\partial^2 f}{\partial V^2} \sigma^2 V^2 + rV \frac{\partial f}{\partial V} - rf, \tag{29}$$

where $f(V,t)$ is the value of the contingent claim as a function of V and t. Thus, the convertible bond price is the solution to (29) where $B(V,t) \equiv f(V,t)$ subject to (28). Again applying the above solution technique yields the following integral:

$$B = e^{-rT} \left[\int_0^X V^* L'(V^*) \, dV^* + \int_X^{X/\alpha} X L'(V^*) \, dV^* + \int_{X/\alpha}^\infty \alpha V^* L'(V^*) \, dV^* \right]. \tag{30}$$

These integrals can be rewritten as

$$B = e^{-rT} \left[\int_0^X V^* L'(V^*) \, dV^* + \int_X^\infty X L'(V^*) \, dV^* + \int_{X/\alpha}^\infty (\alpha V^* - X) L'(V^*) \, dV^* \right]. \tag{31}$$

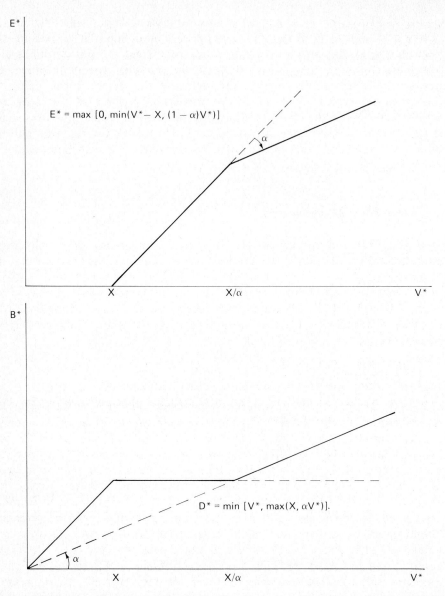

Figure 4.4. Dollar payoffs to a convertible bond with a face value of X and the option to convert the debt into a fraction α of the equity of the firm, as a function of the value of the assets of the firm's assets at the maturity of the convertible bonds, $B^* = \min[V^*, \max(X, \alpha V^*)]$; and dollar payoffs to equity as a function of the value of the assets of the firm, $E^* = \max[0, \min(V^* - X, (1-\alpha)V^*)]$.

The first two terms are the value of a nonconvertible discount bond,[11] $D(V,X,T,\sigma^2,r)$. The third term is just a call option on the α fraction of the firm with exercise price equal to the face value of the bond issue, X.[12] Thus, the convertible bond, B, is equivalent to a nonconvertible bond, D, plus a call option:

$$B(V,X,T,\alpha,\sigma^2,r) = D(V,X,T,\sigma^2,r) + c(\alpha V,X,T,\sigma^2,r), \tag{32}$$

where

$$\frac{\partial B}{\partial V} \equiv \frac{\partial D}{\partial V} + \alpha\frac{\partial C}{\partial \alpha V} > 0,$$

$$\frac{\partial B}{\partial \alpha} \equiv V\frac{\partial C}{\partial(\alpha V)} > 0,$$

$$\frac{\partial B}{\partial X} \equiv \frac{\partial D}{\partial X} + \frac{\partial C}{\partial X} > 0,$$

$$\frac{\partial B}{\partial T} \equiv \frac{\partial D}{\partial T} + \frac{\partial C}{\partial T} \gtrless 0,$$

$$\frac{\partial B}{\partial \sigma^2} \equiv \frac{\partial D}{\partial \sigma^2} + \frac{\partial C}{\partial \sigma^2} \gtrless 0,$$

$$\frac{\partial B}{\partial r} \equiv \frac{\partial D}{\partial r} + \frac{\partial C}{\partial r} < 0.$$

If the value of the firm's assets, V, increases, both the "bond" and "call" portion of the convertible debt become more valuable. If the fraction of the firm received through conversion, α, increases, then the "call" portion of the bond becomes more valuable without reducing the "bond" portion. If the face value of the debt increases (from X to X'), the payoff to the bondholders increases. When the value of the firm's assets is between the old face value and the new minimum conversion value (when V^* is between X and X'/α) other payoffs are unaffected. If either the time to maturity or the variance rate increases, the "bond" portion becomes less valuable while the "call" portion becomes more valuable. Either effect can dominate. If the interest rate increases, the present value of the promised repayment is reduced. Since in this bond there is no required dollar outlay at conversion, this is the only effect that must be considered.

For an analysis of callable convertible bonds and convertible preferred stock, see Ingersoll (1977).

---

[11]This can be seen by using the above theorem with $\psi=1, \phi=1, \lambda=\exp(-rT), \gamma=0$ for the first integral and $\psi=1, \phi=\infty, \lambda=0, \gamma=-\exp(-rT)$ for the second. This yields (18).

[12]Again employ the above theorem with $\psi=1/\alpha, \phi=0, \lambda=\alpha\exp(-rT), \gamma=\exp(-rT)$.

3.3. The pricing of subordinated debt

Black and Cox (1976) analyze the pricing of subordinated debt. They assume that, instead of one debt issue, there are two, one senior and one junior. The issues contain restrictions against dividend payments until after both the bond issues are paid off. Both bonds are discount bonds and both mature at t^*. If the value of the firm at t^* is greater than the face value of the senior debt, X_s, then the senior bondholders receive their promised repayment; if not, the senior bondholders receive the assets of the firm and the junior bondholders and stockholders receive nothing. If the value of the firm is greater than the sum of the face value of the senior debt plus the face value of the junior debt, X_j, then the junior bondholders receive their promised payment, and the stockholders receive the residual. If the value of the firm at t^* is between X_s and $X_s + X_j$, the junior bondholders receive the difference between the value of the firm and the X_s. Thus, the boundary conditions for the equity and respective debt issues are

$$E^* = \max[0, V^* - (X_s + X_j)], \tag{33}$$

$$D_s^* = \min[V^*, X_s], \tag{34}$$

$$D_j^* = \max[\min(V^* - X_s, X_j), 0]. \tag{35}$$

Fig. 4.5 illustrates the payoff function to the equity and junior and senior bonds.

Again, (28) can be applied to define the appropriate differential equation with $E(V,t) \equiv f(V,t)$, $D_s(V,t) \equiv f(V,t)$, or $D_j(V,t) \equiv f(V,t)$, subject to (33), (34) or (35), respectively. These equations can again be solved using the above technique. In a risk neutral world, the value of the equity, senior debt, and junior debt can be expressed as

$$E = e^{-rT} \int_{X_s + X_j}^{\infty} (V^* - (X_s + X_j)) L'(V^*) dV^*, \tag{36}$$

$$D_s = e^{-rt} \left[\int_0^{X_s} V^* L'(V^*) dV^* + \int_{X_s}^{\infty} X_s L'(V^*) dV^* \right], \tag{37}$$

$$D_j = e^{-rT} \left[\int_{X_s}^{X_s + X_j} (V^* - X_s) L'(V^*) dV^* + \int_{X_s + X_j}^{\infty} X_j L'(V^*) c V^* \right]. \tag{38}$$

Inspection demonstrates that the pricing of the senior debt is unchanged. The value of the equity is unchanged with $X \equiv X_s + X_j$. Eq. (38) can be solved to

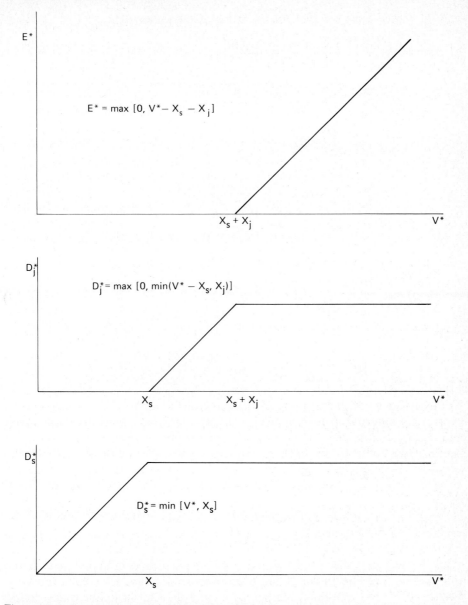

Figure 4.5. Dollar payoffs to a senior debt issue with a face value of X_s as a function of the value of the firm's assets at the maturity date of the bonds, $D_s = \min[V^*, X_s]$; dollar payoffs to a junior debt issue with a face value of X_j as a function of the value of the firm's assets, $D_j = \max[0, \min(V^* - X_s, X_j)]$; and dollar payoffs to the equity as a function of the value of the assets of the firm, $E^* = \max[0, V^* - X_s - X_j]$.

yield the closed-form solution for the value of the junior debt:

$$D_j = V \left[N \left\{ \frac{\ln(V/X_s) + (r + \sigma^2/2)T}{\sigma\sqrt{T}} \right\} \right.$$

$$\left. - N \left\{ \frac{\ln(V/(X_s + X_j)) + (r + \sigma^2/2)T}{\sigma\sqrt{T}} \right\} \right]$$

$$- X_s e^{-rT} \left[N \left\{ \frac{\ln(V/X_s) + (r - \sigma^2/2)T}{\sigma\sqrt{T}} \right\} \right.$$

$$\left. - N \left\{ \frac{\ln(V/(X_s + X_j)) + (r - \sigma^2/2)T}{\sigma\sqrt{T}} \right\} \right]$$

$$+ (X_s + X_j) e^{-rT} N \left\{ \frac{\ln(V/(X_s + X_j)) + (r - \sigma^2/2)T}{\sigma\sqrt{T}} \right\}. \tag{39}$$

In general form this can be expressed as

$$D_j = D_j(V, X_s, X_j, T, \sigma^2, r), \tag{40}$$

where

$$\frac{\partial D_j}{\partial V}, \frac{\partial D_j}{\partial X_j}, > 0; \qquad \frac{\partial D_j}{\partial X_s}, < 0 \quad \text{and} \quad \frac{\partial D_j}{\partial T}, \frac{\partial D_j}{\partial \sigma^2}, \frac{\partial D_j}{\partial r} \gtreqless 0.$$

The ambiguity of the response of the value of the junior debt with respect to the time to maturity of the bonds, the variance rate, and the riskless rate arises because of the dual debt/equity behavior of the instrument. If the value of the firm is "close to" the face value of the senior debt, the junior debt is virtually equivalent to an equity claim. Conversely, if the value of the firm is "close to" the sum of the face values of the junior and senior debt, then it behaves like a debt issue.

Absolute priority. Note that throughout the analysis of the firm's liabilities, the assumptions involving the distribution of the firm's assets among the claimants in the event of bankruptcy has been very clearcut. Here, if the value of the firm is below the face value of the senior debt, the senior debtholders get all the firm's assets and the junior debtholders and equity holders receive nothing. Warner (1977) has examined the law as it is applied to these issues and found that this is not strictly true. In bankruptcy, reorganization is often accompanied by issuance of new claims. The courts have consistently refused to consider the actual market value of the new claims as compared to the old and instead consider the claims satisfied if the face value of the new claim is not less than the face value of the old claim. This suggests that the above closed form solutions will overstate the value of the more senior debt and understate the value of the equity. The value of the junior debt may be over- or understated.

3.4. Pricing of warrants and rights

Smith (1977) employs the Black–Scholes (1973) option pricing framework to derive the equilibrium value for a warrant or rights issue under the standard assumptions plus:

(1) The only liabilities issued by the firm are its common stock and the warrants.

(2) The total proceeds if the warrants are exercised is X (the exercise price per share times the total number of shares sold through the rights issue). The warrants expire after T time periods. If the warrants are exercised, the shares sold through the offering will be a fraction, α, of the total number of shares outstanding ($\alpha \equiv Q_W / Q_S + Q_W$), where Q_W is the number of shares sold through the warrant issue and Q_S is the existing number of shares). Any assets acquired with the proceeds of the warrant issue are acquired at competitive prices.[13]

Given these assumptions, the value of the warrants at the expiration date, W^*, will be either zero, in which case the warrants will not be exercised or, if the warrants are valuable and are exercised, their value is their claim on the total assets of the firm, $\alpha(V^* + X)$ (where V^* is the value of the firm's current assets and X is the proceeds of the exercise of the rights) minus the payment the warrant holders must make, X:

$$W^* = \max[0, \alpha(V^* + X) - X], \tag{41}$$

where W^* is the value of the warrant issue at the expiration date of the issue, t^*, V^* is the value of the firm's assets at the expiration date of the issue, X is the proceeds to the firm of the exercise of the warrants, and α is the fraction of new shares issued through the warrant issue to the total shares of the firm (both old and new) presuming the warrants are exercised.

Given the above assumptions, (29) can again be applied with $W(V,t) \equiv f(V,t)$ to define the differential equation

$$\frac{\partial W}{\partial t} = \frac{1}{2} \frac{\partial^2 W}{\partial V^2} \sigma^2 V^2 + rV \frac{\partial W}{\partial V} - rW, \tag{42}$$

subject to the boundary condition in (41).

---

[13]This last assumption is necessary to avoid the problem of the dependence of the dynamic behavior of the stock price on the probability of the rights being exercised. This problem is similar to that described by Long (1974).

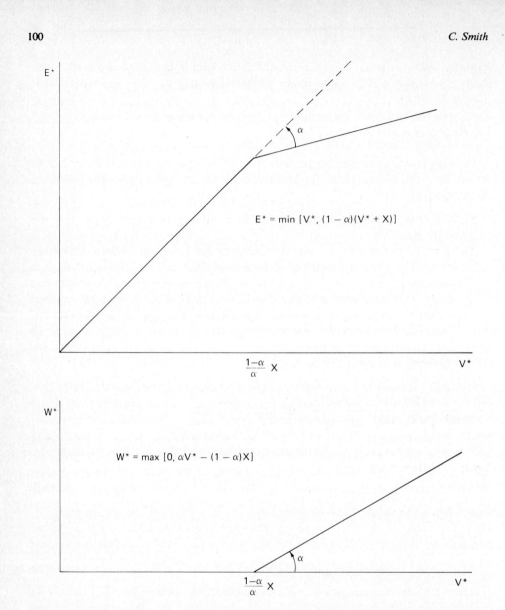

Figure 4.6. Dollar payoffs to a warrant (or rights) issue with exercise price X, representing a claim to a fraction α of the firm's equity, $W^* = \max[0, \alpha V^* - (1-\alpha)X]$; and dollar payoffs to equity as a function of the value of the assets of the firm, $E^* = \min[V^*, (1-\alpha)(V^* + X)]$.

To solve the equation, again assume that the market is composed of risk-neutral investors. In that case, the equilibrium rate of return on all assets will be equal; specifically, the expected rate of return on the firm, and the warrants will equal the riskless rate. Then the current warrants price must be the discounted terminal price:

$$W = e^{-rT} \int_{[(1-\alpha)/\alpha]X}^{\infty} [\alpha V^* - (1-\alpha)X] L'(V^*) dV^*, \tag{43}$$

where $L'(V^*)$ is the log normal density function. Fig. 4.6 illustrates the payoff function to the equity and warrant holders.

Eq. (43) can be solved employing the above theorem with $\psi = (1-\alpha)/\alpha$, $\phi = \infty$, $\lambda = \gamma e^{-rT}$, and $\gamma = (1-\alpha)e^{-rT}$ to yield:

$$W = \alpha V N \left\{ \frac{\ln(\alpha V/(1-\alpha)X) + (r+\sigma^2/2)T}{\sigma \sqrt{T}} \right\}$$

$$- e^{-rT}(1-\alpha)X N \left\{ \frac{\ln(\alpha V/(1-\alpha)X) + (r-\sigma^2/2)T}{\sigma \sqrt{T}} \right\}$$

$$\equiv c(\alpha V, T, (1-\alpha)X, \sigma^2, r) = W(V, T, X, \alpha, \sigma^2, r), \tag{44}$$

where

$$\frac{\partial W}{\partial V}, \frac{\partial W}{\partial T}, \frac{\partial W}{\partial \alpha}, \frac{\partial W}{\partial \sigma^2}, \frac{\partial W}{\partial r} > 0 \quad \text{and} \quad \frac{\partial W}{\partial X} < 0.$$

The indicated partial effects have intuitive interpretations. Increasing the value of the firm, decreasing the exercise price (holding the proportion of the firm's shares offered through the warrant issue constant), or increasing the proportion of the firm's shares offered through the warrant issue (holding the total proceeds of the issue constant) increase the expected payoff to the warrants and thus increase the current market value of the warrants. An increase in the time to expiration or the riskless rate lowers the present value of the exercise payment, and thus increases the value of the warrants. Finally, an increase in the time to expiration or the variance rate gives a higher probability of a large increase in the value of the firm and increases the value of the warrants.

4. The pricing of other contingent claims

4.1. The pricing of underwriting contracts

Smith (1977) analyzes the appropriate compensation to an underwriter for the risk he bears in underwriting the sale of additional equity of an all equity firm. In addition to the standard assumptions, make the following assumptions about the underwriting contract:

Underwriters submit a bid, $\hat{B}$, today which specifies that on the offer date, T time periods from now, the underwriter will pay $\hat{B}$ dollars and receive shares of stock representing fraction α of the total shares of the firm. He can sell the securities at the offer price and receive Ω, or (if the share price is below the offer price) at the market price, $\alpha(V^* + \hat{B})$. If his bid is accepted, he will be notified immediately.

Again, (29) can be employed where $f(V,t)$ is the function representing the value of the underwriting contract (i.e. $U = U(V,t)$). To be well posed, the appropriate boundary condition must be specified. At the offer date the under-writer will pay the firm $\hat{B}$ dollars. The shares which the underwriter receives represent a claim to a fraction γ of the total assets of the firm, $V^* + \hat{B}$. If the offer price is greater than the value of the shares, $\gamma(V^* + \hat{B})$, then the under-writer will sell the shares at the offer price and receive Ω. If, at the offer date the offer price is less than the value of the shares, the underwriter receives the value of the shares. Therefore, the boundary condition is that at the offer date the underwriting contract is worth the minimum of the market value of the shares minus the bid, $\hat{B}$, or the proceeds of the sale at the offer price minus the bid:

$$U^* = \min\left[\alpha(V^* + \hat{B}) - \hat{B}, \Omega - \hat{B} \right]. \tag{45}$$

Again, the above solution technique can be employed to solve (29) subject to (45). In a risk-neutral world, the expected value of the underwriting contract can be expressed as[14]

$$U = \int_{0}^{\Omega/\alpha - \hat{B}} \left[\alpha(V^* + \hat{B}) - \hat{B} \right] L'(V^*) dV^* + \int_{\Omega/\alpha - \hat{B}}^{\infty} \left[\Omega - \hat{B} \right] L'(V^*) dV^*. \tag{46}$$

Note that this can be rewritten as

$$U = \int_{0}^{\infty} \left[\alpha(V^* + \hat{B}) - \hat{B} \right] L'(V^*) dV^* - \int_{\Omega/\alpha - \hat{B}}^{\infty} \left[V^* - \left(\frac{\Omega}{\alpha} - \hat{B} \right) \right] L'(V^*) dV^*$$

$$\tag{47}$$

Eq. (47) can be solved for the risk-neutral case to yield[15]

$$U = e^{rT}\alpha V - (1 - \alpha)\hat{B} - e^{rT}\gamma VN \left\{ \frac{\ln(\alpha V/(\Omega - \alpha\hat{B})) + (r + \sigma^2/2)T}{\sigma\sqrt{T}} \right\}$$

$$+ (\Omega - \hat{B}\alpha)N \left\{ \frac{\ln(\alpha V/(\Omega - \alpha\hat{B})) + (r - \sigma^2/2)T}{\sigma\sqrt{T}} \right\}. \tag{48}$$

---

[14]Since the contract calls for the payment only at t^*, to find the current value of the underwriting contract does not require discounting.

[15]Use theorem 1 with $\psi X = 0$, $\phi X = \infty$, $\lambda S^* = \alpha V^*$, $\gamma X = (1 - \alpha)\hat{B}$. And for the second term, let $\psi X = \Omega/\alpha - \hat{B}, \phi X = \infty, \lambda S^* = \alpha V^*, \gamma X = (\Omega/\alpha) - \hat{B}$.

Eq. (48) is equivalent to a long position in the firm, a cash payment, and writing a call on α of the firm with an exercise price equal to $(\Omega - \alpha \hat{B})$:

$$U = e^{rT}\alpha V - (1-\alpha)B - e^{rT}c(\alpha V, T; \Omega - \alpha \hat{B}),$$

$$= e^{rT}\alpha V - (1-\alpha)B - e^{rT}\alpha c\left(V, T; \frac{\Omega}{\alpha} - \hat{B}\right). \tag{49}$$

If the process of preparing and submitting a bid is costless, then in a competitive equilibrium, the value of the underwriting contract must be zero.[16] Therefore, the bid which would represent a normal compensation for the risk he bears is implicitly defined by the equation[17]

$$\hat{B} - e^{rT}\frac{\alpha}{1-\alpha}\left[V - C\left(V, T; \frac{\Omega}{\alpha} - \hat{B}\right)\right] = 0. \tag{50}$$

The firm generally receives less than the market value of the stock[18] because, given the underwriting contract, if the equilibrium stock price at the offer date is above the offer price then the initial purchaser of the issue receives "rents"; he obtains the shares for less than the market value of the shares. Therefore, if the offer price in the underwriting agreement represents a binding constraint to the underwriter, then in a perfect market underwriting is a more expensive method of raising additional capital than are pre-emptive rights. Therefore, under these conditions underwriting would not be employed.

The above analysis implicitly assumes that the terms of the underwriting contract represent a binding constraint to the underwriter: if the security price is above the offer price, then the offer price presents a constraint to the underwriter and a pure profit opportunity to the potential investor. However, in a market without transactions costs, this should not be the case. If the security price is above the offer price there will be excess demand for the issue. To the extent that the underwriter can, through the rationing process, extract those profits, they will accrue to the underwriter rather than to the initial purchaser. Furthermore, if the underwriter can *systematically* extract those profits, then competitive underwriter bidding would insure that the profits were in fact garnered by the firm. In that case the offer price presents no effective constraint and the competitive bid becomes simply

$$\hat{B} = e^{rT}\left(\frac{\alpha}{1-\alpha}\right)V. \tag{51}$$

Therefore, if through tie-in sales or other means the offer price in an underwriting agreement can be circumvented, then underwriting is no more expensive a

---

[16]If this were not the case, arbitrage profits could be earned by acquiring an underwriting contract and establishing the above hedge.

[17]This equation implicitly defines the bid because $\hat{B}$ appears twice in the equation. The explicit solution for equilibrium bid can be found by standard numerical analysis techniques.

[18]A sufficient condition for the bid to be less than the market value of the shares is that $(1-\alpha)$ be less than e^{rT}. Since T is generally a matter of days, this condition should be met.

method of raising additional capital than a rights offering. However, indirect evidence suggests underwriters are unable to systematically extract these profits.[19]

4.2. The pricing of collateralized loans

The same analysis used to value the debt of a levered firm can also be employed to value collateralized loans. To derive an explicit pricing equation for the equity and debt, make the following assumptions:

(1) There are homogeneous expectations about the dynamic behavior of the value of the collateral. The distribution at the end of any finite time interval is log normal. The variance rate of return is constant.

(2) The collateral provides a continuous flow of service to the borrower. The net value of the flow of services, S, is a constant fraction, s, of the market value of the assets: $s = S/V$.

(3) The dynamic behavior of the value of the assets is independent of the value of the probability of bankruptcy.

(4) There are no costs to voluntary liquidation or bankruptcy. Bankruptcy is defined as the state in which the borrower's assets are less than the promised repayment amount of a maturing loan.

(5) Capital markets and the market for the collateral are perfect. There are no transactions costs or taxes. All participants have free access to all available information. Participants are price takers.

(6) There is a known constant riskless rate, r.

This loan contract is equivalent to the sale of the collateral to the lender by the borrower for a package containing: (1) the proceeds of the loan, D, (2) a lease which allows the borrower to use the assets over the life of the loan, plus (3) a call option to repurchase the assets at the maturity date of the loan, t^*, with an exercise price equal to the promised repayment amount of the loan, X. Thus, the value of the borrower's equity is like a call option plus a lease, and those techniques which have been developed to price options can also be employed to value loans.

Given these assumptions, Merton (1974) has shown that this contingent claim must satisfy the partial differential equation:

$$\frac{\partial D}{\partial t} = rD + (sV + rV)\frac{\partial D}{\partial V} - \tfrac{1}{2}\sigma^2 V^2 \frac{\partial^2 D}{\partial V^2}, \tag{52}$$

where sV is that portion of the flow accruing to this particular contingent claim, and σ^2 is the variance rate on the value of the assets.[19]

---

[19]For example, the underwriter's compensation for debt issues is significantly lower than for a comparable equity issue. Since the debt is less risky, the implicit option would be less valuable.

Employing the above solution technique, the value of the debt can be expressed as

$$D = e^{-rT} \left[\int_0^X V^* L'(V^*) dV^* + \int_X^\infty X L'(V^*) dV^* \right]. \tag{53}$$

Employing the above theorem, the closed-form solution to this integral, assuming that the total return on the collateral, $\rho + s$, equals the riskless rate, r, can be expressed as

$$D = V e^{-sT} N \left\{ \frac{-\ln(V/X) - (r - s + \sigma^2/2)T}{\sigma \sqrt{T}} \right\}$$

$$+ X e^{-rT} N \left\{ \frac{\ln(V/X) + (r - s - \sigma^2/2)T}{\sigma \sqrt{T}} \right\}, \tag{54}$$

$$= D(V, X, T, \sigma^2, s, r), \tag{55}$$

where

$$\frac{\partial D}{\partial V}, \frac{\partial D}{\partial X} > 0 \quad \text{and} \quad \frac{\partial D}{\partial T}, \frac{\partial D}{\partial \sigma^2}, \frac{\partial D}{\partial s}, \frac{\partial D}{\partial r} < 0.$$

The partial effects are the same as those for the corporate bonds with the addition of $\partial D/\partial s > 0$. If the net service flow (for example, for a mortgage loan, s would be the value of the rental services minus the maintenance, insurance and tax expenditures) increases, the expected price appreciation, ρ, falls. Thus, the expected value of the loan at the expiration of the loan will be less, and default is more likely. This decreases the value of the debt.

4.3. The pricing of leases

As was suggested above, the value of the borrower's equity in the collateral is equivalent to a call option to purchase the collateral with the exercise price equal to the promised repayment on the loan, plus a lease. Therefore, the value of the lease equals the value of the collateral minus the value of the debt minus the value of the call:

$$L = V - D - C$$

$$= V - \left[e^{-rT} \int_0^X V^* L'(V^*) dV^* + e^{-rT} \int_X^\infty X L'(V^*) dV^* \right]$$

$$- \left[e^{-rT} \int_X^\infty (V^* - X) L'(V^*) dV^* \right]$$

$$= V - \left[e^{-rT} \int_X^\infty V^* L'(V^*) dV^* \right]. \tag{56}$$

Notice that this equation has an intuitive interpretation: the value of the lease equals the value of the asset minus a claim on the value of the asset T periods from now. Eq. (56) can be solved to yield

$$L = V[1 - e^{-sT}]. \tag{57}$$

This explicitly points out that, given our assumptions, the value of the lease is independent of any financing decisions.

4.4. The pricing of insurance

Mayers and Smith (1977) and Merton (1977) examine the pricing of insurance contracts and loan guarantees. They assume

(1) The insurance contract calls for the payment of a premium, P, at the current date, t. If at the expiration date of the contract, t^*, the market value of the insured asset, V^*, is less than its insured value, X, then the insurance contract will pay the holder of the policy the difference, $X - V^*$. If the market value of the insured asset is greater than its insured value, then there is no payment.

Thus, at the expiration date the value of the insurance contract, P^*, will be the maximum of either the difference between the insured value and the market value of the asset, or zero:

$$P^* = \max[X - V^*], 0]. \tag{58}$$

This contract is equivalent to a European put option on the asset with an exercise price set at the insured value of the asset. Thus, with the following additional assumptions, the Black–Scholes put pricing solution also yields the general equilibrium price for the above insurance contract:

(2) There are homogeneous expectations about the dynamics of the value of the insured asset, V. The distribution of the value at the end of any finite time integral is log normal. The variance rate, σ^2, is constant.
(3) There is a known constant instantaneously riskless rate, r, which is the same for borrowers and lenders.
(4) Capital markets are perfect: there are no transactions costs or taxes and all traders have free and costless access to all available information. Borrowing and perfect short sales are allowed. Traders are price takers in the capital markets.
(5) Trading takes place continuously, price changes are continuous and assets are infinitely divisible.
(6) The insured asset generates no pecuniary or nonpecuniary flows.

The Black–Scholes European put pricing solution and thus the insurance pricing solution can be expressed as

$$P = - VN \left\{ \frac{-\ln(V/X) - (r + \sigma^2/2)T}{\sigma\sqrt{T}} \right\}$$

$$+ Xe^{-rT}N \left\{ \frac{-\ln(V/X) - (r - \sigma^2/2)T}{\sigma\sqrt{T}} \right\}, \tag{59}$$

where P is the insurance premium, V is the current market value of the insured asset, X is the insured value of the asset, T is the time to the expiration of the contract ($\equiv t^* - t$), r is the riskless rate of interest, σ^2 is the variance rate on V, and $N\{\cdot\}$ is the cumulative standard normal density function.

If the insured value of the property can be obtained on demand any time while the policy is in force, not just at the expiration date, then the policy is equivalent to an American put. Although the closed form solution to the American put is not known, the general form solution can be expressed as

$$P = P(V, X, T, \sigma^2, r), \tag{60}$$

where

$$\frac{\partial P}{\partial V}, \frac{\partial P}{\partial r} < 0; \qquad \frac{\partial P}{\partial X}, \frac{\partial P}{\partial T}, \frac{\partial P}{\partial \sigma^2} > 0.$$

These partial derivatives have intuitive interpretations: if the value of the insured asset, V, rises, the asset is less likely to have a value below the insured value. Thus, the insurance policy has a smaller expected payout and the required premium is less. If the insured value of the asset, X, is increased, the expected payout is higher and the required premium is higher. If the expiration date of the policy, T, is increased, the required premium increases, for it is more likely that the policy will be employed.[20] If the variance rate, σ^2, increases, there is a higher probability of a large negative change in the value of the asset and a large payout; thus the required premium rises. If the riskless interest rate, r, rises, the present value of any payoffs falls, thus the required premium falls.

The assumptions employed in deriving (59) are fairly restrictive; however, in the special case of mortgage insurance they are generally met. Assume that a loan is secured by a house and that the loan is to be repaid in one lump sum. The insurance premium is paid by the borrower at the origination of the loan and the policy agrees to pay the difference between the promised repayment and the market value of the house if the borrower defaults. If there were no default costs for the borrower, he would default if the market value of the house were less than the promised repayment at the expiration of the loan contract. Thus,

---

[20]For the simpler contract which was only exercisable at the expiration date (and for European puts) this sign is ambiguous. This is the only partial effect that differs in sign between the two cases.

for the lender a mortgage insurance policy is equivalent to a policy insuring that the value of the house, V^*, will be no less than the promised repayment amount of the loan (see fig. 4.7).

This approach to the analysis of insurance contracts points out that the traditional economic analysis of the supply of insurance is but a special case. It has been established that when events are independent competitively supplied insurance is priced at the "actuarily fair" price, i.e. the price is set equal to the discounted (at the riskless rate) expected payout. The analysis presented above suggests that this is only a special case. The option pricing equations of Black and Scholes (1973) are consistent with the continuous time capital asset pricing model. Specifically, the put is priced according to its marginal risk. Furthermore, the marginal risk of a put is related to the marginal risk of the underlying asset:

$$\beta_p = \varepsilon(P, V)\beta_V, \tag{61}$$

where β_p is the beta of the put, $\varepsilon(P, V)$ is the partial elasticity of the value of the put with respect to the value of the underlying asset, $(\partial P/\partial V)(V/P)$, and β_V is the beta of the underlying asset. Thus, since the elasticity is algebraically less than minus one, the beta of the insurance policy will be zero, and therefore the equilibrium rate of return on the insurance contract will equal the riskless rate, *only if* the marginal risk of the underlying asset is zero. This may be the case for life insurance, but probably not for mortgage or fire insurance. Any systematic risk is not insurable risk; the insuror must be compensated for bearing that risk.

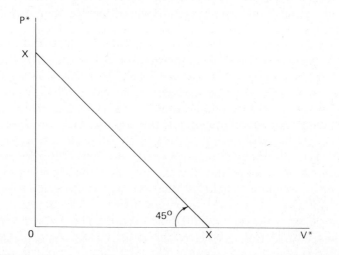

Figure 4.7. Dollar payoffs to a mortgage insurance policy where the promised repayment amount of the loan and the insured value of the loan is X, $P^* = \max[X - V^*, 0]$.

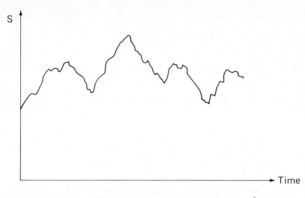

Figure 4.8. sample path of S where S follows an Itô process.

Appendix: An introduction to stochastic calculus

Itô's lemma is a differentiation rule by which functions of certain random variables can be differentiated — specifically, random variables whose movement can be described as an Itô process. An Itô process is a continuous Markov process in continuous time.[21] The sample path of such a process will be continuous (can be drawn without picking the pen up from the paper). Fig. 4.8 illustrates the sample path of a random variable, S, which follows an Itô process through time.

All Itô processes can be prepresented as[22]

$$dS = \mu(S,t)\,dt + \sigma(S,t)\,dZ, \tag{A.1}$$

where dZ is introduced as the Itô differential of a standard Gauss–Wiener process. In many recent finance articles, the return to financial assets is expressed as a differential equation like (A.1). For the understanding of the equation and its implications, it is necessary to understand the meaning of the differential dZ and observe its peculiarities.

If, for example, $q(t)$ is an ordinary (nonrandom) variable, then for any real number k, $k > 1$:[23]

$$(dq(t))^k = 0. \tag{A.2}$$

---

[21]A Markov process depends at most on the most recent observation.

[22]This can be generated so that S, μ, and σ, are N vectors and $dZ(t)$ is an N vector of standard normal random variables. In that case $Z(t)$ is a multidimensional Wiener process.

[23]This is not strictly true. More precisely what is meant is that if differentials of magnitude $dq(t)$ are the magnitudes of interest, then $(dq(t))^k$ for $k > 1$ will be of a smaller order of magnitude and may be ignored. For the purposes of this exposition, the above, somewhat imprecise, terminology will be employed.

However, it will be shown that a similar statement about dZ is not true. In fact, if $Y = F(t, Z)$ is a function of t and Z, then

$$dY = \left(\frac{\partial F}{\partial t} + \frac{1}{2} \frac{\partial^2 F}{\partial Z(t)^2} \right) dt + \frac{\partial F}{\partial Z(t)} dZ(t). \tag{A.3}$$

While if $y = G(t, q)$ is a function of t and a nonrandom variable, q, the differential is

$$dy = \frac{\partial G}{\partial t} dt + \frac{\partial G}{\partial q(t)} dq(t). \tag{A.4}$$

Eq. (A.4) is a well-known result from ordinary calculus, while (A.3) is a special case of Itô's lemma from stochastic calculus.

Unfortunately, references on stochastic calculus are often written in a form inaccessible to the nonspecialist interested in the application of these concepts. This note represents an attempt to reintroduce these concepts in a simplified and intuitive way.

First, recall two computationally useful results from statistics.

Result 1. Let X be a normal random variable with probability distribution function

$$f(x) = \frac{1}{\sqrt{(2\pi)}\sigma} \exp\left[-(x - x_0)^2 / 2\sigma^2 \right]. \tag{A.5}$$

Then for any positive integer n,[24]

$$E\left[(X - x_0)^n \right] = \begin{cases} (n-1)!!\sigma^n, & \text{if } n \text{ is even,} \\ 0, & \text{if } n \text{ is odd.} \end{cases} \tag{A.6}$$

Result 2. Let X be a random variable with distribution function $f_1(x)$ and let $M_n = E(X^n)$, for any positive integer n, let Y be a random variable with conditional distribution function[25]

$$f_2(y|x) = f_2(y|X = x) = \frac{1}{\sqrt{(2\pi)}\sigma} \exp\left[-(y - x)^2 / 2\sigma^2 \right]. \tag{A.7}$$

For any integer $k \geqslant 0$ the following are true:

Result 2a. $\quad E(YX^k) = M_{k+1}$ (A.8)

---

[24]The double factorial notation means multiply all the odd numbers: $R!! = R(R-2)(R-4)\cdots 3 \cdot 1$, where R is odd.

[25]Note that the conditional mean of Y is x: $E(y|x) = x$.

Proof.
$$E(YX^k) = \int\int_{x\dot{y}} [yf_2(y|x)\,dy]x^k f_1(x)\,dx$$

$$= \int_x E[y|x]x^k f_1(x)\,dx$$

$$= \int_x xx^k f_1(x)\,dx$$

$$= M_{k+1}.$$

Result 2b. $E[Y^2X^k] = \sigma^2 M_k + M_{k+2}.$ (A.9)

Proof.
$$E[Y^2X^k) = \int\int_{x\dot{y}} [y^2 f_2(y|x)\,dy]x^k f_1(x)\,dx$$

$$= \int_x E[y^2|x]x^k f_1(x)\,dx$$

$$= \int_x (\sigma^2 + x^2)x^k f_1(x)\,dx$$

$$= M_k\sigma^2 + M_{k+2}.$$

Note:
$$\sigma^2 = E[((y|x) - x)^2]$$
$$= E[(y^2|x) - 2x(y|x) + x^2]$$
$$= E[y^2|x] - 2xE[y|x] + x^2$$
$$= E[y^2|x] - 2xx + x^2$$
$$= E[y^2|x] - x^2.$$

Therefore: $E[y^2|x] = \sigma^2 + x^2.$

Result 2c. $E[Y^3X^k] = 3\sigma^2 M_{k+1} + M_{k+3}.$ (A.10)

Proof.
$$E[Y^3X^k] = \int\int_{x\dot{y}} [y^3 f_2(y|x)\,dy]x^k f_1(x)\,dx$$

$$= \int_x E[y^3|x]x^k f_1(x)\,dx$$

$$= \int_x (3\sigma^2 x + x^3)x^k f_1(x)\,dx$$

$$= 3\sigma^2 M_{k+1} + M_{k+3}.$$

Note: $\sigma^3 = E[(y|x) - x)^3]$

$$= E[(y^3|x) - 3(y^2|x)x + 3(y|x)x^2 - x^3]$$
$$= E[y^3|x] - 3xE[y^2|x] + 3x^2E[y|x] - x^3$$
$$= E[y^3|x] - 3x(\sigma^2 + x^2) + 3x^3 - x^3$$
$$= E[y^3|x] - 3x\sigma^2 - x^3.$$

Therefore: $E[y^3|x] = 3x\sigma^2 + x^3 + \sigma^3$
But from (A.6), $\sigma^3 = 0$. Then, $E[y^3|x] = 3x\sigma^2 + x^3$.

Result 2d. $\quad E[Y^4X^k] = \sigma^4 M_k + 6\sigma^2 M_{k+2} + M_{k+4}.$ $\qquad$ (A.11)

Proof. $\quad E[Y^4X^k] = \int_x \int_y [y^4 f_2(y|x)\,dy]x^k f_1(x)\,dx$

$$= \int_x E[y^4|x]x^k f_1(x)\,dz$$

$$= \int_x (3\sigma^4 + 6x^2\sigma^2 + x^4)x^k f_1(x)\,dx$$

$$= 3\sigma^4 M_k + 6\sigma^2 M_{k+2} + M_{k+4}.$$

Note: $3\sigma^4 = E[((y|x) - x)^4]$

$$= E[(y^4|x) - 4(y^3|x)x + 6(y^2|x)x^2 - 4(y|x)x^3 + x^4]$$
$$= E[y^4|x] - 4xE[y^3|x] + 6x^2E[y^2|x] - 4x^3E[y|x] + x^4$$
$$= E[y^4|x] - 4x(3x\sigma^2 + x^3) + 6x^2(\sigma^2 + x^2) - 4x^3x + x^4$$
$$= E[y^4|x] - 6x^2\sigma^2 - x^4.$$

Therefore: $E[y^4|x] = 3\sigma^4 + 6x^2\sigma^2 + x^4$.

In the simplest terms, a standard Gauss–Wiener process can be defined as a stochastic process $Z(t)$, such that for any t and t_0, where $t > t_0$, the conditional distribution function of $Z(t)$, given $Z(t_0)$, is given by[26]

$$f(z|z_0) = f_{Z(t)}(z|Z(t_0) = z_0) \qquad (A.12)$$

$$= \frac{1}{\sqrt{(2\pi)(t - t_0)}} \exp\left[-(z - z_0)^2/2(t - t_0)\right]. \qquad (A.13)$$

For such a process, the Itô differential, $dZ(t)$ is defined as

$$dZ(t) = \lim_{h \to 0} (Z(t + h) - Z(t)), \qquad h > 0, \qquad (A.14)$$

---

[26]Note that the variance of Z is $(t - t_0)$.

or in terms of the differential dt as

$$dZ(t) = Z(t + dt) - Z(t), \qquad dt > 0. \tag{A.15}$$

Proposition 1. Let $dZ(t)$ be as defined in (15), then

$$E[dZ(t)] = 0 \tag{A.16}$$

and

$$E[dZ(t)^2] = dt. \tag{A.17}$$

Proof. (A.16) follows from (A.13) and (A.6). To show (A.17) observe that

$$E[dZ(t)^2] = E[(Z(t + dt) - Z(t))^2]$$
$$= E[Z(t + dt)^2] - 2E[Z(t + dt)Z(t)] + E[Z(t)^2]. \tag{A.18}$$

If $M_0 = 1$ and $M_k = E[Z(t)^k]$, for k a positive integer then from (A.9): $E[Y^2 X^k]$ $= \sigma^2 M_k + M_{k+2}$. Let $Y = Z(t + dt)$ and $X^0 = 1$. Then

$$E[Z(t + dt)^2] = dt + M_2. \tag{A.19}$$

From (A.8): $E[YX^k] = M_2$. Let $Y = Z(t + dt)$ and $X^k = Z(t)^1$. Then:

$$E[Z(t + dt)Z(t)] = M_2. \tag{A.20}$$

Finally, from (5):

$$E[Z(t)^2] = M_2. \tag{A.21}$$

Substituting (A.19)–(A.21) into (A.18) yields:

$$E[dZ^2] = (dt + M_2) - 2M_2 + M_2$$
$$= dt.$$

Thus (A.17) is proved.

Proposition 2. Let $dZ(t)$ be as defined above, then $dZ(t)^2$ is nonrandom and in fact

$$dZ(t)^2 = dt. \tag{A.22}$$

Proof. To prove proposition 2, it will first be shown that the variance of $dZ(t)^2 = 0$. If the variance is zero then $dZ(t)^2$ is nonrandom and the expected value, $E[dZ(t)^2]$, is $dZ(t)^2$. But first, a useful intermediate result will be proved:

$$E[dZ(t)^4] = 0. \tag{A.23}$$

To show this, substitute from (A.15):

$$E[dZ(t)^4] = E[(Z(t+dt) - Z(t))^4]$$

$$= [Z(t+dt)^4] - 4E[Z(t+dt)^3 Z(t)] + 6E[Z(t+dt)^2 Z(t)^2]$$

$$- 4E[Z(t+dt)Z(t)^3] + E[Z(t)^4]. \quad\quad (A.24)$$

From (A.11): $E(Y^4 X^k) = 3\sigma^4 M_k + 6\sigma^2 M_{k+2} + M_{k+4}$. Let $Y = Z(t+dt)$ and $X^k = Z(t)^0$. Then:

$$E[Z(t+dt)^4] = 3dt^2 + 6M_2 dt + M_4. \quad\quad (A.25)$$

From (A.10): $E(Y^3 X^k) = 3\sigma^2 M_{k+1} + M_{k+3}$. Let $Y = Z(t+dt)$ and $X^k = Z(t)^1$. Then:

$$E[Z(t+dt)^3 Z(t)] = 3M_2 dt + M_4. \quad\quad (A.26)$$

From (A.9): $E(Y^2 X^k) = \sigma^2 M_k + M_{k+2}$. Let $Y = Z(t+dt)$ and $X^k = Z(t)^2$. Then:

$$E[Z(t+dt)^2 Z(t)^2] = M_2 dt + M_4. \quad\quad (A.27)$$

From (A.8): $E(YX^k) = M_{k+1}$. Let $Y = Z(t+dt)$ and $X^k = Z(t)^3$. Then:

$$E[Z(t+dt)Z(t)^3] = M_4. \quad\quad (A.28)$$

Finally, from (A.5):

$$E[Z(t)^4] = M_4. \quad\quad (A.29)$$

Substituting (A.25)–(A.29) into (A.24) and noting from (A.2), $dt^2 = 0$, yields (A.23):

$$E[dZ(t)^4] = (3dt^2 + 6M_2 dt + M_4) - 4(3M_2 dt + M_4)$$

$$+ 6(M_2 dt + M_4) - 4M_4 + M_4$$

$$= 0. \quad\quad (A.30)$$

Now, to see that $dZ(t)^2$ is nonrandom, notice that the variance of $dZ(t)^2$ is zero.

$$\text{var}[dZ(t)^2] = E[(dZ(t)^2 - E[dZ(t)^2])^2]$$

$$= E[dZ(t)^4] - 2E[dZ(t)^2]^2 + E[dZ(t)^2]^2.$$

From (A.23): $E[dZ(t)^4] = 0$; from (A.17): $E[dZ(t)^2] = dt$; and from (A.2): $dt^2 = 0$. Substituting into the above expression yields $\text{var}[dZ(t)^2] = 0$. Consequently, $dZ(t)^2$ is a nonrandom variable, and for nonrandom variables the value of the variable equals the expected value of the variable. From (A.17): $E[dZ(t)^2] = dt$; therefore, since $\text{var}[dZ(t)^2] = 0$, $dZ(t)^2 = E[dZ(t)^2] = dt$. This proves proposition 2.

Proposition 3. For any integer $k \geqslant 3$:

$$E\left[dZ(t)^k\right] = 0. \qquad (A.31)$$

Proof. From (A.6), for all odd powers, $E[dZ(t)^k]=0$. Therefore, it must be shown that $E[dZ(t)^k]=0$ for $k \geqslant 4$ where k is even. For $k \geqslant 4$ and k even:

$$E\left[dZ(t)^k\right] = E\left[\left(dZ(t)^2\right)^{k/2}\right].$$

From (A.22):

$$E\left[dZ(t)^k\right] = E\left[dt^{k/2}\right].$$

If $k \geqslant 4$, then $(k/2) \geqslant 2$, thus, from (A.2):

$$E\left[dZ(t)^k\right] = 0.$$

This proves proposition 3.

Proposition 4. The stochastic process $dZ(t)$ is stationary, since for all t, $dZ(t)$ have the same statistics.

Proposition 5. For $dZ(t)$ as defined in (A.15):

$$dZ(t)dt = 0. \qquad (A.32)$$

Proof. It will be first shown that the variance of $(dZ(t))(dt)$ is zero, implying that $(dZ(t))(dt)$ is nonstochastic. Then for a nonstochastic variable, the value equals the expected value:

$$\begin{aligned}
\mathrm{var}\left[dZ(t)dt\right] &= E\left[\left(dZ(t)dt - E\left[dZ(t)dt\right]\right)^2\right] \\
&= E\left[dZ(t)^2 dt^2\right] - 2E\left[dZ(t)dt\right]^2 + E\left[dZ(t)dt\right]^2 \\
&= dt^2 E\left[dZ(t)^2\right] - dt^2 E\left[dZ(t)\right]^2.
\end{aligned}$$

From (A.2): $dt^2 = 0$; consequently

$$\mathrm{var}\left[dZ(t)dt\right] = 0.$$

The expected value of $(dZ(t))(dt)$ is

$$E\left[dZ(t)dt\right] = dt E\left[dZ(t)\right].$$

From (A.16): $E[dZ(t)]=0$. Therefore

$$E\left[dZ(t)dt\right] = 0.$$

Since the variance of $(dZ(t))(dt)$ is zero, $dZ(t)dt$ equals its expected value:

$$dZ(t)dt = E\left[dZ(t)dt\right] = 0.$$

Thus, proposition 5 is proved.

Proposition 6. Let $t>s$. Then $dZ(t)$ and $dZ(s)$ are uncorrelated, i.e.

$$E[dZ(t)dZ(s)]=0. \tag{A.33}$$

Proof. Let h be a real number, $0<h<t-s$. Let $M_k = E[Z(s)^k]$ and $M'_k = E[Z(s+h)^k]$. Then, from (A.8), we have:

$$E[Z(t)Z(s)]=M_2, \tag{A.34}$$

$$E[Z(t+h)Z(s)]=M_2, \tag{A.35}$$

$$E[Z(t)Z(s+h)]=M'_2, \tag{A.36}$$

$$E[Z(t+h)Z(s+h)]=M'_2. \tag{A.37}$$

Then expanding $E[dZ(t)dZ(s)]$ and substituting (A.34)–(A.37) yields

$$\begin{aligned}
E[dZ(t)dZ(s)] &= E[(Z(t+h)-Z(t))(Z(s+h)-Z(s))] \\
&= E[Z(t+h)Z(s+h)] - E[Z(t+h)Z(s)] \\
&\quad - E[Z(t)Z(s+h)] + E[Z(t)Z(s)] \\
&= M'_2 - M_2 - M'_2 + M_2 \\
&= 0. \tag{A.38}
\end{aligned}$$

This proves (A.33).

Let $X(t)$ and $X_2(t)$ be two Gauss–Wiener processes. Unless $dX_1(t)$ and $dX_2(t)$ are uncorrelated, $E[dX_1(t)dX_2(t)]$ will be nonzero. In that case its value can be computed. However, before that result is derived the following useful intermediate result will be proved.

Proposition 7. If $Z_1(t)$ and $Z_2(t)$ are standard Gauss–Wiener processes and the differentials $dZ_1(t)$ and $dZ_2(t)$ are defined as in (A.15), then $[dZ_1(t)dZ_2(t)]$ is nonrandom, and can be expressed as

$$dZ_1(t)dZ_2(t)=\rho_t dt, \tag{A.39}$$

where ρ_t is the correlation coefficient between $dZ_1(t)$ and $dZ_2(t)$.

Proof. The expected value of $dZ_1(t)dZ_2(t)$ is

$$\begin{aligned}
E[dZ_1(t)dZ_2(t)] &= E[dZ_1(t)]E[dZ_2(t)] + \operatorname{cov}[dZ_1(t),dZ_2(t)] \\
&= 0 + \operatorname{cov}[dZ_1(t),dZ_2(t)].
\end{aligned}$$

The covariance between $dZ_1(t)$ and $dZ_2(t)$ can be written

$$\begin{aligned}
\operatorname{cov}[dZ_1(t),dZ_2(t)] &= \rho_t \sqrt{\{\operatorname{var}[dZ_1(t)]\}} \sqrt{\{\operatorname{var}[dZ_2(t)]\}} \\
&= \rho_t \sqrt{(dt)}\sqrt{(dt)} \\
&= \rho_t\, dt. \tag{A.40}
\end{aligned}$$

Therefore:

$$E[dZ_1(t)dZ_2(t)] = \rho_t dt.$$

The variance of $dZ_1(t)dZ_2(t)$ is zero:

$$\text{var}[dZ_1(t)dZ_2(t)] = E[(dZ_1(t)dZ_2(t) - E[dZ_1(t)dZ_2(t)])^2]$$

$$= E[dZ_1(t)^2 dZ_2(t)^2] - E[dZ_1(t)dZ_2(t)]^2$$

$$= dt^2 - \rho_t^2 dt^2$$

$$= 0.$$

Since the variance is zero, then $dZ_1(t)dZ_2(t)$ is nonstochastic and its value equals its expected value. Therefore

$$dZ_1(t)dZ_2(t) = \rho dt, \tag{A.41}$$

thus proving (A.39).

There is no reason to believe that ρ_t is independent of t. If for all $t, \rho_t = \rho$, then $dZ_1(t)$ and $dZ_2(t)$ are jointly stationary.

Another observation which should be noted is that regardless of whether $dZ_1(t)dZ_2(t)$ is zero or not, for $t \neq s, dZ_1(s)dZ_2(t)$ could be either zero or nonzero. In typical finance applications, t usually represents time and $dZ_1(t)$ and $dZ_2(t)$ are the returns for two assets in period t. Typical finance applications assume that $dZ_1(s)$ and $dZ_2(t)$ for $t \neq s$ are uncorrelated. It should be stressed that this does not follow from the definition of $dZ_1(t)$ and $dZ_2(t)$, nor does it follow from our knowledge of $E[dZ_1(t)dZ_2(t)]$. If the economics of a problem suggests that $dZ_1(s)dZ_2(t) = 0$ for $t \neq s$, then it should be explicitly stated. If it is not zero, then[27]

$$dZ_1(s)dZ_2(t) = \rho_{st} dt. \tag{A.42}$$

In general, ρ is a function of s and t. If it is only a function of $t - s$ (or $s - t$) or it is constant, then it should be so stated.

Proposition 8. If $X(t)$ is a nonstandard Gauss–Wiener process such that

$$dX(t) = \mu(X,t)dt + \sigma(X,t)dZ(t), \tag{A.43}$$

where $Z(t)$ is a standard Gauss–Wiener process, then the expected value of $dX(t)$ is

$$E[dX(t)] = \mu(X,t)dt, \tag{A.44}$$

and the variance of $dX(t)$ is

$$\text{var}[dX(t)] = \sigma^2(X,t)dt. \tag{A.45}$$

---

[27]For example, let $Z_1(s) = Z_2(t)$ (i.e. let Z_1 be Z_2 lagged by $s - t$). Then $dZ_1(s)dZ_2(t) = dt$ because by construction $\rho_{st} = 1$.

Proof. From (A.16), $E[dZ(t)] = 0$. Thus, (A.44) follows immediately. The variance of $dX(t)$ can be expressed as

$$\text{var}[dX(t)] = E\Big[\big(\mu(X,t)dt + \sigma(X,t)dZ(t)$$
$$- E[\mu(X,t)dt + \sigma(X,t)dZ(t)]\big)^2\Big]$$
$$= E\big[(\mu(X,t)dt + \sigma(X,t)dZ(t) - \mu(X,t)dt)^2\big]$$
$$= E[\sigma(X,t)dZ(t)]^2$$
$$= \sigma^2(X,t)dt.$$

Thus, (A.45) is proved.

Proposition 9. If $X_1(t)$ and $X_2(t)$ are nonstandard Gauss–Wiener processes such that

$$dX_j(t) = \mu_j(X_1, X_2, t)dt + \sigma_j(X_1, X_2, t)dZ_j,$$

then

$$dX_1(t)dX_2(t) = \rho_t\sigma_1\sigma_2\, dt. \tag{A.46}$$

Proof. The expected value of $dX_1(t)dX_2(t)$ is

$$E[dX_1(t)dX_2(t)] = E[dX_1(t)]E[dX_2(t)] + \text{cov}[dX_1(t), dX_2(t)]$$
$$= \mu_1\mu_2 dt^2 + \text{cov}[dX_1(t), dX_2(t)]$$
$$= \text{cov}[dX_1(t), dX_2(t)].$$

The covariance between $dX_1(t)$ and $dX_2(t)$ can be written as

$$\text{cov}[dX_1(t), dX_2(t)] = \rho_t\sqrt{\{\text{var}[dX_1(t)]\}}\sqrt{\{\text{var}[dX_2(t)]\}}$$
$$= \rho_t\sqrt{(\sigma_1^2 dt)}\sqrt{(\sigma_2^2 dt)}$$
$$= \rho_t\sigma_1\sigma_2 dt.$$

Therefore

$$E[dX_1(t)dX_2(t)] = \rho_t\sigma_1\sigma_2 dt.$$

The variance of $dX_1(t)dX_2(t)$ is zero:

$$\text{var}[dX_1(t)dX_2(t)] = E\big[(dX_1(t)dX_2(t) - E[dX_1(t)dX_2(t)])^2\big]$$
$$= E[dX_1(t)^2 dX_2(t)^2] - E[dX_1(t)dX_2(t)]^2$$
$$= \mu_1 dt\mu_2 dt - (\rho_t\sigma_1\sigma_2 dt)^2$$
$$= 0.$$

Therefore, since the variance of $dX_1(t)dX_2(t)$ is zero $dX_1(t)dX_2(t)$ equals the expected value of $dX_1(t)dX_2(t)$. This proves (A.46).

Itô's lemma. Let F be a twice differentiable nonrandom function of t and two stochastic processes $X_1(t)$ and $X_2(t)$ where

$$dX_j(t) = \mu_j(X_1, X_2, t)\,dt + \sigma_j(X_1, X_2, t)\,dZ_j.$$

And if (A.46) holds, then

$$dF[t, X_1(t), X_2(t)] = \left(\frac{\partial F}{\partial t} + \frac{1}{2}\frac{\partial^2 F}{\partial X_1^2}\sigma_1^2 + \frac{\partial^2 F}{\partial X_1 \partial X_2}\rho_t\sigma_1\sigma_2 + \frac{1}{2}\frac{\partial^2 F}{\partial X_2^2}\sigma_2 \right)dt$$

$$+ \frac{\partial F}{\partial X_1}dX_1(t) + \frac{\partial F}{\partial X_2}dX_2(t). \tag{A.47}$$

Proof. If $X_1(t)$ and $X_2(t)$ were nonrandom functions, then from ordinary calculus we know that

$$dF = \frac{\partial F}{\partial t}dt + \frac{\partial F}{\partial X_1}dX_1 + \frac{\partial F}{\partial X_2}dX_2 + \frac{1}{2}\frac{\partial^2 F}{\partial t^2}dt^2 + \frac{1}{2}\frac{\partial^2 F}{\partial X_1^2}dX_1^2$$

$$+ \frac{1}{2}\frac{\partial^2 F}{\partial X_2^2}dX_2^2 + \frac{\partial^2 F}{\partial t\partial X_1}dt\,dX_1 + \frac{\partial^2 F}{\partial t\partial X_2}dt\,dX_2 + \frac{\partial^2 F}{\partial X_1\partial X_2}dX_1\,dX_2.$$

$$\tag{A.48}$$

Of course, from (A.2) it follows that all but the first three terms of (A.48) are zero. However, for $X_1(t)$ and $X_2(t)$ stochastic processes, eqs. (A.22), (A.32), and (A.42) must be used for terms containing dX_j^2, $dX_j\,dt$, and $dX_1\,dX_2$:

$$dF = \frac{\partial F}{\partial t}dt + \frac{\partial F}{\partial X_1}dX_1 + \frac{\partial F}{\partial X_2}dX_2 + 0 + \frac{1}{2}\frac{\partial^2 F}{\partial X_1^2}\sigma^2 dt$$

$$+ \frac{1}{2}\frac{\partial^2 F}{\partial X_2^2}\sigma_2^2 dt + 0 + 0 + \frac{\partial^2 F}{\partial X_1\partial X_2}\rho_t\sigma_1\sigma_2 dt.$$

Rearrangement of terms yields (A.47). The case of more or less than two stochastic processes can be treated similarly.

Example: the Black–Scholes option pricing model. Assume that the returns to the stock are represented by

$$dS/S = \mu\,dt + \sigma\,dZ. \tag{A.49}$$

Then

$$dS = \mu S\,dt + \sigma S\,dZ. \tag{A.50}$$

From (A.44) the expected value of dS is

$$E[dS] = \mu S\,dt. \tag{A.51}$$

From (A.45) the variance of dS is

$$\mathrm{var}[dS] = \sigma^2 S^2\,dt. \tag{A.52}$$

Let the value of a call option written on the stock be a function of the stock price and time

$$C = C(S, t).$$ (A.53)

Then (A.47) can be used to express the change in the call price[28]

$$dC = \left(\frac{\partial C}{\partial t} + \frac{1}{2} \frac{\partial^2 F}{\partial S^2} S^2 \sigma^2 \right) dt + \frac{\partial F}{\partial S} dS.$$ (A.54)

References

Black, F. and J. C. Cox (1976) "Valuing Corporate Securities: Some Effects of Bond Indenture Provisions", *Journal of Finance* 31, 351–367.

Black, F. and M. Scholes (1973) "The Pricing of Options and Corporate Liabilities", *Journal of Political Economy* 81, 637–659.

Cox, J. C. and I. A. Ross (1976) "The Valuation of Options for Alternative Stochastic Processes", *Journal of Financial Economics* 3, 145–166.

Friedman, A. (1975) *Stochastic Differential Equations and Applications* (Academic Press, New York).

Galai, D. and R. W. Masulis (1976) "The Option Pricing Model and the Risk Factor of the Stock", *Journal of Financial Economics* 3, 53–81.

Geske, R. (1977) "The Valuation of Corporate Liabilities as Compound Options", *Journal of Financial and Quantitative Analysis* 12, 541–552.

Jensen, M. C. and W. H. Meckling (1976) "Theory of the Firm: Managerial Behavior, Agency Costs and Capital Structure, *Journal of Financial Economics* 3, 305–360.

Ingersoll, J. (1976) "A Theoretical and Empirical Investigation of the Dual Purpose Funds: An Application of Contingent Claims Analysis", *Journal of Financial Economics* 3, 83–123.

Ingersoll, J. E. (1977) "A Contingent-Claims Valuation of Convertible Securities", *Journal of Financial Economics* 4, 289–322.

Long, J. B. (1974) "Discussion", *Journal of Finance* 29, 485–488.

Mayers, D. and C. W. Smith (1977) "Toward a Theory of Financial Contracts: The Insurance Policy", unpublished, University of Rochester.

Merton, R. C. (1973) "Theory of Rational Option Pricing", *Bell Journal of Economics and Management Science* 4, 141–183.

Merton, R. C. (1974) "On the Pricing of Corporate Debt: The Risk Structure of Interest Rates", *Journal of Finance* 29, 449–470.

Merton, R. C. (1976) "Option Pricing When Underlying Stock Returns Are Discontinuous", *Journal of Financial Economics* 3, 125–144.

[28]Note that (A.54) is the same expression that is derived if $C(S+\Delta S; t+\Delta t)$ is expanded using a Taylor series with the series truncated after the $(dS)^2$ term:

$$C(S+\Delta S, t+\Delta t) = C(S, t) + \frac{\partial C}{\partial t} \Delta t + \frac{\partial C}{\partial S} \Delta S + \frac{1}{2} \frac{\partial^2 C}{\partial S^2} (\Delta S)^2 \ldots.$$

Therefore

$$\Delta C = C(S+\Delta S, t+\Delta t) - C(S, t)$$

$$= \frac{\partial C}{\partial t} \Delta t + \frac{\partial C}{\partial S} \Delta S + \frac{1}{2} \frac{\partial^2 C}{\partial S^2} (\Delta S)^2 + \ldots.$$

Utilizing the above multiplication rules to express $(\Delta S)^2$ as $\sigma^2 S^2 \Delta t$ yields (A.54). This suggests that for short time intervals when examining functions of random variables which follow an Itô process, that quadratic approximations are exact.

Merton, R. C. (1977) "An Analytic Derivation of the Cost of Deposit Insurance and Loan Guarantees: An Application of Modern Option Pricing Theory", *Journal of Banking and Finance* 1, 3–12.

Mikkleson, W. (1978) "An Examination of the Agency Cost of Debt Rationale for Convertible Bonds and Warrants", unpublished, University of Rochester.

Modigliani, F. and M. A. Miller (1958) "The Cost of Capital, Corporation Finance, and the Theory of Investment", *American Economic Review* 48, 261–297.

Myers, S. C. (1977) "Determinants of Corporate Borrowing", *Journal of Financial Economics* 5, 147–175.

Smith, C. W. (1976) "Option Pricing: A Review", *Journal of Financial Economics* 3, 3–51.

Smith, C. W. (1977) "Alternative Methods for Raising Capital: Rights Versus Underwritten Offerings", *Journal of Financial Economics* 5, 273–307.

Smith, C. W. and J. B. Warner (1978) "On Financial Contracts and Optimal Capital Structure: An Analysis of Bond Covenants", unpublished, University of Rochester.

Sprenkle, C. M. (1964) "Warrant Prices as Indicators of Expectations and Preferences", in: P. Cootner, ed., *The Random Character of Stock Market Prices* (MIT Press, Cambridge, Mass.) pp. 412–474.

Warner, J. B. (1977) "Bankruptcy, Absolute Priority, and the Pricing of Risky Debt Claims", *Journal of Financial Economics* 4, 239–276.

Chapter 5

THE TERM STRUCTURE OF INTEREST RATES: THEORIES AND EVIDENCE

CHARLES R. NELSON
University of Washington

1. Introduction

The yield or interest rate quoted on a bond depends on numerous characteristics including the term to maturity, coupon size, tax treatment, default risk, transactions costs, and the like. The relationship between maturity and yield, holding other factors constant, is called the term structure of interest rates and the literature dealing with the term structure is one of the most extensive literatures in financial economics. There are at least two good reasons for this. One is that interest rates plotted against maturity invariably suggest a smooth relationship with rates flattening out as maturity is extended. This gives the unmistakable impression that there is a pervasive phenomenon to be explained. Another reason for the extensive literature is the compelling theoretical base on which most of it rests. That base is the idea that long term interest rates must to a considerable extent reflect expectations of future short term rates. This is because a bondholder always has the option of extending or contracting the maturity of a bond portfolio and will do so if the return from doing so is much greater or less, respectively, than the return that is expected to prevail in the spot market when the long term bond matures. How much of a "premium" of long rates over expected short rates is enough to establish equilibrium is the subject of considerable theorizing in the literature. Empirical tests of competing hypotheses about the behavior of term premiums require that observed long term interest rates somehow be decomposed into the parts attributable to expectations of future short term rates and the parts due to term premiums. Much of the literature is concerned with trying to construct such decompositions and exploit their implications for empirical testing.

A thorough review of the term structure literature would occupy a volume in itself and will not be attempted here. The objective is rather to examine the foundations of the body of existing theory and to discuss and illustrate alternate approaches to testing competing hypotheses using actual market data. Section 2

James L. Bicksler, Editor, Handbook of Financial Economics
© *North-Holland Publishing Company – 1979*

reviews several basic concepts essential to the topic. Section 3 develops the main themes in term structure theory. Section 4 illustrates a number of empirical tests and discusses the methodological issues involved. A list of suggested references for further reading is given at the end.

2. Basic concepts: discount rates, yield to maturity, forward rates

The US Treasury issues bills which promise to pay a single lump sum on a specific date in the future. The term to maturity of these bills extends only up to one year but bills of any maturity could in principle be issued. The risk that the Treasury will default on its obligations is essentially zero, so these bills come very close to being a direct exchange of dollars today for dollars in the future. How much will a future dollar sell for today? Let us call the price of a dollar delivered i periods (days, months, years, or whatever) in the future as P_i. Obviously P_0 is $1.00 since a dollar now is worth no more or less than a dollar. We also know that P_1 is less than or equal to $1.00 since the investor always has the option of holding cash instead of buying the bill. Furthermore, it must be that $P_{i+k} \leqslant P_i (k \geqslant 0)$ since the investor has the option of buying the i period bill and then holding cash between periods i and $i+k$ instead of buying the $i+k$ period bill.

Money invested in the one-period bill will grow at rate R_1 given by $(1 + R_1)P_1 = \$1.00$ or $\$1.00/(1 + R_1) = P_1$. Thus, R_1 is the rate at which the future $1.00 payment is discounted in order to arrive at its present value in today's market. Similarly, money invested in the i period bill grows at rate R_i where $(1 + R_i)^i P_i = \$1.00$ or $P_i = \$1.00/(1 + R_i)^i$. Thus, R_i is the rate at which dollars paid i periods hence are discounted in today's market and is called the i period *discount rate* or the i period *interest rate*. A graph of interest rates against term to maturity i is called the *yield curve*.

Bonds are more complex than bills and promise to pay not only a "face value" amount at maturity but also smaller "coupon" payments at regular intervals in the meantime. A bond can be viewed as a bundle of bills with the coupon payments being small bills and the face value payment being a large bill. The value of this bundle on the market today is simply the sum of the values of all these bills and is given by

$$\text{bond price} = \text{coupon}_1 \times P_1 + \text{coupon}_2 \times P_2 + \dots$$
$$+ (\text{coupon}_M + \text{face value}_M) P_M,$$

for an M period bond. In terms of discount rates R_i the price can be expressed as

$$\text{bond price} = \frac{\text{coupon}_1}{(1 + R_1)} + \frac{\text{coupon}_2}{(1 + R_2)^2} + \dots + \frac{(\text{coupon}_M + \text{face value}_M)}{(1 + R_M)^M},$$

so that there is not single discount rate for the bond but rather M different discount rates are involved. What then is the single "yield to maturity" quoted in the bond market?

Yield to maturity is a single discount rate R_M which discounts all the coupon payments and the final payment to today's price. Therefore it is a solution to the equation

$$\text{bond price} = \frac{\text{coupon}}{\left(1+\bar{R}_M\right)} + \frac{\text{coupon}}{\left(1+\bar{R}_M\right)^2} + \ldots + \frac{\text{coupon}+\text{face value}}{\left(1+\bar{R}_M\right)^M}.$$

Comparing the expressions for the price of the bond in terms of $R_1,\ldots,R_M$ and in terms of $\bar{R}_M$ it is clear that $\bar{R}_M$ is a mixture of the individual discount rates and would only by coincidence be equal to the pure M period discount rate. Thus, different bonds of the same maturity which differ only in the size of their coupons will generally have different yields to maturity. This of course does not imply any inconsistency in the market or that an investor is better off shifting to the bond with the higher yield. The bonds are just different bundles of fairly-priced bills.

How can discount rates be calculated if only bonds are available in the market? As long as a full range of maturities is quoted we can proceed as follows. Calculate R_1 from a one period bond which is effectively a bill. Using that discount rate we can evaluate the present value of the first coupon on a two-period bill and solve

$$\text{bond price} - \frac{\text{coupon}}{1+R_1} = \frac{\text{coupon}+\text{face value}}{(1+R_2)^2}$$

for the two-period discount rate. Continuing in the same fashion we can solve sequentially for R_3, R_4, etc. Fortunately, for coupons of the size usually encountered in US markets the actual differences between discount rates and yields to maturity are small and we will not bother to distinguish between them for expository purposes.

How will an investor choose between bonds of different maturities? If the two-year interest rate is 6 percent and the one-year rate is 5 percent, does this imply that two-year bonds are a better investment than one-year bonds if the other characteristics of the bond are identical? What is the opportunity cost of buying a two-year bond instead of a one-year bond? It is the lost opportunity of investing the proceeds of the one-year bond for the second year. The actual return to reinvesting during the second year will depend on market rates a year from now and is therefore subject to uncertainty. What is the actual return on the two-year bond during the second year of its life? The concept of *forward rates* is the key to making these comparisons.

By holding a two-year bond instead of a one-year bond the investor gives up $(1+R_1)$ dollars at the end of year one which is the amount which *would have been received* for each dollar invested in a one-year bond. In its place the two year investor receives $(1 + R_2)^2$ dollars at the end of two years. The return on this exchange of dollars through time is calculated in the usual way by discounting the terminal payment to the cost

$$\text{cost} = (1 + R_1) = \frac{(1 + R_2)^2}{1 + \text{second year return}}$$

and is called a forward rate. In effect, a market in bonds or bills of different maturities is at the same time a futures market because definite rates of return for future periods can be "locked up" simply by extending maturity. A two-year bond is a one-year bond followed by another one year bond the second year and the locked up return for the second year is given by the forward rate calculated above.

Note that the forward rate for the second year is neither the one year rate for the first year, nor is it the two year rate. In fact, R_2 is the geometric average of R_1 and the forward rate. Before calculating other forward rates we introduce the rotation $r_{1,1}$ for this forward rate to indicate that it is the forward rate for a one-year future bond to begin one year from now. The relevant choice for the investor is clearly not between R_1 and R_2 but between $r_{1,1}$ and the one-year rate expected to prevail in the spot market one year hence.

By extending maturity from two to three years the investor locks up a one-year return for the third year in the future. The return is again calculated by discounting the terminal payment to the amount which is given up by not buying the alternative investment (the two-year bond). Hence

$$(1 + R_2)^2 = \frac{(1 + R_3)^3}{1 + r_{1,2}}$$

gives the forward rate two years in the future. The three-year bond also of course contains a future two-year bond during the second and third years of its life. The return on that future bond is simply $r_{2,1}$ given by

$$(1 + R_1) = \frac{(1 + R_3)^3}{(1 + r_{2,1})^2}.$$

If we solve each of these expressions for the forward rate it is easy to see that the general formula for the forward rate on a k year bond to begin j years from now is

$$r_{k,j} = \left[\frac{(1 + R_{k+j})^{k+j}}{(1 + R_j)^j} \right]^{1/k} - 1.$$

It is also easy to see that any long rate is just the geometric average of all its constituent forward rates

$$(1 + R_M) = [(1 + R_1)(1 + r_{1,1})\dots(1 + r_{1,M-1})]^{1/M},$$

noting that $r_{1,0}$ is just the spot market one year rate (R_1) today.

3. Theories of the term structure of interest rates

The motivation behind the concept of forward rates contains the seed of an important behavioral hypothesis about the term structure of interest rates, namely the *expectations hypothesis*. A rational (wealth maximizing) investor will compare forward rates with the short term rate expected to prevail over the corresponding time period in the future. For example, if the one-year rate is 5 percent and the two-year rate is 6 percent, then the forward rate on a one-year bond one year hence is roughly 7 percent. If one-year rates are expected to be greater than 7 percent one year hence there will be an incentive for rational investors to hold one-year rather than two-year bonds in order to take advantage of spot one-year yields which are expected to be in excess of the 7 percent forward rate. Note that it is not sufficient that one-year rates be expected to rise for investors to have an incentive to hold one-year rather than two-year securities. Rates have to be expected to rise *by more* than 2 percent. For example, if one-year rates are expected to rise from 5 to only 6 percent, then the second year of the two-year bond with its forward yield of 7 percent offers an incentive to hold the larger term bond. If the one-year rate expected one year hence is 7 percent, the same as the forward rate, will all investors then be indifferent between one- and two-year bonds? Presumably not, because the forward rate is fixed for certain and the expected rate is just an expectation. However, if some investors are willing to shift funds from one bond to the other as long as there is any discrepancy between forward and expected rates then market equilibrium can occur only when all forward rates have been equated to corresponding expected future rates. That this condition holds is called the *expectations hypothesis*. Thus, if the expected one-year rate one year hence is 6 percent, the price of our hypothetical two-year bond must rise until its forward rate is reduced from 7 to 6 percent.

How is the analysis affected if investors do not intend to hold longer term bonds to maturity? It is not necessary to hold the longer bond to maturity to profit from a differential between forward rates and expected future spot rates. Suppose again that the one-year rate is 5 percent, the two-year rate is 6 percent so the one-year ahead one year forward rate is 7 percent, and the expected one year next year is 6 percent. An investor with a one-year holding period still has an incentive to hold the two-year bond. If expectations prove correct the price of the two-year bond after one year will be $(1/(1+0.06))$ since after one year the two-year bond becomes a one-year bond and will be priced at the then prevailing one-year rate. The return on holding the two-year bond for one year will have been

$$\text{holding period return} = \frac{(1+0.06)^{-1}-(1+0.06)^{-2}}{(1+0.06)^{-2}} \times 100\% = 6\%,$$

which is in excess of the 5 percent offered over the same period by the one-year bond even though "interest rates are rising". Therefore one-year holding period investors will in general also have an incentive to shift between one- and two-year bonds if forward rates differ from expected rates. (The statistically inclined reader will note that some additional assumptions are necessary if the above holding period return is to be properly interpreted as an expected holding period return.)

The expectations hypothesis implies that the forward rates observed in the market are simply expected future spot rates, or

$$E_t(_{t+n}R_k) = {}_t r_{k,n},$$

where $E_t(\cdot)$ means "the expectation of" as of period t, $_{t+n}R_k$ is the future k-period spot rate for period $t+n$, and $_t r_{k,n}$ is the forward rate for a k-period bond to be issued n periods after period t. But whose expectation are we talking about? Not any individuals, of course, but in some sense the best expectation which can be formed on the basis of current information. To make the theory testable we need to make specific assumptions about expectations and this problem is taken up in the next section.

Expectations are of course only that, and actual future spot will turn out differently than market participants had expected. This means that actual returns are uncertain and it is reasonable to suppose that risk-averse investors will require compensation for bearing such risk. If investors typically have short investment horizons then long term bonds will be viewed as risky relative to short term bonds therefore long term yields should carry a risk premium over term yields. Reasoning along these lines J. R. Hicks (*Value and Capital*, 1939) hypothesized that forward rates will contain a *liquidity premium* above the expected future spot rate and that these liquidity premiums will rise with term to maturity. The Hicksian hypothesis can therefore be expressed as

$$_t r_{1,n} = E_t(_{t+n}R_1) + L_n,$$

which says that the one-period forward rate n periods hence will be equal to the corresponding expected future spot rate plus the liquidity premium L_n where

$$L_n > L_{n-1} > \dots > 0.$$

In this case forward rates contain an upward bias as forecasts of future spot rates and that bias increases with horizon.

A number of authors have pointed out that the case for investors having short horizons is not at all compelling and that many investors may be more concerned with returns over a long time horizon. In this case long term bonds might be viewed as being less risky than short term bonds. The long term investor can purchase a long term bond offering a certain return over the investment horizon. On the other hand, a strategy of sequential reinvestment in short term bonds would be risky over a long horizon. It can readily be argued therefore that if risk premiums do exist they may be either positive or negative. More generally, different market participants have different *preferred habitats* on the term to maturity scale and the distribution and strength of these preferences will determine the pattern of premiums consistent with market equilibrium. These premiums might therefore be renamed *term premiums* and are defined by

$$_tT_n = {}_tr_{1,n} - E_t({}_{t+n}R_1),$$

where the t subscript on the premium indicates the possibility that it may vary over time as well as across maturity.

At the opposite extreme from the expectations hypothesis is the view that maturity preferences are so strong that investors and borrowers cannot be induced to move along the maturity scale so that complete *market segmentation* occurs. If this is the case, then expectations are irrelevant and the long and short term markets are as unrelated as the markets for apples and autos.

4. Testing theories of the term structure

As we have seen in the previous section, the competing hypotheses concerning the behavior of the term structure of interest rates can be translated into statements concerning the term premium T. According to the expectations hypothesis, T is identically zero and forward rates are just expected future spot rates. According to the liquidity premium hypothesis T_n is positive and increases with n. According to the preferred habitat hypothesis, the term premiums may be either positive or negative, but T_n as a function of n will be smooth because investors and borrowers can be induced to move to adjacent maturities. According to the market segmentation hypothesis, no particular statement can be made concerning term premiums since forward rates have nothing to do with expectations. To test these and related hypotheses we need to make some assumptions about the behavior of expectations, otherwise we would be unable to draw any observable implications from these hypotheses and without observable implications we would have no way of testing the hypothesis against real world data.

One assumption we make about expectations is that they are unbiased, that is, on average the forecast error will be zero. Sometimes spot rates will turn out higher than expected and sometimes lower, but the difference will average out to zero over a long enough history. Now the difference between the forward rate and the actual corresponding future spot rate will reflect not only the error in expectations but also any term premiums in the forward rate, since

$$[_{t+n}R_1 - _{t-n}r_{1,n}] = [_{t+n}R_1 - E_t(_{t+n}R_1)] - _tT_n.$$

If we average this difference over many periods we will find that

$$\bar{R}_1 - \bar{r}_{1,n} \cong -\bar{T}_n,$$

where bars denote average quantities. Therefore, the difference between the average of one-period spot rates and the average of one-period forward rates for horizon n periods is an estimate of the n-period term premium. Thus, if forward rates have historically been higher than one-period spot rates, we can conclude that term premiums are on average positive. If this difference increases with maturity n then term premiums increases with n and yield curves will on average be upward sloping. The fact that yield curves usually have sloped upward historically has been interpreted therefore as strong evidence for the existence of liquidity premiums, i.e. positive term premiums which increase monotonically with M.

It is hasty to conclude, however, that this implies that holders of long term bonds receive a premium over the return earned by holders of short term bonds as predicted by Hicks' theory. To explain this seemingly paradoxical statement we need to compare the expected return on holding and short bonds. For mathematical simplicity consider the return on a three-year bond held to maturity versus the return on a sequence of one-year bonds. At the end of the three years the long bond holder has

$$(1 + _tR_3)^3 = (1 + _tR_1)(1 + _tr_{1,1})(1 + _tr_{1,2})$$

dollars for each dollar invested. The short bond holder cannot know how much will be earned at the end of three years but the expected value is

$$(1 + _tR_1)[(1 + E_t(_{t+1}R_1) + E_t(_{t+2}R_1) + E_t(_{t+1}R_1_{t+2}R_1)].$$

Under the expectations hypothesis the forward rates in the first expression are just expected rates, and the difference between the two expressions would be

$$E_t(_{t+1}R_1)E_t(_{t+2}R_1) - E(_{t+1}R_1_{t+2}R_1) = \text{cov}(_{t+1}R_1, _{t+2}R_1),$$

so that the holder of short bonds could expect to earn more if spot rates covary positively over time. This implies that some positive term premium would have to be included in forward rates just to even up the two returns. Therefore, the existence of positive term premiums is not necessarily indicative of the existence of liquidity premiums as conceived in Hicks' theory.

The Durand yield curve data from 1900 to 1958 provides a long history over which average term premiums can be estimated. The average premium does rise with forward rate horizon to a limit of about one half a percentage point for horizons over eight years. The covariance effect described above also rises with horizon and a statistical analysis of the covariance structure of spot rates provides an estimated limiting effect that is also about half a percentage point. Therefore, it would seem that holders of very long term bonds do not receive extra compensation for risk contrary to the liquidity premium theory.

Expectations cannot be observed directly or measured, but it may be possible to draw observable implications from an assumption about how they are revised. For example, it would seem reasonable that investors learn from their mistakes. The *error-learning hypothesis* states that the revision in an expectation will be proportional to the most recent error, thus

$$E_t({}_{t+n}R_1) - E_{t-1}({}_{t+n}R_1) = \beta_n [{}_tR_1 - E_{t-1}({}_tR_1)],$$

where β_n is presumably (but not necessarily) some positive fraction which gets smaller as horizon n increases. Under the expectations hypothesis the observed forward rates are expected rates so that β can be estimated from the regression equation

$$({}_tr_n - {}_{t-1}r_{n+1}) = \alpha_n + \beta_n({}_tR_1 - {}_{t-1}r_1),$$

where all the forward rates are one-period rates. Note that both forward rates on the left pertain to future period ${}_{t+n}$ while the forward rate on the right is a forecast of ${}_tR_1$ made last period. Estimates of α and β using the Durand data 1901–1958 are given in table 5.1. The estimates of α are not statistically significant while the estimates of β are significant. The data would therefore appear to give strong support to the expectations hypothesis. On the other hand, we cannot exclude the possibility of term premiums because the expectations theory by itself does not provide strong predictions regarding the values of the α's and β's.

To pursue this further, consider the possibility that term premiums are not simply constant through time but rather vary over the business cycle. A number of authors have proposed, for example, that term premiums will vary with the level of interest rates. The services of short term instruments as substitutes for money would suggest that term premiums will rise with the level of interest rates.

Table 5.1

n (years)	α	β	R^2
1	0.0039	0.71	0.91
2	0.0036	0.54	0.76
3	-0.0001	0.41	0.60
4	-0.0215	0.34	0.48
5	-0.0048	0.29	0.43
6	0.0022	0.24	0.41
7	-0.0078	0.25	0.42
8	0.0158	0.22	0.37

On the other hand, protection offered by longer term instruments against risk from fluctuation in short term rates would be less important when interest rates are low suggesting that term premiums fall as interest rates rise. Business confidence may also affect the willingness of market participants to enter into long term lending agreements and if so the term premium might be expected to vary negatively with a measure of the business cycle. These possibilities can be summarized by

$$_tT_n = a_n + b_n I_t + c_n Z_t,$$

where I_t measures the level of interest rates and Z_t the strength of the business cycle.

If we now substitute into the error-learning relation using the identity $r = E(R) + T$ and the above equation for T we obtain the regression equation

$$(_t r_n - {}_{t-1} r_{n+1}) = \alpha_n + \beta_n(R_t - {}_{t-1} r_1) + b_n I_t + (\beta_n b_1 - b_{n+1}) I_{t-1}$$
$$+ c_n Z_t + (\beta_n c_1 - c_{n+1}) Z_{t-1},$$

where the constant α_n is equal to $(a_n - a_{n+1} + \beta_n a_1)$. Note that a constant of zero does not necessarily imply that a_n, a_{n+1} and a_1 are all zero. We have one such equation for each value of n. This implies that there are multiple estimates of the parameters since b_1 and c_1 appear in each equation, and b_n and b_{n+1} and c_n and c_{n+1} appear in the equations for n and $n+1$. To exploit these relationships to reduce the number of parameters estimated it is advantageous to use Zellner's "seemingly unrelated regressions" framework.

The resulting estimates from the Durand data, $n = 1, \ldots, 5$ years, use the negative of the unemployment rate to represent the level of the business cycle (see table 5.2). Estimates of the β, b, and c are statistically significant. These estimates suggest that term premiums fall about six basis points for each 1 percent rise in the level of interest rates and rise about three basis points for each one percentage point rise in the unemployment rate. Note that the β coefficients for error-learning are larger as a result of including the term premium variables. This suggests that the previous estimates were attenuated as a result of omitting relevant variables from the regression.

The monthly data on US Treasury bonds assembled by Van Horne for 1955–1965 provides another and historically later data set on which to test the

Table 5.2

n (years)	α	β	b	c
1	0.0009	0.72	−0.03	−0.01
2	0.0086	0.58	−0.06	−0.02
3	0.0412	0.48	−0.07	−0.03
4	−0.0567	0.41	−0.06	−0.03
5	0.0223	0.40	−0.08	−0.02

Table 5.3

n (years)	α	β	b	c
1	0.22	0.91	−0.17	−0.06
2	0.31	0.70	−0.20	−0.06
3	0.18	0.57	−0.15	−0.04
4	0.15	0.38	−0.11	−0.03

term premium model. The corresponding results are shown in table 5.3, with all but the last two c coefficients being statistically significant. It would seem that the Treasury data offer stronger evidence of the existence of a constant component in the term premium and of a negative response to the general level of interest rates.

One of the problems in interpreting the error-learning model is that we have no prior basis on which to say whether the estimated β coefficients are reasonable. To do this we need a theory of expectations which implies error-learning from which some estimates of "reasonable" β's can be derived. The theory of discrete linear stochastic process is such theory.

According to Wold's theorem any nondeterministic stationary time series, say Y_t, can be represented as a weighted sum of past Y's plus a purely random zero-mean error u_t, thus

$$Y_t = \pi_1 Y_{t-1} + \pi_2 Y_{t-2} + \ldots + u_t.$$

Equivalently, Y_t can be expressed in terms of past u's as

$$Y_t = u_t + \psi_1 u_{t-1} + \psi_2 u_{t-2} + \ldots.$$

Now the variable of interest might be the spot one-period interest rate. A forecast of $_{t+n}R_1$ at time t is given by

$$E_t(_{t+n}R_1) = E_t(u_{t+n} + \psi_1 u_{t+n-1} + \ldots)$$
$$= \psi_n u_t + \psi_{n+1} u_{t-1} + \ldots,$$

since future u's are purely random with mean zero. If we now write down the previous forecast and subtract it from the above expression we obtain the *optimal* error-learning rule

$$E_t(_{t+n}R_1) - E_{t-1}(_{t+n}R_1) = \psi_n[_tR_1 - E_{t-1}(_tR_1)].$$

Therefore the β's can be interpreted as the ψ's in a representation of one-period spot rates as a linear stochastic process. To implement this analysis empirically we need only estimate the parameters of the linear process, compute the ψ's, and compare them with the β coefficients estimated from forward rates.

A linear stochastic process which fits the Durand one year rates $_tR_1$ is

$$_tR_1 = 0.80 _{t-1}R_1 + 0.13 _{t-2}R_1 + 0.22 + u_t,$$

Table 5.4

n (years)	ψ_i
1	0.80
2	0.77
3	0.72
4	0.68
5	0.64
6	0.60
7	0.57
8	0.53

which implies ψ weights (see table 5.4). Comparing these ψ's with the β's estimated previously we note that the ψ weights are larger than the β's estimated from the Durand data, but that the discrepancy is smaller when term premium variables are included. This suggests that additional variables may still be omitted from the term premium model and/or that the expectations mechanism in the market is more complex than the simple error-learning model.

We can also use the stochastic process model of one-year rates to calculate estimated expected future rates. The one-year ahead forecast is given by

$$_{t+1}\hat{R}_1 = 0.80\,_tR_1 + 0.13\,_{t-1}R_1 + 0.22$$

and the two-year ahead forecast by

$$_{t+2}\hat{R}_1 = 0.80\,_{t+1}\hat{R}_1 + 0.13\,_tR_1 + 0.22$$

and so forth. There is no reason to believe that these estimates correspond exactly to actual market expectations. However, as long as the discrepancy between actual and estimated expectations is uncorrelated with determinants of term premiums, then the estimated expectation can be employed as a proxy for the actual expectation. An estimate of the term premium is then

$$_t\hat{T}_n = {}_tr_n - {}_{t+n}\hat{R}_1$$

and we can estimate b_n and c_n in the regression

$$_t\hat{T}_t = a_n + b_n I_t + c_n Z_t.$$

Using again the Durand data and after correcting for serial correlation in residuals the results are shown in table 5.5. All coefficients are statistically significant and the percentage of variation explained by I and Z's is about 70 percent. These estimates suggest a significant fixed component in the term premium as well as a substantial negative response of term premiums to a rise in the general level of interest rates. Thus, term premiums are estimated to drop roughly 20 basis points for each one percentage point rise in the level of interest rates, but only by about three basis points for each one percentage point fall in the unemployment rate.

Table 5.5

n (years)	a_n	b_n	c_n
1	0.15	−0.09	−0.02
2	0.23	−0.18	−0.03
3	0.26	−0.21	−0.03
4	0.27	−0.22	−0.03
5	0.32	−0.23	−0.03

Another available proxy for the expected future spot rate is the *actual* future spot rate. Denoting the market's forecast error by $_t e_n$ for the expectation at time of $_{t+n}R_1$ we have

$$({_t}r_n - {_{t+n}}R_1) = a_n + b_n I_t + c_n Z_t - {_t}^e n$$

as another regression equation from which a, b, and c can be estimated. The forecast error $_t e_n$ is simply part of the regression disturbance. Least squares estimates will be consistent only if $_t e_n$ is uncorrelated with the variables I_t and Z_t. This will be the case as long as the market expectation incorporates all available information at time t including any information contained in I_t and Z_t. Expectations of this sort are called *rational expectations* and a market in which expectations are rational is called an *efficient market*. Thus, if we *assume* that the bond market is efficient we can use the actual as a proxy for the expectation. Resulting estimates of a, b, and c are given in table 5.6. The signs and magnitudes of the estimated b's and c's are consistent with those estimated by other approaches although the negative values of the constant term a_n would suggest that forecast errors were on balance positive (actual above expected) during the 1900–1958 sample period. Note that the Durbin–Watson statistic does not indicate serial correlation in the regression residuals for $n=1$, but it does for n greater than one. Does this indicate that the model is misspecified or that expectations are somehow irrational? Not at all. The error $_t e_1$ should be serially random since any serial correlation in one-step-ahead errors would be exploited by a rational expectation. Errors for more than one step ahead, however, are quite naturally autocorrelated. The easiest way to see this is in the case of a linear stochastic process being forecasted from its own past. The one-step-ahead error is just u_{t+1} which is serially random. The two-step-ahead

Table 5.6

n (years)	a	b	c	Durbin–Watson
1	−0.35	−0.02	−0.08	2.2
2	−0.46	−0.06	−0.12	1.3
3	−0.50	−0.09	−0.15	0.9
4	−0.67	−0.06	−0.17	0.9
5	−0.53	−0.08	−0.17	0.6

error is $(u_{t+2} + \psi_1 u_{t+1})$ which is serially correlated; for example

$$\operatorname{cov}({}_te_2, {}_{t+1}e_2) = \psi_1 \operatorname{var}(u).$$

Similarly, ${}_te_n$ will be serially correlated and generally more strongly as n increases since

$$\operatorname{cov}({}_te_n, {}_{t+1}e_n) = \left(\sum_{i=0}^{n-2} \psi_i \psi_{i+1}\right) \operatorname{var}(u),$$

with $\psi_0 = 1$. Therefore the pattern of Durbin–Watson statistics is quite consistent with the fact that ${}_te_n$ is part of the regression disturbance.

It is difficult to assess the statistical significance of parameter estimates when the actual future rate is used as a proxy for the expected since t-statistics are unreliable in the presence of the serially correlated disturbances which occur for $n > 1$. Furthermore, statistical efficiency is reduced because ${}_te_n$ adds substantially to the *variance* of the regression disturbance. For the case $n = 1$ where serial correlation is not indicated only the estimate of c_1 is significant.

The results presented thus far would not seem to be consistent with the hypothesis of constant liquidity premiums which increase monotonically with horizon but rather suggest that term premiums are more consistent with the preferred habitat view modified to allow for cyclical movement in term premiums. If the liquidity premium model were correct then the expected rate and the forward rate would differ only by a constant so that

$$_{t+n}R_1 = -L_n + {}_tr_n + {}_te_n,$$

and therefore in a regression of the form

$$_{t+n}R_1 = -a_n - b_n I_t - c_n Z_t + d_n {}_tr_n$$

we should find that b_n and c_n are close to zero, d_n is close to unity, and a_n would just be an estimate of L_n. Note that again ${}_te_n$ becomes part of the regression disturbances so that we cannot expect great precision in parameter estimates and for horizons greater than one year the Durbin–Watson statistic will be low. If the term premium model is correct, there we have put ${}_tr_n$ on the "wrong" side of the regression (which is why a, b, and c have been given negative signs) and least squares estimates of the parameters will not be consistent. The results are shown in table 5.7. The estimates of a_n are negative, the d coefficient declines sharply with n, and c_1 is significant, all contrary to the liquidity premium model. If the term premium model is the more appropriate model, as appears to be the

Table 5.7

n (years)	a	b	c	d	Durbin–Watson
1	−0.44	−0.11	−0.07	0.87	2.27
5	−1.98	−0.41	−0.12	0.19	0.74

case, then we should put the forward rate back on the left-hand side of the regression where it belongs.

A simple test of the liquidity premium model again uses the assumption that expectations are rational. If the forward rate is simply the expected rate plus a constant premium we should not be able to construct from readily available information an alternative forecast which produces errors with a smaller variance. The calculated $_{t+n}\hat{R}_1$ is an alternative forecast which uses only past spot rates, which are pieces of information readily available to the market and therefore would be taken into account in any rational expectation. The variances of errors made by the forward rates in the Durand data are 0.53, 2.38 and 3.28 percentage points for horizons $n = 1$, 5 and 9 years, respectively. These compare with corresponding variances of 0.40, 1.56 and 2.45 for the simple $\hat{R}$ predictor. This would seem to be strong evidence against the constant liquidity premium hypothesis. It is not evidence against the hypothesis that expectations are rational since the larger variance of forward rate errors is entirely consistent with the presence of varying term premiums which act to pollute the forward rate as a predictor of future spot rates. We conclude then that term premiums do exist, but that they vary with the general level of interest rates and with the business cycle.

The reader will have noticed that all of the empirical tests discussed here required some assumptions about the properties of the expectations embodied in market yields; that they are unbiased, are revised in accordance with forecast errors, or that they are rational. It should be apparent from the structure of these tests that some assumptions about expectations are required if the tests are to be operational. In fact *any* test will require such assumptions as long as expectations themselves remain unobservable. Can these assumptions be tested? They can be tested as hypotheses only in conjunction with a hypothesis about the behavior of term premiums. If the *joint* hypothesis fails, as in the above case of the joint hypothesis that liquidity premiums are constant and expectations are rational, then this may be because either individual hypothesis is wrong. The rationality of expectations per se is not testable any more than is the liquidity premium hypothesis per se. The point is a general one. Unfortunately, much of the "efficient markets" literature leaves the impression that market efficiency, i.e. the rationality of expectations, per se can be tested. Market efficiency is instead an assumption which makes operational tests of other hypotheses about the behavior of financial markets.

References

Culbertson, J. M. (1957) "The Term Structure of Interest Rates", *Quarterly Journal of Economics* 71, November, 485–517.
Fama, E. F. (1976) "Inflation Uncertainty and Expected Returns on Treasury Bills", *Journal of Political Economy* 84, June, 427–448.

Hicks, J. R. (1939) *Value and Capital* (Oxford Clarendon Press, London), 2nd edn. 1946.

Kessel, R. A. (1965) *The Cyclical Behavior of the Term Structure of Interest Rates* (National Bureau of Economic Research, New York).

Malkiel, B. G. (1966) *The Term Structure of Interest Rates: Expectations and Behavior Patterns* (Princeton University Press).

Meiselman, D. (1962) *The Term Structure of Interest Rates* (Prentice-Hall, Englewood Cliffs).

Modigliani, F. and R. Sutch (1966) "Innovations in Interest Rate Policy", *American Economic Review* 56, May, 178–197.

Modiglianim F. and R. Sutch (1967) "Debt Management and the Term Structure of Interest Rates", *Journal of Political Economy* 75, August, 569–589.

Modigliani, F. and R. J. Schiller (1973) "Inflation, Rational Expectations, and the Term Structure of Interest Rates", *Economica* 40, February, 12–43.

Muth, J. (1961) "Rational Expectations and the Theory of Price Movements", *Econometrica*, July, 315–335.

Nelson, C. R. (1972) *The Term Structure of Interest Rates* (Basic Books, New York).

Nelson, C. R. (1973) *Applied Time Series Analysis—for Managerial Forecasting* (Holden-Day, San Francisco).

Roll, R. (1970) *The Behavior of Interest Rates* (Basic Books, New York).

Rutledge, J. (1974) *A Monetarist Model of Inflationary Expectations* (Lexington Books).

Sargent, T. J. (1972) "Rational Expectations and the Term Structure of Interest Rates", *Journal of Money, Credit, and Banking*, February, 74–97.

Van Horne, J. (1965) "Interest Rate Risk and the Term Structure of Interest Rates", *Journal of Political Economy* 73, August, 344–351.

Chapter 6

ECONOMIC FOUNDATIONS OF STOCK MARKET REGULATION

IRWIN FRIEND*
University of Pennsylvania

1. Introduction

Before considering the economic impact of stock regulation in the US, the country which pioneered in this area, it is desirable to review briefly the general purposes of such regulation. The two basic aims of the original legislation — the Securities Act of 1933 and the Securities and Exchange Act of 1934 — were the protection of investors and the promotion of the broader public interest, since this interest is affected by trading in securities. The first aim has an equity orientation, and the second an economic orientation since the public interest in the area of securities regulation relates largely to the impact of regulation on the economic performance of securities markets.

These two aims were to be achieved largely by policies designed to require full disclosure of material facts on securities sold in the primary and secondary markets, to prevent manipulation of securities prices, to curb unfair trading practices, to maintain orderly and liquid markets, and to control "excessive" use of credit. This listing of the main categories of policies is not intended to indicate mutually exclusive groups since there can be broad overlapping. Similarly, while some of the specific policies followed are directed primarily to either an equity or an economic objective, others are directed to both. Some apply to the market for new issues, a number to the market for outstanding issues, and still others to both.

The period subsequent to the original legislation which set up the US Securities and Exchange Commission (SEC) to implement these objectives and policies has seen that agency, both through new legislation and new regulations, greatly expand its powers and assume a much more active and direct role in the

*Richard K. Mellon Professor of Finance, University of Pennsylvania. The author wishes to acknowledge the financial support of the Rodney L. White Center for Financial Research. This paper was presented at the Buckingham Conference, London, 23 June 1975.

James L. Bicksler, Editor, Handbook of Financial Economics
© *North-Holland Publishing Company – 1979*

regulation of securities issuance and trading. This trend has culminated in the recently enacted Securities Act Amendments of 1975 which gives the SEC substantial new powers to structure the central market system and represents another major move away from industry self-regulation.

My comments in this paper will be directed first to the economic rationale of stock market regulation and secondly to the available evidence relating to the economic impact of such regulation. I shall largely confine my attention to economic effects though equity considerations are obviously also relevant. I shall not consider here several peripheral areas of securities regulation, including mutual funds, holding companies, and the recent extension of corporate disclosure requirements to social policy issues.

Before considering the technical materials to follow, I should point out that it is my belief that securities legislation in the US has, as a whole, had a beneficial impact on the economy totally apart from its effect in reducing inequities among different participants in the securities markets. This does not mean that the economic case for every major facet of securities legislation has been proved beyond doubt, but simply that the economic case for some major facets is rather strong and that for other facets the case for seems to be stronger than the case against.

It has always amused me that the most vociferous economic critics of securities legislation have taken the tack that the case for such legislation must rest on irrefutable evidence that it has benefited the economy, not that the evidence for should be stronger than the evidence against. I would further argue that even if this legislation, with due consideration given to the costs involved, were neutral in its effect on the economy, much of it would be desirable on equity grounds.

To summarize my own views as to the effectiveness of different facets of securities regulation, the evidence that fuller disclosure has benefited the market for new securities issues seems to me rather strong. The position that fuller disclosure has improved the market for outstanding issues seems more defensible on the basis of the available evidence than the position that it has not, though the case is not as strong as for new issues. My evaluation of the success of the policies designed to maintain orderly and liquid markets and to control "excessive" use of credit in the stock market is that they probably have done more economic good than harm, but the case again is not very strong. The economic rationale for some specific measures taken by the SEC to prevent manipulation of securities prices and to curb unfair trading practices might be questioned, without much empirical support either way, but such policies can frequently be justified on equity grounds. In the subsequent discussion of the available evidence relating to the economic impact of securities regulation, I shall present only selected highlights and refer to the literature for further support of my position.

The remainder of this paper will discuss in turn the ways in which the stock market might be expected, at least in theory, to impinge on the economy (section 2), the economic rationale for believing that stock market regulation would favorably affect the market (section 3), and the empirical evidence relating to the performance of such regulation in furthering its economic goals (section 4). Parts of these sections rely heavily on earlier studies by myself and others but new material is also presented including a brief discussion of some recent, relevant literature.

2. Theory of market impact on economy [1]

The stock market affects the functioning of the economy in two principal ways. First, market developments may affect the national income through their influence on the aggregate propensities to consume, to save, and to invest. Secondly, even with a given level of saving and investment, market arrangements can affect the efficiency of the allocation of investment funds. This paper will be concerned primarily with the second of these two potential influences, namely the impact of the market on economic efficiency — the type of impact to which economists have directed most of their attention.

It might be noted here, however, that economists have given inadequate consideration to the fact that a highly volatile stock market may decrease aggregate investment by increasing the cost of capital to business enterprises [2] and may also result in substantial swings in the level of consumption and hence income through an asset effect. Thus, a less volatile stock market might stimulate a higher secular level of investment and less pronounced cyclical swings in the level of consumption and income. Presumably, since all available evidence suggests that people are risk averse, their expected utility would be increased by smaller cyclical fluctuations, perhaps even if the average level of the national income were lowered somewhat in the process.

Concepts of market efficiency

Economic theorists have shown that making assumptions they consider reasonable — including management acting in the stockholders' interests and the costless and immediate availability of all information to all investors — a firm's output decisions under capital market equilibrium will be optimal for all its stockholders and will also be optimal in the sense that in long-run equilibrium

---

[1] Part of this discussion is based on Friend (1972).

[2] In completely efficient markets the volatility may of course simply reflect the influence of different economic forces affecting investment risks and prospective returns.

each firm will be operating at minimum average costs.[3] Perhaps the most common conception of an efficient market in recent studies of stock market phenomena is one in which every price fully reflects all the available information so that any new relevant information is reflected in prices extremely rapidly (and cannot be used to make abnormal returns). There are, however, a number of difficulties with this definition.

First, the market must in some fashion reflect all available information. The important question is the relevance of the information to the subsequent earnings or riskiness of the stock. How is information to be distinguished from misinformation? Secondly, is a market in which prices fully reflect the scanty information available as efficient as a market in which much more information is available and reflected in stock prices? In other words, what is the justification for considering the information set fixed? Thirdly, is the efficiency of the market independent of the costs incurred? It seems desirable to have two measures of efficiency, one measuring the quality of the service rendered (sometimes referred to as "allocational efficiency"), the other its cost (or "operational efficiency").

Finally, even if the markets are efficient according to any reasonable definition, this would not ensure a flow of economic resources into the most productive real investment. However, efficient markets should ensure that the markets are providing the appropriate guidelines for the flow of capital.

Another approach to appraising market efficiency has been to set up two standards: (1) the extent to which short-run fluctuations in price — that is, those not matched by changes in equilibrium price — are eliminated, or alternatively, the extent to which transaction costs to the public are minimized; and (2) the success with which changes in equilibrium prices are anticipated (Stigler (1964)). The first of these standards may be considered to lead to an appropriate measure of the market's operational efficiency. For a given volume and quality of services, and for given factor costs, operational efficiency may be measured by, and is an inverse function of, underwriting and other flotation costs of new issues and transaction costs in the public transfer of outstanding issues (including any relevant regulatory costs). The transaction costs in the transfer of outstanding issues from a public buyer to a public seller include not only two commissions but also either all or part of the bid–ask spread.

The second of these standards, which is addressed to the market's allocational efficiency, introduces all of the difficulties in defining, and in attempting to measure, equilibrium price. (See Friend and Herman (1964/1965).) The latter is apparently taken to represent the intersection of the investors' demand schedule for a security with the amount outstanding — no matter how temporary or ill-advised retrospectively that price turns out to be. Again, no consideration is given to the market role of misinformation or of the adequacy of the information set.

---

[3]See, for example, Leland (1974) and also Merton and Subrahmanyam (1974).

Probably the most satisfactory way of evaluating the allocational efficiency of decisions made in the securities markets is to inquire whether the outcomes are the best obtainable with the information that was available at the time the decisions were made or that could have been made available at that time (with the costs involved reflected in the measurement of operational efficiency). The best outcomes would be obtained if the markets maintained equivalent rates of return and hence equivalent costs of financing on comparable investments. This quality of the markets would help to ensure that funds are channeled from savers to those users who will apply them most profitably and that portfolio shifts can be made to the mutual advantage of different investors. The efficiency of this allocation process can be assessed in retrospect by the extent to which there are variations in market return and by the extent to which these variations can be explained by differentials in risk.

While it is not too difficult to obtain a retrospective view of allocational efficiency by analyzing returns and risks associated with different investments, it is virtually impossible to tell how the outcomes compare with the best obtainable at the time the decisions were made. Retrospective data permit an absolute appraisal of the optimality of outcomes only with the benefit of hindsight. Yet they do provide an indication of the departure of outcomes from ex post optimality. If ex ante measures of return and risk at the beginning of a period bear little relationship to ex post measures at the end of the period, the value of the ex ante magnitudes would be quite limited.

In spite of the deficiencies in reliance on retrospective data to supply an adequate measure of absolute market efficiency, they probably do provide a reasonably satisfactory index of relative market efficiency which can be used to analyze the impact on efficiency of different financial developments and practices, including the impact of securities regulation.

3. Economic rationale of market regulation

The economic justification for disclosure, which is perhaps the most basic mechanism of securities regulation, is the belief that the provision of information to prospective investors is a necessary condition for efficient markets.

> With full disclosure we would expect less drastic shifts in estimates of expected profitability of a given issue as a result of the greater initial level of economic information (and, presumably, the reduction in the possibility of surprises from this source), a greater scope for scientific investment analysis, a diminished reliance on and use of rumors, and a reduction in the scale of manipulative practices (Friend and Herman (1964/1965)).

Information is a basic ingredient for rational economic behavior. We would therefore expect improved disclosure to increase allocational efficiency. Less important, it might increase operational efficiency as a result of greater public knowledge concerning underwriting and other transaction costs, and the reduction in private expenses of investigation facilitated by the required disclosure of information. However, the provision of new information entails additional costs which may offset some or all of the operational savings referred to. Most people would also regard disclosure as enhancing equity among different groups in the market.

The economic as well as noneconomic justification of regulations designed to prevent the more flagrant types of manipulation of securities prices requires little explanation. Theoretically, such regulations might be expected to improve both efficiency and equity in the capital markets, and perhaps also general economic stability, even though empirical evidence is required to assess whether the benefits achieved are worth the cost. Restrictions on certain types of speculation to maintain orderly and liquid markets and limitations on the use of securities credit are frequently rationalized on similar grounds, but even the existence of economic benefits from such policies is not clear from theory alone and must depend on evidence. For example, it is easy enough to use theoretical considerations to "demonstrate" that under plausible conditions speculators on the average must stabilize stock prices so long as it is assumed that their activities do not affect the demand schedules of investors. This, however, is a heroic assumption and requires direct or indirect empirical verification.

4. Economic performance of market regulation[4]

Some of the most convincing evidence on the SEC's accomplishments in the markets for new and outstanding issues is provided in the Pecora hearings (US Congress (1933–34)), two other US Government pre-World War II studies (US Congress (1935; 1939–42)), and the postwar SEC *Special Study* (1963), with their documentation of the massive securities abuses of the earlier period and the much healthier post-SEC experience. This evidence provides substantial reason for believing that the effects of disclosure and related aspects of securities legislation have been beneficial. Vast amounts of money were demonstrably lost in the pre-SEC period as a result of activities which have been greatly reduced by securities legislation. These amounts would appear to dwarf any reasonable estimate of the costs of such legislation.

Stock market pools, bucket shop operation, misuse of insider information and other types of manipulation and fraud, which frequently relied on the deliberate use of misinformation and the absence of full disclosure, were widespread in the pre-SEC period, involved vast sums of money and seem less prevalent today. In the earlier period, enormous losses were absorbed by the public in excessively

---

[4]Part of this discussion is based on Friend (1969).

leveraged, highly speculative, and frequently manipulated new issues of public utility holding companies, investment companies, and foreign bonds, each of which was frequently sold under disclosure conditions bordering on fraud. It is undoubtedly true that a substantial share of the blame for such losses lies elsewhere, but an important share is attributable to inadequate and deliberately misleading information, and widespread violations of fiduciary responsibilities by market and corporate insiders.

The Pecora investigation catalogued 107 issues on the New York Stock Exchange and 71 issues on the New York Curb in which members of these exchanges participated in pools in 1929. It also documented an impressive number of cases of new issue sales in the mid- to late 1920s with inadequate disclosure and disastrous results. Both the nature of the facts and statements by the investment bankers involved make it quite clear that with a modicum of disclosure of known facts these issues could not have been sold.

4.1. Impact on new issues

There is additional evidence in the postwar *Special Study* suggesting a beneficial effect on new issues of the full disclosure requirement under the SEC. For example, during 1960–61 a law firm representing 17 issuers filed 13 Regulation A statements, which do not require full disclosure, and four registration statements which do. Eleven of the 13 Regulation A statements but none of the four registration statements became effective. Of the 11 Regulation A issues subsequently marketed, all went to a premium immediately after the offering but by November 1962 eight were no longer mentioned in the quotation sheets and there were quoted below their offering price. Through a variety of arrangements, the public monies raised through these offerings were substantially siphoned off to persons affiliated with the law firm representing the 17 issuers. The *Special Study* also shows that while Regulation A issues in 1959–61 fared better than registered issues in the immediate post-offering period (up to one month after offering), they fared worse by 30 September 1962. This can be construed as suggesting that in the short run full disclosure may prevent unwarranted price rises and in the longer run ensure a closer coincidence between initial price and intrinsic value.

One of several tests of the effect of full disclosure which I carried out in the past in conjunction with Edward Herman is provided by a comparison of the market experience from 1958 to 1963 of unregistered new industrial common stock below $300,000 in size issued in 1958 with the smaller registered issues over $300,000 where both groups of stocks are adjusted by movements in the market averages (Friend and Herman (1964/1965)). Only nonrights, publicly offered, primary issues were included to maintain comparability. While this test was of rather limited scope, it pointed to a superior after-issue price performance of the registered issues. The price relatives for the registered small issues were not very different from those typically found for the larger issues, but they were appreciably better than the price relatives for the very small issues not subject to registration.

Another test of the effect of full disclosure which we carried out in connection with our criticism of a similar earlier test by George Stigler (Stigler (1964)) is to compare the price performance relatives of comparable large new stock issues in the pre-SEC 1923–28 and post-SEC 1949–55 periods over a five-year period subsequent to their offering (Friend and Herman (1964/1965)). These price performance relatives were obtained by adjusting the price trends of new issues for the price trends of outstanding issues (as measured by the Standard and Poor's Industrial Index) in an attempt to eliminate the effects of general market conditions. Such a test assumes that any differences in the relation of the markets for new and outstanding issues in the two periods were mainly a reflection of the SEC, with the disclosure provisions for new issues likely to be particularly important.[5] The deficiencies in this assumption are obvious, but the results of this test are still of interest.

In this comparison of the 1923–28 and 1949–55 periods, we found that the price performance of new issues was inferior to that of outstanding issues, but was closer to outstanding issues in the post-SEC than in the pre-SEC period suggesting an increase in allocational efficiency. The price performance of new issues relative to outstanding issues was, as a result, superior in the post-SEC period. This superiority was least marked in the first year or so after the issue date, but this finding can be explained by two facts (1) the extensive price pegging and numerous manipulative pools in the 1920s which might be expected to be particularly active in the first year after the public sale of a new issue; and (2) the extreme difficulty of securities valuation in the absence of full disclosure until there is some record of operating experience. In connection with the first of these two points, it might be noted that a sample of new issues which according to the Pecora hearings were subject to pool operations in the 1920s had an above-average price performance in the first year after the issue date (Friend and Herman (1964/1965)).

We extended the pre-SEC and post-SEC comparisons, in which we had covered the same time period and size categories of issues used by Stigler, to include 1958 and the first half of 1959 and also to include small issues for 1923, the first half of 1928 and the first half of 1958. Again we obtained the same qualitative results when comparing the pre-SEC and post-SEC periods.

Another significant result of this comparison of pre-SEC and post-SEC price performance of new common stock issues relative to outstanding issues is that the variances of the price ratios for each of the five years after issue date were

---

[5]While the SEC has effected significant increases in disclosure for both new and outstanding issues, the disclosure requirements for new issues are more extensive and started in the pre-SEC period at a much lower base.

much larger in the pre-SEC period. In other words, there was much less dispersion in relative price performance of new issues in the post-SEC period, which is another result consistent with the theoretical expectations of the effects of improved information and a reduction of manipulative activity. This again could be construed as evidence that securities legislation has improved the structure of stock prices.

In a subsequent analysis, we pointed out that another measure of performance advanced by Stigler suggested a statistically significant improvement in the structure of new issue prices from the pre-SEC to post-SEC periods (Friend and Herman (1964); Stigler (1964b)). Thus, the correlation in the pre-SEC period between new issue prices and prices one year later (with all new issue prices deflated by the price index for outstanding issues) seems to have been significantly lower than the average correlation for adjacent pairs of years after issue, whereas these correlations are identical (and higher) in the post-SEC period.

The only comprehensive data updating the comparative performance of new and outstanding issues appears in an unpublished Ph.D. dissertation by Roger Ibbotson (1973). That study, which covers the price performance of SEC registered underwritten unseasoned common stock issued during each month of the period 1960–69 over a post-issuance five-year period through 1971, finds that after a short-lived initial premium these new issues are indistinguishable from other outstanding stock. If these results are taken at face value, they would seem to suggest the virtual disappearance in the post-SEC period of the inferior performance of new issues. Thus, to the extent such data are relevant, they support an improvement in the efficiency of the new-issue market in the post-SEC period.

In the light of all these findings, it is not surprising that Randolph Westerfield and I stated in June 1975 that "We interpret the evidence on the 1933 Act as clearly favorable to disclosure" (Friend and Westerfield (1975)). It may be useful, therefore, to consider a different evaluation by George Benston which appeared in that same issue (Benston (1975)), both to examine its validity and perhaps its conformance with elementary standards of full disclosure. Benston in referring to the papers by Stigler, Herman, and myself, which cover all the results summarized above except those obtained by Ibbotson, states that

The data presented in these papers indicate an insignificant difference in the mean rate of return (relative to the market) on stocks floated in the years 1923–27 compared to flotations in the period 1949–55. However, the standard deviations of the returns are higher in the pre-Securities and Exchange Commission (SEC) period, which F-W assume is favorable.

He then proceeds to attack the relevance of the standard deviations and concludes that from such evidence "one should not interpret the evidence as clearly favorable to disclosure".

Benston clearly states (1) that the 1923–27 and 1949–55 comparisons provide insignificant differences in mean rates of return and strongly implies (2) that these are the only relevant results available and (3) that our conclusion is exclusively or primarily based on the respective standard deviations, which do not constitute terribly relevant evidence. The first point is grossly misleading, the second and third false. I can begin to understand Benston's distaste for full disclosure.

Turning to the first point, both Stigler and Friend and Herman make two different comparisons of the pre-SEC and post-SEC performance of new issues. The first covered 1923–28 for the pre-SEC period and included Class A stock as common, following Stigler's original procedures. The second covered 1923–27 and excluded Class A stock from common, following Stigler's revision of his original procedures when we pointed out that the original results appropriately corrected suggested a favorable SEC effect in the new issue market.

What Benston does not point out — and this would seem to be a glaring omission — is that for the first set of comparisons the post-SEC period was superior in the performance of new issues for each of the five years tested subsequent to their offering and was significantly superior (at the 5 percent level) for four of the five years. When the pre-SEC period is terminated at 1927, which had the best relative price experience of the pre-SEC years included, instead of 1928 which had the worst, *and* when Class A stock is excluded, it is true that the differences between the pre-SEC and post-SEC results for the five years subsequent to the offering are not statistically significant in any year, but Benston neglects to point out that the post-SEC performance is superior in four of the five years. While the differences in two of the five years are quite small, they range from 6 to 17 percent in the other three, with the post-SEC results superior in these years. If 1928 is retained in the earlier period, but Class A stock still omitted, the post-SEC performance of new issues in all of the five years rose by from 9 to 37 percent a year. Moreover, even for the pre-SEC comparison which is least unfavorable to Benston's position, a serial correlation measure of performance commented on earlier in this paper seems to show a statistically significant superiority of the post-SEC period.[6]

Turning to the second point implied by Benston, that the 1923–27 and 1949–55 comparisons to which he refers are the only evidence in the papers cited on mean relative rates of return on new issues, I have already indicated that this view is without any foundation. Totally apart from the several other 1923–27 and 1923–28 comparisons to which I have just referred, and the comparison of standard deviations of returns to which Benston does refer, it may be recalled that I previously discussed five other reasonably independent

---

[6]I will not comment here on the appropriateness of a longer vs. a shorter period for assessing the performance of new issues since Benston does not raise it, and it is fully covered in Friend and Herman (1964).

statistical tests and a substantial amount of qualitative information all favorable to the efficacy of the 1933 Act disclosure requirements and all cited in the literature referred to by Benston.

The last point implied by Benston, that our favorable conclusion on 1933 Act disclosure depended basically on the comparison of standard deviations of returns in the pre-SEC and post-SEC periods, is thus completely incorrect. As for the relevance of such a comparison, the reduction in the variance of the new issue price ratios from the pre-SEC to the post-SEC periods, since it was clearly not associated with a reduction in relative return, can be regarded from the investor's viewpoint as a positive achievement of the SEC, making the usual assumption that investors are risk averse. Benston advances the strange argument that such evidence has no relevance to the effectiveness of the SEC, relative to private individuals, in screening out fraudulent issues and, apparently in view of the covariance problems, in measuring potential risk. The evidence would seem to be directly relevant to the effectiveness of the securities regulation in screening out fraudulent issues, and I would assume that in the theoretical world to which covariances apply any desired level of risk could be obtained by a suitable combination of the market portfolio and the "risk-free" asset. If Benston is implying that the variance of the market portfolio has increased over this period as a result of covariance developments in the new issues markets, this seems far-fetched and in any case the available data do not support this hypothesis.[7]

A question might be raised as to the effect of securities regulation on the costs of new issues. In other words, has the apparent increase in allocational efficiency been offset by a reduction in operational efficiency or an increase in new issue costs, including the costs of the SEC as well as private costs? To the extent of course that registration costs are already reflected in price performance, our performance relatives have already adjusted for any difference in registration costs in the pre-SEC and post-SEC periods. However, in any case the evidence suggests a decline in underwriting compensation from the pre-SEC and the early SEC to the subsequent period (Friend et al. (1967)), and other information points to an inconsequential upward movement — in the aggregate a fraction of 1 percent — in other expenses associated with new issues (Friend and Herman (1964/1965)). The cost of SEC registration activities is estimated at well under one-tenth of 1 percent of the proceeds of registered issues. There are some other social costs as well as savings associated with required disclosure but these are not readily quantified, are not clear in direction and, in my opinion, are not very large. The costs of disclosure would seem to be a small fraction of the savings suggested by the various tests referred to earlier.

---

[7]See Friend and Blume (1975). The data there indicate that the standard deviation of return on New York Stock Exchange stocks as a whole was smaller in each of the decades 1942–51, 1952–61 and 1962–71 than for the decades 1922–31 and 1932–41 or than for the entire period 1872–1971 or for the period 1926–71 for which the data are much more reliable.

4.2. Impact on market for outstanding issues[8]

Several direct tests of the market's relative allocational efficiency in different periods have been derived from market equilibrium theory which demonstrates that under plausible assumptions the return on an individual stock over time should bear a simple linear relation to the return on the stock market as a whole (or on all risky assets), while the return of an individual stock in a cross section should be linearly related to its risk as measured by the covariance of its return with that on the market. The residual variation in these relationships provides a basis for assessing the efficiency implications of changes in the market structure. Thus, a study which regresses the monthly individual returns for 251 New York Stock Exchange (NYSE) stocks against the average market return for all of them finds that the variance of the residuals for 247 issues was smaller in the post-World War II period than in the period from 1926 through the 1930s (Blume (1967)). The total variance of return on these 247 issues, which measures variance in the market return as well as residual variance, was also smaller in the postwar period.

A supplementary analysis which I carried out several years ago (Friend 1972)) regresses on time the standard deviation of residuals from a series of cross-section relationships of portfolio monthly return and risk for 21 periods of 24 months each from July 1926, through June 1968. Each of the 21 cross-section relationships regressed the average monthly return on the estimated beta[9] of ten or so portfolios, each consisting of approximately 80 NYSE stocks stratified by beta in a preceding period. The 21 standard deviations of residuals obtained from these relationships were then regressed on time. A significant downward time trend was found in these standard deviations.

Both of these last two tests derived from market equilibrium theory suggest an improvement in market structure from the 1920s to the period after World War II. Since they abstract from factors affecting return on the market as a whole, they supply some support to the thesis that changes in securities regulation may have improved efficiency in the market for outstanding stock. However, the evidence here is not very strong.

There are moreover two more recent studies which purport to provide evidence that securities regulation in the market for outstanding stock has had no significant impact on market efficiency. The first, carried out by Officer (1973), concludes that the decline from the pre-SEC to the post-SEC periods in the one year standard deviation of monthly returns on the NYSE stock as a whole was "not attributable to the SEC". The second by Benston (1975) concludes that empirical evidence provides no support for the belief that the disclosure and

---

[8]Part of this discussion is based on Friend (1972).
[9]Beta is a measure of an asset's risk based on the covariance of its rate of return with that on the market (normalized by dividing this covariance by the variance of the market's rate of return).

related provisions of the Securities and Exchange Act of 1934 had any effect on the market for outstanding issues.

The conclusion by Officer, which as he notes differs from that reached in earlier analyses of the variability of returns of NYSE stocks as a whole, is to a substantial extent dependent on an extension back to February 1897 of the series on NYSE average returns from the reasonably satisfactory data covering all NYSE stocks starting with January 1926 back to January 1915 on the basis of a 20-stock Dow Jones index and then prior to 1915 on the basis of a 12-stock Dow Jones index. In view of the major incomparabilities between the data before and after January 1926, and presumably the much higher quality of the Dow Jones stocks as compared to the market as a whole, the new evidence by Officer does not appear at all cogent, though he asserts that the biases introduced by these incomparabilities are relatively unimportant. Moreover, it should be noted that Officer addresses himself only to variance in the market return and not at all to variance in residual returns.

The analysis by Benston is of somewhat greater interest since it is directed specifically at measuring the impact of SEC-mandated disclosure on the market for outstanding stocks on the basis of two tests of the impact of the 1934 Act disclosure. The first estimates the impact of changes in accounting data on common stock prices by deriving cross-sectional regressions in the year 1964 between changes in prices of individual stocks on the New York Stock Exchange (adjusted for movements in the market) and "unexpected" changes in each of a number of different financial variables (net sales, cash flow, net operating income and adjusted net income). Expected changes in these financial variables were obtained from several simple autoregressive models based on past data and then compared with subsequent published data to obtain estimates of unexpected changes. A similar but more limited analysis was carried out for 1963.

As Westerfield and I pointed out in a comment on this analysis (Friend and Westerfield (1975)), Benston for reasons which are obscure does not use more than one of these unexpected changes in financial variables in the same regression, but only one at a time. Even so, his findings point to statistically significant relations between price changes and the unexpected changes in each of these financial variables. Nevertheless, in view of what he considers the small size of the regression coefficients, he concludes that "this evidence is not consistent with the underlying assumption, that the financial data made public are timely or relevant, on average". There does not seem to be any justification for his willingness to dismiss out of hand the economic importance of these statistically significant results. Thus, he in effect considers not too relevant for stock prices knowledge about changes in financial variables in spite of the fact that he finds an increase of 100 percent in the annual rate of net sales is associated with an increase in price of 10.4 percent in the month of the announcement, and that changes in other variables are also associated with significant though proportionally smaller changes in price.

Moreover, it seems clear that Benston's regressions considerably understate the usefulness of published financial statements. They do not allow for the joint effects of unexpected changes in the different financial variables, and they make no adjustment for the substantial understatement of the relevant regression coefficients arising from the very large random measurement errors associated with any empirical measures of unexpected change.

Finally, we pointed out that on the basis of independent analyses "...many writers have concluded that published accounting profile variables can be useful in making investment decisions and contribute to market efficiency". We cited two articles as examples, one by Martin (1971), the other by May (1971). Benston had alleged that almost all previous empirical work relating published accounting data to stock price changes also leads to the conclusion that the data are not useful or are redundant.

In attempting to refute our comments on the first of his two tests discussed immediately above, Benston's rejoinder (Benston (1975)) advances six arguments (2–7) of which three (2, 3 and 5) might be regarded as substantive and will be considered here. In reply to our above quotation on earlier analyses of the utility of published accounting profiles, Benston states categorically that "No such conclusions are drawn in the articles they cite." Since Benston has a propensity for interpreting not only financial and statistical theory but also the English language differently from the way I do, let me quote directly from the Martin article we cited. Martin concludes (pp. 20–21)

> We have presented empirical evidence in support of the decision-relevance of accounting annual report data for investment decisions. In our view, this evidence is complementary to evidence provided by existing studies examining various aspects of accounting information utility. This study uniquely provides an explicit test of the usefulness of a series of accounting variables taken together.... Finally, we consider legislation to increase the scope and amount of reported data as potentially beneficial to investors, based on the ability of current information to explain investor expectations....

Clearly Benston's categorical assertion is unwarranted. May's summarization of the two implications of his results (p. 151) again seems consistent with the above quotation to which Benston takes exception.

Interestingly enough, even Nicholas J. Gonedes whom Benston cites in his continued refutation of the above quotation, and indeed at several different points in his rebuttal, concludes in a recent paper (Gonedes (1974a)),

> The results of our tests — which involved tests on means, variances, and covariances — are consistent with the statement that special accounting items convey information pertinent to establishing firms' equilibrium values. Also, our results are not consistent with the statement that no effect is associated with the disaggregation represented by the separate disclosure treatment accorded to special accounting items....

In reply to our criticism that "...Benston does not use more than one of these expected changes in financial variables in the same regression...," he agrees this criticism is correct but says that Gonedes in an unpublished manuscript dated September 1973 obtained similar results when he used a number of accounting data ratios simultaneously. Surely, it is disingenuous of Benston to make such a statement without pointing out the main conclusion which Gonedes reached (Gonedes (1974b)): "Our major purpose was to determine whether the accounting numbers jointly reflect new information. The results of our multivariate tests assign a high probability to the statement that the numbers do jointly provide information pertinent to assessing equilibrium expected returns."

From the viewpoint of statistical theory and elementary logic, perhaps the strangest point made by Benston is in response to our reference to the "...substantial understatement of the relevant regression coefficients arising from the very large random measurement errors associated with any empirical measures of unexpected change". The clear import of this reference is that under plausible and well-known statistical assumptions substantial random errors in an independent variable in a regression will bias substantially downward the absolute value of the coefficient of that variable. As a result the impact of disclosure which Benston found statistically significant in spite of this problem is clearly understated in his analysis, and probably substantially. Benston's reply, apart from referring again to the unpublished study by Gonedes which uses a grouping technique to reduce this measurement error, is that we "should question why the SEC has done so little to reduce these errors, or even to provide investors with some indication of their magnitude and effect". Nothing in Benston's analysis casts any light on the SEC's accomplishments in these areas since this would require comparable results for the pre-SEC period.

Benston's second set of tests of the impact of SEC-mandated disclosure on the market for outstanding stocks is similarly flawed. This set attempts to determine whether a large sample of individual NYSE stocks which were affected by sales disclosure provisions of the 1934 Act subsequently behaved "better" relative to the market as a whole than stocks for which such sales data were already available prior to the Act. The deficiencies in these tests were spelled out in some detail in the comment by Westerfield and myself in the June 1975 issue of *The American Economic Review* referred to earlier and were responded to in the rejoinder by Benston in the same *Review*. I shall not here repeat the arguments pro and con made in that issue except again to point out the errors in the more important relevant points made in Benston's rejoinder.

First, he objects to our statement that "We have indicated that Benston's analysis suggests that the 1934 Act did improve estimates of expected return." He goes on to state "I have been unable to detect where in their analysis F-W so indicate." I am afraid that Benston here is forgetting his first set of tests where, as I indicated earlier, he does find a statistically significant effect of accounting disclosure of such financial items as sales and net income on stock prices. If we assume as Benston does that the effect of disclosure on risk evaluation is marginal, then the effect on stock prices must reflect change in expected return.

Secondly, Benston states that "F-W then somewhat overstate the reported usefulness of accounting data [in several external studies] for forecasting betas". This point is significant since his finding that the market evaluation of risk as measured by beta did not change more in the post-SEC period for pre-SEC "nondisclosure" firms than for pre-SEC "disclosure" firms is essentially the only evidence Benston has to support his position that disclosure had no effect. We pointed out that "there are several external studies showing that current accounting data can be used to make at least as good and possibly superior forecasts of future asset risk (as measured by beta) than forecasts dependent only on historically estimated asset risks..." and "The accounting data which turn out to be useful for this purpose are balance sheet and income account items other than sales." Sales it will be recalled is the only variable Benston used in estimating the value of disclosure in this second set of tests. Benston's rejoinder is that the analysis in the external studies we referred to is flawed and again refers to the unpublished study by Gonedes which asserts that some of the results we relied on may reflect "spurious correlation".

Nothing Benston says or that we have seen in the literature is inconsistent with our assertion that the available external studies[10] can be used to make "as good and *possibly* superior forecasts of future asset risk" as can be obtained from past market derived betas. Our view was and is that there is some weak evidence to support the position that disclosure can and does help in the assessment of risk of outstanding stock as measured by beta, and stronger evidence that disclosure affects stock price in the theoretically expected and desired direction. Such a price effect even in the absence of a beta effect would be sufficient to justify 1934 Act disclosure unless associated costs were excessive.

The last consequential point in Benston's rejoinder takes issue with our statement (quoted here more fully): "Contrary to Benston's assertions, none of the assumptions that the portfolio approach depends upon appears strictly correct and empirical evidence on the validity of the beta coefficient is not conclusive. Therefore, it might have been illuminating to have included total variability estimates to supplement the analysis." Benston objects both to our criticism of the assumptions and to our evaluation of the empirical evidence. Both the simple capital asset pricing theory which he relies on and the portfolio approach he uses to justify almost exclusive reliance on beta assume that investors will attempt to minimize risk of their portfolio for given expected rate of return. The relevant measure of risk is total variability of return on the portfolio they hold. If investors hold a perfectly diversified portfolio of risky assets as is implied by the capital asset theory, each will hold a microcosm of all

---

[10]The most comprehensive listing (and summary) I have seen of such studies appears in Myers (1975).

stock and other risky assets in the same proportion to the total of their risky assets. Under these circumstances, the total variability in the portfolio would be mainly determined by the betas of the individual assets held, but this is no longer true for portfolios which are not well diversified so that for such investors the average standard deviation or some other measure of total variability of returns on individual assets is also important.

Therefore, it is highly relevant to point out that convincing statistical evidence is available which indicates that a high proportion of portfolios are dominated by a small number of assets and thus are not well diversified (Blume et al (1974); Blume and Friend (1975)). Nearly one-third of all stock owned by US individuals in 1971 was held in portfolios with fewer than five stocks, over 55 percent in portfolios with less than ten stocks, and one or two stocks dominated not only such portfolios but a surprisingly high proportion of portfolios with a larger number of stocks. To assume that investors with such portfolios would use beta to the exclusion of total variability as the measure of risk is to assume they are irrational and to vitiate both capital asset pricing and portfolio theory.

Turning to Benston's objections to our evaluation of the empirical evidence on the desirability of a total variability measure "to *supplement* the analysis", he quotes or paraphrases Miller and Scholes (1971) (whom we also cited), Jensen (1972), and Fama and MacBeth (1973) to the contrary. He clearly misinterprets Miller and Scholes and Fama and MacBeth and presumably also Jensen. Miller and Scholes and Fama and MacBeth state in reasonably clear language that it is *possible* though not proved that the empirical data they investigate are consistent with capital asset pricing theory which implies that beta of an individual stock if we could properly measure it is the only relevant measure of its risk. Jensen whom Benston quotes out of context (see rest of footnote 35, p. 367 to which Benston refers) is making the statement quoted about portfolios rather than individual securities and depends on Fama and MacBeth for its extension to individual assets. It seems to me, at the present state of the arts in capital asset pricing theory, that if we are concerned with realistic explanation of real world phenomena — not the most elegant theory which may or may not be applicable — it is unfortunate that Benston did not examine total variability estimates.

4.3. Impact of margin regulation

Of the various regulatory policies which have been directed towards the maintenance of orderly markets, the one of perhaps greatest interest to the general economist is the regulation of margin trading, which originally reflected Congressional concerns about the possibly excessive use of securities credit on the economy as a whole as well as on the stock market itself. Neoclassical economists in the US seem to consider this type of securities regulation as especially distasteful presumably because it interferes with the freedom of behavior of the beneficient speculators, substitutes selective credit controls for the free market, and has no obvious strong equity rationale.

I have indicated in an earlier paper (Friend (1972)) that my casual empiricism led me to the conclusion that margin requirements have probably tended to reduce stock price volatility and increase market efficiency, though such evidence is obviously not at all convincing. I also pointed out in that study that a rather comprehensive analysis of margin trading completed a little earlier (Moore (1966)), which concluded that "margin requirements have failed to achieve any of their objectives", was subject to deficiencies which when corrected appear to present a more favorable case for margin regulation.

Since that time, I have seen three other studies of the effectiveness of margin regulation, two of them — one by Douglas (1969) and the other by Largay (1973) — presenting favorable evidence, the third by Officer (1973) arguing for the ineffectiveness of such regulation. The Officer argument is based on two annual time-series regressions, apparently over the 1934–68 period, between each of two forms of the standard deviation of stock market return and both margin requirements and the standard deviation of industrial production. The two forms of the market return variable lead the margin requirements in one regression and follow them in the other, with the lead and lag both one year in duration. The lead form turns out to have a much higher correlation and the margin requirement variable is statistically insignificant in both, with the same negative coefficient and a t-value of somewhat over one.

The Douglas analysis regresses the standard deviation of the rate of change in price both on the standard deviation of the rate of change in dividends and on margin requirements for the period 1926–60, where each observation is a subperiod of five-year length (with the exception of four-year for the last) for each of 100 stocks. The coefficient of margin requirements is again negative but now highly significant which according to the author "suggests that margin requirements tend to reduce price volatility".

The Largay paper analyzes the price and volume characteristics of 71 NYSE and 38 AMEX stocks placed under special margin requirements during 1968–69. The price and volume characteristics of these stocks are explained both around the times when 100 percent margins were imposed and, subsequently, when they were removed. The author concludes that "The empirical results support the *a priori* hypothesis that banning the use of credit for transactions in individual issues is associated with a moderation or 'cooling off' of speculative activity in these stocks." This conclusion is based on several key findings: imposition of 100 percent margin was associated with the termination of the marked upward price movement and a reduction of the heavy volume of trading, both of which had typically preceded the new margin restriction. As the author notes, the NYSE stocks actually declined in price after they were placed under this restriction. Prices of the restricted stocks generally declined preceding removal of the special margin requirement. After removal only prices of the AMEX stocks tended to rise again though the volume of trading began to accelerate both for the NYSE and AMEX stocks.

My own appraisal of this material is that the evidence of a favorable effect of margin regulation on at least stock market volatility is stronger than the evidence on the other side. However, this assessment may reflect my personal biases, and I would agree that the evidence is far from conclusive.

4.4. Impact of other restrictions on trading activity

I will comment only briefly on the other major restrictions on trading activity effected by securities regulation apart from margin requirements, namely restrictions on short sales, on ordinary floor trading by members of an exchange, on stock specialists' activities, and on trading by corporate insiders (officers, directors and principal stockholders) in stocks of the corporations with which they are affiliated. Since specialists are considered as having a responsibility for helping to maintain fair and orderly markets, their trading activity has not been subjected to as severe regulatory restrictions as those imposed on the other types of speculative activity.

In the paper referred to earlier (Friend (1969)), I pointed out that my interpretation of the available evidence was that the trading activity of NYSE floor traders appeared as a whole more likely to be destabilizing than stabilizing; the reverse was true of NYSE specialists, and perhaps also of corporate insiders, at least in the post-SEC period; the evidence on short selling was mixed; and that none of this evidence was terribly strong. I also noted that even if restrictions on insider trading did not have a favorable impact on stock market volatility and market efficiency, they might be justified on equity grounds.

Since that earlier paper, an interesting new analysis of insider trading has been published by Jaffe (1974) which indicates that three legal actions which might have been expected to lead corporate insiders to expect stricter enforcement of the SEC insider trading rules (specifically SEC Rule 10(B)-5) did not in fact have a statistically significant effect on the profitability and volume of insider trading. Actually, the two legal actions which might have been expected to have the largest impact (the Cady, Roberts and Texas Gulf Sulphur decisions) *were* associated with drops in insider profitability while the third (the Texas Gulf Sulphur indictment) was associated with an increase in profitability. However, the changes were not statistically significant and the volume of insider trading increased slightly after all three actions (again without statistical significance). As a result, at least these specific changes in the prospects for implementation of regulatory constraints on insider trading seemed to have very little effect on the profitability and volume of such activity.

While this new evidence is certainly relevant to the effectiveness of these three legal actions all involving the SEC, it is not clear how much relevance it has for the broader effectiveness of Section 16B of the 1934 Act (relating to corporate recovery of shortterm profits by insiders) and it would seem to have very little relevance for the effectiveness of Section 16A (relating to full disclosure provisions for insiders).[11] Thus, if these provisions of the 1934 Act had been extremely effective well in advance of the first of the three legal actions, i.e. the November 1961 Cady, Roberts decision, Jaffe would have obtained the results he did, but the interpretation of his results would be radically different. Given the extreme variability of stock price changes and rates of return, it would not be surprising to find apparently little effect of new evidence of stricter enforcement of the SEC insider trading rules. Even prior to Cady, Roberts, there were both the prospect and I suspect actuality of private litigation for recovery of insider profits.

Clearly what is required for a more convincing answer to the overall effect of insider regulation is a careful comparison of pre-SEC and post-SEC insider behavior from the scattered pieces of evidence available. My own reaction to a reading of the major US Government investigations of the stock market and related abuses of the 1920s cited earlier in this paper makes me believe that insider abuses have declined substantially subsequent to that period, and I think that this is attributable at least in part to the disclosure provisions and restrictions imposed on insiders by the 1934 Act. A careful documentation of all such evidence would provide more relevant evidence than we now have available for assessing the effectiveness of the insider provisions of the 1934 Act.

Finally, I have not commented here on the ultimate type of interference with free market processes in the securities markets when trading in individual stocks or on rare occasions in the market as a whole is temporarily stopped in the face of major disruptions in the market. I have indicated elsewhere that under certain extreme circumstances (e.g. the assassination of President Kennedy) I consider such action desirable (Friend (1969)).

To conclude, it is my view that securities legislation in the US has, as a whole, benefited the stock market and the economy. However, as I have stated in the past, it is not yet clear whether a number of specific policies have been beneficial, and further exploration of the impact of such policies would be highly desirable.

[11]Actually Cady, Roberts involved activities which did not require corporate insider disclosure.

References

Benston, G. J. (1975) "Required Disclosure and the Stock Market: Rejoinder", *The American Economic Review*, June.

Blume, M.E. (1967) "The Assessment of Portfolio Performance: An Application to Portfolio Theory", Ph.D. Dissertation, University of Chicago.

Blume, M.E. and I. Friend (1975) "The Asset Structure of Individual Portfolios and Some Implications for Utility Functions", *Journal of Finance*, May.

Blume, M.E., I. Friend and J. Crockett (1974) "Stockownership in the United States: Characteristics and Trends", *Survey of Current Business*, November.

Fama, E.F. and J. MacBeth (1973) "Risk, Return and Equilibrium: Empirical Tests", *Journal of Political Economy*, May.

Friend, I. (1969) "The SEC and the Economic Performance of Securities Markets", in: H.G. Manne, ed., *Economic Policy and the Regulation of Corporate Securities* (American Institute for Public Research).

Friend, I. (1972) "The Economic Consequences of the Stable Market", *The American Economic Review*, May.

Friend, I. and M.E. Blume (1975) "The Demand for Risky Assets", *The American Economic Review*, December.

Friend, I. and E.S. Herman (1964) "Professor Stigler on Securities Regulation: A Further Comment", *Journal of Business*, January.

Friend, I. and E.S. Herman (1964/1965) "The SEC Through a Glass Darkly", *Journal of Business*, October, 399; January, 109.

Friend, I. and R. Westerfield (1975) "Required Disclosure and the Stock Market: Comment", *The American Economic Review*, June.

Friend, I., J. Longstreet, M. Mendelson, E. Miller and A. Hess, Jr. (1967) Investment Banking and the New Issues Market (The World Publishing Company).

Gonedes, N.J. (1974a) *Risk Information and the Effects of Special Accounting Items in Capital Market Equilibrium*, Report 7429 (Center for Mathematical Studies in Business and Economics, University of Chicago).

Gonedes, N.J. (1974b) "Capital Market Equilibrium and Annual Accounting Numbers: Empirical Evidence", *Journal of Accounting Research*, Spring.

Ibbotson, R.G. (1973) "Prices Performance of Common Stock New Issues", University of Chicago.

Jaffe, J. F. (1974) "The Effect of Regulation Changes on Insider Trading", *The Bell Journal of Economics and Management Science*, Spring.

Jensen, M. (1972) "Capital Markets: Theory and Evidence", *Bell Journal of Economics*, Autumn.

Leland, H.E. (1974) "Production Theory and the Stock Market", *The Bell Journal of Economics and Management Science*, Spring.

Martin, A. (1971) "An Empirical Test of the Relevance of Accounting Information for Investment Decisions", *Journal of Accounting Research, Empirical Research in Accounting: Selected Studies*.

May, R. G. (1971) "The Influence of Quarterly Earnings Announcements on Investor Decisions as Reflected in Common Stock Price Changes", *Journal of Accounting Research, Empirical Research in Accounting: Selected Studies*.

Merton, R. C. and M. G. Subrahmanyam (1974) "The Optimality of a Competitive Stock Market", *The Bell Journal of Economics and Management Science*, Spring.

Miller, M.H. and M. Scholes (1971) "Rates of Return in Relation to Risk: A Re-examination of Some Recent Findings", in: M.C. Jensen, ed., *Studies in the Theory of Capital Markets* (Praeger, New York).

Myers, S. C. (1975) "The Relation Between Real and Financial Measures of Risk and Return", in: I. Friend and J. Bicksler, eds., *Risk and Return in Finance* (Ballinger Publishing, Cambridge).

Officer, R.R. (1973) "The Variability of the Market Factor of the New York Stock Exchange", *Journal of Business*, July.

SEC (1963) *Report of Special Study of Securities Markets of the Securities and Exchange Commission* (US Government Printing Office, Washington, D.C.).

Stigler, G.J. (1964a) "Public Regulation of the Securities Market", *Journal of Business*, April, 117.
Stigler, G.J. (1964b) "Comment", *Journal of Business*, October.
US Congress (1933–34) *Stock Exchange Practices: Hearings before the Senate Committee on Banking and Currency* (72d and 73d Cong., Parts 1–17) (Washington, D.C.).
US Congress (1935) *Report of the Federal Trade Commission on Utility Corporations* (70th Cong., 1st Sess., Sen. Doc. 92) (Washington, D.C.).
US Congress (1939–42) *Report of the Securities and Exchange Commission on Investment Trusts and Investment Companies* (Washington, D.C.).

PART II

OPTIMAL FINANCIAL STRATEGIES FOR THE FIRM

Chapter 7

ON THE THEORY OF THE FIRM IN A CAPITAL ASSET PRICING MODEL WORLD

GAILEN L. HITE*
Ohio State University

1. Introduction

The primary purpose of this paper is to provide some linkage between the microeconomic theory of the firm and modern capital market theory of financial economics. These bodies of literature have proceeded along surprisingly distinct lines. The traditional theory of the firm has little to say about uncertainty and even less to say about the existence of a market for corporate securities. On the other hand, the literature of finance has concentrated on the pricing of securities and deriving implications for capital budgeting without explicitly introducing production, pricing, and output decisions.[1] One is left to wonder if and how capital market variables and firm financing methods affect not only corporate investment decisions but also output and input decisions as well.

In what follows we will attempt to provide some integration of the theory of the firm and capital market theory. We suppose the firm produces output by combining capital and labor inputs. We introduce uncertainty by assuming demand is stochastic as is the end of period price of capital goods. Claims to the resulting stochastic cashflow are sold to investors in the securities market. Market prices, then, guide the firm in its production and investment decisions since we assume the firm maximizes profit, or equivalently, its discounted net present value. This model allows us to assess the impact of capital market variables such as systematic risk, the price of risk, and the risk-free rate on the production and output decisions. Furthermore, in our single period model we are able to identify systematic risk as the result of uncertainty in product and used capital goods markets.

*I wish to thank W. W. Alberts, M. C. Jensen, K. B. Leffler, J. B. Long, L. E. Morris, G. A. Racette, C. A. Shoemaker, C. W. Smith, and H. M. Weingartner for many helpful discussions but I retain sole responsibility for any errors or omissions.

[1]A notable exception is presented by Fama and Miller (1972, ch. 3) who treat production and output in the case of perfect certainty.

James L. Bicksler, Editor, Handbook of Financial Economics
© *North-Holland Publishing Company – 1979*

The plan of the paper involves two approximations: with and without corporate taxes. In section 2 we ignore corporate taxes and capital structure mix. We derive an objective function of maximization of profit which utilizes the certainty-equivalent notions of the capital asset pricing model. After deriving several comparative statics results, we compare our model which uses an objective market-determined profit function to models which assume utility functions for a "personified" firm. Finally, we observe that the firm's "cost of capital" is not invariant to scale.

Section 3 introduces corporate taxes and capital structure becomes relevant by virtue of the tax deductibility of interest payments on debt. By comparing a levered and unlevered firm facing the same product and factor markets, we find that financial leverage will influence factor mix, capital utilization, output, profit, and the firms overall discount rate. Finally, section 4 provides a brief summary of our conclusions.

2. First approximation: no tax case

The optimization process we are about to describe involves a firm which is being organized to exploit an investment opportunity. The firm's securities will be sold in a perfect capital market described by the Sharpe (1964), Lintner (1965), and Mossin (1966) tradition. The proceeds will be used to purchase a stock of capital which in conjunction with a complementary amount of labor will be used to produce a quantity of output. The output will be sold at the end of the production period at a price which is unknown as of the planning date. The revenues are collected, the capital stock is liquidated, labor is paid, and the residual is distributed to security holders.[2] The decisions to be made at the beginning of the period include the quantity to be produced and the efficient choice of inputs to be acquired.

2.1. The value of the firm

The securities market is described by the single period equilibrium capital asset pricing models of Sharpe (1964), Lintner (1965), and Mossin (1966). Both firms

---

[2]The requirement of liquidation at the end of the period is primarily for the sake of convenience. However, if (i) the market for physical capital is perfect for new and second-hand capital goods, (ii) there are no adjustment costs, (iii) the firm holds no inventory of outputs as with a perishable product, and (iv) the demand schedules are not functionally dependent through time, then optimization can be done myopically. That is, the decision to continue after the current period is a separate investment decision that need not be made until next period and therefore has no bearing on the current decisions.

and individuals are price-takers in frictionless markets. In such a world, the value of the firm is simply the present value of its end-of-period cashflow and is given by[3]

$$V = \frac{E(\tilde{Y}) - \lambda \operatorname{cov}(\tilde{Y}, \tilde{M})}{1 + r}, \qquad (1)$$

where

$V =$ the value of the firm at the beginning of the period,
$\tilde{Y} =$ the end-of-period (random) cashflow,
$E(\cdot) =$ the expectation operator,
$\operatorname{cov}(\cdot, \cdot) =$ the covariance operator,
$\tilde{M} =$ the end-of-period rate of return on the market portfolio,
$r =$ the risk-free rate of interest, and
$\lambda =$ the market price of systematic risk.

In eq. (1), the equilibrium value of the firm depends on the market prices λ and r and the distribution of cashflow.

It is tempting to think of the valuation process in (1) as one of simply "forecasting" cashflows and for many problems in finance such an abstraction is appropriate.[4] However, for a more general set of problems one may want to take explicit recognition that the distribution of cashflow is *conditional* on the decision variables of the firm. For example, we shall deal with an uncertain product demand and resale price of capital goods. The distribution of $\tilde{Y}$ will depend not only on these two exogenous random variables but also on the choice of output and input mix. We suppose the market fully understands the internal decision model so that investors infer the correct conditional distributions to forecast.[5] The next task is to provide a detailed specification of the firm and an objective function.

---

[3]We shall use ~ to denote a random variable, ⁻ to denote an expected value of a random variable, and ˆ to denote a certainty equivalent. The numerator of (1) could also be written as $[\bar{Y} - \lambda \operatorname{cov}(\tilde{Y}, \tilde{M})]$ or even more simply as just $\hat{Y}$. The latter two symbols will be employed primarily for functions of random variables.

[4]Sometimes in capital budgeting one considers a "project" which is economically independent of the firm's other projects and attempts to infer an accept/reject decision rule from (1). Presumably such a project is of absolutely fixed scale with a unique labor requirement and output level with no factor substitution or marginal expansion possibilities. To evaluate such a project by (1) would be a matter of simple forecasting since the only firm decision variable is whether the project is accepted or rejected.

[5]It would be possible to introduce uncertainty into the reaction of the firm to exogenous variables as well but this is beyond the scope of our current effort. We suppose later that the goal is to maximize the net present value of the firm so that we are ignoring any problems of agency which might result in divergence between the goals of owners, managers, and bondholders. See the important advances by Jensen and Meckling (1976) and Myers (1977).

2.2. The environment of the firm

2.2.1. Demand

The firm is assumed to be a quantity-setter facing a demand schedule which is stochastic when viewed from the planning date. As described by Leland (1972) we may represent the demand relationship as

$$\tilde{P} = D(Q, \tilde{\Psi}) \tag{2}$$

which relates product price $\tilde{P}$, via the demand function D, to the quantity of output Q and to a random state of nature variable denoted $\tilde{\Psi}$.[6] We assume D is continuous and differentiable, slopes downward with respect to Q for a specific outcome of $\tilde{\Psi}$, and increases with larger values of $\tilde{\Psi}$ for any given output. By assumption, the distribution of $\tilde{\Psi}$ is independent of Q but $\tilde{P}$ is dependent on both Q and the distribution of $\tilde{\Psi}$.

Fig. 7.1 shows several possible outcomes. Suppose, for example, that ψ_1 represents the minimum value of $\tilde{\Psi}$ and ψ_2, the maximum. Should the output be Q the price will be P_1 if ψ_1 obtains and P_2 for ψ_2. It is in this sense that $\tilde{\Psi}$ represents a "shift" in demand such that higher prices are received at a given output for larger values of $\tilde{\Psi}$. On the other hand, for a given value of $\tilde{\Psi}$ price will decline with output. Should the output be at the level denoted by Q' and $\tilde{\Psi}$ take on, say, ψ_1 the price would be P_1', lower than P_1. Finally, even with $\tilde{\Psi}$ being independent of Q, the distribution of $\tilde{P}$ is not independent of Q, in general. In fig. 7.1 the price range is drawn to increase with output. While this need not be the case, it clearly demonstrates that the probability density function of $\tilde{P}$ may vary with output.[7]

2.2.2. Production

The production process is described by a technological constraint of the form

$$Q = f(K, L) \tag{3}$$

which relates output to the amount of labor input, L, and capital stock, K. The function, f, is assumed to be a "well-behaved", neoclassical production function. It requires positive levels of both inputs to produce any output, is continuous

---

[6] $\tilde{\Psi}$ might represent some aggregate variable such as weather or consumer tastes. The important point is that it is unaffected by Q.

[7] One class of demand functions exhibiting identical distributions of $\tilde{P}$ independent of Q is the additive form $\tilde{P} = D(Q) + \tilde{\Psi}$. (The perfectly competitive case is of this variety with $D(Q)$ being a constant; see Alberts (1977).) This form results in parallel shifts as $\tilde{\Psi}$ changes. We have used the more general form in (2) which allows for both shifts and changes of slope as shown in fig. 7.1.

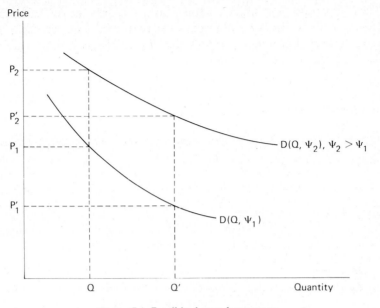

Figure 7.1. Possible demand outcomes.

and twice differentiable, has positive marginal products, and is strictly concave. The technology is fixed during the period of analysis and there is no uncertainty in the production process.

2.2.3. Input markets

The firm is assumed to be a price-taker in the labor market and in the market for new and used capital goods. Labor is contracted at the beginning of the period at a known wage, w, but the total payment wL is not paid until after the output is sold. We implicitly assume even with the worst possible demand conditions that sufficient cashflows will be available to pay wages. Hence there is no default on payments to labor.

The production process requires a stock of homogeneous capital which is purchased with the proceeds of the security issues and after production has been completed this capital is liquidated in a perfect second-hand market.[8] For simplicity we choose capital as our numeraire and take its initial price to be

---

[8]Recall that the firm will be operated for just one period. Alternatively, one could view a decision to stay in business as one of simultaneous liquidation and repurchase of capital since there are no transactions costs.

unity. Thus, K is both a monetary value and a physical measure of the capital stock. However, the end-of-period price is stochastic, so if we represent the price change or "rate of depreciation" as $\tilde{\delta}$ then the resale price is $(1-\tilde{\delta})$ and the proceeds of liquidation are $(1-\tilde{\delta})K$.

2.2.4. Objective function

We can express the cashflow in the absence of taxes on corporate income as

$$\begin{aligned} \tilde{Y} &= R(Q,\tilde{\Psi}) - wL + (1-\tilde{\delta})K \\ &= \left[R(Q,\tilde{\Psi}) - wL - \tilde{\delta}K \right] + K, \end{aligned} \tag{4}$$

where $R(Q,\tilde{\Psi})$ the stochastic total revenue function resulting from the product of Q and $\tilde{P}$ in (2).[9] The term in brackets in (4) may be thought of as "accounting" income in the sense of being the residual of revenue after wage payments and an allowance for "depreciation", $\tilde{\delta}K$. The final term, K, represents "return of capital".

The market value of $\tilde{Y}$ is from (1)

$$V = \frac{\left[\hat{R}(Q) - wL - \hat{\delta}K \right] + K}{1+r}, \tag{5}$$

where

$$\begin{aligned} \hat{R}(Q) &\equiv E\left[R(Q,\tilde{\Psi}) \right] - \lambda \operatorname{cov}\left[R(Q,\tilde{\Psi}), \tilde{M} \right] \\ &= Q\left[E(\tilde{P}) - \lambda \operatorname{cov}\left[\tilde{P}, \tilde{M} \right] \right] \end{aligned} \tag{6}$$

and

$$\hat{\delta} \equiv E(\tilde{\delta}) - \lambda \operatorname{cov}(\tilde{\delta}, \tilde{M}). \tag{7}$$

The function $\hat{R}(Q)$ in (6) is a certainty equivalent total revenue function and $\hat{\delta}$ in (7) is the certainty-equivalent depreciation rate.

The revenue function $\hat{R}(Q)$ depends on output level, expected price, and covariation between price and the market portfolio. It is important to note that the distribution of price is conditional on output as seen from the demand function in (2). Thus, expected price, $E(\tilde{P})$, and the risk premium per unit,

---

[9]It is always possible that the actual demand curve which obtains will be inelastic at the chosen output level. In this case total revenue could be increased by disposing of part of the output. Thus, we would have to complicate the model to distinguish quantity produced from quantity sold. The simpler case we follow is to suppose that over the relevant range of outputs we consider the ex post demand curve will be elastic. Intuitively we are considering regions for which the absolute values of demand elasticities exceed unity and have small variances.

$\lambda \operatorname{cov}(\tilde{P}, \tilde{M})$, will both depend on Q [10] so the certainty-equivalent of price will change with output. Therefore, we are *not* assuming that risk increases linearly with output.

Liquidation of the firm's capital stock at the end of the period is assumed to leave the price of capital goods, $1 - \tilde{\delta}$, unchanged. Hence, the certainty-equivalent $\tilde{\delta}$ in (7) is independent of the size of the capital stock. The portfolio risk of the liquidation, $\operatorname{cov}(1 - \tilde{\delta}, \tilde{M})K$, increases linearly with K. On the other hand the systematic risk of depreciation, $\operatorname{cov}(\tilde{\delta}, \tilde{M})K$, also increases linearly with K. These two covariances have opposite signs such that if the price of capital goods is positively correlated with the market then depreciation is negatively correlated with the market and either notion would add to the firm's systematic risk.[11]

The expression in (5) is more explicit than (1) and focuses attention on the fact that the value of the firm depends on three sets of arguments: (i) the distributions of the random variables $\tilde{\Psi}$ and $\tilde{\delta}$ which are exogenous to the firm; (ii) the market prices λ and r which are parametric to the firm[12]; and (iii) the decision variables Q, K, and L which are the result of an optimization process to be specified shortly. We assume that decisions will be made so as to maximize the net present value[13] of the firm so that the maximand is

$$\max_{Q,K,L} \{V - K\} = \max_{Q,K,L} \left\{ \frac{\hat{R}(Q) - wL - (\tilde{\delta} + r)K}{1 + r} \right\}, \tag{8}$$

subject to the production constraint of (3).

One should note that (8) is developed within the context of a capital market equilibrium. Thus, the adjustment for time preference is made with the *market* price r and the adjustment for risk involves the *market* price λ. In a perfect

---

[10] Again the issue is how the stochastic disturbance term affects the demand curve. The additive form, $\tilde{P} = D(Q) + \tilde{\Psi}$, mentioned previously, would have the price risk term as $\operatorname{cov}(\tilde{\Psi}, \tilde{M})$ which is independent of Q since $\tilde{\Psi}$ is independent of Q. For this case, revenue risk would increase linearly with output.

[11] That is $\operatorname{cov}(1 - \tilde{\delta}, \tilde{M}) = -\operatorname{cov}(\tilde{\delta}, \tilde{M})$. Hence, the liquidation form in the first line of (4) or the depreciation form in the bottom line produce identical results.

[12] We assume the firm is a price-taker in the securities market by which we mean that the firm acts "as if" it has no impact on λ, r, and the distribution of $\tilde{M}$. That is to say that if there already exists a stream identical to $\tilde{Y}$ then the firm assumes that $\tilde{Y}$ will sell for the same price as the already existing stream. Thus, for example, if another firm already owned $\tilde{Y}$ then our firm believes that its own equilibrium market value would be the same whether it merges with the other firm or simply produces $\tilde{Y}$ itself. In other words we ignore changes in the aggregate supply of risk. For a rigorous investigation of this issue see Long (1972) and Merton and Subrahmanyam (1974).

[13] We have no reason at this point to consider how the investment is financed whether by debt, inside equity, or outside equity because we are assuming away any problems and costs of agency (see Jensen and Meckling (1976)) and corporate taxes (see Hamada (1969)). Later, when we introduce taxes, we will be forced to consider the financing method explicitly. Presumably this residual between the value of the firm's securities and the initial outlay for capital assets is captured by the promoters or founders.

capital market there is no reason to introduce a firm utility function[14] and use *internal* prices for risk aversion and time preferences. In general, it would be impossible to assess an aggregate stockholder utility function guaranteeing unanimity but here there is no need to do so. In fact, failure to use market prices would be disciplined by the market in the same fashion as failure to use any other market price. Thus, our development takes full advantage of the separation theorem resulting from our perfect capital market setting.

Another important insight can be gained by focusing on the numerator of (8) which we shall designate by Π where

$$\Pi = \hat{R}(Q) - wL - (\hat{\delta} + r) \cdot K. \tag{9}$$

Since the discount factor $(1 + r)$ is parametric, maximization of (8) will maximize (9) also. In fact, we view Π as *economic profit*[15] under uncertainty. The first term $\hat{R}(Q)$, is the certainty-equivalent of total revenue. The second term is a deduction for wage payments to labor, wL. The final term, $(\hat{\delta} + r)K$, represents the cost of utilizing the capital stock. The cost per unit is $(\hat{\delta} + r)$ which is the sum of the certainty-equivalent of depreciation, $\hat{\delta}$, and the pure (riskless) opportunity cost, r, of capital is often called the "user cost" or implicit rental rate of capital.[16] This notion of profit is directly analogous to that in the timeless certainty model of the microeconomic theory of the firm except that uncertainty is introduced and adjusted for with market prices. We could develop the optimization process by either maximizing profit in (9) or its discounted value, i.e. net present value in (8), but we will focus on the profit form.

It is important to note that we are using "profit" in the sense of that which is to be maximized. Consequently, profit is an ex ante concept which depends on the *distribution* of end-of-period cashflows but does not depend on the ex post *results* per se. That is, profits are maximized at the beginning of the period such that once the decisions are made profit is known. Ex post outcomes are not something that can be "maximized" but the ex ante certainty equivalents can be. Hence, from a decision-making point of view we have no interest in the actual ex post results.[17] We shall have more to say about this later when we assess the impact of uncertainty on the real decisions of the firm.

----

[14]For example, see Leland (1972), Sandmo (1971), etc.

[15]To avoid the confusion of Π with business profit we might follow standard convention and employ the label "rents" for Π. In any case, it is Π that is to be maximized. Note also that the concept here is quite different from "Knightian profit".

[16]The term "user cost" of capital is not the same as the weighted average "cost of capital" as the latter term is normally used in finance to mean the firm's overall discount rate. The term $(\hat{\delta} + r)$ would be the rate at which one could lease a unit of capital in a competitive rental market. Note also that the riskless rate is appropriate without any added premium for risk since all risk adjustments are made separately in the certainty equivalents of the individual cashflow components.

[17]In a multiperiod context, ex post results might be of some interest to the extent that they offered some predictive capability.

2.3. Firm equilibrium

With the objective function in (9) we turn to the optimization problem which may be partitioned into two sequential subproblems: (1) cost minimization for each level of output which yields the cost function, and (2) profit maximization given the cost function. By rewriting (8) we have

$$\max_{Q,K,L} \{\Pi\} = \max_{Q} \left\{ \hat{R}(Q) - \min_{K,L} \left[wL + (\hat{\delta} + r)K \right] \right\}. \tag{10}$$

$$\text{subject to } Q = f(K,L) \qquad \text{subject to } Q = f(K,L)$$

We proceed with the nested problem first.

2.3.1. Input determination

The minimization problem within (10) can be represented by forming the Lagrangian expression C^* with underdetermined Lagrange multiplier c as

$$C^* = \hat{C}(K,L) + c[Q - f(K,L)]$$

$$= wL + (\hat{\delta} + r)K + c[Q - f(K,L)], \tag{11}$$

where C^* is to be minimized and $\hat{C}(K,L)$ is the certainty-equivalent cost function which depends on the level of output and the levels of the two factor inputs. In equilibrium, the constraint will be zero so minimizing C^* will minimize total production cost.

The first-order necessary conditions for minimizing (11) are

$$\frac{\partial C^*}{\partial L} = w - cf_L = 0, \tag{12a}$$

$$\frac{\partial C^*}{\partial K} = (\hat{\delta} + r) - cf_K = 0, \tag{12b}$$

$$\frac{\partial C^*}{\partial c} = Q - f(K,L) = 0, \tag{12c}$$

where f_L and f_K are the marginal products of labor and capital, respectively, and where (12c) is the production constraint in (3). The Lagrange multiplier c should be interpreted as the certainty equivalent of marginal production cost[18] and this shadow price will normally vary with output. In anticipation of the full optimization process presented later, we might note that c is also equal to the certainty-equivalent of marginal revenue. The second-order conditions sufficient

---

[18]See, for example, Henderson and Quandt (1971, ch. 3).

for a "regular" solution to (11) is that the matrix of cross-partials D, where

$$D = \begin{bmatrix} -cf_{LL} & -cf_{LK} & -f_L \\ -cf_{KL} & -cf_{KK} & -f_K \\ -f_L & -f_K & 0 \end{bmatrix}, \tag{12d}$$

be positive definite subject to (12c).

The conditions in (12) are quite similar to the traditional theory of the firm under certainty. Rearrangement yields

$$w = cf_L, \tag{13a}$$

$$(\hat{\delta} + r) = cf_K \tag{13b}$$

or

$$\frac{f_L}{f_K} = \frac{w}{\hat{\delta} + r}. \tag{14}$$

As mentioned previously, c is marginal cost, which in equilibrium will be equal to marginal revenue, so (13) can be interpreted as requiring that each factor be utilized to the point where (the certainty-equivalent of) the factor's marginal revenue product just equals its (certainty-equivalent) wage. Furthermore, (14) shows the rate of technical substitution between factors so we have the familiar tangency between isoquants and the (certainty-equivalent) isocost line. The adjustment for risk in a capital market setting requires that the rental rate, $\hat{\delta} + r$, include a certainty-equivalent (not just an expected value) for depreciation. Four distinct variables affect this user cost: (i) the riskless rate of interest, r; (ii) the expected rate of depreciation, $E(\hat{\delta})$; (iii) the market price of risk, λ; and (iv) the systematic risk of price changes for physical capital goods, $\text{cov}(\tilde{\delta}, \tilde{M})$. An *increase* in the first two or a *decrease* in the last will increase the implicit factor price. However, changes in λ are dependent on the sign of $\text{cov}(\tilde{\delta}, \tilde{M})$. If the covariance is positive then increasing the price of risk is the same as an increase in systematic risk but a negative covariance will produce opposite effects. We are particularly interested in the impact of λ and $\text{cov}(\tilde{\delta}, \tilde{M})$ since they are absent from the traditional theory of the firm.

To investigate the effects of depreciation risk we differentiate the first-order identities in (12) with respect to $\hat{\delta}$ to yield

$$D \begin{bmatrix} dL/d\hat{\delta} \\ dK/d\hat{\delta} \\ dc/d\hat{\delta} \end{bmatrix} = \begin{bmatrix} 0 \\ -1 \\ 0 \end{bmatrix}. \tag{15}$$

Solving for the effect on capital we have

$$\frac{\mathrm{d}K}{\mathrm{d}\hat{\delta}} = -\frac{D_{22}}{|D|} < 0, \tag{16}$$

where D_{22} is the second principal minor and $|D|$ is the determinant of the matrix D defined in (12d). Since D is positive definite we find the factor demand in (16) is downward sloping. Hence, an *increase* in $\mathrm{cov}(\tilde{\delta}, \tilde{M})$ will *increase* the utilization of capital at each level of output by lowering the factor cost. The same result holds for λ only if the covariance term is positive. If, however, capital good depreciation is negatively related to the market (i.e. salvage value positively related) then an increase in the price of risk would decrease capital utilization.

At first glance it might appear strange that an increase in the (systematic) riskiness of depreciation would increase the usage of capital. Recall that liquidation of capital adds $(1 - \tilde{\delta})K$ to cashflow. Hence, for a given $E(\tilde{\delta})$ an increase in the $\mathrm{cov}(\tilde{\delta}, M)$ will reduce the systematic risk of *total* cashflow since $\tilde{\delta}K$ is a cost.[19] Similarly, a higher price of risk will increase capital's importance in producing any level of output[20] for a positive covariance term or decrease it for a negative covariance.

The impact of risk on marginal cost can be seen by solving (15) to yield

$$\frac{\mathrm{d}c}{\mathrm{d}\hat{\delta}} = \frac{D_{23}}{|D|}, \tag{17}$$

which is of indeterminate sign since we have no restrictions on the off-diagonal minor D_{23}. However, had we differentiated (12) with respect to Q[21] and solved for the effect of output expansion on capital we would have found

$$\frac{\mathrm{d}K}{\mathrm{d}Q} = \frac{D_{32}}{|D|}. \tag{18}$$

Since the matrix D is symmetric we see that (17) and (18) are identical. Thus, if capital is a normal input[22] which increases with output then (18) is positive and

---

[19]The crucial covariance involves the liquidation value per unit which is $\mathrm{cov}(1 - \tilde{\delta}, \tilde{M}) = -\mathrm{cov}(\tilde{\delta}, \tilde{M})$. Hence, an increase in the risk of depreciation will decrease the systematic risk of the salvage value and capital goods are then available on more favorable terms.

[20]Notice that the foregoing comparative statics results are derived for a fixed level of output and for a single firm in isolation. It is not clear that effects of changes in aggregate economic variables such as λ can be analyzed in such a framework. The results here are not intended as general equilibrium statements.

[21]This would yield the system of equations

$$[D] \begin{bmatrix} \mathrm{d}L/\mathrm{d}Q \\ \mathrm{d}K/\mathrm{d}Q \\ \mathrm{d}c/\mathrm{d}Q \end{bmatrix} = \begin{bmatrix} 0 \\ 0 \\ -1 \end{bmatrix}.$$

[22]For a full explanation see Bear (1965).

so is (17). We assume this to be the case so marginal cost will shift in the same direction as changes in $\hat{\delta}$.[23] Since as increase in $\text{cov}(\hat{\delta}, M)$ decreases $\hat{\delta}$, it would *reduce* marginal cost. The effect of λ will again depend on the sign of the covariance term. The conclusion, then, is that increases in the systematic risk of depreciation will shift the marginal cost curve downward. On the other hand, increases in the expected rate of depreciation or the risk-free rate will shift marginal cost upward. Finally, the price of risk has an effect conditional on the sign of the risk term.

We suppose that for any set of factor prices the inputs will be chosen to satisfy (12). Thus, for a given set of prices we summarize the cost function in terms of Q by

$$\hat{C}(Q) = wL^* + (\hat{\delta} + r)K^*, \tag{19}$$

where L^* and K^* are the factor demand equations from solving (11). We shall call $\hat{C}(Q)$ the "total cost" function and its derivatives, $\hat{C}'(Q)$, the "marginal cost" function but the reader should keep in mind that each is a certainty-equivalent.

2.3.2. Output determination

The derivation of the cost function is crucial to solving the output problem. The other necessary function is the certainty-equivalent total revenue function $\hat{R}(Q)$ introduced in (6). In anticipation of the subsequent development, we concentrate on the properties of this function before solving the output problem.

The certainty-equivalent of revenue will change with output through both the expectation term and the risk premium term as can be seen from differentiating (6) with respect to Q to yield

$$\hat{R}'(Q) = \frac{\partial E[R(Q, \tilde{\Psi})]}{\partial Q} - \lambda \frac{\partial \text{cov}[R(Q, \tilde{\Psi}), \tilde{M}]}{\partial Q}$$

$$= E\left[\frac{\partial R(Q, \tilde{\Psi})}{\partial Q}\right] - \text{cov}\left[\frac{\partial R(Q, \tilde{\Psi})}{\partial Q}, \tilde{M}\right]. \tag{20}$$

The expression in (20) is the marginal certainty-equivalent of total revenue with respect to changes in output. Alternatively, it can be interpreted as the certainty-equivalent of marginal revenue which is the derivative in brackets.[24]

---

[23]Of course, total cost will change in the same direction as $\hat{\delta}$ since by differentiating (11) and using (12) we have

$$dC^*/d\hat{\delta} = \partial C^*/\partial \hat{\delta} = K > 0.$$

[24]The derivative in (20) results from the distribution of $\tilde{\psi}$ being functionally independent of Q. Thus, under the current set of assumptions, the derivative of an expectation of a function is the expected value of the derivative of the function. See Cramér (1946).

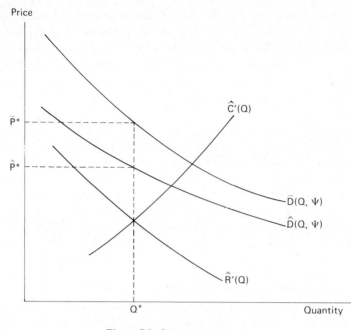

Figure 7.2. Output determination.

Bringing together the revenue and cost equations we can rewrite (10) as

$$\max_{Q} \{ \Pi \} = \max_{Q} \{ \hat{R}(Q) - \hat{C}(Q) \}, \tag{21}$$

which requires

$$\hat{R}'(Q) = \hat{C}'(Q) \tag{22}$$

in equilibrium.[25] Eq. (22) is simply the requirement that marginal cost equals marginal revenue except now those terms imply certainty-equivalent risk adjustment and not simply expected values. This equality is shown in fig. 7.2 and results in output Q^*.

The illustration involves three downward sloping curves: (i) the "expected demand curve", $\bar{D}(Q, \tilde{\Psi})$;[26] (ii) the certainty-equivalent demand curve, $\hat{D}(Q, \tilde{\Psi})$; and (iii) the certainty-equivalent marginal revenue curve $\hat{R}'(Q)$. The intersection of the last curve with the certainty-equivalent marginal cost curve $\hat{C}'(Q)$ gives

---

[25]The second-order sufficiency condition which is assumed to hold would have $\hat{R}''(Q) < \hat{C}''(Q)$ which shows that marginal revenue curve cannot cut the marginal cost curve from below at the optimum. While these are local conditions we also require $\Pi > 0$ to insure positive output.

[26]This expected demand curve will not, in general, be the curve $D(Q, \tilde{\Psi})$ "evaluated" at the expected value of the random demand component $\tilde{\Psi}$.

the profit-maximizing output as Q^*. The resulting expected price is $\bar{P}^*$ and, after adjustment for the amount of price risk at this level of output, the certainty-equivalent price is $\hat{P}^{*27}$ which is $\bar{P}^* - \lambda \operatorname{cov}(\tilde{P}, \tilde{M})$

2.4. Comparative statics with risk

With output determination as shown in fig. 7.2 we can address the issue of how uncertainty affects the operating decisions of the firm. This question was addressed previously by Leland (1972) and Sandmo (1971) who explicitly introduce utility functions for a personified "firm". They provide comparative statics results for the risk-averse, risk-neutral, and risk-seeking cases. By way of contrast, we have assumed wealth maximization in a capital market equilibrium using market-determined prices of risk. What is relevant in our model is not the mere existence of uncertainty but instead the contribution of the firm to the risk of the market portfolio. Hence, our comparative statics results deal with changes in the signs of the covariance terms instead of changes in the sign of the risk-aversion parameter.

To compare the certainty and uncertainty cases, one must replace the distribution of each random variable with a single value. Which value should one use? One approach has been to use the expected values for the comparable certainty case. Meaningful questions can then be asked as follows: How would the decision variables change if the values of the random variables were revealed in advance and the revealed values just happened to be the mathematical expectation of the original distributions? In our case we could achieve the same situation by assuming the covariance terms were zero so we could simultaneously compare certainty versus uncertainty and zero versus nonzero *systematic* risk. Uncertainty per se would have no impact since there would be no systematic risk in the cashflows. Leland and Sandmo also considered a case in which uncertainty had no impact but their result was due to their assuming a risk-neutral "firm" whereas we are assuming wealth maximization given market prices for risk.

There are three variables in our model which deal with risk: (i) $\operatorname{cov}(\tilde{P}, \tilde{M})$ in (6); (ii) $\operatorname{cov}(\tilde{\delta}, \tilde{M})$ in (7); and (iii) λ in both (6) and (7). In a capital market dominated by risk-averters we know that λ will be positive but there is no a priori reason to constrain the signs of the two risk terms. As our base case we

---

[27]These curves are drawn to show demand being positively correlated with the market portfolio. Furthermore, the certainty-equivalent curve is drawn in such a way that price uncertainty, $\operatorname{cov}(\tilde{P}, \tilde{M})$, declines with higher outputs and lower expected prices. There is nothing in our analysis that requires either of these. If demand had negative covariance risk then $\hat{D}(Q, \tilde{\Psi})$ would actually lie above $\bar{D}(Q, \tilde{\Psi})$. Finally, the covariance risk could even change signs at different outputs and cause $\bar{D}$ and $\hat{D}$ to intersect.

consider the unlikely event that neither product demand nor the liquidation value of the particular capital good has any systematic risk, i.e. the covariances are zero.

The base case is shown in fig. 7.3. If the covariances were indeed zero then we would have the expected marginal cost curve $\overline{C}'(Q)$ and expected marginal revenue curve $\overline{R}'(Q)$. This would result in output Q_0 and expected price $\overline{P}_0$.

Let us introduce price risk by assuming that $\mathrm{cov}(\tilde{P}, \tilde{M})$ is nonzero. If greater demand is associated with above average returns on the market portfolio then the certainty-equivalent marginal revenue curve $\hat{R}'(Q)$ will lie below the expectation curve $\overline{R}'(Q)$ and for a given marginal cost schedule would reduce output. On the other hand, if the price of capital goods varies positively with the market portfolio then we have $\mathrm{cov}(\tilde{\delta}, \tilde{M}) < 0$ and the risk adjustment would shift the marginal cost curve upward from its expectation $\overline{C}'(Q)$ to its certainty-equivalent provided that capital is a normal input. This would tend to reinforce the price risk effect and reduce output further to Q_1 and increase expected price to $\overline{P}_1$.

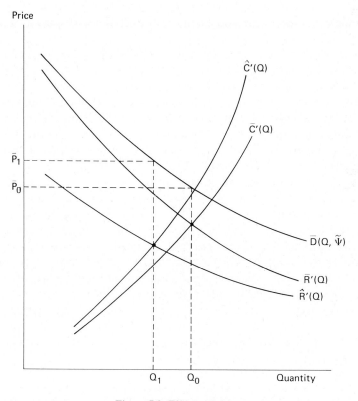

Figure 7.3. Effects of risk.

Compared to the base case in which uncertainty had no impact, we find that output will be smaller and price (expected and ex post) will be higher. These results were derived by Leland and Sandmo under the assumption that the "firm" was risk-averse. However, these are by no means the only possibilities. If we suppose that product demand and the price of the capital good were negatively related to the market portfolio then the curves would have shifted down and output would have increased causing a lower price than the certainty case. Since Leland and Sandmo do not introduce the notion of portfolio risk they would predict this larger output only in the case of a risk-preferent "firm".

At this point we conclude that the impact of uncertainty on the output decision depends on the stochastic relationship between product demand (and depreciation) on the one hand and the returns on assets in the market portfolio on the other. A positive covariance between demand and the market portfolio would, ceteris paribus, reduce output. If securities are priced in equilibrium according to the capital asset pricing model and if managers make decisions so as to maximize the wealth of stockholders, then the relevant feature of uncertainty lies in its stochastic relationship with the market portfolio. That is to say, the important feature is the stochastic nature of the distribution and not the nature of the firm which possesses it.

Our view contrasts quite sharply with the work of Leland and Sandmo who employ utility functions for "firms". In their world, two firms with identical production functions, the same distribution of demand, and equivalent factor market conditions might well make very different output decisions if they had different utility functions. Thus, two such firms could earn different profits, or rates of return, in "equilibrium".[28] Such results could not persist in our model since we have introduced a perfect market for trading claims to risky income streams. Separation obtains in our world so the appropriate price of risk is the external market price of risk λ instead of an internal one.

The implication of the two types of models will contrast sharply. For example, Leland examines the impact of a fixed cost, such as a lump sum tax on output. Since the fixed cost would reduce profit the "firm's" Pratt–Arrow measure of absolute risk aversion would change. With decreasing absolute risk-aversion and risk increasing with output, the "firm" would move to a lower level of risk and hence lower output. He concludes that fixed costs are not neutral with respect to output decisions. Retracing our development one finds that a fixed cost would reduce the absolute profit of the firm but would not change the marginal conditions in (12) or (22).[29] Hence, we would conclude that fixed costs are neutral so long as they do not cause the firm to become unprofitable and reduce output to zero.

---

[28]Incidentally, both assume a competitive firm in the sense that while price is stochastic it is unaffected by the output of the individual firm. Sandmo addresses the current issue and finds the conclusions palatable. Note, of course, his notion of profit is not risk-adjusted as ours is.

[29]However, the "cost of capital" will rise, as we will show later.

This last result is the same result that obtains under certainty. In fact, we find that when capital markets are as described by the capital asset pricing model the introduction of uncertainty into the theory of the firm changes the exposition in a predictable way: certainty-equivalents using market risk measures and the market price of risk replace the known values in the traditional analysis. Imposing a utility function for the firm seems quite unnecessary unless one is willing to assert substantial capital market imperfections which result in the failure of the separation theorems.[30]

2.5. The cost of capital

In our development we have taken into account the changes in the risk premia when assessing the marginal conditions for equilibrium. One might wonder what is happening to the firm's overall discount rate or "cost of capital" as it is often referred to in the finance literature. We can formally define the cost of capital, denoted k, by the single period equation

$$V = \frac{E(\tilde{Y})}{1+k}. \tag{23}$$

This alternative valuation equation calls for discounting the expected cashflow at an appropriate risk-adjusted rate. By combining (23) and the capital asset pricing equation in (1) we can solve explicitly for k to yield

$$k = r + (1+r) \frac{\lambda \mathrm{cov}(\tilde{Y}, \tilde{M})/E(\tilde{Y})}{1 - \lambda \mathrm{cov}(\tilde{Y}, \tilde{M})/E(\tilde{Y})}. \tag{24}$$

Here we see that for cashflow streams which have positive systematic risk the discount rate is an increasing function of the risk-reward ratio $\mathrm{cov}(\tilde{Y}, \tilde{M})/E(\tilde{Y})$.

In general, there is no reason to believe that the risk–reward ratio would be invariant to changes in output. Long and Racette (1974) first suggested that the cost of capital could change with output although they were unable to determine meaningful conditions under which the direction of change could be determined. From (24) we can determine for a positive covariance

$$\mathrm{sign}\left[\frac{\mathrm{d}k}{\mathrm{d}Q} \right] = \mathrm{sign}\left[\frac{\mathrm{d}}{\mathrm{d}Q} \frac{\mathrm{cov}(\tilde{Y}, \tilde{M})}{E(\tilde{Y})} \right]$$

$$= \mathrm{sign}\left[\frac{\mathrm{d}\,\mathrm{cov}(\tilde{Y}, \tilde{M})/\mathrm{d}Q}{\mathrm{d}E(\tilde{Y})/\mathrm{d}Q} - \frac{\mathrm{cov}(\tilde{Y}, \tilde{M})}{E(\tilde{Y})} \right]. \tag{25}$$

[30]Leland derives this result for the case of constant absolute risk aversion. One might argue all along that our model is the same as his except we simply employ a "utility" function with constant absolute risk aversion. We would argue the difference is far greater since we require the existence of a market for trading financial claims whereas he eschews the market completely.

The first term in brackets is the risk–return ratio at the margin whereas the second term is the average risk–return ratio.

Long and Racette examine the case of a price-taking firm facing a stochastic price independent of output and a known cost function. Systematic risk would increase linearly with output but expected cashflow is subject to positive but diminishing marginal returns. Hence, the marginal risk reward ratio exceeds the average risk reward ratio[31] so from (25) we can see that the cost of capital will rise for a competitive firm in the region of the profit-maximizing output.

While the Long and Racette case seems plausible it need not be the case when we introduce uncertain cost and downward-sloping demand functions. Still, we suggest that the cost of capital need not be invariant to output levels. This variation may not be of much practical significance but it does demonstrate that minimizing the cost of capital is not consistent with the profit, or net present value, maximization model we present here. This is perhaps more important once we introduce corporate taxes in the next section.

3. Second approximation: corporate tax case

In the first approximation we ignored taxes on corporate income. As a result, there was no reason to distinguish between debt and equity financing in our frictionless world. In this section we suppose the firm is subject to a proportional income tax. Furthermore, we assume the firm issues both debt and equity securities and that interest payments are tax deductible. Under these assumptions we will show that the value of the firm is dependent on capital structure in the same spirit as Modigliani and Miller (1958, 1963) and Hamada (1969). Furthermore, we will show the impact of capital structure on the operating decisions of the firm.

3.1. The model with taxes

The original valuation equation in (1) is still valid except that we must now interpret Y as total after tax cashflow to all security holders. We assume that the fraction γ of the capital stock is financed by riskless bonds. Thus, bonds will be issued in the amount γK and the interest payments will be $r\gamma K$. Assuming a proportional tax rate τ we can compute total taxes $\tilde{T}$ as

$$\tilde{T} = \tau\left[R(Q, \tilde{\Psi}) - wL - \delta K - r\gamma K \right], \tag{26}$$

where wages wL, depreciation $\tilde{\delta}K$, and interest payments $r\gamma K$ are deducted from

---

[31]Alternatively we could speak of the expected return per unit of systematic risk. Here, with returns expanding less than proportionately but systematic risk increasing proportionately the return per unit risk is falling. Hence, the firm is moving up the security market line.

revenue before taxes are levied. The cashflow equation is now

$$\tilde{Y} = R(Q, \tilde{\Psi}) - wL + (1-\tilde{\delta})K - \tilde{T}$$
$$= (1-\tau)\left[R(Q, \tilde{\Psi}) - wL - \tilde{\delta}K\right] + \tau r\gamma K + K. \tag{27}$$

The first term $(1-\tau)[R(Q, \tilde{\Psi}) - wL - \tilde{\delta}K]$ in (27) is net income as if the firm were all equity financed. The term $\tau r\gamma K$ represents the tax shield on debt and the final term K is "return of capital".

Substituting the new expression for cashflow in (27) into (1) we have

$$V = \frac{(1-\tau)\left[\hat{R}(Q) - wL - \hat{\delta}K\right] + \tau r\delta K + K}{1+r}. \tag{28}$$

The new maximand corresponding to (8) is

$$\max_{Q,K,L} \{V - K\} = \max_{Q,K,L} \frac{(1-\tau)\left[\hat{R}(Q) - wL - \hat{\delta}K\right] + \tau r\gamma K - rK}{1+r} \tag{29}$$

subject to the production constraint of (3). Again, we concentrate on the numerator of (29) and call it "profit" which we denote as

$$\Pi = (1-\tau)\left[\hat{R}(Q) - wL - \hat{\delta}K\right] + \tau r\gamma K - rK. \tag{30}$$

The first term is simply the after-tax certainty-equivalent of net income. The next term is the tax subsidy on debt and the final term is the riskless opportunity cost on funds invested.

Eq. (30) should not be viewed as meaning that taxes are levied on only the certainty-equivalent of income since risk premia are not deductible. However, since taxes are proportional to net income which is stochastic, the tax receipts have systematic risk as well. The recipients of the tax receipts receive the fraction τ of income so they must bear the same fraction of the total systematic risk. Security holders receive the residual fraction of cashflow so they bear only the fraction $(1-\tau)$ of the total systematic risk.[32]

While the tax recipients share proportionally in the systematic risk, they do not share in the opportunity cost on capital in quite the same manner since the opportunity cost rK is not deductible. However, owners can share at least some portion of this cost with tax recipients by using debt financing and deducting the interest for tax purposes. That is, since the interest expense is deductible, the tax recipients bear the fraction $\tau\gamma$ of the total opportunity cost by providing the tax subsidy $\tau r\gamma K$ in (30). This subsidy is, of course, the sole motive for levering up in the world we are describing.

If we manipulate (30) somewhat we have

$$\Pi = (1-\tau)\left[\hat{R}(Q) - wL - (r+\hat{\delta})K\right] - \tau(1-\gamma)rK. \tag{30'}$$

---

[32]As Myers (1972, p.91) states, "It is simply that a part of the risk is absorbed by 'we the people' via fluctuations in the corporate income tax revenues."

The term in brackets is identical to eq. (9) for profit in the no tax case which included an appropriate allowance rK for the opportunity cost of capital. If taxes were levied as the proportion τ of this term, then taxes would simply change profits by the fraction $(1-\tau)$ as we move from the no-tax to the tax case. Since the objective function would change only by a constant of proportionality, none of the operating decisions would change. Taxes would be neutral with the full deductibility of the opportunity cost. But under our assumptions about taxation we see that taxes are not neutral for less than 100 percent debt financing. Since (30′) includes the tax subsidy, the final term shows the fraction $(1-\gamma)$ of the total opportunity cost rK which is *not* deductible. In fact, the term $\tau(1-\gamma)rK$ shows the extra taxes paid compared to the case of deductibility of opportunity costs.

The important point of this discussion is the impact of taxation on the operating decisions of the firm. The payments to the two factors of production are treated quite differently for tax purposes. Wage payments wL are fully deductible but for capital the opportunity cost rK is not. This creates a downward bias in the relative factor price of labor. However, this distortion may be reversed somewhat by debt financing and deducting γrK of the opportunity cost of capital. The deductibility of interest provides the incentive (in our model, anyway) for using debt and this, in turn, removes part of the downward bias in the relative factor price of labor. We examine these effects in the next section.

3.2. The impact of tax deductibility of interest [33]

From eq. (30) we saw the tax subsidy on interest payments provides an incentive to use debt financing. In this section we investigate the impact of financial leverage on the real decisions of the firm. A simple way to think about our development would be to envision a scenario starting with an unlevered firm (i.e. $\gamma=0$) and suppose that managers "suddenly realize" the tax advantage of debt. Then, as debt financing is employed and $\gamma>0$, we might ask how the operating decisions change. We admit that our model is not sufficiently detailed to describe the choice of an optimal γ.[34] Thus, we simply take as given some degree

---

[33]Many of the comparative statics results in this section have been developed elsewhere in Hite (1977). Therefore we see no advantage in duplicating involved mathematical arguments. Instead, we shall present the results with the rationale for their validity and we will attempt to draw some further implications.

[34]Taking our equations literally, the optimal debt ratio seems to call for 100 percent debt financing. Just as M–M (1963, section V) hedge their bets on "the maximum possible amount of debt in their capital structure" we want to hedge ours. The use of riskless debt is an abstraction to allow us to get at the real decisions more easily. This abstraction also ignores agency costs and bankruptcy costs (see Jensen and Meckling (1976) and Myers (1977)) which must be considered in the study of the "limits of leverage". Our development is silent on the issue of optimal capital structure.

of leverage and compare the results to the unlevered case. We are investigating the *partial* impact of financial policy on real decisions while ignoring any feedback of real policies on financial decisions.

Perhaps a more meaningful view of our work would be as an extension of the Modigliani–Miller (M–M) tax case. Their work compared an unlevered and levered firm under the assumption that the only difference between the two lay in their financial policy. One might think of their case as having an unlevered firm substitute debt for equity in the capital structure while holding inputs and output constant. We shall refer to this M–M case as the "pure leverage effect". In our case, we suppose the firm substitutes debt for equity and simultaneously adjusts inputs and output to the new profit-maximizing levels. We shall refer to our case as the "total leverage effect" which incorporates both the M–M effect and the effect of reoptimization over Q, K, and L. We find, in general, that the operating decisions which are optimal for the unlevered firm would no longer be optimal when the firm employs debt in its financing method.[35]

3.2.1. Factor proportions

Once again we partition the problem into the two subproblems of minimizing production cost for a given level of output followed by output determination. We form the Lagrange cost expression comparable to (11) as

$$C^* = (1-\tau)wL + \left[(1-\tau)\hat{\delta} + r - \tau r\gamma\right]K + c\left[Q - f(K,L)\right]. \tag{31}$$

Note that in (31) the new user cost of capital is $[(1-\tau)\hat{\delta} + r - \tau r\gamma]$ which reflects the deductibility of only the fraction γ of the total opportunity cost of capital. The after-tax factor price of labor is $(1-\tau)w$ reflecting the full deductibility of wages.

The new first order conditions are

$$\frac{\partial C^*}{\partial L} = (1-\tau)w - cf_L = 0, \tag{32a}$$

$$\frac{\partial C^*}{\partial K} = \left[(1-\tau)\hat{\delta} + r - \tau r\gamma\right] - cf_K = 0, \tag{32b}$$

$$\frac{\partial C^*}{\partial c} = Q - f(K,L) = 0. \tag{32c}$$

The second-order sufficiency conditions remain the same as described in (12d).

---

[35]While M–M did not explicitly treat the adjustments we are dealing with, they did suggest them indirectly. In eq. (7) of M–M (1963) they show the cut-off rate is lower for the levered firm which would expand investment beyond that of the unlevered firm. They state, "...[the] required rate of return cannot be defined without reference to financial policy".

If we rearrange (32a) and (32b) we have

$$\frac{f_L}{f_K} = \frac{(1-\tau)w}{(1-\tau)\hat{\delta}+r-\tau r\hat{\gamma}}. \tag{33}$$

We see the ratio of marginal products in (33) is positively related to the leverage ratio. The denominator of the right-hand side of (33) is the user cost of capital which decreases with leverage and increases the equilibrium ratio of marginal products as the firm substitutes capital for labor in the two factor case. Leverage would partially offset the factor distortion created by the difference in the deductibility of capital and labor costs.[36]

3.2.2. Investment and output

Since leverage reduces the implicit factor price of capital we would expect an impact on investment scale and output as we found in section 2.3. If we differentiate (32) with respect to γ and solve for the effect on capital we have

$$\frac{\mathrm{d}K}{\mathrm{d}\gamma} = \tau r \frac{D_{22}}{|D|} > 0, \tag{34}$$

where D_{22} and $|D|$ are identical to the no tax case. The effect shown in (34) states that since leverage reduces the implicit factor cost, then an increase in leverage will increase capital utilization. In other words, increased leverage reduces the marginal factor cost of capital and investment expands. (See Modigliani and Miller (1963, eq. (7)).)

The impact on marginal cost is now

$$\frac{\mathrm{d}c}{\mathrm{d}\gamma} = -\tau r \frac{D_{23}}{|D|} < 0, \tag{35}$$

which again has an ambiguous sign but the expansion effect on capital is still given by (18). Therefore, if capital is a normal input then an increase in leverage will shift the marginal cost schedule down and output will increase. In such a case both investment and output would expand.[37] The final effect is that the levered firm would be more capital intensive, have larger investment, and produce greater output then in the case where it remained unlevered.

[36]In fact, if the firm could set $\gamma = 1$ and still obtain the tax deduction of interest, then the tax factor would drop out of (33) and the right-hand side would be $w/(\delta+r)$, the same as the no tax case in (14). In this case taxes would be neutral with respect to the factor mix at any given level of output.

[37]In the unlikely case that capital is an inferior input, capital utilization will increase with leverage but output would decline. We assume capital is normal in the remainder of the discussion but in either case *total* cost will fall.

3.2.3. Profit

We may now examine the impact of leverage of profit in (30). The pure leverage effect would vary only γ while all other variables remain unchanged so Π would increase by $\tau r \gamma K$ as the levered firm issues γK of bonds. Hence, the marginal contribution of a unit of bonds would add the subsidy τr as in the pure M–M case.[38] Our complete adjustment would increase profit by at least this amount and in most cases by a larger amount since we have three distinct adjustments: (i) the pure tax effect, (ii) the factor substitution of the now relatively less costly capital for labor, and (iii) the expansion effect resulting in larger output as total and marginal cost decline. For any finite change in γ, the last two effects must be non-negative so we conclude the complete adjustment to leverage increases profit by at least as much as M–M suggest.[39] As usual, one would expect a more "elastic" response of profits the more variables that are allowed to adjust to the reduction in a factor price. (See Samuelson (1972, pp. 35–36).)

3.2.4. Cost of capital

One might wonder what would happen to the cost of capital as a firm levers up since this has received so much attention in the literature. The pure leverage effect was developed by M–M and leverage unambiguously lowers the firm's discount rate. The tax subsidy is less risky[40] than the other cashflows. This reduces the systematic risk per unit of expected cashflow and so the discount rate would fall. The crucial element in this result is that the cashflow *excluding* debt subsidy is unchanged and therefore has the same systematic risk with or without leverage.

The total leverage effect has a less clear-cut impact on the cost of capital. In addition to the tax subsidy, leverage will change the optimal scale of investment and output. In the case that capital is a normal input, leverage will increase output. In section 2.5 we argued that the systematic risk of cashflow would probably vary with output. In the case that the risk–reward ratio of the unlevered stream (excluding tax subsidy) increases with output then there will be two counteracting forces influencing the discount rate: (i) leverage will increase capital and output resulting in more systematic risk per unit of expected cashflow; and (ii) the tax subsidy is riskless and reduces the risk–reward ratio. If

---

[38]Our model is in "flow" terms whereas M–M used "stock", or present value, terms. In a present value sense, a unit of debt would add $\tau r/(1+r)$ to the value of the firm for Q, K, and L constant. In the perpetuity case of M–M this would reduce to τ per unit of debt since the perpetuity discount factor r would replace our single period factor $1/(1+r)$.

[39]In some sense, the pure leverage effect would be thought of as short-run analysis holding the real decisions fixed. This seems to be the case suggested by Hamada (1969, esp. fn. 9).

[40]In fact, in our simple model it is riskless just as the bonds are.

the tax effect dominates the discount rate, it will decline as suggested by M–M. On the other hand, if the output expansion effect dominates, then the discount rate would actually rise even in perfect capital markets.[41] We have no a priori reason to suggest which effect would dominate or that one factor would dominate in all cases. This is clearly an empirical issue and the output expansion effect may complicate interpretation of empirical results regarding the relationship between leverage and the discount rate.

While there is no reason to suggest that the cost of capital increases or decreases with leverage, there is also no reason to suggest it is invariant to leverage. In fact, the possibility of the discount rate varying with output and investment suggests that its interpretation as the "cost of capital", or cut-off rate, for marginal investment is a tenuous one in that expansion may not be of the same "risk class" even if the leverage ratio γ is always at the firm's "target level". While the practical significance of this suggestion is unknown, there is no reason to believe that using a target debt ratio and then treating the "cost of capital" as a constant will be consistent with profit-maximizing behavior.

4. Summary and conclusions

We have attempted to add to the theory of the firm by incorporating uncertainty, taxes, and financial policy in a world in which securities are priced according to the capital asset pricing model. In section 2 we ignored taxes and capital structure and we found that uncertainty changed the decision model of the firm in one very predictable way: certainty-equivalents (and not just expected values) replaced prices known with perfect certainty in the traditional theory. Furthermore, we investigated several previous results which suggested the certainty and uncertainty cases were vastly different and we found these counterintuitive results were due to personification of the firm by introducing a utility function with varying risk aversion. We argued that a more appealing approach in a perfect capital market would involve using a market price of risk. Use of this external price as opposed to an internal, utility-derived price yields an exposition of the theory of the firm which is fundamentally consistent with the theory of the firm under certainty.

In the third section we introduced taxes and found that taxes do not have a neutral impact on corporate decisions in two fundamental respects: (i) wage payments and capital costs are treated differently with respect to tax deductibility, and (ii) the tax shelter on interest payments creates a well-known incentive for a leveraged capital structure. This combination of debt and taxes was investigated by M–M while implicitly assuming the operating decisions of the "equivalent" levered and unlevered firms were the same. We expanded upon this

[41]Hite (1977) presents a numerical example of this case.

"pure leverage effect" by allowing for changes in operating decisions as leverage changed. In general, we found our "total leverage effect" would change input mix, investment, and output decisions along with profit and the cost of capital. In fact, the adjustment of all variables to increases in leverage may alter the precise relationship postulated by M–M regarding leverage and the declining cost of capital.

References

Alberts (1977)

Bear, D. V. T. (1965) "Inferior Inputs and the Theory of the Firm", *Journal of Political Economy* 73, 287–289.

Borch, K. B. (1968) The *Economics of Uncertainty* (Princeton University Press, Princeton, New Jersey).

Cramér, H. (1946) *Mathematical Methods of Statistics* (Princeton University Press, Princeton, New Jersey).

Fama, E. F. and M. H. Miller (1972) *The Theory of Finance* (Holt, Rinehart, and Winston, New York).

Haley, Charles W. (1969) "Comments on the Valuation of Risk Assets...", *Review of Economics and Statistics* 51, 220–221.

Haley, C. W. and L. D. Schall (1973) *The Theory of Financial Decisions* (McGraw-Hill, New York).

Hamada, R. S. (1969) "Portfolio Analysis, Market Equilibrium, and Corporation Finance", *Journal of Finance* 24, 13–31.

Henderson, J. M. and R. E. Quandt (1971) *Microeconomics Theory – A Mathematical Approach* (McGraw-Hill, New York).

Hite, G. L. (1977) "Leverage, Output Effects, and the M–M Theorems", *Journal of Financial Economics* 4, 177–203.

Jensen, M. C. and J. B. Long, Jr. (1972) "Optimality of Capital Markets", *The Bell Journal of Economics and Management Science* 3, 151–174.

Jensen, M. C. and W. H. Meckling (1976) "Theory of the Firm; Managerial Behavior, Agency Costs and Capital Structure", *Journal of Financial Economics* 3, 305–360.

Jones, R. W. (1971) Distortions in Factor Markets and the General Equilibrium Model of Production", *Journal of Political Economy* 79, 437–459.

Koehl, D. (1978) "Relationships Between Investment and Financing Decisions of Firms in Regulated Industries", Unpublished manuscript, Ohio State University, Columbus, Ohio.

Korkie, R. M. (1975) "Theory of the Firm Facing Uncertain Demand: Comments", *American Economic Review* 65, 245–247.

Leland, H. E. (1972) "Theory of the Firm Facing Uncertain Demand", *American Economic Review* 62, 278–291.

Leland, H. E. (1975) "Theory of the Firm Facing Uncertain Demand: Reply", *American Economic Review* 65, 248.

Lintner, J. (1965) "The Valuation of Risk Assets and the Selection of Risky Investments in Stock Portfolios and Capital Budgets", *Review of Economics and Statistics* 47, 13–37.

Long, J. B. Jr. (1972) "Wealth, Welfare, and the Price of Risk", *Journal of Finance* 27, 419–453.

Long, M. S. and G. A. Racette (1974) "Stochastic Demand, Output and the Cost of Capital", *Journal of Finance* 29, 499–506.

McCall, J. J. (1971) "Probabilistic Microeconomics", *The Bell Journal of Economics and Management Science* 2, 403–433.

Merton, R. C. and M. G. Subrahmanyam (1974) "The Optimality of a Competitive Stock Market", *The Bell Journal of Economics and Management Science* 5, 145–170.

Modigliani, F. and M. H. Miller (1958) "The Cost of Capital, Corporation Finance, and the Theory of Investment", American Economic Review 48, 261–297.

Modigliani, F. and M. H. Miller (1963) "Corporate Income Taxes and the Cost of Capital: A Connection", *American Economic Review* 33, 433–443.

Mossin, J. (1966) "Equilibrium in the Capital Markets", *Econometrica* 34, 768–783.

Myers, S. C. (1977) "Determinants of Corporate Borrowing", *Journal of Financial Economics* 5, 147–175.

Pratt, J. W. (1964) "Risk Aversion in the Small and in the Large", *Econometrica* 32, 122–136.

Robichek, A. A. and S. C. Myers (1966) "Problems in the Theory of Optimal Capital Structure", *Journal of Financial and Quantitative Analysis* 1, 1–35.

Samuelson, P. A. (1948) *Foundations of Economic Analysis* (Harvard University Press, Cambridge, Mass.).

Sandmo, A. (1971) "On the Theory of the Competitive Firm under Price Uncertainty", *American Economic Review* 61, 65–73.

Sharpe, W. F. (1964) "Capital Asset Prices: A Theory of Market Equilibrium under Conditions of Risk", *Journal of Finance* 19, 425–442.

Silberberg, E. (1978) *The Structure of Economics – A Mathematical Approach* (McGraw-Hill, New York).

Vickers, D. (1968) *The Theory of the Firm: Production, Capital and Finance* (McGraw-Hill, New York).

Zabel, E. (1970) "Monopoly and Uncertainty", *Review of Economics Studies* 37, 205–219.

Zabel, E. (1971) "Risk and the Competitive Firm", *Journal of Economic Theory* 3, 109–133.

Chapter 8

CAPITAL BUDGETING

JAMES L. BICKSLER
Rutgers University

1. Some preliminary matters[1]

Probably, the most important financial decision of the firm is that of capital budgeting.[2] There are at least four important tasks associated with this decision. They are:

(1) deriving the set of investment opportunities to be evaluated;

(2) forecasting the relevant dimensions of cash flows associated with the project;

(3) choosing the appropriate criterion or framework for calculating the economic value of the project; and

(4) deriving the operational dimensions of the appropriate capital budgeting criterion.

As to the first task, finance has, unfortunately, little in the way of practical, meaningful advice except to suggest that, if possible, the firm should take advantage of any monopolistic power it possesses or any imperfections that may exist in the factor markets. In regard to assessing the relevant dimensions of future cash flows, there is a rich body of knowledge, namely Bayesian statistics, which offers some useful and well-defined guidelines. The essence of the Bayesian approach is structuring one's assessments so that they are (1) coherent and (2) consistent with empirical reality.[3] The Bayesian approach has the desirable feature of being able to capture and effectively utilize any systematic and coherent knowledge about the particular project that the decision-maker or

---

[1]This article is not intended to be a complete encyclopedic treatment of all of the many issues of capital budgeting. Instead, a few of the more central and traditional issues and topics are discussed.

[2]The primary financial decisions facing the firm are the optimal choice of the sources and uses of funds. In efficient markets, the capital structure question is irrelevant. This means that the choice of the optimal capital budgeting vector is the major financial decision of the firm.

[3]For a further discussion of this, see Tversky and Kaheman (1973). Discussion of the methods and techniques for deriving subjective probability distributions is contained in Winkler (1967) and Savage (1971). See also the chapter by Winkler in this volume.

James L. Bicksler, Editor, Handbook of Financial Economics
© *North-Holland Publishing Company – 1979*

his staff may have. Indeed, Bayes' theorem sets forth a specific manner in which a decision-maker's prior knowledge is revised with the arrival of new sample information to obtain one's posterior probability.[4] It should be emphasized that Bayesian estimation is operational and central to a systematic inductive process inasmuch as "learning from experience" is consistent with the scientific method.[5]

Concerning the conceptually appropriate criterion or framework for calculating the economic value of a project, finance has a great deal to offer about this microdecision problem.[6] Microfinance, like microeconomics generally, has as its central normative underpinning the maximization of expected utility for the individual.[7] While there are some unique conditions under which individual utility functions can be aggregated into a composite corporate utility function, such would be atypical.[8] Hence, utility maximization would generally represent an ambiguous guide for optimal corporate decision making. However, given perfect capital markets, market value maximization leads precisely to the same managerial finance decisions that would result if the firm was operated individually by each single shareholder.[9, 10] That is, the optimum consumption–savings–borrowing–investment decision for an individual is the same via either the

[4]Bayes' theorem, commonly referred to as the principle of inverse probability, utilizes information from sample data and combines it with prior information to make inferences about the parameters of a stochastic process. Thus, the posterior distribution makes inferences about parameters based on both the likelihood function and the prior probability density function.

[5]For a discussion of the conceptual underpinnings of Bayesian statistics within the context of science, see Zellner (1971a, b).

[6]An appropriate capital budgeting rule is conceptually mandatory if firm value is maximized. This is in contrast to the assessment of net cash inflows wherein even if there are errors the errors can be diversified away within an investor's portfolio provided such forecasting errors are not systematically biased.

[7]An axiomatic development of the expected utility maxim is contained in von Neumann and Morgenstern (1947). Space limitations prohibit the delineation of the decision under uncertainty framework of the individual which underlies the investment theory under uncertainty for the firm. Suffice it to say that the investment decision for the individual consists of the choice of (1) the optimal consumption-savings mix and (2) the optimal investment (i.e. portfolio selection) of these allocated savings. Utility maximization is a necessary and sufficient condition for both subdecisions. The two most utilized economic theories of portfolio selection are the time-state preference framework of Arrow and Debreau and the mean-variance framework of Markowitz and Tobin.

[8]Preference ordering for group decision-making and the inapplicability of the expected utility rule for the firm is discussed in Borch (1968). The "impossibility theorem" from which this argument is derived was first proven in Arrow (1951).

[9]This rules out a number of behavioral managerial organizational goals and management–shareholder conflicts. For a discussion of such, see Simon (1959); Donaldson (1963) and Marris (1964).

[10]A possibly important distinction is whether firm value maximization and social welfare maximization are simultaneous solutions. Specifically, Jensen and Long and Stiglitz have claimed to show that even if firms are competitive, value maximization by firms will not in general lead to a Pareto optimum. However, under conditions of competitive mean-variance equilibrium where firms are price takers, Merton and Subrahmanyam maintain that there is an implicit error in the Jensen–Long and Stiglitz reasoning and that social welfare and value maximization are consistent. See Jensen and Long (1972); Stiglitz (1972); and Merton and Subrahmanyam (1974).

expected utility maxim or the market value rule. A demonstration of this follows:

$$\max_{c,k} U(C)$$

subject to

$$V(C) = V(Y) + V(K),$$
$$T(K) = 0,$$

where C = the vector of consumption expenditures, $V(C)$ = the present value of lifetime consumption, $V(Y)$ = the present value of lifetime's earnings plus initial wealth, $V(K)$ = the present value of the firm.

This is equivalent to the following unconstrained maximization equation stated in lagrangian form:

$$\max_{c,k} \left[U(C) - \lambda_1(V(C) - V(Y) - V(K)) - \lambda_2 T(K) \right],$$

where λ_1 and λ_2 are lagrangian multipliers.

Via solving the following two equations, the solution to the maximization of firm's market value is derived.

$$\max_{K} \left[V(K) - \lambda_3 T(K) \right],$$

and

$$\max_{c} \left[U(C) - \lambda_1(V(C) - V(Y) - V^*(K)) \right].$$

This conclusion of utility maximization being equivalent to firm market value maximization is generalized from a single-owner to a multi-owner firm by subdividing $V(K)$ into proportional shares equal to an individual's relative ownership of the firm.[11]

Two other points should be noted. First, while the market value rule has been shown to be optimal under perfect capital markets under certainty, there is (are) no formal proof(s) for the uncertainty and imperfect capital markets cases. Indeed, decision-making under imperfect financial markets constitutes an almost infinite array of different scenarios. That is, imperfect financial markets can be of many different kinds and therefore imply quite different solutions. Hence, finance does not offer a unified solution to decision-making in imperfect markets but, at best, can simply arrive at ad hoc solutions to specific imperfect financial market scenarios.

Secondly, for the uncertainty case, the firm having a multi-security financial structure, certain valuation paradoxes and conflicts between shareholders and

---

[11]This line of reasoning is taken from Fama and Miller (1972, pp. 72, 73).

bondholders may occur. They arise from the fact that if bondholders are not protected by "me first" rules and shareholders are not protected from the possibility of the retirement of priority debt rather than secondary debt, then redistribution of wealth between classes of security holders may occur. More specifically, if debt is risky and if side payments between classes of security owners are ruled out, then different investment–production strategies may result in quite different terminal wealths for various stock–bondholder classes. However, in the two-parameter market equilibrium scenario, with homogeneous expectations, all investors hold the market portfolio of all risky assets wherein investor wealth remains unchanged even if the market value of the composition of the claims changes.[12]

2. Traditional issues in capital budgeting

The essence of the capital budgeting problem is choosing those physical investment projects which will maximize the market value of the firm. Traditionally, capital budgeting has been an issue of much attention in microfinance. One useful classification schema of capital budgeting rules is:

(1) Ad hoc rules of thumb;

(2) Investment criteria based on asset valuation under conditions of certainty; and

(3) Investment criteria based on asset valuation of a capital market equilibrium scenario under uncertainty.

The above schema offers some useful insights into the conceptual appeal of alternative capital budgeting rules.[13,14]

Inasmuch as time and uncertainty are the two dimensions that account for microfinance being a nontrivial subject matter, many discussions of capital budgeting focus on the limitations of criteria which do not integrate or properly integrate these dimensions. For example, one popular commonly used capital

---

[12]An insightful qualitative analysis of the potential conflict between shareholders and bondholders and the likelihood of such is detailed in Fama and Miller (1972, pp. 150–156 and 178–180). Additional insightful analysis is contained in Galai and Masulis (1976) and Jensen and Meckling (1976).

[13]There are at least two aspects of the corporate investment which differentiate it from the portfolio selection problem for the individual. First, for the individual, only linear resource allocations among securities are presumed while for the firm selecting physical projects nonlinear production technologies are indeed feasible. Secondly, the individual, but not the firm, is permitted negative investments. The reasoning here is the availability of short sale opportunities in securities but the absence of such for production technologies.

[14]A project is viewed as a series of net cash flows received at the end of a year, $X_1, X_2, X_3, \ldots, X_n$. The net cash flows can be either positive or negative and they represent the after tax operating income from the net new investment. Specifically, net cash inflows represent revenues less costs adding back taxes and depreciation.

Table 8.1. Summary of rankings.

Measure of investment worth	Investments			
	A	B	C	D
Payback period	1*	1*	4	3
Proceeds per dollar of outlay	4	3	1*	1*
Average annual proceeds per dollar of outlay	1	4	2*	2*
Average income on book value or cost	4	3	1*	1*
Yield of an investment	4	1*	3	1*
Present value: at 6 percent	4	3	2	1
at 3 percent	3	1	4	2

*Indicates tie between projects.
Source: Bierman and Smidt (1966, p. 31).

budgeting text analyzes and ranks projects according to a variety of different criteria (see table 8.1).

According to the Bierman–Smidt text,

> the most striking conclusion to be drawn from Table 1 [our table 8.1] is the tendency for each measure of investment worth to give a different ranking to the identical set of investments. This emphasizes the need to give careful consideration to the choice of measures used to evaluate proposed investments. Obviously all these measures cannot be equally valid. By considering specific pairs of investments, we have shown that the measures of investment worth that do not involve the use of the discounted cash flow method can give rankings of investments that are obviously incorrect. For this reason these measures will be excluded from further consideration (Bierman and Smidt (1966, pp. 31–32)).

A commonly espoused ad hoc capital budgeting criterion is payback. The payback method tells the years necessary to recoup the initial project investment. For example, if the project investment is I, then the number of years necessary to equate the net cash flows $X_1, X_2, \ldots, X_n$ with I is the payback period. Via this method, projects are ranked on their desirability in terms of the quickest time to recoup the reinvestment. Sometimes, a cut-off rate for accepting projects is detailed via a maximum acceptable payback period.

There are, at least, three important limitations to the payback method. First, project risk is not integrated into the analysis. This means that differential risk between projects is not accounted for. Secondly, the timing of the net cash flows and their time value of money is disregarded. Third, post-payback net cash flows are disregarded. For these reasons, the payback method does not necessarily reflect the economic impact of a project on the market value of the firm.[15]

[15]An interesting article discussing the reasons for the popularity of the payback method is Weingartner (1969).

Alternatively stated, economists dismiss payback, as well as other investment criteria, which do not effectively account for the price of time and the price of risk. Further, this means that many, if not most, of the textbook discussion of optimal capital budgeting frameworks deals with the net present value and internal rate of return investment criteria.

The internal rate of return technique is a two-step decision process whereby:

(1) The internal rate of return (*IRR*) is calculated.

(2) The internal rate of return is compared to the cutoff rate (i.e. cost of capital). If the *IRR* is higher (lower) than the cut-off rate, the project is accepted (rejected).

The internal rate of return is that rate (see eq. (1)) which equilibrates the present value of the cash inflows with the present value of the cash outflows. This is equivalent to algebraically finding the root of a *n*th order polynomial whereby the net present value of the investment is zero:

$$I = \frac{X_1}{1+i} + \frac{X_2}{(1+i)^2} + \ldots + \frac{X_n}{(1+i)^n}. \tag{1}$$

It is termed an internal rate of return inasmuch as this yield is dependent only upon the time pattern of cash inflows and outflows and not upon any market determined equilibrium cost rate.

Three limitations and an often cited criticism of the *IRR* technique will be discussed. First, from a formal standpoint, there may be multiple solutions (i.e. more than one internal rate of return) to the *n*th order polynomial. Indeed from Descartes' rule of signs, it is known that there can be no more solutions (i.e. positive roots) than there are changes in signs of the net cash inflows.[16] Secondly, the DCF framework postulates that the discount rate is the same for each of the *N* periods. If this is not a "good" approximation to reality, then the *IRR* technique should not be used as a basis for screening investment projects. Thirdly, in the case of mutually exclusive investment projects all of which meet the acceptance criterion, it is commonly asserted that the rankings should be from highest to lowest in terms of *IRR*. However, the *IRR* technique cannot properly handle scale aspects of investment projects. This results in a basic deficiency of the *IRR* – namely that it always leads to acceptance of a higher *IRR* project even if the scale is trivial (i.e. $1.00). Therefore, since the *IRR* criterion cannot trade-off higher (lower) rates and lower (higher) scales in terms of impact on market values, it cannot be viewed as a completely appropriate technique for screening mutually exclusive projects.

[16]In their classic article Lorie–Savage showed that there may be multiple internal rates of return. See Lorie and Savage (1955). For further analyses of the multiple roots problem, see Teichroew et al. (1965).

These criticisms of the *IRR* technique in perfect capital markets are quite straightforward but become more forceful under imperfect capital markets. As Fama and Miller (1972, p. 143) indicate

> Objections to rate of return ranking are perhaps obvious enough in the case of perfect capital markets, in which the simple accept or reject decision is all that we need; but the idea of ranking by rate of return becomes doubly nonsensical in the presence of financial constraints. It is more than just a matter of an inconsistency between the maximand and the constraints of the kind discussed earlier in connection with the constrained version of the present value rule. In this case, it was case, it was at least clear what was being maximized, if not why, and the indirect contributions of the projects by way of their effects on the constraints were also taken into account. If, however, we merely march down a rate of return ranking until we run out of money without taking into account the indirect effects on later constraints, we have something like the disembodied smile of the Cheshire cat — a maximizing condition, but one not derived from or even related to any known maximand.

Also, the *IRR* technique assumes that the reinvestment rate is equal to the project rate. Sometimes, this is argued not to be a reasonable approximation to reality (see, for example, van Horne (1974)). If the reinvestment rate(rates) is(are) not equal to the project rate, then the *IRR* rate is biased and the technique may lead to "incorrect" decisions. While part of this argument may be correct, the major implications are incorrect. Indeed, inasmuch as the lowest reinvestment rate is always the market equilibrium yield, reinvestment considerations would never lead to a change or reversal in signs (i.e. negative–positive net present values) of the economic value of the project. Hence, this criticism does not per se limit the conceptual validity of the *IRR* rule in screening capital projects. In summary, the *IRR* technique even though it integrates the elements of time and risk has the inherent limitations of (1) possible multiple roots, (2) assuming constant period-to-period discount rates, and (3) providing ambiguous solutions for the case of mutually exclusive investment projects.

The net present value criterion is also a capital budgeting framework that integrates futurity and uncertainty. The net present value method is a two-step technique whereby:

(1) the present value of the inflows and the present value of the outflows are calculated separately; and

(2) if the present value of the inflows is greater(less) than the present value of the outflows, the project is accepted(rejected).

Formally, the net present value rule is

$$NPV = -I + \sum_{t=1}^{N} \frac{X_t}{(1+k)^t}$$

Table 8.2

Project	Present value of outflows	Present value of inflows	Present value index	Net present value
A	$1 million	$2 million	2	$1 million
B	$5 million	$7 million	14	$2 million

or equivalently

$$NPV = PV_{\text{inflows}} - PV_{\text{outflows}},$$

where

NPV = the net present value,

   I = the present value of the investment expenditures,

   X = the net cash inflows associated with the project,

   k = the discount rate for both futurity and uncertainty, and

 PV = present value.

The cost of capital, k, is a securities market determined rate of return. It reflects the market uncertainty for the project. Typically k is assumed to be constant from period to period. However, if the assessment is that the market reinvestment rate will change in the future, then different values or magnitudes of k can be specified. A key query with regard to the net present value criterion is the conceptual counterpart of the market determined discount rate. This issue will be discussed in a subsequent section of the paper.

Frequently, a present value index (i.e. ratio of present value of inflows to present value of outflows) is espoused for capital projects. For example, via the present value index, the choice would be project A is preferred to project B (see table 8.2). Some people would apparently argue that project A would be obviously more desirable than project B inasmuch as the "rate of return" and ratio of present values received per dollar spent is higher for A rather than B. However, in perfect capital markets the scale factor does not act as a binding constraint. Furthermore, the present value ratio would clearly be nonoptimal since it is the maximum absolute difference between present value streams that maximizes market values and not the ratio of the present values. However, for independent projects the present value index would be the cut-off point for projects having a value of greater than one for the index.

3. Market equilibrium theory and capital budgeting

Both the NPV and IRR are tautological valuation relationships. In order to derive the appropriate conceptual counterparts to the cost of capital or the cut-off rate, a model of capital market equilibrium risk-expected return relationships must be specified. As Mossin (1969, p. 749) correctly notes

The most general and universally acceptable formulation of company objectives is maximization of the market value of the company's equity. Through its actions management can influence the market value, but is clearly unable to determine it completely. The market value is determined by the simultaneous interplay of supply and demand in the capital markets, where other companies also participate in the demand for these securities. No theory of finance can give a satisfactory explanation of security valuation or investment behavior if it fails to take into account the relationships that exist with individual investors' portfolio decisions. This means that all the investment alternatives open to the investor must be taken into account if we want to understand his evaluation of any one of them. Market values are determined by the demand by all investors, and this leads us to establish a theory of general equilibrium in capital markets. For without such a model, management is unable to foresee the effects of alternative investment and financing decisions.

Furthermore,

in view of the fundamental theoretical role that the analysis of capital markets should play for the study of the corporate decisions, it is remarkable to what limited extent such an analysis has been brought explicitly into existing financial literature. Even in modern and reputable introduction to the theory of finance, the market plays a highly indirect role. A number of hypotheses are advanced concerning the way in which the market evaluates and reacts (e.g. with respect to discounting for time and uncertainty), but these hypotheses are entirely ad hoc and quite arbitrary, since they are not derived from any fundamental assumptions describing market equilibrium.[17,18]

A commonly used market equilibrium valuation scenario is the Sharpe–Lintner–Mossin two-parameter valuation model or its extensions. The basic assumptions underlying the market equilibrium relationship of security prices in a mean-variance world are as follows.

(1) All investors are risk averse and choose portfolios in a manner consistent with maximizing expected utility of single-period terminal wealth.

(2) Portfolio investment opportunities can be described solely in terms of means and variances (or standard deviations) of the ex ante distribution of one-period portfolio returns.

(3) Investors have homogeneous expectations regarding means, variances, covariances of returns for all securities in the investment opportunity set and, in addition, all investors have identical investment opportunity sets.

---

[17]The Sharpe–Lintner–Mossin two-parameter model of capital market equilibrium derived one of its generic names from its originators. See Sharpe (1964); Lintner (1965); and Mossin (1966).

[18]The assumptions of the Black zero-beta version are identical to those enumerated previously except that there is no riskless asset and hence no riskless borrowing or lending. See Black (1972).

(4) Capital markets are efficient in the sense that borrowing and lending rates are equal. There are no restrictions to short sales, no taxes, no transactions costs, and capital assets are perfectly divisible.

(5) The supply of all capital assets is given.

Under these, and other less restrictive conditions, equilibrium relationships for risky capital assets have been derived. The fundamental result of risk, return, and market equilibrium at the level of the individual asset or security is:

$$E(\tilde{R}_i) = R_f + B_i[E(\tilde{R}_m) - R_f],$$

where $E(\tilde{R}_i)$ is the expected return on the individual security for the single period being considered, $E(\tilde{R}_m)$ is the expected return on the market portfolio, R_f is the riskless rate of return, and B_i is the systematic risk of the ith security. The above equation says that the equilibrium expected return on an asset equals the riskless rate of return (the rate of time preference) plus a risk premium.

The beta of a security or capital asset measures the marginal contribution of that individual risky asset to the dispersion or variance of the ex ante return distribution of the market portfolio, $\tilde{R}_m$. Formally, beta or the marginal risk of an asset is:

$$B_i = \text{cov}(\tilde{R}_i, \tilde{R}_m) / o^2(\tilde{R}_m).$$

From the above two equations, it follows that

$$E(\tilde{R}_i) = R_f + \frac{[E(\tilde{R}_m) - R_f](\text{cov}\,\tilde{R}_i, \tilde{R}_m)}{o^2(\tilde{R}_m)}.$$

This is the equivalent to saying that the equilibrium expected return for a risky asset is equal to a riskless rate of interest plus a linear risk premium equal to the product of the risk premium per unit of risk, commonly called the proportionality factor or $[E(\tilde{R}_m) - R_f] / o^2(\tilde{R}_m)$, and the asset's covariance with the market portfolio, or $\text{cov}(\tilde{R}_i, \tilde{R}_m)$.

This linear expected risk–return relationship for securities was derived from a market scenario where investors choose only mean-variance efficient portfolios and market conditions imply a set of clearing prices for all assets in the investment opportunity set. Under these conditions the expected risk–return market equilibrium relationship for such portfolios can be described by the capital market line

$$E(\tilde{R}_p) = R_f + \lambda(o[\tilde{R}_p])$$

where $(o^2\tilde{R})_p$ is the standard deviation of the expected return distribution for efficient portfolios and is the price of risk reduction and is equal to

$$(E(\tilde{R}_p) - R_f) / o(\tilde{R}_m).$$

It is clear that under conditions of mean-variance market equilibrium and given a world of positive but not perfectly correlated securities' returns, an individual security's contribution to the risk of an efficient portfolio is not the asset's variance of return. Instead, the asset's variance of return can be dichotomized into two components: (1) systematic risk or the asset's covariation with the return on the market portfolio, and (2) the unsystematic risk or the asset's variation due to residual elements. This relationship can be expressed as

$$o^2(\tilde{R}_i) = B_i^2 o^2(\tilde{R}_m) + o^2(\tilde{e}_i),$$

where $o^2(\tilde{e}_i)$ is that portion of $o^2(\tilde{R}_i)$ which is uncorrelated with the market portfolio. This is the diversifiable or unsystematic risk. The unsystematic risk component of the variance of returns of a security is eliminated in the formation of efficient portfolios. Hence, the total risk of an efficient portfolio is equal to the portfolio's systematic risk. Alternatively stated, any portfolio having unsystematic or residual risk is nonefficient inasmuch as there is always an alternative portfolio having equivalent expected return and less risk.

The above briefly indicates that the risk of an asset must be measured from a portfolio viewpoint and that the mean-variance equilibrium model of market prices implies that beta is the appropriate measure of a risky asset's volatility or sensitivity.[19]

Restating the CAPM in terms of market values gives

$$V^{(0)} = \frac{E[\tilde{V}^{(1)}] - \lambda^{(0)} \operatorname{cov}(\tilde{V}^{(1)}, \tilde{V}_m^{(1)})}{1 + r_f^{(0)}}$$

where $\tilde{V}^{(1)}$ = the uncertain end-of-period value of the firm (including any dividends paid over the period), and $\tilde{V}_m^{(1)}$ = the uncertain end-of-period value of all firms.

Presume a given project has a current cash outflow of $I_{(0)}$ and an expected incremental cash inflow of X_1. This project has a market value, disregarding investment outlays, to the firm equal to $\Delta V^{(0)}$ where

$$\Delta V^{(0)} = \frac{E[\tilde{C}^{(1)}] - \lambda^{(0)} \operatorname{cov}(\tilde{C}^{(1)}, \tilde{V}_m^{(1)})}{1 + r_f^{(0)}}.$$

[19]It is at the level of both the capital markets and the investor's portfolio where diversification has its meaning in terms of pricing of assets and risk and optimal portfolio choice. Furthermore, there is substantial evidence that the capital markets do not pay a risk premium for bearing unsystematic risk. Thus, from an investor viewpoint what is important is not that some fraction of the individual's portfolio (e.g. a firm) does have unsystematic risk. Therefore, attempts, such as by Cohen and Elton and Van Horne, to apply normative portfolio selection models at the level of the firm are in error. (See Cohen and Elton (1967) and van Horne (1966).) Alternatively stated, investment criteria that view the firm "similar" to the individual and ascribe it a utility function are in error.

The decision rule for project selection is to accept the project if $\Delta V^{(0)} > I_0$ and reject the project if $I_0 > \Delta V$. Hence, the two-parameter equilibrium model provides specifics to the net present value rule for the one-period case. That is, it indicates that the expected cash flows from the project and the project's beta should be assessed and then utilizing the market price of risk and risk-free rate, a net present value estimate should be derived.[20-23]

This single-period analysis can be generalized to the multiperiod capital budgeting scenario provided there are perfect secondary markets (Fama and Miller (1972, pp. 122–125)). For example, assume a project having uncertain cash flows over n periods. Its cash flows for the next period should be forecasted and converted via the prices of risk and time into a present value figure. The decision to accept the project depends only on the current cost (present value) of the project and the sum of its one period present value of cash inflows and the present value of the forecasted end-of-period price.

The decision to accept or reject the project is invariant to whether the firm will continue to utilize the plant or not. That is, the perfect secondary market assumption results in the resale price being equal to its discounted cash flows from the start of period $t + 1$ on. Thus, the perfect secondary market assumption is the explanation of why a one-period horizon of the equilibrium model is sufficient even though the asset will be generating cash flows for a number of periods.[24] Furthermore, a recent extension by Merton (1973), using continuous time version of the Sharpe–Lintner formulation and an additional risk premium to incorporate changes in the investment opportunity set, suggests that the traditional asset pricing models may not lead to substantially different choices than via multiperiod models (Constantinides (forthcoming)).[25]

---

[20]While there is a certain superficial similarity, particularly in jargon, between a market equilibrium valuation approach and a valuation under certainty framework of traditional finance, the discount rates for the Sharpe–Lintner–Mossin framework are derived from a market equilibrium scenario and are not simply ad hoc definitions without any testable and meaningful empirical implications.

[21]The essence of these points can also be stated in terms of the *IRR* technique. Specifically, if a project plots above (below) the security market line (a locus of equilibrium costs of capital for projects of varying risk), then it should be accepted (rejected).

[22]Inasmuch as, strictly speaking, the market portfolio of all risky assets does change when firms undertake investment projects, such impact should be integrated into the analysis. Quantitatively, in almost all cases, it would result in trivial changes and implications for cost of capital-equilibrium return calculations. Hence, it is not formally integrated into this presentation. For a discussion regarding this issue, see Mossin (1973).

[23]Capital budgeting in the context of the two-parameter equilibrium model was first developed by Tuttle and Litzenberger (1968) and Mossin (1969). See also Hamada (1971); Rubenstein (1973); and Weston (1973).

[24]The multiperiod capital budgeting problem using a continuous time capital asset pricing model is detailed in Brennan (1973).

[25]Constantinides, within the Merton intertemporal continuous-time capital asset pricing framework, derives formal valuation expressions for corporate project selection.

If there are imperfect secondary markets for assets, then the multiperiod solution involves backward optimization of a dynamic programming formulation of the path changing the incremental value of the firm. The change in value of the firm under imperfect secondary markets is, according to Bogue and Roll, identical to that under perfect secondary markets.[26]

4. Estimation of discount rates via state preference – contingent claims analysis

Banz and Miller (forthcoming) in a provocative paper set forth "a method for making risk adjustments in applied capital budgeting that is at least as good as any of the available alternatives". This approach assumes that (1) possible future outcomes can be categorized into a set of mutually exclusive and exhaustive states of the world; (2) the decision-maker can assess the expected value of the cash flows in each of the states; (3) there is a set of pure securities whose payment is contingent upon whether a single state of nature occurs; and (4) that state prices exist for these pure securities and are known. If these above assumptions hold, then the gross present value of a project can be calculated by summing the product of the expected value of the cash flows of each state and the state price. This means that the Banz–Miller state-contingent claims approach specifies the value of the project as weighted sums across both time and states. Presumably, projects that have payouts in states that are countercyclical (cyclical) would have low (high) relative risk and consequently low (high) present values. While a number of approaches are operationally possible to arrive at the appropriate state price, Banz–Miller recommend the Black–Scholes option pricing formula.

In fact, most capital budgeting proposals result in multiperiod cash flows. The conversion of the present values from a single period to a multiperiod is a result of assuming that the dynamics of the required inputs can be described by a stationary Markov chain. The resulting matrix describes the temporal structure for each state of the present values. Using data from the simulated predictive distributions of Ibbotson and Sinquefield, Banz-Miller derive state prices for a number of alternative (three, five, and twenty) states and years. These tables of estimated state prices represent the equivalent of the traditional discount rate tables for taking uncertainty into account. That is, given the estimated cash flows from the hypothesized states and given the requisite state prices a risk adjusted present value figure can be calculated for the project being evaluated.[27]

---

[26]For further discussion of various aspects of the multiperiod equilibrium valuation, see Bogue and Roll (1964).

[27]Such an illustrative capital budgeting computation is contained in Banz and Miller (forthcoming).

5. Capital rationing

One interesting paradigm of capital budgeting is choice under conditions of funds constraints. A quite extensive literature, mathematical programming solutions to capital budgeting, has arisen in an attempt to find the optimal project mix under funds constraints.

The case of the capital rationing problem is, given that the firm has an upper limit restriction on the funds imposed upon it from the capital market, what projects should be accepted to maximize the value of the firm? The solution is to impose a binding constraint to the optimization process which would ensure that the specified available funds are not exceeded and which simultaneously maximizes the value of the objective function of total present value.

However, even given a mathematical programming solution to a capital budgeting under financial constraints problem, a fundamental paradox would appear to question the economic meaning of such a solution. Specifically, if you view the financial markets as efficient, this would imply the nonexistence of any financial funds constraint. Furthermore, if one argues that the firm faces a financial constraint, then there is no economic rationale for the present value rule. That is, there is a logical inconsistency between using the present value rule to determine "fair" or equilibrium market values and arguing that the financial markets are not efficient (i.e. set "unfair" or nonequilibrium prices). As Fama and Miller note, "given this rationale for the maximand, what sense can we make of the constraints?". If the firm really does face approximately perfect markets, the financial constraints are arbitrary impositions of the management contrary to the best interests of the owners. The solution from their point of view would not be optimal, although it had been formally derived by a "maximization" process. On the other hand, "if the constraints were genuine and the firm really faced limitations on outside funds, it is the maximand that would be purely arbitrary. For what point is there in discounting a stream with market interest rates that do not represent actual opportunities for the firm in question? The firm might just as well use the rates of a foreign country or any other set of numbers plucked out of the air".[28]

However, the use of mathematical programming models may still be useful for capital budgeting decisions. That is, if the constraints are engineering (i.e. technological) or involve other factor inputs rather than financial market conditions, such methodology may serve to alleviate potential bottleneck problems that may occur during construction.[29]

---

[28]See Fama and Miller (1972, p. 136). This point has also been recognized by Weingartner in a recent review article whereby it is argued that the proposition that a firm's investment outlays are constrained by externally imposed conditions of the capital markets is "inconsistent with its internal assumptions and its consequences are at variance with observation", as well as being "massively counterproductive". See Weingartner (1977).

[29]An excellent treatment of mathematical programming and capital budgeting in the context of factor input constraints is contained in Weingartner (1963).

6. Summary

There has been a great deal of progress in finance, both theoretical and empirical, in the last few decades. This has had a spill-over effect for capital budgeting wherein elements of the discount rate can now be specified within a market equilibrium price context. Research via capital asset pricing and state preference theory-contingent claims analyses likely will result in further understanding of the complexities of normative and operational issues in capital budgeting.

References

Arrow, K. (1951) *Social Choice and Individual Values* (Wiley, New York).

Banz, R. and M. Miller (forthcoming) "Prices for State Contingent Claims: Some Estimates and Applications", *Journal of Business*.

Bierman, H. and S. Smidt (1966) *The Capital Budgeting Decision* (Macmillan, New York).

Black, F. (1972) "Capital Market Equilibrium with Restricted Borrowing", *Journal of Business*, July.

Bogue, M. and R. Roll (1964) "Capital Budgeting of Risky Projects with 'Imperfect' Markets for Physical Capital", *Journal of Finance*, May.

Borch, K. (1968) *The Economics of Uncertainty* (Princeton University Press).

Brennan, M. (1973) "An Approach to the Valuation of Uncertain Income Streams", *Journal of Finance*, June.

Cohen, K. and E. Elton (1967) "Inter-Temporal Portfolio Analysis Based on Simulation of Joint Returns", *Management Science*, September.

Constantinides, S. (forthcoming) "Market Risk Adjustment in Project Valuation", *Journal of Finance*.

Donaldson, G. (1963) "Financial Goals: Management vs. Stockholders", *Harvard Business Review*, May–June.

Fama, E. and M. Miller (1972) *The Theory of Finance* (Holt, Rinehart & Winston, New York).

Hamada, R. (1971) "Investment Decisions with a Mean–Variance Approach", *Quarterly Journal of Economics*, November.

Jenson, M. and J. Long (1972) "Corporate Investment under Uncertainty and Pareto Optimality in the Capital Markets", *Bell Journal of Economics and Management Science*, Spring.

Lintner, J. (1965) "The Valuation of Risk Assets and the Selection of Risky Investments in Stock Portfolios and Capital Budgets", *Review of Economics and Statistics*, February.

Lorie, J. and Savage, L. (1955) "Three Problems in Rationing Capital", *Journal of Business*, October.

Marris, R. (1964) *The Economic Theory of Managerial Capitalism* (Macmillan, London).

Merton, R. (1973) "An Intertemporal Capital Asset Pricing Model", *Econometrica*, September, 867–887.

Merton R. and M. Subrahmanyan (1974) "The Optimality of a Competitive Stock Market", *Bell Journal of Economics and Management Science*, Spring.

Mossin, J. (1966) "Equilibrium in a Capital Asset Market", *Econometrica*, October.

Mossin, J. (1969) "Security Pricing and Investment Criteria in Competitive Markets", *American Economic Review*, December, 749.

Mossin, J. (1973) *Theory of Financial Markets* (Prentice-Hall, Englewood Cliffs).

Rubenstein, M. (1973) "A Mean-Variance Synthesis of Corporate Financial Theory", *Journal of Finance*, March.

Savage, L. J. (1971) "The Elicitation of Personal Probabilities and Expectations", *Journal of the American Statistical Association*, March, 783–801.

Sharpe, W. (1964) "Capital Asset Prices: A Theory of Market Equilibrium under Conditions of Risk", *Journal of Finance*, September.

Simon, H. (1959) "Theories of Decision Making in Economic and Behavioral Science", *American Economic Review*, June.

Stiglitz, J. (1972) "On the Optimality of the Stock Market Allocation of Investment", *Quarterly Journal Of Economics*, February.

Teichroew, D., A. Robichek and M. Montalbano (1965) "An Analysis of Criteria for Investment and Financing Decisions under Uncertainty", *Management Science*.

Tuttle, D. and R. Litzenberger (1968) "Leverage, Diversification, and Capital Market Effects on a Risk-Adjusted Capital Budgeting Framework", *Journal of Finance*, June.

Tversky, A. and D. Kaheman (1973) "Judgement under Uncertainty: Heuristics and Biases", presented at 4th Conference on Subjective Probability, Utility, and Decision Making, Rome, pp. 1–6.

Van Horne, J. (1966) "Capital Budgeting Decisions Involving Combinations of Risky Investments", *Management Science*, October.

Van Horne, J. (1974) *Financial Management and Policy* (Prentice-Hall, Englewood Cliffs).

Von Neumann, J. and O. Morgenstern (1974) *Theory of Games and Economic Behavior* (Princeton University Press).

Weingartner, H. M. (1963) *Mathematical Programming and the Analysis of Capital Budgeting Problems* (Prentice-Hall, Englewood Cliffs).

Weingartner, M. (1969) "Some New Views on the Payback Period and Capital Budgeting Decisions", *Management Science*, August.

Weingartner, H. M. (1977) "Capital Rationing: *n* Authors in Search of a Plot", *Journal of Finance*, December, 1403–1431.

Weston, J. F. (1973) "Investment Decisions using the Capital Asset Pricing Model", *Financial Management*, Spring.

Winkler, R. (1967) "The Assessment of Prior Distributions in Bayesian Analysis", *Journal of the American Statistical Society*, 776–800.

Zellner, A. (1971a) *An Introduction to Bayesian Methods in Economics* (Wiley, New York).

Zellner, A. (1971b) "The Bayesian Approach and Alternatives in Econometrics", in: M. Intrilligator, ed., *Frontiers of Quantitative Economics* (North-Holland, Amsterdam), pp. 178–193.

Chapter 9

CASH MANAGEMENT

EDWIN J. ELTON and MARTIN J. GRUBER
New York University

1. Introduction

One function of the financial officer of a firm is to decide on the optimal amount of cash (or demand deposits) to keep on hand in order to meet the needs of his firm. There have been three alternative formulations of the cash problem.

In the most common formulation, the aggregate amount of cash and marketable securities is assumed to be exogenous and the cash problem is to determine the split between cash and marketable securities. The decision-maker is seen as determining this allocation in order to maximize the revenues from the marketable security portfolio less both the transaction costs from changing the size of this portfolio and the cost of running out of cash. Furthermore, the decision-maker is assumed to have no control over inflows and outflows from the pool of liquid assets. Rather, these are assumed to be exogenously determined usually by a stochastic process. An alternative to this is presented by Robichek, Teichrow and Jones (1965) and by Orgler (1970). The earliest work was done by Robichek, Teichrow and Jones. However, the Orgler formulation has been developed in more detail and hence will be discussed here. Orgler presents a linear programming solution to the short term working capital problem that includes cash as one variable. The most important difference in the Orgler approach is that the decision-maker does not react to exogenous cash flows; rather, the cash flows are part of the solution. In Orgler's view, cash inflows and outflows are in part results of policy decisions (such as whether or not to take discounts on payables) and in order to decide how much to put in cash, one must simultaneously decide on receivables and payables policies. Many of the inflows and outflows in Orgler's formulation are fixed by previous policy. Examples would be the timing of the payment to labor and the credit policies which determine the amount customers pay in cash. Other payments or receipts are determined in solutions such as whether or not to take discounts on payables. The amount to hold in cash is one decision and is affected by all the

James L. Bicksler, Editor, Handbook of Financial Economics
© *North-Holland Publishing Company – 1979*

other decisions concerning receivables and payables. While this approach is more general than the first approach, the generality is bought by increasing the demands on the decision-maker and having the cash flows deterministic.

The third approach to the cash problem is presented by Pogue, Fawcett and Busard (PFB). PFB view the cash decision as the choice of how much to hold in demand deposits in order to purchase services offered by the banks in which the demand deposits are kept. Banks provide a variety of services such as loans, credit investigation, check clearing and foreign transactions. Corporations pay for these services, in part, by maintaining demand deposits at their banks. Money earned on the demand deposits are a source of income to the bank that compensates them for the services. PFB determine cash balances by balancing the benefits they provide from these services with the costs of maintaining these services. Once again the problem is solved as a linear programming problem.

Each of these formulations is useful for some situations. We will concentrate on the first. We have made this choice primarily because the literature here is so extensive that a review is important, but also because there are a number of situations where this is the appropriate formulation.

This form of the cash management problem, which is called the cash balance problem, is a realistic description of a type of problem faced by many firms. For example, it captures the nature of the problem faced by the financial officer of an industrial corporation who has the job of managing the company's day-to-day cash position given that the financing and investment decisions are either determined by others or fixed over a reasonable period of time. It also captures the problem, faced by the treasurer, of many types of financial intermediaries (e.g. mutual funds, pension funds, college endowment funds, and insurance companies). In each case the inflows and outflows of cash are beyond the control of the decision-maker. In each case the decision-maker must decide how much of the liquid assets to hold in cash to meet transaction demands and how much to place in the institution's portfolio of securities. For example, the cash demand faced by the treasurer of a mutual fund is largely determined by the net of redemptions, new contributions, and inflows from investments. Although he may affect the inflows from new investments, it is reasonable to assume that the other net cash flows to the firm are beyond his control.

2. The optimum allocation between cash and marketable securities – general solution

The cash balance problem involves the decision on the optimal level of cash with which to start each period (j) given (1) an initial cash position (i); (2) a set of transfer costs; (3) understock and holding costs, and (4) a density function for stochastic changes in cash flows. The solution to this problem is similar to a dynamic programming solution to the inventory problem in that both involve the balancing of understock, holding and transaction costs, so as to minimize the present value of expected future costs. However, there are major differences in that: (a) stochastic changes in the level of cash can be positive or negative, and (b) the manager can either increase or decrease the amount of inventory (cash) at the start of each period.

We can represent the transfer costs of changing the cash level of the firm i to j as

$$\text{transfer costs } T(i,j) = \begin{bmatrix} T_u + t_u(j-i), & \text{if } j > i \\ 0, & \text{if } j = i \\ T_d + t_d(i-j), & \text{if } j < i \end{bmatrix}. \tag{1}$$

In this expression T_u and T_d represent, respectively, any fixed costs involved in increasing or decreasing the level of the cash balance, while t_u and t_d represent the marginal costs per dollar of change.

Holding and understock costs can be assumed to be a function of the level of cash at the beginning or the end of each period, or they can be assumed to be a function of some intermediate or average cash position during the period. It is difficult to choose among these assumptions and in fact the best choice depends on the circumstances facing the firm.[1] Fortunately, the choice of assumption does not affect the type of analysis or conclusions contained in this paper, although it will affect the numerical calculations for any problem. In order to make the analysis generally useful, we will define the costs associated with the level of cash, $L(i)$ (holding and understock costs) in two different ways: first in terms of beginning cash balance levels, then in terms of ending cash balance levels. For both these cases, let: $h(\cdot)$ be the function that represents the opportunity cost associated with having a positive cash balance of any size, and $u(\cdot)$ be the function that represents the understock costs associated with having a negative cash balance of any size. At this point we have made no assumption as to the functional form of $h(\cdot)$ and $u(\cdot)$.

If we assume that the argument of these functions is the cash level at the beginning of the period, then

$$L(j) = \begin{cases} -u(j), & \text{if } j < 0 \\ 0, & \text{if } j = 0 \\ h(j), & \text{if } j > 0 \end{cases}. \tag{2}$$

In order to define $L(j)$ when costs depend on the cash balance with which we end a period, we must describe the distribution of changes in cash balance. We will treat cash outflows as an independently distributed random variable with a

[1]Alternative assumptions have been made by articles discussing the cash management problem. See Eppen and Fama (1969a, b), Girges (1968), Neave (1970).

density function $P(e)$.[2] With this definition expected understock costs will be

$$\int_{+j}^{\infty} u(e-j)P(e)\,de.$$

The expected opportunity cost of having too much cash is

$$\int_{-\infty}^{j} h(j-e)P(e)\,de.$$

Finally, the cost associated with starting a period with a level of cash, j, is the sum of these costs or[3]

$$L(j) = \int_{-\infty}^{j} h(j-e)P(e)\,de + \int_{j}^{\infty} u(e-j)P(e)\,de. \tag{3}$$

The analysis contained in the remainder of this chapter is appropriate under either of these definitions of $L(j)$, (2) or (3), unless an exception is explicitly noted.

The recursive relationship representing the optimal cash management problem can now easily be constructed. The optimal cash balance to move to (j), given any starting cash balance (i) at time t is going to be that value which minimizes the sum of:

(a) the transfer cost of going from a cash balance of i to one of j or $T(i,j)$;

(b) the holding–understock cost which is associated with a cash balance of j or $L(j)$; or

(c) the present value of the expected minimum cost of managing cash from period $t+1$ until the horizon given a move to state j at time t.[4]

If we let $\alpha =$ the appropriate discount factor and $f_t(i) =$ the minimum expected cost of managing cash from period t until the horizon given that the opening cash balance is i in period t, then the recursive relationship becomes

$$f_t(i) = \min_{j} \left[T(i,j) + L(j) + \alpha \int_{-\infty}^{\infty} f_{t+1}(j-e)P(e)\,de \right]. \tag{4}$$

---

[2]In solving any problem, management will treat e as a discrete variable with finite bounds. Management can define upper and lower limits for cash flows during any period and management will deal with possible cash flows in discrete quantities. While all of the analysis in this chapter could be performed by treating e as a discrete variable with finite bounds, without a change in results, the analysis is facilitated by treating e as a continuous variable.

[3]The firm may be operating under constraints (e.g. need for compensating balances) which make a new level for holding and understock costs occur at some positive cash position m rather than at a zero cash balance. Under this assumption, eq. (3) becomes

$$L(j) = \int_{-\infty}^{j-m} h[(j-m)-e]P(e)\,de + \int_{j-m}^{\infty} u[e-(j-m)]P(e)\,de.$$

[4]We are numbering periods forwards in time. The horizon is period T, the period before the horizon is period $T-1$, etc.

This relationship can be used to solve any cash balance problem. However, the special structure of many cash balance problems allow us to employ this relationship to both define the form of an optimal cash balance policy and to simplify the calculations needed to reach such a policy. Furthermore, knowing the form of the optimum cash balance policy is often more important than the numeric solution to a particular problem.

3. Exploiting special structure

Our ability to deduce the form of the optimum policy from the dynamic programming formulation depends on the special structure of the components of the dynamic programming equation. If these cost components are convex or concave functions, we can gain insights into the problem. In particular, we can simplify the solution to the cash management problem because $L(j)$ can reasonably be assumed to be a convex function of j. The function $L(j)$ is convex if holding costs increase at least proportionately (or faster) with increases in cash balances for positive cash balances, understock costs increase at least proportionately with decreases in cash balances for negative cash balances, and $h(0) = u(0) = 0.$[5] The actual composition of holding and understock costs are consistent with the convexity of $L(j)$. Holding costs are the interest forgone by holding cash rather than marketable securities. These should be directly proportional to the size of the cash balance. Understock costs are costs associated with the delay and embarrassement caused by an inability promptly to meet obligations. These should increase more than proportionately with the size of the unpaid obligation. Finally, note that $L(j)$ has a finite minimum equal to or greater than zero, the cost of having a cash balance of zero.

Once the convexity of $L(j)$ is accepted, one can proceed to derive the optimum form of the cash balance policy. We shall start by studying the case where the fixed component of transaction costs is assumed equal to zero. Then we shall study cases where the fixed components has a positive value.

3.1. Optimal models with only fixed transaction costs

A number of cash balance models have been developed under the assumption that the transfer cost per transaction does not vary with the amount of funds transferred. While we believe that this is the least realistic assumption with

[5]The convexity of $L(j)$ under the assumption stated in the text can be seen by examining eqs. (2) and (3).

respect to transaction costs, these models are worth examining for the following two reasons.[6]

(1) They have received a lot of attention in the literature.

(2) The authors who have constructed these models have generally *assumed* the form of the optimal policy and simply solved for the parameters of the model. The general dynamic programming model developed earlier in eq. (4) can be used to show whether the assumed form of the policy is indeed optimum.

In this section we shall examine three models developed by Baumol (1952), Sastry (1970), and Miller and Orr (1966, 1968) which assume that transaction costs are fixed.

3.1.1. Baumol's model

The first model for the cash balance problem which treated transaction costs as fixed was developed by Baumol (1952).[7]

He assumed that:

(1) the outflow of cash per period (e) is a positive constant known with certainty;

(2) management is concerned with an infinite horizon;

(3) management will never incur a cash shortage (stockout costs are infinite);

(4) the holding cost of cash equals h dollars per dollar of average inventory held during a period; and

(5) all transactions increase the cash level and if a transaction takes place the cost is T_u independent of the size of the transaction.

In terms of previously defined symbols we have[8]

(1) $T(i,j) = T_u,$ if $j > i,$

$\quad\quad\quad = 0,$ if $j = i;$

(2) $L(j) = \dfrac{j + (j - e)}{2} h,$ if $j \geqslant e,$

$\quad\quad\quad = \infty,$ if $j < e;$

(3) $P(e) = 1,$ for $e = \bar{e},$

$\quad\quad P(e) = 0,$ for $e \neq \bar{e}.$

---

[6]The total cost of a transaction should vary with the size of the transaction simply because of the structure of brokerage commissions in effect. The size of these commissions is likely to be quite large relative to the fixed cost of planning and executing a transaction.

[7]Tobin (1956) developed a similar formulation.

[8]j cannot be less than i under Baumol's assumption.

If we now rewrite eq. (4) using these new definitions, we have

$$f(i) = \min \begin{bmatrix} \min_{j} \left[T_u + \dfrac{j + (j - e)}{2} h + \alpha f(j - e) \right], & \text{if } j > i \\[2mm] \dfrac{i + (i - e)}{2} h + \alpha f(i - e), & \text{if } j = i \end{bmatrix}.$$

The time subscript can be dropped since all costs are assumed to be stable over an infinite horizon.

An examination of the above equation shows that the same problem is being faced repeatedly: over an infinite horizon a stationary policy exists. Therefore, letting K equal the number of periods between voluntary changes in the cash balance, the recursive relationship can be reformulated to solve for the optimum time between transactions or[9]

$$f_t = \min_{K} \left[T_u + h \sum_{y=1}^{K} \alpha^y \frac{e(2K - 2y + 1)}{2} + \alpha^K f_{t+K} \right].$$

To arrive at Baumol's results, we must make the assumption that $\alpha = 1$. Then we can state the recursive relationship in terms of equivalent average return, or[10]

$$f = \min_{K} \left[\frac{T_u + he \sum_{y=1}^{K} \dfrac{2K - 2y + 1}{2}}{K} \right].$$

The terms in the brackets are convex with respect to K and thus a minimum exists.[11] The presence of an unique minimum implies that there is an optimum

[9]Holding costs are based on average inventory and so are equal to

$$h \left[\alpha_K \frac{Ke + (Ke - e)}{2} + \alpha^2 \frac{(Ke - e) + (Ke - 2e)}{2} + \ldots + \alpha^K \frac{e + 0}{2} \right]$$

or

$$h \sum_{y=1}^{K} \alpha^y \frac{e(2K - 2y + 1)}{2}.$$

[10]For a discussion of the properties of equivalent average return, see Wagner (1969, pp. 367–370). For α less than 1 and large K, this solution is not necessarily optimum.

[11]The convexity of f can be shown by proving that an average of the above expression evaluated at $K + 1$ and $K - 1$ is greater than this expression evaluated at K, that is

$$\left[T_u + he \sum_{y=1}^{K+1} \frac{2(K+1) - 2y + 1}{2} \right] \Big/ 2(K + 1)$$

$$+ \frac{T_u + he \sum_{y=1}^{K-1} \dfrac{2(K-1) - 2y + 1}{2}}{2} > \left[\frac{T_u + he \sum_{y=1}^{K} \dfrac{2K - 2y + 1}{2}}{K} \right].$$

Simplifying yields

$$\frac{T_u}{K(K-1)(K+1)} > 0.$$

time between reorders or equivalently an optimum order size. Employing the sum of an arithmetic progression and simplifying yields

$$f = \min_{K} \left[\frac{T_u}{K} + \frac{heK}{2} \right].$$

Differentiating the above formula and setting it equal to zero yields, as the optimum time between orders,[12]

$$K = \sqrt{\left(\frac{2T_u}{he} \right)}.$$

The optimum order size is ke or

$$Ke = \sqrt{\left(\frac{2T_u e}{h} \right)},$$

which is Baumol's formula for cash management.

3.1.2. Sastry's model

Sastry (1970) has modified Baumol's model to allow cash shortage at a cost u per average dollar of cash shortage per period. If we let $(K-k)$ equal the optimum number of periods for which there is a cash shortage, then

$$f_t = \min_{K,k} \left[T_u + h \sum_{y=1}^{k} \frac{\alpha^y e(2k - 2y + 1)}{2} \right.$$
$$\left. + u \sum_{y=1}^{K-k} \alpha^{k+y} \frac{e[2(K-k) - 2y + 1]}{2} + \alpha^K f_{t+K} \right].$$

For the infinite case, if we assume that $\alpha = 1$, we can write this in terms of the equivalent average return

$$f = \frac{\min_{K,k} \left[\frac{Tu}{K} + he \sum_{y=1}^{k} \frac{(2k - 2y + 1)}{2} \quad ue \sum_{y=1}^{K-k} \frac{(2(K-k) - 2y + 1)}{2} \right.}{K} + \frac{}{K}.$$

Employing the formula for the sum of an arithmetic progression and simplifying

$$f = \min_{K,k} \left[\frac{Tu}{K} + \frac{hek^2}{2K} + \frac{ue(K-k)^2}{K} \right].$$

[12]We have followed Baumol (1952) in treating K as a continuous variable.

Taking the partial derivative of f with respect to K and k, setting the partial derivatives equal to zero and solving yields

$$k = \sqrt{\left(\frac{2T_u}{he}\right)} \sqrt{\left(\frac{u}{h+u}\right)} \, ,$$

or the optimum amount of cash to hold immediately after increasing the cash position is

$$ke = \sqrt{\left(\frac{2T_u e}{h}\right)} \sqrt{\left(\frac{u}{h+u}\right)} \, ,$$

which is Sastry's result.

3.1.3. Miller and Orr's model

Miller and Orr (1966, 1968) have modified the above analysis by making the demand for cash a stochastic variable (e) which can take on either positive or negative values.[13] They assume, as did the other models in this section, that the time horizon is infinite and transaction costs, per transaction, are a fixed quantity. In terms of previously defined symbols

$$L(j) = \frac{j+(j-e)}{2}, \quad \text{if } j > e$$

$$\qquad = \infty, \qquad \text{if } j < e;$$

$$T(i,j) = T_u, \qquad \text{if } j > i,$$

$$\qquad = 0, \qquad \text{if } j = i,$$

$$\qquad = T_d, \qquad \text{if } j < i.$$

The recursive relationship is:

$$f_t(i) = \min \begin{bmatrix} T_d + \min\limits_{j>i} \left[\int_e \frac{j+(j-e)}{2} hP(e) + \alpha \int_e f_{t+1}(j-e)P(e) \right] \\ \int_e \frac{i+(i-e)}{2} hP(e) + \alpha \int_e f_{t+1}(i-e)P(e) \\ T_u + \min\limits_{i>j} \left[\int_e \frac{j+(j-e)}{e} hP(e) + \alpha \int_e f_{t+1}(j-e)P(e) \right] \end{bmatrix}.$$

[13]They further specify that the probability distribution of e is symmetrical.

Since there is an infinite horizon the subscript on the f_t can be dropped. Dropping the subscript and simplifying yields

$$f(i) = \min \begin{bmatrix} T_d + \min_{j>i} \left[\dfrac{j+(j-\bar{e})}{2} h + \alpha \int_e f(j-e)P(e) \right] \\[2mm] \dfrac{i+(i-\bar{e})}{2} h + \alpha \int_e f(i-e)P(e) \\[2mm] T_u + \min_{i>j} \left[\dfrac{j+(j-e)}{2} h + \alpha \int_e f(j-e)P(e) \right] \end{bmatrix}.$$

The above is a discrete formulation while Miller and Orr's (1966, 1968) is continuous. However, by letting the time interval go to zero, the continuous form is approximated. Terms which are to be minimized with respect to j in the top and bottom part of the recursive relationship are identical. This implies that once the fixed charge is incurred, the cash level after the transaction will be identical whether the original cash level was too high or too low. A little reflection shows that this is sensible. There are no variable transaction costs. Once the fixed cost is incurred, any cash level can be selected without further cost. This is true whether T_d or T_u is paid. Consequently, the same decision problem is being faced in both cases and they must have a common optimum.[14]

Consider that there is an optimum set of decision rules that determine whether to increase or decrease cash. For the ease of understanding one could imagine an upper bound that determined when cash is turned into securities, a lower bound that determined when securities were sold and a common return point. What happens when these decisions points are lowered by a constant amount? The number of transactions and the time between a transaction would be unchanged since these depend only upon the shape of the pattern (width of boundaries and location of return point) and the shape is unchanged by a constant decrease. However, holding costs are reduced since the whole channel within which the cash position can move and so the average level of cash held has been reduced. Carried to an extreme, this implies that the securities should be sold only when the cash level reaches minus infinity. What prevents this from happening is Miller and Orr's assumption that cash cannot be reduced below a certain level, which is determined exogenously from their cash management model. Given this external level specified as the minimum cash balance, the argument presented above shows that cash should only be increased when the

---

[14]Miller and Orr (1966, pp. 419) state that it may not be so if $T_u \neq T_d$. The equality of T_d and T_u is not important, what is important is that there are no variable costs.

minimum is reached.[15] If we let L_B be the externally determined level, then we can state that the lower branch is selected when $i = L_B$.

Up to this point we have used the dynamic programming formulation to show that there is a unique lower bound and that there is a common return point to which the firm moves once a transaction cost is incurred. Why might there be a unique upper bound? First, there must be at least one upper bound since without one, holding costs can go to infinity. If the return point is fixed then an increase in the upper bound leads to a constant increase in holding costs, while transaction costs should decrease at a decreasing rate (since we are going further and further into the tail of the distribution of cash levels). At some point the changes are equal and a unique optimum exists. If the return point is then increased, holding costs increase linearly while transaction costs should decrease at a decreasing rate, since the distribution of cash levels becomes more centered. Both of these processes have the same effect with the result that through such an iterative process a unique minimum could be determined. Given the knowledge of such a unique bound, it could, of course, also be determined by equating the upper and middle part of the recursive relationship.[16]

In short, from the dynamic programming framework we can show that the policy assumed by Miller and Orr does appear to be optimal. Once this form of policy is determined as optimum, Miller and Orr's analysis of the location of the upper bound and return point follows logically.

3.2. Variable costs but no fixed costs

The assumption that the fixed cost per transaction approaches zero seems to be a reasonable assumption for the cash balance problem of many firms. For example, a mutual fund in transferring funds from cash to its portfolio will incur a transaction cost on purchase or sale which is roughly proportional to the amount of funds involved. There are some fixed costs involved in writing a check and processing the paperwork, but these should be negligible compared to the variable components.[17] A special case of this form of the problem has been studied by Eppen and Fama (1969b). They assumed that there were constant marginal holding and understock costs. While several of our results are similar to theirs, our proofs are significantly different and our results are more generally applicable.

---

[15]Miller and Orr (1966) assume this is true but express concern that such a policy need not be optimal (p. 419). There is no basis for their concern.

[16]See Miller and Orr (1966) for an exact formula.

[17]To the extent that these functions are performed by employees with slack time, they are not a real cost of the decision.

If we accept the fixed component in the transaction cost as being equal to zero, eq. (4) can be rewritten as

$$f_t(i) = \min \begin{bmatrix} \min_{j>i} \left[t_u(j-i) + L(j) + \alpha \int_{-\infty}^{\infty} f_{t+1}(j-e)P(e)\,de \right] \\ L(i) + \alpha \int_{-\infty}^{\infty} f_{t+1}(i-e)P(e)\,de \\ \min_{i>j} \left[t_d(i-j) + L(j) + \alpha \int_{-\infty}^{\infty} f_{t+1}(j-e)P(e)\,de \right] \end{bmatrix}. \tag{5}$$

3.2.1. Optimal policy for the final decision period

For the last decision point, eq. (5) can be rewritten as[18]

$$f_{T-1}(i) = \min \begin{bmatrix} -t_u i + \min_{j>i} \left[t_u j + L(j) \right] \\ L(i) \\ t_d i + \min_{i>j} \left[-t_d j + L(j) \right] \end{bmatrix}. \tag{6}$$

Consider the upper part of the recursive relationship.

Since $L(j)$ is a convex function and $t_u j$ is a linear function of j, their sum is a convex function of j. Therefore, there is a minimum which can be denoted by D_{T-1} such that[19]

$$\min_{j} \left[t_u j + L(j) \right] = t_u D_{T-1} + L(D_{T-1}). \tag{7}$$

Furthermore, by the properties of convexity a local optimum value of D_{T-1} is also a global optimum.

Assume $i \geqslant D_{T-1}$. Values of j greater than i do not contain D_{T-1} and i is closer to D_{T-1} than any value of j. Since we are assuming convex functions, we have

$$\min_{j>i} \left[t_u j + L(j) \right] > t_u i + L(i).$$

---

[18]The final decision period is $T-1$ and $f_T=0$.

[19]This function will usually have a unique minimum and the treatment in the text is based on this case. It is possible that the function has a minimum value over some range of i. If this occurs, D_{T-1} should be defined as the lowest value of i for which the equality holds. In this case, all of the results stated below still hold. All proofs would remain valid except that some of the equalities of the greater than form would have to be replaced with inequalities of the equal to or greater than form.

In the proofs involving upper limits if a minimum value of the cost function occurs over a range of i, U_{T-1} should be defined as the largest value of i for which the minimization equality holds. These statements pertain not only to the proof in this section, but to all proofs involving the determination of upper and lower limits for cash balances throughout this paper.

Rearranging terms:

$$- t_u i + \min_{j>i} \left[t_u j + L(j) \right] > L(i).$$

The left-hand side of this expression is the same as the top choice in eq. (6). Since $L(i)$ is smaller the middle choice is preferable to the top choice and we have: if $i \geqslant D_{T-1}$ then the value of j which minimizes $f_{T-1}(i)$ is equal to i and $f_{T-1}(i) = L(i)$.

Assume $i < D_{T-1}$. If we examine all j greater than i, setting $j = D_{T-1}$ is one possible choice. Since

$$t_u D_{T-1} + L(D_{T-1}) < t_u i + L(i).$$

Then

$$- t_u i + t_u D_{T-1} + L(D_{T-1}) < L(i).$$

The top choice in eq. (6) is preferred and we have: if $i < D_{T-1}$ set $j < D_{t-1}$. By an analogous argument it can be shown that

$$\min_{j} \left[- t_d j + L(j) \right] = - t_d U_{T-1} + L(U_{t-1})$$

and that the optimal policy becomes:[20]

for $i \leqslant U_{T-1}$, set $j = i$ and therefore $f_{T-1}(i) = L(i)$;

for $i > U_{T-1}$, set $j = U_{T-1}$ and therefore $f_{T-1}(i) = t_d(i - U_{T-1}) + L(u_{T-1})$.

A general policy can now be stated for time $T-1$. If the cash position is below D_{T-1} sell enough securities to bring the cash position up to D_{T-1}. If the cash position is above U_{T-1} buy enough securities to restore the cash position to U_{T-1}. If it is between these two limits take no action. Notice that we can state the optimal policy independent of the starting position of cash D_{T-1} and U_{T-1} are not functions of i.

The costs involved in following this policy are a function of i. They can be presented as

$$f_{T-1}(i) = \begin{bmatrix} t_u(D_{T-1} - i) + L(D_{T-1}), & \text{if } i < D_{T-1} \\ L(i), & \text{if } D_{T-1} \leqslant i \leqslant U_{T-1} \\ t_d(i - U_{T-1}) + L(U_{T-1}), & \text{if } i > U_{T-1} \end{bmatrix}. \qquad (8)$$

3.2.2. Optimal policy for earlier decision periods

We have now formulated an optimum policy for the last decision period. In order to extend this analysis to earlier periods we must be able to make

---

[20]For this policy to be optimum, it is necessary that $U_{T-1} \geqslant D_{T-1}$. In a later section we shall prove that for any t, $U_t \geqslant 0$ and $D_t \leqslant 0$. Therefore, $U_{T-1} \geqslant D_{T-1}$.

statements about the form of $f_{T-1}(i)$. As is shown in Appendix B, $f_{T-1}(i)$ is a convex function. The expression

$$\int_{-\infty}^{\infty} f_{T-1}(j-e)P(e)\,de$$

is also convex because the sum of convex functions is a convex function and integration, a summation operation, preserves convexity.

Eq. (5) can now be rewritten to define f_{T-2} as

$$f_{T-2}(i) = \min \begin{bmatrix} -t_u i + \min_{j>1}\left[t_u j + L(j) + \alpha \int_{-\infty}^{\infty} f_{T-1}(j-e)P(e)\,de \right] \\[2mm] L(i) + \alpha \int_{-\infty}^{\infty} f_{T-1}(i-e)P(e)\,de \\[2mm] t_d i + \min_{i>j}\left[-t_d j + L(j) + \alpha \int_{-\infty}^{\infty} f_{T-1}(j-e)P(e)\,de \right] \end{bmatrix}. \qquad (10)$$

Consider the top expression in eq. (10). Since $L(j)$ is a convex function of j, $t_u j$ is a linear function of j and

$$\int_{-\infty}^{\infty} f_{T-1}(j-e)P(e)\,de$$

is a convex function of j, their sum is a convex function of j. Therefore, there is a minimum which can be denoted by D_{T-2} such that

$$\min_{j}\left[t_u j + L(j) + \alpha \int_{-\infty}^{\infty} f_{T-1}(j-e)P(e)\,de \right]$$

$$= t_u D_{T-2} + L(D_{T-2}) + \alpha \int_{-\infty}^{\infty} f_{T-1}(D_{T-2}-e)P(e)\,de.$$

Since D_{T-2} is a global optimum for this function one can proceed directly paralleling the steps of the proof in section 2 to show that the optimum policy for period $T-2$ is described as

if $i < D_{T-2}$, $j = D_{T-2}$,

if $D_{T-2} \leqslant i \leqslant U_{T-2}$, $j = i$,

if $U_{T-2} < i$, $j = U_{T-2}$.

One can then proceed by paralleling the steps in the proof of convexity of $f_{T-1}(i)$ to show that $f_{T-2}(i)$ is also convex.

This procedure can then be repeated for periods $T-3$, $T-4$, $T-5$, etc. to show that for any period the costs of following an optimum policy can be represented as

$$f_t(i) = \begin{bmatrix} t_u(D_t - i) + L(D_t) + \alpha \int_{-\infty}^{\infty} f_{t+1}(D_t - e)P(e)\,de, & \text{for } i < D_t \\ L(i) + \alpha \int_{-\infty}^{\infty} f_{t+1}(i - e)P(e)\,de, & \text{for } D_1 \leqslant i \leqslant U_t \\ t_d(i - U_t) + L(U_t) + \alpha \int_{-\infty}^{\infty} f_{t+1}(U_t - e)P(e)\,de, & \text{for } U_t < i \end{bmatrix},$$

(11)

and the optimum policy can be represented as[21]

if $i < D_t$, $j = D_t$,

if $D_i \leqslant i \leqslant U_t$, $j = i$,

if $U_t < i$, $j = U_t$.

We have now exploited the cost structure of the cash balance problem to define the form of an optimum cash management policy. Note that, as shown in eq. (11), this policy can be stated to hold *regardless* of the cash balance of the firm at any moment in time. The limits U_t and D_t are not affected by the cash balance at any time. The independence of U_t and D_t from i leads to a vast reduction in calculations for the following reasons.

(1) U_t and D_t need only be determined once in any period. Furthermore, that determination is simplified by the fact that the functions are convex and each possess a minimum.

(2) Once U_t and D_t are determined, $f_t(i)$ is a simple linear function of i for $i < D_t$ and $i > U_t$ (see eq. (11)).

Before leaving this section we will show how the form of the recursive relationship can be used to define an optimal policy in more detail. In particular, we will show that if $L(j)$ is defined as in eq. (2), D_t must be nonpositive and U_t must be non-negative for all t.

Given any level of cash, the marginal cost of increasing the cash balance by one unit (see eq. (5)) is

$$t_u + \Delta L(i) + \alpha \Delta \int_{-\infty}^{\infty} f_{t+1}(i - e)P(e)\,de,$$

where Δ represents the value of the term which follows it evaluated at $i+1$ minus the value of the term evaluated at i. In order for the increase in cash

---

[21]It can further be shown that if the cost functions and probability distribution of cash demands are stationary over time, and management has an infinitely long time horizon, then stationary values exist for D_T and U_T.

balance to be profitable, this expression must be no larger than zero. Or rearranging terms

$$\Delta L(i) + \alpha \Delta \int_{-\infty}^{\infty} f_{t+1}(i-e) P(e) \, \mathrm{d}e \leqslant -t_u. \tag{12}$$

The second term can be evaluated from

$$\Delta f_{t+1}(i) = \begin{bmatrix} -t_u, & \text{for } i < D_t \\ \Delta L(i) + \alpha \Delta \int_{\infty}^{\infty} f_{t+2}(i-e) P(e) \, \mathrm{d}e, & \text{for } D_t \leqslant i \leqslant U_t \\ t_d, & \text{for } i > U_t \end{bmatrix}.$$

Since we have established that $f_{t+1}(i)$ is convex, $\Delta f_{t+1}(i)$ is monotone nondecreasing with a minimum value of $-t_u$. Since

$$\Delta f_{t+1}(i) \geqslant -t_u, \text{ for any } i,$$

then

$$\Delta \int_{-\infty}^{\infty} f_{t+1}(i-e) P(e) \, \mathrm{d}e$$

must be greater or equal to $-t_u$. Furthermore, since α is a number smaller than one,

$$\alpha \Delta \int_{-\infty}^{\infty} f_{t+1}(i-e) P(e) \, \mathrm{d}e \geqslant -t_u.$$

So, for the left-hand side of eq. (12) to be less than or equal to $-t_u$, $\Delta L(i)$ must be negative or equal to zero. From eq. (12) this can only happen if i is less than or equal to zero. Thus, it will not pay to raise the level of cash if the level of cash is above zero and $D_t \leqslant 0$.[22]

By an analogous proof, we can show that $U_t \geqslant 0$ for all t.

Up to this point we have assumed that the fixed cost component of transaction costs was equal to zero. While we believe this is a reasonable assumption for may cash management problems, in the next section of this paper we shall briefly explore the form of optimum policies when fixed costs are present.

3.3. Optimum policies with variable and fixed transaction costs

The fixed component of transaction costs is likely to be small relative to the variable component. However, these costs are often positive, since any transaction in securities involves a certain amount of a financial officer's time, plus

---

[22]If we had employed eq. (3) as the definition of $L(j)$ then an upper limit on D_t could be established as that value of i for which $\Delta L(i)$ first became negative.

clerical costs (e.g. cost of entering the transactions on the books, and recording receipts).

Let us take the simplest case where a fixed cost is present on one side of the transaction, but not on the other. This case has been analyzed by Girges (1965) and our results are identical to his though there are differences in the analysis. In particular, let us assume that there is a fixed cost T_u of selling securities. Then for the last period, eq. (4) can be written as

$$f_{T-1}(i) = \min \begin{bmatrix} T_u - t_u i + \min_{j>i} [t_u j + L(j)] \\ L(i) \\ t_d i + \min_{i>j} [-t_u j + L(j)] \end{bmatrix}. \tag{13}$$

Consider the top part of the recursive relationship. From the convexity of $t_u j + L(j)$ there is a minimum which can be denoted by D_{T-1} such that

$$\min_j [t_u j + L(j)] = t_u D_{T-1} + L(D_{T-1}).$$

Now suppose $i \geqslant D_{T-1}$. Values of $j > i \geqslant D_{T-1}$ do not contain D_{T-1}. Since we are assuming convex functions, the minimum occurs at the feasible value nearest D_{T-1} or i. Therefore

$$\min_{j>i} [t_u j + L(j)] > t_u i + L(i).$$

Rearranging terms

$$-t_u i + \min_{j>i} [t_u j + L(j)] > L(i).$$

Adding T_u to the left-hand side would not change the inequality. With this addition the left-hand side of the inequality is identical to the top of the recursive relationship and the right-hand side is the same as the middle part. The implication of the inequality is that if the level of cash balance is greater than D_{T-1} do not raise it.

Now suppose $i < D_{T-1}$. Then D_{T-1} is a feasible choice and the minimum cost is less than or equal to the cost at an arbitrary level i or

$$\min_{j<i} [t_u j + L(j)] \leqslant t_u i + L(i).$$

Rearranging terms

$$-t_u i + \min_{j<i} [t_u j + L(j)] \leqslant L(i).$$

The inequality is the same as the top and middle of the recursive relationship with the addition of T_u to the left-hand side. The addition of T_u to the left-hand side may or may not reverse the inequality.

Let d_{T-1} be the smallest value of i that reverses the inequality. That is, d_{T-1} is the smallest value of i for which

$$- T_u i + \min_{j<i} \left[t_u j + L(j) \right] < L(i)$$

Then we have: if $i \geqslant d_T$ do not raise the cash balance and $j = i$.[23] If $i < d_T$ then the inequality is retained and the optimal policy is to raise the level of cash to the value D_{T-1}, a value of which minimizes the top part of the recursive relationship.[24]

The proof for an upper limit on the cash balance is exactly the same as in section 3.1 and the optimum last period policy can be stated as

if $i < d_{T-1}$,   set $j = D_{T-1}$,

if $d_{T-1} \leqslant i \leqslant U_{T-1}$,   set $j = i$,

if $U_{T-1} < i$,   set $j = U_{T-1}$.

The cost of following this policy can be stated as

$$f_{T-1}(i) = \begin{bmatrix} T_u + t_u(D_{T-1} - i) + L(D_{T-1}), & \text{for } i < d_{T-1} \\ L(i), & \text{for } d_{T-1} \leqslant i \leqslant U_{T-1} \\ t_d(i - U_{T-1}) + L(U_{T-1}), & \text{for } U_{T-1} < i \end{bmatrix}.$$

To proceed to the analysis of earlier periods, we must first understand the properties of $f_{T-1}(i)$. We show below that a simple form of the optimal policy exists if $f_{T-1}(i)$ is right-hand T_u-convex. A function is right-hand T_u-convex if

$$f^*(i) = f(i+a) - f(i) + t_u - \frac{a}{b} \left[f(i) - f(i-b) \right] \geqslant 0, \tag{14}$$

for all values of i, and all positive values of a and b. Employing the expression for $f_{T-1}(i)$, using the properties of D_{T-1} and eq. (14), it can easily be shown that $f_{T-1}(i)$ is everywhere right-hand T_u-convex.[25]

[23] Because of the convexity of $t_u i + L(i)$, increasing i makes the difference between the left- and right-hand side smaller.

[24] By contrasting this proof with the discussion in section 3.2.1, the reader can see how the presence of a fixed cost has modified the analysis.

[25] Right-hand T_u-convexity has been proven by Girges (1968). To demonstrate right-hand T_u-convexity eq. (14) must be shown to hold over the following regions:
  (a) $i + a < d_{T-1}$;
  (b) $d_{T-1} \leqslant i - b < i < i + a \leqslant U_{T-1}$;
  (c) $U_{T-1} < i - b$;
  (d) $i = d_{T-1}$ and $i + a \leqslant U_{T-1}$; and
  (e) $i = U_{T-1}$ and $i - b > d_{T-1}$.

We can proceed to prove the optimal policy for earlier periods by employing the same steps needed to find the optimal policy for time period $T-1$. The first step is to note that

$$L(j) + \alpha \int_{-\infty}^{\infty} f_{T-1}(j-e)P(e)\,de$$

is a right-hand T_u-convex function of j.[26] The optimal policy for any period can then be defined as

$$\text{if } i < d_t, \qquad j = D_t,$$

$$\text{if } d_t \leqslant i \leqslant U_t, \qquad j = i,$$

$$\text{if } U_t < i, \qquad j = U_t,$$

and the associated optimum cost can be found by

$$f_t(i) = \left[\begin{array}{ll} T_u + t_u(D_t - i) + L(D_t) & \\ \quad + \alpha \int_{-\infty}^{\infty} f_{t+1}(D_t - e)P(e)\,de, & \text{for } i < d_t \\ L(i) + \alpha \int_{-\infty}^{\infty} f_{t+1}(i-e)P(e)\,de, & \text{for } d_t \leqslant i \leqslant U_t \\ t_d(i - U_t) + L(U_t) & \\ \quad + \alpha \int_{-\infty}^{\infty} f_{t+1}(U_t - e)P(e)\,de, & \text{for } U_t < i \end{array} \right].$$

Again, the optimal policy can be determined independently of the cash balance i at any moment in time. Computations can be facilitated by a procedure directly analogous to that described in section 3.1 except that after determining D_t one tries alternative values of d_t progressively smaller than D_t until

$$T_u + t_u(D_t - d_t) + L(D_t) + \alpha \int_{-\infty}^{\infty} f_{t+1}(D_t - e)P(e)\,de$$

$$\leqslant L(d_t) + \alpha \int_{-\infty}^{\infty} f_{t+1}(d_t - e)P(e)\,de.$$

[26]This is true since $L(j)$ is right-hand zero-convex (ordinary convexity) and the sum of a right hand T_u convex function and a zero-convex function is right hand T_u-convex. This is a special case of the general rule that the sum of a right hand T_u-convex function and a right hand K-convex function is right hand $(T_u + K)$ convex.

Directly analogous results can be derived if $T_u = 0$ and $T_d > 0$.[27] In this case, it can be shown that the optimal policy is

if $i < D_t$, $j = D_t$,

if $D_t \leqslant i \leqslant u_t$, $j = i$,

if $u_t < i$, $j = U_t$,

and the associated cost of following that policy is

$$f_t(i) = \left[\begin{array}{ll} t_u(D_t - i) + L(D_t) + \alpha \int_{-\infty}^{\infty} f_{t+1}(D_t - e) P(e)\, de, & \text{if } i < D_t \\[4mm] L(i) + \alpha \int_{-\infty}^{\infty} f_{t+1}(i - e) P(e)\, de, & \text{if } D_t \leqslant i \leqslant u_t \\[4mm] T_d + t_d(i - U_t) + L(U_t) + \alpha \int_{-\infty}^{\infty} f_{t+1}(U_t - e) P(e)\, de, & \text{if } u_t < i \end{array} \right].$$

One might think that the methodology presented above could easily be used to derive the optimal policy for $T_u > 0$ and $T_d > 0$ and that the optimal policy would be:

if $i < d_t$, $j = D_t$,

if $d_t \leqslant i \leqslant u_t$, $j = i$,

if $u_t < i$, $j = U_t$.

However, as shown by Neave (1970), this form of policy is not in general optimum. In fact, a policy which determines any type of limits independent of cash balance (i) is not in general optimum. The reason for this is that the cost functions generally contain both concave and convex regions when T_d and T_u are positive.[28] In this case, while some simplification of the optimal policy is possible, it is generally necessary to return to eq. (4) for the solution of the cash management problem. In the infinite case, computations can be simplified by employing the linear programming transformation of eq. (4) presented in Appendix A of this paper.

---

[27]The proof requires that functions be proved left handed convex.

[28]Neave (1970) has demonstrated that a simple policy involving decision points which are independent of (i) is generally nonoptimal when fixed and variable costs are present. The problem arises because the cost functions are not everywhere zero-convex nor right-hand K-convex, nor left hand K-convex. Neave has further shown that it is possible *partially* to define a policy in terms of fixed decision points.

Appendix A: the linear programming model of the infinite horizon cash management problem with Markovian transition probabilities

Let us consider a general dynamic programming problem of the form

$$f_t(i) = \min_{j} \left[C_{ij} + \alpha \sum_k f_{t+1}(k) P(k|i,j) \right], \qquad (A.1)$$

where

$f_t(i)$ = the minimum cost from period t until the horizon given that we are in state (i) at time t,
j = a decision made at time t,
C_{ij} = the cost of decision j given that we are in state i,
$P(k/i,j)$ = the probability of starting the subsequent period in state k, given that we started period t in state i and made decision j,
α = the appropriate discount factor.

If eq. (A.1) represents a problem with an infinite horizon, if $\alpha < 1$, and transition probabilities can be described by a Markov process then a stationary policy is optimal. That is the same decision j should be made any time we are in a particular state i.[29] Therefore the time subscript can be deleted and the optimal policy must satisfy the following extremal equation:

$$f(i) = \min_{j} \left[C_{ij} + \alpha \sum_k f(k) P(k|i,j) \right].$$

Let us now define r_k as the probability that the system is in state k at the beginning of the first time period. Let N designate the number of states the system can enter. Then

$$r_k \geqslant 0, \quad \text{for } k = 1, 2, \ldots, N,$$

$$\sum_{k=1}^{N} r_k = 1.$$

Let us further designate J_i as the set of all possible decisions (j) which we can make when in state i.

Then the dynamic programming problem presented in (A.1) has been shown to be identical to the following linear programming model.[30]

---

[29]For a proof of this statement, see Wagner (1969, pp. 747—748).
[30]See Wagner (1969) and Ghellinck and Eppen (1967).

Minimize

$$\sum_{i=1}^{N} \sum_{j \in J_i} C_{ij} X_{ij}$$

subject to

$$\sum_{j \in J_k} X_{kj} - \alpha \sum_{i=1}^{N} \sum_{j \in J_k} X_{ij} P(k|i,j) = r_k, \quad \text{for } k = 1, 2, \ldots, N$$

$$X_{ij} \geqslant 0, \quad \text{for } i = 1, 2, \ldots, N, \quad j \in J_i.$$

The optimal basic solution will contain one and only one X_{ij} greater than zero for each i. The optimal policy is to make a particular decision j whenever the system is in state i. The expected present cost of following this policy is given by the value of the objective function.

By defining k as equal to $j - e$ and recognizing that there are finite limits on the level of the cash balance and that the cash level changes by discrete amounts, we can rewrite eq. (4) in the body of this paper as

$$f_t(i) = \min_j \left[T(i,j) + L(j) + \alpha \sum_{k=1}^{N} f_{t+1}(k) P(k|j) \right]. \tag{A.2}$$

Let

$$C_{ij} = T(i,j) + L(j),$$

and j represents one of the N states defined as possible for the system. Then (4) has the same form as eq. (A.1). Utilizing the previous analysis, we can write the linear programming model of the cash management problem as:[31]

Minimize

$$\sum_{i=1}^{N} \sum_{j=1}^{N} [T(i,j) + L(j)] X_{ij}$$

subject to

$$\sum_{j=1}^{N} X_{kj} - \alpha \sum_{i=1}^{N} \sum_{j=1}^{N} X_{ij} P(k|j) = r_k, \quad \text{for } k = 1, 2, \ldots, N,$$

$$X_{ij} \geqslant 0, \text{ for } i = 1, 2, \ldots, N \text{ and } j = 1, 2, \ldots, N.$$

---

[31] Alternative forms of this problem which allow some savings in computation time can be found in Ghellinck and Eppen (1967) and Eppen and Fama (1969a).

This can easily be demonstrated. Since $U_{T-1} > i$ write U_{T-1} as $i + c$. Because $L(\cdot)$ is a convex function $L(i + c) > L(i) + cL'(i)$. Substituting U_{T-1} for $i + c$ and $U_{T-1} - i$ for c we have $L(U_{T-1}) - L(i) > L'(i)(U_{T-1} - i)$.

Appendix B: Proof of the convexity of $f_{T-1}(i)$ for the case of no fixed transaction costs

A function $f(i)$ is convex if

$$f^*(i) = f(i+1) + f(i-1) - 2f(i) \geqslant 0, \tag{9}$$

for all values of i. Below, we show that $f_{T-1}(i)$ is convex for all values of i by employing eqs. (7), (8) and (9).

Eq. (8) consists of three separate functional forms. In order to show convexity, it is necessary to show that each functional form is convex and that convexity is maintained across each intersection of the functions. We will examine five sections of the function $f_{T-1}(i)$; the region below D_{T-1}, the region between D_{T-1} and U_{T-1}, the region above U_{T-1}, and the region in the neighborhood of U_{T-1} and D_{T-1}.

(i) $i+1 < D_{T-1}$:

$$f^*_{T-1}(i) = t_u[D_{T-1} - (i+1)] + L(D_{T-1}) + t_u[D_{t-1} - (i-1)]$$
$$+ L(D_{T-1}) - 2[t_u(D_{t-1} - i) + L(D_{T-1})] = 0.$$

(ii) $U_{T-1} \geqslant i-1$ and $i+1 \geqslant D_{T-1}$:

$$f^*_{T-1}(i) = L(i+1) + L(i-1) - 2L(i) \geqslant 0.$$

This holds since $L(\cdot)$ is a convex function.

(iii) $i-1 > U_{T-1}$:

$$f^*_{T-1}(i) = t_d[(i+1) - U_{T-1}] + L(U_{T-1}) + t_d[(i-1) - U_{T-1}]$$
$$+ L(U_{T-1}) - 2[t_u(i - U_{T-1}) + L(U_{T-1})] = 0.$$

(iv) $i = D_{T-1}$:

$$f^*_{T-1}(i) = L(i+1) + t_u[D_{t-1} - (i-1)] + L(D_{T-1}) - 2L(D_{T-1}).$$

Since $i = D_{T-1}$ we have

$$f^*_{T-1}(i) = L(i+1) + t_u - L(i).$$

Adding and subtracting $t_u i$ we have

$$f^*_{T-1}(i) = L(i+1) + t_u(i+1) - L(i) - t_u(i).$$

This is greater than zero since $D_{T-1} = i$ and since by the definition of D_{T-1} in eq. (7)

$$L(j) + t_u(j) \geqslant L(D_{T-1}) + t_u(D_{T-1}), \qquad j \neq D_{T-1}$$

and one possible value for j is $i+1$.

(v) $i = U_{T-1}$:

$$f^*_{T-1}(i) = t_d[(i+1) - U_{T-1}] + L(U_{T-1}) + L(i-1) + 2L(U_{T-1})$$

Since $i = U_{T-1}$

$$f^*_{T-1}(i) = t_d + L(i-1) - L(i).$$

Subtracting and adding $t_d i$, we have

$$f^*_{T-1}(i) = -t_d(i-1) + L(i-1) - [-t_d(i) + L(i)].$$

This is greater than zero, since $D_{T-1} = i$ and since by definition of U_{T-1}

$$-t_d(j) + L(j) \geqslant -t_d U_{T-1} + L(U_{T-1}), \qquad j \neq U_{T-1}.$$

and one possible value for j is $i-1$.

References

Baumol, W. (1952) "The Transaction's Demand for Cash: An Inventory Theoretic Approach", *Quarterly Journal of Economics* 56, November, 545–556.

Beranek, W. (1968) *Working Capital Management* (Wadsworth Publishing Co., Belmont, California).

Daellenbach, H. and S. Archer (1969) "The Optimal Bank Liquidity: A Multi-Period Stochastic Model", *Journal of Financial and Quantitative Analysis* 4, September, 329–343.

Elton, E. J. and M. J. Gruber (1971) "Dynamic Programming Applications in Finance", *Journal of Finance* 26, May, 473–505.

Elton, E. J. and M. J. Gruber (1974a) "On the Cash Balance Problem", *Operations Research Quarterly* 25, 553–572.

Elton, E. J. and M. J. Gruber (1974b) *Finance as a Dynamic Process*, (Prentice-Hall, Englewood Cliffs, New Jersey).

Eppen, G. and E. Fama (1969a) "Solutions for Cash Balance and Simple Dynamic Portfolio Problems", *Journal of Business* 61, January, 94–112.

Eppen, G. and E. Fama (1969b) "Cash Balance and Simple Dynamic Portfolio Problems with Proportional Costs", *International Economic Review* 10, June, 119–133.

Ghellinck, G. and G. Eppen (1967) "Linear Programming Solutions for Separable Markovian Decision Problems", *Management Science* 13, January, 371–394.

Girges, N. (1968) "Optimal Cash Balance Levels", *Management Science* 15, November, 130–140.

Miller, M. and D. Orr (1966) "A Model of the Demand for Money by Firms", *Quarterly Journal of Economics* 80, August, 413–435.

Miller, M. and D. Orr (1968) "The Demand for Money by Firms: Extensions and Analytical Results", *Journal of Finance* 23, December, 735–759.

Neave, E. (1970) "The Stochastic Cash Balance Problem with Fixed Costs for Increases and Decreases", *Management Science* 16, March, 472–490.

Orgler, Y. (1970) *Cash Management: Methods and Models* (Wadsworth Publishing Co., Belmont, California).

Robichek, Teichroew and Jones (1965) "Optimal Short Term Financing Decision", *Management Science* 12, September, 1–36.

Sastry, A. S. R. (1970) "The Effect of Credit on Transaction Demand for Cash", *Journal of Finance* 25, September, 743–760.

Sethi, S. and G. Thompson (1970) "Applications of Mathematical Control Theory to Finance: Modeling Simple Dynamic Cash Balance Problems", *Journal of Financial and Quantitative Analysis* 5, 381–394.

Tobin, J. (1956) "The Interest-Elasticity of Transaction Demand for Cash", *Review of Economics and Statistics* 38, August, 241–247.

Wagner, H. (1969) *Principle of Operations Research* (Prentice-Hall, Englewood Cliffs, New Jersey).

Chapter 10

FINANCIAL DECISION-MAKING FOR THE FIRM IN AN OPEN ECONOMY*

MICHAEL ADLER
Columbia University

and

BERNARD DUMAS
E.S.S.E.C., France

1. Introduction

This paper undertakes to survey a largely nonexistent literature. The extension of the theory of the firm to the open economy is still in its nascence. Consequently, this paper makes an attempt to fill in gaps by defining and discussing issues which have not yet received systematic treatment elsewhere.

The traditional theory of the firm assumed profit maximization which is Pareto-optimal under certainty. Early attempts to model the international firm (e.g. Stevens (1969), Horst (1971) and Adler and Stevens (1974)) all employed this paradigm. The neoclassical approach, however, breaks down under uncertainty. Profit maximization no longer ranks alternative decisions since profits are no longer under the firm's complete control. Value maximization is then the most practicable option, despite the likelihood that it will not be unanimously preferred. The paper therefore examines the possibility for and nature of value maximizing decisions for open-economy firms.

The paper stops short of addressing empirical questions such as, say, the impact of a change in exchange risk on international corporate financial behavior and the implications for capital flows. Such issues are a matter of the comparative statics (or dynamics) of optimal decisions. Our concern is with the logically-prior question of whether such decision rules exist and can be characterized.

Section 2 examines the validity of value maximization and the assumptions under which it is Pareto-optimal. Section 3 reviews the two competing models of

*Financial support from the Rockefeller Foundation is gratefully acknowledged. This article is adapted from the *American Economic Review* 67, February 1977, 180–189.

James L. Bicksler, Editor, Handbook of Financial Economics

the international structure of risky financial asset-prices and indicates desirable characteristics for a synthetic model not yet built. Section 4 links real decisions to financial market decisions via the financing and capital budgeting decision rules which can prospectively be derived. Section 5 examines the interface of the theory of the firm with monetary theory, i.e. the firms short-term decisions as to its liquid assets and liabilities.

2. The objective of the firm: general considerations

A logical prerequisite to the computation of firms' decisions is the specification of an objective function which the firm can reasonably be postulated to maximize. It was long taken for granted that the corporate firm ought to maximize the sum of the market values of the securities it has issued and issues currently, and of the current cash flow distribution to its capital suppliers; an objective which we shall henceforth refer to as "value maximization". But since the firm is owned by stockholders, we must ask whether this objective is to their satisfaction. More precisely, since it is preferable not to have to resolve possible conflicts between stockholders, one might simply ask: when will the firms' decisions be Pareto-optimal from the standpoint of stockholders? Assuming that the welfare of nonstock securities holders is protected by covenants and the law,[1] we can rephrase the question one more time: when will firms' decisions be Pareto-optimal from the standpoint of all investors?

After a long debate, the definitive answer to this question was provided by Nielsen's dissertation (1974).[2] According to this rendering, the main distinction to be introduced is whether or not the set of securities available in the capital market (for a given production decision of firms) affords an unconstrained Pareto-optimal (UPO) allocation of consumption among households.

If the market is UPO, Nielsen proves two important theorems. First, the principle of conservation of investment value (CIV) obtains; that is to say, if one transforms linearly the cash flows of securities without affecting the total cash flows, the market value of the new securities is equal to the same linear transformation of the old securities' market values. Secondly, value maximizing firms make Pareto-optimal production decisions provided only that they behave as price takers with respect to the prices of existing securities. The CIV result provides us with sufficient conditions for cash flow preserving decisions to be irrelevant; among these are the merger, debt–equity-mix and forward-contracting decisions as well as the currency-denomination (c-d) decision for the debt in the absence of taxes and bankruptcy costs. The second result provides us with a convenient maximand to reach the optimal level of these decisions which

---

[1] See Fama–Miller (1972, p. 151), and Scott (1976).
[2] The interpretation of Nielsen's results provided here is solely our responsibility.

do modify total cash flows such as the production and investment decisions as well as the merger, debt–equity-mix, debt-denomination and forward-contracting decisions in the presence of taxes and bankruptcy costs.[3]

Unfortunately, the market is UPO under circumstances which cannot reasonably be expected to obtain. One sufficient condition for UPO is completeness in the Arrow–Debreu sense but it would require a prohibitively large number of securities and would imply astronomical market-making costs. Other sufficient conditions under which the market is UPO without being complete are spelled out in various so-called portfolio separation theorems.[4] They usually assume that all investors share homogeneous probability beliefs regarding the purchasing power of the future returns from securities. If investor-consumers have diverse consumption tastes or face different commodities prices, homogeneity cannot obtain; for, even if they held identical expectations regarding returns, the corresponding purchasing powers of returns would nevertheless differ for various investors. This difficulty may be more acute internationally if tastes differ between nations more than they differ within nations. The only separation theorem so far which handles diversity of tastes is that of Solnik (1974); but one of his assumptions (see section 3) is particularly difficult to accept.

When, on the other hand, the market is constrained Pareto-optimal (CPO), Nielsen had to introduce additional restrictions in order to preserve CIV and to prove that value maximizing firms make *constrained* Pareto-optimal production decisions. He assumed essentially that the basis of the linear state-of-nature subspace spanned by existing securities was not modified by the linear transformation (in the case of the CIV theorem) or by the firm's decision (in the case of the value-maximization theorem). This means that the cash flows of all pretransformation (resp. predecision) securities must be perfectly correlated with a linear combination of post-transformation (resp. post-decision) securities' cash flows and vice-versa. But, just to take an example, this condition is violated as a firm changes its debt–equity ratio even if there are no bankruptcy costs; indeed, since the probability of bankruptcy is usually affected, the state-dependent cash flow pattern of the debt and the equity is modified in a manner which will usually prevent replication of the old pattern by means of linear combinations. That is to say, securities have been created or eliminated which are not substitutable with others; this modification of the security–space dimensions implies *discrete changes* in securities values; under such circumstances CIV is violated and we do not know what the correspondence is between value maximization and Pareto-optimality.

---

[3]The value-maximization theorem was established in the absence of taxes and bankruptcy costs. Because the latter involve complex problems of uncompensated social redistribution, it is not at all clear that the theorem is applicable in their presence. This remark casts a shadow over the discussion of the financing decision in section 4.

[4]See Cass–Stiglitz (1970), Ross (1976), and Black (1973).

The theory of the firm in the open economy which we shall now review postulates value maximization as the only practicable objective. At the present state of our knowledge, it must therefore rest on an assumption of UPO of the capital market or on the assumption that whatever is done to securities' cash flows preserves the basis of the linear state–space.

3. The objective of the firm in the open economy

Maximization of the value of the firm's securities frequently calls for the use of a model which gives securities' market values as a function of the probability distribution of their cash flows. In the international (i.e. multicurrency) sphere,[5] two such international asset pricing models (IAPMs) are currently in existence: that of Solnik (1974) and that of Grauer, Litzenberger and Stehle (1976) (GLS).

The GLS model depends on the assumptions that all goods are traded (so that they are priced at parity everywhere) and that all investors have the same consumption preferences. These assumptions permit a straightforward extension of the closed-economy capital asset pricing model to the world as a whole. Exchange rates in this model can fluctuate only as a result of pure monetary factors and not as a result of relative price fluctuations. The model conveys therefore solely the impact of what can be called "monetary exchange risk".

Solnik, by contrast, assumes that in each country the rate of inflation is zero (or nonrandom). Contrary to GLS's allegations, Solnik's assumption does not imply any money illusion or any inconsistency with the assumed randomness of exchange rates. So long as consumption preferences differ from country to country, exchange rates can fluctuate if the relative prices of national consumption baskets fluctuate. Furthermore, some goods may not be traded internationally and may therefore not be priced at parity everywhere. Solnik's model conveys therefore the impact of that component of exchange risk which results from relative-price uncertainty – a component which could perhaps be called "real exchange risk". Unfortunately, Solnik's mathematical derivations rely on the asssumption that nominal securities' returns are stochastically independent of exchange rates. While this assumption is introduced only for technical reasons, it is nonetheless disturbing economically: since exchange rates in this model represent relative prices it is unreasonable to assume that they will not

[5]The multiplicity of currencies is not the only additional problem to be tackled by international financial theory. Partial segmentation of capital markets is another, see Banz (1976). The presence of large oligopolistic firms such as multinational corporations is yet another; see the literature on direct investment which unfortunately draws very little on financial theory (see Hufbauer (1975) and the references therein).

affect the value of firms' outputs and therefore the nominal returns.

To date no IAPM exists which incorporates both monetary and real exchange risks, and yet remains usable. Indeed, the most general model with heterogeneous consumption tastes would necessarily involve the investors' risk aversions individually[6] and, since the latter are almost impossible to measure, would be virtually useless. The quest today is for a special case which allows treatment of both types of exchange risk, which yields a usable model and which nonetheless remains relevant.

The impact of exchange risk on the firm's valuation maximand and on its decisions is a question which remains to be worked out precisely and which has a meaning within a partial-equilibrium framework only. Indeed, in general equilibrium, future exchange rates are endogenous and it is meaningless to discuss their impact. The framework must keep the variability of exchange rates exogenous, which implies either that expectations are not at all constrained to be rational or that they are rational in the first-moment sense only (Muth's sense); in either case there must also not exist a sufficient number of commodities and currencies futures markets to iron out the irrationality in advance. Finally, the Pareto-optimality of capital markets would have to be defined with reference to the expected utilities of economic agents, *and relative to the given set of expectations*.

Within this cramped paradigm, one may be tempted to make two tentative statements and one definitive but trivial statement. Real exchange risk presumably has an impact on first-period equilibrium: an increase in real exchange risk should cause a fall in welfare, a rise in current consumption, a decrease in inputs and, therefore, a fall in firms' values. Monetary exchange risk will also have an impact because of the existence of nominally defined financial claims: money, debt, etc.; an increase in nominal exchange risk amounts to a redefinition of these securities much as would a change in their denomination. But a redefinition of securities, although it always leads to a rebalancing of investors' portfolios, may or may not affect first-period consumption and production decisions; if there is no money, if the capital market is and remains UPO in the above sense, if there are no taxes and bankruptcy costs or other imperfections, and if expectations, although irrational, do take account of future-spot-market arbitrage relations, then an increase in pure monetary risk amounts only to a redefinition of the numeraire which will have no effect. If the market is or becomes CPO, the redefinition will have unpredictable effects. If there are taxes or bankruptcy costs, the firm will change its financing decision and perhaps consequently also its production decision, as a result of the change in bankruptcy risk.

[6]See Rubinstein (1974).

4. Long-term decisions: financing and capital budgeting

We proceed to examine the financing, capital-budgeting and foreign-acquisition decisions of the international firm.[7] In a unified and perfect world capital market where CIV can be assumed to hold, the financing, the currency denomination of debt and foreign acquisition decisions, as we saw, are irrelevant. In the absence of currency-transaction costs, there will also be no optimal choice of currencies in the liquid asset portfolio. The firm need not do what investors can do for themselves. However, when these decisions may change cash flows, as they will in the presence of bankruptcy costs or taxes, optimal decision rules can be derived. To illustrate this let us discuss the financing decision: other decisions follow identical principles. The total value of the firm is decomposed into three terms:

$$V = \sum_i V_i = V_0 + \sum_i t_i D_i - BC\left(\ldots \sum D_i, \sum V_i \ldots\right), \tag{1}$$

where

V_i = the total market value of the ith, fully owned corporate subentity (subsidiary or parent) *including* current cash flow.

D_i = face value of the debt issued by the ith subunit.

t_i = effective tax-rate applicable to the debt of the ith subentity.

BC = the present market value of the anticipated bankruptcy costs.

In eq. (1) V_0 is the market value of the whole firm when no debt is issued. The second term represents the value of the tax savings owing to the deductibility of interest payments everywhere. The third term, the market value of the many kinds of costs accruing in the event of bankruptcy, is therefore a function of many variables of which two are especially important: $\sum D_i$ and $\sum V_i$.[8] $\sum D_i$ determines the promised interest and sinking fund payments which constitute a cash drain, while $\sum V_i$ is a proxy for the ability to meet fixed financial changes. If subsidiaries are not allowed to go bankrupt independently, bankruptcy will occur when the market value of the whole corporate entity's stock reaches zero.[9]

---

[7]With an IAPM in hand, it will no longer be necessary to assert a utility function for the firm as Sandmo (1971) did for the closed economy, Kenen (1966) and Ethier (1973) for the trading firm, and Prachowny (1972) for the MNC. In a recent paper Baron (1976) derived unanimously preferred decision rules for an international firm. The adoption of this more general objective was costly analytically. Had he assumed price-taking behavior, value maximization would have yielded identical decisions while being simpler to use. Moreover, in his model the only source of uncertainty was the exchange rate and there were no taxes or bankruptcy costs.

[8]These costs include lawyers fees, reorganization costs, lost production and/or market position and capital losses if illiquid assets must be sold at a discount. Expropriate costs could also be added to this term.

[9]Bankruptcy will occur at the end of a period if that period's cash throw-offs plus liquid assets on hand are so adverse as to make it unprofitable for the stockholders to prevent bankruptcy by investing further to secure the future cash flow stream. We assume for the multiunit corporation that bankruptcy involves the whole. Bankruptcy of parts involve contractual nuances which we cannot discuss here.

Once the problem is thus formulated, the optimal financing decision can be found. As borrowing increases, the value of bankruptcy costs increases slowly at first and then rapidly as the probability of bankruptcy increases. Their difference should reach an optimum. The optimum will be reached at some optimal debt/value ratio, $(\Sigma D_i / V)^*$. Individually $(D_i / V_i)^*$ should be greater the higher the subsidiary's effective tax rate. An open question is the effect of constraints which prevent $(D_i / V_i) > 1$ if this were otherwise optimal.

Subsidiaries need not borrow in their own local currencies. The borrowing decision therefore possesses one additional dimension which becomes relevant in the presence of possibly costly bankruptcy, namely, its currency denomination. However, no models exist that determine the c–d mix for long-term debt which would (partially) minimize the present value of bankruptcy costs. As in the choice of the optimal c–d mix of short-term instruments, discussed below, it is a portfolio problem the solution to which is probably *not* the mix that best matches the c–d mix of assets.

We now turn to the capital budgeting decision and leave the financial decision, having determined an optimal debt ratio. To avoid the problem of simultaneity between the financing and investment decision which is not resolved even in the one-country setting, we assume without justification that firms invest in projects which do not affect firms' costs or risks of bankruptcy.[10] In that case, the preinvestment optimal debt ratio is not changed and can be used as a target for the financing mix of the project. Investment decision rules can be contrived in two cases. In the first, which requires no knowledge of an IAPM, the random, after-tax cash flows from the marginal project, $d\tilde{X}$, are perfectly correlated with a linear combination of cash flows yielded by existing securities, $\tilde{X}_j, j = 1, \ldots, n$:

$$d\tilde{X} = \sum_j d\delta_j \tilde{X}_j,$$

where $d\delta_j =$ an infinitely small weight.

By CIV, the marginal contribution of the project to the value of the firm is equal to the *same* linear combination of the *prices* of existing securities *plus* the value of the tax saving due to the project's debt:

$$dV = \sum_j d\delta_j V_j + \sum_i t_i dV (D_i / V)^*.$$

Accept the project if $dV \geqslant dI =$ the present cost of the project, i.e. if

$$\sum_j V_j \frac{d\delta_j}{dI} \geqslant 1 - \sum_i t_i \left(\frac{D_i}{V}\right)^*.$$

[10]See Weiss (1976) and the references therein.

This decision rule can be recast in cost-of-capital terms. Compute the weighted average, ρ, of the yields, ρ_j, on existing securities:

$$\rho = \frac{\sum_j \mathrm{d}\delta_j \rho_j V_j}{\sum_j \mathrm{d}\delta_j V_j},$$

where $\rho_j = E(X_j)/V_j - 1$. Then, accept if

$$\frac{E(\mathrm{d}\tilde{X})}{\mathrm{d}I} \geqslant (1+\rho)\left[1 - \sum_i t_i \left(\frac{D_i}{V}\right)*\right]$$

The after-tax, zero-debt, rate of return on the project must be larger than its cost of capital adjusted for taxes. These criteria, which generalize Modigliani–Miller, are not essentially different from what they would be in the closed economy.[11] Only the target debt ratios have an international dimension. For a given pattern of bankruptcy risks and costs and, therefore, a preset c-d decision, these decision criteria will be independent of exchange risk.[12] Clearly, also, firms which have different bankruptcy costs and risks will generally evaluate a given project differently. But it is unlikely, pending further research, that decision criteria will vary systematically across countries. We do not mean to imply, however, that project decisions themselves will be independent of locational factors, for project cash flows, $\mathrm{d}\tilde{X}$, will generally vary by location. Equally, these cash flows will be affected by exchange risk to the extent that projects employ cash balances.

In the second case, the project is not perfectly correlated with a linear combination of existing securities. Assuming that sufficient conditions for UPO are met, investment decision criteria like those above can be derived from a relevant IAPM, of the type discussed in section 3, following well known procedures, initiated by Hamada (1969). The additional problems with this approach are familiar: the market adjustment for risk varies with the assumed characteristics of investors' utility functions; and the projects' risk characteristics must be measured prospectively – in practice a difficult task.

To complete the discussion of long-term decisions let us move briefly to a world of completely segmented capital markets: investors do not invest abroad at all. If firms can bridge the gulf between national segments, CIV no longer obtains, and there appears a one-to-one correspondence between the market which is segmented and the decision which becomes relevant: if the bond

---

[11]Modigliani and Miller (1958) restricted their criteria to projects in the firm's risk class: their weighted average cost of capital consequently included only the firm's own debt and equity. Our criteria are not so restricted.

[12]To be sure, changes in exchange rate variances would change the values of all securities and of the market's risk adjustment (the market price of risk). But price-taking firms would take these as given.

market is segmented, the choice of the locus of borrowing is relevant; if the stock market is, the foreign acquisition decision becomes relevant. Let us review the latter.

Assume that each national market, separately, is UPO and that within each segment exchange and inflation risks are perceived similarly by all. Assume further, following Adler–Dumas (1975) and Lee–Sachdeva (1976) that the firms of only one country are permitted to invest abroad, but behave as price takers in both markets. Value maximization will be Pareto-optimal from the point of view of home market investors who take the prices of foreign securities as given, but not from that of foreigners. The optimal aggregate acquisition decision can then be derived from a capital asset pricing model (CAPM) into which the post-acquisition cash flows of home firms are substituted. It satisfies three conditions: (a) foreign securities are priced as if they were valued by the home CAPM; (b) foreigners' excess demand at those prices is filled by the aggregate acquisition decision; and (c) the allocation of the aggregate among individual firms is indeterminate. Because the home market is already capable of an optimal allocation of risk bearing, foreign securities provide no diversification advantage.[13] No results are presently available for the more general case which would permit foreign acquisitions by firms everywhere.

5. The short-term decisions

The short-term decisions of the firm are the area of overlap between the theory of the firm and monetary theory, since they involve, among other things, the firm's demand for cash and other liquid assets and liabilities. But the relationship of these decisions to value maximization is not yet clear in the closed economy, much less the open economy. When attempting to maximize the market value of its securities with respect to short-term decisions, the firm should presumably take three categories of costs into consideration: opportunity costs, transaction costs and bankruptcy costs. The opportunity costs arise out of the fact that short-term assets such as cash have a rate of return lower than fixed assets; keeping a larger proportion of short-term assets therefore reduces the long-term profitability of the firm and thereby also, paradoxically, increases the probability of future bankruptcy.[14] Transaction costs have been neglected in the context of long-term decisions; to the extent that short-term decisions involve

---

[13]In this case value-maximizing investment decisions by both the parent and the acquired subsidiary will be Pareto-optimal for home-country investors (though not for foreigners). Adler (1974) examined the case where the home market is UPO but, conversely, the home firm does not act as a price taker in the foreign market. The home firm has an optimal acquisition to make for home-country investors. However, value maximization by the foreign subsidiary with respect to its own decisions ceases to be Pareto-optimal for investors in either capital market.

[14]This point is made by Weiss (1976) in his Columbia University, Ph.D., dissertation.

more frequent transactions, however, it is possible that these costs will no longer be negligible. Finally, bankruptcy costs have already been described; one of these is the loss if assets must be liquidated at a discount: short-term assets usually carry a smaller liquidation discount (they are more "liquid") than do long-term assets. Hence, increasing the proportion of short-term assets reduces bankruptcy costs. Following from these considerations, an optimal short-term decision generally exists.

Unfortunately no model has yet been built which maximizes a firm's value taking all three categories of costs into account. To date there are two strands of models each of which accommodates, wholly or in part, pairs of cost items. In the first strand, opportunity costs (not, however, explicitly linked to firms' costs of capital as defined above) plus transactions costs are minimized. These are usually inventory theoretic models, related to monetary theory in the spirit of the pioneering work of Baumol (1952) and Tobin (1956). The approach has been extended by Tsiang (1969) to incorporate uncertainty but has not been applied internationally although it could fruitfully be used to derive propositions regarding the degree of substitutability of currencies' balances with each other and with short-term instruments of various denominations, depending on the level of transactions costs and the degree of fluctuation of exchange rates. A model which seeks to minimize the proportional transactions costs of maneuvering liquid assets internationally is that of Rutenberg (1970); it is designed to optimize not the level of liquid assets in each location, but rather their flows among corporate subunits. The transportation algorithm is used and uncertainty is not taken into acoount.

The second strand of models minimize bankruptcy costs and opportunity costs, in a portfolio choice approach. Since this approach is characteristic of financial theory and has already found tentative international application, we pursue it below.

Consider first the short-term decision problem in the closed economy. Assuming for simplicity that investors are risk-neutral, the impact of bankruptcy costs on the value of the firm is simply equal to the probability of bankruptcy multiplied by the expected costs conditional on the event of bankruptcy. Suppose that the dominant component of bankruptcy cost is the discount contingent upon the liquidation of assets; each asset is then characterized by its rate of discount and the total rate on the whole portfolio of the firm's assets and liabilities is equal to a weighted average of the individual discount rates.

Following the definition of bankruptcy in footnote 9, there exists in each period a required minimum rate of return $\tilde{R}^*$ on the firm's total portfolio of assets and liabilities, below which the firm is bankrupt. If rates of return are all normally distributed, the probability of bankruptcy is a function only of the coefficient of variation (expected value over standard deviation) of the firm portfolio's excess rate of return over the required rate. In that case we can write the firm's portfolio choice in the following way:[15]

$$\text{maximize } E(R_p) - \phi \left[\frac{-E(\tilde{R}_p) + E(\tilde{R}^*)}{\sqrt{\{\sigma^2(\tilde{R}_p) + \sigma^2(\tilde{R}^*) - 2\operatorname{cov}(\tilde{R}_p, \tilde{R}^*)\}}} \right] C,$$

where:

$\tilde{R}_p = \Sigma_j x_j \tilde{R}_j$,
$C = \Sigma_i x_i b_i = $ bankruptcy cost,
$b_i = $ liquidation discount on asset or liability i,
$x_i = $ relative weight of the asset or liability in the portfolio;
$\quad x_i > 0$ for an asset, and
$\quad x_i < 0$ for a liability,
$\phi = $ area under the normal curve.

Besides the obvious constraint $\Sigma_i x_i = 1$, there may be others. For instance, there is a minimum required amount of cash to be kept for transactions purposes. Accounts receivable and accounts payable may be related rigidly to sales if the firm is forced by its competitors to adopt a specific credit or payment period. Finally, the x_i values corresponding to long-term assets and long-term debt are not objects of choice since they have been determined previously on other grounds;[16] their presence nevertheless would influence the short-term portfolio choice.[17] The above problem can be solved by sequential quadratic programming in the manner of Markowitz (1959) and by varying the value of C whose definition would serve as a constraint at each step. The value of C and of the corresponding portfolio which maximizes the objective is easily selected.[18]

Extension of this framework to the multicurrency world is promising. Section 3 indicated that exchange risk would affect the probability of bankruptcy and therefore in the presence of bankruptcy costs the value of a firm which holds nominal financial claims: there will be an optimal c-d mix in this situation for short-term as well as long-term financial decisions. One can therefore hope in the future to link studies such as Lietaer's (1971), which arbitrarily seeks to

---

[15]This objective is applicable only when investors are risk-neutral. In the case of risk aversion, one should subtract a risk penalty on the portfolio return R_p and add back a risk premium on the costs of bankruptcy in order to reconstitute the value-maximization objective.

[16]The level of long-term debt presumably cannot be altered as frequently as the portfolio of short-term assets and short-term liabilities. This, as well as the tax advantage of the debt, would be the chief differences between the above program and that which determined the long-term debt; but ideally the two should be solved simultaneously: cf. Weiss (1976).

[17]See Mayers' (1971) treatment of the "nontraded-asset" problem. The long-term assets and long-term debt would act as a nontraded asset with respect to the choice of the short-term portfolio.

[18]All the short-term decisions would fall out of this program. In particular the decision to enter forward contracts, and the choice of denomination of all short-term assets and liabilities to the extent that they can be chosen, would thus be determined. The optimal denomination of accounts receivable leads to the choice of a currency for invoicing.

minimize losses due to exchange risk subject to rate of return constraints, via the bankruptcy cost nexus to the valuation objective.[19] In applying the quadratic programming approach to the multicurrency case, however, one must beware of the assumption of universal normality of returns. If the returns are normal in one currency, they are not in another because of multiplication by the random exchange rate. Since the distribution assumption should preferably not favor one particular currency, it is necessary, whenever possible, to formulate the program on the basis of "real" returns (i.e. returns expressed in units of a consumption basket) and to assume that these are normally distributed.

Any prospective solution to the above portfolio choice problem, whether exactly or approximately specified, will undoubtedly call for diversification of the currency portfolio. This conclusion runs counter to the practice of some corporate treasurers who hedge returns denominated in currencies other than the parent's in an attempt to reduce their "exchange-risk exposure" (cf. Kenen (1966)). In fact, when structuring such portfolio-choice models, a change of variable is sometimes convenient. This amounts to defining a variable which is the sum of the firms balance-sheet weights corresponding to assets and liabilities denominated in the same currency. This is exactly what accountants refer to as "exposure". There is no reason, however, to institute the changed variable as a target to be minimized for some currencies.

This argument extends further. Lietaer (1971) introduces a totally different definition of exposure which seems more useful than the accountants' in the case where $\tilde{R}$ is not independent of $\tilde{S}$. Exposure may intuitively be identified with the partial regression coefficient, b_{ij}, of $\tilde{S}_i(1 + \tilde{R}_{ij})$ with respect to $\tilde{S}_i$, where $\tilde{S}_i$ is the exchange rate (units of reference currency/unit of currency i) and $\tilde{R}_{ij}$ is the return on asset j expressed in terms of currency i. If $b_{ij} = 0$, the returns are not exposed; if $b_{ij} = 1$, they are totally exposed.[20] The firm's total exposure is a weighted average of the individual exposures. While this notion can serve as a fine descriptive tool, it is in no way implied that it represents a quantity to be reduced. Furthermore, in multiperiod models exposure will remain a concept describing cash returns of each period separately. It is usually impossible to define an aggregate over several periods which could be called the exposure of an asset or liability taken as a whole.

---

[19]Dumas (1978) has so formulated the optimal forward contracting decision of the firm.

[20]This definition is unfortunately not invariant to the choice of the reference currency. It would have been preferable to use real returns, all expressed in terms of a unique consumption basket.

References

Adler, M. (1974) "The Cost of Capital and Valuation of a Two Country Firm", *Journal of Finance*, March.

Adler, M. and B. Dumas (1975) "Optimal Internal Acquisitions", *Journal of Finance*, March.

Adler, M. and G. V. G. Stevens (1974) "The Trade Effect of Direct Investment", *Journal of Finance* 29, May, 655–676.

Banz, R. (1976) "Capital Asset Pricing in Partially Segmented Markets", University of Chicago, Graduate School of Business.

Baron, D. P. (1976) "Flexible Exchange Rates, Forward Markets, and the Level of Trade", *American Economic Review* 66, June, 253–267.

Baumol, W. J. (1952) "The Transactions Demand for Cash: An Inventory Theoretical Approach", *Quarterly Journal of Economics* 26, November, 545–556.

Black, F. (1973) "Capital Market Equilibrium with Restricted Borrowing", *Journal of Business*, March.

Cass, D. and J. Stiglitz (1970) "The Structure of Investor Preferences and Assets Returns, and Separability in Portfolio Selection: A Contribution to the Pure Theory of Mutual Funds", *Journal of Economic Theory* 2, 122–160.

Dumas, B. (1978) "The Theory of the Trading Firm Revisited", *Journal of Finance*, May.

Ethier, W. (1973) "International Trade and the Forward Exchange Market", *American Economic Review* 63, June, 494–503.

Fama, E. F. and M. H. Miller (1972) *The Theory of Finance* (Holt, Rinehart and Winston, New York).

Grauer, F., R. H. Litzenberger and R. Stehle (1976) "Sharing Rules and Equilibrium in an International Capital Market Under Uncertainty", *Journal of Financial Economics* 3, June, 233–256.

Hamada, R. S. (1969) "Portfolio Analysis, Market Equilibrium and Corporation Finance", *Journal of Finance* 24, March, 13–32.

Horst, T. (1971) "The Theory of the Multinational Firm: Optimal Behavior Under Different Tariff and Tax Rates", *Journal of Political Economy*, September/October, 1059–1072.

Hufbauer, G. C. (1975) "The Multinational Corporation and Direct Investment", in: P. B. Kenen, ed., *International Trade and Finance*, (Cambridge University Press) pp. 253–320.

Kenen, P. B. (1966) "Trade, Speculation and the Forward Exchange Rate", in: Baldwin et al., *Trade Growth and the Balance of Payments* (Rand McNally, Chicago).

Lee, W. Y. and K. S. Sachdeva (1976) "The Role of the Multinational Firm in the Integration of Segmented Capital Markets", Indiana University, School of Business.

Lietaer, B. A. (1971) *Financial Management of Foreign Exchange* (MIT Press, Cambridge, Mass.).

Markowitz (1959) *Portfolio Analysis* (Wiley, New York).

Mayers, D. (1971) "Non Marketable Assets and Capital Market Equilibrium Under Uncertainty", in: M. C. Jensen, ed., *Studies in the Theory of Capital Markets* (Praeger, New York) pp 223–248.

Modigliani, F. and M. H. Miller (1958) "The Cost of Capital, Corporation Finance and the Theory of Investment", *American Economic Review* 48, June, 261–297.

Nielsen, N. C. (1974) "The Firm as an Intermediary Between Consumers and Production Functions Under Uncertainty", Ph.D. Dissertation, Stanford University.

Prachowny, M. F. J. (1972) "Direct Investment and the Balance of Payments of the United States: A Portfolio Approach", in: Machlup et al., *International Mobility and Movement of Capital* (Columbia University Press, New York).

Ross, S. A. (1976) "Mutual Fund Separation in Financial Theory — The Separation Distributions", University of Pennsylvania, R. White Center.

Rubinstein, M. (1974) "An Aggregation Theorem for Securities Market", *Journal of Financial Economies* 1, September, 225–244.

Rutenberg, D. P. (1970) "Maneuvering Liquid Assets in a Multi-National Company: Formulation and Deterministic Solution Procedures", *Management Science* 17, June.

Sandmo, A. (1971) "On the Theory of the Competitive Firm Under Price Uncertainty", *American Economic Review* 61, March, 65–73.

Scott, J. H. (1976) "On the Theory of Conglomerate Mergers", Columbia University, Graduate School of Business, Working Paper 135, June.

Solnik, B. H. (1974) "An Equilibrium Model of the International Capital Market", *Journal of Economic Theory* 8, August, 500–524.

Stevens, G. V. G. (1969) "Fixed Investment Expenditures of Foreign Manufacturing Affiliates of U.S. Firms: Theoretical Models and Empirical Evidence", *Yale Economic Essays*, Spring.

Tobin, J. (1956) "The Interest-Elasticity of Transactions Demand for Cash", *Review of Economics and Statistics* 38, August, 241–247.

Tsiang, S. C. (1969) "The Precautionary Demand for Money: An Inventory Theoretical Analysis", *Journal of Political Economics* 77, January/February, 99–117.

Weiss, N. (1976) "A Simultaneous Solution to the Real and Financial Decisions of the Firm Under Uncertainty: An Integration of the Neoclassical Theory of the Firm and Finance Theory", Columbia University, Graduate School of Business.

Chapter 11

UNCERTAIN INFLATION AND OPTIMAL CORPORATE INVESTMENT DECISIONS

ANDREW H. CHEN
Ohio State University

1. Introduction

Perhaps one of the most important and challenging tasks confronting the modern corporate managers is to derive the general criteria and rules for making capital investment decisions in the environment with uncertain inflation. With the exception of the recent work by Chen and Boness (1975), the literature on corporate investment has not provided rigorous analysis of the impact of uncertain inflation on a firm's capital investment decisions.[1] Within the framework of equilibrium capital asset pricing model under uncertain inflation, Chen and Boness have derived the risk-adjusted "hurdle rate" for project selection under uncertain inflation. However, the criterion is only applicable to the problem of selecting a single risky project with a fixed size of investment. It is not applicable to the problem of determining the optimal level of corporate investment, nor is it applicable to the problem of selecting among multiple interrelated risky projects.

The purpose of this paper is to derive the general criteria for determining the optimal level of corporate investment and for selecting the optimal set of interrelated risky projects under uncertain inflation. The joint effects of uncertain inflation and taxation on the corporate investment decisions will also be examined. It is assumed that value maximization is an appropriate criterion for financial decisions for a firm under uncertainty. Explicit recognition of the role of uncertain inflation in the equilibrium capital asset pricing model is provided.

The paper is organized as follows. Section 2 provides the capital asset pricing model under uncertain inflation. The model, which is an extended version of the Sharpe–Lintner–Mossin capital asset pricing model, explicitly takes into account uncertain inflation in the evaluation of capital assets. In section 3 we

---

[1] The effects of inflation on capital budgeting in the context of perfect certainty have recently been studied by Nelson (1976).

James L. Bicksler, Editor, Handbook of Financial Economics
© *North-Holland Publishing Company – 1979*

derive the optimal level of corporate investment under uncertain inflation and analyze some properties of inflation effects. In section 4 we derive the general criteria for selecting a group of interrelated risky projects, combining the capital asset pricing model and the mathematical programming technique. Section 5 examines the joint effects of corporate income taxes and uncertain inflation on a firm's investment decisions. Summaries and implications of our analysis are presented in the final section.

2. The capital asset pricing model under uncertain inflation

In this section we present a capital asset pricing model adjusted for uncertain inflation, which will be used to analyze the effects of inflation and corporate income taxes on a firm's optimal investment decisions. Under the assumptions that only a nominal risk-free rate of interest exists in a perfectly competitive capital market and that all investors are risk-averse and single-period expected utility of *real* terminal wealth maximizers, Chen and Boness (1975) have derived the following equilibrium risk–return relationship for an asset:[2]

$$E(\tilde{R}_j) = R_f + \lambda \left[\operatorname{cov}(\tilde{R}_j, \tilde{R}_m) - \operatorname{cov}(\tilde{R}_j, \tilde{R}_a) \right], \tag{1}$$

where

$E(\tilde{R}_j) =$ the expected value of $\tilde{R}_j$, the random *nominal* rate of return on the jth risky asset;

$R_f =$ the *nominal* risk-free rate of interest;

$\operatorname{cov}(\tilde{R}_j, \tilde{R}_m) =$ the covariance between the *nominal* rate of return on asset j and that of the market portfolio, $\tilde{R}_m$, which has expected value $E(\tilde{R}_m)$ and variance $\operatorname{var}(\tilde{R}_m)$;

$\operatorname{cov}(\tilde{R}_j, \tilde{R}_a) =$ the covariance between the *nominal* rate of return on asset j and the rate of inflation;

$\lambda = [E(\tilde{R}_m) - R_f]/[\operatorname{var}(\tilde{R}_m) - \operatorname{cov}(\tilde{R}_m, \tilde{R}_a)]$
$=$ the market price per unit of risk.

Eq. (1) shows that the structure of the equilibrium risk–return relationship for an asset under uncertain inflation is still linear, the same as that in the traditional capital asset pricing model developed by Sharpe (1964), Lintner (1965) and Mossin (1966). However, the relevant measure of an asset's riskiness (i.e. the systematic risk) in the modified model of capital asset prices consists of two elements: (1) the *volatility risk*, represented by the covariance between the nominal rate of return on the asset and that of the market portfolio; and (2) the

---

[2] In their recent paper, Friend and Landskroner (1975) have, using a continuous time model, derived the same result.

inflation risk, represented by the covariance between the nominal rate of return on the asset and the rate of inflation. Therefore, as pointed out by Chen and Boness (1975) the traditional capital asset pricing model *overstates* the asset's systematic risk if its return is positively correlated with the rate of inflation, and it *understates* the asset's systematic risk if its return is negatively correlated with the rate of inflation.

In order to analyze the corporate investment decisions under uncertain inflation, it is more convenient to express the valuation equation in terms of cash flows. From eq. (1) the equilibrium value of the jth firm under uncertain inflation is given by

$$V_j = \frac{1}{r}\left\{\overline{D}_j - \lambda^*\left[\mathrm{cov}\left(\tilde{D}_j, \tilde{D}_m\right) - \mathrm{cov}\left(\tilde{D}_j, \tilde{D}_a\right)\right]\right\}, \tag{2}$$

where

$\overline{D}_j = E(\tilde{D}_j) =$ the expected value of the total end-of-period cash flows to the shareholders of firm j;

$r = 1 + R_f$;

$\mathrm{cov}(\tilde{D}_j, \tilde{D}_m) = \sigma_{jm} =$ the covariance between the total cash flows of firm j and the total cash flows of all firms (including firm j), $\tilde{D}_m$;

$\mathrm{cov}(\tilde{D}_j, \tilde{D}_a) = \sigma_{ja} =$ the covariance between the total cash flows of firm j and the total value of random inflation, $\tilde{D}_a = V_m \tilde{R}_a$, where V_m is the total market value of all firms;

$\lambda^* = \lambda / V_m$
$= [E(\tilde{D}_m) - r V_m]/[\mathrm{var}(\tilde{D}_m) - \mathrm{cov}(\tilde{D}_m, \tilde{D}_a)]$.

Thus, in equilibrium the value of firm j is the present value of the certainty equivalent of the firm's random cash flow, $\tilde{D}_j$. The certainty equivalent is obtained by adjusting the firm's risk premium (the product of the market price risk and the systematic risk) from its expected cash flow.

3. The optimal corporate investment under uncertain inflation

Starting with a simpler case of no corporate income tax, we will derive the optimal level of corporate investment under uncertain inflation in this section, and in the next section we will show that the modified capital asset pricing model can be used to determine the risk-adjusted net present value (*RANPV*) of a risky project and that the general rules for capital budgeting can be obtained. In section 5, the analysis of corporate investment decisions under uncertain inflation will be extended to take into account the impact of the existence of corporate income taxes.

3.1. The optimal level of corporate investment

To analyze the effects of uncertain inflation on the optimal level of investment of a value-maximizing firm, let us assume that there is a *new* investment opportunity which promises a random return per dollar invested, $\tilde{\rho}$, with

$$E(\tilde{\rho}) = \bar{\rho},$$

$$\text{var}(\tilde{\rho}) = \sigma_\rho^2,$$

$$\text{cov}(\tilde{\rho}, \tilde{D}_j) = \sigma_{\rho j}, \tag{3}$$

$$\text{cov}(\tilde{\rho}, \tilde{D}_m) = \sigma_{\rho m},$$

$$\text{cov}(\tilde{\rho}, \tilde{D}_a) = \sigma_{\rho a}.$$

We further assume that the new investment opportunity has constant returns to scale. Let I_j be the amount to be invested in the new investment opportunity by firm j and, for simplicity, it will be raised through the sale of additional common stock.[3] Furthermore, let us denote the *post-investment* total cash flows of firm j by $\tilde{D}'_j = \tilde{D}_j + I_j\tilde{\rho}$ and the *post-investment* total cash flows of all firms by $\tilde{D}'_m = \tilde{D}_m + I_j\tilde{\rho}$. Thus, the new equilibrium value of the firm is given by

$$V'_j = \frac{1}{r}\left\{ \bar{D}'_j - \lambda^*\left[\text{cov}(\tilde{D}'_j, \tilde{D}'_m) - \text{cov}(\tilde{D}'_j, \tilde{D}_a) \right] \right\}$$

$$= \frac{1}{r}\left\{ (\bar{D}_j + I_j\bar{\rho}) - \lambda^*\left[\sigma_{jm} + I_j\sigma_{\rho m} + I_j\sigma_{\rho j} + I_j^2\sigma_\rho^2 - \sigma_{ja} - I_j\sigma_{\rho a} \right] \right\}. \tag{4}$$

Therefore, the net increase in the value of firm j (i.e. the change in the value of the firm brought about by the new investment after subtracting the cost of the investment) is given by

$$\Delta V_j = \frac{I_j}{r}\left[(\bar{\rho} - r) - \lambda^*\left(\sigma_{\rho m} + \sigma_{\rho j} + I_j\sigma_\rho^2 - \sigma_{\rho a} \right) \right]. \tag{5}$$

The optimal level of investment for a value-maximizing firm can be derived by differentiating eq. (5) and setting the result equal to zero. The solution is[4]

$$I_j^* = \max\left\{ 0, \frac{1}{2\lambda^*\sigma_\rho^2}\left[(\bar{\rho} - r) - \lambda^*(\sigma_{\rho m} + \sigma_{\rho j} - \sigma_{\rho a}) \right] \right\}. \tag{6}$$

Before we analyze the effects of uncertain inflation on the optimal level of the firm's investment, it should be noted that the optimal level of investment under

---

[3]In the absence of bankruptcy cost and corporate income taxes, the value of a firm is independent of its financial structure; see, for example, Modigliani and Miller (1958). Chen and Boness (1975) have shown that Modigliani and Miller's irrelevancy theorem holds even under uncertain inflation in the absence of corporate income taxes. In section 5 of this paper the effect of financing decision on a firm's investment decision in the presence of corporate income taxes will be discussed in detail.

uncertain inflation depends upon the particular firm making such a decision. This can be seen from (6) where the covariance between the return on the new investment and the firm's cash flows, $\sigma_{\rho j}$, is one of the factors determining the optimal level of investment.[5] Accordingly, the investment decision criteria are likely to be different among firms, even though it has been assumed that the stochastic nature of the return on the new investment is independent of which firm undertakes it.

As pointed out by Chen and Boness (1975) the optimal level of a firm's investment could be biased if the firm ignores the inflation factor in its investment decisions. More specifically, a firm, without considering the inflation factor, tends to underinvest in the inflation-preferred (i.e. $\sigma_{\rho a} > 0$) projects and to overinvest in the inflation-averse (i.e. $\sigma_{\rho a} < 0$) projects. To see this more clearly, let us express the optimal level of new investment of a firm without an explicit consideration of uncertain inflation in the following:[6]

$$ I_j^{**} = \max \left\{ 0, \frac{1}{2\lambda^{**}\sigma_\rho^2} \left[(\bar{\rho} - r) - \lambda^{**}(\sigma_{\rho m} + \sigma_{\rho j}) \right] \right\}, \tag{7} $$

where $\lambda^{**} = [E(\tilde{D}_m) - rV_m]/\text{var}(\tilde{D}_m)$.

Using (6) and (7), we can derive the difference in a firm's optimal levels of investment, with and without incorporating uncertain inflation, as follows:

$$ \Delta I_j = I_j^* - I_j^{**} = \frac{1}{2\lambda^*\lambda^{**}\sigma_\rho^2} \left[\lambda^*\lambda^{**}\sigma_{\rho a} + (\lambda^{**} - \lambda^*)(\bar{\rho} - r) \right]. \tag{8} $$

The magnitude of ΔI_j in (8) is determined in part by the sign of $(\lambda^{**} - \lambda^*)$. Several empirical studies (e.g. Chen (1976) and Lintner (1975)) have shown that $\text{cov}(\tilde{R}_m, \tilde{R}_a)$ is in general mildly negative. Thus, it is not unreasonable for us to postulate that $\text{cov}(\tilde{R}_m, \tilde{R}_a) \leqslant 0$ and to conclude that $\lambda^{**} \geqslant \lambda^*$. Therefore, eq. (8) indicates that $\Delta I_j \geqslant 0$ if $\sigma_{\rho a} \geqslant 0$, which implies that a firm, ignoring the inflation factor, will result in an underinvestment in the inflation-preferred projects. We can also see from (8) that a firm, without an explicit consideration of uncertain inflation, will overinvest in the inflation-averse investments (i.e. the projects with

---

[4]The optimal amount of investment which maximizes the social welfare can be derived as

$$ I_w^* = \max \left\{ 0, \frac{1}{\lambda^*(\sigma_\rho^2 - \sigma_{\rho a})} \left[(\bar{\rho} - r) - \lambda^*\sigma_{\rho m} \right] \right\}. $$

The problem of optimality in the capital market is beyond the scope of this paper; however, it should be noted that Merton and Subrahmanyam (1974) have shown that the private value maximization and the social welfare maximization criteria on investment, with proper interpretation, are consistent in the context of no uncertain inflation.

[5]As pointed out in Jensen and Long (1972) and Merton and Subrahmanyam (1974) also, this is in contrast with that of Myers (1968), Rubinstein (1973) and Schall (1972).

[6]This is the same result given in Jensen and Long (1972) and Merton and Subrahmanyam (1974).

$\sigma_{\rho a} < 0)$ if

$$|\sigma_{\rho a}| > \frac{(\lambda^{**} - \lambda^*)(\bar{\rho} - r)}{\lambda^* \lambda^{**}}. \tag{9}$$

3.2. The effects of changes in inflation risk and anticipation

In what follows we will employ the comparative statics to analyze the effects of changes in inflation risk and inflation anticipation on the optimal level of corporate investment under uncertain inflation.

3.2.1. Effects of inflation risk

A change in the risk of inflation perceived by investors in the economy affects the optimal level of investment of a value-maximizing firm. Differentiating I_j^* in (6) with respect to the standard deviation of inflation, σ_a, we obtain

$$\frac{\partial I_j^*}{\partial \sigma_a} = \frac{\gamma_{\rho a}}{2\sigma_\rho} - \frac{(\bar{\rho} - r)(\bar{R}_m - R_f)\gamma_{ma}\sigma_m}{2[\lambda^* \sigma_\rho(\sigma_m^2 - \sigma_{ma})]^2}, \tag{10}$$

where $\gamma_{\rho a}$ = the correlation coefficient between $\tilde{\rho}$ and $\tilde{R}_a$, and γ_{ma} = the correlation coefficient between $\tilde{R}_m$ and $\tilde{R}_a$.

The second term in the right-hand side of (10) without the sign is negative under our postulate that $\mathrm{cov}(\tilde{R}_m, \tilde{R}_a) < 0$. Therefore,

$$\partial I_j^*/\partial \sigma_a > 0, \quad \text{for } \gamma_{\rho a} \geqslant 0. \tag{11}$$

Thus, other things being equal, an increase in inflation risk will result in a greater amount of the firm's investment in the noninflation averse projects (i.e. the inflation-preferred or the inflation-neutral projects). However, an increase in inflation risk will increase the firm's investment in the inflation-averse projects, only if

$$\frac{\gamma_{\rho a}}{\gamma_{ma}} < \frac{(\bar{\rho} - r)(\bar{R}_m - R_f)\sigma_m}{\sigma_\rho[\lambda^*(\sigma_m^2 - \sigma_{ma})]^2}. \tag{12}$$

3.2.2. Effects of inflation anticipation

Depending upon the different utility functions used to derive the equilibrium valuation equation, a change in the anticipated level of inflation will have different impact on the optimal level of a firm's investment. Differentiating (6) with respect to the expected rate of inflation, we have

$$\frac{\partial I_i^*}{\partial \bar{R}_a} = \left[\frac{-(\bar{\rho}-r)}{2\lambda^{*2}\sigma_\rho^2} \right]\left(\frac{\partial \lambda^*}{\partial \bar{R}_a} \right). \tag{13}$$

It can be shown that the market price of risk, λ^*, in (6) is the harmonic mean of the investors' expected absolute risk-aversion coefficients. (See Chen and Boness (1975).) That is, $\lambda^* = (\Sigma_i \theta_i)^{-1}$, where $\theta_i = E(A_i^{-1})$ and A_i is the ith investor's Pratt–Arrow absolute risk-aversion coefficient. Therefore, it is easy to see that

(a) $\partial \lambda^*/\partial \bar{R}_a > 0$, for quadratic utility function (increasing absolute risk-aversion);
(b) $\partial \lambda^*/\partial \bar{R}_a = 0$, for negative exponential utility function (constant absolute risk-aversion); and
(c) $\partial \lambda^*/\partial \bar{R}_a < 0$, for logarithmic utility function (decreasing absolute risk-aversion).

It is clear from the above that an increase in the anticipated level of inflation will result in a higher, unchanged or lower optimal level of investment of a firm under uncertain inflation, if the investors' utility functions exhibit decreasing, constant or increasing absolute risk-aversion. Thus we can see that Nelson's (1976) conclusion regarding the effect of anticipated inflation on a firm's investment is only a special case of the more general results we have shown here.

4. Project selection rules under uncertain inflation

Under the condition of certainty, the project selection rules in a firm's capital budgeting decision are quite simple. Applying the net-present-value (*NPV*) method, a single investment proposal should be accepted if the *NPV* of the project is positive, and it should be rejected if its *NPV* is negative. Between any two mutually exclusive investment projects, the one with a higher *NPV* should be selected. Furthermore, the problem of selecting among a set of multiple projects with capital rationing can be solved by mathematical programming techniques. The set of investment projects which yield the largest *NPV* and do not exceed the ceiling of the firm's capital budget should be selected.

Under the condition of uncertainty, the project selection rules in capital budgeting decisions are the same as those under the condition of certainty. The *NPV* criterion for capital budgeting can be applied under the conditions of certainty as well as uncertainty. However, under the condition of uncertainty the riskiness of a project has to be taken into account in the determination of the project's net present value.

Using the equilibrium capital asset pricing model under uncertain inflation, we can unambiguously determine the risk-adjusted net present value of a risky investment project. Assume that an investment proposal under consideration by firm j requires a cash outlay of I_k and will generate uncertain end-of-period cash flows of $\tilde{D}_k$, with expected value $\bar{D}_k$. The risk-adjusted net present value of the project (i.e. the net increase in the value of firm j to be brought about by the project) is given by

$$\Delta V_j^k = NPV_k = \frac{1}{r}\left\{\bar{D}_k - \lambda^*\left[\text{cov}(\tilde{D}_k, \tilde{D}_m) + \text{cov}(\tilde{D}_k, \tilde{D}_j)\right.\right.$$

$$\left.\left. + \text{var}(\tilde{D}_k) - \text{cov}(\tilde{D}_k, \tilde{D}_a)\right]\right\} - I_k. \tag{14}$$

Thus, the risk-adjusted *NPV* of the project is the present value of the certainty-equivalent of its expected future cash flow, minus its initial cash outlay. A new investment project is acceptable to a value-maximizing firm only if its *RANPV* as expressed in (14) is greater than zero. Note that the above project selection criterion under inflation does depend on the particular firm making the evaluation and selection decisions. Furthermore, note that the inflation risk of an investment project, measured by the covariance between the cash flow of the project and the uncertain inflation, influences the value and the desirability of the project to the firm. For example, an inflation-preferred project (i.e. $\text{cov}(\tilde{D}_k, \tilde{D}_a) > 0$) is protected against the inflation risk, hence it should be more favorably treated and valued higher. Thus, a firm ignoring the inflation-risk component of the investment projects could result in an incorrect project-selection decision due to biases in the evaluation of projects.

To see how the equilibrium capital asset pricing model and the mathematical programming technique can be combined[7] to solve the problem of selecting multiple risky investment projects under capital rationing, let us denote CEQ_k as the certainty-equivalent of the expected cash flow of project k. For simplicity, we assume that the cash flows among the new projects are uncorrelated. Thus, we have

$$CEQ_k = \bar{D}_k - \lambda^*\left[\text{cov}(\tilde{D}_k, \tilde{D}_m) + \text{cov}(\tilde{D}_k, \tilde{D}_j) + \text{var}(\tilde{D}_k) - \text{cov}(\tilde{D}_k, \tilde{D}_a)\right]. \tag{15}$$

The risk-adjusted net present value of the kth project is given by

$$b_k = \frac{1}{r}(CEQ_k) - I_k \quad \text{(all } k). \tag{16}$$

Once the risk-adjusted net present values of all the projects under consideration are determined, the capital budgeting problem with capital rationing faced by a value-maximizing firm can easily be formulated and solved by the follow-

---

[7]Combining the traditional capital asset pricing model and the mathematical programming techniques for capital budgeting without inflation has been discussed by Thompson (1976).

ing mathematical programming model:

$$\max_{\langle X_k \rangle} \sum_{k=1}^{n} b_k X_k$$

subject to

$$\sum_{k=1}^{n} I_k X_k \leqslant C, \tag{17}$$

where $X_k =$ proportion of the kth project invested, and $C =$ the ceiling of the firm's capital budget.

The above formulation can also be used to handle the problem of selecting among economically interrelated projects. For mutually exclusive projects, say the kth and the lth projects, we simply add one additional constraint that $X_k X_l = 0$ to the above maximization model. For the contingent projects, for example, project l is a prerequisite for project k, we simply add the constraint that $X_k \leqslant X_l$ to the maximization problem presented in (17).

5. The effects of taxation and inflation on corporate investment decisions

In this section we examine the joint effects of taxation and uncertain inflation on a firm's investment decisions. The existence of corporate income taxes has significant impact on a firm's investment decisions because under the US tax code both the payment of interest and the depreciation charges are tax deductible. Furthermore, under the US tax code the depreciation deductions for tax purpose are based on the historical costs of capital investments, uncertain inflation affects the firm's investment decision in additional dimensions in the existence of corporate income taxes. Fortunately, incorporating both uncertain inflation and corporate income taxes into corporate investment decisions merely complicates the determination of the after-tax cash flows; it will not change the decision criteria we have described in the previous sections.

5.1. The optimal level of corporate investment with taxation

The cash flows after taxes are relevant factors in the evaluation of investment proposals if a firm is subject to corporate income taxes. In making corporate investment decisions, a firm should take into account both the incremental tax savings on payment of interest and the incremental tax savings on depreciation charges brought about by the new investment.

To see how taxation and uncertain inflation jointly affect a firm's optimal level of investment, let us assume that the new investment under consideration by firm j requires an initial cash outlay of I_j and promises a random before-tax return per dollar invested of $\tilde{\rho}$. Assume further that the jth firm's current debt–assets ratio is β and that the new investment is to be financed with the same proportion of debt capital at an interest cost of R_f. Thus, the tax savings to the firm on the payments of interest resulted from the new investment is $tR_f\beta I_j$, where t is the marginal (and average) corporate income tax rate. Let α be the fraction of the cost of new capital investment allowable for depreciation deduction for tax purpose, the tax savings on depreciation charges from the new investment will be $t\alpha I_j$. Therefore, the after-tax cash flow of the new investment to the firm is given by

$$\tilde{D}_I(t) = I_j\left[\tilde{\rho}(1-t) + tR_f\beta + t\alpha\right]. \tag{18}$$

Thus, the net increase in the value of firm j, after subtracting the cost of the investment is

$$\Delta V_j(t) = \frac{I_j(1-t)}{r}\left\{\left[\bar{\rho} - \frac{r}{1-t} + \frac{R_f\beta t}{1-t} + \frac{\alpha t}{1-t}\right]\right.$$

$$\left. -\lambda^*\left[(1-t)\left(\sigma_{\rho m} + \sigma_{\rho j} + I_j\sigma_\rho^2\right) - \sigma_{\rho a}\right]\right\}. \tag{19}$$

Using (19) we can derive the optimal level of investment for firm j as follows:

$$I_j^*(t) = \max\left\{0, \frac{1}{2\lambda^*\sigma_\rho^2}\left[\frac{\bar{\rho}}{1-t} - \frac{r}{(1-t)^2} + \frac{R_f\beta t}{(1-t)^2} + \frac{\alpha t}{(1-t)^2}\right]\right.$$

$$\left. -\lambda^*\left[\sigma_{\rho m} + \sigma_{\rho j} - \frac{\sigma_{\rho a}}{1-t}\right]\right\}. \tag{20}$$

Note in (20) that in the presence of corporate income taxes the inflation risk of the capital investment (measured by $\sigma_{\rho a}$) plays a more important role (relative to $\sigma_{\rho m}$ and $\sigma_{\rho j}$) in the determination of the relevant risk of the investment. Furthermore, note that, other things being equal, a firm with a higher degree of financial leverage (i.e. with a larger value of β) tends to have a higher optimal level of investment, since it receives larger tax savings on the payments of interest in maintaining the current financial policy of the firm.

Some comparative statics can be used to analyze the effect of a change in the corporate income tax rate on the optimal level of a firm's investment. Differentiating (20) with respect to the corporate income tax rate yields (λ^* remains constant if investors' utility functions exhibit constant absolute risk-aversion)

$$\frac{\partial I_j^*(t)}{\partial t} = \frac{1}{2\lambda^*\sigma_\rho^2(1-t)^3}\left\{\bar{\rho}(1-t) - 2r + R_f\beta(1+t)\right.$$

$$\left. + \alpha(1+t) + \lambda^*\sigma_{\rho a}(1-t)\right\}. \tag{21}$$

It is evidently clear from (21) that the effect of an increase in the corporate income tax rate on the optimal level of a firm's investment cannot be stated a priori. We can see from (21) that

$$[\partial I_j^*(t)/\partial t] > 0,$$

if and only if

$$[(1-t)(\bar{\rho}+\lambda^*\sigma_{pa})+(1+t)(R_f\beta+\alpha)] > 2r.$$

Thus, an increase in the corporate income tax rate is more likely to induce a firm with relatively higher financial leverage to invest more in the inflation-preferred projects. This reverse effect of corporate income taxes on a firm's investment is based on considerations different from that discussed by Haley (1971).

We know from (20) that $[\partial I_j^*(t)/\partial \alpha] > 0$. This indicates that the existence of uncertain inflation has not materially changed the result that increasing the allowable portion of historical cost for depreciation deduction makes the capital investments more desirable.

5.2. Taxation and project selection rules

A firm which is subject to corporate income taxes cannot ignore the impact of taxation in capital budgeting decisions. As mentioned above, the existence of corporate income taxes affects the after-tax cash flows of capital investments, because the payments of interest from financing the new investment and the depreciation charges on the new investment are both tax-deductible under the US tax code. However, incorporating corporate income taxes into a firm's capital budgeting will not alter the basic rules in project selection under uncertain inflation. In order to see the joint effects of corporate income taxes and uncertain inflation on the criteria for capital budgeting of a firm, let us assume that a new investment proposal requires a cash outlay of I_k and that it will generate a random cash income of $\tilde{D}_k$. Let us further assume that the firm attempts to maintain its current financial policy of having a debt–assets ratio of β_j, and hence $\beta_j I_k$ of the investment cost is to be financed with debt capital at an interest cost of R_f. Given these assumptions, the after-tax cash flow of the project available to the security-holders of the firm is defined as

$$_t\tilde{D}_K = (1-t)\tilde{D}_k + tR_f\beta_j I_k + t\alpha I_k, \tag{22}$$

where $\alpha =$ the fraction of the cost of capital investment allowable for depreciation deduction.

Thus, using the equilibrium capital asset pricing model under uncertain inflation, we can derive the risk- and tax-adjusted net present value (RTANPV) of the investment project as follows:

$$NPV_k(t) = \frac{1}{r}\left\{(1-t)\overline{D}_k + tR_f\beta_j I_k + t\alpha I_k - \lambda^*\left[\text{cov}(_t\tilde{D}_k, _t\tilde{D}_m) + \text{cov}(_t\tilde{D}_k, _t\tilde{D}_j)\right.\right.$$

$$\left.\left. + \text{var}(_t\tilde{D}_k) - \text{cov}(_t\tilde{D}_k, \tilde{D}_a)\right]\right\} - I_k, \qquad (23)$$

where $_t\tilde{D}_j =$ the after-tax cash flows of firm j, and $_t\tilde{D}_m =$ the after-tax cash flows of all firms.

After the appropriate NPV (adjusted for tax and risk) of a project has been determined by using (23), the simple NPV decision criterion for capital budgeting can then be applied to decide whether or not the project is acceptable to the firm. An investment project should be accepted by the firm if its NPV (adjusted for tax and risk) as expressed in (23) is greater than zero, and it should be rejected otherwise.

It is important to note that the adjusted net present value of an investment project and hence its acceptability to a firm depend upon the particular firm which contemplates on undertaking it, since β_j as well as $\text{cov}(_t\tilde{D}_k, _t\tilde{D}_j)$ in (23) are in general different among firms. A project is more valuable to a firm with relatively higher financial leverage in its current capital structure. This implies that a firm's investment decision is in general not independent of its financing decision. Furthermore, a project is worth more, other things being equal, to a firm with a lower value of $\text{cov}(_t\tilde{D}_k, _t\tilde{D}_j)$, implying there is a portfolio diversification effect in capital budgeting decision.

As for the problem of selecting among multiple interrelated projects, we can first use (23) to compute the risk and tax adjusted NPVs of all projects under consideration, and then solve the problem by applying the mathematical programming formulation discussed in section 4.

6. Conclusion

In this paper we have attempted to show the effects of uncertain inflation and corporate income taxes on the optimal investment decisions of a firm — an important but neglected aspect of corporate investment in the modern theory of financial management. Based upon a modified capital asset pricing model, we have derived and analyzed the optimal level of corporate investment under uncertain inflation for cases without and with the existence of corporate income taxes. We have also shown that the modified valuation model can be used to determine investment projects' net present values adjusted for risk as well as corporate income taxes, and hence derived criteria for capital budgeting under uncertain inflation. In the presence of corporate income taxes, a firm's financing decision has been shown to influence its investment decisions under uncertain inflation.

Our analyses have indicated that the financial managers, in making corporate investment decisions, should not ignore the importance of the inflation-risk component of investment alternatives. Furthermore, our results imply that public policies changing the investors' estimates of the nature of uncertain inflation could well be an effective means of influencing the firms' capital investments. Finally, the analytical framework presented in this paper can be extended to study the investment decisions of a regulated firm under uncertain inflation. Thus, further research in this direction is called for.

References

Arrow, K. J. (1965) *Aspects of the Theory of Risk Bearing* (Helsinki).

Baumol, W. J. and R. E. Quandt (1965) "Investment and Discount Rates Under Capital Rationing — A Programming Approach", *The Economic Journal*, June.

Chen, A. H. and A. J. Boness (1975) "Effects of Uncertain Inflation on the Investment and Financing Decisions of A Firm", *Journal of Finance*, May.

Chen, E. T. (1976) "Capital Asset Prices Under Uncertain Inflation", unpublished Ph.D. dissertation, University of California, Berkeley.

Fama, E. F. (1972) "Perfect Competition and Optimal Production Decision Under Uncertainty", *Bell Journal of Economics and Management Science*, Autumn.

Friend, I. and Y. Landskroner (1975) "The Demand For Risky Assets Under Uncertain Inflation", Working Paper, The Wharton School, University of Pennsylvania.

Haley, C. W. (1971) "Taxes, The Cost of Capital, and the Firm's Investment Decisions", *Journal of Finance*, September.

Hamada, R. S. (1969) "Portfolio Analysis, Market Equilibrium, and Corporation Finance", *Journal of Finance*, March.

Jensen, M. C. and J. B. Long (1972) "Corporate Investment Under Uncertainty and Pareto Optimality in the Capital Market", *Bell Journal of Economics and Management Science*, Spring.

Leland, H. E. (1974) "Production Theory and the Stock Market", *Bell Journal of Economics and Management Science*, Spring.

Lintner, J. (1965) "The Valuation of Risk Assets and the Selection of Risky Investments in Stock Portfolios and Capital Budgets", *Review of Economics and Statistics*, February.

Lintner, J. (1975) "Inflation and Security Returns", *Journal of Finance*, May.

Litzenberger, R. H. and A. P. Budd (1970) "Corporate Investment Criteria and the Valuation of Risk Assets", *Journal of Financial and Quantitative Analysis*, December.

Merton, R. C. and M. G. Subrahmanyam (1974) "The Optimality of A Competitive Stock Market", *Bell Journal of Economics and Management Science*, Spring.

Modigliani, F. and M. H. Miller (1958) "The Cost of Capital, Corporation Finance, and the Theory of Investment", *American Economic Review*, June.

Modigliani, F. and M. H. Miller (1963) "Corporate Income Taxes and the Cost of Capital: A Correction", *American Economic Review*, June.

Mossin, J. (1966) "Equilibrium in a Capital Asset Market", *Econometrica*, October.

Mossin, J. (1969) "Security Pricing and Investment Criteria in Competitive Markets", *American Economic Review*, December.

Myers, S. C. (1968) "Procedures for Capital Budgeting Under Uncertainty", *Industrial Management Review*, Spring.

Nelson, C. R. (1976) "Inflation and Capital Budgeting", *Journal of Finance*, June.

Pratt, J. W. (1964) "Risk Aversion in the Small and in the Large", *Econometrica*, January.

Rubinstein, M. E. (1973) "A Mean-Variance Synthesis in Corporate Financial Theory", *Journal of Finance*, March.

Sharpe, W. F. (1964) "Capital Asset Prices: A Theory of Market Equilibrium Under Condition of Risk", *Journal of Finance*, September.

Schall, L. D. (1972) "Asset Valuation, Firm Investment, and Firm Diversification", *Journal of Business*, January.

Stiglitz, J. E. (1972) "On the Optimality of the Stock Market Allocation of Investment", *Quarterly Journal of Economics*, February.

Thompson, H. E. (1976) "Mathematical Programming, The Capital Asset Pricing Model and Capital Budgeting of Interrelated Projects", *Journal of Finance*, March.

Tuttle, D. L. and R. H. Litzenberger (1968) "Leverage, Diversification and Capital Market Effects on a Risk-Adjusted Capital Budgeting Framework", *Journal of Finance*, June.

Weingartner, H. M. (1963) *Mathematical Programming and the Analysis of Capital Budgeting Problems* (Prentice-Hall).

Chapter 12

THE TRADE CREDIT DECISION

ROBERT A. SCHWARTZ
New York University

and

DAVID K. WHITCOMB
Rutgers University

1. Introduction

Trade credit is short-term unsecured financing extended by nonfinancial institutions and linked to the purchase of goods or services; in other words, it is financial intermediation by nonfinancial firms. Its closest counterpart is revolving credit, since both are customarily "rolled over", but may be cancelled by either party on appropriate notice. Trade credit usually flows from sellers to buyers, although prepayment for the construction of buildings, machinery and transportation equipment is fairly common.

At the end of the first quarter of 1976, the trade debt of US manufacturing, mining and wholesale trade corporations totalled $106.9 billion, over twice the amount of short-term liabilities to banks, making trade credit the largest single source of short-term corporate debt. At the same date, corporate receivables from other than the US government were $186.8 billion, or 1.75 times aggregate trade debt. The ratio of manufacturer's receivables to trade debt rose almost monotonically with asset size.[1] Thus, there is a net flow of trade credit from corporations to retailers and unincorporated businesses, and from large to small firms.

The magnitude and direction of trade credit flows raise interesting questions for the financial economist. Anyone familiar with the sizeable literature on the irrelevance of capital structure and maturity structure would presume that under perfect capital markets trade credit would be a matter of indifference to seller and buyer alike. If anything, economies of scale and specialization might appear

---

[1]See table 12.1 for these ratios. Source of aggregate amounts: US Federal Trade Commission, *Quarterly Financial Report for Manufacturing, Mining and Trade Corporations*, Second Quarter 1976, Tables G-2 and K-2.

James L. Bicksler, Editor, Handbook of Financial Economics
© *North-Holland Publishing Company – 1979*

to give the financial sector an advantage over nonfinancial corporations in retailing credit.

Despite its quantitative importance, trade credit, unlike most subjects studied in this volume, has received scant attention in the literature of modern financial economics. Most of the existing literature concentrates on the monetary policy implications of trade credit, although Wrightsman (1969) and Schwartz (1974) present models of optimal trade credit terms, Schwartz and Whitcomb (1978) discuss financial and product market imperfections which provide motives for trade credit, and Pringle and Cohn (1974) state an indifference proposition between holding and factoring receivables. The collection of articles in section 3 of Smith, K. V. (1974) summarizes the present state of the corporate finance literature on the subject. The literature contains no full demonstration of an indifference proposition regarding the existence and terms (i.e. credit period) of trade credit.

This paper deals with four interrelated issues. (1) In section 3 we build a base for our analytic framework by presenting a trade credit indifference proposition which holds under the standard perfect markets assumptions. (2) In sections 4–6 we develop an optimization model for setting trade credit terms in light of financial and product market imperfections. (3) Section 7 focuses on the effect of monetary conditions on trade credit terms. (4) The economic implications the trade credit model has for the direction of trade credit flows, the discriminatory impact of market imperfections, and the incidence of prepayment are considered in section 8.

2. Background discussion

In this section we specify the traditional trade credit terms and identify the underlying motives which might explain the existence of trade credit flows. The terms of seller-to-buyer trade credit typically constitute a two-part offer: a discount for payment within a relatively short discount period, and a longer net period at the end of which full payment is required. The offer, expressed in conventional shorthand, is

$$d/D, \text{net } N,$$

where d = percent discount for payment within discount period, D = length of discount period in days, and N = length of net period in days. Frequently, a discount is not offered, and the terms are simply "net N". Net N trade credit is equivalent to N-day revolving credit where the balance is divided into N units, each maturing and cancellable on a different day.

When there is a two-part trade credit offer, the buyer's opportunity cost of forgoing the discount (i.e. borrowing $1-d$ times the list price P_{L}, for $N-D$

days) may be expressed as a continuously compounded rate per day by solving

$$(1-d)P_{\rm L}e^{r(N-D)}=P_{\rm L}$$

for r:

$$r=\ln(1-d)/D-N. \tag{1}$$

For terms of 2/10, net 30, r is 0.00101/day or 0.369/annum continuously compounded; 2/15, net 60 gives 0.00045 and 0.164, respectively. Seiden (1964) provides evidence that sellers frequently allow buyers to extend the credit period beyond the stated terms (and discount periods are sometimes extended as well), so the effective rates often differ from the stated terms. In this paper we take N to be the actual, rather than the stated, period.

The trade credit offer alters the effective price paid by the buyer and the effective price received by the seller. The effective price to a buyer is the lesser of the present value of the discount price to be paid in D days or the present value of the list price to be paid in N days:

$$P_{{\rm B}j}=\min\{(1-d)P_{\rm L}\exp[-r_{{\rm B}j}(D)D],P_{\rm L}\exp[-r_{{\rm B}j}(N)N]\}, \tag{2}$$

where $r_{{\rm B}j}(D)$ and $r_{{\rm B}j}(N)$ represent the value to the jth buyer of D-day and N-day credit, respectively. (That is, they represent the maximum daily interest rate he would pay for the credit.) We will shortly consider how these rates vary with the credit period, referring to $r_{{\rm B}j}(N)$ only for compactness.

We have elsewhere identified three "motives" for the trade credit offer: a transactions motive, a financing motive (Schwartz (1974)), as well as a pricing motive (Schwartz and Whitcomb (1978)).

The transactions motive reflects the fact that buyers' transaction costs are reduced if invoices are allowed to accumulate for periodic payment. This may partially explain very short term trade credit (e.g. "net 15" or perhaps the d/D part of a two-part credit offer). As electronic banking lowers the costs of rapid funds transfers, we may expect this motive to diminish in relative importance, and it plays no part in the models considered in this paper. The financing motive exists if firms can profitably link financial intermediation to the sale of a product due to capital market imperfections. The pricing motive exists if product market imperfections make trade credit an effective means for disguised price reductions or discriminatory pricing.

3. The value of trade credit to buyers, the cost to sellers, and a perfect markets indifference proposition

This section identifies the value of N-day trade credit to a jth buyer–recipient $[r_{{\rm B}j}(N)]$, the cost to a seller extending credit to the jth buyer $[r_{{\rm S}j}(N)]$, and establishes an indifference proposition that holds for trade credit loans under perfect capital markets. First, recognize that from the buyer's side trade credit may be used to finance additional investments and/or to substitute for other sources of funds.[2] Because of differing risks and maturity structures of interest rates, we cannot simply take the interest rates applicable to these uses to be the value of the trade credit loan to the buyer.

We structure the problem in the following way. We take account of differing risk by adjusting all returns to a risk equivalent to that of the N-day revolving credit loan. Then, to take account of the maturity structure, we adjust all rates of return to an N-day revolving rate equivalent. Because the maturity structure is generally positive, $r_{Bj}(N)$ will, ceteris paribus, be an increasing function of N. Hence, for the financing of additional investments we take the risk adjusted return on a revolving N-day investment which would be of equivalent value to the buyer (i.e. the buyer would be indifferent between the actual and the N-day "fictitious" investment, since both would result in the same market value of the firm). Similarly, for funds retirement, the value of trade credit to the buyer is identified as the interest rate on N-day revolving credit which would cause the buyer to be indifferent between not receiving that credit and taking it for the purpose of retiring the alternative funds (i.e. it is the N-day equivalent cost of the replaced source). Because the total amount of trade credit received is a positive function of N, and since additional funds might (in imperfect investment and credit markets) be put to less productive uses, it is possible for $r_{Bj}(N)$ to be a decreasing function of N.

From the seller's side, the effective price received depends on the buyer's choice of credit terms:

$$P_{Sj} = \begin{cases} (1-d)P_L \exp\left[-r_{Sj}(D)D\right], & \text{if } j \text{ selects } D \\ P_L \exp\left[-r_{Sj}(N)N\right], & \text{if } j \text{ selects } N \end{cases}, \tag{3}$$

where $r_{Sj}(D)$ and $r_{Sj}(N)$ are the daily required returns on the extension of D-day and N-day credit, respectively, to the jth buyer. Now, introducing the convenient fiction that the seller may sell any of his receivables each period at price V_{jt} on a competitive market,[3] the required return on the N-day trade credit

---

[2] Either use of trade credit will generally change both the maturity and leverage structures of capital. In perfect capital markets the capital source for which trade credit is substituted is a matter of indifference to the buyer, since the value of the firm is unaltered by changes in the maturity or leverage structure (see, e.g., Rubenstein (1973) and Stiglitz (1974)), although this is not generally the case under capital market imperfections. For demonstrations of the maturity, leverage, and risk structures of interest rates propositions under perfect capital market assumptions, see, respectively, Nelson (this volume), Arzac, Schwartz and Whitcomb (1979b), and Merton (1973).

[3] The methodology in this paragraph loosely follows that used by Miller and Upton (1976) to establish the required return on a lease. The one-period construction is necessary to avoid the truncation of returns distributions on debt held to maturity. The fiction of a sales opportunity is made realistic in cases where factoring is continuously available; one possibility is that the seller operates a decentralized division (such as GMAC) to which it sells all receivables.

investment may be expressed in terms of the (log form of the) CAPM:

$$r_{Sj}(N) = i + \beta_j(N)[E(r_m) - i],$$ (4)

where i = riskless return; r_m = return on market portfolio; $\beta_j(N) = \text{cov}(g_{jt}, r_{mt})/\text{var}(r_{mt})$; and $g_{jt} = \ln(V_{jt}/V_{jt-1})$.

It follows that the seller's required return on a trade credit investment depends on the riskiness of the company receiving the trade credit, but not on the special characteristics of the company extending the credit. Hence, a bank (we use "bank" as a compact reference to "any financial sector institution") making an N-day revolving credit loan to the same firm j (and facing identical transaction costs) would require the same return as the seller and in competitive credit markets the seller and the bank would both charge $r_{Sj}(N)$. Given an increasing maturity structure of interest rates, $r_{Sj}(N)$ is positively related to N.

If the buyer operates in perfect capital markets, he is indifferent among all sources of capital including N-day revolving credit. Hence, $r_{Bj}(N)$, the value of any source (arbitrarily) replaced by trade credit expressed as an N-day equivalent rate, equals the rate a bank or the seller would actually change, $r_{Sj}(N)$. We have that $r_{Sj}(N) = r_{Bj}(N)$ for all N (with a similar result for D), the seller's effective price (given by (3)) equals the buyer's effective price (given by (2)), and the seller is unable to profit by the act of retailing credit. (The seller's indifference to N is, given discount rate equivalence, proved in another way in the formal model of section 4.) This result constitutes the trade credit indifference proposition.

Proposition 1. In perfect capital markets, the seller's required return on trade credit equals the maximum interest rate the buyer would pay for trade credit for all credit periods and, absent a pricing motive, both seller and buyer are indifferent as to credit period.

Conversely, if the buyer faces an imperfect credit market, banks may charge a rate exceeding $r_{Sj}(N)$ for N-day revolving credit and the buyer may be unable to substitute another source of capital at an N-day equivalent rate as low as $r_{Sj}(N)$, so we would have $r_{Bj}(N) > r_{Sj}(N)$ over some range of N. This provides the seller with a financial motive for trade credit; we shall state optimality conditions for N in the next section.

4. Optimal trade credit terms when sellers' and buyers' discount rates diverge

Schwartz (1974) presented a model that specifies a firm's optimal quantity sales, product list price, and net N trade credit period. In this section, we shall restate this model (altering some assumptions) in a way that enables us directly to arrive at marginal conditions for an optimum which satisfy the necessary curvature conditions on the $r_B(N)$ and $r_S(N)$ functions.

Assumption 1. The seller maximizes the present value of profit.

Assumption 2. The seller faces a known[4] concave revenue function (i.e. buyers are price takers and competitors' reactions, if any, are known), and a known convex cost function. One of these functions must be nonlinear.

Assumption 3. The seller makes only a net N trade credit offer (i.e. $d = D = 0$).

Assumption 4. Buyers are homogeneous with respect to the discount rate for a given N. (This will be relaxed in footnote 7 and section 6, but it simplifies exposition here.)

Assumption 5. r_S and r_B are functions of N but not of Q.[5] (This implies an assumption of buyer/seller insignificance in credit markets: as the buyer/seller expands, maturity, leverage and risk constant, his cost of capital does not rise.) $r_S(N)$ and $r_B(N)$ are taken to be continuous and twice differentiable. We write the present value of the seller's profit as:

$$\pi = QP_L(Q)\exp[-r_S(N)N] - C(Q). \tag{5}$$

Since buyers are willing to pay a higher list price as N increases, the list price may be rewritten in terms of buyers' present value ("payment on delivery") demand function

$$P_L(Q) = P_B(Q)\exp[r_B(N)N], \tag{6}$$

and (5) becomes

$$\pi = QP_B(Q)\exp[R_B(N) - R_S(N)] - C(Q), \tag{7}$$

where $R_B(N) = r_B(N)N, R_S(N) = r_S(N)N$ for compactness.

The first order conditions for maximizing π with respect to Q and N are

$$\pi_Q = \left[Q\frac{dP_B(Q)}{dQ} + P_B(Q)\right]\exp[R_B(N) - R_S(N)] - \frac{dC(Q)}{dQ} = 0, \tag{8}$$

$$\pi_N = QP_B(Q)\exp[R_B(N) - R_S(N)][R_B'(N) - R_S'(N)] = 0. \tag{9}$$

---

[4]The model could be extended to the case of uncertain demand with known parameters, as done by Sandmo (1970), but no additional insight into the trade credit issue would be gained.

[5]We will show that the extension of credit can generate an output effect. However, the expansion of output induced by a credit offer does not generate the credit to finance additional investment or to replace other sources of funds, and hence does not imply a relationship between r_B and Q.

Eq. (8) states the equality of discounted marginal revenue with marginal cost. For (9) to hold we must also have

$$R_B'(N^*) = R_S'(N^*). \tag{10}$$

That is, at N^* the buyers' marginal interest rate

$$\left[R_B'(N) = r_B(N^*) + N^* \frac{dr_B(N)}{dN^*} \right]$$

must equal the seller's marginal interest rate.[6] Intuitively (for some N such that $r_B(N) > r_S(N)$), if an increase in N raises the value buyers assign to trade credit ($R_B(N)$) more than it raises the seller's cost, the seller can gain by so increasing N, because he can increase P_L by more than enough to cover his cost.[7] Optimal Q in eq. (7) may in general depend on N; that is, there may be an output effect of optimal trade credit. Having determined P_B^* and N^*, the seller sets P_L^* by substituting these in eq. (6).

Note that if $r_S(N) = r_B(N)$ for all N, as in perfect credit markets, any N satisfies eq. (9) and the seller is indifferent as to trade credit policy. For imperfect capital markets with $r_S(N) < r_B(N)$, we have (given satisfaction of the second order conditions) $0 < N^* < \infty$ (a delayed payment credit offer) and, for $r_S(N) > r_B(N)$, we have $-\infty < N^* < 0$ (a prepayment request).

[6]Writing the optimality conditions as

$$r_B(N)[1 + \eta_{r_B(N)N}] = r_S(N)[1 + \eta_{r_S(N)N}]$$

we see that at N^* for $r_B(N) > r_S(N)$ we must have

$$\eta_{R_B(N)N} < \eta_{r_S(N)N}.$$

[7]If S charges the same list price to n heterogeneous-with-respect-to-discount-rate buyers, it is easy to show that the profit function

$$\pi = \sum_{j=1}^{n} Q_j P_{Bj}(\Sigma Q_j) \exp\left[R_{Bj}(N_j) - R_{Sj}(N_j) \right] - C(\Sigma Q_j)$$

implies the optimality conditions

$$R_{Bj}'(N_j) - R_{Sj}'(N_j) = 0, \qquad j = 1, \ldots, n,$$

if the seller can set differing N_j, and

$$\sum_{j=1}^{n} Q_j P_{Bj}(\Sigma Q_j) \exp[R_{Bj}(N) - R_{Sj}(N)][R_{Bj}'(N) - R_{Sj}'(N)] = 0$$

(i.e. that the sum of net marginal interest rates weighted by revenue equal 0 at N^*) for common N.

It is shown in the footnote[8] that, given assumption 2, the second order conditions for a maximum at N^* will be satisfied if and only if

$$R_B''(N^*) - R_S''(N^*) < 0. \tag{11}$$

That is, for the "typical" case of a unique optimum at a finite positive N, we must have that the seller's marginal interest rate function intersects the buyers' from below as $N \to N^*$. In the next section we examine whether several commonly accepted credit market imperfections would generate interest rate functions that satisfy (10) and (11).

5. Credit market imperfections

5.1. Institutional restrictions on lending

There is a substantial literature explaining the existence of credit rationing, i.e. the practice of limiting loan amounts to risky customers instead of charging higher interest rates. All credit rationing models assume that lenders are forced, or choose, to charge the same interest rate to all borrowers. Jaffee and Modigliani (1969) show that under this condition, a monopolistic lender will ration credit to customers desiring higher leverage (but will not if he is free to price differentiate). They present empirical evidence of widespread credit rationing. Smith, V. (1972) and Arzac, Schwartz and Whitcomb (1979a) demonstrate (under differing assumptions concerning to whom the risk asset is available) that competitive lenders required to charge the same rate to all borrowers will ration loans such that each borrower's leverage is the same. Baltensperger (1976) shows that if competitive lenders are not required to set a uniform borrowing rate, and that if an equilibrium leverage structure of interest rates exists, credit rationing will not occur.

[8]The second order conditions for a maximum of π at N^* are: $\pi_{NN} < 0$ and $\pi_{NN}\pi_{QQ} - (\pi_{NQ})^2 > 0$:

$$\pi_{NN} = QP_B(Q)\exp[R_B(N) - R_S(N)]\{[R_B'(N) - R_S'(N)]^2 + [R_B''(N) - R_S''(N)]\},$$

$$\pi_{QQ} = \left[Q\frac{d^2P_B}{dQ^2} - 2\frac{dP_B}{dQ}\right]\exp[R_B(N) - R_S(N)] - C''(Q),$$

$$\pi_{NQ} = \left[Q\frac{dP_B}{dQ} + P_B(Q)\right]\exp[R_B(N) - R_S(N)][R_B'(N) - R_S'(N)].$$

Since $R_B'(N^*) - R_S'(N^*) = 0$, we must have for finite $N^* \pi_{NQ} = 0$ and $\pi_{NN} < 0$ iff $[R_B''(N) - R_S''(N)] < 0$. Assumption 2 implies $\pi_{QQ} < 0$, so the second order conditions are satisfied iff $R_B''(N) - R_S''(N) < 0$.

It thus seems clear that interference in the adjustment of interest rates to differences in leverage causes rationing of credit to firms desiring high leverage. Among the sources of interference may be usury laws. While many large states do not limit the interest rate which may be charged corporations, unincorporated businesses are more often "protected". Moreover, credit rationing is directly legislated where certain financial institutions (e.g. insurance companies) are prohibited from lending to risky customers.

Now suppose a firm, B, is subject to some form of credit rationing on loans from financial sector firms, but that one of its suppliers, S, is not. In a world of corporate taxes and bankruptcy costs, B would be forced to choose a second best leverage or maturity composition of capital and B's value would be increased if it could obtain N-day credit at an interest rate equal to a bank's or S's required return. Thus, B would be willing to substitute trade credit for some of its present capital at a rate $r_B(N) > r_S(N)$ for some $N > 0$. As N increases, B approaches an optimal capital composition, and there is some N_0 where $r_B(N_0) = r_S(N_0)$. Thus, we have that $R_B(N)[= r_B(N)N]$ strictly exceeds $R_S(N)$ over $0 < N < N_0$. If $r_S(N)$ and $r_B(N)$ are continuous and twice differentiable, there must be some $N^* < N_0$ such that $R_B'(N^*) = R_S'(N^*)$ and $R_B''(N^*) < R_S''(N^*)$. Uniqueness of N^* requires stronger assumptions than we have made here.

A similar argument could be made when the seller rather than the buyer faces credit rationing; this would lead to $R_S(N) > R_B(N)$ over $N_0 < N < 0$, and some amount of prepayment would be optimal. Credit rationing would also suggest the possibility of loans between nonfinancial firms where there is no other exchange of goods or services.

5.2. Loan transaction costs and sales activity

Information on customers' creditworthiness may be a joint product of sales activities involving analysis of customer demand and ability to buy. Clearly, this can occur only in imperfectly competitive product markets where there is a rationale for sales activity. Buyers' purchasing activities would usually not generate credit information because they concentrate on the product rather than the producer (except where the product is very long lived and failure of the specific producer would be injurious). Thus, oligopolistic sellers may be able to obtain credit information on their customers at lower cost than can banks and specialized credit investigation firms.

We might expect a market for credit information to arise where sellers could sell credit information to financial sector firms at a price equaling or exceeding its value to the seller. However, such a market would be highly imperfect due to costs of information transmission and verification, and the loss of good will if the confidentiality of a customer's financial status were violated. In relation to the costs of information verification, Leland and Pyle (1977) show that, under informational asymmetries, the willingness of one individual (e.g. a seller) to extend funds to another (e.g. a buyer), may be necessary to signal the true creditworthiness of the borrower to some third party lender (e.g. a bank). The Leland–Pyle model leads these authors to suggest that informational asymmetries might be a primary cause for financial intermediation; their formulation is complementary to the trade credit optimization model of this paper.

We expect that the cost of the joint sales activity–credit investigation would not vary appreciably with N. Thus, any unit cost advantage would diminish as N rises, and might even be reversed if banks enjoy greater economies of scale and specialization in lending. Thus, there would again be some positive N^*, where $R'_S(N)$ intersects $R'_B(N)$ from below.

Before leaving this section, it should be pointed out that any source of financial market imperfections creates an arbitrage opportunity that tends to reduce the imperfection. If there are many sellers (of the same or different products) offering trade credit to the same buyers in order to profit from a difference in discount rates, $r_B(N)$ and $r_S(N)$ will shift toward each other at every N. As the number of competing sellers of trade credit increases without bound, $r_B(N)$ and $r_S(N)$ must become coincident, although for their identity to hold, substantial trade credit may have to be used in equilibrium. So, while trade credit may, under perfect product markets, eliminate financial market imperfections, it cannot itself be eliminated in the process. Evidence of a difference in discount rates would therefore suggest both financial and product market imperfections.

6. Product market imperfections

In this section we examine the pure pricing motive for trade credit. That is, we assume perfect financial markets ($r_{S_j}(N) = r_{B_j}(N)$ at any N, $j = 1,\ldots,n$), and consider how trade credit may be used as a means of disguising price reductions or increases, or of concealing price discrimination.[9]

6.1. Evasion of administered prices

Suppose the seller is an oligopolist who knows his demand function, but is constrained by his rivals' potential reactions to charge a list price of $\bar{P}_L$.[10] If the

---

[9]Although their primary focus is on financial aspects, Miller and Upton (1976) note that price discrimination is frequently mentioned as a motive for leasing.

[10]A number of models of oligopolistic price behavior would generate such a situation. Schwartz and Whitcomb (1978), for example, assumed the familiar kinked demand curve model, but an overt or covert cartel arrangement would also generate a price floor. It is not uncommon for an oligopolist who would benefit from setting a lower price to offer under the table discounts from the common list price. Trade credit is simply one means of effecting such a discount.

seller has n customers who, in general, have differing discount rate functions and if the seller is free to set each N_j at any level he may costlessly evade the constraint by setting the N_j such that

$$P_B(Q)\exp R_{Bj}(N_j) = \bar{P}_L \qquad (j=1,\ldots,n), \tag{12}$$

(where we have used $r_{Sj}(N_j) = r_{Bj}(N_j)$). Substituting $P_B^*(Q^*)$ from the seller's usual $MC = MR$ first order conditions for maximum profit into (12), solving for the $R_{Bj}(N_j^*)$ and rewriting, we obtain

$$r_{Bj}(N_j^*)N_j^* = \ln(\bar{P}_L/P_B^*(Q)) \qquad (j=1,\ldots,n). \tag{13}$$

Clearly, the greater the common price discount to be given, the longer must be the credit period, although buyers with high discount rates must be given smaller N_j^*. Of course, when the seller is subverting a collusive price-fixing agreement, he must announce reasonable nominal credit terms, keeping the actual terms a secret between himself and the buyer. This mechanism would appear to offer a rational explanation for the widespread practice of allowing trade debtors to stretch their credit periods.

The same mechanism can also work in reverse. If the government introduces price controls to reduce the rate of inflation, an oligopolistic trade creditor who makes a practice of offering lengthy de facto credit periods, can achieve an increase in effective price by shortening the credit periods. Schwartz (1974) notes that this tightening of trade credit would come at just the time when increased trade credit is needed to counter the effects of greater bank credit rationing which occurs during periods of monetary restraint.

6.2. Price discrimination

Suppose the seller wishes to price discriminate, but is constrained legally or otherwise to charge the same list price to all buyers. If he is free to vary credit periods, he may evade the constraint by setting N_j^* to satisfy (12) above. The procedure is as follows: The monopolist solves the standard $MR_j = MC$ condition for optimal discrimination, finding P_{Bj}^* which differ in general across buyers. P_L^* may then be set (by an iterative procedure) such that one buyer gets the customary nominal net period, N_0 (e.g. 30 days), and all other buyers get effective $N_j^* \geqslant N_0$. Then using the convenient definition $MR = P(1-1/\epsilon)$, sign ϵ $= -\text{sign}\,dQ/dP$, we must have at the optimum

$$P_L\exp\left[-R_{B1}(N_1^*)\right]\left(1-\frac{1}{|\epsilon_1|}\right) = \ldots = P_L\exp\left[-R_{Bj}(N_j^*)\right]\left(1-\frac{1}{|\epsilon_j|}\right) = \ldots$$

$$= C'\left(\sum_{j=1}^{n}Q^*_{\ j}\right). \tag{14}$$

Rearranging, solving for $R_{Bj}(N_j^*)$ and rewriting we have

$$r_{Bj}(N_j^*)N_j^* = ln\left[P_L\left(1 - \frac{1}{|\epsilon_j|}\right)/MC \right] \qquad (j=1,\dots,n). \qquad (15)$$

Thus, we have that (to the extent that discount rate functions are similar across buyers at an N), buyers with greater demand elasticity should be given longer credit periods so as to make their effective prices lower.

Where N_j cannot be differentiated freely among buyers, (15) shows that some price discrimination will still be achieved if buyers with relatively high discount rates at the common N also have high demand elasticity. Schwartz and Whitcomb (1978) speculate that this may be so for two reasons. (a) If certain firms have high $r_B(N)$ because they are subject to credit rationing, they may appropriately have higher hurdle rates and reject physical capital and inventory investments which would be attractive to other firms. Thus, a discriminatory lower price may be necessary to induce purchases. (b) High discount rates are generally associated with high risk of failure, and such firms would be quite sensitive to small price differences. We have also noted that a positive association between elasticity and buyer discount rates can explain the two-part trade credit offer; the terms can be set so that the opportunity cost of forgoing the discount (see eq. (1)) is small enough to imply a lower effective price to those buyers with higher discount rates.

7. Cyclical and monetary influences on trade credit terms

A number of writers, including Meltzer (1960), Brechling and Lipsey (1963), and Jaffe (1971), report evidence that credit periods are lengthened in times of restrictive monetary policy. The most detailed study is Jaffe's time series regression of the net trade credit (receivables less payables) to sales ratio on a credit rationing proxy using a four-quarter distributed lag. Jaffe reports results for each of six asset size classes in his table 6.1. While most individual coefficients are insignificant, their pattern is suggestive: the largest corporations increase their net receivables in the quarters following an increase in credit rationing, while smaller corporations reduce net receivables. Jaffe also reports survey data showing that small firms most often face credit rationing and, when rationed, are more likely to turn to trade credit as an alternative source of funds.

The optimization model of section 4, together with the discussion of the effect of credit rationing on the $R_S(N)$ and $R_B(N)$ functions, suggest an explanation of these observations regarding cyclical trade credit variations. Suppose we have a seller offering the credit period N_0 satisfying (10) and (11) to buyers facing moderate credit rationing. If monetary policy becomes restrictive, the evidence of the credit rationing literature suggests those firms already rationed must bear the brunt of the increased rationing, while low risk customers primarily sustain a rise in interest rates. In this situation, $r_B(N)$ would shift up by a greater amount than would $r_S(N)$. The seller's optimum would now be at some $N_1 > N_0$.

Clearly, the seller would raise his list price to compensate for both higher $r_S(N_0)$ and higher N. Thus, Schwartz (1974) notes that restrictive monetary policy may cause a high *perceived* rate of inflation. To the extent that wages, for example, are tied to list price indexes, this contributes to the wage price spiral. Jaffe (1971), Laffer (1970), and Schwartz (1974) also conclude that the cyclical revision of trade credit flows reduces the dampening effect of monetary stringency on real expenditures, making any given degree of stringency less effective, but allowing the monetary authorities to pursue a generally tighter policy than would otherwise be possible.

8. Economic implications and conclusions

8.1. Size distribution of extenders and recipients of trade credit

The credit market imperfections that generate a financial motive for trade credit suggest a net extension of trade credit by the financially strong to the weaker firms. The credit rationing literature holds that firms with high leverage (and by extension, high risk from whatever source) are subject to credit rationing, while those with low leverage are not. Also, where usury laws limit interest rates on loans to unincorporated businesses (and in some states to corporations), and where laws and regulatory practices directly prohibit loans to risky customers, high risk firms will have unsatisfied loan demand. Thus, a flow of trade credit (and prepayment, where it occurs) should predominantly be from the financially strong firms to the weaker, as the stronger seek to profit from interest rate arbitrage. To the extent that financial strength is associated with size, the flow will also be from large to small firms. A large-to-small firm flow will also occur when information on customers' creditworthiness is obtained as a byproduct of sales activities, since such activities should be substantial only among oligopolistic sellers.

The pricing motive suggests the same direction of trade credit flows. Disguised price reductions would be employed only by oligopolistic firms, and an ability to price discriminate implies market power. When a two-part credit offer is used to achieve price discrimination, the buyers with the highest discount rate (the weakest financially) elect to receive the most trade credit.

The literature does not contain a thorough microempirical study of the association between trade credit flows, and size, concentration and risk, but some evidence corroborating these hypotheses is presented in table 12.1. As manufacturing corporations' asset sizes increase, the ratio of receivables/ trade debt rises and trade debt/all current liabilities falls. Durable goods manu- facturers (which are generally larger due to scale economies) have greater receivables/trade debt and lower trade debt/current liabilities than other manufacturers. In wholesale trade (where firms are probably the smallest of all our categories) trade debt forms the largest part of all short term funds.

These data do not enable us to separate the effect of financial strength from that of size, since equity/debt ratios are closely associated with asset size. However, we expect that at least some of the relationship between size and trade credit flows is indeed due to banks credit rationing firms with high leverage.

8.2. Explanation of the rarity of prepayment

Aggregate figures are not available, but it is well known that prepayment (a credit flow from buyer to seller) is uncommon relative to delayed payment. This is at first puzzling, since one would also expect to observe financially strong buyers facing credit rationed sellers. In this case, we could have $r_B(N) < r_S(N)$ over a wide range of $N \geqslant 0$; with no reason for the inequality to be reversed, no

Table 12.1. Trade credit and risk ratios by corporate size and type, first quarter 1976.[a]

	Receivables	Trade debt	Total equity
	Trade debt	Current liabilities	Total debt
Manufacturers by asset size ($MM)			
All	2.01	0.338	2.40
Under 1	1.57	0.495	1.81
1–5	1.65	0.447	1.94
5–10	1.87	0.396	2.02
10–25	2.12	0.368	2.31
25–50	2.20	0.370	2.07
50–100	2.38	0.347	2.04
100–250	2.48	0.317	2.06
250–1,000	2.39	0.319	2.10
1,000 and over	1.91	0.299	2.79
Corporations by type			
Durable manufacturers	2.14	0.297	2.36
Non-durable manufacturers	1.88	0.390	2.44
Mining	1.64	0.331	1.71
Wholesale trade	1.32	0.510	1.42
Retail trade	1.00[b]	0.420	1.47

[a]*Source*: U S Federal Trade Commission (1976).
[b]The numerator of this ratio is largely consumer credit, not trade credit.

positive N would satisfy eqs. (12) and (13), the first and second order conditions for N^*. In such a case, both the seller and buyer could benefit from agreeing to negative N (prepayment); given that $r_S(N)$ approaches $r_B(N)$ from above as $|N|$ becomes larger and the seller's capital composition improves, there is an optimal $N^* < 0$.

The infrequency of $N^* < 0$ may be partly explained by our discussion of transaction costs. Presumably, financial institutions (including factors, finance companies, and others able and willing to lend to high risk firms) usually have a cost advantage over nonfinancial institutions due to economies of scale and specialization in lending. As we suggested in section 5, this advantage may be outweighed when sales activities generate credit information as a byproduct. As we noted, it is rare that purchasing activities would generate much credit information. Exceptions are long lived products where the buyer would be hurt if the producer failed to deliver the product or spare parts; it is in just such industries (ship-building, construction, machinery) where we observe substantial prepayment.

It would be wrong to conclude that the preponderance of delayed payment over prepayment refutes the credit rationing hypothesis. Jaffe's (1971) evidence of a cyclical connection between monetary stringency and trade credit is fairly persuasive. We suggest that trade credit is most likely to flow where two conditions are met: (1) sales activity generates credit information, and (2) the buyer but not the seller is subject to credit rationing.

Our discussion of the pricing motive might also appear to suggest a reason for prepayment. If a small group of buyers (oligopsonists) conspire to extract a low price from a product's sellers, one buyer may benefit (i.e. obtain additional supply at a marginal factor cost less than marginal revenue product) by offering a sub rosa prepayment. This would suggest common use of prepayment if oligopsony were as prevalent as oligopoly. However, while there has been relatively little work on buyer market imperfections, Guth, Schwartz and Whitcomb (1977) report buyer concentration ratios that are substantially less than seller concentration ratios for the same products; hence, relatively few products appear to have oligopsonistic markets.

8.3. Welfare effects of trade credit

In several ways, trade credit may serve partially to alleviate the allocational inefficiencies and discriminatory effects of imperfect credit and product markets. As we showed in section 5, with imperfect credit but perfect product markets, the $r_B(N)$ and $r_S(N)$ functions will tend to shift toward each other and become coincident, with substantial trade credit necessarily being extended in equilibrium. Among those benefiting are the (generally small) firms subject to credit rationing. The benefit will be greatest in periods of restrictive monetary policy.

However, we cannot conclude that the financial market imperfections are eliminated unless financial sector firms enjoy no unrealized economies of scale and specialization. If "banks" do have such an advantage over nonfinancial lenders, their required returns on loans to credit rationed firms will be below those of sellers, and a Pareto optimality condition will be violated. Clearly, however, actual and potential competition from trade credit limits the ability of financial sector firms to credit ration and creates opportunities to circumvent legal restrictions on interest rates and loans to risky borrowers. In imperfect product markets, trade credit may be a vehicle for disguised price competition and may thus bring effective prices closer to those which would prevail in perfectly competitive equilibrium. However, at conventional interest rates it would take extremely long credit periods to effect a substantial reduction in effective price.

8.4. Trade credit policy

Our emphasis on perfect market indifference propositions and reduction of market imperfections by trade credit extension might leave the impression that in "workably competitive" markets the trade credit decision (like the capital structure decision) may be made arbitrarily, at least within a wide range of N. This would not be a correct impression because, even in perfect markets, it is possible to make a wrong trade credit decision. If the seller sets any $N > 0$, he must estimate the $r_B(N)$ function so as to avoid setting a list price which is not optimal. That is, by eq. (6), determining P_L^* given an N chosen arbitrarily or otherwise requires knowledge of P_B^* and $r_B(N)$. We have suggested that, in perfect credit markets, the CAPM provides a means of estimating $r_B(N)$ $[= r_S(N)]$.

In imperfect credit markets where the seller is not subject to credit rationing, he may use the CAPM to estimate $r_S(N)$, but must obtain $r_B(N)$ by other means. We have not investigated this problem; it is very likely that the somewhat arbitrary and traditional terms of trade credit are explained by the difficulty of obtaining accurate estimates of $r_B(N)$.

Probably the most important implication of the examination of pricing motives for trade credit is that trade credit policy is not simply a financial decision, as most finance texts take it to be. In imperfect product markets the trade credit decision is an integral part of the firm's general pricing policy. Also, it is important to recognize that the financing motive provides a direct link between aggregate monetary conditions and the pricing decisions of individual firms.

References

Arzac, E., R. Schwartz and D. Whitcomb (1979a) "A Theory and Test of Credit Rationing: Some Further Results", Working Paper, January.

Arzac, E., R. Schwartz and D. Whitcomb (1979b) "The Leverage Structure of Interest Rates", Working Paper, February.

Baltensperger, E. (1976) "The Borrower–Lender Relationship, Competitive Equilibrium, and the Theory of Hedonic Prices", *American Economic Review* 66, 401–405.

Brechling, F. and R. Lipsey (1963) "Trade Credit and Monetary Policy", *Economic Journal* 73, 619–641.

Guth, L., R. Schwartz and D. Whitcomb (1977) "Buyer Concentration Ratios", *Journal of Industrial Economics* 25, 241–258.

Jaffe, D. (1971) *Credit Rationing and the Commercial Loan Market* (Wiley, New York).

Jaffe, D. and F. Modigliani (1969) "A Theory and Test of Credit Rationing", *American Economic Review* 59, 850–872.

Laffer, A. (1970) "Trade Credit and the Money Market", *Journal of Political Economy* 78, 239–267.

Leland, H.E. and D. H. Pyle (1977) "Informational Asymmetries, Financial Structure, and Financial Intermediation", *Journal of Finance* 32, 371–387.

Meltzer, A. (1960) "Mercantile Credit, Monetary Policy, and Size of Firms", *Review of Economics and Statistics* 42, 429–437.

Merton, R. (1974) "On the Pricing of Corporate Debt: The Risk Structure of Interest Rates", *Journal of Finance* 29, 449–470.

Miller, M. H. and C. W. Upton (1976) "Leasing, Buying, and the Cost of Capital Services", *Journal of Finance* 31, 761–786.

Pringle, J. J. and R. A. Cohn (1974) "Steps Toward an Integration of Corporate Financial Planning", in: K. V. Smith, ed., *Management of Working Capital* (West, New York) pp. 369–375.

Rubenstein, M. (1973) "A Mean-Variance Synthesis of Corporate Financial Theory", *Journal of Finance* 27, 167–181.

Sandmo, A. (1971) "On the Theory of the Competitive Firm Under Price Uncertainty", *American Economic Review* 61, 65–73.

Schwartz, R.A. (1974) "An Economic Model of Trade Credit", *Journal of Financial and Quantitative Analysis* 8, 643–657.

Schwartz, R.A. and D.K. Whitcomb (1978) "Implicit Transfers in the Extension of Trade Credit", in K. Boulding and T. Wilson, eds., *The Channels of Redistribution Through the Financial System: The Grants Economics of Money and Credit* (Praeger, New York).

Seiden, M. (1964) *The Quality of Trade Credit*, Occasional Paper 87 (National Bureau of Economic Research).

Smith, K.V. (1974) *Management of Working Capital* (West,

Smith, K.V. (1974) *Management of Working Capital* (West, New York).

Smith, V. (1972) "A Theory and Test of Credit Rationing: Some Generalizations", *American Economic Review* 62, 477–483.

Stiglitz, J.E. (1974) "On the Irrelevance of Corporate Financial Policy", *American Economic Review* 64, 851–866.

US Federal Trade Commission (1976) *Quarterly Financial Report for Manufacturing, Mining and Trade Corporations*, Second Quarter.

Wrightsman, D. (1969) "Optimal Credit for Accounts Receivable", *The Quarterly Review of Economics and Business* 9, 59–66.

Chapter 13

A THEORY OF CORPORATE BANKRUPTCY AND OPTIMAL CAPITAL STRUCTURE

ANDREW H. CHEN*
Ohio State University

1. Introduction

In their pathbreaking article, Modigliani and Miller (MM) (1958) relied on the risk–class assumption and the familiar arbitrage argument to prove that in the absence of corporate income taxes and bankruptcy risk the value of a firm was invariant to its capital structure. In their later work, MM (1963) showed that in the presence of corporate income taxes but in the absence of bankruptcy risk there would be a linear relationship between the value of a firm and that of its debt. The well known implication of the MM tax model for financial management is that a firm should maximize its use of debt in order to capture the benefit of tax subsidy on interest payments on the debt. Several subsequent studies have shown that the MM results can be obtained under more general conditions. (See, for example, Baron (1974), Hamada (1969), Rubinstein (1973) and Stiglitz (1969, 1974).) In an empirical study, MM (1966) concluded that their empirical results were consistent with their propositions on the theory of financial leverage. However, the MM empirical study was criticized by some authors on the empirical procedures as well as interpretations of the empirical results. (See, for example, Crockett and Friend (1967), Gordon (1967), and Robichek et al. (1967).)

Recently several authors have argued that in the presence of both corporate income taxes and costly bankruptcy there might exist an optimal capital structure for a firm. (See for example, Robichek and Myers (1966), Baxter (1967), Hirschleifer (1970), Kraus and Litzenberger (1973), Scott (1976), Kim (1978), Elton et al. (1976), Lee and Barker (1977), and Chen (1977, 1978).) The debt is utilized up to the point where the gain from tax savings on the debt is just offset by the expected cost of bankruptcy. With the exception of Scott (1976) and

*The author wishes to thank A. J. Boness, J. L. Bicksler, M. J. Gordon, E. J. Kane, E. H. Kim, G. A. Racette and J. H. Scott for valuable comments on this paper.

James L. Bicksler, Editor, Handbook of Financial Economics
© *North-Holland Publishing Company – 1979*

Elton et al. (1976), all the previous studies on the optimal capital structure with corporate income taxes and costly bankruptcy are within the framework of one-period models. Since it is impossible to make distinction between corporate reorganization and liquidation in the single-period framework, the one-period models are inadequate for analyzing the dynamic characteristics of the capital structure problem.

Although Scott has made an important contribution to the theory of optimal capital structure by incorporating a more realistic definition of bankruptcy for an on-going firm advanced by Stiglitz (1972) into a multiperiod model, his study suffers the following major limitations: (1) risk-neutrality is assumed for investors in the capital market; (2) bankruptcy cost is narrowly defined; and (3) the model of firm valuation is not expressed in a way that direct comparisons with the MM model can easily be done. In their paper, Elton et al. (1976) have applied the time–state preference theory to study the effect of corporate bankruptcy on the optimal capital structure of a firm within a multiperiod framework. Although the transfer of ownership upon bankruptcy-reorganization is considered in the paper, they have failed to specify a bankruptcy criterion so firm value has not been expressed as a function of the probability of bankruptcy. In other words, they have analyzed ex post rather than ex ante effects of bankruptcy on the value of a firm.

The purpose of this paper is to provide a more complete analysis of optimal capital structure with corporate income taxes and costly bankruptcy. The models of equity, debt and firm valuation are derived with explicit considerations of *bankruptcy-reorganization* and *bankruptcy-liquidation* alternatives. Furthermore, the more generally defined bankruptcy costs are incorporated into models. The important feature of the current models is that they are directly comparable with the MM results.

Section 2 of this paper discusses briefly the multiperiod capital asset pricing model — a proper way to evaluate an uncertain income stream, and discusses the criterion of corporate bankruptcy. Section 3 derives and analyzes the valuation equations for equity, debt and the firm with corporate income taxes and costly bankruptcy. The models of firm valuation are formulated for the purpose of direct comparison with the MM tax model. The final section briefly concludes the paper.

2. Key elements in a multiperiod model of financial decisions

We have to specify the form of firm's objective function for financial decisions before the optimal leverage policy of an on-going firm can be meaningfully studied. Under the assumption that the managers of a firm follow the market-value rule and maximize the market value of the firm in their financial decisions, it is then important to start our discussion of the optimal leverage policy by examining how a stream of uncertain future cash flows can be properly evaluated. Furthermore, the bankruptcy of an on-going firm has to be properly and realistically defined before we can address ourselves to the important issues of optimal capital structure of a firm in a multiperiod setting. Thus, a multiperiod capital asset pricing model under uncertainty and the definition of bankruptcy for an on-going firm will be briefly discussed in what follows.

2.1. A multiperiod CAPM

Under conditions of perfect capital markets, the market value of a firm under certainty is equal to the sum of discounted certain net cash flows of the firm. However, under uncertainty the future stream of cash flows of a firm is uncertain. Thus, the uncertainty in a firm's future cash flows has to be taken into account in the determination of the market value of the firm. Several authors, for example, Bogue and Roll (1974), Stevens (1974), Fama (1977) and Myers and Turnbull (1977), have recently extended the single-period Sharpe–Lintner–Mossin capital asset pricing model (CAPM) into a multiperiod framework for the purpose of evaluating a stream of uncertain cash flows. Fama has pointed out that under the assumption that the Sharpe–Lintner–Mossin CAPM holds in every period the only admissible risk is the uncertainty associated with the reassessments of expectations and that the market parameters (the market price of risk and the future risk-free interest rates) should be nonstochastic. Therefore, using the risk-adjusted discount rate approach, Fama has shown that the value of any future cash flow is the current expected value of the flow discounted at nonstochastic risk-adjusted discount rates for each of the periods until the flow is realized. Myers and Turnbull, on the other hand, have applied the certainty-equivalent approach to derive their asset valuation model and to show that the risk associated with revision of expectations complicates the real determinants of beta in capital budgeting decisions.

For our present purpose to study the effects of financial leverage on the value of a firm and the cost of capital we can conveniently assume that the parameters of expectations are known in all earlier periods, since for a given investment plan the firm's *basic* cash flows are not affected by its financial choices. Therefore, we assume that the market value of a stream of uncertain cash flows is equal to the sum of discounted certainty-equivalent (CEQ) of the cash flows. The risk-adjustment factor is simply a product of the market price of risk and the relevant risk measure of the cash flows (the covariance between the asset's cash flows and that of all cash flows in the economy). Specifically, the market value of an asset at time $t=0$ can be written as

$$V(0) = \sum_{t=1}^{\infty} \{ E[\tilde{C}(t)] - \lambda(t)[CV(\tilde{C}(t), \tilde{M}(t))] \} \prod_{s=1}^{t} [1 + r(s)]^{-1}, \qquad (1)$$

where

$\tilde{C}(t) =$ the random cash flow of the asset at time t;
$\tilde{M}(t) =$ the random cash flows of all assets in the economy at time t;
$\lambda(t) =$ the market price of risk at time t. $\lambda(t) = E[\tilde{M}(t) - (1 + r(t)) M(t-1)]/\sigma^2[\tilde{M}(t)]$; and
$E(\cdot)$ and $CV(\cdot)$ denote expectation and covariance, respectively.

2.2. Definition of bankruptcy for an on-going firm

The definition of bankruptcy for a firm in a single-period model is relatively simple. A firm is declared bankrupt at the end of the period if the terminal value of the firm is less than its total fixed obligations to the creditors. (See, for example, Kraus and Litzenberger (1973), Lee and Barker (1977), Kim (1978) and Chen (1977).) However, this definition of bankruptcy is not appropriate for an on-going firm. Stiglitz (1972) defines the bankruptcy criterion in a multiperiod model as follows: "A firm is bankrupt if the value of its equity is zero (it cannot be negative under conditions of limited liability), or equivalently, if the value of its future income streams, assuring it does not go bankrupt, is less than the value of its outstanding debt."[1] Therefore, the income of an on-going firm can be less than its fixed obligations and yet it remains solvent, since it can obtain funds in a perfect capital market to pay current obligations. Thus, an on-going firm can only be declared bankrupt if it is unable to meet its current obligations to the creditors. Let us describe the bankruptcy criterion for an on-going firm more precisely in the following paragraph.

At time t, if the firm's net operating income $X(t)$ exceeds the interest payments, $I(t)$, and if θ is the constant proportional corporate income tax rate, then $(1-\theta)[X(t) - I(t)]$ is the after-tax net income available to the firm's stockholders. Let the equilibrium ex-dividend market value of equity at time t be $V_E(t)$, then the wealth of stockholders at time t is equal to $V_E(t) + (1-\theta)[X(t) - I(t)]$. On the other hand, if $X(t)$ is less than $I(t)$, the stockholders of the firm must raise enough money to meet the interest payments or the firm will be declared bankrupt. A firm can sell additional equity in an efficient and perfect securities market to meet its interest payments as long as the total value of

---

[1]See Stiglitz (1972, p. 460). Scott (1976) has recently applied this definition of bankruptcy in his study of the optimal capital structure of a firm.

stockholder wealth is positive, that is $V_E(t)+(1-\theta)[X(t)-I(t)]>0$.[2] However, there is a limit on which additional equity can be sold to meet the after-tax losses. If the firm's net operating loss is so large that the total value of stockholder wealth becomes zero or negative, it will not be possible for the firm to sell any additional equity to meet the obligations of interest payments, and hence the firm is declared bankrupt and the stockholders receive nothing. Therefore, within a multiperiod framework, an on-going firm is declared bankrupt at time t if

$$X(t) \leqslant I(t) - V_E(t)(1-\theta)^{-1}. \tag{2}$$

3. The valuation models

To examine the effect of corporate leverage on the value of a firm, it is assumed that firms issue equity and only one type of senior debt, both of which have limited liability and are traded in a perfect securities market. All investors in the securities market are assumed to be risk-averse and to have all relevant information. Therefore, both equity and debt of the firm are priced in the capital market according to the multiperiod capital asset pricing model under uncertainty described in the previous section. We shall assume that firms are subject to a constant income tax rate and that interest payments are tax-deductible. Since bankruptcy is possible, in the event the stockholders are unable to meet the fixed obligations the firm is declared bankrupt. Upon bankruptcy, the stockholders' claim on the firm is lost and the ownership of the firm is transferred to the creditors.

In what follows we shall first derive the market value of an all-equity firm. We then derive the market values of equity and risky debt for three cases, namely a bankrupt firm can only be reorganized, can only be liquidated, and can either be reorganized or liquidated. The sum of the market values of equity and debt is the market value of the firm upon which the impact of corporate leverage will be analyzed.

3.1. The market value of an all-equity firm

In the presence of business risk and short-term creditors, it is assumed that the unlevered firms are also subject to the risk of bankruptcy. Under the assumption that corporate securities are traded in a perfect capital market, the impact of

---

[2]See Scott (1976) for discussions of why issuing additional equity is preferred to issuing additional debt or selling assets of the firm.

future possible bankruptcy is fully reflected in the security prices. Since the stockholders receive nothing if a firm is declared bankrupt, they will first attempt to avert bankruptcy by issuing additional equity as long as stockholder wealth is positive. An on-going unlevered firm is declared bankrupt if the wealth of stockholders is equal to or less than zero. Thus, the wealth of stockholders of the unlevered firm at the end of period t is given by

$$\tilde{Y}(t) = \begin{cases} (1-\theta)\tilde{X}(t) + V(t), & \text{if } X(t) > -V(t)(1-\theta)^{-1} \equiv Z(t), \\ 0, & \text{otherwise}, \end{cases} \tag{3}$$

where $\tilde{X}(t)$ denotes the before-tax earnings in period t and $V(t)$ the ex-dividend market value of the unlevered firm at the end of period t, respectively.

The equilibrium market value of the unlevered firm at the beginning of period t (or equivalently, at the end of period $t-1$) is

$$V(t-1) = \frac{1}{1+r(t)} \left\{ CEQ[\,\tilde{Y}(t)\,] \right\}$$

$$= \frac{1}{1+r(t)} \left\{ (1-\theta)[\, E_{Z(t)}(\tilde{X}(t)) - \lambda(t)CV_{Z(t)}(\tilde{X}(t),\tilde{M}(t)) \,] \right.$$

$$\left. + V(t)[\, 1 - F(Z(t)) \,] \right\} \tag{4}$$

where

$$r(t) = \text{the risk-free rate of interest in period } t;$$

$$E_{Z(t)}(\tilde{X}(t)) = \int_{Z(t)}^{\infty} \tilde{X}(t) f(\tilde{X}(t)) \mathrm{d}\tilde{X}(t);$$

$$CV_{Z(t)}[\,\tilde{X}(t),\tilde{M}(t)\,] = \text{the partial covariance between } \tilde{X}(t) \text{ (truncated from } Z(t) \text{ upward) and } \tilde{M}(t);[3] \text{ and}$$

$$F(Z(t)) = \int_{-\infty}^{Z(t)} f(\tilde{X}(t)) \mathrm{d}\tilde{X}(t) = \text{the probability of bankruptcy at time } t.$$

In general, the following notation will be used:

$$E_a^b(\tilde{X}) = \int_a^b \tilde{X} f(\tilde{X}) \mathrm{d}\tilde{X}$$

and

$$CV_a^b(\tilde{X},\tilde{M}) = E\{[\,\tilde{X}_a^b - E_a^b(\tilde{X})\,][\,\tilde{M} - E(\tilde{M})\,]\}.$$

The absence of a subscript (or superscript) implies that the limit of integration or the limit of partial covariance is $-\infty$ (or ∞).

---

[3] Several useful properties of the partial moments are presented in Lintner (1977).

Using the recursive relations in dynamic programming, we can express the *current* equilibrium market value of the unlevered firm as

$$V = \sum_{t=1}^{\infty} \frac{\prod_{s=1}^{t} \{1 - F[Z(s-1)]\} \{(1-\theta)[E_{Z(t)}[\tilde{X}(t)] - \lambda(t)CV_{Z(t)}(\tilde{X}(t), \tilde{M}(t))]\}}{\prod_{s=1}^{t} [1 + r(s)]}.$$

(5)

For expositional simplicity, we shall assume in the following analysis a zero-growth firm with net operating incomes identically and temporally independently distributed.[4] We further assume that the term structure of interest rates is flat and that the market price of risk is constant over time. As a result, the expression for the market value of the unlevered firm in (5) can be greatly simplified to[5]

$$V = \frac{(1-\theta)[E_Z(\tilde{X}) - \lambda CV_Z(\tilde{X}, \tilde{M})]}{r + F(Z)},$$

(6)

where $F(Z) = \int_{-\infty}^{Z} f(\tilde{X}) d\tilde{X}$, the identical probability that the firm will not survive at the end of each period, and $Z = -V(1-\theta)^{-1}$.

The numerator on the right-hand side of (6) is the per period risk-adjusted expected net income to the stockholders of the unlevered firm. The first term in the denominator is the risk-free interest rate and the second term is the probability of bankruptcy which can be regarded as a bankruptcy premium.

Define $E(\tilde{R}_e)$ as the equilibrium expected rate of return on the securities of the zero-growth all-equity firm such that

$$V = \frac{(1-\theta)E_Z(\tilde{X})}{E(\tilde{R}_e) + F(Z)}$$

(7)

---

[4]Note that a systematic growth rate in the firm's net operating incomes can be easily incorporated into the analysis.

[5]Under the simplifying assumptions, eq. (5) can be written as

$$V = \sum_{t=1}^{\infty} \frac{[1 - F(Z)]^{t-1} \{(1-\theta)[E_Z(\tilde{X}) - \lambda CV_Z(\tilde{X}, \tilde{M})]\}}{(1+r)^t}$$

$$= \frac{(1-\theta)[E_Z(\tilde{X}) - \lambda CV_Z(\tilde{X}, \tilde{M})]}{(1+r)} \left[1 + \frac{[1 - F(Z)]}{(1+r)} + \frac{[1 - F(Z)]^2}{(1+r)^2} + \frac{[1 - F(Z)]^3}{(1+r)^3} + \ldots \right]$$

$$= \frac{(1-\theta)[E_Z(\tilde{X}) - \lambda CV_Z(\tilde{X}, \tilde{M})]}{(1+r)} \left[\frac{1}{1 - [1 - F(Z)]/(1+r)} \right]$$

$$= \frac{(1-\theta)[E_Z(\tilde{X}) - \lambda CV_Z(\tilde{X}, \tilde{M})]}{r + F(Z)},$$

which is (6) in the text.

From (6) and (7), we can derive

$$E(\tilde{R}_e)=[r+F(Z)][1-\lambda CV_Z(\tilde{X},\tilde{M})/E_Z(\tilde{X})]^{-1}-F(Z). \tag{8}$$

Therefore, the *cost of equity capital* for an all-equity zero-growth firm is a function of its systematic business risk $(CV(\tilde{X},\tilde{M},))$, its bankruptcy premium $(F(Z))$ and the risk-free interest rate.

3.2. *The market value of equity of the levered firm*

Since common stock has limited liability and stockholders receive nothing if a firm is declared bankrupt, the stockholders of a levered firm will first attempt to avoid bankruptcy by issuing additional equity as long as stockholder wealth is positive. If the wealth of stockholders is equal to or less than zero, the firm is declared bankrupt and the stockholders receive nothing. For expositional simplicity, we maintain the stationarity assumptions in the previous section to derive the market value of equity of the levered firm. We further assume that the firm's debt is a perpetual bond with a coupon interest, I, which is tax-deductible.[6] Under these circumstances, the wealth of stockholders of the levered firm at the end of any period is given by

$$\tilde{Y}_E \begin{cases} (1-\theta)(X-I)+V_E, & \text{if } X>I-V_E(1-\theta)^{-1} \\ 0, & \text{otherwise.} \end{cases} \tag{9}$$

We can derive the current market value of the levered firm's equity as follows:

$$V_E=\frac{1}{1+r}[CEQ(\tilde{Y}_E)]$$

$$=\frac{1}{1+r}\{(1-\theta)[E_b(\tilde{X}-I)-\lambda CV_b(\tilde{X},\tilde{M})]+[1-F(b)]V_E\},$$

or

$$V_E=(1-\theta)[E_b(\tilde{X}-I)-\lambda CV_b(\tilde{X},\tilde{M})]/[r+F(b)], \tag{10}$$

where

$$F(b)=\int_{-\infty}^{b}f(\tilde{X})d\tilde{X}, \text{ the identical probability of bankruptcy for the levered firm at the end of each period;}$$

$$E_b(\tilde{X}-I)=\int_{b}^{\infty}(\tilde{X}-I)f(\tilde{X})d\tilde{X}; \text{ and}$$

$$b=I-V_E(1-\theta)^{-1}.$$

---

[6]Note that there is no problem with respect to the maturity structure of the firm's debt, since the firm, if it does not go bankrupt, can refinance any maturing debt by issuing new debt on the same terms in the efficient capital market.

Thus, the value of a levered firm's equity is simply the risk-adjusted expected net income available to the stockholders divided by the sum of the risk-free interest rate and the bankruptcy premium. Note that (10) reduces to the same equity valuation equation in Scott (1976) if investors are assumed to be risk-neutral.

Using the equity valuation equation in (10), we can derive the cost of equity capital for a levered firm as

$$E(\tilde{R}_e) = [r + F(b)]\{1 - \lambda CV_b(\tilde{X}, \tilde{M}) / [E_b(\tilde{X}) - I(1 - F(b))]\}^{-1} - F(b).$$

$$(11)$$

3.3. The market values of risky debt and the firm

If the firm remains solvent, the wealth of bondholders is equal to $I + V_D$, where V_D is the market value of the bond. However, in the event the stockholders of the firm are incapable of meeting the fixed obligations to the bondholders, one of the following two possible situations will occur to the bankrupt firm: (1) straight, or ordinary bankruptcy, or (2) corporate reorganization. These are two different events in which the bondholder wealth is not the same. Upon a straight bankruptcy the assets of the firm are liquidated privately or publicly and the proceeds are distributed to the claimholders according to the priority of claims. Thus, a straight bankruptcy means the termination of a business enterprise. A corporate reorganization, however, provides the means by which the business enterprise and its value as a going concern are preserved. Therefore, in deriving the valuation formulae for risky debt and the firm, we shall make a distinction between *bankruptcy-reorganization* and *bankruptcy-liquidation*.

3.3.1. The case of bankruptcy-reorganization

In the event stockholders are unable to meet the fixed obligations and the firm is declared bankrupt, the stockholders lose all their claims on the firm. If corporate reorganization is chosen for the bankrupt firm, the stockholders should be excluded in principle from the participation in the reorganized firm. However, they are often allowed by the court settlements to participate in the reorganized firm in certain ways. Therefore, *bankruptcy-reorganization* will be examined in two different ways. First, upon bankruptcy the entire ownership of the bankrupt firm is transferred to the bondholders. Secondly, upon bankruptcy only a partial transfer of ownership of the firm to the bondholders will occur.

(1) *Total Transfer of Ownership*. Upon bankruptcy-reorganization, it is assumed that the bondholders take over the entire ownership of the bankrupt firm under the plan of reorganization and bear all losses and expenses incurred during reorganization proceeding. Furthermore, assume for simplicity that the

firm's future earnings will not be affected by reorganization, so the value of the reorganized firm is the same as that of the on-going firm and can be denoted by V. Therefore, upon bankruptcy-reorganization bondholder wealth can be expressed as $V+(1-\theta)X-C$, where C is the explicit cost of reorganization.[7] Thus, bondholder wealth at the end of the period is given by

$$\tilde{Y}_D = \begin{cases} I+V_D, & \text{if } X > I - V_E(1-\theta)^{-1} \equiv b, \\ V+(1-\theta)\tilde{X}-C, & \text{if } b \geqslant X > (C-V)(1-\theta)^{-1} \equiv h_1, \\ 0, & \text{if } h_1 \geqslant X, \end{cases} \tag{12}$$

The equilibrium market value of the firm's risky debt is given by

$$V_D = \frac{1}{1+r}\left[CEQ(\tilde{Y}_D)\right]$$

$$= \frac{1}{1+r}\left\{E_b[I+V_D]+E_{h_1}^b[V+(1-\theta)\tilde{X}-C]-\lambda(1-\theta)CV_{h_1}^b(\tilde{X},\tilde{M})\right\},$$

or

$$V_D = \frac{[1-F(b)]I+(1-\theta)\left[E_{h_1}^b(\tilde{X})-\lambda CV_{h_1}^b(\tilde{X},\tilde{M})\right]+[F(b)-F(h_1)][V-C]}{r+F(b)}. \tag{13}$$

It can be shown from (13) that the *cost of debt capital* for the levered firm is given by

$$E(\tilde{R}_d)=[r+F(b)]\left(\frac{Q}{Q-q}\right)-F(b), \tag{14}$$

where

$$Q=[1-F(b)]I+[F(b)-F(h_1)](V-C)+(1-\theta)E_{h_1}^b(\tilde{X}),$$

$$q=(1-\theta)\lambda CV_{h_1}^b(\tilde{X},\tilde{M})$$

It can be easily seen from (13) that if the probability of bankruptcy is zero the market value of the riskless perpetual debt is simply $V_D^*=I/r$.

Adding up the market value of equity in (10) and the market value of debt in (13), we derive the market value of the levered firm as follows

$$V_L = V_E + V_D$$

$$= \frac{(1-\theta)CEQ_{h_1}(\tilde{X})+[1-F(b)]\theta I+[F(b)-F(h_1)](V-C)}{r+F(b)}, \tag{15}$$

where $CEQ_{h_1}(\tilde{X})=E_{h_1}(\tilde{X})-\lambda CV_{h_1}(\tilde{X},\tilde{M})$.

---

[7]We are assuming here that the computation of corporate income taxes remains the same upon bankruptcy-reorganization. The loss of tax credit upon bankruptcy will be explicitly treated in the case of bankruptcy-liquidation to be analyzed below.

In the following, we shall rewrite V_L in (15) in a way that a more direct comparison between the current result and that of MM can be made.

From the expression of the market value of an unlevered firm in (6), we have

$$V[r+F(Z)]=(1-\theta)CEQ_Z(\tilde{X})$$

$$=(1-\theta)CEQ_Z^{h_1}(\tilde{X})+(1-\theta)CEQ_{h_1}(\tilde{X}), \tag{16}$$

and hence

$$(1-\theta)CEQ_{h_1}(\tilde{X})=V[r+F(Z)]-(1-\theta)CEQ_Z^{h_1}(\tilde{X}). \tag{17}$$

Substituting (17) into (15) and defining the value of riskless debt, V_D^*, as I/r, we can express the market value of the levered firm as follows:

$$V_L=V+\theta V_D^*+H_1,$$

where

$$H_1=-[r+F(b)]^{-1}\{\theta IF(b)(1+1/r)+[F(b)-F(h_1)]C$$
$$+[F(h_1)-F(Z)]V+(1-\theta)CEQ_Z^{h_1}(\tilde{X})\}. \tag{18}$$

Note that θV_D^* is the present value of the tax subsidy on interest payments on a riskless perpetual bond, and the term H_1 arises because (1) the interest payments and consequently the tax subsidy are eliminated upon bankruptcy-reorganization; (2) there exists an explicit cost of reorganization; and (3) the bondholders are protected by limited liability. Thus, the market value of the levered firm is equal to the market value of the otherwise identical unlevered firm, plus the market value of the tax subsidy on interest payments on a perpetual riskless bond, and plus an adjustment term arises because of changes in bondholder wealth upon bankruptcy-reorganization.

The following points are worth noting from the examination of the market value of the levered firm as given in (18).

First, if the probability of bankruptcy is zero, the value of the levered firm in (18) reduces to $V_L=V+\theta V_D^*$, which is the same result as that given in the MM (1963) model. The implication of such a model on the firm's financial policies is well known in the literature.

Secondly, if there is no *explicit* cost of bankruptcy-reorganization (i.e. $C=0$), the value of the levered firm can be expressed as

$$V_L=V+\theta V_D^*-[r+F(b)]^{-1}\{\theta IF(b)(1+1/r)$$
$$+[F(h_1)-F(Z)]V+(1-\theta)CEQ_Z^{h_1}(\tilde{X})\}. \tag{19}$$

Thus, increasing the use of risky debt will increase the value of the firm by an amount smaller than that given in the MM tax model. Since upon bankruptcy-reorganization, the tax subsidy on interest payments is assumed to be eliminated. The possible loss of tax subsidy upon bankruptcy reduces the benefit of debt capital and implies the existence of an optimal capital structure for a firm even in the absence of bankruptcy-reorganization cost.

Only in a very special case in which there is no cost of bankruptcy in the real sense (i.e. no cost of reorganization and no elimination of the tax subsidy on interest payments), then $V_L = V + \theta V_D^*$ and the validity of the MM tax model will be upheld.

Thirdly, in the presence of tax subsidy on corporate interest payments and in the presence of bankruptcy risk and bankruptcy costs, there exists an optimal capital structure less than 100 percent debt for the firm in terms of the level of contractual coupon interest payments which maximizes the value of the firm.[8]

(2) *Partial transfer of ownership.* Let us examine the case of reorganization in which there is only a partial transfer of ownership of the firm from stockholders to bondholders and there is no explicit costs of corporate reorganization. In this situation bondholder wealth at the end of any period is given by

$$\tilde{Y}_D = \begin{cases} I + V_D, & \text{if } X > I - V_E(1-\theta)^{-1} \equiv b, \\ I' + \alpha[V + (1-\theta)(\tilde{X} - I')], & \text{if } b \geqslant X > W, \\ 0, & \text{if } X \leqslant W, \end{cases} \tag{20}$$

where α denotes the fraction of ownership of the bankrupt firm transferred to the bondholders, I' is the per period interest payment to the bondholders upon bankruptcy-reorganization, and $W = I' - [I'/\alpha + V](1-\theta)^{-1}$.

The equilibrium market value of the firm's risky debt is given by

$$V_D = \frac{1}{1+r}[CEQ(\tilde{Y}_D)]$$

or

$$V_D = \frac{[1 - F(b)]I + [F(b) - F(W)](1-\alpha)I' + \alpha(1-\theta)CEQ_W^b(\tilde{X}) + \alpha[F(b) - F(W)][V + \theta I']}{r + F(b)} \tag{21}$$

The sum of the first two terms in the numerator on the right-hand side of (21) represents the expected per period coupon payments to the bondholders and the sum of the next two terms represents the fraction of the risk-adjusted expected value of the bankrupt firm which belongs to the bondholders upon corporate reorganization.

---

[8]Using the procedures in Scott (1976), we can differentiate (18) with respect to I to derive the necessary conditions for the existence of a maximum. Note that V_L in (18) is a concave function of I and the interior maximum is reached at the point where the marginal expected increment in tax subsidy on interest payments is equal to the marginal expected increment in bankruptcy costs resulting from promising one additional dollar of coupon interest payments.

Similarly, we can derive the market values of equity and the firm under the assumption that a partial transfer of ownership from shareholders to bond-holders will take place upon bankruptcy-reorganization. The market value of the firm is given by

$$V_L = V + \theta V_D^* + H_2, \tag{22}$$

where

$$H_2 = [r + F(b)]^{-1}\{[F(b) - F(h_2)]\theta I' - \theta IF(b)(1 + 1/r)$$
$$+ [F(Z) - F(h_2)]V + (1-\theta)CEQ_{h_2}^Z(\tilde{X})\},$$

$$h_2 = -(V + \theta I')(1-\theta)^{-1}.$$

Thus, under the assumption that a partial transfer of ownership will take place in the event the firm is declared bankrupt, the market value of the levered firm is again equal to the market value of the unlevered firm, plus the market value of tax subsidy on interest payments on a perpetual riskless bond, and plus an adjustment term. However, the adjustment term in this case is different from that in the previous case of total transfer of ownership, mainly because a partial payment of coupon interest and the associated tax subsidy are preserved in the current case.

Therefore, in the absence of explicit bankruptcy costs, if upon bankruptcy-reorganization the bondholders receive a partial ownership of the firm and a partial payment of coupon interest, the market value of the firm will increase with debt more slowly than what has been suggested in the MM analysis.

3.3.2. The case of bankruptcy-liquidation

In this section it is assumed that upon bankruptcy the total assets of the firm are liquidated and the business enterprise is terminated. Thus, upon bankruptcy-liquidation, the bondholders receive the net proceeds from the liquidation of assets and will have to cover the losses which the firm has incurred and the expenses associated with bankruptcy proceedings. The costs associated with bankruptcy-liquidation consist of the following major components:[9] (a) the costs of liquidating assets in distress; (b) the various direct administrative expenses incurred during the bankruptcy proceedings; (c) the loss of tax credit on operating losses; and (d) the loss of tax subsidy on interest payments due to the termination of business enterprise.

Let k be the proportional liquidation costs of selling assets in distress and K be the fixed administrative costs associated with bankruptcy-liquidation. Then

---

[9]Some of these costs have been discussed extensively in the literature. See, for example, Baxter (1967), Stanley and Girth (1971), Van Horne (1975) and Kim (1978).

bondholder wealth at the end of a given period can be expressed as

$$\tilde{Y}_D = \begin{cases} I + V_D, & \text{if } X > I - V_E(1-\theta)^{-1} \equiv b, \\ V(1-k) + \tilde{X} - K, & \text{if } b \geqslant X > K - V(1-k) \equiv h_3, \\ 0, & \text{if } X \leqslant h_3. \end{cases} \tag{23}$$

Therefore, the market value of the firm's risky debt is given by

$$V_D = \frac{[1 - F(b)]I + [F(b) - F(h_3)][V(1-k) - K] + CEQ_{h_3}^b(\tilde{X})}{r + F(b)}. \tag{24}$$

The first term in the numerator on the right-hand side of (24) represents the expected per period coupon interest payments to the bondholders, and the sum of the second and the third terms in the numerator represents the expected net liquidation value of the bankrupt firm to the bondholders.

Adding up V_E in (10) and V_D in (24), we can derive the market value of the levered firm as follows:

$$V_L = V + \theta V_D^* + H_3, \tag{25}$$

where

$$H_3 = -[r + F(b)]^{-1} \{ \theta IF(b)(1 + 1/r) + [F(b) - F(h_3)](kV + K)$$

$$+ [F(h_3) - F(Z)]V + (1 - \theta)CEQ_Z^{h_3}(\tilde{X}) - \theta CEQ_{h_3}^b(\tilde{X}) \}.$$

Note that the costs of bankruptcy-liquidation enter the adjustment term in the market value of the levered firm given in (25) as expected.

3.3.3. The case of bankruptcy-reorganization / liquidation

It is certainly more profitable for bondholders to reorganize and to continue a bankrupt firm than to liquidate it if the market value of the reorganized firm is greater than the net liquidation value of the bankrupt firm. Therefore, unless the operating losses are so substantial that the business enterprise has no value of being preserved, a bankrupt firm will in general be reorganized. However, this will not preclude the possibility of liquidating a bankrupt firm. In what follows we derive the market value of a firm under the assumption that it is possible for the bankrupt firm to be reorganized as well as to be liquidated. Depending upon the different states the firm is in (solvent, reorganization or liquidation), bondholder wealth at the end of a given period is given by the following

$$
\tilde{Y}_{\mathrm{D}} = \begin{cases} I + V_{\mathrm{D}}, & \text{if } X > b, \\ V + (1-\theta)\tilde{X} - C, & \text{if } b \geqslant X > h_1, \\ V(1-k) + \tilde{X} - K, & \text{if } h_1 \geqslant X > h_3, \\ 0, & \text{if } X \leqslant h_3, \end{cases} \tag{26}
$$

where h_1 and h_3 are given in (12) and (23), respectively.

Given the random end-of-period bondholder wealth specified in (26), we can easily derive the market value of risky debt under the assumption that a bankrupt firm can be reorganized as well as liquidated. Furthermore, the market value of the firm can be expressed as

$$V_{\mathrm{L}} = V + \theta V_{\mathrm{D}}^* + H_4,$$

where

$$
\begin{aligned}
H_4 = & -[r + F(b)]^{-1} \{ \theta IF(b)(1 + 1/r) + [F(b) - F(h_1)]C \\
& + [F(h_1) - F(h_3)](kV + K) + [F(h_3) - F(Z)]V \\
& + (1-\theta)CEQ_Z^{h_3}(\tilde{X}) - \theta CEQ_{h_3}^{h_1}(\tilde{X}) \}
\end{aligned}
$$

in which $F(b)$ = the probability of bankruptcy; $[F(b) - F(h_1)]$ = the probability of bankruptcy-reorganization; and $[F(h_1) - F(h_3)]$ = the probability of bankruptcy-liquidation.

Thus, the market value of the levered firm is equal to the market value of the unlevered firm, plus the market value of tax subsidy on interest payments on a perpetual riskless bond, and plus an adjustment term which includes both the expected reorganization cost and the expected liquidation cost. Again, in the presence of tax subsidy on interest payments and the bankruptcy costs (reorganization as well as liquidation costs), the linear relationship between the market value of the firm and the market value of debt given in the MM analysis does not hold. There is an optimal capital structure which maximizes the market value of the firm.

4. Conclusions

In this paper we have derived models of firm valuation in a multiperiod framework with corporate income taxes and costly bankruptcy. The distinction between bankruptcy-reorganization and bankruptcy-liquidation has been explicitly incorporated into the models of firm valuation. Thus, we have generalized the MM model to show that an optimal capital structure exists in the presence of corporate income taxes and costly bankruptcy in a rather general setting. With the more complete models we have developed, we believe that some significant propositions regarding the theory of financial leverage can be obtained and more meaningful empirical investigations can be conducted. Furthermore, the models of firm valuation presented in the paper should provide a better analytical framework for studying the theory of conglomerate merger.

References

Baron, D. P. (1974) "Default Risk, Homemade Leverage, and the Modigliani-Miller Theorem", *American Economic Review*, March.

Baxter, N. (1967) "Leverage, Risk of Ruin and The Cost of Capital", *Journal of Finance*, September.

Bogue, M. and R. Roll (1974) "Capital Budgeting for Risky Projects with 'Imperfect' Markets for Physical Capital", *Journal of Finance*, May.

Chen, A. H. (1977) "Bankruptcy and Corporate Investment-Financing Decisions", Working Paper, Ohio State University.

Chen, A. H. (1978) "Recent Developments in The Cost of Debt Capital", *Journal of Finance*, June.

Crockett, J. and I. Friend (1967) "Some Estimates of the Cost of Capital to the Electric Utility Industry, 1954–57: Comment", *American Economic Review*, December.

Elton, E. J., M. J. Gruber and J. B. Lightstone (1976) "The Impact of Bankruptcy on the Firm's Capital Structure, the Reasonableness of Mergers and the Risk Independence of Projects", Working Paper, Graduate School of Business Administration, New York University.

Fama, E. F. (1977) "Risk-Adjusted Discount Rates and Capital Budgeting Under Uncertainty", *Journal of Financial Economics*, August.

Gordon, M. J. (1967) "Some Estimates of the Cost of Capital to the Electric Utility Industry, 1954–57: Comment", *American Economic Review*, December.

Hamada, R. S. (1969) "Portfolio Analysis, Market Equilibrium and Corporate Finance", *Journal of Finance*, March.

Hirschleifer, J. (1970) *Investment, Interest and Capital* (Prentice-Hall, Englewood Cliffs).

Kim, E. H. (1978) "A Mean–Variance Theory of Optimal Capital Structure and Corporate Debt Capacity", *Journal of Finance*, March.

Kraus, A. and R. Litzenberger (1973) "A State-Preference Model of Optimal Financial Leverage", *Journal of Finance*, September, 911–922.

Lee, W. Y. and H. H. Barker (1977) "Bankruptcy Costs and the Firm's Optimal Debt Capacity: A Positive Theory of Capital Structure", *Southern Economic Journal*, March.

Lintner, J. (1977) "Bankruptcy Risk, Market Segmentation, and Optimal Capital Structure", in: I. Friend and J. L. Bicksler, eds., *Risk and Return in Finance* (Ballinger Publishing Co., Massachusetts).

Modigliani, F. F. and M. H. Miller (1958) "The Cost of Capital Corporation Finance, and the Theory of Investment", *American Economic Review*, June.

Modigliani, F. F. and M. H. Miller (1963) "Corporation Income Taxes and the Cost of Capital: A Correction", *American Economic Review*, June.

Modigliani, F. F. and M. H. Miller (1966) "Some Estimates of the Cost of Capital to the Electric Utility Industry, 1954–57", *American Economic Review*, June.

Myers, S. C. and S. M. Turnball (1977) "Capital Budgeting and the Capital Asset Pricing Model: Good News and Bad News", *Journal of Finance*, May.

Robichek, A. A. and S. C. Myers (1966) "Problems in the Theory of Optimal Capital Structure", *Journal of Financial and Quantitative Analysis*, June.

Robichek, A. A., J. G. McDonald and R. C. Higgins (1967) "Some Estimates of the Cost of Capital to the Electric Utility Industry, 1954–57: Comment", *American Economic Review*, December.

Rubinstein, M. (1973) "A Mean–Variance Synthesis of Corporate Financial Theory", *Journal of Finance*, March.

Scott, J. H. (1976) "A Theory of Optimal Capital Structure", *The Bell Journal of Economics and Management Science*, Spring, 33–54.

Stanley, D. and M. Girth (1971) *Bankruptcy: Problem, Process, Reform* (The Brookings Institution, Washington, D. C.).

Stevens, G. V. G. (1974) "On the Impact of Uncertainty on the Value and Investment of the Neoclassical Firm", *American Economic Review*, June, 319–336.

Stiglitz, J. (1969) "A Re-Examination of the Modigliani–Miller Theorem", *American Economic Review*, December, 784–793.

Stiglitz, J. (1972) "Some Aspects of the Pure Theory of Corporate Finance: Bankruptcies and Takeovers", *The Bell Journal of Economics and Management*, Autumn, 458–482.

Stiglitz, J. (1974) "On the Irrelevance of Corporate Financial Policy", *American Economic Review*, December, 851–866.

Van Horne, J. C. (1975) "Corporate Liquidity and Bankruptcy Costs", Research Paper no. 205, Stanford University.

Chapter 14

LEASING AS A FINANCIAL INSTRUMENT

CHARLES UPTON
Rutgers University

1. Introduction

The financial literature on leasing has focused for many years on equations for evaluating the relative attractiveness of leasing and buying. The various equations computed the present value of the cash flows associated with leasing and buying as a function of risk, tax liabilities, salvage value, maintenance and the like. Because the equations that constituted the prescription of the trade were not simple, an army of MBAs rose to prominence, wealth and power within corporations by virtue of their facility with rent-or-buy calculations. And from the perspective of professors of finance, development of lease or buy equations represented two possible sources of gain: first, by creating a demand for publication of new and refined formulae for these calculations and secondly, by creating a market for their students in applying the equations to corporate decisions (and perhaps a market for themselves as consultants in the application of the equations).

Having thus created the market, the profession now seems prepared to destroy it. Recent studies (Miller and Upton (1976) and Lewellen et al. (1976)) have argued that the lease-or-buy decision can be made independent of such exercises. It can be shown that most firms will be indifferent between buying or leasing in a competitive leasing market. Furthermore, the special cases where some firms will have a definite preference for leasing or buying can be identified in terms of the characteristics of the firm without resort to an error-prone calculation of cash flows. Indeed, the focus of recent studies is to determine precisely when those special cases arise.

2. Leasing as a factor of production

Before turning to an analysis of the financial aspects of leasing, it should be noted that there are nonfinancial factors to be considered in making the lease-or-buy decision. As an example, consider the problem faced by a firm that wants to acquire the services of a machine for a period of one year. One factor

James L. Bicksler, Editor, Handbook of Financial Economics
© *North-Holland Publishing Company – 1979*

to be considered is the impact of lease-or-buy on maintenance expenditures. To determine the optimum level of maintenance expenditures during that year it is necessary to estimate the value of the services, S, of the machine during that year as well as the (appropriately) discounted resale value of the machine, R, both as functions of the level of maintenance, M. The optimum level of maintenance is then found by setting $C'(M) = S'(M) + R'(M)$, where $C(M)$ is the cost of providing a given level of maintenance M.

If the company purchases its equipment, it may well lack the specialized knowledge necessary to determine and provide the optimal level of maintenance expenditures; that is, it may not know what the functions $C(M)$, $S(M)$, and $R(M)$ look like. It could remedy in part this deficiency by purchasing maintenance services from an outside vendor but it will still face the problem of ensuring that the vendor has the right incentives to provide the right level of service.

An alternative solution to the problem of imperfect knowledge would be to lease the equipment, with the leasing company providing "free" maintenance service at the level which it, with its specialized knowledge, believes optimal. Even this solution presents difficulties, for the leasing company does not have a natural incentive to consider the impact of maintenance on the level of services S during the life of the lease and thus has an incentive to undersupply maintenance services.[1]

Moreover, other real costs arise because of the different costs in legal fees and taxes to transfer ownership in a property than to transfer a lease.[2]

In what follows these issues will be waived so that the discussion can focus on the financial aspects of the lease-versus-buy question. But this brief discussion should serve as a reminder that the rent-or-buy question depends in part on factors other than which arrangement minimizes the present value of acquiring capital equipment.

3. Lease rates in a model without taxes

3.1. The basic proposition

These issues aside, let us now turn our attention to considering how lease rates will be set. To take the easy case first, let us first consider the rent-or-buy decision under the following assumptions.

[1]This proposition is well known to anyone who has patiently awaited the arrival of a computer repairman. On the other hand, "free" maintenance service from the leasing company gives the user little incentive to protect the machine from abuse that will affect its resale value.

[2]For example, Hertz could sell cars rather than rent them; the user's costs of searching for a buyer at the end of the day could presumably be avoided by including in the sales contract a repurchase agreement effective at the end of the day. But such a procedure would necessitate two filings of a title transfer. Another nonfinancial factor militating against the use of sales-cum-repurchase agreements is the cost of enforcement. Failing to return a rented car is a criminal offense, and the lessor has access to police powers to recover the car; failing to honor a repurchase agreement is a civil offense for which the only remedy available to Hertz would be an expensive civil suit.

(1) The machines in question are produced by a perfectly competitive industry at a constant cost of Π_t per unit. The same machines will be produced by the industry next period, again at a constant cost of Π_{t+1} not necessarily equal to Π_t. Technological innovation, for example, may result in production costs declining over time. The deterioration of these machines is assumed to be of the "evaporation" type, so that each machine produced in period t is equivalent in productive power to $1 - \delta$ new machines in period t.

(2) Maintenance and repair of the machines during use are obtained by purchase of a service policy from a competitive specialized service industry. Let there initially be one and only one level of maintenance expenditures that is technologically feasible and let the law be that this amount of maintenance must be purchased by the user firm whether it chooses to rent or buy.

(3) Second-hand machines can be bought, sold or sublet by leasing companies in unlimited quantities in perfect markets.

(4) Leasing companies can borrow or lend indefinitely in a perfect capital market at a known one-period rate of interest of r. Leasing, moreover, is a business that anyone is free to enter and requires the use of no real resources.

(5) There are no taxes to be paid, either by the leasee or the leasor.

Given these simplifying assumptions, the equilibrium one-period rental L_t^* can easily be shown to be the familiar

$$L_t^* = \Pi_t(r_t + d_t) = \prod_t \left[r_t + \frac{\Pi_{t+1}}{\Pi_t} \delta_t + \left(1 - \frac{\Pi_{t+1}}{\Pi_t} \right) \right]. \tag{1}$$

That is to say, the equilibrium rental is equal to the interest forgone on the capital invested in the machine, $\Pi_t r_t$, plus the depreciation of the machine $\Pi_t d_t$. In this case, the depreciation consists of two parts: a "deterioration" and an "obsolescence", whenever the new machines can be produced in period $t + 1$ at a lower cost than during period t. No leasing firm need ever contract for a rental less than L_t^* because it always has the opportunity to sell the machine for Π_t and invest the proceeds in the capital market to earn the rate r_t. And if the going rental rate were to rise to $L_t' > L_t^*$, leasing firms would earn a rate of return greater than r_t. New leasing companies would enter the industry, buying the equipment from the manufacturers at its cost of Π_t per unit and cutting rentals until the market's quoted rental rate returned to L_t^*. The user actually faces two decision problems: (1) given the market rental of L_t^*, how many machines is it optimal to rent; and (2) given L_t^*, r_t, δ_t, Π_t and Π_{t+1}, does it pay to buy or lease? The first of these decisions is the core of neoclassical production theory and need not be discussed here. As to the second decision note that a decision to buy is equivalent to setting up a leasing subsidiary which purchases machines for lease either to the firm or possibly to others. If it does set up a leasing subsidiary, the appropriate lease rate for internal transfer purposes would be L_t^*, the rate it could earn by leasing to outsiders. Stating the problem in this manner, of course, provides the solution. The assumption of a competitive leasing industry, with no costs of entry or exit, means that there are no economic profits to be earned from setting up a leasing subsidiary, whether it leases only to the firm or to outsiders as well. In sum, a user firm would have no *financial* incentive to purchase machines for lease either to itself or to others.[3]

So far, it has been assumed that the machine in question will have a market or "salvage" value equal to $(1-\delta_t)\Pi_{t+1}$ at the end of the lease. It is also possible to consider life-of-the-product leases, where the residual value of the property at the end of the lease is zero. In practice, recent IRS regulations rule out such leases. Among other things, a leasing company must retain a claim to some expected positive residual salvage value at the end of the lease to take any of the tax advantages of ownership, which it clearly may for machines which it owns and leases out on a short-term basis. The effect of these regulations is to treat long-term leases of the type described here as equivalent to secured mortgages, at least for tax purposes.[4]

However, long-term leases still have useful expository value, and it is useful to establish the same indifference propositions in this case as well. For this purpose, consider a lease in which the user agrees to pay the lessor a series of annual payments, $L(t,j)$, in years $j=t+0,\ldots,t+T$ for the right to use the machine; the machine is assumed to have zero salvage value at the end of the lease. For simplicity, we also assume that the lease is noncancellable, with the lease payments therefore treated as riskless. The leassee does, however, have the privilege of subleasing.

The equilibrium lease rates are constrained by first finding the present value of the T one-period rentals, given as

$$V(t) = \sum_{j=t}^{t+T} \frac{L(t,j)}{(1+r)^{j-1}} \qquad (2)$$

assuming, for simplicity, a constant interest rate over time. Competition will, of course, force the present value of the rentals, $V(t)$ to be equal to Π_t, the cost of a new machine. No rational leasing company would charge less and competition among potential lessors will not admit of higher rates.

To be sure, the zero profit constraint does not require a unique pattern of lease payments, for there are infinitely many possible payment patterns with an equivalent present value. What is important is that from the perspective of a user, any lease payment pattern must have a present value equal to the purchase price, thus making him indifferent between buying and taking a long-term lease.

Moreover, the user is indifferent as to the choice of buying a short-term lease or a long-term lease *independent of the size of the first year lease payment under a long-term lease*. To see this consider a user firm that plans to use the machine for

[3]The discussion suggests the essential difference between what we have referred to as "financial" and "nonfinancial" costs. Differences in financial costs create arbitrage opportunities whereas nonfinancial differences do not.

[4]The argument of whether one purchases equipment with a mortgage or with a long-term "financing" lease thus hinges on which minimizes the nonfinancial costs of obtaining credit.

a single period. The actual first year outlay is only one part of the cost of acquiring the capital services for the year, since a sublessee will have to be found to take over the remaining years of the lease. As a consequence, the compensation that must be paid to the sublessee to assume the obligations of the lease must be added to obtain the true cost of owning and using the machine for a year. The sublessee must be paid an amount equal to the difference between the present value of the $T-1$ lease payments as of the start of the next period,

$$\sum_{j=t+1}^{t+T} \frac{L(t,j)}{(1+r)^{j-t-1}},$$

(3)

and the present value of the rental rates on one-period old machines. Because equilibrium in the rental market for used machines requires that the present value of those lease payments be equal to the market value of the equipment, $\Pi_{t+1}(1-\delta_t)$, the required compensation will be given by

$$\sum_{j=t+1}^{t+T} \frac{L(t,j)}{(1+r)^{j-t-1}} \Pi_{t+1}(1-\delta_t).$$

(4)

Discounting (4) and adding $L(t,1)$, we obtain the true opportunity cost of using a machine for one year:

$$\frac{1}{1+r}\left(\sum_{j=t+1}^{t+T} \frac{L(t,j)}{(1+r)^{j-t-1}}\right) - \Pi_{t+1}(1-\delta_t) + L(t,1).$$

(5)

Because $L(t,1)$ has been set so that $V(t)=\Pi_t$, eq. (5) can be rewritten as

$$\Pi_t - \Pi_{t+1}(1-\delta_t)\frac{1}{1+r}.$$

(6)

Some final rearrangement of terms permits the cost of use to be written as

$$\frac{1}{1+r}\Pi_t\left[r + \frac{\Pi_{t+1}}{\Pi_t}\delta_t + \left(\Pi_t - \frac{\Pi_{t+1}}{\Pi_t}\right)\right].$$

(7)

The bracketed term in the right-hand side of (7) is, of course, L_t^*, the one-period lease. That is, the cost of using the machine is independent of the terms of the lease.

3.2. Some extensions and qualifications to the basic proposition

Further generality can be obtained, at least in principle, by relaxing the very severe restrictions imposed in assumption (1) on the conditions under which new machines are produced. Treating machine producers as a competitive constant-cost industry makes it possible to take the prices of machines now and in all subsequent periods as parameters in the valuation expressions, independent of the demand for the machines. The demand by users affects only the equilibrium stocks of machines of various types, not their prices.[5] If we were to permit the costs of production of the machines to vary with industry output or if we were to consider a monopoly producer of machines, the scenario needed to describe the emergence of the equilibrium rental would have to be broadened to allow for the determination of the selling price for the machines as well as their rental terms. Such a scenario will clearly be a good deal more complicated, involving as it does the simultaneous solution of a very large number of equations. But when the dust has settled we must have exactly the same relation as before between the equilibrium rental rates and market prices of machines, whatever those market prices turn out to be. Otherwise, leasing firms would be able to exploit any departures from the relation to earn abnormal profits from renting out or subletting equipment.[6]

Although relaxing the assumptions about the production of machines leads to no change in the presumption that user firms will be indifferent between leasing or buying, some possible grounds for distinction emerge when we turn to other assumptions on the list. Assumption (2), it will be recalled, makes the convenient simplification that the maintenance required for any machine is given exogenously. As has already been noted, the level of maintenance is itself an economic decision which might depend on who happens to have the legal title to the machine.

A nonfinancial advantage to leasing is a likely consequence of weakening our assumption (3) — that the purchase and rental markets for second-hand equipment are perfect. The twist is imparted not so much by the search costs which, though they may well be substantial, are little different in principle whether one is searching for a buyer or a subtenant.[7] The difference comes rather from the fact that it often costs considerably more in legal fees and taxes to transfer ownership in a property than to transfer a lease. The transfer costs are particularly high, of course, where land is concerned. This assumption does, however, serve the useful purpose of allowing us to concentrate on the financial aspects of leasing without taking up the thorny nonfinancial aspects discussed earlier.

Consider also the consequences of weakening our assumption (4), that of perfect capital markets, to allow for one company having a lower effective borrowing rate than that built into the rental rates. It is true that such a company, looking only at the conventional formulae, might find it profitable to

---

[5]To treat the value of a new machine as its cost of production, independent of current and future demands, we must, however, rule out certain extreme cases. We cannot, for example, allow demand for the services of machines of type i in any future year to fall so far that the production of new machines falls to zero.

[6]It is sometimes argued that monopolists engage in leasing because it offers greater possibilities for price discrimination than an outright sale. Since concern in this paper is primarily with the financial aspects of leasing, these and related issues of optimum price and marketing policy are not explored in any detail.

[7]However, there may be nonfinancial advantages in having leasing firms that specialize in bearing these search costs, thereby obtaining whatever economics of specialization may exist.

buy rather than rent. But it would find it even more profitable, under those circumstances, to enter the leasing business! We can presume, therefore, that the leasing business will gravitate eventually to the firms whose efficiency in fund raising leads to the lowest cost of borrowing. They will be or will become "financial intermediaries". The fact that some (or even all) of these intermediaries may be subsidiaries of user firms does not alter the fundamental point that the typical user firm making its investment decisions can safely proceed on the assumption that renting will not be an option inferior to buying.

4. The impact of taxes

Now let us turn to assumption (5). Like many corporate decisions, the rent-or-buy decision is frequently justified in terms of the implications for the corporation's tax bill. The advertisements of some leasing companies continue to argue that lease payments are deductible in full, whereas the owner of a machine can only deduct its depreciation plus that part of capital cost represented by interest payments. While this is a false argument, there are important asymmetries in the tax law that do affect the decision and which will be explored below. These asymmetries lead to the conclusions that, when the implications of tax laws are taken into account, a taxable corporation is unlikely to find it financially advantageous to buy rather than to rent, while tax exempt institutions and individuals will probably find leasing financially unattractive.

4.1. The effect of deductibility on corporate leasing

To see that differences in deductibility do not, by themselves, bias the rent-or-buy decision, let us consider first the case in which there is no corporate borrowing. All corporations, including leasing companies, must finance themselves entirely with equity capital, and thus none of the payments made to security holders are deductible from taxable corporate income. The corporate tax rate itself τ_c is a constant taken to be independent of the level of profits and the same for all taxable corporations.

The equilibrium single-period rental will be the before-tax rental rate that leaves leasing companies just indifferent between renting their machines and selling them and investing the proceeds in assets of equivalent risk. Under the lease strategy, the leasing company's after-tax earnings, y_t, will be

$$y_t = L_t(1 - \tau_e) - d_t \Pi_t + \tau_c d_t \Pi_t,$$ (8)

where L_t is the one-period lease payment and

$$d_t = \frac{\Pi_{t+1}}{\Pi_t} \delta_t + \left(1 - \frac{\Pi_{t+1}}{\Pi_t}\right)$$ (9)

is, as before, depreciation due to deterioration and obsolescence. We assume for the moment that the amount of depreciation allowed as a deduction for tax purposes is exactly the same as the decline in the market value of the machine (i.e. economic depreciation).

Since equilibrium in the corporate leasing market will require that $L/\Pi = r$, the after-tax rate of return to investors, we have as the equilibrium one-period rental

$$L^{**} = \left[d + \frac{1}{1-\tau_c} r \right], \tag{10}$$

which can be seen to differ from the corresponding value for the no-tax case, L^* only in that the term representing the return on the capital invested must now be "grossed up" by the factor $1/(1-\tau_c)$.[8]

Given that the market sets the (before-tax) equilibrium rental at L^{**} user firms that happen to have opted for a buy policy will have no purely financial incentive to switch. They will gain an after-tax return of $r\Pi$ on the funds released, plus the depreciation avoided, $d\Pi$ plus the tax shield on the lease, $\tau_c L^{**}$. But they will lose the tax shield on the depreciation, $\tau_c d\Pi$ and incur the rental expense L^{**}. From (10) it is clear that these gains and losses must exactly balance.

4.2. The effect of deductibility of interest payments

With interest payments fully deductible from taxable corporate income and with corporate rates in the neighborhood of 50 percent, corporations would appear to have powerful incentives to use debt financing to the maximum extent allowable. Yet the typical manufacturing corporation today has debt equal to only about a quarter of its book assets.[9] Conventional wisdom in finance attributes this seeming paradox to certain offsetting deadweight costs of debt financing. For example, the conflict of interest between lender and borrower creates a moral hazard that the lender can protect against only by incurring surveillance costs — costs that are normally passed on to the borrower in the form of stated interest rates higher than necessary to compensate for the systematic risk. Hence, the increasing burden of these costs as the debt ratio rises will eventually impose an upper limit on the amount of borrowing that any firm can profitably support.

An alternative view is that equity capital has a sufficiently lower before-tax cost than debt capital that corporations are indifferent to the debt/equity mix. The supply equity capital by the capital market is explained by the differential

---

[8]Note that, for simplicity, the time subscript has been dropped.
[9]See the 1970 *Statistics of Income-Corporate Tax Returns*.

tax treatment on debt and equity capital *after* it leaves the hands of the corporation.[10] While interest payments on debt capital are fully deductible for corporate tax purposes, interest income from corporate bonds are fully subject to the personal income tax, at rates ranging up to 70 percent. Similarly, while "interest payments" on equity capital (in the guise of corporate profits) are fully subject to corporate income taxes, earnings on equity securities often receive preferential treatment for personal income tax purposes. A case in point is, of course, the capital gains component of equity returns. The tax liability may be deferred until the stock is sold and, even then, is taxed at a rate never more than half of the personal tax rate. Hence individuals with high tax rates have, ceteribus paribus, a preference for equity capital, and individuals and organizations with zero or low tax rates (e.g. tax-exempt universities) have a preference for equity capital.

For the moment, it is not necessary to explore which of these alternative explanations is correct. And, if we are to accept the conventional line, it is not necessary to explore the determinants of the optimal debt/equity ratio; the rent-or-buy issue can be analyzed without raising this issue.

For our purposes, we will assume that the market rate on equity capital is given by r^e and that the rate on debt capital is given by r^d_α, where α is the fraction of the firm's capital structure represented by debt. We will further assume that the firm has either found – by processes not described here – the optimal value of α or that, at minimum, it is indifferent between alternative values of α. Given these assumptions, the after-tax earnings of a leasing company from a one-period lease at the rate L will be

$$y = L(1 - \tau_c) - (d\Pi + \alpha r^d_\alpha \Pi)(1 - \tau_c). \tag{11}$$

Instead of leasing the equipment, the firm could sell it for Π and then invest the proceeds in financial assets with a return of r^e, the return on equity capital.[11] To keep the degree of leverage constant, we will assume that the firm still borrows an amount $\alpha\Pi$ which it distributes to its shareholders as a return of capital. Its books then show financial assets of Π and liabilities of $\alpha\Pi$ for indebtedness plus $(1 - \alpha)\Pi$ of stockholders' equity. The firm's after-tax income will now be

$$y' = \Pi(r^e - \alpha r^d_\alpha). \tag{12}$$

---

[10] This argument is stated more fully in Miller (1977).

[11] It would be possible to modify this analysis to allow for the riskiness of the underlying assets. If the firm leases the equipment, it holds title to an asset whose value next period $(1 - \delta_t)\Pi_{t+1}$, is uncertain. Similarly, most financial assets the firm might acquire would also involve similar risk. In either case, that risk would be borne by the firm's shareholders, with a corresponding impact on the expected value of the return r^e. It has been shown (Miller and Upton (1976)) that introducing risk into this analysis does not affect the results presented here and, for the purposes of this paper, we will not undertake an explicit risk analysis. The reader should bear in mind, however, that there is an implicit assumption that the capital equipment and the alternative financial assets have equivalent risk.

Equating (12) and (13), the equilibrium value of a one-period lease L is

$$L = \Pi \left[(r^e) \frac{1}{1 - \tau_c} + d - \frac{\tau_c}{1 - \tau_c} (r_\alpha^d) \alpha \right].$$ (13)

It is an easy matter to show that the expected after-tax cost to a user company of owning the machine, assuming that it too borrows a fraction of the purchase price equal to $(1 - \tau_c)L^\alpha$. Thus, the deductibility of interest payments obtained earlier for taxable firms in the no-borrowing case.

5. The impact of tax subsidies and tax exemptions

So far it has been assumed that the depreciation deductions allowed for tax purposes equal the true economic depreciation. In practice, this is rarely the case. The investment tax credit and accelerated depreciation have been introduced precisely to make tax deductions larger than economic depreciation, and should be viewed as a means of reducing the effective tax on income from capital. For present purposes, however, it is more convenient to model them as tax subsidies rather than rate reductions, though this will in no way change the essential conclusions.

5.1. Tax subsidies

The use of the term tax subsidy, rather than simply subsidy, is intended as a reminder that the full benefit of tax subsidies cannot be obtained unless the affected firm has enough income from other sources to utilize the tax shields. A company contemplating a large capital expansion project could find the investment tax credit on that project exceeding the current permissible deduction of 50 percent of gross tax liabilities.[12] In that event its effective tax subsidy would be lower than that of a leasing company which presumably can take full advantage of the tax subsidy.

To see the effects of tax subsidies, let s_L be the first-period, flow-equivalent after-tax value of the tax subsidies to leasing companies. That is, assume that the leasing company has somehow computed the present value of all tax subsidies over the optimal period of ownership of the machine, and that it has allocated to

---

[12]As this article was being prepared, the administration was considering proposals to allow investment tax credits up to 100 percent of tax liability. Such a change would not affect the argument presented here, though it would reduce the potential for tax subsidies to have differential values for leassee and lessor.

its first year's income an amount that can appropriately be attributed to the first year's ownership.[13] The precise details of this calculation and allocation need not concern us at this point. And let s_B, which may or may not be equal to s_L, be the first-period flow-equivalent value of the subsidies to a using company that chooses to buy the equipment. Then it is a straightforward matter to show that the equilibrium, one-period rental rate will be

$$L^\alpha(s_L) = \left[r^e \frac{1}{1-\tau_L} + d - \frac{\tau_L}{1-\tau_L} \alpha r_\alpha^d - \frac{s_L}{1-\tau_L} \right] \Pi_t, \tag{14}$$

and that the after-tax cost to a user-owner will be

$$C^\alpha(s_B) = \left[(r^e) + (1-\tau_B)d - \tau_B \alpha r_\alpha^d - s_B \right] \Pi_t, \tag{15}$$

where τ_L and τ_B represent the tax rates of the leasing and buying companies. The difference between the after-tax cost of leasing and owning will be

$$\Delta = \left[\frac{\tau_L - \tau_B}{1-\tau_L} r^e - \frac{1-\tau_B}{1-\tau_L} + s_B - \frac{\tau_L - \tau_B}{1-\tau} r_\alpha^d \alpha \right] \Pi_t. \tag{16}$$

Thus, if the tax rate were the same for both parties (implying $\tau_L = \tau_B$) and if both had equal ability to utilize the tax subsidies (so that $s_L = s_B$), the choice between renting or buying would remain a matter of indifference for the user firm. But where the user firm cannot take full advantage of the tax subsidy, it will pay to rent. That way the firm can still get the indirect advantage of the congressional largesse that competition among leasing companies will build into rental rates.

Our tax laws in sum have created a new source of gains from specialization over and above those considered in the standard neoclassical analysis. Whether eliminating the waste of lost tax subsidies is a social gain is far from clear as indeed is the case for the subsidies themselves. But the private gains are substantial, as witness the explosive growth of the equipment leasing industry after the introduction of the investment tax credit in 1962.

The presumption in favor of renting is weakened, and in some circumstances even reversed, when the tax rate on income from the use of the property is smaller for the user than for the leasing company. Such might be the case, for example, for a user firm which, for any of a number of reasons, finds itself with a net loss carry-forward. Both its tax payments and receipts of tax subsidies will then cease until it has worked off these losses and once again become taxable. We can express this temporary cessation of taxes and subsidies for the user firm by setting $\tau_B < \tau_L$ and $s_B < s_L$; and from (16) it can then be shown that buying will become the superior policy over a wide range of values.

---

[13]We have to define s_L in this somewhat convoluted way because, under present tax laws, some kinds of tax subsidies can be lost or recaptured if the property is sold after a short period of time.

5.2. Rent-or-buy strategies for tax-exempt organizations

The most extreme case of this asymmetry in the tax treatment of users and lessors is that of tax-exempt organizations. Consider, for example, a university that is deciding whether to buy a computer whose current one-period rental rate is the $L^\alpha(s_L)$ of eq. (14). Since the university is tax exempt we have $\tau_B = 0$; and since s_B is a tax subsidy, we must also therefore have $s_B = 0$. Thus, the difference in cost between leasing and buying becomes

$$\Delta = \left[\frac{\tau_L}{1 - \tau_L} r^e - \frac{1}{1 - \tau_L} s_L - \frac{\tau_L}{1 - \tau_L} r_\alpha^d \alpha \right] \Pi_t. \tag{17}$$

Hence, as long as $\tau_L r^e - \alpha r_\alpha^d > s_L$ it will pay the university to buy rather than rent.

As a matter of arithmetic, of course, it is possible for s_L to exceed $\tau_L(r^e) - \alpha r_\alpha$. But this would imply that the subsidies collected by a leasing company, s_L, would be greater than the taxes it paid on its rental income, given by

$$\tau_L r_\alpha^d \Pi - \tau_L d\Pi - \tau_L r_\alpha^d \Pi = \Pi\left(r_\alpha^d \frac{\tau_L}{1 - \tau_L} - \frac{\tau_L}{1 - \tau_L} r^e - \frac{\tau_L s_L}{1 - \tau_L} \right) = \Delta.$$

And this, in turn, would violate our premise that s_L and s_B are intended as tax subsidies. The word *intended* should be emphasized since ingenious tax-payers constantly search for (and sometimes find) new ways of expanding tax exemptions and subsidies. Our premise asserts only that such successful subversions of the intent of the law are transitory and will be eliminated by regulations or new legislation if they threaten to become widespread.

5.3. Rent-or-buy strategies for individuals

Another much discussed case in which the tax on the user is smaller than that on the leasing company is that of consumer durables. Under US law, the services provided by consumer durables such as housing and automobiles are not considered part of taxable income. Lease payments are not deductible if the product is used for personal consumption; an exception is made for durables used by an individual in an unincorporated business. Consideration of rent-or-buy strategies for individuals must consider two questions:

(a) Should an individual rent or buy consumption durables?

(b) Should an unincorporated business subject to personal tax rates rent or buy?

5.3.1. Consumer durables

In the case of consumer durables, the after-tax cost of ownership depends on whether debt or equity securities offer a better investment for the individual.

That is, it is equal to the maximum of

$$\left[r^d(1-\tau_{pd}) + (d-s_B) \right] \Pi \tag{18a}$$

and

$$\left[r^e(1-\tau_{pe}) + (d-s_B) \right] \Pi_t, \tag{18b}$$

where τ_{pd} and τ_{pe} are the effective personal tax rates on income from debt and equity capital, respectively, and s_B is the after-tax value of any further specific tax subsidies to consumer durables, such as the right to deduct local property taxes. Assuming that (18b) is the maximum, the excess of leasing cost over ownership cost will be

$$\Delta = \left[r^e\left(\frac{\tau_{pe} + \tau_L - \tau_{pe}\tau_L}{1-\tau_L} \right) - \left(\frac{\tau_L \alpha r_\alpha^d}{1-\tau_L} \right) + s_B - \frac{s_L}{1-\tau_L} \right] \Pi_t. \tag{19}$$

If (18a) is the appropriate measurement of ownership cost, then eq. (19) is a lower bound on Δ. In either case, as long as we continue to rule out cases of $s_L > \tau_L(r^e - \alpha r^d)$, Δ is greater than zero for nonzero values of τ_L, implying that buying is preferable to leasing.

5.3.2. *Unincorporated business*

There is a significant shift in tax policy when we move from the case of durables acquired for personal use to that of durables acquired for business use. Both lease payments on machines rented and depreciation on machines owned by the user now becomes deductible. As every tax accountant is well aware, the distinction between the tax treatment of assets owned or used for business purposes and those owned or used for personal purposes creates strong incentives to consider all consumer durables as having been acquired for business purposes. For our purposes, we need not raise the issue of how one determines whether, say, the car in the garage is to be treated as a business expense. Instead, we shall focus on the lease-or-buy question for a consumer durable, given that lease and/or depreciation costs can be treated as a deductible expense for tax purposes.

Tax deductibility reduces both the cost of leasing and the cost of owning. In the case of leasing the after-tax cost now becomes $(1-\tau_{pd})L^\alpha$, where L^α is given by eq. (19). (Note that we assume lease payments are deductible against income otherwise taxable at the rate on income from bonds, which is higher than the rate on income from capital income. This assumption certainly seems consistent with US tax practice.) Similarly, the cost of ownership is reduced with eqs. (18a) and (18b) being replaced by

$$C = \left[r^d(1-\tau_{pd}) + d(1-\tau_{pd}) - s_B \right] \Pi_t \tag{20a}$$

and

$$C = \left[r^e(1 - \tau_{pe}) + d(1 - \tau_{pd}) - s_B \right] \Pi_t. \tag{20b}$$

(Again, note the assumption that depreciation expenses are assumed deductible against income otherwise taxed at the rate on interest income.)

Using these values, it is straightforward to calculate the excess of the cost of leasing over buying, given by

$$\Delta = (1 - \tau_{pd})L - C, \tag{21}$$

$$\Delta = \left[r^e \frac{\tau_L - \tau_{pd} + \tau_{pe}(1 - \tau_L)}{1 - \tau_L} - \frac{\tau_L}{1 - \tau_L} \alpha r_\alpha^d (1 - \tau_{pd}) - s_L \left(\frac{1 - \tau_{pd}}{1 - \tau_L} \right) + s_B \right] \Pi_t. \tag{22}$$

In turn, it can be shown that $\tau_{pd} > \tau_{pe}$ implies that

$$\Delta > \left[\frac{r_e - \tau_L(1 - \tau_{pd})}{1 - \tau_L} - \frac{\tau_L}{1 - \tau_L} r_\alpha^d \alpha (1 - \tau_{pd}) - s_L \frac{(1 - \tau_{pd})}{1 - \tau_L} + s_B \right] \Pi_t. \tag{23}$$

Our assumption that $s_L > \tau_L(r^e - \alpha r_\alpha^d)$ implies that the right-hand side of eq. (20) is positive, meaning that leasing is more expensive than buying.

6. Summary

As we have seen, equilibrium in the capital market ensures that it can be determined for a wide range of circumstances whether leasing is a preferable financial alternative to buying without reference to explicit financial calculations. Under most circumstances, corporations will find it financially advantageous to lease and individuals will find it financially advantageous to buy. These financial considerations must, however, be tempered by consideration of whether leasing or buying has the lower nonfinancial costs of acquisition, maintenance and disposal.

References

Lewellen, W. G., M. S. Long and J. J. McConnell (1976) "Asset Leasing in Competitive Markets", *Journal of Finance*, June.

Miller, H. M. (1977) "Debt and Taxes", *Journal of Finance*, July.

Miller, H. M. and C. W. Upton (1976) "Leasing, Buying, and the Cost of Capital Services", *Journal of Finance*, June.

PART III

PORTFOLIO CHOICE

Chapter 15

MEAN–VARIANCE PORTFOLIO SELECTION STRATEGIES

GEORGE C. PHILIPPATOS
Pennsylvania State University

1. Perspectives

During the past two decades, the literature on financial analysis and management has been enriched by a wealth of articles, monographs, and textbooks devoted to the topic of diversification[1] — with its concommitant complementary research on methodology, implications, testing, and applications. Central to this research activity has been the Mean–Variance (E–V) methodology for the selection of asset portfolios under conditions of market risk and/or uncertainty, orginally articulated by Markowitz (1952) and later extended by Tobin (1958), Sharpe (1964), Lintner (1965), and others.

The Mean–Variance (E–V) approach, although predominant in research and practice, is, of course, one of several competing or complementary methodologies[2] employed in the construction of asset combinations. For example, on the macroportfolio selection level of capital markets, the two main approaches[3] are (a) the mean–variance (E–V) due to Markowitz, and (b) the State Preference (S–T) proposed by Arrow (1965), and extended by Hirshleifer (1965, 1966), and others. The State Preference or Time-State Preference (T–S–T) framework provides an elegant analytical structure for studying the allocation of risk in capital markets, but its empirical structure has eluded researchers to date. On the other hand, the mean–variance (E–V) is sufficiently general analytically, and allows extensive empirical testing and experimentation. And, both methodologies have evolved from generalizations of Irving Fisher's work on interest rate theory. Similarly, on the microportfolio selection level, there are four well-known methodologies.[4] (a) The mean–variance (Markowitz (1952), Sharpe (1964), Tobin (1958)); (b) the Stochastic Dominance (S–D) approaches (Hadar and Russell (1969), Hanoch and Levy (1969), Levy and Hanoch (1970)); (c) the Chance-Constrained or Safety-First (S–F) techniques (Naslung and

---

[1]See, for example, Brealey and Pyle (1974) and Jensen (1972a) or Fama (1976) for some recent bibliography on the topic.
[2]The E–V framework under conditions of risk and partial ignorance, along with some extensions will be reviewed in this chapter. Several other approaches will be reviewed in another chapter under the title "Alternatives to Mean–Variance for Portfolio Selection".
[3]See Jensen (1972b) for a similar classification.
[4]See Hakansson (1971) for another classification.

James L. Bicksler, Editor, Handbook of Financial Economics
© *North-Holland Publishing Company – 1979*

Whinston (1962), Roy (1952)); and (d) the Geometric Mean (G–M) or Capital
Growth methodologies (Latané (1959), Latané and Young (1969), Latané and
Tuttle (1967), Hakansson (1971), Breiman (1961)).

The motivational assumption for the E–V and S–D methodologies delineates
a decision-maker who attempts to maximize expected one-period utility under
conditions of risk. Similarly, for the G–M, which is a multiperiod approach, the
individual attempts to maximize end-of-period wealth for $n \geqslant 2$ holding periods
or equivalently he strives to maximize the expected geometric mean. Finally, the
S–F methodology is couched in terms of the probability of failing to obtain a
minimum level of return — a disaster level.

The E–V criterion states that for any two portfolios F and G with single-
period expected returns $E(R_F) = \mu_F$, $E(R_G) = \mu_G$, and variances $V(R_F) = \sigma_F^2$,
$V(R_G) = \sigma_G^2$, respectively, portfolio F is preferred to portfolio G when $\mu_F \geqslant \mu_G$
and $\sigma_F^2 \leqslant \sigma_G^2$ — not both equalities holding simultaneously.

In this chapter we shall review E–V portfolio selection strategies with particular emphasis on microeconomic considerations. Section 2 concentrates on microportfolio selection under risk and reviews the basic Markowitz model. Section 3
deals with the generalization of the basic model into the diagonal, single-index
framework by Sharpe (1963, 1964, 1970), and the multi-index extensions by
Cohen and Pogue (1967) and others (Wallingford (1967)). Section 4 covers
microportfolio selection under conditions of partial ignorance, beginning with
the work of Mao and Särndal (1966), and continuing with the studies of Fried
(1970), and Kalymon (1971), Frankfurter et al. (1971, 1974), Dhingra (1973),
Barry (1974), Dickinson (1974), Gressis (1975), and others (Winkler (1973,
1975)). Section 5 discusses the microportfolio generalization of the E–V framework by Sharpe (1964, 1965, 1966), Lintner (1965a, b), Fama (1968), and others
into what is commonly known as capital markets theory. Section 6 reviews
briefly some recent extensions of the asset pricing model, while section 7
concludes with a selective discussion of several empirical tests of the Markowitz
E–V approach in its various forms.

2. E–V portfolio selection under risk[5] – early developments

In the basic formulation of the E–V criterion, we define a set of N assets with
expected returns μ_i, variances σ_i^2, and covariances σ_{ij}, where $i, j = 1, 2, \ldots, N$.

---

[5]In statistical decision theory, which provides the methodological support for the normative
microportfolio selection models, the external decision-making environment is classified into four
broad categories, as follows: (1) *Environmental certainty*, where each specific action results invariably
in a specific outcome, known to the decision-maker in advance. (2) *Environmental risk*, where each
specific action by the decision-maker results in one of several possible outcomes, with known
probabilities of occurrence attached to each outcome and known to the decision-maker in advance.
(3) *Environmental uncertainty*, where a set of specific actions leads to a set of possible specific
outcomes whose probabilities are either unknown or nonmeaningful. (4) *Environmental partial
ignorance*, where uncertainty may be reduced to risk through the use of experimental evidence, as in
the case of statistical inference. See for example, Luce and Raiffa (1957, p. 13).

Then, the expected return from the portfolio is

$$\mu_p = \sum_{i=1}^{N} X_i \mu_i,$$ (1)

where X_i, $X_j =$ the proportion of the portfolio invested in assets i and j, respectively, and

$$\sum_{i=1}^{N} X_i = 1, \quad \text{and } X_i \geq 0, \quad \text{for all } i.$$

The variance of portfolio return is given by

$$\sigma_p^2 = \sum_{i=1}^{N} \sum_{j=1}^{N} X_i X_j \sigma_{ij}$$ (2)

The locus of efficient combinations (efficient frontier) will be obtained by[6]

$$\min(-\lambda\mu + \sigma_p^2)$$ (3)

or, by substitution of (2.1) and (2.2) into (2.3),

$$\min\left(-\lambda \sum_{i=1}^{N} X_i \mu_i + \sum_{i=1}^{N} \sum_{j=1}^{N} X_i X_j \sigma_{ij}\right)$$ (3′)

for all non-negative values of λ, which serves as a proxy for the trade-off between return and risk. In effect, the parametric quadratic programming algorithm that yields the optimal decision vector $X' = [X_1, X_2, \ldots, X_n]$ of each value of λ, also computes the corresponding values for μ_p and σ_p^2.

Since the investor in the Markowitz E–V framework acts to maximize his expected utility, given in the form $E(u) = U(\mu, \sigma^2)$, the optimal portfolio will obtain at the point of tangency between the efficient frontier and the investor's indifference curve, as shown in 1ig. 15.1 below. In fact, given indifference curves of the form

$$\sigma_p^2 = \alpha + \lambda\mu_p$$ (4)

the investor's goal is to obtain the particular feasible portfolio that is also the point of tangency with the most desirable indifference curve. Hence, minimizing

[6]See, for example, Sharpe (1970, p. 57).

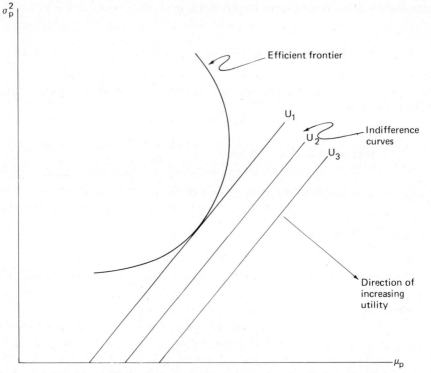

Figure 15.1. Portfolio choice based on expected return (μ_p) and risk (σ_p^2).

the function

$$\alpha = -\lambda\mu_p + \sigma_p^2 \tag{4'}$$

is equivalent to minimizing the objective function (3') and, obviously, similar to the equilibrium solution in consumer choice.[7]

The Markowitz model

The development of the mean-variance approach began in 1952 with the publication of an article by Markowitz (1952). Beginning with the apparently innocuous assumption that rational investors will prefer certain (less uncertain) returns to uncertain (more uncertain) ones, Markowitz both specified a framework for the analysis of choices under risk and provided a workable algorithm for its utilization. The analytical framework of the model is based upon the following behavioral assumptions.

[7]See Henderson and Quandt (1971, ch.2).

(1) The investor views expected returns as being desirable and, given the opportunity, prefers high returns to low ones.

(2) The investor considers variability of returns undesirable and prefers less to more. Variability is associated with risk and measured by the variance or standard deviation of returns.

(3) The investor bases his portfolio decisions upon the principle of utility maximization.

(4) The actions of the investor are defined by the rules of rational behavior.

Markowitz utilized the measure of covariance between two securities to demonstrate that the total variance of the portfolio could be reduced by the judicious selection of securities with specific properties. The original formulation proceeds basically in two steps. First, the investor selects a set of efficient portfolios from a universe of N securities; an efficient portfolio, P_e, is a subset of the N-security universe that possesses the following characteristics:[8]

(1) It is a legitimate portfolio, i.e. it excludes short sales;

(2) If another legitimate portfolio promises a higher expected return, it must also be characterized by a larger variance than P_e; and

(3) If another legitimate portfolio possesses a smaller variance of returns, it must also be characterized by a smaller expected return than P_e.

Secondly, the investor selects the particular efficient portfolio which provides him with the most suitable combination of risk and return. That is, the investor chooses from among many efficient portfolios the one that maximizes his utility, given his wealth constraint.

Let us now define the return from a given security (asset) i in period t, R_{it}, by

$$R_{it} = \frac{P_{it+1} + D_{it}}{P_{it}} = 1 + r_{it}, \qquad i = 1, 2, \ldots, N, \tag{5}$$

where

P_{it} = market price at beginning of period t,
D_{it} = cash dividend (or interest) for period t, and
r_{it} = rate of return in period t.

Then we can define portfolio return for period t, R_{pt}, by

$$R_{pt} = X_1 R_{1t} + X_2 R_{2t} + \ldots + X_N R_{Nt} = \sum_{i=1}^{N} X_i R_{it}, \tag{6}$$

where X_i = proportion of portfolio wealth invested in security i, and

$$\sum_{i=1}^{N} X_i = 1, \qquad X_i \geq 0. \tag{7}$$

The first constraint, above, implies full investment in risky assets by excluding

[8]See Markowitz (1959, p. 140).

cash holdings, and the second constraint ensures the legitimacy of the portfolio by excluding short sales. Thus, the return from a portfolio of securities is a linear combination of the individual security returns in proportion to their participation, or a weighted sum of the random variables, R_i. Similarly, the variance of the portfolio by

$$\sigma_p^2 = \sum_{i=1}^{N} \sum_{j=1}^{N} X_i X_j \sigma_{ij}, \tag{8}$$

where $\sigma_{ij} =$ the covariance between the returns of the ith and jth securities.

Now, the E–V criterion requires that the investor choose that particular portfolio with minimum variance (V) for a given return (E) or, conversely, maximum (E) for a given (V), where $E = \mu_p$ and $V = \sigma_p^2$. Properly stated, the E–V criterion will yield efficient combinations of assets by solving the following quadratic programming problem:[9]

$$\min \left(\sum_{i=1}^{N} \sum_{j=1}^{N} X_i X_j \sigma_{ij} \right)$$

subject to

$$\sum_{i=1}^{N} X_i \mu_i = E_0, \tag{9}$$

$$\sum_{i=1}^{N} X_i = 1.$$

The E–V criterion, being a single-period[10] decision framework is, of course, a static model which, according to Markowitz can be augmented by combining standard statistical methodology with the judgement of market experts.[11] Moreover, Markowitz (1959) viewed portfolio selection as a two-step procedure whereby the investor first constructed an efficient frontier and then utilized his preference structure to obtain the optimal portfolio.[12]

[9]The E–V criterion is the most commonly utilized efficiency criterion for portfolio selection. It is a sufficient (but not a necessary) condition for dominance when either the investor's utility function is quadratic or the probability distributions of the resultant portfolios can be fully described by only two parameters that are independent of each other. While some criticism of the E–V criterion will be presented in section 7 of this chapter and in the chapter entitled "Alternatives to Mean–Variance for Portfolio Selection" the reader may refer to Feldstein (1969), Hanoch and Levy (1969), Levy and Hanoch (1970) and Tobin (1969) for more elaborate discussions.

[10]Markowitz (1959) also developed a "long-run growth" model which was later extended by Latané (1959, 1967, 1969), Breiman (1961), Hakansson (1971a, 1971b) and others.

[11]The Bayesian approach proposed by Markowitz will be discussed in section 4 of this chapter.

[12]The two-step E–V to the selection of the optimal portfolio was improved by Farrar (1962), who reformulated the parametric quadratic programming model in terms of maximizing the utility function of the decision maker. In this case, the investor specifies the appropriate risk-aversion coefficient and obtains the corresponding optimal portfolio. It should be noted here that Farrar's original intention was to test the explanatory power of the E–V strategy by utilizing data from mutual fund companies. And, while he concluded in the affirmative, his results were challenged by Friend and Vickers (1965), and gave rise to a host of similar studies.

3. E–V portfolio selection under risk–index models

The basic Markowitz E–V technique, known as the full covariance model, posed both conceptual and computational problems. For this reason Markowitz had suggested that the relationship between securities be portrayed by relating each security to some common index, and then deriving the covariance implicitly from this new relationship.[13]

A number of important observations should be made at this juncture. First, the index proposed by Markowitz need not be confined to one indicator of general economic activity. Indeed, a number of indices could (and should) be constructed to indicate the correlations in the levels of economic activity within industries, between industries, the overall economy, and so forth. Secondly, the relationship between the performance of a security and the relevant index need not be assumed linear. Thirdly, the actual probability distribution of index changes can be expected to have different degrees of variability at high and low points of the index.

Sharpe (1963) seized upon the index concept and developed the so-called diagonal or single-index model, whose eventual modification by Sharpe (1964, 1965, 1966), Lintner (1965a, b), and Fama (1968), led to a macroeconomic theory of equilibrium in capital markets. The standard formulation of the single-index stochastic model is as follows:

$$R_i = \beta_{0i} + \beta_{1i} R_m + u_i, \tag{10}$$

where R_i = random return on security i, β_{0i} = intercept, a constant, β_{1i} = the slope of the linear regression model specific to security i, R_m = random return from a market index, and u_i = a random variable with an expected value of zero and zero correlation with m and the other u_i's.

If we let μ_m be the expected return on R_m, and σ_m^2, σ_{ui}^2 denote the variance of R_m and u_i, respectively, the portfolio selection problem reduces to the minimization of

$$-\lambda \left(\sum_{i=1}^{N} \beta_{0i} X_i + \beta_m \mu_m \right) + \beta_m^2 \sigma_m^2 + \sum_{i=1}^{N} X_i^2 \sigma_{ui}^2, \tag{11}$$

subject to

$$\sum_{i=1}^{N} \beta_{1i} X_i = \beta_m,$$

$$\sum_{i=1}^{N} X_i = 1,$$

$$X_i \geqslant 0, \qquad i = 1, 2, \ldots, N.$$

[13]See Markowitz (1959, p. 100).

Hence, in terms of its original motivation, the cumbersome covariance matrix of the basic E–V model has now been reduced to a diagonal matrix — one step removed from the final solution. It should also be stated in passing that some of the assumptions of the Sharpe model may not obtain in general. For example, it is assumed that return covariances can be estimated indirectly through the return on the index rather than through a pairwise comparison of security returns. Indeed, the diagonal model assumes that $E(u_i, u_j) = 0$ — an assumption not made by the Markowitz full-covariance model.[14]

Since one of the strongest assumptions made by the single-index model is the homogeneity of assets in the market, with a dominant market factor, attempts have also been made to construct multi-index models that would capture the potential heterogeneities generated by such factors as restricted competition or industry effects. These models can also be utilized to verify the marginal improvement in the portfolio as we increase the number of indices. Conversely, they also measure the marginal cost of reducing the number of indices, in an N-security portfolio. There are two types of multi-index models.[15]

(1) The covariance form of the multi-index model, which maintains the basic single-index formulation within each class of securities, but allows for the covariability among class indices. The covariance form assumes components from M-classes of securities, where the return for each individual security is linearly related to the level of the index derived from the class. The covariance matrix can be partitioned into four submatrices, two with zero and two with non-zero elements.

(2) The diagonal form of the multi-index model, which employs a hierarchy of indices, of which the first relates to the yield of the securities in their respective class. Thus, the relationship is expressed among class (or industry) indices. The basic structure of this model is similar to the covariance form, but it assumes in addition that each class (industry) index is itself linearly related to an overall market index.

4. E–V portfolio selection under partial ignorance[16]

The selection of portfolios under conditions of risk – outlined in sections 2 and 3 — basically assumes that the parameters are known with certainty. However, the estimation of the required parameters is the cornerstone of sound portfolio selection practice. Thus, if we were to utilize time series data for the

[14]Early empirical tests by Sharpe (1965, 1966) lent support to the empirical content of the diagonal single-index model. However, later tests by McEnally (1973), Cohen and Pogue (1967), Wallingford (1967) and others yielded conflicting results.

[15]See Wallingford (1967) and Cohen and Pogue (1967) for details on the construction of these models.

[16]This section follows the general outline presented in Gressis (1975).

estimation of the parameters in the objective functions (3) and (3′), we would rewrite them as follows:

$$-\lambda \overline{R}_p + S_p^2 = -\lambda X' \overline{R} + X' S X, \tag{12}$$

where

$$X = [X_1, X_2, \ldots, X_N]', \text{ is an } N \times 1 \text{ decision vector,}$$
$$\overline{R} = [\overline{R}_1, \overline{R}_1, \overline{R}_2, \ldots, \overline{R}_N]', \text{ is an } N \times 1 \text{ sample mean vector,}$$
$$S = \{s_{ij}\}, \text{ is an } N \times N \text{ sample covariance matrix,}$$
$$(\overline{R}_p, S_p^2(\overline{R}_p, S_p^2) = \text{estimates of } (\mu_p, \sigma_p^2), \text{ and}$$
$$(\overline{R}_i, S_{ij}) = \text{estimates of } (\mu_i, \sigma_{ij}), \ i,j = 1, 2, \ldots, N.$$

The problem arising from the estimation of parameters is, of course, not confined to the construction of the efficient frontier. Indeed, as there exists exact mapping between the arguments (parameters) in the expectations function (efficient frontier) and the preference function (indifference curves), the recognition of stochasticity in one function carries over to the other. Unfortunately, very few researchers have studied the problem of uncertainty in the parameters as it applies to portfolio selection models. Among these researchers, Mao and Särndal (1966), Kalymon (1971), Fried (1970), Frankfurter et al. (1971, 1974), Dhingra (1973) have concentrated on the effects of such uncertainty upon the efficient frontier, while Gressis (1975) has attempted to study both stochastic frontiers and stochastic preferences. However, all researchers have concluded that the effects of the sampling are serious, and in the remainder of this section we shall review some of these studies.

4.1. Estimation of parameters — Bayesian models

Mao and Särndal (1966) expanded on an earlier suggestion by Markowitz[17] and attempted to reconstruct the portfolio selection problem in terms of statistical decision theory. Beginning with the premise that the estimates of the security analyst about probable future returns are subjective and conditional upon several environmental state variables, they proposed a method for including these effects in the analysis.

Let us begin the analysis by restricting the external environmental factors to the influence of general economic activity upon investment decisions. The investor has assigned a probability p to the prospect of good business conditions and a probability q to the expectation of poor conditions. These beliefs are known as a priori probabilities. Within this framework, he has also adjusted the information about the returns from each of m securities, to be conditional upon

---

[17]See Markowitz (1959, p. 27).

Table 15.1.

Good business conditions, ψ_1	Poor business conditions, ψ_2
E_i	E_i'
σ_{ii}	σ_{ii}'
σ_{ij}	σ_{ij}'

the two expected states of the economy, as shown in table 15.1, where E_i, E_i' = the expected return from security i, under states ψ_1 and ψ_2, respectively, σ_{ii}, σ_{ii}' = the variance of returns from security i, under states ψ_1, and ψ_2, respectively, and σ_{ij}, σ_{ij}' = the covariance of returns from securities i and j, under states ψ_1 and ψ_2, respectively.

Now, assume that the individual through the observation of some experimental process, y, is able to obtain more information about the true state of the world, ψ, and revises his a priori probabilities p and q. The new probabilities – known as a posteriori probabilities – are denoted by p^* and q^*, and can be evaluated by *Bayes' theorem*, as follows:

$$p^* = P(\Psi = \psi_1|y) = \frac{P(y|\psi_1)P(\psi_1)}{P(y|\psi_1)P(\psi_1) + P(y|\psi_2)P(\psi_2)}, \tag{13}$$

$$q^* = P(\Psi = \psi_2|y) = \frac{P(y|\psi_2)P(\psi_2)}{P(y|\psi_1)P(\psi_1) + P(y|\psi_2)P(\psi_2)}, \tag{14}$$

where $P(y|\psi_1)$; $P(y|\psi_2)$ = the probabilities of observing outcome y under states ψ_1 and ψ_2, respectively, and $P(\psi_1)$; $P(\psi_2)$ = the a prior probabilities of the states of the world.

The decision theory framework proposed by Mao and Särndal requires the construction of a payoff matrix. The payoff matrix for the portfolio model is constructed in the standard fashion of computing the expected returns and variances under each of the two states, ψ_1 and ψ_2. Substitution of the computed values for E_i, E_i', and σ_{ii}, σ_{ii}', into the investor's objective preference function will determine the payoff of the portfolio under any state of the world. When the complete payoff matrix has been constructed, an admissible set is selected by eliminating all the portfolios that are dominated by other portfolios. Finally, the optimal portfolio is selected by the *Bayesian strategy*; this strategy yields the portfolio that maximizes the weighted average of payoffs.

When we apply the Bayesian strategy to the Markowitz framework, the portfolio selection problem is recast in the following form:

$$\left(\sum_{i=1}^{N} X_i(p^*E_i + q^*E_i') - A \sum_{i=1}^{N} \sum_{j=1}^{N} X_i X_j (p^*\sigma_{ij} + q^*\sigma_{ij}') \right), \tag{15}$$

subject to

$$\sum_{i=1}^{N} X_i = 1$$

and

$$X_i \geqslant 0, \qquad i = 1, 2, \ldots, N,$$

where A = the investor's risk-aversion coefficient, and all other symbols are as defined throughout the chapter.

In perspective the Mao and Särndal decision theoretic approach to portfolio selection is an improved version of the Farrar (1962) framework for obtaining the optimal portfolio from the efficient frontier. The allowance for multiple states of the world — through the influence of environmental conditions— improves the flexibility and generality of portfolio selection methodology.

Interesting extensions of Bayesian methodology have also been applied recently to the problem of estimation risk by Barry (1974), Winkler (1973, 1975), and others. We shall briefly review the work of Barry who also considers the problem of uncertainty associated with the covariance matrix of security returns, Σ. Barry considers three states of prior knowledge about the population mean, $\hat{\mu}$, and covariance matrix, Σ.

(a) μ and Σ are both known. This is the standard case where the analyst utilizes the sample mean, $\hat{\mu}$, and sample covariance matrix, S, to estimate μ and Σ, respectively.

(b) μ is unknown and Σ is known. This is a case in which the portfolio variance is affected and will be dealt with when we review the earlier work by Kalymon (1971).

(c) μ and Σ are both unknown, which is by far the most interesting case.

In all three cases the portfolio return is the same, while the variance increases as the standard assumption of known μ and Σ is relaxed, with the largest portfolio variance associated with case (c).[18] Moreover, efficient portfolios obtained under one set of assumptions say, case (a), are inefficient under the other two sets.[19]

4.2. Estimation of parameters — non-Bayesian models

Fried (1970), utilizing standard statistical techniques, developed a framework for obtaining a priori distributions for the Markowitz E–V portfolio selection method. Beginning with the case of a single asset, Fried defines the return, R_{it},

---

[18]It should be noted that these works utilizing a Bayesian decision theory framework basically assume that the sample estimates are the true population parameters, in effect sidestepping rather than resolving the estimation problem.

[19]Similar conclusions for cases (b) and (c) were reached earlier by Kalymon (1971), which the Barry study attempted to extend within the Bayesian framework.

of the ith security in period t as follows:

$$R_{it} = Y_t\Gamma_i + U_{it},$$ (16)

where $Y_t = [y_{1t}, \ldots, y_{st}]$ is a row vector of s fixed known independent variables; $\Gamma_i' = [\gamma_{1i}, \ldots, \gamma_{si}]$ is a vector of coefficients describing the effect of Y_t on R_{it}; and U_{it} is a disturbance term, assumed independent of Y_t, with a distribution having an expected value of zero and variance $\sigma_{u_{ii}}$. It follows that

$$E(R_{it}) = \mu_{it} = Y_t\Gamma_i = \sum_{j=1}^{s} y_{it}\gamma_{ji}$$ (17)

and

$$E(R_{it} - \mu_{it})^2 = \sigma_{ii} = \sigma_{u_{ii}}.$$ (18)

On the basis of the above, Fried proceeds to establish the bias generated by the utilization of historical measures of risk and return. For example, given n historical observations for R_i, we can compute the average return and variance by

$$\underline{R}_i = \frac{1}{n}\sum_{t=1}^{n} R_{it} = \frac{1}{n}\sum_{t=1}^{n}(Y_t\Gamma_i + U_{it})$$

$$= \underline{Y}\Gamma_i + \underline{U}_i,$$ (19)

where

$$\underline{Y} = \frac{1}{n}\sum_{t=1}^{n} Y_t$$

is the calculated mean value of past values of Y,

$$\underline{U}_i = \frac{1}{n}\sum_{t=1}^{n} U_{it}$$

is the calculated mean value of past values of U_i; and

$$\underline{\sigma}_i^2 = \frac{1}{n}\sum_{t=1}^{n}(R_{it} - \underline{R}_i)^2$$

$$= \Gamma_i'\underline{\Sigma}_y\Gamma_i + \frac{2}{n}\sum_{t=1}^{n}(U_{it} - \underline{U}_i)(Y_t - \underline{Y})\Gamma_i + \underline{S}u_{ii},$$ (20)

where

$$\underline{\Sigma}_y = \frac{1}{n}\sum_{t=1}^{n}(Y_t - \underline{Y})'(Y_t - \underline{Y})$$

is the matrix of average calculated squared deviations of the explanatory variables about their means, and

$$\underline{S}u_{ii} = \frac{1}{n}\sum_{t=1}^{n}(U_{it} - \underline{U}_i)^2$$

is the average of the calculated squared deviations of the disturbance term about its mean.

Taking expected values for (19) and (20) we obtain (19') and (20') below, indicating that the former are not correct estimates[20] of the expected return and risk for investment in the current period, $\tau = n + 1$:

$$E(R_i) = \underline{\mu}_i = \underline{Y}\Gamma_i + E(\underline{U}_i) = \underline{Y}\Gamma_i \tag{19'}$$

and

$$E(\underline{\sigma}_i^2) = \Gamma_i' \underline{\Sigma}_y \Gamma_i + \frac{n}{n-1} \sigma_{U_{ii}}. \tag{20'}$$

Generalization of the analysis to the case of N assets leads to similarly biased estimates.

If the matrix of coefficients Γ_i is not known, then estimates must be obtained. Thus, given a sample of n observations on R_i,

$$R_i' = [R_{i1}, R_{i2}, \ldots, R_{in}],$$

since

$$E(U_{it}) = 0, \qquad \text{for all } t,$$
$$E(U_{it}, U_{is}) = 0, \qquad \text{for all } s \neq t,$$
$$E(U_{it}, U_{it}) = \sigma_{U_{ii}}, \quad \text{for all } t,$$

and, as we know, $Y' \equiv [Y_1', Y_2', \ldots, Y_n']$ is a matrix of fixed numbers with rank $s < n$, the best linear unbiased estimate of Γ_i obtained by the method of least squares will be

$$\hat{\Gamma}_i = (Y'Y)^{-1} Y' R_i. \tag{21}$$

Because $\hat{\Gamma}_i$ is unbiased

$$E(R_{it}) = \mu_{it} = Y_t \hat{\Gamma}_i. \tag{22}$$

Hence, in such cases the risk associated with R_{it} cannot be captured through an estimate of $\sigma_{U_{ii}}$ along, since we also need an additional measure of the degree of confidence in the estimate of Γ_i.

A combined estimate of the uncertainty attached to the forecast of R_{it} is given by

$$\sigma_{iit} = S_{Uii} \left[\overline{Y}_t (\overline{Y}' \overline{Y})^{-1} \overline{Y}_t' + \frac{1}{n} + 1 \right], \tag{23}$$

where

$$S_{Uii} = \frac{e_i' e_i}{n - S},$$
$$e_i' = [e_{i1}, \ldots, e_{in}], \tag{24}$$
$$e_{it} = R_{it} - Y_t \hat{\Gamma}_i,$$

[20] The estimate of the variance will always have a positive bias, and in general, $\mu_{it} \neq \underline{\mu}_i$.

and the bars signify deviations about the sample mean. It should be noted here that the first two terms within the brackets of (23) reflect the analyst's confidence in the estimate of the matrix of coefficients, Γ_i, while the last term represents the unexplained variation. Moreover, the Fried forecasting model can be recast in a form analogous to Sharpe's model, with greater flexibility in capturing changing expectations.[21]

Kalymon (1971) actually had developed the first formal model for the incorporation of estimation risk into the Markowitz E–V framework and for the assessment of portfolio risk when both objective and subjective information is employed. He considered two kinds of risk: (a) the risk generated by the fluctuation of security returns, and (b) the risk attributed to incomplete information about the parameters of the model. The combined measure of total risk is the variance about the estimate of the mean.

In applying the quadratic programming model (eq. (9)) for decision-making under risk with historical data, the investor must obtain a portfolio with vector weights

$$X^* = [X_1^*, X_2^*, \ldots, X_N^*]$$

such that

$$X^* \Sigma X'^* = \min(X\Sigma X' \mid X\mu = E_0) \tag{25}$$

for some required expected return E_0. For a sample of n vector observations, and if $\hat{\mu}$ is an unbiased estimator of μ, we have

$$E(X\hat{\mu}) = XE(\hat{\mu}) = X\mu = E(R_p) \tag{26}$$

and

$$V(X\hat{\mu}) = XV(\hat{\mu})X' = X\Sigma^*X'. \tag{27}$$

Moreover, Kalymon claims that, for the investor who is concerned about the deviation of actual portfolio returns from predicted returns, then $V(R_p - X\hat{\mu})$ is the appropriate measure of portfolio risk.[22]

Another interesting analysis was performed by Dickinson (1974) who questioned the reliability of the results obtained from the E–V portfolio selection approach. Considering just the simple case of a two-security portfolio, with normally distributed security returns and $\sigma_{12} = 0$, Dickinson reached the follow-

---

[21]It should be noted that most of the approaches to decision-making under partial ignorance implicitly refute the so-called "semi-strong form of efficient capital markets" (Fama (1970)). In the case of Fried, he considers the assumption that prices fully reflect all publicly available information as untenable (Fried (1970)).

[22]Kalymon (1971) further shows that minimization of $X\Sigma X'$ will yield efficient portfolios and, hence, there is no need to solve for the full risk matrix. This latter conclusion is drawn on the basis of two assumptions: (a) the distributions of returns are stationary, and (b) the covariances of the returns are known. Under these assumptions the variances yielded by the two procedures will differ by a known value.

ing conclusions: (a) the distributions of the estimated portfolio weights. $\tilde{X}_1$, $\tilde{X}_2$ are very complex; (b) the estimated weights for the two-security, equal-risk ($\sigma_1^2 = \sigma_2^2$) portfolio are not reliable, even in the case of a large number of historical observations; and (c) the reliability of the estimate obtained for the minimum-risk portfolio is very low, even for $n = 40$.

4.3. Estimation of parameters — simulation models

As was shown by Kalymon (1971), the estimation error is an important component of risk in portfolio selection. However, an additional impact is generated when we allow for uncertainty in the variances and covariances of the participating securities. In the remainder of this section we shall review briefly three studies that utilized simulation experiments to assess the joint effects of uncertain means, variances, and covariances.

In the first study, Frankfurter et al. (1971, 1974) utilized a Monte-Carlo simulation with a universe of three securities, whose returns they assumed to be multivariate normally distributed. They obtained time-series estimates of the mean vector and covariance matrix, which they utilized to generate samples of three-tuples of returns of size $M = 5$, 10, 25, and 50. Estimates of portfolio means and variances for each sample were obtained, and by varying the proportions of security participation the authors defined 66 distinct portfolios. On the basis of their results, the authors reached the following conclusions: (a) The composition of the efficient set varies substantially among sample trials, and portfolios which are inefficient in terms of the true parameters may frequently appear efficient. (b) In general, both the truly efficient and the truly inefficient portfolios appear on the efficient frontier with approximately the same relative frequencies. However, as the sample size increases, the relative frequency with which inferior portfolios appear on the efficient frontier decreases, but still remains significantly large.

In another study, Dhingra (1973) also employed a Monte-Carlo simulation on a sample of 100 securities from the New York Stock Exchange (NYSE) and the S&P Industrial Index, to assess the effects of estimation error on the stability of portfolios generated by the Sharpe diagonal model for selected target mean returns. Dhingra utilized the following conditional stochastic form of eq. (10), which assumes that R_m is known with certainty:

$$\tilde{R}_i | R_m = \beta_{0i} + \beta_{1i} R_m + \tilde{u}_i, \tag{27}$$

where R_m = the mean value of return on the market factor for next time period, and $\tilde{R}_i | R_m$ = conditional return on security i, i.e. the random return on i for the next time period given that the return on the market factor will be R_m. Then, the efficient frontier is obtained by solving the standard quadratic programming problem given by (11), which yields an optimal choice decision vector for prespecified values of λ^*:

$$X^* = [X_1^*, X_2^*, \ldots, X_N^*]' \tag{28}$$

It is obvious that the sample estimates of the true model parameters are such that the resulting efficient frontier will actually be an efficient band.

Dhingra drew the following conclusions from his study: (a) for a target portfolio's mean return, the degree of diversification does not vary among sample periods; (b) the variance of the distribution of S^{*2} varies directly with the portfolio mean return and inversely with the degree of diversification; (c) the distributions of S^{*2} for all sample periods are negatively skewed, while the stability of X^* varies directly with the degree of diversification; (d) the stability of S^{*2} and X^* of an efficient portfolio varies directly with the length of the time period used, up to a critical level of diversification; and (e) for given target portfolio mean returns, the securities that do not enter the true efficient portfolio have a low tendency to enter the sampling distribution of the sample efficient portfolios.

In the last study to be reviewed, Gressis (1975) applied simulation methodology to assess the sampling error (estimation risk) in the Markowitz E–V portfolio selection model. Using a sample of ten common stocks, and assuming normality of returns distributions and quadratic utility functions, Gressis draws the following conclusions:[23] (a) the effects of sampling error upon the reliability of the E–V model solutions are serious; (b) even for relatively large sample sizes, all portfolio related estimators, i.e. $\bar{R}_p$, $\bar{S}_p^2$, and X are not very reliable; (c) the portfolio related estimators, above, are also biased; and (d) the effects of sampling error are magnified when we allow for the existence of stochastic utility functions.

5. E–V capital market theory–the asset pricing model[24]

The original E–V portfolio selection framework, as proposed by Markowitz (1952, 1959), was both restricted and normative in nature.[25] In its basic form it constitutes a sufficient (but not a necessary) condition for dominance when either the investor's utility function is quadratic or the probability distributions

---

[23]The Gressis study was broader in scope than the assessment of the estimation risk, and a fair review of its implications is beyond the limits of this chapter.

[24]The presentation in this section follows the outline presented in Jensen (1969, 1972a) and Fama (1976). The general topic and its empirical content is also reviewed in Fama (1970), Fama and MacBeth (1974), Fama and Miller (1972), Merton (1973), Mossin (1968), Mayers (1972), Roll (1977), and Sharpe (1961, 1965).

[25]It should be noted here that Markowitz was well aware of some of the problems involved and proposed several extensions. Indeed, as has already been discussed earlier, the basic extensions by Sharpe (1963) and Mao and Särndal (1966) were inspired from Markowitz's suggestions. Moreover, as will be seen in the follow-up chapter, other extensions, e.g. the semivariance approach, were also outlined by Markowitz.

of the asset combinations can be fully described by two parameters that are independent of each other (Hanock and Levy (1969), Hadar and Russell (1969)). However, several economists seized upon the opportunity to transform the E–V framework into a positive hypothesis for the equilibrium structure of prices in the capital markets. Among the early contributors, Tobin (1965, 1969) employed the portfolio selection approach to derive implications about the demand for cash balances, followed by a series of research papers on the portfolio behavior of financial institutions (Hester and Tobin (1967a, b)). But, the E–V approach did not really become a generalizable hypothesis of market behavior until the works of Sharpe (1963), Lintner (1965a, b), Fama (1968), and others[26], reformulated the Sharpe (1963) diagonal, single index model into an equilibrium model of capital asset prices. We shall devote this section of the chapter to the basic asset pricing model and the other two sections to some of its extensions, tests, and limitations.

The one-period asset pricing model is predicated upon the following assumptions, applicable to all investors and market assets.

(a) Investors in the market act to maximize expected utility of single-period terminal wealth.

(b) Investors select portfolios on the basis of two summary statistical measures of central tendency and dispersion–namely, the mean and variance (or standard deviation).

(c) Investors can borrow or lend unlimited amounts of funds at a risk-free rate of interest (exogenously determined).

(d) Investors can engage in short-sales activity.[27]

(e) Investors possess identical subjective estimates of the means, variances, and covariances of returns among market assets.

(f) Market assets are perfectly divisible.

(g) Market assets are perfectly liquid (marketable).

(h) There are no transaction costs.

(i) There are no taxes.

(j) Investors are price takers.

(k) The supply of market assets is given.

Now let us define the model variables, as follows. Let

$$R_F = \text{the riskless rate of interest,}$$
$$E(\tilde{R}_j) = \text{the expected return on asset } j,\text{[28]}$$
$$E(\tilde{R}_m) = \text{the expected return on the market portfolio,[29]}$$

---

[26]There are, of course, several other contributors to the capital asset pricing model, e.g. Treynor and Mossin. For a more detailed review the reader is referred to Fama (1976), Fama and Miller (1972), Jensen (1972a), and Roll (1977).

[27]Following the original framework of E–V, Sharpe, (1963, 1964) excludes short-sales.

[28]The tildes denote random variables.

[29]The market portfolio, whose exact composition is otherwise both elusive and controversial, is here defined as a portfolio invested in every asset outstanding, exactly in proportion to its fraction of the total value of assets. See Jensen (1972b, p. 359).

$\sigma(\tilde{R}_m)$ = the standard deviation of return on the market portfolio,[30] and
$\text{cov}(\tilde{R}_j, \tilde{R}_m)$ = the covariance between the return on asset j and the market portfolio.

Then, the equilibrium expected return on a given asset j, $E(\tilde{R}_j)$, is given by the following expression:

$$E(\tilde{R}_j) = R_F + \frac{\left[E(\tilde{R}_m) - R_F\right]\text{cov}(\tilde{R}_j, R_m)}{\sigma(\tilde{R}_m)}, \tag{29}$$

or, letting

$$\lambda = \frac{\left[E(\tilde{R}_m) - R_F\right]}{\sigma(\tilde{R}_m)} \tag{30}$$

be the market price of risk, we have

$$E(\tilde{R}_j) = R_F + \frac{\text{cov}(\tilde{R}_j, \tilde{R}_m)}{\sigma(\tilde{R}_m)}. \tag{31}$$

Reference to fig. 15.2 will clarify the meaning of the market portfolio. For example, the opportunity (feasible) set is defined by the boundary line *CDME*, which also defines the meaningful area of diversification, i.e. the efficient frontier. In terms of the original E–V formulation,[31] the risk-averse investor will maximize his expected utility by selecting efficient portfolio D, yielding a level of expected utility U_1, and defined by $[E(\tilde{R}_D), \sigma(\tilde{R}_D)]$. However, when the investor is allowed to hold some of his funds in the form of cash or other noncash risk-free assets, the efficient set changes. Assume a riskless asset with a certain future return, R_F. Then the investor can form any combination of the riskless and risky assets along a straight line that connects the two opportunities. And, by virtue of assumption (c), above, the straight line is defined as $R_F MQ$.

Now, any point below M along the straight line $R_F M$, defined by

$$E(\tilde{R}) = R_F + \frac{E(\tilde{R}_M) - R_F}{\sigma(\tilde{R}_M)} \sigma(\tilde{R}), \tag{32}$$

where $\sigma(\tilde{R}) < \sigma(\tilde{R}_M)$, is clearly more efficient than the corresponding points along the old efficient frontier. And, by similar reasoning for points along the MQ segment, we conclude that the straight line $R_F MQ$ is the new efficient frontier, also referred to as the "capital market line". Hence, the investor may now choose portfolio P, yielding a level of expected utility U_2, and defined by $[E(\tilde{R}_p), \sigma(\tilde{R}_p)]$. Given assumptions (a) through (k), all investors who wish to hold both risky and the riskless assets will hold portfolios along the capital market line $R_F MQ$, which will be combinations of R_F and M,[32] the latter being the

[31]See Tobin (1969).

[30]The mean–standard deviation formulation yields results identical to the mean–variance approach.

[32]This is, of course, Tobin's (1969) separation theorem.

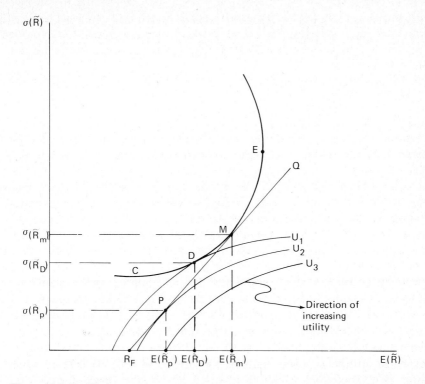

Figure 15.2. Equilibrium market portfolio with same riskless borrowing and lending rates.

so-called market portfolio. Of course, given the definition for the market price of risk (risk premium) λ in (30) and the definition for expected return in (32), we can rewrite (29) as follows:

$$E(\tilde{R}_p) = R_F + \lambda \sigma(\tilde{R}_p), \tag{29'}$$

which states the exact relationship between the returns on any efficient portfolio on the capital market line and the market portfolio.[33]

6. E – V asset pricing model–some extensions

The robustness of any analytical structure like the capital asset pricing model can only be tested by allowing other structures, i.e. institutional, empirical,[34] etc.

---

[33]See Jensen (1972, pp. 361–363) for an interesting derivation of the equation for the equilibrium expected returns on an individual asset *j*. See also his appendix (pp. 392–395) for an alternative derivation of the equilibrum asset pricing model.

[34]Some of the tests on analytical robustness are the direct result of empirical tests, which are reviewed in the final section of this chapter.

to influence it. In the case of the asset pricing model, one can relax some of the assumptions and investigate the extent to which they are crucial to the model. In this section we shall review briefly several such developments and extensions of the basic framework.

6.1. Multiperiod asset pricing

Assumption (a), above, requiring that all investors be single-period expected utility of terminal wealth maximizers is, obviously, overly restrictive in terms of market realities. For this reason several discrete and continuous multiperiod versions have been constructed as alternatives to the basic asset pricing model.[35] In one of the early papers Fama (1970) formalized the simultaneous nature of the consumption and investment decisions in a multiperiod framework. By establishing the motivational assumption as the maximization of expected life-time utility of consumption, Fama formulates the decision as the standard dynamic programming problem with the property of recursive optimality. Thus, the problem becomes one of optimizing the consumption–investment decision for period 1, provided that all future contingent decisions are also known. Thus, the risk-averse maximizer of expected lifetime utiltiy of consumption acts much like the risk-averse, single-period expected utility maximizer.[36]

Other attempts to multiperiod portfolio selection have also been made. For example, Long (1972) has developed a more general discrete, multiperiod portfolio selection model, which enabled him to derive some implications for the term structure of interest rates. Similarly, Black and Scholes[37] and Merton (1973)[38] have derived continuous-time versions of the basic asset pricing model.

6.2. Restrictions on riskless borrowing and lending

Various efforts to test the analytical robustness of the asset pricing model when either riskless borrowing and/or lending are restricted have resulted in some

[35]Two of the earliest works on lifetime portfolio selection by Mossin (1968) and Samuelson (1969) will not be discussed here.

[36]In a recent paper, however, Gressis et al. (1976), dealing directly with multiperiod portfolio selection, reached the following conclusions. (a) In the case of risky assets only, single-period E–V efficiency criterion also yields K-period E–V efficient frontiers. However, in the case of expected quadratic utility maximizers, investment horizon affects portfolio choice. (b) When both riskless and risky assets are considered, the one-period and K-period portfolios differ in composition. (c) When we relax the assumption on the uniformity of the planning horizon length, the overall, clearing, market portfolio is likely to be inefficient.

[37]See (Jensen (1972b), pp. 385–388).

[38]An interesting byproduct of Merton's intertemporal continuous time model is his conclusion that under certain conditions all investors will hold their funds in three different portfolios: (a) the market portfolio, (b) the riskless asset, and (c) a portfolio whose returns are perfectly negatively correlated with changes in the risk-free interest rate.

interesting implications, For example, Fama (1976) has shown that in the absence of the riskless asset, the assumptions of homogeneity of expectations and short-selling suffice to relate the equilibrium return on any asset linearly to its systematic risk.[39] Black (1972) has also shown that, in the absence of riskless borrowing and lending, but with allowance for short-selling, the portfolios of all investors will consist of linear combinations of the market portfolio and another portfolio whose returns have zero covariance with the market portfolio. Further refinements were subsequently made by allowing riskless lending but no borrowing or, as in the case of Brennan (1971), by allowing differential borrowing and lending rates.

6.3. Other extensions

Other extensions of the asset pricing model have included the effects of differential rates of taxation on dividends and capital gains (Black (1972)), the existence of transactions costs and nonmarketable assets (Mayers (1972)), and the presence of heterogeneous expectations (Brennan (1971), Fama (1976), and Lintner (1965b, 1969)). And, in nearly all cases, it has been shown that the basic two-factor capital asset pricing model is relatively robust.[40]

7. E–V portfolio selection–some empirical tests

The E–V portfolio selection criterion, whether in its basic form proposed by Markowitz and Tobin, or the single-index diagonal form derived by Sharpe, or its more general hypothesis of asset pricing developed by Sharpe, Lintner, Fama, and others, has been subjected to extensive empirical testing. In this final section of the chapter we review very briefly some representative studies of the model in each of its three stages of development.

7.1. Tests on the full-covariance model

The earliest direct test of the Markowitz full-covariance E–V selection criterion was performed by Farrar (1962). Farrar chose the mutual fund industry as his universe of interest, since it was the least constrained by legal and cost limitations. Utilizing monthly data and postulating an arbitrary one-year investment

---

[39]Of course, in the absence of a risk-free asset, the meaning of the intercept in (29) is no longer clear.

[40]Since the nature and scope of this chapter confine it to "strategies", we cannot review several interesting works on extensions of the basic model.

horizon, Farrar addressed the following two questions:[41]

(a) Are mutual fund portolios efficient?

(b) Are the computed attitudes toward risk by the funds consistent with their stated investment objectives?

The inputs for the portfolio were generated by a simple simulator of expectations, which consisted of three separate "naive" assumptions:

(a) Dividends and prices will behave as in the past.

(b) Dividends will behave as in the past, but prices will follow the linear trend fitted to the changes over the last 12 months.

(c) Dividends will behave as in the past but prices will follow the exponential trend of the last 12 months.

Farrar concluded that the E–V model is insensitive to the method by which actual mutual fund managerial expectations are formed. Furthermore, in computing the E–V combinations for portfolios actually held by 23 mutual funds, he found that all these portfolios lie close to the E–V efficient frontier derived from the same universe of securities held by the mutual funds.[42] Farrar's findings suggest that mutual fund managers act on the belief that the future performance of secrities is well approximated by past behavior.[43]

7.2. Tests on the diagonal, index model

Portfolio efficiency tests attracted greater attention after the development of the diagonal model by Sharpe (1963). Sharpe posited a linear approximation to the variance of the portfolio return–namely the product of the weighted responsiveness of the securities to the index and the variability of the index. He tested this approximation in 1967 using 63 securities, from which he chose 30 portfolios by the linear method; exactly 21 securities were included in each portfolio. A comparison of Sharpe's results with those of the full-covariance model indicated that, of the 34 securities chosen by the approximation, 32 were also selected by the full-covariance model. Furthermore, a comparison of the true variance of

[41]As discussed in an earlier section, the motivational assumption in Farrar's model is the maximization of expected utility, approximated by a quadratic curve. As Samuelson (1969) has shown, if the total initial wealth of the investor is high relative to risk, then the quadratic utility function is a good approximation to most utility functions and consequently the E–V analysis is useful as a practical criterion for portfolio allocation.

[42]The Farrar study was later challenged by several researchers on grounds ranging from methodology to its implications for mutual fund performance. See, for example, Friend and Vickers (1965).

[43]Several other tests on the efficiency and/or the assumptions of the full-covariance E–V portfolio selection model have resulted in the construction of alternative efficiency criteria. Such criteria as the mean-semivariance (Mao (1970)), stochastic-dominance (Hadar and Russell (1969), Hansch and Levy (1969), Levy and Hanoch (1970)), geometric mean (Latané (1959), Latané and Young (1969), Latané and Tuttle (1967)), and third and fourth moments of a distribution (Levy and Hanoch (1970)), will be discussed in the chapter entitled "Alternatives to Mean–Variance for Portfolio Selection".

each of the portfolios, computed by the two methods, showed that the variance of the portfolios selected by the approximation was greater, but by not more than 1 percent. Typically, the variance was about 0.5 percent greater, thus supporting the efficiency of Sharpe's linear approximation.

In 1966 Cohen and Pogue (1967) performed the most thorough test of Sharpe's diagonal model, compared its performance to the Markowitz approach, and expanded the analysis by formulating and testing several multi-index models. They took samples of 75 and 150 security groups over a period of 17 years (1947–1964), and generated efficient portfolios for each of four models. The 17-year horizon was broken into two segments so that they could make an ex-post comparison of actual results, i.e. actual relative performance after the efficient frontiers had been attained. Moreover, a universe of 543 securities was selected and divided into ten industry subgroupings, computing one aggregate index, and one index for each industry.

The interesting feature of the results was that the single-index model dominated the multi-index models over a wide range of expected returns. Cohen and Pogue attributed this result to the fact that only common stocks were used and that their high intercorrelation made the group more amenable to a single-index model. They also found that the larger universe size tended to give more efficient frontiers. The upper bound restrictions were decreased with the larger universe size, and the authors found that this effect was less of a factor than universe size in affecting the efficiency of the portfolios.

In addition, Cohen and Pogue drew the following conclusions. (a) The ex-post performance of the efficient portfolios selected by the models, and by mutual funds, clearly dominated that of random portfolios. (b) The ex-post performance of the efficient portfolios tended to dominate mutual funds for returns over 15 percent. (c) There was no strong evidence for the absolute dominance of any of the models over the total range of returns available. The Markowitz model, however, tended to out-perform the others over restricted ranges, followed by the covariance form of the multi-index models.

Wallingford (1967) in a related study tested the single-index and two-index models for dominance, using both actual and simulated data. However, Wallingford made some modifications, and as a result his study was not quite comparable to the one by Cohen and Pogue. He used a universe of only 20 securities, which precluded the use of constraints limiting the maximum investment in a security. This reduction in universe size, and the resultant elimination of the investment constraints, is a major deviation from the Cohen and Pogue analysis and may help to explain some of the differences in conclusions.

Another major deviation by Wallingford was his sole use of the simple two-index model as the only multi-index formulation. He first used only common stocks and found the results to be similar to those reached by Cohen and Pogue, with the single-index model dominating. He then tested a combination of common and preferred stocks–fourteen chosen randomly and six from a single industry. An overall index, along with one for each subgroup, were computed, and for this group the two-index model dominated the single-index model, throughout almost the entire range of returns and variances.

Wallingford proceeded to introduce preferred stocks in place of the six common in the small group, while retaining the original fourteen stocks. The test was conducted again, and the two-index model again out-performed the single-index algorithm. These results were a major deviation from those obtained by Cohen and Pogue. However, his changing of the conditions may well be responsible for the difference. The major deviations in Wallingford's methods were his drastic reduction in the sample size, the omission of institutional constraints, and the computation of indices from the samples rather than from the population. All of these factors would tend to reduce the correlation between the indices, thereby improving the relative performance of the two-index model. Moreover, MacEnally (1973), in a more recent study, concluded that the diagonal form of the multi-index model is a relatively inefficient estimator of the correlation between returns of broad types of securities.[44]

7.3. Tests on the asset pricing model

Most direct tests of the capital asset pricing model regress the average cross-sectional sample returns against each asset's covariance with a selected market index. The earliest such test was performed by Lintner,[45] followed by Douglas (1969), who regressed average cross-sectional sample returns against their own variances, as well as on their covariances with a sample-based index. Utilizing five-year intervals (1926–1960), Douglas found a significant positive correlation between the realized returns and the variance of the returns over time, but not to their covariance with the sample index.[46]

Black et. al. (1972) have argued that, for a specific process of generating asset returns, cross-sectional tests of the asset pricing model will yield misleading results. And, in time-series tests of the model under a different specification (the two-factor random coefficient model), they have concluded that the individual security variances contribute little to the explanation of the mean portfolio returns. Finally, in what appears to be the latest and most comprehensive test of

---

[44]Several worthwhile studies are obviously excluded from this review. See, for example, Hester and Tobin (1967a, b).

[45]Cited in Douglas (1969).

[46]The results by Douglas and Lintner cast serious doubt on the predictive power of the model, as given by (29). According to this form of the model, the variance term for the individual security returns should have a coefficient of zero, whereas the above results indicate that the individual variances (asset risk) are more important than the covariances (portfolio risk). Miller and Scholes (1972) attempted to explain these cross-sectional results in terms specification errors. However, another suggestion offered, i.e. the presence of skewness, which results in interdependence of distributional moments, is a more plausible explanation of the results.

the model, Fama and MacBeth (1974) extended the Black et.al. two-factor model into a four-factor random coefficient model. Fama and MacBeth tested four hypotheses that derive from the Markowitz E–V portfolio selection model.

(a) The risk–return relationship is linear.

(b) The only measure of risk related systematically to expected returns is the β-risk.

(c) The trade-off between expected return and risk is linear.

(d) The expected return on the so-called β-factor, $E(\tilde{\gamma}_{0t}) = R_{Ft}$.

On the basis of the overall sample and of five-year subperiods, Fama and MacBeth conclude that the data are consistent with (a) through (c), above. However, as with Black et. al., they found $E(\tilde{\gamma}_{0t}) \neq R_{Ft}$, and concluded that the basic Sharpe–Lintner formulation is inconsistent with the data.

In closing this chapter on the Markowitz E–V portfolio selection criterion, it will be worth raising the following question: "Is the two-parameter asset pricing model testable?" This question has in reality been raised lately by Roll (1977), one of the early supporters of the framework, who concluded that the pricing model "is testable *in principle*: but arguments are given here that: (a) No correct and unambiguous test of the theory has appeared in the literature, and (b) there is practically no possibility that such a test can be accomplished in the future" (see Roll (1977) pp. 129–130).[47]

References

Adler, M. (1969) "Stock Prices, Inflation, and the Term Structure of Interest Rates", *Journal of Financial and Quantitative Analysis*, December, pp. 493–512.

Arrow, K. J. (1965) *Aspects of the Theory of Risk Bearing*. (Y. Johnsson Lectures, Helsinki).

Barry, C. B. (1974) "Portfolio Analysis under Uncertain Means, Variances, and Covariances", *Journal of Finance*, May, 515–522.

Becker, G. M., M. H. De Groot and J. Marshak (1964) "Measuring Utility by a Single-Response Sequential Method", *Behavioral Science*, July, 226–232.

Bicksler, J. L and J. R. McGuigan (1971) "Utility Functions: A Priori Thoughts and Empirical Fact", ASA, *Proceedings of the Business and Economic Statistics Section*, 297–301.

Black, F. (1972) "Capital Market Equilibrium with Restricted Borrowing", *Journal of Business*, July, 444–454.

Black, F. and M. Scholes (1974) "The Effects of Dividend Yield and Dividend Policy on Common Stock Prices and Returns", *Journal of Financial Economics*, May, 1–22.

Black, F., M. C. Jensen and M. Scholes (1972) "The Capital Asset Pricing Model: Some Empirical Tests", in: M. Jensen, ed., *Studies in the Theory of Capital Markets* (Praeger, New York).

Blume, M. and I. Friend. (1973) "A New Look at the Capital Asset Pricing Model", *Journal of Finance*, March, 19–33.

Borch, K. H. (1968) *The Economics of Uncertainty* (Princeton University Press).

[47]Roll in a wide-ranging three-part study delineates the only testable hypothesis of the two-parameter asset pricing model of Black (1972) i.e. "the market portfolio is mean–variance efficient" —a mere analytical tautology since by definition the market portfolio is on the E–V efficient frontier. In addition, Roll raises questions about the identification (measured composition) of the market portfolio, as well as questioning some of the common uses of the two-parameter asset pricing model.

Brealey, R. A and C. Pyle (compilers) (1974) *A Bibliography of Finance and Investment* (The MIT Press, Cambridge, Mass.).

Breiman, L. (1961) "Optimal Gambling Systems for Favorable Games, in: *Proceedings of the Fourth Berkeley Symposium on Mathematical Statistics and Probability* (University of California Press).

Brennan, M. J. (1971) "Capital Market Equilibrium with Divergent Borrowing and Lending Rates", *Journal of Financial and Quantitative Analysis*, December, 1197–1205.

Cohen, K. J. and J. A. Pogue (1967) "An Empirical Evaluation of Alternative Portfolio-Selection Models", *Journal of Business*, April, 166–193.

Dhingra, H. L. (1973) "Stability of Efficient Portfolios Under Uncertainty", Working Paper WP 73-02, College of Commerce, University of Saskatchewan, Saskatoon, Canada.

Dickinson, J. P. (1974) "The Reliability of Estimation Procedures in Portfolio Analysis", *Journal of Financial and Quantitative Analysis*, June, 447–462.

Douglas, G. W. (1969) "Risk in the Equity Markets: An Empirical Appraisal of Market Efficiency", *Yale Economic Essays*, Spring, 3–45.

Dragomirescu, M. (1972) "An Algorithm for the Minimum-Risk Problem of Stochastic Programming", *Operations Research*, January–February, 154–164.

Dyckman, T. R. and R. Salomon (1972) "Empirical Utility Functions and Random Devices: An Experiment", *Decision Sciences*, April, 1–13.

Enis, P. and S. Geisser (1971) "Estimation of the Probability that $Y < X$", *Journal of the American Statistical Association*, March, 162–168.

Fama, E. F. (1965) "The Behavior of Stock-Market Prices", *Journal of Business*, January, 34–105.

Fama, E. F. (1968) "Risk, Return and Equilibrium: Some Clarifying Comments", *Journal of Finance*, March, 29–40.

Fama, E. F. (1970a) "Multiperiod Consumption-Investment Decisions", *The American Economic Review*, March 163–174.

Fama, E. F. (1970b) "Efficient Capital Markets: A Review of Theory and Empirical Work", *Journal of Finance*, May 383–417.

Fama, E. F. (1976) *Foundations of Finance* (Basic Books, New York).

Fama, E. F. and J. D. MacBeth (1974) "Tests of the Multiperiod Two-Parameter Model", *Journal of Financial Economics*, May, 43–66.

Fama, E. F. and M. H. Miller (1972) *The Theory of Finance* (Holt, Rinehart and Winston, New York).

Farrar, D. E. (1962) *The Investment Decision Under Uncertainty* (Prentice-Hall, Englewood Cliffs).

Feldstein, M. (1969) "Mean Variance Analysis in the Theory of Liquidity Preference and Portfolio Selection", *Review of Economic Studies*, January, 5–12.

Feller, W. (1968) *An Introduction to Probability Theory and Its Applications*, vol. 1, 3rd edn. (John Wiley, New York).

Fishburn, P. C. (1967) "Methods of Estimating Additive Utilities", *Management Science*, March, 435–453.

Frankfurter, G. M., H. E. Phillips and T. P. Seagle. (1971) "Portfolio Selection: The Effects of Uncertain Means, Variances, and Covariances", *Journal of Financial and Quantitative Analysis*, December, 1251–1262.

Frankfurter, G. M., H. E. Phillips and T. P. Sealge (1974) Bias in Estimating Portfolio Alpha and Beta Scores", *The Review of Economics and Statistics*, August, 412–414.

Frederick, D. G. (1971) "An Industrial Pricing Decision Using Bayesian Multivariate Analysis", *Journal of Marketing Research*, May, 199–203.

Freeman, P. and A. E. Gear (1971) "A Probabilistic Objective Function for R & D Portfolio Selection", *Operational Research Quarterly*, September, 253–265.

Fried, J. (1970) "Forecasting and Probability Distributions for Models of Portfolio Selection", *Journal of Finance*, June, 539–554.

Friend, I. and M. Blume (1970) "Measurement of Portfolio Performance under Uncertainty", *The American Economic Review*, September, 561–575.

Friend, I. and D. Vickers (1965) "Portfolio Selection and Investment Performance", *Journal of Finance*, September, 291–315.

Gressis, N. (1975) "The Effects of Sampling Error on the EV Portfolio Selection Model", Unpublished Ph.D. Thesis, The Pennsylvania State University, August.

Gressis, N., J. Hayya and G. C. Philippatos (1974) "Multiperiod Portfolio Efficiency Analysis via the Geometric Mean", *Financial Review*, 46–63.

Gressis, N., G. C. Phillippatos and J. Hayya (1976) "Multiperiod Portfolio Analysis and the Inefficiency of the Market Portfolio", *Journal of Finance*, September, 1115–1126.

Glustoff, E. and N. Nigro (1972) "Liquidity Preference and Risk Aversion with Exponential Utility Function", *Review of Economic Studies*, January, 113–115.

Gonedes, N. J. (1973) "Evidence on the Information Content of Accounting Numbers: Accounting-Based and Market-Based Estimates of Systematic Risk", *Journal of Financial and Quantitative Analysis*, June 407–443.

Hadar, J. and W. R. Russell (1969) "Rules for Ordering Uncertain Prospects", *American Economic Review*, March, 25–34.

Hakansson, N. H. (1971a) "Captial Growth and the Mean-Variance Approach to Portfolio Selection", *Journal of Financial and Quantitative Analysis*, January, 517–557.

Hakansson, N. H. (1971b) "Multiperiod Mean-Variance Analysis: Toward a General Theory of Portfolio Choice", *Journal of Finance*, September, 857–884.

Hamada, R. S. (1969) "Portfolio Analysis, Market Equilibrium and Corporation Finance", *Journal of Finance*, March, 13–32.

Hanoch, G and H. Levy (1969) "The Efficiency Analysis of Choices Involving Risk", *Review of Economic Studies*, July, 335–346.

Henderson, T. M. and R. E. Quandt (1971) *Microeconomic Theory: A Mathematical Approach*, 2nd edn. (McGraw-Hill, New York).

Hester, D. D. and J. Tobin, eds. (1967a) *Risk Aversion and Portfolio Choice* (John Wiley, New York).

Hester, D. D. and J. Tobin, eds. (1967b) *Studies of Portfolio Behavior* (John Wiley, New York).

Hirschleifer, J. (1965) "Investment Decision Under Uncertainty: Choice-Theoretic Approaches", *Quarterly Journal of Economics*, November, 509–536.

Hirschleifer, J. (1966) "Investment Decision Under Uncertainty: Applications of the State Preference Approach", *Quarterly Journal of Economics*, May, 252–277.

Hirschleifer, J. (1971) "The Private and Social Value of Information and the Reward to Inventive Activity", *American Economic Review*, September, 561–574.

Hsu, D., R. B. Miller and D. W. Wichern (1974) "On the Stable Paretian Behavior of Stock-Market Prices", *Journal of the American Statistical Association*, March, 108–113.

Jacob, N. (1971) "The Measurement of Systematic Risk for Securities and Portfolios: Some Empirical Results", *Journal of Financial and Quantitative Analysis*, March, 815–834.

Jensen, M. (1969) "Risk, the Pricing of Capital Assets, and the Evaluation of Investment Portfolios", *Journal of Business*, April 167–247.

Jensen, M. C., ed. (1972a) *Studies in the Theory of Capital Markets* (Praeger, New York).

Jensen, M. (1972b) "Capital Markets: Theory and Evidence", *Bell Journal of Economics and Management Science*, Autumn, 357–398.

Joy, O. M. and R. B. Porter (1974) "Stochastic Dominance and Mutual Fund Performance", *Journal of Financial and Quantitative Analysis*, January, 25–31.

Kalymon, B. A. (1971) "Estimation Risk in the Portfolio Selection Model", *Journal of Financial and Quantitative Analysis*, January, 559–582.

Kraus, A. and R. H. Litzenberger (1975) "Market Equilibrium in a Multiperiod State Preference Model with Logarithmic Utility", *Journal of Finance*, December, 1213–1227.

Kuark, J. Y. T. (1972) "Bayesian Decision Model for Portfolio Selection", *Occasional Studies no. 7* (Division of Research, College of Business Administration, The University of Denver).

Latané, H. (1959) "Criteria for Choice among Risky Ventures", *Journal of Political Economy*, April, 144–155.

Latané, H. A. and D. L. Tuttle (1967) "Criteria for Portfolio Building", *Journal of Finance*, September, 359–373.

Latané, H. and W. E. Young (1969) "Test of Portfolio Building Rules", *Journal of Finance*, September, 595–612.

Lerner, E. M. and R. E. Machol (1969) "Risk, Ruin, and Investment Analysis", *Journal of Financial and Quantitative Analysis*, December, 473–492.

Levy, H. and G. Hanoch (1970) "Relative Effectiveness of Efficiency Criteria for Portfolio Selection", *Journal of Financial and Quantitative Analysis*, March, 63–76.

Lintner, J. (1965a) "The Valuation of Risk Assets and the Selection of Risky Investments in Stock Portfolios and Capital Budgets", *Review of Economics and Statistics*, February, 13–37.

Lintner, J. (1965b) "Security Prices, Risk and Maximal Gains from Diversification", *Review of Economics and Statistics*, December, 587–616.

Lintner, J. (1969) "The Aggregation of Investors' Diverse Judgments and Preferences in Purely Competitive Securities Markets", *Journal of Financial and Quantitative Analysis*, December, 347–400.

Litzenberger, R. H. and A. P. Budd (1971) "A Note on Geometric Mean Portfolio Selection and the Market Prices of Equities", *Journal of Financial and Quantitative Analysis*, December, 1277–1281.

Long, J. B., Jr. (1972) "Consumption-Investment Decisions and Equilibrium in the Securities Markets", in: M. Jensen, ed., *Studies in the Theory of Capital Markets* (Praeger, New York).

Long, J. B., Jr. (1974) "Stock Prices, Inflation, and the Term Structure of Interest Rates", *Journal of Financial Economics*, 131–170.

Luce, R. D. and H. Raiffa (1957) *Games and Decisions* (John Wiley, New York).

Mao, J. C. T. (1970) "Survey of Capital Budgeting: Theory and Practice", *Journal of Finance*, May, 349–360.

Mao, J. C. T. and C. E. Särndal (1966) "A Decision Theory Approach to Portfolio Selection", *Management Science*, April, (B-323)–(B-334).

Markowitz, H. M. (1952) "Portfolio Selection", *Journal of Finance*, March, 77–91.

Markowitz, H. M. (1959) *Portfolio Selection* (John Wiley, New York).

Mayers, D. (1972) "Nonmarketable Assets and Capital Market Equilibrium under Uncertainty", in: M. Jensen, Ed., *Studies in the Theory of Capital Markets* (Praeger, New York).

McEnally, R. W. (1973) "Some Portfolio-Relevant Risk Characteristics of Long-Term Marketable Securities", *Journal of Financial and Quantitative Analysis*, September, 565–585.

Merton, R. C. (1973) "An Intertemporal Capital Asset Pricing Model", *Econometrica*, September, 867–887.

Mossin, J. (1968) "Optimal Multiperiod Portfolio Policies", *Journal of Business*, April, 215–229.

Mosteller, F. and P. Nogee (1951) "An Experimental Measure of Utility", *Journal of Political Economy*, October, 371–404.

Murray, M. L. (1973) "Empirical Utility Functions and Insurance Consumption Decisions", *Journal of Risk and Insurance*, March, 31–41.

Naslung, B. and A Whinston (1962) "A Model of Multi-Period Investment under Uncertainty", *Management Science*, January, 184–200.

Neumann, J. von and O. Morgenstern (1964) *Theory of Games and Economic Behavior* (John Wiley, New York).

Officer, R. R. (1972) "The Distribution of Stock Returns", *Journal of the American Statistical Association*, December, 807–812.

Peles, Y. (1971) "A Note on Risk and the Theory of Asset Value", *Journal of Financial and Quantitative Analysis*, January, 643–647.

Phillips, H. E. and J. P. Sealge (1973) "Data: A Blessing or a Curse in Portfolio Selection", in Hopfe, M. W. ed., *1973 AIDS Proceedings*.

Porter, R. B. (1973) "An Empirical Comparison of Stochastic Dominance and Mean Variance Portfolio Choice Criteria", *Journal of Financial and Quantitative Analysis*, September, 587–608.

Porter, R. B. and R. P. Bey (1974) "An Evaluation of the Empirical Significance of Optimal Seeking Algorithms in Portfolio Selection", *Journal of Finance*, December, 1479–1490.

Porter, R. B. and J. E. Gaumnitz (1972) "Stochastic Dominance vs. Mean-Variance Portfolio Analysis: An Empirical Evaluation", *American Economic Review*, June, 438–446.

Praetz, P. D. (1972) "The Distribution of Share Price Changes", *Journal of Business*, January, 49–55.

Pratt, J. (1964) "Risk Aversion in the Small and in the Large", *Econometrica*, January–April, 122–136.

Press, S. J. (1972) *Applied Multivariate Analysis* (Holt, Rinehart and Winston, New York).

Raiffa, H. (1968) *Decision Analysis: Introductory Lectures on Choices Under Uncertainty* (Addison-Wesley, Reading, Mass.).

Reilly, F. K. (1972) "Evidence Regarding a Segmented Stock Market", *Journal of Finance*, June, 607–625.

Roll, R. (1969) "Bias in Fitting the Sharpe Model to Time Series Data", *Journal of Financial and Quantitative Analysis*, September, 271–289.

Roll, R. (1973) "Evidence on the Growth Optimum Model." *Journal of Finance*, June 1973, 551–566.

Roll, R. (1977) "A Critique of the Asset Pricing Theory's Tests-I", *Journal of Financial Economics*, May, 129–176.

Roy, A. D. (1952) "Safety-First and the Holding of Assets", *Econometrica*, July, 431–449.

Royama, S. and K. Hamada (1967) "Substitution and Complementarity in the Choice of Risky Assets", In: D. D. Hester and J. Tobin, eds., *Studies of Portfolio Behavior* (John Wiley, New York).

Rubinstein, M. (1973) "A Mean Variance Synthesis of Corporate Financial Theory", *Journal of Finance*, March, 167–181.

Samuelson, P. A. (1960) "The St. Petersburg Paradox as a Divergent Double Limit", *International Economic Review*, January, 31–37.

Samuelson, P. A. (1969) "Lifetime Portfolio Selection by Dynamic Stochastic Programming", *Review of Economics and Statistics*, August, 239–246.

Samuelson, P. A. (1970) "The Fundametnal Approximation Theorem of Portfolio Analysis in Terms of Means, Variances and Higher Moments", *Review of Economic Studies*, October, 537–542.

Sarnat, M. (1974) "Capital Market Imperfections and the Composition of Optimal Portfolios", *Journal of Finance*, September, 1241–1253.

Savage, L. J. (1954) *The Foundations of Statistics* (John Wiley, New York).

Schilbred, C. M. (1972) "An Experiment with Bonds and Risk", *Swedish Journal of Economics*, September, 344–355.

Sharpe, W. F. (1963) "A Simplified Model for Portfolio Analysis", *Management Science*, January, 277–293.

Sharpe, W. F. (1964) "Capital Asset Prices: A Theory of Market Equilibrium Under Conditions of Risk", *Journal of Finance*, September, 425–442.

Sharpe, W. F. (1965) "Risk Aversion in the Stock Market: Some Empirical Evidence", *Journal of Finance*, September, 416–422.

Sharpe, W. F. (1966) "Mutual Fund Performance", *Journal of Business*, Supplement, January, 119–138.

Sharpe, W. F. (1970) *Portfolio Theory and Capital Markets* (McGraw-Hill, New York).

Suppes, P. (1961) "Behavioristic Foundations of Utility", *Econometrica*, 29, 186–202.

Swalm, R. O. (1966) "Utility Theory–Insights Into Risk Taking, *Harvard Business Review*, November–December, 123–136.

Tarascio, V. J. and J. L. Murphy (1972) "Uncertainty, Learning, and Dynamic Utility Theory", *Quarterly Review of Economics and Business*, Autumn, 19–33.

Tobin, J. (1958) "Liquidity Preference as Behavior toward Risk", *Review of Economic Studies*, February, 65–86.

Tobin, J. (1965) "The Theory of Portfolio Selection", in: F. H. Hahn and F. P. R. Brechling, eds., *The Theory of Interest Rates* (Macmillan, London).

Tobin, J. (1969) "Comment on Borch and Feldstein", *Review of Economic Studies*, January, 13–14.

Tomasini, L. M. (1971) "Teorie delle Decisioni e Teorie dell'Utilita", *Rivista Internasionale di Scienze Economiche e Commerciali*, September, 851–866.

Wallingford, B. A. (1967) "A Survey and Comparison of Portfolio Selection Models", *Journal of Financial and Quantitative Analysis*, June, 85–104.

Whitmore, G. A. (1970) "Third-Degree Stochastic Dominance", *American Economic Review*, June, 457–459.

Winkler, R. L. (1973) "Bayesian Models for Forecasting Future Security Prices", *Journal of Financial and Quantitative Analysis*, June, 387–405.

Winkler, R. L. and C. B. Barry (1975) "A Bayesian Model for Portfolio Selection and Revision", *Journal of Finance*, March, 179–192.

Wippern, R. F. (1975) "Utility Implications of Portfolio Selection and Revision", *Journal of Finance*, March, 179–192.

Chapter 16

THE SELECTION OF OPTIMAL PORTFOLIOS: SOME SIMPLE TECHNIQUES

EDWIN J. ELTON, MARTIN J. GRUBER and MANFRED W. PADBERG
New York University

1. Introduction

Modern portfolio theory dates from Markowitz's (1952, 1959) pioneering article and subsequent book. Markowitz's suggestions were intended to be practical and implementable. It is ironic that the primary outgrowth has been normative and theoretical and that modern portfolio theory has rarely been implemented.

There are three major reasons why portfolio theory has not been implemented. These are

(1) the difficulty in estimating the type of input data necessary (particularly correlation matrices);

(2) the time and cost necessary to generate efficient portfolios (solve a quadratic programming problem); and

(3) the difficulty of educating portfolio managers to relate to risk return tradeoffs expressed in terms of covariances as well as returns and standard deviations.

Several techniques have been suggested for forecasting the correlation structure between securities. These include single-index models, multi-index models, and several types of models which forecast by averaging past data. In section 2 we review some of the empirical work which has been done on forecasting correlation coefficients. We shall then proceed to show that the techniques which work best as forecasters of correlation structures also allow the development of simple selection rules for optimal portfolios. These rules go a long way towards solving the second and third problem discussed above. In particular they allow the selection of optimum portfolios in a manner so simple that it can be done with pencil and paper. Furthermore, as we shall see, these optimal selection rules call for the ranking of securities in a manner which should be intuitively appealing to both security analysts and portfolio managers.

James L. Bicksler, Editor, Handbook of Financial Economics
© *North-Holland Publishing Company – 1979*

2. Forecasting correlation structures

Any portfolio selection problem involves the simulation of the expected return for each security, the variance of return for each security, and the matrix of correlation coefficients between all securities. While the problem of estimating means and variances is not a trivial one, it is one that has received much attention. The random walk literature specifies that the best estimate of future mean returns and variances for any stock is historical means and variances (the random walk theory assumes that the distribution of returns for any stock in stable overtime). On the other hand, most analysts believe that they can form expectations about future mean returns (how well a stock will perform) and variances (how sure they are about their forecasts).

While a great deal of attention has been paid to estimating means and variances, less attention has been paid to the problem of estimating correlations. The analyst has a difficult time in producing direct estimates of correlations for two reasons. First, because of the large number of estimates involved. To obtain efficient portfolios from among 200 stocks, 19,800 correlation coefficients would have to be produced. Secondly, and perhaps more important, because there is no nonoverlapping organizational structure that will allow security analysts to produce estimates of correlation coefficients between all pairs of stocks. Each analyst in a financial institution follows a subset of the stocks in which the institution has an interest. Who, then, can produce correlations between stocks followed by different analysts? The analyst also has a difficult time in obtaining indirect estimates of correlation coefficients. For example, the analyst could obtain estimates of correlation coefficients by first estimating the parameters of a single or multi-index model. Contained in these estimates is an implied forecast of correlation coefficients. Although some organizations have made attempts in this direction, it seems unlikely that most analysts can think in these terms and even when they are trained to do so that their estimates will necessarily be superior to more mechanical procedures.[1] Despite these problems (except for some indirect tests of the Sharpe model), the literature in finance has paid almost no attention to the accuracy of techniques used for estimating the correlation structure of share prices.[2]

---

[1]It has been shown that even when forecasting a much more familiar concept, i.e. earnings, analysts have not out-performed models based on extrapolation from historical data. See Elton and Gruber (1972) and Cragg and Malkiel (1968).

[2]King (1966) examined the correlation structure of share prices during a period of time, but he did not examine the stability or predictive value of this structure over time. Cohen and Pogue (1967) examined the predictability of several portfolio models, but did not examine the accuracy of their correlation projections nor attempt to separate errors caused by misestimating correlation coefficients from errors in misestimating mean returns or variances. Blume (1971) has analyzed the stability of β over time. Since β's are related to correlation coefficients (see section 2), this is an indirect test of the predictability of the correlation coefficients produced by the Sharpe model. However, Blume's results cannot be used directly to estimate the errors in forecasting correlation coefficients.

A relevant question then becomes how can one obtain good estimates of future correlation coefficients from historical data? One obvious answer is to use the past historical correlation matrix as an estimate of the future correlation matrix. It is likely that the past correlation matrix contains information about the future correlation matrix plus random noise. If this is true then techniques should exist which by either averaging past correlation coefficients to reduce random noise or extracting some simple underlying structure produce better estimates of the future.

2.1. Averaging models

The most naive forecasting model which can be used is one which assumes that the historic correlation matrix only contains information about the average correlation between securities. That is, the future correlation between any two securities is predicted to be equal to the correlation between any other two securities and is set equal to the average historic correlation between all paired securities.

A second technique is to assume that the industry structure contains some information about future correlation coefficients. In this case the correlation between any two stocks in the same industry is set equal to the average historical correlation coefficient between all paired stocks in that industry. Similarly, any stock in one industry (say, steel) and another (say, chemical) is set equal to the average of the historical correlation between stocks in one industry and stocks in the second.

A technique directly analogous to the industry grouping can be used where pseudo-industries (groups of stocks which have behaved alike) rather than traditional industries are used as the averaging units.[3]

2.2. Simple structure – index models

The most widely used technique for forecasting future correlation matrices is the well known Sharpe single-index model. In this model correlation between stocks arises only because of common correlation with the market.

In addition to the single-index model, several multi-index models have been suggested which attempt better to forecast correlation coefficients by introducing additional indexes to capture common influences beyond the market. For example, the most commonly used multi-index model uses industry indexes in addition to a market index.

[3]See Elton and Gruber (1970, 1971, 1972) for discussion of statistical techniques for the formation of pseudo-industries.

2.3. *Some empirical results*

While most of the models discussed above were developed to simplify the amount and type of data needed for portfolio analysis, they have been shown to do a better job of forecasting future correlation matrices than the historical correlation matrix itself. Elton and Gruber (1973) have investigated the performance of these models in two ways: first by the statistical significance of their forecast errors, and secondly by examining the differences in rates of return that would have been earned had each of these techniques been used to forecast portfolios. The Sharpe single-index model, the overall average correlation model, the group average correlation model, and some forms of the multi-index model consistently out-performed the full historical correlation matrix as an estimate of future correlations on both statistical and economic grounds. While previous studies (see Cohen and Pogue (1967)) have reported on the excellent forecasting ability of the single-index model, the results reported by Elton and Gruber (1973) indicate that the overall mean correlation model, the group mean correlation model, and to a lesser extent, some forms of the multi-index model, are worth considering as ways of generating forecasts of correlation coefficients between security returns.

The rest of this paper will show that if any of these simple models are taken as the best estimate of future correlation coefficients, simple rules can be found which allow portfolio selection to be performed without the use of large scale programming models. Furthermore, the results which are derived are not approximations but represent the true optimum portfolios under the respective assumptions about correlation coefficients.

In the next five sections of this paper we shall derive rules for optimal portfolio selection under each of five models. The Sharpe single-index model the constant correlation model, the multigroup model, and two forms of the multi-index model. In all five sections we shall solve the portfolio problem given a riskless lending/borrowing rate. The set of efficient portfolios can be traced out by varying the riskless lending and borrowing rate. However, it is more efficient to solve directly for corner portfolios. We show how this can be done for the case of the Sharpe single-index model and the constant correlation model. The analysis can be extended to the other cases.

3. The single-index model and the construction of optimal portfolios

In this section we shall assume that the standard single index model is an accurate description of reality. That is

(1) $R_i = \alpha_i + \beta_i I + \varepsilon_i,$

(2) $I = \alpha_{N+1} + \varepsilon_{N+1},$

(3) $E(\varepsilon_{N+1}\varepsilon_i) = 0,$ $i = 1, \ldots, N,$

(4) $E(\varepsilon_i\varepsilon_j) = 0,$ $i = 1, \ldots, N; \quad j = 1, \ldots, N; \quad i \neq j,$

where

R_i = the return on security i (a random variable),
 I = a market index (a random variable),
 β_i = a measure of the responsiveness of security i to change in the market index,
 α_i = the return on security i that is independent of changes in the market index,
 ε_i = a variable with a mean of zero and variance $\sigma_{\varepsilon i}^2$, and
 σ_m^2 = the variance of the market index.

The last two equations characterize the approximation of the standard single index model to the variance–covariance structure. The assumption implied by these equations is that the only joint movement between securities comes about because of a common response to a market index.

We show that under these assumptions one can solve for optimal portfolios with simple decision criteria without resorting to mathematical programming. The methods we derive for finding optimal portfolios are more accurate than the linear programming approximations which have been put forth and in fact reach the same solution to the portfolio problem as the exact quadratic programming method.[4]

We study two cases involving different degrees of complexity. In the first case we assume that short-selling is allowed while in the second case we do not allow short-selling. For each case we solve for the efficient portfolio when riskless lending and borrowing can take place in unlimited amounts and for the relevant portion of the efficient frontier when lending and borrowing is not allowed.

We start this section by deriving the expression for the optimal portfolio when unlimited lending and borrowing can take place at the riskless rate R_f and short-selling is allowed. Lintner (1965) has proved that the optimal portfolio to hold in this case is that portfolio which has the highest excess return to standard deviation. Thus, we want to find a set of relative weights to place on each security (X_i's) in order to maximize

$$\theta = \frac{\bar{R}_p - R_f}{\sigma_p}, \tag{1}$$

where $\bar{R}_p$ = the expected value of the return on a portfolio, and σ_p = the standard deviation of return on a portfolio. Then we wish to scale the X_i's to ensure that we are fully invested.

---

[4]Sharpe (1971) presents a linear programming *approximation* to the quadratic programming problem.

Employing the single-index assumptions outlined above and eq. (1)[5]

$$\theta = \frac{\displaystyle\sum_{i=1}^{N} X_i(\bar{R}_i - R_f)}{\left[\displaystyle\sum_{i=1}^{N} X_i^2 \beta_i^2 \sigma_m^2 + \sum_{i=1}^{N} \sum_{\substack{j=1 \\ j \neq i}}^{N} X_i X_j \beta_i \beta_j \sigma_m^2 + \sum_{i=1}^{N} X_i^2 \sigma_{\epsilon_i}^2\right]^{1/2}}.$$

To find that set of X_i's which maximize θ we take the derivative of θ with respect to each X_i and set it equal to zero:[6]

$$\frac{d\theta}{dX_i} = (\bar{R}_i - R_f) - \frac{\displaystyle\sum_{j=1}^{N} X_j(\bar{R}_j - R_f)}{\sigma_p^2}\left[X_i \beta_i^2 \sigma_m^2 + \sum_{\substack{j=1 \\ j \neq i}}^{N} \beta_i X_j \beta_j \sigma_m^2 + X_i \sigma_{\epsilon_j}^2\right] = 0.$$

Defining

$$Z_i = \frac{\bar{R}_i - R_f}{\sigma_p^2} X_i$$

and solving this expression for Z_i yields[7]

$$Z_i = \frac{\bar{R}_i - R_f}{\sigma_{\epsilon_i}^2} - \frac{\beta_i \sigma_m \displaystyle\sum_{j=1}^{N} Z_j \beta_j}{\sigma_{\epsilon_i}^2}. \tag{2}$$

[5]X_i can be negative for short sales. We are following Lintner's (1965) suggestion in treating short sales. That is the short seller pays any dividends which accrue to the person who lends him the stock and gets a capital gain (or loss) which is the negative of any price appreciation. In addition the short seller is assumed to receive interest at the riskless rate on both the money loaned to the owner of the borrowed stock and the money placed in escrow when the short sale is made. See Lintner (1965) for a full discussion of these assumptions.

[6]Since the denominator appearing in θ is defined with respect to a positive-definite quadratic form, θ is continuously differentiable everywhere except for the point X with all coordinates $X_i = 0$ for $i = 1, \ldots, N$. It is not difficult, however, to verify that θ is bounded in zero. For $X \neq 0$, it follows from the Cauchy–Schwartz inequality that θ is bounded from above and that the maximum is unique to a multiplicative factor. Consequently, the calculation outlined above produces a maximum. See also Lintner (1965). Note, furthermore, that the maximum value of θ and thus the transformation of X to Z below involves a positive factor. This follows since the standard deviation and excess return of the optimal portfolio are both positive since otherwise the investor holds the riskless asset.

[7]A problem could occur if residual risk is zero. If only one security has a zero residual risk then

$$\sigma_p^2 \sum_{i=1}^{N} \beta_i Z_i = \frac{\bar{R}_i - R_f}{\beta_i}.$$

If more than one security has zero residual risk then a riskless portfolio can be found since

$$\sigma_p^2 = (x_1^2 \beta_1^2 \sigma_f^2 + x_2^2 \beta_2^2 \sigma_f^2 + 2x_1 x_2 \beta_1 \beta_2 \sigma_f^2) = (x_1 \beta_1 + x_2 \beta_2)^2 \sigma_f^2.$$

This equals zero if $x_1 \beta_1 = x_2 \beta_2$. This riskless portfolio is an alternative to the riskless asset. The analysis proceeds after any adjustments in R_f. In practice one would not expect zero residual risk.

The equation for each Z_i contains the term $\sum_{j=1}^{N} Z_j \beta_j$. If this can be expressed in terms of known quantities, then (2) is the solution. This can be accomplished by multiplying (2) by β_j summing over all N equations and rearranging. This yields

$$\sum_{j=1}^{N} Z_j \beta_j = \frac{\displaystyle\sum_{j=1}^{N} \left[\frac{\bar{R}_j - R_f}{\sigma_{\varepsilon_j}^2} \beta_j \right]}{1 + \sigma_m^2 \displaystyle\sum_{j=1}^{N} \frac{\beta_j^2}{\sigma_{\varepsilon_j}^2}}.$$

Letting ϕ_N denote the expression

$$\phi_N = \sigma_m^2 \frac{\displaystyle\sum_{j=1}^{N} \left[\frac{\bar{R}_j - R_f}{\sigma_{\varepsilon_j}^2} \beta_j \right]}{1 + \sigma_m^2 \displaystyle\sum_{j=1}^{N} \frac{\beta_j^2}{\sigma_{\varepsilon_j}^2}}. \tag{3}$$

We obtain from (2)

$$Z_i = \frac{\beta_i}{\sigma_{\varepsilon_i}^2} \left[\frac{\bar{R}_i - R_f}{\beta_i} - \phi_N \right]. \tag{4}$$

In order to determine the optimal amount to invest in each security (X_i^o) the above has to be divided by the absolute value of the sum of the Z_i. The optimal amount is thus

$$X_i^o = \frac{Z_i}{\displaystyle\sum_{j=1}^{N} |Z_i|}. \tag{5}$$

The advantage of formulae like (4) and (5) is that they can be easily calculated and the optimal arrived at for any population of stocks. Since the last term in brackets in eq. (4) is a constant for all stocks it need only be calculated once and the value of Z_i for any stock can be calculated simply by one subtraction and one multiplication. Furthermore, we can infer immediately from eq. (4) that the attractiveness of any stock and the amount held is determined by the ratio of its excess return to β.

Notice that θ is the slope of a line tangent to the efficient frontier. Up to now we have assumed a unique R_f and solved for the composition of the optimal portfolio given the ability of the investor to borrow and lend unlimited amounts of funds at that riskless rate. Now if such borrowing and lending is disallowed the concept of a riskless rate can still stand as an artifact to trace out the efficient frontier. The efficient frontier can be traced out by solving (4) for a sequence of arbitrarily selected R_f. For example, R_f could start at zero and vary by 0.1 to maximum R_i.[8]

If instead one wished to trace out corner portfolios a different procedure is needed. To understand the procedure first note that the sign of Z_i depends on the term in the brackets in eq. (4). Note also that the term ϕ_N in the brackets of eq. (4) is a constant independent of i. Hence, for positive β_i if $(\overline{R}_i - R_f)/\beta_i$ is greater than the constant the security is purchased long; if it is less it is purchased short; and if it is equal it drops out of the portfolio.[9] It is this latter condition which determines a corner portfolio. For any security this can occur only once. This holds because $(\overline{R}_i - R_f)/\beta_i$ is a linear function of R_f. Likewise, the second term in the brackets is also linear in R_f. Two linear functions will have at most one intersection in the range of interest.

Therefore to determine the corner portfolios we have the following steps.

(1) For each security i solve eq. (4) for the value of R_f which makes Z_i and hence X_i^o zero. Each distinct value of R_f greater than the lower bound will be uniquely associated with one corner portfolio.

(2) For each value of R_f defined in step 1 we use eqs. (4) and (5) to determine the value of all X_i^o in that corner portfolio.

(3) Solve for the return and risk for each corner portfolio determined in step 2.

Portfolios with R_f between corner portfolios can be determined in the usual way.[10]

4. Optimal portfolios when short sales are not allowed

Once again we will start by examining the case where a unique riskless rate R_f exists at which unlimited lending and borrowing can take place. If we restrict management prerogatives by disallowing short sales we must modify the solution presented in the last section. In particular, if short selling is disallowed then we must introduce the constraints that all $X_i \geqslant 0$. This requires employing the Kuhn–Tucker conditions. Since the variance–covariance matrix is positive definite, the Kuhn–Tucker conditions are both necessary and sufficient for an

---

[8]Throughout the analysis of the efficient frontier one must deal with the problem of establishing the lowest point on the frontier which is of interest. Since most analysis is performed in nominal terms and since the investor is always free to hold cash, the lowest point on the efficient frontier of interest will usually be that associated with a lending rate of zero. However, nothing in the analysis restricts the user from defining lower regions on the efficient (stock) frontier by considering values of R_f below zero. In fact in the limit R_f can be examined as it approaches infinity.

[9]The opposite set of statements can be made for negative β.

[10]One desires corner portfolio since intermediate portfolios can be determined by calculating portfolios consisting of adjacent corner portfolios. This is also true when the R_p's are arbitrarily selected if adjacent portfolios differ by at most one security.

optimum. The equivalent of eq. (2) using the Kuhn–Tucker conditions is[11]

$$Z_i = \frac{\bar{R}_i - R_f}{\sigma_{\varepsilon_i}^2} - \frac{\beta_i}{\sigma_{\varepsilon_i}^2} \sigma_m^2 \sum_{j=1}^{N} \beta_j Z_j + \frac{\mu_i}{\sigma_{\varepsilon_i}^2}, \tag{6}$$

where

$$Z_i > 0, \mu_i > 0, \text{ and } \mu_i Z_i = 0 \text{ for all } i.$$

Now let us assume for a moment that we can find all stocks which would be in an optimal portfolio and call the set of such stocks k. For the subpopulation of stocks that make up the optimal portfolio

$$Z_i = \frac{\bar{R}_i - R_f}{\sigma_{\varepsilon_i}^2} - \frac{\beta_i}{\sigma_{\varepsilon_i}^2} \sigma_m^2 \sum_{j \in k} Z_j \beta_j \text{ and } \mu_i = 0.$$

Multiplying both sides by β_i, summing over all stocks in k and rearranging yields

$$\sum_{j=1}^{k} Z_j \beta_j = \frac{\displaystyle\sum_{j \in k} \left[\frac{\bar{R}_j - R_f}{\sigma_{\varepsilon_j}^2} \beta_j \right]}{1 + \sigma_m^2 \displaystyle\sum_{j \in k} \frac{\beta_j^2}{\sigma_{\varepsilon_j}^2}}. \tag{7}$$

Notice since the set k contains all stocks with positive Z_i's

$$\sum_{j=1}^{N} Z_j \beta_j = \sum_{j \in k} Z_j \beta_j \tag{8}$$

and let

$$\phi_k = \sigma_m^2 \frac{\displaystyle\sum_{j \in k} \frac{\bar{R}_j - R_f}{\sigma_{\varepsilon_j}^2} \beta_j}{1 + \sigma_m^2 \displaystyle\sum_{j \in k} \frac{\beta_j^2}{\sigma_{\varepsilon_j}^2}}. \tag{9}$$

[11] A complication could occur if residual risk were zero. In this case

$$\sum_{i=1}^{k} \beta_i Z_i$$

equals the maximum $(\bar{R}_i - R_f)/\beta_i$ with zero residual risk. The rest of the analysis follows. It should be noted that the Kuhn–Tucker multipliers μ_i appearing in (5) as well as elsewhere in this paper are the usual multipliers up to multiplication by the constant σ_p for the optimal portfolio.

Using (9) we obtain, after substitution and rearranging from eq. (6), the following expression for Z_i:

$$Z_i = \frac{\beta_i}{\sigma_{\varepsilon_i}^2}\left[\frac{\bar{R}_i - R_f}{\beta_i} - \phi_k\right] + \mu_i. \tag{10}$$

Since $\mu_i \geqslant 0$, including μ_i can only increase the value of Z_i. Thus, if Z_i is positive with $\mu_i = 0$, the inclusion of μ_i can never make it zero. Hence, if Z_i is positive when $\mu_i = 0$ the security should be included. The contrary holds if Z_i is negative when $\mu_i = 0$.

Using (10) one can establish a procedure for determining the efficient frontier. We note that for $\mu_i = 0$ the sign of Z_i as defined by (10) depends on the sign of β_i and the sign of the term in the brackets. More precisely, the following rules determine an optimal portfolio.

(1) If a security with a particular value $(\bar{R}_i - R_f)/\beta_i$ and $\beta_i > 0$ is included in the optimum portfolio, any security with a greater value $(\bar{R}_j - R_f)/\beta_j$ will also be included provided that β_j is positive. Similarly, if β_j is negative.[12]

(2) If a security with a particular value $(\bar{R}_i - R_f)/\beta_i$ and $\beta_i > 0$ is excluded from the optimum portfolio, any security with a lower value $(\bar{R}_j - R_f)/\beta_j$ will also be excluded from the optimum portfolio provided that $\beta_j > 0$. Similarly, if β_i is negative.

(3) If a particular security can be "included" in the optimal portfolio with $Z_i = 0$, then it can as well be excluded and vice versa.

Whereas the first two rules are immediate consequences of the Kuhn–Tucker conditions, the third requires the following line of reasoning. Suppose that security i is such that $(\bar{R}_i - R_f)/\beta_i - \phi_k = 0$, where ϕ_k is defined by (9) and is calculated for the optimum portfolio. Denote by $\phi_{k+\{i\}}$ the expression resulting from (9) if the summation in (9) is extended to include security i. Then by straightforward algebraic manipulations we find that

$$\phi_{k+\{i\}} - \phi_k = \frac{\sigma_m^2 \beta_i^2}{\sigma_{\varepsilon_i}^2\left[1 + \displaystyle\sum_{j \in k} \frac{\beta_j^2}{\sigma_{\varepsilon_j}^2} + \frac{\beta_i^2}{\sigma_{\varepsilon_i}^2}\right]}\frac{\bar{R}_i - R_f}{\beta_i} - \phi_k$$

and consequently, $\phi_{k+\{i\}} = \phi_k$ and rule 3 follows. This latter observation greatly simplifies the process of tracing the entire efficient frontier.

Before addressing ourselves to the problem of tracing the entire efficient frontier, we will describe a ranking procedure that permits us to determine an optimal portfolio from the above rules for a particular riskless rate R_f. Suppose, first that all, that β_j are positive. Then all we have to do to arrive at an optimal

---

[12] If β_i is negative the above rules are reversed. For example, for negative β_i if a security with a particular $R_i - R_f/\beta_i$ is included all lower ranking securities are also included.

portfolio is to rank from 1 to N all securities by $(\overline{R}_i - R_f)/\beta_i$. Then compute a value for eq. (9) as if the set k only contained the first security. Next we calculate Z_i from eq. (10) setting $i = 2$. If $Z_2 \leqslant 0$, we stop. The optimal portfolio contains only the first security. Otherwise we compute ϕ_k from (9) letting the set k contain the first two securities. We proceed for $i = 3, 4, \ldots$ until Z_i computed from eq. (10) with $\mu_i = 0$ turns negative. If it turns negative for the $j + 1$st security then the set k contains the first j securities $(i = j)$. Since the set k arrived at this way satisfies the Kuhn–Tucker conditions, we have found a simple and fast way to define all securities in the set k. Once these securities are found the X_i^o value for all securities in the set can be found simply by calculating the Z_i for each security from eq. (10) with μ_i set equal to zero and dividing each Z_i by the sum of the Z_i over the set k. Once again a simple and very quick procedure has been found for designing an optimal portfolio. Furthermore, note that from eq. (10) the desirability of any security and the amount we invest in it will be uniquely related to its excess return to the β ratio.

If stocks with both negative and positive β's are present then we should follow the procedure outlined above to see which of the positive stocks should be included in the portfolio. When no more positive stocks are included stocks with negative β's should be tried (starting with the one with the smallest $((\underline{R}_i - R_f)/\beta_i)$ until no more enter. If any negative β stocks enter it may decrease the size of the term in brackets in (9) and so the highest excess return to positive β stocks previously rejected should be checked to see if it now enters. If more positive β stocks enter then the negative β stock list should be checked and the procedure repeated iteratively until no more stocks enter. In actual practice this iterative procedure will converge almost instantaneously because of the very small number of stocks with negative β's.[13]

If we are willing to accept a riskless borrowing and lending rate, then we are finished at this step. The procedure is so simple that it can be done with the aid of a desk calculator. Furthermore, the above makes clear that excess return and β are the characteristics of a security that are of interest to a portfolio manager. New securities with a positive β would be included if they had an excess return to β ratio above the last accepted security. New securities with a positive β need not be considered if they have an excess return to β below the highest rejected positive β security.[14]

If lending and borrowing at a riskless rate are disallowed it becomes appropriate to define the efficient frontier. Once again the analysis performed for

---

[13]The last problem left to deal with is the problem of stocks with zero β. From eq. (9) if any stocks exist with zero β then they should be included in the optimal portfolio if their expected return exceeds the riskless rate of interest. Hence, when the first positive stocks (and all other stocks) are checked to see if they belong in the optimal portfolio all zero β stocks with an expected return above the riskless rate should be included in the portfolio since they do not alter the value of ϕ_k given by (8).

[14]An analagous set of statements holds for negative B stocks.

the lending and borrowing case can be extended by treating R_f as an artifact. The general shape of the efficient frontier can be traced out by repeating the above analysis for alternative values of R_f. Owing to rule 3 this task is simplified since we can thereby reduce the problem to finding all "corner" portfolios along the efficient frontier. A corner portfolio is one where a security either enters or leaves an efficient portfolio (or both) as we vary the riskless rate R_f parametrically. We can start with the efficient portfolio at the lowest R_f of interest and look at efficient portfolios at higher values of R_f.

In order to determine critical values of the riskless rate R_f which determine a different set k of securities to be included in an optimal portfolio we write $R_f = R_f^o + \lambda$, where R_f^o is the riskless rate for which we have determined an optimal portfolio. We are then interested in R_f for values of $\lambda \geqslant 0$. We observe that, by using (9), relation (10) can be rewritten for Z_i as follows:

$$Z_i(\lambda) = \alpha_i - \Psi_i \lambda, \tag{11}$$

where $\alpha_i = Z_i(o) - \mu_i$ and Ψ_i is given by

$$\Psi_i = \frac{1}{\sigma_{\varepsilon_i}^2} - \beta_i \frac{\sigma_m^2}{\sigma_{\varepsilon_i}^2} \left(\frac{\displaystyle\sum_{j \in k} \frac{\beta_j}{\sigma_{\varepsilon_j}^2}}{1 + \sigma_m^2 \displaystyle\sum_{j \in k} \beta_j^2 / \sigma_{\varepsilon_j}^2} \right). \tag{12}$$

In particular, $Z_i(\lambda)$ is a linear function of λ. Consequently, if for $R_f = R_f^o$ the optimal portfolio contains security i at a positive level Z_i, then security i will remain in an optimal portfolio with $R_f = R_f^o + \lambda$ for a sufficiently small positive change λ provided that $\Psi_i \leqslant 0$. If, however, $\Psi_i > 0$, then security i is a candidate for leaving the optimal portfolio when a small positive change in λ is considered. More precisely, letting K^+ denote the set of securities that are in the optimal portfolio at strictly positive level, we are interested in security j having

$$\frac{\alpha_j}{\Psi_j} = \min \left\{ \frac{\alpha_i}{\Psi_i} \middle| \Psi_i > 0, \quad i \in K^+ \right\},$$

since it is the first candidate to leave the optimal portfolio. Similarly, letting K^- denote the set of securities having $\mu_i > 0$, i.e. for which

$$Z_i = \frac{\beta_i}{\sigma_{\varepsilon_i}^2} \left[\frac{\bar{R}_i - R_f}{\beta_i} - \phi_k \right] < 0$$

the first security to enter the optimal portfolio is given by the security e for which

$$\frac{\alpha_e}{\Psi_e} = \min \left\{ \frac{\alpha_i}{\Psi_i} \middle| \Psi_i < 0, \quad i \in K^- \right\}.$$

Consequently, if $\Psi_j > \Psi_e$, security e will enter the optimal portfolio prior to security j leaving the optimal portfolio, whereas if $\Psi_j < \Psi_e$ security j will leave the optimal portfolio before e is considered for inclusion. So far we have not yet discussed securities for which $Z_i = 0$ which, according to rule 3, may or may not be included in the optimal portfolio at zero level. Let us call the set of these securities K^0. Obviously, if Ψ_i as defined by (12) are all positive or zero for securities in K^0, we will not include any of these securities in the optimal portfolio. However if $\Psi_i < 0$, some of these securities should enter the optimal portfolio. Prior to determining the next corner portfolio, one has to establish which securities in K^0 should enter the optimal portfolio at zero level. Once this is done, we can then determine the next critical value

$$\lambda' = \min\left\{ \frac{\alpha_j}{\Psi_{j,}} \frac{\alpha_e}{\Psi_e} \right\},$$

where now Ψ_j and Ψ_e are calculated with respect to the possibly enlarged optimal portfolio.

The preceding readily defines a procedure for tracing out the entire efficient frontier. Starting with minimum R_f determine the optimal portfolio by the ranking procedure outlined above.[15] Classify all securities as "belonging" to the optimal portfolio or "not belonging" to the optimal portfolio including those for which formula (10) results in $Z_i = 0$ for $\mu_i = 0$. (In the Appendix we describe a procedure for carrying out this classification.) Determine λ' and repeat.

Finally, the proportions in the optimal portfolio are calculated at every critical value of λ in the usual way, whereas optimal portfolios for "in between" values of λ are obtained by simple linear interpolation, i.e. as convex combinations of the respective corner portfolios.

5. Constant correlation coefficients and the construction of optimal portfolios

In this section we will assume that all pairwise correlation coefficients are equal. While this probably does not represent the true pattern, we find in the economy it is very difficult to obtain a better estimate. Elsewhere (Cohen and Pogue (1967)) we have shown that this assumption produces better estimates of future correlation coefficients than do historical correlation coefficients or those produced from the single-index approximation discussed in section 2. In fact, the assumption of a constant correlation coefficient produced forecasts which were

---

[15]Zero is normally the lowest lending rate of interest since cash can be held. The analysis does not assume that funds can be borrowed at this rate since the efficient portfolio at all higher rates will be traced out. If the analysis is being conducted in real terms an appropriate lower level must be selected.

about as accurate as any of nine techniques we tried. If we allow lending and borrowing at the riskless rate of interest, as discussed earlier, the optimum portfolio is that which maximizes the ratio of excess return on the portfolio to its standard deviation of returns. Letting

(1) σ_{ij} = covariance between security i and security j,

(2) σ_i^2 = the variance of security i,

(3) ρ = the correlation coefficient between any two securities, and

(4)   all other terms as before,

then excess returns on an N security portfolio is

$$\bar{R}_p - R_f = \sum_{i=1}^{N} X_i(\bar{R}_i - R_f),$$

And the standard deviation is

$$\sigma_p = \left[\sum_{i=1}^{N} X_i^2 \sigma_i^2 + \sum_{i=1}^{N} \sum_{\substack{j=1 \\ j \neq i}}^{N} X_i X_j \sigma_{ij} \right]^{1/2}.$$

Notice from the above expression that there is a direct relationship between the variance of a portfolio under the Sharpe single-index model and the constant correlation coefficient model. In fact, if we define the following transformations:

(a) $\sigma_{\epsilon_i}^2 = \sigma_i^2(1-\rho)$,

(b) $\beta_i = \sigma_i$,

(c) $\sigma_m^2 = \rho$,

the expressions for the variance of any portfolio and the θ value of a portfolio are identical under the two models, since we can safely assume that ρ is in fact positive.

The advantage of these transformations is that they will allow us directly to utilize the results from section 2 to solve the portfolio problem with constant correlation coefficients.

5.1. Optimal policies when short sales are allowed

If we allow short sales then we maximize $\theta = (\bar{R}_p - R_f)/\sigma_p$ without restricting the sign of X_i. The first order conditions necessary for a maximum were presented by Lintner (1965) and are

$$Z_i \sigma_i^2 + \sum_{\substack{j=1 \\ j \neq i}}^{N} Z_j \sigma_{ij} = \bar{R}_i - R_f, \qquad i = 1, \dots, N.$$

In section 2 eqs. (3) and (4) were derived as a solution when the single index model was assumed. Substituting transformations *a*, *b*, and *c* into eqs. (3) and (4) yields

$$\phi = \frac{\rho}{1 - \rho + N\rho} \sum_{j=1}^{N} \frac{\bar{R}_j - R_f}{\sigma_j}, \qquad (13)$$

$$X_i = \frac{Z_i}{\sum\limits_{j=1}^{N} |Z_j|} = \frac{1}{\sum\limits_{j=1}^{N} |Z_j|} \frac{1}{\sigma_i(1-\rho)} \left[\frac{\bar{R}_i - R_f}{\sigma_i} - \phi \right]. \qquad (14)$$

All of the conclusions of section 2 follow, except that the standard deviation σ_i serves the function in this section that β_i served in the last. If anything eqs. (13) and (14) are even simpler. ϕ defines a cutoff rate. All securities with excess return to standard deviation above ϕ are purchased long and all securities with excess return to standard deviation ratios below ϕ are sold short.

To construct the full efficient frontier one could vary the riskless rate from the lowest possible lending rate usually zero to the return on the highest return security and repeat the previous procedure.[16] Alternatively, one can determine the critical points exactly as discussed in section 2.

5.2. Optimal policies when short sales are not allowed

Once again we will start our analysis by assuming that unlimited lending and borrowing can take place at a riskless rate of interest. If short selling is not allowed then we have to rely on the Kuhn–Tucker conditions. Since the optimization problem involves the maximization of a concave function, they are both necessary and sufficient. The Kuhn–Tucker conditions for maximizing θ are

1. $\bar{R}_i - R_f - Z_i \sigma_i^2 - \sum\limits_{\substack{j=1 \\ j \neq i}}^{N} Z_j \sigma_{ij} + \mu_i = 0,$

2. $Z_i \geqslant 0, \ \mu_i \geqslant 0,$

3. $Z_i \mu_i = 0.$

---

[16]The discussion in the first section dealing with $\beta_i < 0$ can be ignored since σ_i must be non-negative.

Recognizing that this equation is the same as the one given in section 2, and employing the relationships given by a, b, and c the expression for Z_i is

$$Z_i = \frac{1}{1-\rho} \frac{1}{\sigma_i} \left[\frac{\bar{R}_i - R_f}{\sigma_i} - \phi_k \right] + \mu_i, \tag{15}$$

where

$$\phi_k = \frac{\rho}{1-\rho+k\rho} \sum_{j \in k} \frac{\bar{R}_j - R_f}{\sigma_j}.$$

Recognizing once again that since $\mu_i \geqslant 0$ the term containing μ_i can only increase Z_i. Thus, any security with positive Z_i when $\mu_i = 0$ must be included. The sign of Z_i depends on the terms in the brackets. Since the last term in the brackets is a constant for any k if a security with a particular ratio $(\bar{R}_i - R_f)/\sigma_i$ has a positive Z_i then all securities with a higher ratio must also be included. In addition, if a stock has a negative Z_i all lower ranking stocks will also have a negative Z_i if they are added. These two characteristics determine decision rules for solving the portfolio problem. Rank stocks in decreasing order of excess return to standard deviation, add securities until the term in the brackets becomes negative. Once the term in the brackets is negative for the security added last it will be negative for any additional securities that are added. Finally, the optimum amount to invest in each security is given by the above divided by the sum of Z_i.[17] Thus,

$$X_i^o = \frac{Z_i}{\sum_{i \in k} Z_i}.$$

Thus, once again if we are willing to assume an R_f at which lending and borrowing can take place then the optimum portfolio can be determined by a simple ranking procedure.

As in the case where short sales were allowed the shape of the efficient frontier can be deduced by solving eq. (15) for alternative values of R_f.

[17]It is interesting to note that this procedure considerably simplifies the revision of portfolios as new securities are considered. If a new stock is under consideration it will be included if its excess return to standard deviation ratio exceeds that of the lowest ranking stock included in the portfolio and will be excluded if its excess return to standard deviation ratio is below that of the highest ranking excluded stock. If its excess return to standard deviation ratio falls between these two limits, eq. (13) will have to be used to see if the stock should be included or excluded.

This makes very explicit the characteristics that will make a stock enter and means that the proportions in the optimum portfolio will only have to be recalculated occasionally. Secondly, the introduction of new stock is unlikely to cause a radical change in the stocks included in the optimal portfolio. At most the entry of a new stock should cause a marginal change in the optimal excess return to standard deviation cutoff rate. Thus, using the old cutoff rate as a starting point in determining the new cutoff rate should lead to a quick solution to the problem.

The solution for corner portfolios is somewhat more complex. However, if we redefine Ψ_i as

$$\Psi_i = \frac{1}{\sigma_i(1-\rho)}\left[\frac{1}{\sigma_i} - \frac{\rho}{1-\rho+k\rho}\sum_{j\in k}\frac{1}{\sigma_j}\right].$$

The procedure then follows directly from that outlined in section 2.

6. The multigroup case and the construction of optimal portfolios

In this section we assume that stocks have been partitioned into groups so that (a) the correlations between any two stocks in the same group is assumed to be the same as that between any other two stocks in that group, and (b) the correlation between any stock in one group and a stock in a second group is the same as the correlation between any other stock in the first group and any stock in the second group.

In addition to the notation already introduced, let

ρ_{ii} = the correlation coefficient between any two stocks in group i,
ρ_{ij} = the correlation coefficient between any stock in group i and any stock in group j,
N_i = the number of securities in group i,
X_i = the set of stocks in group i, and
ρ = the number of groups under study.

6.1. Short sales attained

Substituting the correct expression for the correlation between securities in eq. (1), taking the derivative with respect to X_i, and transforming X_i to Z_i as done earlier, we have for a member of group k[18]

$$Z_i = \frac{\bar{R}_i - R_f}{\sigma_i^2(1-\rho_{kk})} - \frac{\rho_{1k}}{1-\rho_{kk}}\frac{1}{\sigma_i}\sum_{j\in X_1}Z_j\sigma_j \cdots - \frac{\rho_{kk}}{1-\rho_{kk}}\frac{1}{\sigma_i}\sum_{j\in X_k}Z_j\sigma_j$$

$$\times \cdots - \frac{\rho_{kp}}{1-\rho_{kk}}\frac{1}{\sigma_i}\sum_{j\in X_p}Z_j\sigma_j. \tag{16}$$

The above would be the solution if we can express summations of the form $\sum_{j\in X_2}Z_j\sigma_j$ in terms of known quantities. This can be accomplished by multiplying each of the above by σ_i and summing over all members of that group.

---

[18]For a detailed derivation, see Elton et al. (forthcoming (b)).

Rearranging this yields

$$(1-\rho_{11}+\rho_{11}N_1)\sum_{j\in X_1} X_j\sigma_j + \ldots + N_1\rho_{1k}\sum_{j\in X_k} X_j\sigma_j + \ldots$$

$$+ N_1\rho_{1P}\sum_{j\in X_p} X_j\sigma_j = \sum_{j\in X_1}\frac{\bar{R}_j - R_f}{\sigma_j},$$

$$\vdots$$

$$N_k\rho_{1k}\sum_{j\in X_1} X_j\sigma_j + \ldots + (1-\rho_{kk}+\rho_{kk}N_k)\sum_{j\in X_k} X_j\sigma_j + \ldots$$

$$+ N_k\rho_{kP}\sum_{j\in X_p} X_j\sigma_j = \sum_{j=1}\frac{\bar{R}_j - R_f}{\sigma_j},$$

$$\vdots$$

$$N_P\rho_{1P}\sum_{j\in X_1} X_j\sigma_j + \ldots + N_P\rho_{kP}\sum_{j\in X_k} X_j\sigma_j + \ldots$$

$$+ (1-\rho_{PP}+\rho_{PP}N_P)\sum_{j\in X_p} X_j\sigma_j = \sum_{j\in X_p}\frac{\bar{R}_j - R_f}{\sigma_j}.$$

This can be written as

$$AX = C,$$

where

$$A = \begin{pmatrix} 1-\rho_{11}+\rho_{11}N_1 & N_1\rho_{12}\ldots N_1\rho_{1P} \\ N_2\rho_{12} & 1-\rho_{22}+\rho_{22}N_2\ldots N_2\rho_{2P} \\ \vdots & \vdots \quad \vdots \\ N_P\rho_{1P} & N_P\rho_{2P}\ldots 1-\rho_{PP}+\rho_{PP}N_P \end{pmatrix},$$

$$X = \begin{pmatrix} \sum_{j\in X_1} X_j\sigma_j \\ \sum_{j\in X_2} X_j\sigma_j \\ \vdots \\ \sum_{j\in X_p} X_j\sigma_j \end{pmatrix}; \quad C = \begin{pmatrix} \sum_{j\in X_1}\frac{\bar{R}_j - R_f}{\sigma_j} \\ \sum_{j\in X_2}\frac{\bar{R}_j - R_f}{\sigma_j} \\ \vdots \\ \sum_{j\in X_p}\frac{\bar{R}_j - R_f}{\sigma_j} \end{pmatrix}$$

The solution to the above equation is, of course,

$$X = A^{-1}C.$$

Substituting this into eq. (16) allows us to calculate the Z_i. Define

(1) $A_i^{-1} = i$th column of A^{-1},

(2) $b_k = (\rho_{1k}\rho_{2k} \cdots \rho_{Pk})$.

Then the solution for a member of group k is

$$Z_i = \frac{1}{\sigma_i(1-\rho_{kk})} \left[\frac{\bar{R}_i - R_f}{\sigma_i} - b_k A_1^{-1} \sum_{j \in X_1} \frac{\bar{R}_j - R_f}{\sigma_j} - b_k A_2^{-1} \sum_{j \in X_2} \frac{\bar{R}_j - R_f}{\sigma_j} \right. $$
$$\left. - \cdots - b_k A_P^{-1} \sum_{j \in X_P} \frac{\bar{R}_j - R_f}{\sigma_j} \right]. \tag{17}$$

Note that this equation can be written as

$$Z_i = \frac{1}{\rho_i(1-\rho_{kk})} \left[\frac{\bar{R}_i - R_f}{\rho_i} - C_k \right], \tag{18}$$

where C_k is a constant which has the same value for all stocks in group k. Since C_k (or the constant for any group) does not depend on the composition of the optimal portfolio, it can be computed before the analysis of the optimal portfolio is begun. Once the C_k for each group is computed, it is a trivial task to calculate Z_i for all securities. It can easily be done with paper and pencil in a few minutes. Note how easy it is to determine if any stock should be held long or short. If the excess return to standard deviation for any stock is higher than its group constant, it should be bought; if it is lower, it should be sold short.

6.2. *Short sales not allowed*

If short sales are not allowed, we can notify the above analysis in a manner analogous to that used in the two cases above. In particular, as shown in Elton et al. (forthcoming (b)), eq. (17) still holds but the summations encompass only those securities included in the optimal portfolio. Since we know that if a security with a particular $(\bar{R}_i - R_f)/\sigma_i$ has a positive Z_i then all securities with a higher ratio must also be included and if a stock has a negative Z_i all lower ranking stocks will also have a negative Z_i. This characteristic can be used to determine decision rules for solving the portfolio problem. The following seems to us to be an efficient method. First, rank stocks in each group by excess return to standard deviation. Since the formula for the cutoff rate in each group depends on the number in the other group arbitrarily fix the number in all groups but one. Then add securities to the one under study starting with the one with the highest excess return to standard deviation ratio, then the next highest and so forth. Continue until the term in the brackets becomes negative. Fix the number in this group at the number that are contained just before the term in the brackets becomes negative. Now optimize the number in one of the previously included groups by adding securities in descending order of excess return to risk or deleting securities in ascending order. Proceed in this fashion across all groups until neither adding a security to any group or deleting one leads to improvement.

The amount to invest in each security is determined by dividing each Z_i by the sum of the Z_i's. A byproduct of the above calculations is a cutoff rate for each group, which is very useful to managers. Any security with a higher excess return to standard deviation ratio than the last accepted security in the same group must be included. Any security with a lower excess return to standard deviation ratio than the first rejected security need not be considered. If a security is to be included, the old optimum should be an excellent starting solution and the optimum should be reached very quickly.

7. The diagonal form of the multi-index model

Cohen and Pogue (1967) have presented a multi-index model that leads to a diagonal form for the covariance structure between securities. The assumptions underlying the model are that each stock is linearly related to one group index and that each group index is linearly related to a market index. This model can be represented as

$$R_i = \alpha_i + \beta_i J_j + \varepsilon_i,$$

$$J_j = \gamma_j + b_j I_m + C_j,$$

$$I_m = a + d,$$

$$E(\varepsilon_i \varepsilon_k) = 0, \quad i = 1,\dots,N, \quad k = 1,\dots,N, \quad i \neq k,$$

$$E(C_j C_l) = 0, \quad j = 1,\dots,P, \quad l = 1,\dots,P, \quad j \neq l,$$

$$E(\varepsilon_i C_j) = 0, \quad i = 1,\dots,N, \quad j = 1,\dots,P,$$

$$E(\varepsilon_i d) = 0, \quad i = 1,\dots,N,$$

$$E(C_j d) = 0, \quad j = 1,\dots,P. \tag{20}$$

where
(1) R_i = the return on security i which is in group j (a random variable),
(2) J_j = the return on the index for group j,

(3) I_m = the market index,

(4) β_i = a measure of the responsiveness of security i to changes in the group index J_j,

(5) α_i = the return on security i that is independent of the group index,

(6) ε_i = a variable with mean of zero and variance $\sigma_{\varepsilon_i}^2$ which measures the variance of security i not associated with changes in the group (or market index),

(7) b_j = a measure of the responsiveness of index j to changes in the market index,

(8) γ_i = the return on index j that is independent of the market index,

(9) C_j = a variable with a mean of zero and a variance of σ_j^2 which measures the variance of group j not associated with changes in the market index,

(10) σ_m^2 = the variance of the market index,

(11) a = the mean return of the market, and

(12) d = a variable with a mean of zero and variance equal to σ_m^2.

These equations make clear the approximations of the diagonal form of the multi-index model to the variance–covariance structure. While each stock is linearly related to one group index and all group indices are linearly related to the market the residuals from any of these relationships are assumed to be uncorrelated.

In this section we shall develop simple decision rules for portfolio composition when this diagonal form of the multi-index model is assumed to be a reasonable way to forecast future correlation coefficients. We shall separate the case where short selling is permitted from the case where it is not allowed.

7.1. Short selling allowed

Once again employing Lintner's eq. (1) for our objective function, substituting for the correct equation for the variance of the portfolio, taking derivatives, and making the transformation from X_i to Z_i we find for a stock which is related to group index k:[19]

$$Z_i = \frac{\overline{R}_i - R_f}{\sigma_{\varepsilon_i}^2} - \frac{\beta_i}{\sigma_{\varepsilon_i}^2} b_1 b_k \sigma_m^2 \sum_{j \in X_1} \beta_j Z_j - \dots - \frac{\beta_i}{\sigma_{\varepsilon_i}^2} \left(b_k^2 \sigma_m^2 + \sigma_{\varepsilon_i}^2 \right) \sum_{j \in X_k} \beta_j Z_j$$

$$- \dots - \frac{\beta_i}{\sigma_{\varepsilon_i}^2} b_p b_k \sum_{j \in X_p} \beta_j Z_j. \tag{21}$$

[19]For a detailed derivation, see Elton et al. (forthcoming (b)).

The above is the solution if we can express the

$$\sum_{j\in X_1} \beta_j Z_j, \dots, \sum_{j\in X_k} \beta_j Z_j, \dots, \sum_{j\in X_p} \beta_j Z_j$$

in terms of known quantities. This can be done by multiplying by β_i and summing. Rearranging this summation yields

$$AX = C,$$

where

$$A = \begin{vmatrix} 1+\left(b_1^2\sigma_m^2+\sigma_1^2\right)\sum\limits_{j\in X_1}\dfrac{\beta_j^2}{\sigma_{\epsilon_j}^2}, & b_1b_2\sigma_m^2\sum\limits_{j\in X_1}\dfrac{\beta_j^2}{\sigma_{\epsilon_j}^2}\dots, & b_1b_p\sum\limits_{j\in X_1}\dfrac{\beta_j^2}{\sigma_{\epsilon_j}^2}, \\[2em] b_1b_2\sigma_m^2\sum\limits_{j\in X_2}^{N_2}\dfrac{\beta_j^2}{\sigma_{\epsilon_j}^2}, & 1+\left(b_2^2\sigma_m^2+\sigma_2^2\right)\sum\limits_{j\in X_2}^{N_2}\dfrac{\beta_j^2}{\sigma_{\epsilon_j}^2}\dots b_2b_p\sum\limits_{j\in X_2}^{N_2}\dfrac{\beta_j^2}{\sigma_{\epsilon_j}^2}, \\[2em] b_1b_p\sigma_m^2\sum\limits_{j\in X_p}\dfrac{\beta_j^2}{\sigma_{\epsilon_j}^2}, & b_2b_p\sum\limits_{j\in X_p}\dfrac{\beta_j^2}{\sigma_{\epsilon_j}^2}\dots 1+\left(b_p^2\sigma_m^2+\sigma_p^2\right)\sum\limits_{j\in X_p}\dfrac{\beta_j^2}{\sigma_{\epsilon_j}^2} \end{vmatrix},$$

$$X = \left(\sum_{j\in X_1} x_j\beta_j, \quad \sum_{j=1}^{N_2} x_j\beta_j, \dots, \quad \sum_{j\in X_p} x_j\beta_j\right),$$

$$C = \left[\sum_{j\in X_1}\frac{\bar{R}_j-R_f}{\sigma_{\epsilon_j}^2}\beta_j, \quad \sum_{j=1}^{N_2}\frac{\bar{R}_j-R_f}{\sigma_{\epsilon_j}^2}\beta_j, \dots, \quad \sum_{j\in X_p}\frac{\bar{R}_j-R_f}{\sigma_{\epsilon_j}^2}\beta_j\right].$$

The solution to the above equation is of course

$$X = A^{-1}C.$$

Substituting this into eq. (21) allows us to calculate Z_i. Define

$$R_k = \left(b_1b_k\sigma_m^2 \dots b_k^2\sigma_m^2 + \sigma_{\epsilon_k}^2 \dots b_p b_k\sigma_m^2\right).$$

Then the solution for a member of group k is

$$Z_i = \frac{\beta_i}{\sigma_{\epsilon_i}^2}\left(\frac{\bar{R}_i-R_f}{\beta_i} - R_k A^{-1}C\right) \tag{22}$$

or

$$Z_i = \frac{\beta_i}{\sigma_{\epsilon_i}^2}\left[\frac{\bar{R}_i-R_f}{\beta_i} - C_k\right],$$

where C_k is a constant for any stock in group k. Once again because the C_k can be calculated before decisions are made on the composition of optimal portfolios, the construction of the optimal portfolio can be done easily. After the constants for each group are computed, simply compare the excess return to β of each stock with its group constant. For positive β securities, hold all stocks with higher excess return to β, sell short all stocks with excess return to β lower than the constant. For negative β stocks, act in the opposite manner. The Z_i can quickly and easily be computed for each stock and the sum of the absolute values forced to add to one.

7.2. Short sales not allowed

As proven in Elton et al. (forthcoming (b)), eq. (22) is the appropriate equation if $N_1, N_2, \ldots, N_\rho$ are defined so as to include only those securities in the optimal portfolio. Once again an optimal portfolio can be obtained by alternatively fixing the number in all but one group and then optimizing in that group. This is directly analogous to the method outlined in the previous section.

8. Simple rules with general multi-index models

The multi-index models discussed earlier have a very special form. Simple rules can be derived for index models with a more general form. The cost of employing a more general form of an index model is a more complex solution. While solutions exist which are simpler than a programming solution, they are more complex than those presented so far and they do not in general lead to an unambiguous ranking of securities. For example, in (13) we derive simple rules when a securities return is related to a series of orthogonal indices. The first index can be thought of as a general market index and subsequent indices can be viewed as industry indices with the market removed. The orthogonality is not a limitation since we can always represent a series of nonorthogonal indices as orthogonal. What is limiting is an assumption that any return has a positive coefficient on only two indices. Thus, a firm's return is related to the market and its own industry but not to other industries. Simple rules similar to those discussed earlier are derived and shown to be optimal.

9. Simple rules with upper bounds

The previous analysis can be extended to incorporate upper limits on the fraction of the portfolio that can be held in any stock. Institutions are often restricted by law (and individuals frequently by choice) from placing more than a certain percentage of their funds in any one security. For example, the Investment Company Act of 1940 states that no more than 5 percent of the funds of an investment company can be invested in any one security. Furthermore, the importance of considering the upper bound constraints can be seen from an empirical study done by Cohen and Pogue (1967). They report that when selecting portfolios from 75 and 150 stock populations, 66–82 percent of the securities selected were at their legally defined upper bounds of 5 percent. Naturally, if management were operating under tighter self-imposed upper bounds (as most managers do), the number of securities at the upper bound would tend to be even larger. Thus, the problem of incorporating upper bounds is a serious one.

The inclusion of upper bounds changes the procedures for solving the portfolio problem by ranking techniques and requires a completely new set of proofs of optimality. Nevertheless, utilizing the particularities of the variance–covariance matrix, one can derive decision rules for optimal portfolio selection with upper bounds which are much more direct and more easily understood than the usual nonlinear programming methods. Furthermore, criteria can be developed for ranking stocks which make clear the risk characteristics of a stock which are important to the portfolio manager.

In (10) we develop simple procedures for two cases: (1) when the single-index model is appropriate, and (2) when one can assume a constant correlation coefficient between all pairs of securities. The same methodology can be used to derive similar procedures for other cases.

Portfolio selection with upper bounds involves two steps: (1) a preranking of stocks which is exactly the same as the ones discussed earlier which determines the order in which stocks enter into the optimal portfolio; and (2) a further ranking which now uses effectively the upper bounds to determine which of the selected stocks are to be invested in at their respective upper bounds. Although our limited computational experience indicates that the latter ranking is a one-short operation, this need not necessarily be so and in order to produce an optimal portfolio it may be necessary to iterate.

Although the proofs of optimality are quite complex, the actual procedure is straightforward. Furthermore, since upper bonds effectively set a minimum number of securities (5 percent bounds require at least 20 securities) the actual computation time with upper bounds may be less than without upper bounds.

10. Conclusion

In this paper we have derived simple decision rules which, under any of the currently accepted predictive models of the correlation structure between securities, lead to the selection of optimal portfolios. These rules are not approximations but are optimum in the sense that they produce answers identical to those that would be produced by solving the quadratic programming problem. Not only are these rules computationally simple, they produce unique rankings of securities in terms to which practitioners should be able to relate.

Appendix

Consider the set K^0 for which $Z_i = 0$ when $\mu_i = 0$. According to rule (3) these can be included or excluded at the R_f being considered since they do not effect ϕ_k. For any security in set K^0 it must be true that $(\bar{R}_i - R_f)/\beta_i$ is the same constant. Consider an increase in R_f by an amount δ. Then from rules (1) and (2) these can be ranked by

$$\frac{\bar{R}_i - R_f - \delta}{\beta_i} = \frac{R_i - R_f}{\beta_i} - \frac{\delta}{\beta_i}.$$

Since $(\bar{R}_i - R_f)/\beta_i$ is the same they can be ranked by $-\delta/\beta_i$.

It follows that positive β securities should be ranked in descending order of β_i and negative β stocks in ascending order. Any remaining ties must be identical securities and the one(s) with the largest $\sigma_{\varepsilon_i}^2$ can be excluded.

If $\Psi_i < 0$ for a security, it should be in the included set since an increase in λ would cause it to have a positive Z_i. Thus, securities in set K^0 should be added to the included set k in decreasing order of β_i for positive β and ascending order for negative β until $\Psi_i \geq 0$ for the next security to be added. Furthermore, an examination of Ψ_i shows that only either positive β securities or negative β securities would be added depending on the sign of

$$\sum_{i=1}^{k} \frac{\beta_i}{\sigma_{\varepsilon_i}^2}.$$

References

Blume, M. (1971) "On the Assessment of Risk", *Journal of Finance* 26 (1), 1–10.
Cohen, K. and J. Pogue (1967) "An Empirical Evaluation of Alternative Portfolio Selection Models", *Journal of Business*, April, 166–193.
Cragg, J. and B. Malkiel (1968) "The Consensus and Accuracy of Some Predictions of the Growth of Corporate Earnings", *Journal of Finance*, March, 67–84.
Elton, E. J. and M. J. Gruber (1970) "Homogeneous Groups and the Testing of Economic Hypotheses", *Journal of Financial and Quantitative Analysis*, January, 581–602.
Elton, E. J. and M. J. Gruber (1971) "Improved Forecasting Through the Design of Homogeneous Groups", *Journal of Business*, October, 432–450.
Elton, E. J. and M. J. Gruber (1972) "Earnings Estimates and the Accuracy of Expectational Data", *Management Science* 18, B409–B424.

Elton, E. J. and M. J. Gruber (1973) "Estimating the Dependence Structure of Share Prices — Implications for Portfolio Selection Models", *Journal of Finance* 27 (5), 1203–1233.

Elton, E. J. and M. J. Gruber (1975) *Finance as a Dynamic Process* (Prentice-Hall, Englewood Cliffs).

Elton, E. J., M. J. Gruber and H. W. Padberg (1976) "Simple Rules for Optimal Portfolio Selection", *Journal of Finance*, December.

Elton, E. J., M. J. Gruber and H. W. Padberg (forthcoming (a)) "Simple Rules for Optimal Portfolio Selection with Upper Bound Constraints", *Operations Research*.

Elton, E. J., M. J. Gruber and H. W. Padberg (forthcoming (b)) "Simple Rules for Optimal Portfolio Selection — the Multi-Group Case", *Journal of Financial and Quantitative Analysis*.

Elton, E. J., M. J. Gruber and M. W. Padberg (n.d.) "Simple Rules for Optimal Portfolio Selection — Tracing the Efficient Frontier", unpublished manuscript.

Elton, E. J., M. J. Gruber and M. W. Padberg (n.d.) "Simple Criteria for Optimal Portfolio Selection — Multi-Index Case", Paper presented at Western Finance Association.

King, B. (1966) "Market and Industry Factors in Stock Price Behavior", *Journal of Business, Supplement*, January, 139–190.

Latané, H. and D. Tuttle (1967) "Criteria for Portfolio Building", *Journal of Finance* 22 (3), 359–374.

Lintner, J. (1965) "The Valuation of Risk Assets on the Selection of Risky Investments in Stock Portfolios and Capital Budgets", *The Review of Ecconomics and Statistics*, February, 13–37.

Mao, J. (1970) "Essentials for Portfolio Diversification Strategy", *Journal of Finance*, December.

Markowitz, H. (1952) "Portfolio Selection", *Journal of Finance*, March, 77–91.

Markowitz, H. (1959) *Portfolio Selection* (Wiley & Sons, Inc., New York).

Sharpe, W. (1963) "A Simplified Model for Portfolio Analysis", *Management Science*, January, 277–293.

Sharpe, W. (1971) "A Linear Programming Approximation for the General Portfolio Selection Problem", *Journal of Financial and Quantitative Analysis*, December, 1263–1276.

Sharpe, W. (1973) "Simple Strategies for Portfolio Diversification: Comment", *Journal of Finance* 27 (1), 127–129.

Chapter 17

ALTERNATIVES TO MEAN–VARIANCE FOR PORTFOLIO SELECTION

GEORGE C. PHILIPPATOS
Pennsylvania State University

1. Perspectives

The Markowitz Mean–Variance (E–V) criterion for the selection of efficient portfolios has been traditionally criticized on several grounds.

(1) It is a static, single-period decision criterion, whose extension (without serious modifications) to long-run decisions may be inappropriate (Gressis (1975), Hakansson (1971a, b), Latané (1959), Latané and Young (1969), Latané and Tuttle (1967), Thorp (1971)).[1]

(2) It relies entirely on the mean and variance (or standard deviation) of the distribution of holding-period-returns (HPRs). However, other moments of the distribution like skewness and kurtosis may also be of interest to investors (Arditti (1968), Jean (1971)); or, perhaps, the entire distribution of returns should be known (Hadar and Russell (1969), Hanoch and Levy (1969, 1970), Whitmore (1970)). Alternatively, to the extent that there exist in the market nonsymmetric expectations and/or preferences, measures for downside risk should be included in the decision process (Mao (1970a, b), Pyle and Turnovsky (1970), Roy (1952)).

(3) It is a sufficient criterion for choice when the HPRs are normally distributed and/or investors' utility functions are quadratic (Hadar and Russell (1969), Hanoch and Levy (1970), Tobin (1969)); however, as recent empirical evidence suggests, stock price changes are better fitted by non-normal distributions (Fama (1976), Officer (1972), Praetz (1972), Press (1972)).

(4) The investors' actual utility can be adequately approximated by quadratic curve only over some relevant range of HPRs (Sharpe (1970)).

---

[1]Some of this criticism has been partially discussed in terms of the multiperiod E–V models discussed in Part 6 of the chapter on "Mean–Variance Portfolio Selection Strategies." However, additional extensions in terms of the growth-optimal or geometric model will be discussed later on this chapter. It should also be noted that the State-Preference framework will not be discussed here, as it falls outside the scope of this paper.

James L. Bicksler, Editor, Handbook of Financial Economics
© *North-Holland Publishing Company – 1979*

(5) Other criticisms ranging from the unigoal structure of the model (Kumar and Philippatos (1977), Kumar et al. (1978), Lee and Lerro (1973)) to the measure of uncertainty utilized (Philippatos and Gressis (1975), Philippatos and Wilson (1972, 1974a,b)), have also been voiced about the E–V criterion.

Some of the criticism must, of course, be appreciated within the context of the prominence that the E–V portfolio selection criterion has attained in the past two decades or so. Beginning as a normative rule for formalized investment decision-making (Markowitz (1952)), it has been expanded into a positive macroeconomic theory of capital market efficiency (Fama (1976) and equilibrium asset-pricing — with intermediate applications from monetary policy (Tobin (1958)), to retailing and farm planning (Hazell (1971), Thomson and Hazell (1973)). However, a good part of the criticism must also be attributed to recent research into the behavior of stock market prices (Fama (1976)), Officer (1972), Praetz (1972), Press (1972)), as well as the decision-making behavior of individual and institutional investors (Schilbred (1972), Swalm (1966), Tarascio and Murphy (1972), Dyckman and Salomon (1972), MacCrimmon and Larsson (1975)). It is, then, within this spirit of evolving knowledge that we shall examine some of the criticisms and review some of the proposed alternative strategies — which in some cases may be no more than extensions or augmentations imposed by market realities. Nevertheless, they differ sufficiently from the basic form of the model to justify the overall nomenclature of "alternative strategies".

In this chapter we shall examine some of the alternative strategies to the E–V portfolio selection criterion. Section 2 will make a brief detour into the simple concepts of utility theory underlying the E–V framework. This detour will set the framework for much of the criticism leveled against the basic E–V approach. Section 3 will deal with what has been called the "General Efficiency Criterion" — a methodology for ordering investment prospects under uncertainty in terms of stochastic dominance (Hadar and Russell (1969), Hanoch and Levy (1969, 1970), Levy (1970, 1973, 1974), Porter (1973), Porter and Gaumnitz (1972), Whitmore (1970)). Section 4 will concentrate on the alternatives proposed for the selection of portfolios when various forms of asymmetries are manifested in market expectations and/or investor preferences. For such cases, we shall review E–V extensions that include additional moments of the distribution of security returns (Suppes (1961), Arditti (1968)), the utilization of semivariance as a nonsymmetric measure of risk (downside risk) (Mao (1970a, b), Porter and Bey (1974)), the employment of a disaster level of return as a measure of risk (Agnew et al. (1969), Gressis (1975), Naslung and Whinston (1962), Roy (1952)), and other types of risk measures (Markowitz (1959), Levy and Sarnat (1970)), as well as the growth optimum (geometric mean) model (Latané (1959), Latané and Young (1969), Latané and Tuttle (1967), Hakansson (1971a,b), Markowitz (1959)). Finally section 5 will discuss some newer and less known, but nevertheless potentially promising approaches, such as goal programming (Kumar and

Philippatos (1977), Kumar et al. (1978), Lee and Lerro (1973)), adaptive and heuristic models (Murphy (1965), Clarkson (1962), Clarkson and Meltzer (1960), Elton et al. (1976, 1977)), as well as information-theoretic approaches (Philippatos and Gressis (1975), Philippatos and Wilson (1972, 1974a, b), Thorp (1971)).

2. Utility aspects of portfolio selection

The locus of efficient combinations (efficient frontier), which reflects the market expectations framework formed by asset-price behavior, provides a partial ordering of portfolios in accordance with the E–V efficiency criterion. However, the final, optimal portfolio that maximizes the investor's utility[2] is obtained at the point of equilibrium between expectations and preferences. Utility theory is the most satisfactory and generally accepted theory of decision-making under uncertainty.[3] The theory assumes that a rational decision-maker has a preference ordering (utility) function with the following properties:

(a) U is defined on the set of all possible outcomes,

(b) outcome X is preferred to outcome Y if and only if $U(X) > U(Y)$, and

(c) If the payoffs of two given outcomes are stated in the form of stochastic distributions $(F(x), F(y))$, then outcome X is preferred to project Y if and only if

$$\int_{-\infty}^{+\infty} \left(U(x)\,df(x) > \int_{-\infty}^{+\infty} U(y)\,df(y). \right. \tag{1}$$

The utility of a probability distribution U_2 is defined as the positive real number $p, (0 < p < 1)$ which ensures that the relation (2) below holds when $U_1 > U_2 > U_3$:

$$U_2 \sim pU_1 + (1-p)U_3. \tag{2}$$

The utility function in (2) can be shown to be a real, order-preserving, monotonically increasing function, which is linear in the probabilities and unique up to a positive linear transformation.

Assume a risk-averse investor who can map out a preference ordering on any combination of assets that are described by the probability distributions of their future returns and conforming to the von Neumann–Morgenstern axioms. If he is given the choice of participating in a lottery with a probability p of receiving

---

[2]In this case, we employ the von Neumann–Morgenstern axioms of utility theory (von Neumann and Morgenstern (1964)).

[3]There are, of course, other distinctively different approaches to decision-making under uncertainty, e.g. adaptive and heuristic, which will be discussed in conjunction with selection techniques in Section 5 of this chapter. In addition, other axiomatic approaches to utility theory are discussed in Raiffa (1968) and Tomasini (1971).

the amount X and a probability $(1-p)$ of receiving the amount 0, or instead receiving the certain amount Y, where $Y=pX$, then the following possibilities exist:

$Y \gtrless pX$,   risk-aversion,
$Y \sim pX$,   risk-indifference,
$pX \gtrless Y$,   risk-attraction.

Pratt (1964) and Arrow (1965) define risk-aversion by

$$r(X) = \frac{U''(X)}{U'(X)} = \frac{d \ln U'(X)}{dX}. \tag{3}$$

The risk-aversion function describes the utility function $U(X)$ completely, since integration of (3) yields[4]

$$U(X) \sim \int \exp\left[- \int r(X) dX \right] dX. \tag{4}$$

In the basic E–V portfolio selection approach the utility function of investors is assumed to be quadratic of the form

$$U'(R) = \frac{dU(R)}{dR} > 0 \tag{5}$$

and

$$U''(R) = \frac{d^2 U(R)}{d^2 R} < 0, \tag{6}$$

where $U(R)$ is the utility derived from a given level of monetary return. Markowitz (1959) has shown that if an investor makes his decisions on the basis of μ and σ^2, and attempts to maximize the expected value of his utility, then his utility function is of the form[5]

$$U(R) = \gamma_0 + \gamma_1 R - \gamma_2 R^2 \tag{7}$$

where $\gamma_2 > 0$ for risk-averse individuals. Moreover, since $U(R)$ is determined only up to a linear transformation, then for the risk-averse decision-maker

$$U(R) = R - AR^2, \qquad A > 0 \tag{8}$$

---

[4]For $r(X) > 0$ the utility function will be concave and for $r(X) < 0$ it will be convex. Alternating convexities and concavities are also admitted.
[5]Decision rules derived from (7) require only the first and second moments of the probability distribution of R, making the variance a measure of risk.

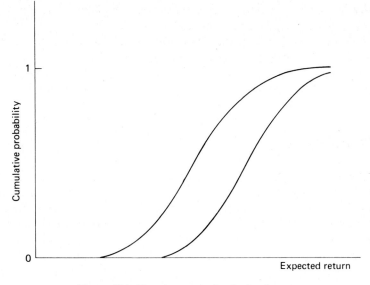

Figure 17.1. First degree stochastic dominance.

the utility function must have $U'(R)>0$ and $U''(R)<0$, $\forall R \in[a,b]$.[13] The SSD relationship for portfolios F and G is shown in fig. 17.2.

The Third Degree Stochastic Dominance (TSD) criterion states, then, that portfolio F dominates portfolio G if

$$\int_a^R \int_a^y \int_a^w [f(z)-g(z)]\,dz\,dw\,dy \leqslant 0 \tag{13}$$

for all $R \in[a,b]$, with strict inequality for at least one value of $R \in[a,b]$, and

$$\int_a^b \int_a^y [f(w)-g(w)]\,dw\,dy < 0, \tag{14}$$

where R varies continuously on the closed interval $[a,b]$. The TSD is appropriate for situations where we assume a decreasing premium associated with an investor's wealth.[14] In such cases the investor's utility function must have

---

[13] See Philippatos and Gressis (1975) for conditions of eqivalence between SSD and other portfolio selection criteria.
[14] See Arrow (1965) and Pratt (1964). Pratt has shown that there are lower levels of wealth ranges where the investor's utility function can exhibit increasing risk-aversion and ranges of higher wealth levels where the utility function exhibits decreasing risk-aversion.

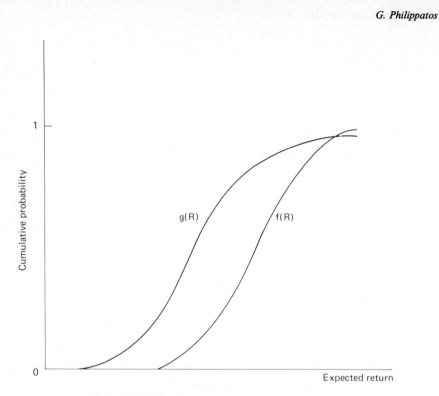

Figure 17.2. Second degree stochastic dominance.

$U'(R)>0$, $U''(R)<0$, and $U'''(R)>0$, $\forall R \in [a,b]$. The TSD relationship for portfolio F and G is shown in fig. 17.3.

The utilization of the stochastic dominance rules on the set of all possible combinations of risky assets should, in principle, partition the set into an efficient subset and an inefficient subset — the latter being of no further interest to the investor. Thus, a portfolio is efficient if and only if it is not dominated by another portfolio. However, whereas the stochastic dominance criterion provides a preference ordering of portfolios (or individual assets) it is not capable of providing an algorithm for constructing asset combinations — owing to the lack of appropriate optimizing algorithms. Indeed, the existing applications of the technique have involved pairwise comparisons of portfolios that contain pre-specified combinations of risky assets.[15]

[15]Several studies have utilized Stochastic Dominance Criteria to rank portfolios ordered by other techniques or individual assets. See Hanoch and Levy (1970), Joy and Porter (1974), Levy (1973), Levy and Hanoch (1974), Levy and Sarnat (1970), Porter (1973), Porter and Bey (1974), Porter and Gaumnitz (1972).

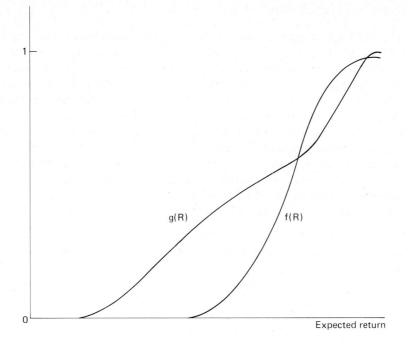

Figure 17.3. Third degree stochastic dominance.

4. Models for nonsymmetric expectations and preferences[16]

The mean–variance approach to portfolio selection, being based on symmetric market expectations (normal distributions of returns) and symmetric preferences (quadratic utility functions) is, obviously, at a disadvantage when put to test in situations where asymmetries prevail. For this reason, several other alternative strategies have been proposed. In this section, we shall review briefly some of these strategies, beginning with the Confidence Limit criterion proposed by Baumol (1963), Levy and Hanoch (1974), Russell and Smith (1966), then continuing with the Mean–Semivariance criterion[17] (Mao (1970a, b)), the Safety-First criterion proposed by Roy (1952) Pyle and Turnovsky (1970), Agnew et al. (1969), as well as some other criteria that attempt to account for various types of asymmetries.

---

[16]Several of the portfolio selection strategies outlined in this section and some in section 5 of this chapter would, under the rules of stochastic dominance be judged to be inefficient. See Levy and Sarnat (1970) [54] and Levy and Hanoch (1974).

[17]The Mean–Semivariance criterion was also proposed by Markowitz (1959, pp. 188–196).

4.1. Baumol's confidence limit criterion—(E–L)

Baumol (1963) has suggested that an investor is usually not interested in the entire efficient set of portfolios yielded by the Markowitz (E–V) framework. Instead, the investor is concerned with a smaller subset of efficient portfolios. He places his emphasis on the proposition that the investor is not just concerned with obtaining a future return while minimizing his risk. Rather, according to Baumol, the individual is concerned with the minimum acceptable return, or maximum acceptable loss. Subsequently, if a portfolio manager is supplied with the investor's coefficient of risk aversion, K—measured in terms of the number of standard deviations below the expected return—he can construct a set of efficient portfolios based on expected gain, E, and a lower confidence limit, L. Baumol calls his method the (E–L) criterion.

Given two investments, F and G, F will be preferred to G if

$$E_F > E_G \quad \text{and} \quad E_F - K\sigma_F \geqslant E_G - K\sigma_G, \tag{15}$$

not both equalities holding simultaneously. The expression $E - K\sigma$ represents the

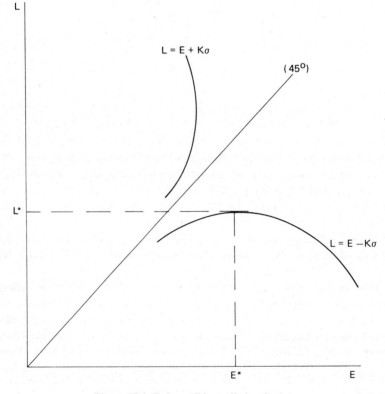

Figure 17.4. E–L confidence limit criterion.

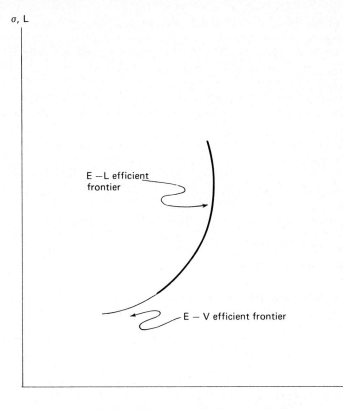

Figure 17.5. Relationship between the E–L and E–V criteria.

"lower confidence limit for the investor's return" (Baumol (1963), p. 177). The critical nature of the risk-aversion coefficient is defined by Tchebycheff's inequality, which states that

$$\Pr\{|F - E_F| > K\sigma_F\} \leqslant 1/K^2. \tag{16}$$

That is, the probability that the actual return from an investment F will be lower than K standard deviations below the expected return of F is bounded[18] by $1/K^2$.

It can be easily shown that Baumol's E–L criterion yields an efficient set which is a subset of the Markowitz Mean–Standard Deviation efficient frontier. Indeed, as $K \to \infty$, the E–L frontier approaches the mean–standard deviation frontier (Russell and Smith (1966)), with the functional relationship between the two shown in figs. 17.4 and 17.5, respectively. For example, focusing on the

---

[18]See Baumol (1963, pp. 177–181), where he also explains his awareness about some peculiarities arising from his approach.

curve defined by $L = E - K\sigma$, we see that each point on it corresponds to an efficient portfolio along the Markowitz mean–standard deviation frontier. When, $dL/dE > 0$, the investor would prefer the portfolio with higher L — ensuring both higher E and L — yielding portfolio (E^*, L^*) along this segment. However, when $dL/dE < 0$, risk–return comparisons must be made.

4.2. The Mean–Semivariance criterion[19] (E–S)

Markowitz (1959), Mao (1970a, b), and others (Porter and Bey (1974), Swalm (1966)), have suggested that investors (and particularly businessmen) may be concerned with the risk of abnormally low returns or downside risk. For this reason, the criterion of mean–semivariance (E–S) was proposed to account for such cases of nonsymmetric expectations and preferences. The semivariance is generally defined as the expected value of the squared deviations of possible outcomes from some point of reference, chosen by the decision-maker as a critical value.

Now, let R be a random variable with a known probability distribution, and let h be some arbitrarily chosen critical value, such that the following relationship holds:

$$(R - h) = \left[\begin{array}{ll} \{(R - h), & \text{if } (R - h) \leqslant 0\} \\ \{0, & \text{if } (R - h) > 0\} \end{array} \right]. \tag{17}$$

Then, the semivariance, S_h, with the critical value h is defined as

$$E[(R - h)^-]^2 \tag{18}$$

or, alternatively,

$$E[\min(R - h, 0)]^2. \tag{18'}$$

The utility function that corresponds to (18) as defined by Markowitz (1959, p. 291) is of the hybrid[20] form given by (19), below

$$U(R) = c + aR + b[\min(R - h, 0)]^2. \tag{19}$$

The utility function in (19) is quadratic in the range $R \leqslant h$ and linear for $R > h$, as shown in fig. 17.6. Now, let s_h stand for the positive square root of the semivariance, which we shall call the semistandard deviation. Then, taking the expected value of (19), we have

$$E[U(R)] = c + a\mu + b(s_h)^2. \tag{20}$$

---

[19]For a detailed analysis and application of the E–S criterion, see Mao (1970a).
[20]This type of utility function depicts an investor who is risk averse for values below the critical point h and risk-neutral above h.

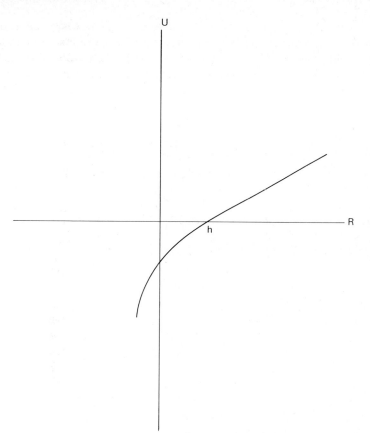

Figure 17.6. Hybrid utility function.

For this function, $b<0, ds_h/d\mu>0$, and $d^2s_h/d\mu^2<0$, indicating indifference curves that are both upward sloping and concave downward.[21]

In perspective, we can draw the following generalizations about the E–S criterion: (1) it implies a hybrid utility function, indicating an investor who acts conservatively for values below some arbitrarily chosen critical point h, and in a "devil may care" fashion for values higher than h; (2) for critical value E, the E–S_E criterion is prejudiced against the investment where distribution of returns is skewed to the left, while it is insensitive to right-skewness;[22] and (3) for critical

---

[21] Although the signs of the first and second derivatives of the $\mu-\sigma$ and $\mu-s$ indifference curves are the same, their shapes will differ. Moreover, for nonsymmetric distributions the two criteria will likely yield different efficient portfolios. However, for symmetric distributions, since $\sigma^2=2S_E$ (E being the mean), the two criteria will yield the same optimal solution. See (Mao, 1970a, p. 661).

[22] The E–V criterion is, of course, sensitive to changes on both sides of the mean, but it is insensitive to the direction (desireability) of the skewness. See Mao (1970a, pp. 663–664) and Markowitz (1959, pp. 290–291).

value zero (0), in the E–S_0 criterion — which is concerned with expected return and distribution of losses — the symmetry of the distributions is not the crucial condition. Rather, it is the scatter of values below zero, and the E–S_0 criterion discriminates against the prospect with the greatest scatter of points below zero.

4.3. Roy's Safety-First criterion (S–F)

Contemporaneously with the original publication of Markowitz's E–V criterion (Markowitz (1952)), another normative selection criterion was proposed by Roy (1952). This approach[23] is also concerned with nonsymmetric preferences, specifically with decision-makers who are concerned with the probability of failing to achieve some desired minimum level of return from their investment—called the disaster level, D.

In the absence of perfect knowledge about the probability density function of portfolio (or asset) returns, Roy utilizes the Tchebycheff inequaliity. Given that the values of $E(R_p) = \mu_p$, σ_p^2, and D are known, the Tchebycheff inequality yields the upper bound, a priori

$$\Pr\left[\,|R_p - \mu_p| \geqslant \left[\,\mu_p - D\,\right]\,\right] \leqslant \frac{\sigma_p^2}{\left(\mu_p - D\right)^2} \tag{21}$$

and a forteriori

$$\Pr\left[\,\mu_p - R_p \geqslant \mu_p - D\,\right] = \Pr\left[\,R_p \leqslant D\,\right] \leqslant \frac{\sigma_p^2}{\left(\mu_p - D\right)^2} \tag{22}$$

Hence, in the absence of perfect information about the probability density function, the best strategy for minimizing $\Pr[R_p \leqslant D]$ is to minimize

$$\frac{\sigma_p^2}{\left(\mu_p - D\right)^2} \quad \text{or} \quad \frac{\sigma_p^2}{\left(\mu_p - D\right)} \quad \text{or} \quad \frac{\sigma_p}{\left(\mu_p - D\right)},$$

because of strict monotonicity.[24]

Geometrically, the optimal S–F portfolio can be obtained by drawing a line from the D intercept in the expected returns axis tangent to the mean–variance or mean–standard deviation frontier, as shown in fig. 17.7. In fact, the slope of

---

[23]Several extensions and applications of the S–F approach have been made by employing the appropriate methodology of chance-constrained programming. See Agnew et al. (1969), Pyle and Turnovsky (1970), and Gressis (1975), who derived some interesting implications.

[24]For normally distributed portfolio returns, minimizing $\Pr[R_p < D]$ is equivalent to minimizing $\sigma_p^2/(\mu_p - D)^2$ or minimizing $\sigma_p/(\mu_p - D)$ (Roy (1952, p. 434)).

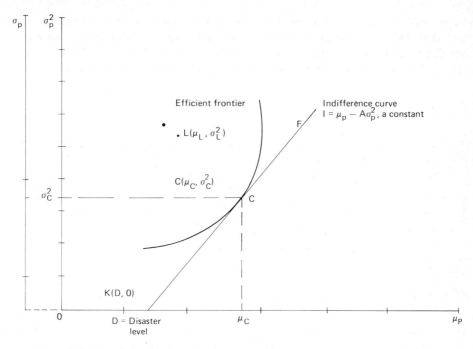

Figure 17.7. The relationship between the E–V and the S–F portfolio selection solutions.

any line from the μ_p intercept D to any point $L(\mu_L, \sigma_L^2)$ in the feasibility region has the value $\sigma_L/(\mu_L - D)$ and the only point which minimizes this slope lies on the efficient frontier and is the point of tangency between the efficient frontier and the straight line KCF. Therefore, the S–F optimal portfolio corresponding to disaster level D is $C(\mu_c, \sigma_c^2)$, because only this portfolio minimizes $\sigma_p^2/(\mu_p - D)^2$ or $\sigma_p/(\mu_p - D)$.

Furthermore, it should be noted that for a disaster level $D_1 < D$, $(D_2 > D)$ the investor's optimal S–F portfolio moves down (up) and to the left (right) along the efficient frontier. The implication of this property of S–F optimal portfolios is that the more conservative the investor the lower his disaster level, D, and vice versa.

Thus, given the disaster level, D, Roy's safety first both explains diversification ·and chooses the optimal portfolio. Moreover, if investors who minimize $\Pr[R_p \leqslant D]$ and investors who maximize $E[U(R_p)] = E(R_p) - A\sigma_p^2$ select the same optimal portfolio, $C(\mu_c, \sigma_c^2)$, then all points on the KCF indifference curve obtain combinations of mean–variance such that $\mu_p - A\sigma_p^2 = $ constant. Specifically, for portfolios $K(D,0)$ and $C(\mu_c, \sigma_c^2)$, we have $D = \mu_c - A\sigma_c^2$. Thus, for normally distributed portfolio returns, the portfolio that maximizes the investor's expected utility also maximizes the probability of obtaining portfolio returns above the specified disaster level, D.

4.4. Other selection strategies

In addition to the selection criteria outlined above, several authors have suggested approaches that account either for known asymmetries or for decision-making under partial ignorance. For example, Arditti (1968) suggested the utilization of the third moment around the mean to account for skewness. His work was later extended to portfolio analysis both for the normative microeconomic framework and for the positive macroeconomic model of asset pricing by Jean (1971). Moreover, Levy and Hanoch (1974) and Hanoch and Levy (1970) have outlined several efficiency criteria for optimal portfolio selection with quadratic and cubic utility functions[25]

Another interesting criterion is concerned with "investment in the long-run" as proposed by Latané (1959), Latané and Young (1969), Latané and Tuttle (1967), Markowitz (1959), and others (Thorp (1971), Hakansson (1971a, b), Gressis (1975)). Whereas one-period portfolio selection is performed by the use of the mean–variance criterion, or any of the alternatives already discussed, the long-run finite multiperiod selection is made through the application of the expected Geometric Mean (G–M) or, equivalently, the long-run capital growth maximization criterion.[26] The expected geometric mean criterion, although limited in scope to special groups of investors, does possess intuitive appeal and has normative implications for institutional investment managers and wealthy investors, whose objective is the long-run maximization of the growth rate on their invested assets.[27] It has been shown that maximizing the geometric mean return is consistent with maximizing the logarithmic utility of wealth function.[28]

---

[25]The limited scope of the chapter prevents us from discussing these strategies here.

[26]The maximization of the geometric mean criterion is based on the following assumptions: (a) the same investment opportunities exist at the end of each period; (b) the outcomes of the projects are independent over time; (c) all income from the investment is reinvested; and (d) there exist no taxes, commissions, illiquidities, and indivisibilities.

[27]The geometric mean criterion has been rather controversial, as can be seen by reference to Latané (1959), Markowitz (1952, 1959), Gressis (1975), Hakansson (1971a, b). Suffice it to say that in tracing out the (E–V) efficient portfolios, it passes through the portfolio that maximizes approximately the expected value of the logarithm of $(1 + R)$. Markowitz (1959) has argued in a recent article (Markowitz (1976)) and proven that under certain conditions, "...this Kelly–Latané point should be considered the upper limit for conservative choice among E–V efficient portfolios, since portfolios with higher (arithmetic) mean give greater short-run variability with less return in the long run" (p. 1274). See also Hsu et al. (1974) for some interesting results about (E–V) and (G–M) in the case of lognormally distributed security (and portfolio) returns and Bernoulli utility maximizers.

[28]Given an infinite number of periods, the Central Limit Theorem ensures the same results, i.e. the geometric mean criterion, is sufficient.

5. Alternative portfolio selection strategies

Several approaches to the portfolio selection problem have been developed to describe situations where investors utilize nonoptimizing, heuristic approaches (Clarkson (1962), Clarkson and Meltzer (1960)) or very complicated optimizing algorithms based on trial-and-error learning patterns—generally known as type-2 adaptive processes. Moreover, efforts have been made recently to account for the multigoal nature of motivational assumptions in the case of some institutional investors, such as dual-fund managers, by utilizing goal-programming methodolgy (Kumar and Philippatos (1977), Kumar et al. (1978), Lee and Lerro (1973)). Finally, alternative methodologies have been proposed that differ radically from existing methods in that the measure of uncertainty is derived from information-theoretic considerations rather than the standard statistical concepts (Philippatos and Gressis (1975), Philippatos and Wilson (1972, 1974a, b)). In this section we shall review briefly some of the alternative strategies that may be utilized for the selection of portfolios.

5.1. Heuristic and goal-programming portfolio selection models

Clarkson (1962) and Clarkson and Meltzer (1960) developed a heuristic simulation model based on the actual, operational portfolio decisions of trust investment officers in a medium-sized bank. The nonoptimizing approach employed, utilized the following phases of the decision process:

(a) the data formation and search;

(b) the establishment of postulates that relate control, primitive information processes, and an unambiguous set of rules;

(c) the delineation of modifiable rules—the modifications based on learning behavior;[29]

(d) the construction of a model of investment behavior through interviews of the decision-makers and understanding of their organizational and clientele constraints; and

(e) the construction of decision-making protocols.

The simulation model also contained a clear specification of the investment goals associated with each of the accounts studied thus giving early recognition to the existence of multigoal motivations in institutional investment behavior.[30]

---

[29]More formal models of learning behavior applications to the investment decision have been constructed by Murphy (1965), who utilized complicated type-2 adaptive control processes to analyze both heuristic and optimizing investor behavior under uncertainty.

[30]Recently Elton et al. (1976, 1977) have proposed a "heuristic" decision criterion that can be utilized for the selection of optimal portfolios. However, this criterion is not a bona fide heuristic rule but rather a method for avoiding the mathematical programming complications, very much based on assumptions about the existence of optimum portfolio inputs.

The results of the simulation were rather surprising in that the models generated portfolio compositions and yields that nearly matched those of the trust investment officers.

The existence of multigoal motivational approaches in portfolio selection was pursued more formally at a later date by Lee and Lerro (1973) and by Kumar and Philippatos (1977) and Kumar et al. (1978). The methodolgy of goal programming, utilized by these authors, is designed to resolve situations where the traditional unigoal motivational assumption typically employed in the standard portfolio selection problem, is replaced by the more realistic appreciation that several conflicting goals may compete in the allocational decision. The technique is best suited for problems where goal "satisficing" rather than optimizing is forced upon the decision-maker by the environment.

Since both goals and constraints are incorporated in the allocation decision, the objective function is constructed in a way that, upon solution, yields a result "as close as possible" to the indicated goals. In addition, the goal-programming approach allows the differential weighting and ordering of the various goals such that they are satisfied sequentially in order of preassigned importance. Several applications of this technique have been made in environments like Dual-Purpose Funds which are legally required to dichotomize their investment goals.

5.2. Entropic models of portfolio selection

The last alternative strategy for portfolio selection to be reviewed in this chapter is the scheme of mean–entropy diversification, originally proposed and tested by Philippatos and Wilson (1972, 1974a, b), and later formalized analytically by Philippatos and Gressis (1975).[31]

Entropy is a well known measure of uncertainty that is freely employed in the dynamic processes analyzed by engineers, communications theorists, and social scientists. The entropy measure is independent of the mean, as well as of the form of the distribution, and it can be used in metric and nonmetric form to incorporate both the variates and the attributes of the assets in the market.

In order to apply mean–entropy diversification in a meaningful way we need the following information: (1) the pairwise joint entropies of the asset-returns, and (2) the pairwise conditional (marginal) entropies of these returns. As it turns out, the entropy of a portfolio, H_p, is the sum of the conditional entropies of the M-security sample.

[31]It should be noted here that earlier efforts to explain long-run investment behavior in terms of information-theoretic measures had been made. For example, the so-called Kelly criterion is based on a new interpretation of the information rate. See, for example, Thorp (1971) for an application of the Kelly criterion to portfolio choice. Moreover, since the information measure is expressed in logarithmic terms, it lends itself as a suitable contender for use in the capital growth model which seeks to maximize the expected value of the logarithm of the wealth variable.

In addition to the above, mean–entropy diversification can be enriched to account for the contingency states of nature as well as the relationship of the asset-returns to an external index. Under the latter modification, the entropy of a single-index portfolio model, H_p, will be defined by

$$(H_p|R_I) = \sum_{i=1}^{m} X_i(R_i|R_I), \tag{23}$$

where R_i and R_I are the returns of the ith security and the market index, respectively. As has been shown in Philippatos and Gressis (1975), mean–entropy diversification is formally equivalent to mean–variance and second degree stochastic dominance diversifications under the following distributions of asset-returns: (a) normal; (b) uniform; (c) lognormal; and (d) Weibull.

Philippatos and Wilson tested the efficiency of mean–entropy diversification algorithms by constructing portfolios from a sample of 50 randomly selected securities for the period from 1957 to 1971. Using monthly relative returns, mean–entropy diversified frontiers were constructed and compared with their counterparts based on the simple (E–V) and the single-index models. On the basis of the results, the efficiency of the mean–entropy model was fully substantiated; hence, given the formal equivalence of the three frontiers, the usefulness of this criterion must be based on its analytical advantages.

References

Agnew, H. H., R. A. Agnew, J. Rasmussen and K. R. Smith (1969) "An Application of Chance Constrained Programming to Portfolio Selection in a Casualty Insurance Firm", *Management Science*, June, B-512–B-520.

Arditti, F. (1968) "Risk and the Required Rate of Return on Security Selection Models", *Journal of Finance*, December, 805–819.

Arrow, K. J. (1965) *Aspects of the Theory of Risk Bearing* (Yrjo Janssonin, Säätiö, Helsinki).

Barry, C. B. (1974) "Portfolio Analysis under Uncertain Means, Variances, and Covariances", *Journal of Finance*, May, 515–522.

Baumol, W. J. (1963) "An Expected Gain-Confidence Limit Criterion for Portfolio Selection", *Management Science*, October, 174–182.

Becker, G. M., M. H. De Groot and J. Marshak (1964) "Measuring Utility by a Single-Response Sequential Method", *Behavioral Science*, July, 226–232.

Bicksler, J. L., and J. R., McGuigan (1971) "Utility Functions: A Priori Thoughts and Empirical Fact", ASA, *Proceedings of the Business and Economic Statistics Section*, 297–301.

Borch, K. H. *The Economics of Uncertainty* (Princeton University Press, New Jersey).

Brealey, R. A. and C. Pyle (Compilers) (1974) *A Bibliography of Finance and Investment* (The M.I.T. Press, Cambridge, Mass.).

Breen, W. and J. Savage (1968) "Portfolio Distributions and Tests of Security Selection Models", *Journal of Finance*, December, 805–819.

Churchman, C. W. (1973) "Reliability of Models in the Social Sciences", *Interfaces*, November, 1–12.

Clarkson, G. P. (1962) *Portfolio Selection: A Simulation of Trust Investment* (Prentice-Hall, Englewood Cliffs).

Clarkson, G. P. and A. H. Meltzer (1960) "Portfolio Selection: A Euristic Approach", *Journal of Finance*, December, 465–480.

Davidson, D., P. Suppes, and S. Siegel (1957) *Decision Making: An Experimental Approach* (Stanford University Press, California).

Dhingra, H. L. (1973) "Stability of Efficient Portfolios Under Uncertainty", *Working Paper WP 73-02* (College of Commerce University of Saskatchewan, Saskatoon, Canada).

Dickinson, J. P. (1974) "The Reliability of Estimation Procedures in Portfolio Analysis", *Journal of Financial and Quantitative Analysis*, June, 447–462.

Dragomirescu, M. (1972) "An Algorithm for the Minimum-Risk Problem of Stochastic Programming", *Operations Research*, January–February, 154–164.

Dyckman, T. R. and R. Salomon (1972) "Empirical Utility Functions and Random Devices: An Experiment", *Decision Sciences*, April, 1–13.

Elton, E. J., M. J. Gruber and M. W. Padberg (1976) "Simple Criteria for Optimal Portfolio Selection", *Journal of Finance*, December, 1341–1357.

Elton, E. J., M. J. Gruber and M. W. Padberg (1977) "Simple Rules for Optimal Portfolio Selection: The Multi Group Case", *Journal of Financial and Quantitative Analysis*, September, 329–345.

Enis, P. and S. Geisser (1971) "Estimation of the Probability that $Y < X$", *Journal of the American Statisical Association*, March 162–168.

Fama, E. F. (1976) *Foundations of Finance* (Basic Books, New York).

Farrar, D. E. (1961) *The Investment Decision Under Uncertainty* (Prentice-Hall, Englewood Cliffs).

Feller, W. (1968) *An Introduction to Probability Theory and Its Applications*, vol. 1, 3rd edn. (John Wiley, New York).

Fishburn, P. C. (1967) "Methods of Estimating Additive Utilities", *Management Science*, March, 435–453.

Frankfurter, G. M. (1974) "Bias in Estimating Portfolio Alpha and Beta Scores", *The Review of Economics and Statistics*, August, 412–4.

Frankfurter, G. M., H. E. Phillips and T. P. Seagle (1971) "Portfolio Selection: The Effects of Uncertain Means, Variances, and Covariances", *Journal of Financial and Quantitative Analysis*, December, 1251–1262.

Glustoff, E. and N. Nigro (1972) "Liquidity Preference and Risk Aversion with Exponential Utility Function", *Review of Economic Studies*, January, 113–115.

Gressis, N. (1975) "The Effects of Sampling Error on the EV Portfolio Selection Model", Unpublished Ph.D. Thesis, The Pennsylvania State University.

Hadar, J. and W. R. Russlell (1969) "Rules for Ordering Uncertain Prospects", *American Economic Review*, March, 25–34.

Hakansson, N. H. (1971a) "Capital Growth and the Mean–Variance Approach to Portfolio Selection", *Journal of Financial and Quantitative Analysis*, January, 517–557.

Hakansson, N. H. (1971b) "Multiperiod Mean–Variance Analysis: Toward a General Theory of Portfolio Choice", *Journal of Finance*, September, 857–884.

Hanoch, G. and H. Levy (1969) "The Efficiency Analysis of Choices Involving Risk", *Review of Economic Studies*, July, 335–346.

Hanoch, G. and H. Levy (1970) "Efficient Portfolio Selection with Quadratic and Cubic Utility", *The Journal of Business*, April, 181–190.

Hazell, P. B. R. (1971) "A Linear Alternative to Quadratic and semivariance Programming for Farm Planning Under Uncertainty", *American Journal of Agricultural Economics*, February, 53–62.

Hirschleifer, J. (1965) "Investment Decision Under Uncertainty: Choice-Theoretic Approaches", *Quarterly Journal of Economics*, November, 509–536.

Hirschleifer, J. (1966) "Investment Decision Under Uncertainty: Applications of the State Preference Approach", *Quarterly Journal of Economics*, May, 252–277.

Hirschleifer, J. (1971) "The Private and Social Value of Information and the Reward to Inventive Activity", *American Economic Review*, September, 561–574.

Hsu, D., R. B. Miller and D. W. Wichern (1974) "On the Stable Paretian Behavior of Stock-Market Prices", *Journal of the American Statistical Association*, March, 108–113.

Jean, W. H. (1971) "The Extension of Portfolio Analysis to Three or More Parameters", *Journal of Financial and Quantitative Analysis*, January 505–515.

Joy, O. M. and R. B. Porter (1974) "Stochastic Dominance and Mutual Fund Performance", *Journal of Financial and Quantitative Analysis*, January, 25–31.

Kalymon, B. A. (1974) "Estimation Risk in the Portfolio Selection Model", *Journal of Financial and Quantitative Analysis*, January, 25–31.

Kraus, A. and R. H. Litzenberger (1974) "Market Equilibrium in a Multiperiod State Preference Model with Logarithmic Utility", *Journal of Finance*, December, 1213–1227.

Kuark, J. Y. T. (1972) "Bayesion Decision Model for Portfolio Selection", *Occasional Studies No. 7* (Division of Research, College of Business Administration, The University of Denver).

Kumar, P. C. and G. C. Philippatos (1977) "A Goal Programming Formulation to the Selection of Portfolios by Dual-Purpose Funds", Paper presented at the XXIII International Meeting of the Institute of Management Sciences, Athens, Greece, 25–27 July.

Kumar, P. C., G. C. Philippatos and J. R. Ezzell (1978) "Goal Programming and the Selection of Portfolios by Dual-Purpose Funds", *Journal of Finance*, March, 303–310.

Latané, H. (1959) "Criteria for Choice among Risky Ventures", *Journal of Political Economy*, April, 144–155.

Latané, H. and D. L. Tuttle (1967) "Criteria for Portfolio Building", *Journal of Finance*, September, 359–373.

Latané, H. and W. E. Young (1969) "Test of Portfolio Building Rules", *Journal of Finance*, September, 595–612.

Lee, S. M. and A. J. Lerro (1973) "Optimizing the Portfolio Selection for Mutual Funds", *Journal of Finance*, December, 1089–1102.

Lerner, E. M. and R. E. Machol (1969) "Risk, Ruin, and Investment Analysis", *Journal of Financial and Quantitative Analysis*, December, 473–492.

Levy, H. (1973) "Stochastic Dominance Among Log-Normal Prospects", *International Economic Review*, October, 601–614.

Levy, H. and G. Hanoch (1974) "Relative Effectiveness of Efficiency Criteria for Portfolio Selection", *Journal of Financial and Quantitative Analysis*, March, 63–76.

Levy, H. and M. Sarnat (1970) "Alternative Efficiency Criteria: An Empirical Analysis", *Journal of Finance*, December, 1153–1158.

Luce, R. D. and H. Raiffa (1957) *Games and Decisions* (John Wiley, New York).

MacCrimmon, K. R. and S. Larsson (1975) "Utility Theory: Axions versus Paradoxes", *Working Paper No. 311* (University of British Columbia).

Mao, J. C. T. (1970a) "Models of Capital Budgeting, E–V vs. E–S", *Journal of Financial and Quantitative Analysis*, January, 657–675.

Mao, J. C. T. (1970b) "Survey of Capital Budgeting: Theory and Practice", *Journal of Finance*, May, 349–360.

Markowitz, H. M. (1952) "Portfolio Selection", *Journal of Finance*, March, 77–91.

Markowitz, H. M. (1959) *Portfolio Selection* (John Wiley, New York).

Markowitz, H. M. (1976) "Investment in the Long-Run: New Evidence for An Old Rule", *Journal of Finance*, December, 1273–1286.

Mossin, J. (1968) "Optimal Multiperiod Portfolio Policies", *Journal of Business*, April, 215–229.

Murphy, R. E. Jr. (1965) *Adaptive Processes in Economic Systems* (Academic Press, New York).

Myers, S. C. (1968) "A Time-State-Preference Model for Security Valuation", *Journal of Financial and Quantitative Analysis*, March, 1–33.

Naslung, B. and A. Whinston (1962) "A Model of Multi-Period Investment under Uncertainty", *Management Science*, January, 184–200.

Neumann, J. von and O. Morgenstern (1964) *Theory of Games and Economic Behavior* (John Wiley, New York).

Officer, R. R. (1972) "The Distribution of Stock Returns", *Journal of the American Statistical Association*, December, 807–812.

Phillips, H. E. and J. P. Seagle (1973) "Data: A Blessing or a Curse in Portfolio Selection", in: M. W. Hopfe, ed., *1973 AIDS Proceedings*.

Philippatos, G. C. and N. Gressis (1975) "Conditions of Formal Equivalence among E–V, SSD, and E–H Portfolio Selection Criteria: The Case for Uniform, Normal, and Lognormal Distributions", *Management Science*, February, 617–625.

Philippatos, G. C. and C. J. Wilson (1972) "Entrophy, Market Risk, and the Selection of Efficient Portfolios", *Applied Economics*, September, 209–220.

Philippatos, G. C. and C. J. Wilson (1974a) "Entrophy, Market Risk, and the Selection of Efficient Portfolios: Reply", *Applied Economics*, March, 77–81.

Philippatos, G. C. and C. J. Wilson (1974b) "Information Theory and Risk in Capital Markets", *OMEGA, The International Journal of Management Science*, December, 523–531.

Porter, R. B. (1973) "An Empirical Comparison of Stochastic Dominance and Mean Variance Portfolio Choice Criteria", *Journal of Financial and Quantitative Analysis*, September, 587–608.

Porter, R. B. and R. P. Bey (1974) "An Evaluation of the Empirical Significance of Optimal Seeking Algorithms in Portfolio Selection", *Journal of Finance*, December, 1479–1490.

Porter, R. B. and J. E. Gaumnitz (1972) "Stochastic Dominance vs. Mean–Variance Portfolio Analysis: An Empirical Evaluation", *American Economic Review*, June, 438–446.

Praetz, P. E. (1972) "The Distribution of Share Price Changes", *Journal of Business*, January, 49–55.

Pratt, J. (1964) "Risk Aversion in the Small and in the Large", *Econometrica*, January–April, 122–136.

Press, S. J. (1972) *Applied Multivariate Analysis* (Holt, Rinehart & Winston, New York).

Pyle, D. H. and J. Turnovsky (1970) "Safety-First and Expected Utility in Mean Standard Deviation Portfolio Analysis", *Review of Economics and Statistics*, February, 75–81.

Quirk, J. and R. Saposnik (1962) "Admissibility and Measurable Utility Functions", *Review of Economic Studies*, October, 140–146.

Raiffa, H. (1968) *Decision Analysis: Introductory Lectures on Choices Under Uncertainty* (Addison-Wesley, Reading, Mass.).

Roy, A. D. (1952) "Safety-First and the Holding of Assets", *Econometrica*, July, 431–449.

Russell, W. R. and P. E. Smith (1966) "Communications to the Editor: A Comment on Baumol (E,L) Efficient Portfolios", *Management Science*, March, 619–621.

Samuelson, P. A. (1970) "The Fundamental Approximation Theorem of Portfolio Analysis in Terms of Means, Variances, and Higher Moments", *Review of Economic Studies*, October, 537–542.

Schilbred, C. M. (1972) "An Experiment with Bonds and Risk", *Swedish Journal of Economics*, September, 344–355.

Sharpe, W. F. (1967) "A Linear Programming Algorithm for Portfolio Selection", *Management Science*, March, 277–293.

Sharpe, W. F. (1970) *Portfolio Theory and Capital Markets* (McGraw-Hill, New York).

Stone, B. K. (1973) "A Linear Programming Formulation of the General Portfolio Selection Problem", *Journal of Financial and Quantitative Analysis*, September, 621–636.

Stone, B. K. (1975) "Constructing a Model for Managing Portfolio Revisions", *Journal of Bank Research*, Spring, 49–60.

Suppes, P. (1961) "Behavioristic Foundations of Utility", *Econometrica*, 29, 186–202.

Swalm, R. O. (1966) "Utility Theory–Insights Into Risk Taking", *Harvard Business Review*, November–December, 123–136.

Tarascio, V. J. and J. L. Murphy (1972) "Uncertainty, Learning, and Dynamic Utility Theory", *Quarterly Review of Economics and Business*, Autumn, 19–33.

Thomson, K. J. and P. B. R. Hazell (1973) "Reliability of Using the Mean Absolute Deviation to Derive Efficient E,V Form Plans", *American Journal of Agricultural Economics*, March, 503–506.

Thorp, E. O. (1971) "Portfolio Choice and the Kelly Criterion", ASA *Proceedings of the Business and Economics Section*, 215–224.

Tobin, J. (1958) "Liquidity Preference as Behavior Toward Risk", *Review of Economic Studies*, February, 65–86.

Tobin, J. (1965) "The Theory of Portfolio Selection", in: F. H. Hahn and F. P. R. Brechling, eds., *The Theory of Interest Rates* (Macmillan, London).

Tobin, J. (1969) "Comment on Borch and Feldstein", *Review of Economic Studies*, January, 13–14.

Tomasini, L. M. (1971) "Teorie delle Decisioni e Teorie dell'Utilita", *Rivista Internazionale de Scienze Economiche e Commerciali*, September, 851–866.

Whitmore, G. A. (1970) "Third-Degree Stochastic Dominance", *American Economic Review*, June, 457–459.

Winkler, R. L. (1973) "Bayesian Models for Forecasting Future Security Prices", *Journal of Financial and Quantitative Analysis*, June, 387–405.

Winkler, R. L. and C. B Barry (1975) "A Bayesian Model for Portfolio Selection and Revision", *Journal of Finance*, March, 179–192.

Wippern, R. F. (1971) "Utility Implications of Portfolio Selection and Performance Appraisal Models", *Journal of Financial and Quantitative Analysis*, June, 913–923.

Chapter 18

EVALUATION OF INVESTMENT PERFORMANCE

PATRICK J. HESS and MARC R. REINGANUM
Ohio State University and University of Southern California

1. Introduction

A question of universal concern to investors is evaluation of investment performance. Evaluation of investment performance is a judgment regarding the
optimality of a particular portfolio for a particular investor. Many authors have
emphasized ex post analysis; it seems more appropriate, however, to consider
investment performance in an ex ante context. See, for example, Sharpe (1966,
1970, ch. 8). In this paper we study investment strategies under alternative
settings. This analysis provides a basis for suggesting investment performance
criteria and demonstrating the inappropriateness of some approaches. Each
setting examined assumes that the portfolio selection problem can be viewed
as a single-period problem.[1] While this assumption is likely to be an overly
simplistic view of the world, it provides a sufficient framework to show the
complex nature of evaluating investment performance. Several investment performance measures of historical interest are presented and analyzed. We close
with a general discussion and conclusion.

2. Settings

The most idealized setting considered in this paper is characterized by the
following:

A1: All investors are single-period expected utility of terminal wealth decision-makers. Their utility functions are concave with continuous first and
second derivatives.

A2: There are no taxes, transaction costs or other barriers to capital markets.
Thus, all assets are marketable and any portfolio position can be costlessly
achieved.

[1]Fama (1970) has examined conditions where a multiperiod portfolio/consumption problem
would be treated as a set of single-period problems.

James L. Bicksler, Editor, Handbook of Financial Economics
© *North-Holland Publishing Company – 1979*

A3: The joint distribution of asset returns is multivariate normal with a nonsingular covariance matrix. All the parameters of the joint distribution are known by all investors.

A4: Investors are able to borrow and lend freely at a riskless rate of interest.

Using assumptions A1 and A3 it can be shown that investors are mean–variance decision-makers.[2] Utilizing A2 and A4 in addition to A1 and A3, the Sharpe–Lintner form of the capital asset pricing model follows (Sharpe (1964), Lintner (1965a, b)). Finally, the uncertain return on any optimal portfolio will be driven entirely by the return on the market portfolio of all risky assets. This implies a clear test of optimality for any portfolio; the observed return on any investor's portfolio must be perfectly positively correlated with the market portfolio of all risky assets. An equivalent test is that the relative asset weights of the investor's risky portfolio (that part of his entire portfolio invested only in risk assets) are identical to the market weights of each asset.

One of the simplest modifications of the assumptions is the elimination of riskless borrowing and lending (A4). Under these conditions, it still holds that the optimal portfolio for any investor must be mean–variance efficient; however, it is no longer true that all optimal portfolios will be perfectly positively correlated with the market portfolio of all risky assets. Similarly, the relative weights of any investor's risky portfolio need not correspond to the market weights for all assets. Fortunately, given assumption A3, the set of mean–variance efficient portfolios can be determined. Any portfolio that does not belong to this set cannot be optimal for any investor.

Given assumption A2, it follows that any convex combination of efficient portfolios is itself efficient.[3] By induction, any linear combination of efficient portfolios with nonzero weights adding up to 1 must also be efficient. Therefore, the market portfolio of all risky assets is efficient. It can be shown that for any minimum variance (except the global minimum variance) and, therefore, efficient portfolio (except the global minimum variance),

$$E(\tilde{R}_i) = E(\tilde{R}_{0,e}) + \beta_{i,e} \left[E(\tilde{R}_e) - E(\tilde{R}_{0,e}) \right], \tag{1}$$

where $E(\tilde{R}_i)$ is the expected return of asset i, $E(\tilde{R}_{0,e})$ is the expected return on a portfolio that has zero covariance with portfolio e, $\beta_{i,e}$ is $\text{cov}(\tilde{R}_e, \tilde{R}_i)/\sigma_{R_e}^2$, and $E(\tilde{R}_e)$ is the expected return of portfolio e, which is any efficient portfolio except the global minimum variance portfolio. Premultiply (1) by n'_p, where n_p is the vector of asset weights for portfolio p, and use the result that the market portfolio is efficient to derive

$$E(\tilde{R}_p) = E(\tilde{R}_{0,m}) + \beta_{p,m} \left[E(\tilde{R}_m) - \tilde{E}(R_{0,m}) \right]. \tag{1a}$$

---

[2]See Fama and Miller (1972, ch. 6) for a discussion and proof of this proposition.
[3]For a discussion of this point and others relating to the efficient set, see Fama (1976, ch. 8).

Thus, we have an expected return–risk relationship between any portfolio (efficient or otherwise) and the market portfolio of all risky assets. Furthermore, with certain assumptions (1a) could easily be used to derive a regression function involving observed returns. In particular,

$$\tilde{R}_{p,t} = \gamma_{0,t} + \beta_{p,m}\gamma_{1,t} + \tilde{u}_{p,t}, \qquad t = 1, 2, \ldots, T, \tag{1b}$$

where $\tilde{R}_{p,t}$ is the return of portfolio p in t, $\gamma_{0,t}$ is the expected return of portfolio $0, m$ in t, $\gamma_{1,t}$ is the expected return of m less the expected return of $0, m$ in t, and $\tilde{u}_{p,t}$ is a random error term. One sample statistic that might be used to judge investment performance is the size of the estimated variance of $\tilde{u}_{p,t}$ for $\beta_{p,m}$. While this measure will not provide a global judgment, it will provide sample evidence on ex post efficiency of competing portfolios. It should be noted, however, that the interest in ex post measures of performance is ruled out by assumption A3.

There are several ways of relaxing the assumption of complete knowledge of the joint distribution (A3). The most superficial is to assume investors act as if they knew the value of the parameters, e.g. assumed they equaled maximum likelihood estimates. This is sometimes identified as the certainty equivalence approach and obviously leads to implications identical to those outlined above.[4] Unfortunately, this is an unattractive approach since it is ad hoc. A Bayesian approach provides techniques for dealing with parameter uncertainty and can be given a rigorous justification. Under appropriate circumstances, however, the portfolio decisions implied by a certainty equivalence rule are identical to those of Bayesian decision-maker. In particular, let the joint distribution be stationary, the prior of the Bayesian be nondogmatic, and the loss function be quadratic (or at least well approximated by a quadratic). Under these conditions, the Bayesian estimators approach the maximum likelihood estimators (see Zellner (1971, pp. 31–34)) and the precision of the posterior distribution goes to infinity as the sample size goes to infinity. In short, the certainty equivalence rule can be given a Bayesian justification in large samples.

If the return distribution is not stationary, it is clear that this asymptotic argument does not apply. In this situation the posterior will not be independent of an informative prior and will not be well approximated by a degenerate distribution if the prior is not dogmatic. The set of portfolios admissible to the Bayesian decision-maker will not in general correspond to the mean–variance efficient set generated from the certainty equivalence rule (see Klein and Bawa (1977)). Clearly, comparing investors' portfolios to the certainty equivalence efficient set is an inappropriate performance measure. The importance of this point is illustrated by considering that some firms may be in the business of producing informative priors. Investors may purchase these priors by payment of a management fee as in the case of mutual funds.

[4]Klein and Bawa (1976, 1977) analyze this problem.

In the case of Bayseian decision-makers, judging the optimality of a particular portfolio for a particular investor requires: (a) identification of the prior used by the investor, and (b) knowledge of the investor's loss function. Without this information there is no way of eliminating portfolios from the set of possible optimums.

The final assumption to be altered is the lack of transaction costs, taxes or other barriers to capital market trades (A2). The most popular form of changing A2 is to assume the existence of a completely nonmarketable asset, e.g. human capital.[5] The popularity of human capital stems from the prohibition of slavery and the inability to detach much of the yield of human capital from consumption of the individual, e.g. the appreciation of art by a trained eye. In the presence of nonmarketable assets, the entire portfolio of an investor need not be mean–variance efficient. The same applies to the proportion of marketable assets as well. Moreover, in the less extreme case of finite transaction costs for some assets, it is easy to imagine cases where the optimal portfolio for an investor need not be mean–variance efficient. The portfolio of marketable assets selected by an investor will depend upon the structure of transaction costs and the endowed assets. As a result, physicians may demand different types of mutual funds from corporate executives. Judging the marketable proportion of a portfolio will generally not provide a relevant investment performance criterion.

3. Historical performance measures

Perhaps the most popular method of evaluating investment performance is comparison of the portfolio return to the return of a New York Stock Exchange index, e.g. Standard and Poor's 500. Sometimes the comparison includes estimates of the mean and variance of the portfolio and the index and others strictly compare the means. The advantage of the technique is the ease of calculation. The disadvantages are many. First of all, the underlying model of investor behavior is left unstated. Thus, it is not possible to dissect the model and examine its reasonableness either theoretically or empirically. Secondly, within the context of the models outlined in the previous section, we see that in general there is no unique optimal portfolio for all investors. As a result there is no unique portfolio to which performance can be compared.

Sharpe (1966) developed and applied a measure of portfolio performance to a group of mutual funds. Utilizing assumptions A1 through A4, Sharpe concludes that investors are mean–variance decision-makers with unrestricted borrowing and lending opportunities. As a result, the expected return on any investor's

---

[5]Mayers (1972) studied the problem of human capital.

portfolio is

$$E(\tilde{R}_p) = \alpha R_f + (1 - \alpha) E(\tilde{R}_e),$$

where $E(\tilde{R}_p)$ is the expected return on the investor's portfolio, R_f is the riskless rate of interest, α is the percent of funds invested in the riskless security, and $E(\tilde{R}_e)$ is the expected return on the risky portfolio the investor combines with borrowing and lending. The standard deviation of the investor's portfolio is

$$\sigma_p = (1 - \alpha)\sigma_e,$$

where σ_e is the standard deviation of portfolio e. Solving for α from both equations and setting the results equal to each other,

$$\frac{E(\tilde{R}_p) - E(\tilde{R}_e)}{R_f - E(\tilde{R}_e)} = \frac{\sigma_e - \sigma_p}{\sigma_e}.$$

Rearranging terms,

$$E(\tilde{R}_p) = R_f + \sigma_p \left(\frac{E(\tilde{R}_e) - R_f}{\sigma_e} \right).$$

From this result, we see that for any mean–variance decision-maker the optimal risky portfolio to combine with borrowing or lending must maximize

$$\frac{E(\tilde{R}_e) - R_f}{\sigma_e}.$$

With this idea in mind, Sharpe proposes the empirical measure

$$(A_i - \bar{R}_f)/\hat{\sigma}_i^2,$$

where A_i is the average return of portfolio i during the sample period, $\bar{R}_f$ is the average "risk"-free rate (a government bill rate for Sharpe) during the sample period, and $\hat{\sigma}_i^2$ is the estimated variance of the portfolio's return. While Sharpe's empirical measure does not correspond to the theoretical measure, it will provide identical rankings in the population for any risky portfolio. Also, it is clear that the performance measure only makes sense for risky portfolios.

Sharpe applies this measure to the Dow–Jones Industrial Average and 34 open-ended mutual funds with annual data during the period 1954–1963. The range of the estimates is approximately 0.78 to 0.43 for the 34 funds (Sharpe (1966, p. 134)). The average for these funds is roughly 0.63 while the observed value for the Dow–Jones Industrial Average is 0.68 (Sharpe (1966, p. 136)). Sharpe presents some test statistics comparing the mutual fund average to the Dow–Jones Industrial Average. Unfortunately, he assumes independence of the estimates cross-sectionally. This is almost certainly not true and therefore renders his tests difficult to interpret. An alternative way of testing the performance of the funds, including any index, would be to write the problem as

$$y_t = \alpha + u_t, \qquad t = 1, \ldots, T,$$

where

$$y_t' = \left(\frac{\tilde{R}_{i,t} - \tilde{R}_{j,t}}{\hat{\sigma}_i^2}, \ldots, \frac{\tilde{R}_{i,t} - \tilde{R}_{f,t}}{\hat{\sigma}_i^2} \right),$$

α is an $n \times 1$ mean vector and u_t is an $n \times 1$ error vector assumed to be NID(O, Σ). With this formulation standard techniques to test any hypothesis of interest, e.g. the α equals the Dow–Jones value or all the values are equal, could be used for say, restricted estimators. These tests would account for the dependency of funds returns.

Even with a proper testing methodology the performance measure has problems. First of all, the measure requires the strictest set of assumptions. Secondly, even if these assumptions are true, there is no reason to believe that the Dow–Jones Industrial Average is representative of the true market portfolio of all risky assets.

Jenson has proposed two measures of investment performance (Jensen (1968, 1969)). Since both measures are quite similar, we only examine the simplest. Beginning with the Sharpe–Lintner form of the capital asset pricing model, Jensen derives the relationship for managed portfolios

$$\tilde{R}_{j,t} - R_{f,t} = \alpha_j + \beta_j \left[\tilde{R}_{m,t} - R_{f,t} \right] + \tilde{u}_{j,t},$$

where $\tilde{R}_{j,t}$ is the return of portfolio j in period t, $R_{f,t}$ is the risk-free rate in period t, α_j and β_j are regression parameters, $\tilde{R}_{m,t}$ is the return of the market portfolio of all risky assets in t, and $\tilde{u}_{j,t}$ is a disturbance assumed to obey the standard normal regression assumptions. Jensen presents α_j as a measure of performance.

Jensen empirically estimates α_j for 59 mutual funds using annual data during the period 1955–64 and for 56 mutual funds with annual data for the sample period 1945–64. The Standard and Poor's 500 is used as a proxy for the market portfolio of all risky assets and the one-year government rate is used for the risk-free rate. The average estimates α_j is less than zero, -0.011. The range is approximately -0.080 to 0.058 (Jensen (1968, p. 403)). Jensen concluded that the market portfolio dominated the mutual fund industry.

There are several criticisms that can be leveled at Jensen's study. First of all, his analysis does not allow him statistically to test the dominance of the mutual fund industry by the market portfolio. Had the problem been set up as a multivariate regression, this industry test would have been possible. Secondly, all the assumptions listed in the previous section, A1 through A4, are required to justify his performance measure. Finally, even if the Sharpe–Lintner model is the best approximation available, using Standard and Poor's 500 as a market proxy is questionable.

4. Summary and conclusions

In this essay we have examined investment performance evaluation under alternative settings. We also considered several historical measures of investment performance. The general conclusion emerging from the analysis is that investment performance evaluation is very difficult in the most realistic settings. Furthermore, the historical measures examined did not provide an adequate basis for judging the performance of the mutual fund industry. It is clear that much fruitful work remains to be done.

References

Fama, E. F. (1970) "Multiperiod Consumption–Investment Decisions", *American Economic Review*, March, 163–174.

Fama, E. F. (1976) *Foundations of Finance* (Basic Books, Inc., New York).

Fama, E. F. and M. Miller (1972) *The Theory of Finance* (Holt, Rinehart & Winston, New York).

Jensen, M. (1968) "The Performance of Mutual Funds in the Period 1945–64", *Journal of Finance*, May, 389–416.

Jensen, M. (1969) "Risk, the Pricing of Capital Assets, and Evaluation of Investment Portfolios", *Journal of Business*, April, 357–398.

Klein, R. W. and V. S. Bawa (1976) "The Effect of Estimation Risk on Optimal Portfolio Choice", *Journal of Financial Economics*, June, 215–231.

Klein, R. W. and V. S. Bawa (1977) "The Effect of Limited Information and Estimation Risk on Optimal Portfolio Diversification", *Journal of Financial Economics*, August, 89–111.

Lintner, J. (1965a) "The Valuation of Risk Assets and the Selection of Risky Investments in Stock Portfolios and Capital Budgets", *Review Economics and Statistics*, February, 13–37.

Lintner, J. (1965b) "Security Prices, Risk, and Maximal Gains from Diversification", *Journal of Finance*, December, 587–616.

Mayers, D. (1972) "Nonmarketable Assets and Capital Market Equilibrium under Uncertainty", in: M. Jensen, ed., *Studies in the Theory of Capital Markets* (Praeger Publishers, New York) pp. 223–248.

Sharpe, W. F. (1964) "Capital Asset Prices: A Theory of Market Equilibrium under Conditions of Risk", *Journal of Finance*, September, 425–442.

Sharpe, W. F. (1966) "Mutual Fund Performance", *Journal of Business*, Part 2, January, 119–138.

Zellner, A. (1971) *An Introduction to Bayesian Inference in Econometrics* (John Wiley and Sons, New York).

Chapter 19

STATISTICAL DECISION THEORY AND FINANCIAL DECISION-MAKING

ROBERT L. WINKLER
Indiana University

1. Introduction

Virtually all financial decisions are made in the face of some uncertainty, and decision-makers need to recognize and take account of this uncertainty when choosing courses of action. Moreover, decision-makers are constantly being bombarded with new information, which must somehow be evaluated and assimilated into the decision-making process. Often the decision-making process is sequential in nature, with decisions at one point in time possibly affecting options at other points in time. For example, consider the selection of an optimal portfolio of investments. An investor is generally uncertain about the returns from various investments, with the "state of uncertainty" changing in reaction to a large volume of pieces of new information readily available on an almost continuous basis (e.g. price changes for securities, earnings reports, news reports concerning individual firms or industries, governmental decisions, international developments, reports from financial analysts concerning specific investments, rumors about possible future events). Because of transactions costs, tax considerations, and similar factors, changing one's portfolio is not a cost-free procedure, which implies that today's portfolio decisions will have some effect upon future portfolio decisions. In short, portfolio selection is a dynamic decision-making problem, as are many other types of financial decision-making problems.

Statistical decision theory (also called Bayesian decision theory or decision analysis) provides a formal framework for modeling decision-making problems involving uncertainty. The uncertainty is represented quantitatively in terms of probabilities, and Bayes' theorem can be used to revise probabilities as new information is obtained. Interrelationships among decisions can be represented in the model, thereby capturing the dynamic nature of the actual decision-making situation.

James L. Bicksler, Editor, Handbook of Financial Economics
© *North-Holland Publishing Company – 1979*

The purpose of this paper is to discuss the interface between statistical decision theory and financial decision-making. Statistical decision theory provides the appropriate framework for modeling financial decision-making problems, and conversely, financial decision-making problems provide an ideal setting for the study of statistical decision theory and the further investigation of some important aspects of statistical decision theory. In section 2 of this paper a brief overview of statistical decision theory is presented, and a model for Bayesian portfolio analysis is reviewed in section 3 to illustrate the decision-theoretic approach in a financial decision-making setting. In section 4 the potential role of statistical decision theory in the study of financial markets is discussed and illustrated by a simple model. Sections 3 and 4 both touch upon some important modeling issues. A brief summary is presented in section 5.

2. Statistical decision theory

The area of statistical decision theory has undergone rapid growth in the past two decades, both in terms of methodological developments and in terms of applications. An extensive and rapidly growing literature exists in the area, with contributions by statisticians, mathematicians, economists, psychologists, and others. In this section only a brief, nontechnical sketch of the basic notions of statistical decision theory is presented. For more extensive discussions of statistical decision theory at an introductory level, see Brown et al. (1974), Lindley (1971), Raiffa (1968), *Readings in Decision Analysis* (1974), Schlaifer (1969), and Winkler (1972). At a more advanced level, DeGroot (1970), LaValle (1970), and Raiffa and Schlaifer (1961) are available, and more specialized books such as Keeney and Raiffa (1976) or Zellner (1971) may also be of interest.

It is important at the outset to emphasize that statistical decision theory is not a "trick" that has been developed in an ad hoc manner. Instead, it is based on quite sturdy foundations. As shown by Savage (1954), the existence of subjective probabilities and utilities and the maximization of expected utility as a decision-making criterion follow logically from a set of axioms of rational behavior, or coherent behavior. An example of such an axiom is that of transitivity: if an individual prefers A to B and prefers B to C, then that individual must also prefer A to C. If a decision-maker wants to be rational in the sense of not violating any of the coherence axioms, then decisions should be made on the basis of expected utility.

To apply statistical decision theory to a problem of decision-making under uncertainty, a decision-maker must determine certain inputs. Once these inputs are determined, the formulation of a decision that is "optimal" in view of the inputs is strictly a computational problem, although it should be noted that this problem is not necessarily an easy one. The real modeling is the determination of the inputs, and most of the emphasis in this section will concern these inputs. First, the necessary inputs will be defined individually, and then some modeling questions inherent in the choice of these inputs will be examined. Modeling questions will also be emphasized in sections 3 and 4.

The first input that is needed is a set of actions. After all, how can a decision-making problem be modeled without a list of the possible decisions, or actions? To avoid a trivial situation, it is assumed that there are at least two actions. Denote the space of actions by A, and let an action be denoted by a, where of course $a \in A$.

The second input to the decision model is a set of events. Remember that the situation handled by the model is that of decision-making under uncertainty. The events of interest are those about which the decision-maker is uncertain. The event space is denoted by Θ, and $\theta \in \Theta$ represents a particular event.

The third input required in statistical decision theory is a probability distribution. The decision-maker's uncertainty about the events of interest should be represented in a formal manner, and probability is the mathematical language of uncertainty. Let $P(\theta)$, which is defined on the event space Θ, represent the probability distribution.

The fourth input is the payoff, or reward, or consequence (which could be good or bad) received by the decision-maker. The decision-maker takes an action, and one of the events in the event space occurs. As a result of the action, over which the decision-maker has control, and the event, over which the decision-maker has no control, something happens that affects the decision-maker in some manner (e.g. a loss or gain of a particular sum of money). This "something" is called a payoff, although it must be emphasized that the term "payoff" is being used in a very broad sense and is not necessarily restricted to monetary payoffs. Since the payoff is a function of both a and θ, it will be denoted by $R(a,\theta)$; the letter P is being used to represent probability, and R can be thought of as a reward function.

The fifth and final input to the model is a utility function. In order to make a decision that is consistent with the tastes and preferences of the decision-maker (e.g. the extent to which the decision-maker wants to avoid certain risks), these tastes and preferences must be included in the model. The payoff, or reward, function R represents the overall payoff received by the decision maker. Thus, the utility function U is a function of R.

Once these five inputs — a set of actions, a set of events, a probability distribution, a payoff function, and a utility function — have been determined, the only thing that is needed is a criterion that specifies how the inputs are to be "put together" to arrive at a decision. The axioms of statistical decision theory imply that the criterion that should be used is the maximization of expected utility. Given the five inputs, then, it is a mathematical problem to find the action a^* that yields the largest expected utility. For example, if the event space

Θ is finite, the expected utility of action a can be expressed in the form

$$EU(a) = \sum_{\theta \in \Theta} U[R(a,\theta)]P(\theta),$$

and a^* must satisfy

$$EU(a^*) \geqslant EU(a), \quad \text{for all } a \in A.$$

There are interesting modeling situations interspersed throughout the problem. To start at the beginning, consider the choice of A, the set of actions. It may seem that the potential actions should be obvious to the decision-maker, but that is not always the case. The choice of a set of actions is indeed a modeling problem. It is probably not the most severe modeling problem encountered in statistical decision theory, but neither is it trivial in all instances. In some situations the appropriate set of actions is fairly obvious, and the portfolio problem provides an example of such a situation. When all possible actions are included, however, one result may be a very large action space A that is difficult to handle. To keep things within bounds, it may be desirable to see if some actions can be eliminated from consideration in order to arrive at a more manageable set of actions. In the other direction, it sometimes happens that the decision-maker simply forgets to include or is completely unaware of some quite appealing actions. For example, strategies involving the purchase of additional information before making the decision of primary interest are often overlooked. Sometimes the very process of modeling the problem suggests new actions that might not have been obvious before or indicates that it might be desirable to attempt to seek or create some new alternatives of a particular nature. Modeling a problem in the statistical decision theory framework forces the decision-maker to think about the various aspects of the problem in a formal, rigorous manner, and this may indeed be the primary benefit of the procedure.

The other four inputs also provide interesting modeling problems. A choice of a set of events is a familiar problem (e.g. consider a regression problem with an unmanageably large set of independent variables). What events are considered sufficiently important to be included in the model, and what events can be excluded? Most decision-making problems, with the exception of simple gambles, have rewards that depend upon all sorts of events, some events in an important way and other events in a less important way. It is necessary to decide which events are "crucial" to the problem. The inclusion of too many events may lead to a very complicated model, while the omission of key events may render the model inapplicable. For example, suppose that an investor is contemplating the purchase of a particular security. Surely the future price performance of that security is an event of interest, but how can that price performance be represented for decision-making purposes? To include as events the daily closing prices of the security for a lengthy time period might be very difficult unless some stochastic model is developed to capture the relationship among these prices. Some alternatives might be weekly closing prices, monthly closing prices, monthly averages of daily closing prices, monthly high and low prices, yearly high and low prices, and so on.

A modeling issue related to both actions and events is the appropriate structuring of sets of actions and sets of events in the overall decision model. For example, if two decisions are to be made and the decision-maker will observe certain events after the first decision is made but before the second decision is made, the model must be structured to reflect these conditions. In terms of a tree diagram, branches representing the possible events must be placed between the sets of branches representing the first and second decisions. This type of structuring often causes difficulties for students and for decision-makers actually using statistical decision theory in practice. A common mistake of this nature is the failure to recognize that in the case of information-seeking strategies, the event branches representing the information to be purchased should be placed before the action branches representing the decision of primary interest.

Once the events are chosen, probabilities are needed. The probability distribution for the events may depend on various sorts of information, including "hard" data in the form of observed past data and "softer" data in the form of the subjective judgments of the decision-maker or of an expert consulted by the decision-maker. Ultimately the probability distribution used in the model is the subjective choice of the decision-maker, so the subjective interpretation of probability seems to be the most useful interpretation in decision-making problems. This does not mean that all of the information on which this distribution is based is subjective; indeed, as noted above, some or all of it may be of a more objective nature, in the form of observed data. Nevertheless, the final choice of a probability distribution rests with the decision-maker. Included among the decision-maker's alternatives is the possibility of using certain widely studied probability models. Questions such as the following typify this possibility. Would a normal distribution provide a good approximation here? Does this process look like a Bernoulli process? Would a Markovian model capture the dependence adequately in this situation? The use of particular probability distributions may simplify the analysis somewhat, but this simplification is only reasonable if it provides a good approximation.

In decision-making models with several sets of events and actions, the decision-maker must be careful to condition the probabilities appropriately. At any given point in the model, probabilities must be conditional upon all preceding actions and events. Bayes' theorem may prove helpful in the determination of some conditional probabilities. In the revision of probabilities via Bayesian techniques, it may be possible to use models such as the normal distribution to represent the likelihood function, which relates the new information to the events of interest. The use of well-known probability models for the likelihood function or the prior probabilities may simplify the probability revision process considerably.

The next input of interest is a set of payoffs. In many financial decision-making problems the payoffs are strictly monetary in nature and are often not difficult to determine. In the portfolio selection problem, for instance, if the composition of the portfolio is known and an action specifies certain changes in the portfolio at a particular future date, the payoff at that time depends in a simple manner upon the prices as of that date for the investments in the portfolio. If these prices are included as events, the payoff for the action in question is a simple linear function of the prices. In general, it is frequently possible to model the relationship between events and payoffs, with linear models providing good approximations in many cases.

When the payoffs in a decision-making problem are multidimensional in nature, they may be difficult to determine or measure. Consider, for example, a decision-making problem concerning pollution. The payoff may involve many dimensions, including cost, the amounts of various pollutants discharged into the atmosphere, loss of goodwill in the community, and so on. Even when all aspects of the problem are purely financial, the payoffs may be multidimensional. For instance, in a decision-making problem where cash flow is a crucial consideration, it may be necessary to keep track of both the net monetary payoff and the cash flow. Along these lines, it is important to keep track of the timing of cash inflows or outflows. Seldom do all such transactions for a given decision-making problem occur at the same time, and questions of comparability arise when they occur at different times. Such questions are inevitably resolved by discounting all cash transactions to a common date, but it must be kept in mind that this is a modeling choice that simplifies the problem but may not always be reasonable. The issue here concerns the decision-maker's time preferences for money and thus relates to the decision-maker's utility function.

The final input to the model is a utility function that represents the decision-maker's preferences. As in the case of probability distributions, certain special mathematical forms for utility functions for money (e.g. linear, exponential, logarithmic, quadratic, cubic) have been widely studied. If some details are known about the decision-maker's attitude toward risk (e.g. the decision-maker's risk-aversion may be a decreasing function of wealth), it may be possible to approximate the decision-maker's utility function by a mathematical function that is reasonably tractable. Of course, if the payoffs are multidimensional, then the utility function must be defined on a multidimensional space, and the modeling problem is much more difficult.

As the above discussion implies, modeling a decision-making problem involves an attempt to reach a satisfactory balance between two often-conflicting desires: the desire to make the model as realistic as possible and the desire to keep the model simple in order to ease the analysis. If the model is not realistic, the results derived from the model are of little value for the real-world decision-making problem. If the model is too complicated and unwieldy, it may be difficult (and quite costly) to analyze the model and to obtain any results. Of course, the need to obtain a reasonable balance between realism and tractability is a general consideration that is encountered in virtually all mathematical modeling of real-world situations and is by no means unique to the modeling of decision-making problems under uncertainty.

In general, modeling should be considered as an iterative process. As a first attempt, a decision-maker might start with a very simple model, perhaps with a small set of actions and a small set of events. The results of the simple model, including a sensitivity analysis to determine how sensitive these results are to variations in some of the inputs, may provide some insight as to what sort of further modeling might be beneficial. For example, it may turn out that some types of actions do not appear to be as appealing as originally thought, while other types of actions look very appealing. As a result, the decision-maker should think carefully about the possibility of the existence of (or the development of) additional actions of the latter type. Similarly, certain events may be found to be quite important, and the decision-maker may want to include more detail about such events and may want to consider more sophisticated probability models for such events. On the other hand, the decision-maker may decide that the initial simple model is adequate for the purposes of the problem and that a more sophisticated, detailed model would not be worth the effort and cost that it would require. The point is simply that the modeling process is a sequential process in which revisions can be made repeatedly concerning any of the aspects of the model.

3. Bayesian portfolio analysis

Portfolio selection is a problem that is faced repeatedly by many different decision-makers. Large sums of money are often involved, and even relatively small improvements in terms of return may be important. As a result, much effort has been invested in the study of portfolio analysis, including the development of mathematical models for portfolio analysis (e.g. Markowitz (1959) and Sharpe (1970)). No attempt will be made here to review the extensive literature in the area of portfolio analysis. The purpose of this section is to indicate how the model-building process discussed in section 2 might be applied to portfolio analysis. For more technical details of some Bayesian models for portfolio analysis, see Winkler and Barry (1975), Barry and Winkler (1976), and Klein and Bawa (1977).

First, consider a relatively simple portfolio-selection problem in which a fixed amount of money w is to be invested for a fixed time period, with no trading occurring during the period. How can the inputs discussed in section 2 be determined? First, a list of all potential investments should be drawn up, since the set of actions consists of all possible combinations of investments. This is a very large set of actions; just considering all securities listed on the New York Stock Exchange provides an unmanageably large set of actions, and a large portfolio would surely include some investments not traded on the New York Stock Exchange (e.g. corporate bonds, public bond offerings, real estate, savings accounts, certificates of deposit, and so on). As a first step, it is necessary to take the huge set of possible investments and to cut it down to manageable size. Generally this is not too difficult to do, since many investments are very similar. For any given decision-maker the choice of possible investments is colored by that decision-maker's experience with and knowledge of different investments. The choice is, of course, an important part of the modeling problem.

The events of primary interest in the portfolio problem are the returns from the potential investments, and the probability distribution of interest concerns these returns. In arriving at the probability distribution of returns, the decision-maker can utilize various sources of information. One such source of information is provided by security analysts who follow certain securities very closely and can provide expert opinions concerning those securities. A small investor generally calls a broker for investment advice, which is given in verbal form rather than explicit probabilistic form (although it may include terms such as "probably", "likely", and "doubtful"). For large portfolios, uncertainties about future returns should be expressed in terms of probabilities.

A second source of information is provided by historical data concerning security returns. Such data can provide information about distributions of price changes. Some alternative families of distributions that have been suggested as models for distributions of price changes are the normal family, the Paretian family (which implies an infinite variance of returns), the t family, and families involving mixtures of normal distributions. For a Bayesian approach to this modeling problem, see Barry and Radcliffe (1977). The normal distribution is considerably more convenient to work with than the others, and in practice it often may provide a reasonably good approximation, although the tradeoff between convenience and the accuracy of the approximation must be kept in mind.

A third source of information is provided by relationships between returns on investments and other variables. Traditionally, investment analysts have tried to look at the "intrinsic value" of a security by considering variables relating to the individual firm (e.g. total assets, earnings), the industry, and the economy as a whole (e.g. gross national product). The relationship of such variables to security returns can be studied empirically. For instance, regression analysis could be used with the return on an investment as the dependent variable and variables such as earnings per share and gross national product as independent variables.

Expert advice, possibly combined with historical data and information concerning relationships between returns and other variables, can provide the basis for the decision-maker's probability distribution of future returns in the portfolio problem. Nevertheless, the probability distribution of returns is perhaps the input that causes the most difficulty in the modeling of portfolio problems. The payoff function, on the other hand, can be obtained in a very straightforward manner.

The payoff function is easy to model because of the direct relationship between returns on individual investments and payoffs for the entire portfolio. Suppose that the list of potential investments has been whittled down to K investments and, as noted previously, the total amount of money available is w. Let v_k represent the amount of money invested in investment k for $k = 1, \ldots, K$. The portfolio of investments can be represented by the vector $v = (v_1, \ldots, v_K)$, where the budget constraint implies that $\sum_{k=1}^{K} v_k = w$. If no short selling of investments is possible, then it is also necessary that $v_k \geqslant 0$ for $k = 1, 2, \ldots, K$.

The amount w is to be invested for a fixed time period, so the payoff of interest is the value of the portfolio at the end of this time period. Let x_k represent the return at the end of the period for each dollar invested in investment k. For example, if investment k is a security that increases in value by 10 percent during the period, then $x_k = 1.10$. The value at the end of the period of the decision-maker's investment is $v_k x_k$ for investment k and $\sum_{k=1}^{K} v_k x_k$ for the entire portfolio. The payoff function, therefore, can be expressed as a weighted average of the returns, with the weights simply being the amounts initially invested: $R(v_1, \ldots, v_K, x_1, \ldots, x_K) = \sum_{k=1}^{K} v_k x_k$.

Next, consider the decision-maker's utility function for the value of the portfolio at the end of the period. If the decision-maker is risk-neutral, then the utility function is linear with respect to money. Since linear utility is the simplest possible utility function, it will be considered first. The reason that linear utility is easy to work with is simply that with a linear utility function, maximizing expected utility, $E[U(R)]$, is the same as maximizing expected payoff, $E(R)$. When decision-makers ignore utility completely and just try to maximize their expected payoffs, they are implicitly using a linear utility function.

With a linear utility function, the decision-maker wants to maximize

$$E[R(v_1, \ldots, v_K, x_1, \ldots, x_K)] = \sum_{k=1}^{K} v_k E(x_k)$$

subject to the constraints $\sum_{k=1}^{K} v_k = w$ and $v_k \geqslant 0$ for all k (assuming no short selling). This is a linear programming problem, and the solution is to put all of the money into the investment with the largest expected return. Thus, under linear utility the optimal portfolio will always consist of only one investment provided that one investment has a larger expected return than all other investments. If a tie exists among investments for the largest expected return, w can be allocated in any fashion among the tied investments.

Empirical evidence suggests that portfolios very seldom consist of just one security, except in the case of very small portfolios (i.e. investors with limited funds to invest). It is possible, of course, that different investments are often perceived as having similar expected returns. Nonetheless, a more reasonable explanation of the existence of diversified portfolios is risk-aversion on the part of investors, implying utility functions that are not linear in money.

Many different utility functions can be used to represent risk-aversion. In fact, any concave utility function implies risk-averse behavior. For the purposes of the model under discussion, consider a quadratic utility function of the form $U(R) = a + bR + cR^2$, where a, b, and c are such that U is a concave, increasing function of R. When expected utilities are computed, a quadratic term $E(R^2)$ is present in addition to a linear term $E(R)$. This inclusion of a second moment in the expression for expected utility implies that the variance of R is now a relevant factor in the portfolio decision. To compare portfolios, the decision-maker must consider both the mean and the variance of R:

$$E(R) = \sum_{k=1}^{K} v_k E(x_k)$$

and

$$V(R) = \sum_{k=1}^{K} v_k^2 V(x_k) + 2 \sum_{j=1}^{k-1} \sum_{k=1}^{K} v_k v_j \text{cov}(x_k, x_j).$$

The maximization of $E[U(R)]$ is a quadratic programming problem, and the optimal solution is a member of the so-called "efficient set" from mean–variance analysis. The efficient set consists of portfolios with minimum variance for a given mean return, and the specific member of the efficient set that is optimal depends on the parameters a, b, and c of the utility function.

Of course, the decision-maker may want to consider a utility function that is neither linear nor quadratic. A quadratic utility function implies that the decision-maker becomes more risk-averse as the decision-maker's wealth increases, and this property (increasing risk-aversion) is considered unreasonable by many individuals. Other widely studied risk-averse utility functions include logarithmic and exponential functions. The amount of detail needed concerning the utility function may depend in part on the assumptions made with respect to the probability distribution of returns. If this distribution can be completely represented in terms of first-order and second-order moments, the optimal portfolio will be on the mean–variance efficient set for any risk-averse investor. Of course, the member of the efficient set that is optimal will vary as the exact form of the utility function varies.

The portfolio problem just discussed is very simple, and the results are in agreement with much of the work that has been done in the area of portfolio analysis. Moreover, various extensions such as short selling, transactions costs, tax considerations, borrowing and lending, and so on, can be considered without much difficulty. Nonetheless, a major shortcoming of the model still remains — it is a static model in which a decision is made for a single, fixed period of time. Investors are seldom constrained to hold investments for a fixed time period. More commonly, a decision-maker makes an investment, obtains some returns and observes changes in values of various investments over time, and revises the portfolio over time. In other words, portfolio selection in practice is a dynamic rather than a static problem.

In a dynamic portfolio selection and revision problem, actions are taken at several different times. Assume for convenience that a time horizon of t periods is considered and that transactions can be made at the end of each period. The starting point is time 0, and the actions at time i $(i=0,1,\ldots,t-1)$ consist of purchases p_k^i and sales q_k^i of security k, with $k=1,2,\ldots,K$. Such purchases and sales at any given time are constrained by the value of the entire portfolio and by the amounts held of various investments, which in turn are affected by previous portfolio decisions as well as by the actual returns realized in preceding time periods. Further restrictions are imposed by the inclusion of transactions costs in the model. The simplest form of transactions cost is a constant per-unit cost, although other cost functions can be considered.

If x_k^i and v_k^i represent the return on security k during period i and the amount held of security k at the end of period i, respectively, then the amount held of security k at the beginning of period $i+1$ is $v_k^i+p_k^i-q_k^i$. The relationship between v_k^i and v_k^{i+1} is thus given by

$$v_k^{i+1} = x_k^{i+1}\left(v_k^i+p_k^i-q_k^i\right).$$

In a single-period model that ignores the dynamic nature of the situation, the decision-maker should choose p_k^i and q_k^i at time i for $k=1,\ldots,K$ in order to maximize the expected utility

$$E_i U\left(\sum_{k=1}^{K} x_k^{i+1}\left(v_k^i+p_k^i-q_k^i\right)\right)$$

subject to constraints such as

$$(1+c) \sum_{k=1}^{K} p_k^i = (1-c) \sum_{k=1}^{K} q_k^i,$$

where c represents a per-unit transactions cost. The argument of the utility function is the value of the portfolio at the end of period $i+1$. The expectation E_i is taken with respect to the distribution, at time i, of $(x_1^{i+1},\ldots,x_K^{i+1})$, the vector of returns during the next period. Of course, a Bayesian model could be used to update this distribution from period to period.

In a multiperiod model that takes into account the dynamic nature of the portfolio selection and revision problem, dynamic programming is used to find optimal solutions. With a fixed time horizon of time t, the decision at time $t-1$ is a single-period decision involving

$$E_{t-1} U\left(\sum_{k=1}^{K} x_k^t (v_k^{t-1} + p_k^{t-1} - q_k^{t-1}) \right),$$

where U is a utility function for the value of the portfolio at time t. The decision at time $t-2$ is affected by prospects for the decision at time $t-1$, and the relevant expected utility is

$$E_{t-2}\left\{ \max E_{t-1} U\left(\sum_{k=1}^{K} x_k^t [x_k^{t-1}(v_k^{t-2} + p_k^{t-2} - q_k^{t-2}) + p_k^{t-1} - q_k^{t-1}] \right) \right\}.$$

Here the decision at time $t-1$ is nested within the expectation taken at time $t-2$. The process of backward induction continues until the initial decision-making problem at time 0 is

$$\max E_0\left\{ \max\left\{ E_1\left\{ \cdots \left\{ \max E_{t-1} U\left(\sum_{k=1}^{K} v_k^t \right) \right\} \cdots \right\} \right\} \right\},$$

where the maximization at time i involves p_k^i and q_k^i for $k=1,\ldots,K$ and is subject to constraints on these decision variables created by transactions costs and other restrictions.

The multiperiod decision-making problem necessitates a probability model that anticipates what the probability distribution of returns will look like in future periods in response to information received in the intervening time. For instance, at time 0 the conditional distribution of $(x_1^{i+1},\ldots,x_K^{i+1})$ given all previous returns x_k^j for $j \leqslant i$, $k=1,\ldots,K$ must be specified. Furthermore, since the returns x_k^j for $j \leqslant i$, $k=1,\ldots,K$ are not yet known at time 0, the decision-maker must be able to specify

$$P_i(x_1^{i+1},\ldots,x_K^{i+1} | x_k^j, \quad \text{for } j \leqslant i, k=1,\ldots,K)$$

for *all possible values* of x_k^j for $j \leqslant i$, $k=1,\ldots,K$. To determine all of these distributions individually is very impractical, and this is where a Bayesian model is needed.

For an example of a Bayesian model for forecasting future security prices, suppose that vectors of returns are assumed to be normal with unknown mean vector μ and known covariance matrix Σ. If the prior distribution of μ at time 0 is a normal distribution, then the Bayesian revision process is relatively simple and conditional distributions of the type discussed in the previous paragraph are normal distributions. If the covariance matrix is also unknown but (μ, Σ) has a normal-inverted-Wishart distribution at time 0, then conditional distributions of the type discussed in the previous paragraph are Student-t distributions.

The above models of returns on investments are stationary in that the parameters of the distribution of price changes, μ and Σ, are assumed to remain constant over time. One unfortunate implication of this assumption is that as information is obtained over time, the uncertainty about μ and Σ will be reduced and new information will have less and less impact upon the distributions of future returns. To avoid this result, nonstationary models might be considered. For instance, if μ_i represents the mean of the normal distribution of returns during period i, suppose that the mean changes stochastically from period to period as follows:

$$\mu_{i+1} = \mu_i + e_i,$$

where e_i is a normally distributed vector of errors with mean zero. Under this model, the expected vector of returns at time i involves an exponentially weighted average of previously observed returns, with more recent returns receiving higher weights than not-so-recent returns. This result seems intuitively appealing, as does the fact that the variance of the mean vector does not approach zero as the number of observations increases.

In practice, past returns on particular investments may provide some information about future returns on the same or similar investments, and Bayesian models relating returns in different periods represent an attempt to incorporate such information into the portfolio problem in a systematic fashion. But other variables, such as those mentioned in section 1 (earnings reports, news reports concerning individual firms or industries, governmental decisions, international developments, reports from financial analysts concerning specific investments, rumors about possible future events) may provide valuable information. Some of these variables (e.g. earnings reports) are observed on a regular basis and can be modeled in a Bayesian fashion, just as the returns are modeled, perhaps using a Bayesian regression model to relate the nonreturn variables to the returns. The net effect of including such variables is essentially to increase the size of the model. Other variables, however, are not observed on a regular basis (e.g. revisions in tax laws), and it may be difficult both to anticipate the occurrence of these irregular events and to build them into the model.

The development of Bayesian methodology for more complex situations (e.g. many variables, nonstationary parameters) makes it possible to consider more realistic models of the portfolio problem. Similarly, in terms of utility, the methodology to deal with time preferences via multidimensional utility functions makes it possible to consider models in which the final payoff at time t is not the only payoff of interest. More information is needed concerning the sensitivity of optimal portfolios to variations in the model inputs and concerning the performance of Bayesian portfolio analysis in practice. Of course, even if statistical decision theory accomplishes no more than forcing the decision-maker to think seriously about the various inputs, it will still serve a useful purpose.

4. Decision theory and financial markets

Statistical decision theory provides a framework for an investor to model financial decisions, incorporating uncertainty about events as well as attitude toward risk. Assuming that the model adequately approximates the structure of the decision-making problem and the investor's judgments and preferences, the decisions generated by the model are rational courses of action for that investor. Of course, the decisions may not seem rational to another investor faced with essentially the same decision-making problem, since different individuals need not share common judgments and preferences. For instance, when an investor purchases some shares of a common stock, some other investor is actually selling the shares, although the two individuals never meet. Selling is exactly the opposite decision from buying, yet it is possible that both investors are making decisions in a perfectly rational manner according to the dictates of statistical decision theory. Perhaps the buyer thinks there is a high probability that the price of the stock will go up, while the seller thinks there is a high probability that the price of the stock will go down. On the other hand, they might agree on the probability distribution for the future price performance of the stock. The distribution might indicate that the stock's price is quite volatile, with large shifts in either direction seeming moderately likely, and the buyer's utility function might indicate a greater willingness to take risk than does the seller's utility function. Another possible explanation for the trade could be that the seller agrees with the buyer that the future prospects for the stock look bright but must sell because of a pressing need for cash.

At any given point in time, then, several investors may be contemplating similar investments. If all of these investors use statistical decision theory to guide their investment behavior, what implications may be drawn regarding the market for the investments in question? Given some assumptions about the probability distributions and utility functions of the investors (and perhaps about other aspects of their models as well), it may be possible to make inferences about the market for the investments and to see how the market is affected by changes in the judgments and preferences of some of the investors.

The role of statistical decision theory in the study of financial markets can be illustrated by a relatively simple model. The model and some results derived from the model will be described briefly here. For more details, see Jaffe and

Winkler (1976). A different approach, which relates a Bayesian model to the capital asset pricing model, is presented in Barry (1977).

Suppose that y_1 and y_2 represent estimates prepared by two investors of the value y of an investment, and let

$$u_1 = y_1 - y \quad \text{and} \quad u_2 = y_2 - y$$

represent the errors of estimation. Furthermore, suppose that the distribution of (u_1, u_2) is normal with mean vector zero, $V(u_1) = \sigma_1^2$, $V(u_2) = \sigma_2^2$, and $\text{cov}(u_1, u_2) = \rho \sigma_1 \sigma_2$. This will not always be an appropriate distribution in practice, but the "normal theory of errors" suggests that it may provide a good approximation in many instances. Moreover, if the two investors have observed their errors of estimation in similar situations, such historical data could be used to estimate the parameters σ_1, σ_2, and ρ of the normal model.

In a sense, an investor's judgments concerning the return on an investment are, at least indirectly, judgments about the reactions of other investors to the investment. When the number of individuals contemplating a particular investment is small, the decisions of the competing investors might be included explicitly as events in an individual's model of the situation. If, in addition, the identities of the competing investors are known (or can be guessed with a reasonable degree of confidence), past observations of their investment behavior can be used to make inferences about their current decisions. In the simple model with two investors and a normal distribution for the errors of estimation, suppose that the investors both use the normal model and arrive at the same values for the model parameters σ_1, σ_2, and ρ.

With no information other than y_1 and the distribution of estimation errors, the first investor's distribution of y is normal with mean y_1 and variance σ_1^2. Furthermore, the first investor's distribution of y_2 is normal with mean y_1 and variance $\sigma_1^2 + \sigma_2^2 - 2\rho\sigma_1\sigma_2$. The second investor's distributions of y and y_1 are normal with common mean y_2 and with variances σ_2^2 and $\sigma_1^2 + \sigma_2^2 - 2\rho\sigma_1\sigma_2$, respectively. Note that the model allows for investors with differing amounts of information concerning y in the sense that the error variances need not be equal. If $\sigma_1^2 < \sigma_2^2$, for example, the first investor might be thought of as having more information, as reflected by a more precise estimate, than the second investor. The dependence between the investors' estimation errors is represented by the correlation, ρ. To the extent that dependence is caused by common training, experience, and information, a positive correlation seems much more reasonable than a negative correlation.

Various schemes for the trading of investments can be investigated. First, consider a situation in which the second investor announces a price for an investment and the first investor can purchase the investment at that price plus a commission c or sell the investment to the second investor at that price minus c. Here the second investor is acting as a market-maker. Given the assumed distribution of estimation errors, the second investor should set the price equal to y_2.

When the second investor announces the price, some information is revealed to the first investor, who can then determine a revised distribution of y after observing y_2. From Bayes' theorem, the revised distribution of y is normal with mean

$$y_1^* = \frac{(\sigma_2^2 - \rho\sigma_1\sigma_2)y_1 + (\sigma_1^2 - \rho\sigma_1\sigma_2)y_2}{\sigma_1^2 + \sigma_2^2 - 2\rho\sigma_1\sigma_2}$$

and variance

$$\sigma_1^{*2} = \frac{\sigma_1^2\sigma_2^2(1-\rho^2)}{\sigma_1^2 + \sigma_2^2 - 2\rho\sigma_1\sigma_2}.$$

Note that y_1^* is a weighted average of y_1 and y_2, with the weights depending on σ_1, σ_2, and ρ.

If the first investor is risk-neutral, the optimal decision rule is to purchase the investment if $y_1^* > y_2 + c$, which simplifies to

$$y_1 - y_2 > \left(\frac{\sigma_1^2 + \sigma_2^2 - 2\rho\sigma_1\sigma_2}{\sigma_2^2 - \rho\sigma_1\sigma_2}\right)c,$$

provided that $\sigma_2 > \rho\sigma_1$. Similarly, the investment should be sold to the second investor if

$$y_2 - y_1 > \left(\frac{\sigma_1^2 + \sigma_2^2 - 2\rho\sigma_1\sigma_2}{\sigma_2^2 - \rho\sigma_1\sigma_2}\right)c.$$

On the other hand, if

$$|y_1 - y_2| < \left(\frac{\sigma_1^2 + \sigma_2^2 - 2\rho\sigma_1\sigma_2}{\sigma_2^2 - \rho\sigma_1\sigma_2}\right)c,$$

then the first investor should refrain from trading. But if the second investor is risk-neutral or risk-averse and really believes that the first investor knows the parameters of the model and will always act rationally to maximize expected payoff, then the second investor should avoid the trading situation since trades will only occur when they are disadvantageous to the second investor.

Risk-aversion on the part of the first investor does not improve matters, since it serves to reduce the chance of a trade. For example, if the first investor's utility function is exponential with risk-aversion coefficient $b > 0$,

$$U_1(R) = -e^{-bR},$$

then the investment should be purchased only if

$$E\{-\exp[-b(y - y_2 - c)]\} > E(-e^{-0}) = -1,$$

which simplifies, given the revised distribution of y, to

$$\exp\left[-b(y_1^*-y_2-c)+(b^2\sigma_1^{*2}/2)\right]<1,$$

or

$$y_1-y_2>\left(\frac{\sigma_1^2+\sigma_2^2-2\rho\sigma_1\sigma_2}{\sigma_2^2-\rho\sigma_1\sigma_2}\right)c+\frac{b\sigma_1^2\sigma_2^2(1-\rho^2)}{2(\sigma_2^2-\rho\sigma_1\sigma_2)}.$$

The impact of the exponential utility function is to increase the difference y_1-y_2 required before the first investor will purchase the investment.

Under the conditions of the model, then, neither investor should be willing to serve as a market-maker. Of course, relaxation of some of the assumptions might change this result. For example, the second investor might believe that the first investor misperceives the distribution of errors or does not make decisions according to the dictates of the decision-theoretic model. Failure to act in an optimal fashion may leave an investor vulnerable to exploitation by a competing investor. Also, factors such as the existence of many other investors who may trade with the market-maker, the availability of several investments, and the consideration of a dynamic situation might change matters somewhat, and further work in these directions would be useful. As the situation becomes more complex, it seems less likely that different investors will arrive at the same model of the siutation.

The use of a market-maker is only one possible mechanism for generating a price. In some cases, particularly when a new investment becomes available, the price is determined via a bidding process. Under the normal model of estimation errors with two investors, investor i's "optimal" bid is

$$y_i-\left[(\pi/2)(\sigma_1^2+\sigma_2^2-2\rho\sigma_1\sigma_2)\right]^{1/2}.$$

Here the term that is subtracted from i's estimate is a "hedge". The winning bidder is very likely to have overestimated y, and the hedge represents an attempt to avoid bidding an amount larger than y while still trying to underbid the other investor. Incidentally, note the quotation marks around "optimal" in this instance. The two investors make their decisions simultaneously without interaction, and game-theoretic notions of optimization are relevant. The solution given above is an equilibrium solution. For more details concerning this model in a bidding situation, see Winkler and Brooks (1978), and for additional work in this area, see Wilson (1975).

Other price-generating mechanisms could be investigated, as could other models to represent the judgments and preferences of the investors. The effects of disagreements among investors regarding the model are of particular interest. Such disagreements might include thinking one's error variance is small when in fact it is large, misperceiving the predictive abilities or utility functions of other investors, failing to incorporate new information into the model in an appropriate manner, and so on. Another interesting possibility is the formation of groups of investors who may pool their information and resources. This raises the important question of group decision-making within the framework of statistical decision theory. In terms of the study of financial markets within the framework of statistical decision theory, many promising directions with challenging modeling questions exist for further work in this area.

5. Summary

As noted in section 1, the purpose of this paper is to discuss the interface between statistical decision theory and financial decision-making. The justification for the use of statistical decision theory in financial decision-making is the same as its justification in other types of decision-making situations. It provides a framework for the structuring of a decision-making problem in a logical manner and for the quantification of the decision-maker's judgments about future events and relative perferences for various payoffs. In requiring the inputs discussed in section 2, statistical decision theory forces the decision-maker to give careful thought to various aspects of the problem, and a major contribution of this approach indeed may be that it provides a logical way of thinking about a decision-making problem and about the factors relevant to the problem. Thus, the emphasis in this paper is on modeling rather than on the derivation of optimal solutions. Careful modeling is the key to successful applications of statistical decision theory.

Portfolio analysis represents a very important and widely-studied class of financial decision-making problems, and the study of financial markets and price formation has received quite a bit of attention in the financial literature recently. But most of the work in these areas has not used a Bayesian decision-theoretic approach. Thus, the models and results in sections 3 and 4 may be of some interest, and the modeling issues brought up in those sections lend additional emphasis to the discussion of modeling in section 2 and provide suggestions for further work on these topics.

References

Barry, C. B. (1977) "Effects of Uncertain and Nonstationary Parameters Upon Capital Market Equilibrium Conditions", *Working Paper 77-77* (Graduate School of Business, University of Texas at Austin).

Barry, C. B. and R. C. Radcliffe (1977) "Bayesian Modeling of Alternative Specifications in Portfolio Analysis", *Working Paper 77-71* (Graduate School of Business, University of Texas at Austin).

Barry, C. B. and R. L. Winkler (1976) "Nonstationarity and Portfolio Choice", *Journal of Financial and Quantitative Analysis* 11, 217–235.

Brown, R. V., A. S. Kahr and C. Peterson (1974) *Decision Analysis for the Manager* (Holt, Rinehart & Winston, New York).

DeGroot, M. H. (1970) *Optimal Statistical Decisions* (McGraw-Hill, New York).

Jaffe, J. F. and R. L. Winkler (1976) "Optimal Speculation Against an Efficient Market", *Journal of Finance* 31, 49–61.

Keeney, R. L. and H. Raiffa (1976) *Decisions with Multiple Objectives: Preferences and Value Tradeoffs* (Wiley, New York).

Klein, R. W. and V. S. Bawa (1977) "The Effect of Limited Information and Estimation Risk on Optimal Portfolio Diversification", *Journal of Financial Economics* 5, 89–111.

LaValle, I. H. (1970) *An Introduction to Probability, Decision, and Inference* (Holt, Rinehart & Winston, New York).

Lindley, D. V. (1971) *Making Decisions* (Wiley, New York).

Markowitz, H. (1959) *Portfolio Selection: Efficient Diversification of Investments* (Wiley, New York).

Raiffa, H. (1968) *Decision Analysis* (Addison-Wesley, Reading, Mass.).

Raiffa, H. and R. Schlaifer (1961) *Applied Statistical Decision Theory* (Graduate School of Business Administration, Harvard University, Boston).

Readings in Decision Analysis (1974) (Stanford Research Institute, Menlo Park, California).

Savage, L. J. (1954) *The Foundations of Statistics* (Wiley, New York).

Schlaifer, R. (1969) *Analysis of Decisions Under Uncertainty* (McGraw-Hill, New York).

Sharpe, W. F. (1970) *Portfolio Theory and Capital Markets* (McGraw-Hill, New York).

Wilson, R. B. (1975) "Price Formation via Competitive Bidding", *Working Paper 64* (Institute for Mathematical Studies in the Social Sciences, Stanford University).

Winkler, R. L. (1972) *An Introduction to Bayesian Inference and Decision* (Holt, Rinehart & Winston, New York).

Winkler, R. L. and C. B. Barry (1975) "A Bayesian Model for Portfolio Selection and Revision", *Journal of Finance* 30, 179–192.

Winkler, R. L. and D. G. Brooks (1978) "Competitive Bidding with Dependent Value Estimates", *Working Paper* (Graduate School of Business, Indiana University).

Zellner, A. (1971) *An Introduction to Bayesian Inference in Econometrics* (Wiley, New York).

Chapter 20

THE DUAL ROLE OF ACCOUNTING: A FINANCIAL ECONOMIC PERSPECTIVE

JOSHUA RONEN
New York University

1. Introduction

Financial management decisions within the business firm, and investment and lending decisions outside the firm, are impossible without informational inputs. In the form of financial reports and periodic financial statements, accounting represents one of the sources of these inputs. Like any economic intelligence, accounting emerged historically as a necessary tool for decision-making by single owners of relatively simple, short-lived ventures. Later, as the business environment increased in complexity and specialization, owners found it increasingly imperative to delegate many of the business conducting functions to professional management. This development, along with the continuous increase in the size and diversity of enterprises, has given the accounting function an additional raison d'etre: a tool for guaranteeing that management appropriately fulfill its stewardship function toward its stockholders. Management is used as an agent of stockholders – it must account to them on how it safeguards and manages the owner's resources. Under this view, accounting evolves as a monitoring mechanism either demanded by stockholders or volunteered by management, so as to minimize nonpecuniary benefits obtained by management. An unresolved issue is whether the resulting accounting intelligence is socially optimal.

Aside from the stewardship function, whether in its old vintage form or under the modern label of agency costs (Jensen and Meckling, (1976)), accounting clearly plays an additional role: providing information for resource allocation – internally within the firm – and externally for consumption investment decisions. From this perspective of the role of accounting, the issue is: do companies have incentives within the free market mechanism to provide correct signals for decision making? Should signalling be regulated because the market does not offer sufficient incentives for correct signalling?

James L. Bicksler, Editor, Handbook of Financial Economics
© *North-Holland Publishing Company – 1979*

It is argued by some (Benston (1969), Watts and Zimmerman (1977)) that there exist sufficient incentives in the market system for firm's management – operating in their own self-interests – to be optimally accountable *and* informative. In what follows I examine the dual function of accounting as:

(1) a means of monitoring for owners of the corporation to guarantee the safeguarding, and effective management of the owners' assets entrusted to agents (management), and

(2) a means of informing stockholders and potential investors about the prospects of investing in the corporation.

A special focus is directed to the issue of whether market failures might disrupt the fulfillment of this function and whether as a result some form of regulation might be necessary.

Unlike the finance discipline for which a modern theory has developed recently, we do not yet have anything approximating an accounting theory. Accounting principles and practice are now regulated by private sector professional bodies whose actions are both directed and constrained by the Securities and Exchange Commission (SEC), which is a governmental body. A normative theory of accounting would be one that facilitates the determination of which accounting principles *ought* to guide accounting practice. In the development of such a normative theory numerous assumptions are made that need to be empirically tested. Some of these assumptions – primarily those pertinent to the usage of accounting information by market transactors – have generally been tested using the efficient market hypothesis framework. But no normative theory of accounting is complete without a complementary descriptive theory – one that elucidates the workings of the market mechanism with respect to the generation and dissemination of accounting information and the determination of equilibrium solutions to information production problems. Such a positive theory is beginning to emerge, but so far, it is still in its infancy. Its salient aspects are summarized and critically evaluated below as the dual function of accounting, and its implications are examined.

First, the agency cost theory's link to the historical concept of stewardship is explored. The implications of the agency cost theory to the voluntary provision of information by corporations is discussed. Arguments are then presented to support the contentions that problems of information asymmetry reduce or eliminate the probability of correct information flowing to the market place as a result of voluntary monitoring and bonding activities. Phenomena such as the formulation of accounting standards, the audit institution and the uniformity of accounting and auditing standards are then explained as means that have evolved in the attempt to deal with the information asymmetry problem, and the implications of these developments to the desirability of regulation through the SEC or other professional organizations are evaluated.

The informativeness role of accounting and the social welfare objective implicit in it are the subjects of the second section of this paper. A reconciliation of this role with the stewardship function is attempted. The possibility of voluntary provision of information by firms' managers is then assessed in the context of signalling in a semistrong efficient capital market. For this purpose, the implications of evidence on the information content of accounting numbers and market efficiency are reviewed and critiqued. And finally, an assessment is made of the implications of the accountability and the informativeness functions of accounting for the regulation of information disclosure.

2. Accountability and agency costs

The concept of accountability has its roots in the stewardship role of management. Management must account for its management of the resources entrusted to it by owners of the firm. The necessity to account to the owners of the firms is not one that emerges out of "fairness". It is, rather, an economic relationship that evolved from delegation of resource allocation to professional management. The separation of ownership from management necessitates accountability by the agent to the owner. Legal enforcements of convenants and contracts between managers (agents) and owners probably came about as a form of seeking to minimize divergence of management from maximization of value of the firm due to the incongruence between management goals and owners' goals. That is, managers would pursue their self-interest – not the owners' – if restrictive covenants were not to be imposed. However, managenent may voluntarily wish to restrict its freedom to avoid pecuniary sanctions that result from the owners taking account of the effect of management freedom on the value of the stock. This requires that owners have confidence in managements' compliance with the covenants intended to restrict their freedom. Jensen and Meckling (1976) have formalized the agency relationship and conclude that even without regulation and legal enforcement, management will contract with stockholders and bondholders to limit its own freedom so as to reduce agency costs. These costs are defined by Jensen and Meckling as the decrement in value of the firm resulting from management's deviation from actions that serve the best interests of owners. Since managers bear the total agency costs, they would be motivated to reduce it to a minimum. (This aspect will be elaborated further below.)

2.1. A brief historical perspective

The accounting literature had always offered accountability as one of the primary objectives of financial reporting. Even though we find a recent shift to the objection of informativeness, i.e. providing information for financial decision-making by market transactors, we do encounter statements such as the following by Grady (1965):

> The separation of ownership from management of the business entity is a
> primary factor in imposing on the entity the fiduciary accountabilities to its
> stockholders (p. 26).

> "Account for" is intended to comprehend the entire fulfillment and corporate
> fiduciary accountabilities to stockholders, creditors and others having bona
> fide interests. Investors have entrusted their capital to the corporation to be
> invested in the kinds of assets and activities required to produce the products
> and services which constitute the corporate economic purposes. The fulfill-
> ment of this trust includes all the planning, selection and training of people,
> the development of products and services and the conduct of purchasing,
> manufacturing, and distribution and administrative functions. Good faith and
> due care on the part of directors and management in the conduct of the
> business are inherent requirements for meeting their fiduciary accountabilities.
> Due care includes attention to the establishment of a system of internal
> control adequate to safeguard the corporation's assets, check the accuracy and
> reliability of its accounting data, promote operational efficiency and en-
> courage adherence to prescribed managerial policies. Thus, "account for" as
> used in this summary of generally accepted accounting principles compre-
> hends the actual performance of the corporate business as well as the
> reporting on the financial status and results of operations (p. 55).

It is, however, safe to say that the concept of accounting for stewardship was far
more dominant in the past than in the latter part of the twentieth century.
Larsen (1967, p. 11) describes an accounting by an agent circulated internally to
a merchant (owner) for a caravan shipment venture in early Mesopotamia. The
document accounts for purchased items and expenses of a return trip. The
account is show below:

> Thus Pilahaja, Irma-Assur, and Mannum-balum-Assur; say to Enlil-bani and
> Kukkulanum: 30 minas of silver — its nishatu-tax added — with your seals
> Kikkulanum has brought. We checked the silver and (found) 2/3 mina of
> silver missing. Thereof: 114 linen-cloths, their (price in) silver: $7\frac{1}{2}$ minas $4\frac{1}{4}$
> sheqels 2 talents 15 minas of sealed tin (at the rate of) $13\frac{1}{4}$ sheqels each; 40
> minas of sealed tin, moreover, 8 minas of sealed tin (at the rate of) 13 sheqels
> each — its (price in) silver: 13 5/6 minas 3 3/4 sheqels 6 black donkeys cost 2
> minas 8 sheqels of silver together with their fodder. 16 sheqels of silver: their
> harness; 37 minas of hand-tin (at the rate of) 13 sheqels each — its (price in)
> silver: 2 5/6 minas 2 1/6 sheqels; 1 mina of silver: the working-capital of 2
> harnessors; 4 sheqels: their clothes; 7 sheqels of silver we added to the
> working-capital of Nabi-Sin; $12\frac{1}{2}$ sheqels: "additions"; $2\frac{1}{2}$ sheqels: of the
> sa'udum; 15 sheqels: departure toll; 6 sheqels of silver we paid on the account

of Assur-malik; 5/6 mina of silver Kukkulanum has taken, thus (he said): 'If the tamkarum will not let silver reach me here I shall take it from this silver!'

Indeed, the agency relationship has been long recognized as a factor explaining observed accounting practice (Yamey (1962)). De Ste Croix (1956), traced the stewardship concept to Greek and Roman accounting; Littleton and Zimmerman (1963) traced it to feudal accounting in England and to the British Companies Act of 1847.

2.2. Incentives for voluntary accountability

Jensen and Meckling (1976) in their formalization of the agency costs, argue that because the manager bears all the agency costs, he has an incentive to reduce them. As a result, he would undertake voluntarily to supply information in financial statements required for the monitoring of contracts that management enters into a reduce the costs. In Jensen and Meckling's own words (p. 338):

> Suppose, for example, that the bondholders "or outside equity holders" would find it worthwhile to produce detailed financial statements such as those contained in the usual published accounting reports as a means of monitoring the manager. If the manager himself can produce such information at lower costs than they (perhaps because he's already collecting much of the data they desire for his own internal decision making purposes), it would pay him to agree in advance to incur the costs of providing such reports and to have their accuracy testified to by an independent outside auditor. This is an example of what we refer to as bonding costs.

Would the implication of this analysis be that regulation of accounting information by the SEC or a private sector body is unnecessary? The answer partially depends on whether the information is only necessary for monitoring and bonding purposes. If accounting information can produce net social benefits aside from its role in facilitating monitoring and bonding activities, then it should be determined whether the financial statements provided by managers as attested to by auditors are sufficient to produce the potential benefits. But before this issue is addressed, it is useful to ask whether, indeed, agency costs, in equilibrium, will be totally borne by the manager.

2.3. The problem of information asymmetry

Unlike Jensen and Meckling (1976), I would argue that agency costs will not always be borne by the manager and, therefore, while the manager still has incentives to reduce his share of the agency costs, he will not be motivated to reduce the share borne by the owners. As a result, the extent of monitoring and bonding contracts the manager will get into will not necessarily result in the flow of information that would otherwise enforce adherence to the same minimal agency costs had such costs been totally borne by the manager.

One of the requirements in Jensen and Meckling's analysis for agency costs to be borne by the manager is that the market anticipates the agency cost effects. In other words, prospective minority shareholders and bondholders should be cognizant of the fact that owner-managers' interests will diverge from theirs so that the price they are willing to pay for the shares will reflect the monitoring costs and the effect of the divergence between the manager's interests and theirs. Specifically, if we consider as an example the case of outside equity, the equity holders are assumed to hold rational expectations such that the buyers are aware that the owner will increase his nonpecuniary consumption when his ownership share is reduced. But equity holders are not only required to be cognizant of the consequent nonpecuniary consumption – they must know the manager-owner's response to the change in his ownership (p. 318). The authors do not explain what mechanism will produce such unbiased estimates; what sources, if any, will supply information on the manager's tastes for nonpecuniary benefits; and if there are such sources of information – whether competitive or monopolistic – what is the price that this information commands?

Indeed, if the equity market holds rational, i.e. unbiased estimates of the manager's response to reduction of ownership and if the estimation errors are independent across firms, the authors are justified in concluding that the risk inherent in whatever uncertainties introduced by the lack of perfect knowledge of the owner-manager's response function is diversifiable and that, as a result, equilibrium prices will equal the expected values. A critical issue is then how are such unbiased estimates to be obtained?

Information on the owner-manager's taste for nonpecuniary benefits and thus on his response to a reduced share in the firm's ownership can only come from two sources: (1) the manager himself, or (2) from observations of the manager's behavior over time and his past responses to reductions in his ownership share. Such observations will have to be made possible through some kind of monitoring scheme that will require the gathering of information. This can be quite costly, especially if the owner-manager does not cooperate in providing the information.

Will the owner-manager – pursuing his own interest – have an incentive to provide the information on his response functions? It could be argued that the cost of obtaining information on the manager's response function will reduce the value of the firm and thus increase agency costs to the manager, thereby motivating him to provide the information regarding his reponse function voluntarily. But what we encounter in this instance is a moral hazard situation characterized by information asymmetry similar to the one analyzed by Akerlof

(1970). This asymmetry will cause some of the agency cost to be borne by minority equity owners.

To illustrate how the agency cost will be shared between the manager-owner and equity-holders, consider fig. 20.1. As in Jensen and Meckling's analysis, the F axis reflects the current market value of the stream of manager's expenditures on nonpecuniary benefits. $\overline{V}F$ represents the constraint which a single owner manager faces in deciding how much nonpecuniary income he will extract from the firm. $O\overline{V}$ is the value of the firm when the amount of nonpecuniary income consumed is zero. The slope of $\overline{V}F$ is -1 to indicate that one dollar of current value of nonpecuniary benefits withdrawn from the firm by the manager reduces

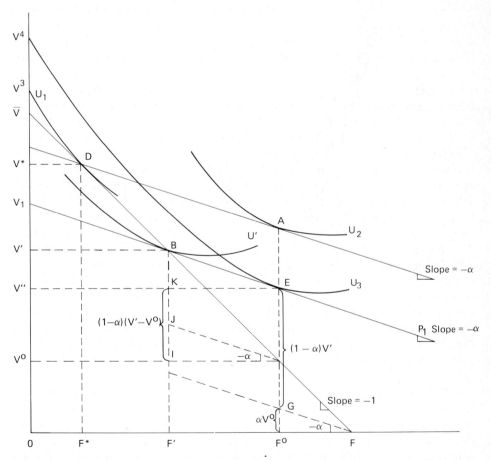

Figure 20.1. The value of the firm (V) and the level of nonpecuniary benefits consumed (F) when the fraction of outside equity is $(1-\alpha)V$. $U_j(j=1,2,3)$ represents owners' "true" indifference curve between wealth and nonpecuniary benefit.

the market value of the firm by one dollar. The convex indifference curves U_1, U_2 and U_3 represent the "true" tradeoff between pecuniary and nonpecuniary benefits – known only to the manager-owner himself. Assume that U' belongs to a map of indifference curves of which U_1 is also a member, erroneously attributed to the manager-owner by the equity holders. Thus, equity-holders, attributing to the manager-owner preferences that differ from his "true" tastes, will derive a *biased* estimate of the change in F triggered by a reduction in the owner's share of the firm.

When the manager is the sole owner, the value of the firm is V^* and the level of nonpecuniary consumed is F^*. Now, suppose a manager sells a fraction $1 - \alpha$ of the firm $(0 < \alpha < 1)$ to an outsider and retains for himself the share α. The cost to the owner-manager of consuming one dollar of nonpecuniary benefits is now $\alpha \times \$1$.

It is easy to show that the new equilibrium will be at the point B, where the indifference curve U' believed by equity owners to characterize the manager's taste for nonpecuniary benefits is tangent to the line $V_1 P_1$ with slope $- \alpha$, such that B lies on the budget line $\overline{VF}$. Equity-holders will agree to pay $(1 - \alpha) \times V'$, where V' corresponds to the point B. The manager is assumed to know that equity-holders attribute to him indifference curve U'. Therefore, if the tangency point were to the left of B on $\overline{VF}$ he will demand more than $(1 - \alpha) V'$ and if the tangency point is to the right of B, the equity-holders will want to pay less than $(1 - \alpha) V'$. In point of fact, however, the manager's consumption of non-pecuniary benefits will be at the point $F°$ corresponding to the value $V°$, where $V' > V°$. The total agency cost is thus $V^* - V°$; however, the manager's share of the agency cost will be only $V^* - [\alpha V° + (1 - \alpha) V']$. The manager's share is represented by the distance $V^* - V''$ where OV'' is composed of the segment $F°G = \alpha V°$ and the segment $GE = (1 - \alpha) V'$. The outside equity-holders will now bear a portion of the agency cost amounting to $(1 - \alpha)(V' - V°)$. This share is represented by the distance $V'' - V° = IK = JB$. Actually, in this particular illustration, in spite of the residual loss to the manager-owner of $V^* - V''$, he gains a net increment in welfare as reflected in the distance $V^4 - V^3$, the difference between the intercepts on the Y axis of the two indifference curves U_3 and U_1. The fact that the manager-owner experiences a net gain in welfare in spite of his pecuniary residual loss is due to the increase in his consumption of nonpecuniary benefits $(F° - F^*)$.

The situation illustrated in fig. 20.1 represents an adverse selection potential. It is easy to draw the analogy with Akerlof's (1970) analysis of the market for "lemons". Managers would not have an incentive to provide correct information about these tastes to potential purchasers of the firm's equity securities. The manager will act like the seller of used cars in Akerlof's model. Since potential buyers do not have the information on these manager's tastes for nonpecuniary benefits, the manager-owners have incentives to sell poor quality securities since the return for good quality securities accrues mainly to the entire group and not to the individual seller. In other words, the manager with a higher taste for nonpecuniary benefits will be selling an inferior security – a "lemon" – to a potential investor uninformed about this particular manager's tastes. As a result, the average quality of securities sold in the market will decrease and so will the size of the market for securities. Moreover, since social and private returns differ, regulation or some government intervention may increase the wealth of society.

To see how the analogy with Akerlof's analysis holds, it is merely necessary to substitute securities for used cars. The security of a company whose manager has low taste for nonpecuniary benefits would resemble the good car, the security of a company whose manager has a great taste for nonpecuniary benefits would resemble the "bad car" or the "lemon". Groups in society are characterized by a utility that is a function of the quality of the securities. Now it is only needed to add the plausible assumption that utility functions of different groups in society differ in the weight attached to security quality and Akerlof's conclusions automatically follow. Clearly, we do have arrangements in the American capital market that minimize the adverse selection bias, but it is precisely these arrangements that some would have us do away with, arguing that in their absence company managers will undertake a sufficient amount of monitoring and bonding activities.

Indeed, if equity-holders were able to estimate unbiasedly the manager's response function, we would be in a situation where the information is symmetrical and where the anomalies encountered in the case of information asymmetry would not arise. The analysis of information asymmetry therefore leads to the conclusion that trade may not take place in spite of the fact that there are given prices at which some manager-owners would be willing to issue securities and at which there would be buyers who are willing to purchase them. And this happens because of the existence of poor quality securities that drive the price below that at which the high quality security suppliers are willing to sell. These adverse effects on trade may well have been one of the underlying factors behind the establishment of the securities law and the regulation of information disclosure. The arguments underlying the disclosure rules and securities regulations typically cite facilitation of trade, the building up of public confidence in the securities market, etc.

Will private institutions come into being in an unregulated market to limit or even eliminate the adverse selection element inherent in the agency relationship? We have seen that the cost of adverse selection (or the cost of dishonesty) lies not only in the potential amount by which a given purchaser is cheated, but also in driving legitimate business out of existence. As in Akerlof's "lemons" model, the presence of manager-owners who are willing to offer inferior goods represents the major cost of dishonesty. The purchaser's problem is to identify the "quality" of the securities, i.e. of the earning streams underlying those securities. In the agency costs case, their problem is to identify the manager's response function to a reduction of his share in the ownership of the company.

In the absence of market regulation, one would in fact expect private institutions to counter the adverse selection effects. In the market for goods, Akerlof mentions a few: prior guarantees, brand names, chains such as hotel or restaurant chains, and licensing practices (such as licensing doctors, lawyers and barbers). What are the likely institutions that would arise in the case of company securities if there were no security regulation and disclosure rules?

2.4. Accounting standards and the audit institution

Clearly, the managers with low taste for perquisites will wish to advertise their "sainthood" attributes, so as to enhance the value of the shares they issue. But nothing prevents managers with more lavish tastes for nonpecuniary benefits from engaging in false advertisement. The good quality managers will need somehow to guarantee to potential purchasers the truth of their advertisement or convince them of its truth through the attestation of an "objective" and "neutral qualified" outsider. They might hire auditors to do the job not because they are required to under a mandatory rule, but because they would be acting in their self-interest by doing so.

But the cost of this particular kind of audit could be exorbitant. Recalling that this is not the kind of audit that company managers expect to result in an attestation that indeed the manager adheres to the consumption of a reduced nonpecuniary benefit in the Jensen and Meckling model, but rather an audit that attests to information about the true response function of managers. Auditors are not likely to elicit the cooperation of managers to the extent that managers have an incentive to advertise less than the planned consumption of nonpecuniary benefits. Auditors would have to be licensed to assure purchasers of the value of their attestations. The licensing imposes penalties on the auditor if he does not conduct his audit job appropriately. Without such penalties the auditor's pursuit of their own self-interests may induce them to collaborate with the "poor quality" management, thus producing an additional source of a new kind of agency costs.

The licensing activities consume social resources and, eventually, the costs of audits themselves will reduce the value of the firm. So, in equilibrium, managers will contract to audit only when the value increment induced by a certified advertisement with respect to the quality of management, exceeds the value decrement caused by the cost of audit. The cost of audits in this case is analagous to the cost incurred by job-seekers in signalling above average productivity when the signal is costly to obtain and when it does not change the individual's productive attributes.

The auditor's attestation will not add much weight unless penalties are imposed on an auditor collaborating with the manager in providing a misleading signal. The auditor, then, in attempting to minimize the private cost to him of providing a misleading statement will have an incentive to apply audit procedures that enable him to detect whatever biases are inherent in management representations. Such a penalty now exists in the form of litigation costs associated with potential suits brought by stockholders, other parties, and regulatory authorities. Moreover, auditors now must be licensed and such licenses could be revoked if the auditor engages in unethical conduct. In addition, since audit costs are likely to be decreased if managers had to apply standard rules of accounting for events and actions, we would expect a social arrangement whereby such standard rules, both for accounting and for auditing, are established. Indeed, this could be the "economic" reason behind the establishment of the accounting and auditing self-regulating professional bodies that took upon themselves the establishment of accounting and auditing standards. If this analysis is correct, the establishment of the Accounting Principles Board and its successor the Financial Accounting Standards Board, as well as the Auditing Standard Executive Committee of the American Institute of Certified Public Accountants has come about in response for an economic need to minimize the monitoring costs in the form of audit so as to attest to signals by management.

2.5. The uniformity of accounting standards

The Securities and Exchange Commission is the governmental body that can enforce the application of the GAAP established by the self-regulating professional Financial Accounting Standards Board. As such, it represents a social arrangement that has set in motion a system of providing assurances with respect to the reliability of signals from management: (1) with respect to the "quality" of management in the sense of consumption of nonpecuniary benefits, and (2) with respect to the adherence of management to certain rules of conducting the business, designed to delimit the consumption of nonpecuniary benefits broadly construed to include the investment in projects that are "too risky" from the standpoint of other stockholders.

The arguments voiced for increasing the uniformity of accounting standards and reducing the flexibility of management in choosing among different accounting treatments could well be explained from an economic standpoint as means for reducing audit (monitoring) costs and for reducing the ambiguity of the resulting signal and the possible effect of such ambiguity on investors reaction. The larger the ambiguity of the signal resulting from an excessive flexibility on the part of management of choosing among accounting means of generating the signal, the lesser the reliability of the inference that can be made by investors on the basis of the signals received.

It is plausible to assume that the demand for securities, apart from being a function of the average quality of earnings as defined above, depends also on the uncertainty surrounding such quality. That is, the greater the uncertainty surrounding the inference on the basis of the signal regarding the manager's behavior, the lesser the demand and the valuation of the securities. Managers with above average quality, expecting such uncertainty-induced decrement in the firm value, will have an incentive to reduce the uncertainty. We would then expect these managers to support a social arrangement that facilitates the kind of monitoring that reduces uncertainty of inferences at minimal costs.

Increasing the uniformity of accounting standards and their application across firms and industries constitutes one way of minimizing the cost of reducing uncertainty surrounding inferences by investors. But increasing the uniformity of standards and of audit procedures is not costless. It reduces the flexibility of management to signal. The more confining the generally accepted accounting principles and the methods of their application, the lesser the flexibility that management can use to convey its expectations regarding the firm's prospects and regarding its own actions within the range of signals attested to be auditors and expected to form a basis for inference by investors. This reduction in the ability of management to signal counteracts the reduction in monitoring cost produced by the enforcement of uniform standards. Thus, as in most economic activities, we conclude, unsurprisingly, that there is an optimal amount of uniformity of accounting standards. An optimum that balances the costs of limiting management flexibility and signalling against the benefits inherent in the reduction of monitoring costs due to uniformity.

An analogy can be drawn with the example of food distribution discussed by Akerlof (1970). He compares the heterogeneity of quality in the street market of underdeveloped countries such as India with the canned qualities of the American supermarket, suggesting that quality variation is a greater problem in underdeveloped countries than in developed countries. For example, "Indian housewives must carefully glean the rice of the local bazaar to sort out stones of the same color and shape which have been intentionally added to the rice" (p. 496). This quality variation explains, in Akerlof's mind, the need for quality control of exports. As an example, Akerlof cites the export quality control and inspection act of 1963 in India, which covers about 85 percent of Indian exports (p. 496). I would argue that there are similarities between the need to classify and distribute food in developed countries by homogeneous, canned quality groups under adequately descriptive labels and the need to establish uniform accounting and auditing standards.

By the same token, we observe a sufficiently large number of different homogeneous quality groups in the supermarkets of the industrialized world to conclude that quality uniformity has not been carried too far. Enough flexibility is accorded to manufacturers to offer different qualities and different prices. The analogy extends to the accounting signals case: uniformity will reduce the ambiguity surrounding the signal; however, some flexibility should be retained so that management can offer a variety of signals (analogous to food products) characterized by different degrees of ambiguity (analogous to quality of products) provided that each signal is provided in conjunction with its associated degree of uncertainty.

2.6. Implications for voluntary engagement of auditors

If companies operated in an environment in which they can decide on whether or not to be audited, we are more likely to observe good quality managers who elect to purchase audit services than poor quality managers. The actual nature of equilibrium will depend on the audit costs, the proportion of good quality managers to all managers, and the extent of the differences between the qualities which in turn determines the benefit to the good quality management from attestation to its reports. Depending on the configuration of these factors, we may even observe all firms electing to purchase audit services if the audits are imperfect in the sense of committing both a "type one" and a "type two" error: attesting to good quality when in fact quality is poor or attesting to poor quality when in fact the quality is good.

It might seem at first that for a diversified portfolio investor the audit institution would be of minimal benefit since the error associated with relying on an unaudited signal can be diversified away. But the ability to diversify away such errors depends on the proportion of poor quality managers to all managers. The larger the proportion, the lesser the ability to diversify a judgmental error away. Note also that the errors are dependent across firms. A poor quality manager's firm will always bias their signals (or the quality of earnings) up, whereas high quality managers will *not* bias their signals downward. Thus, the view that audit costs will only decrease the wealth of diversified portfolio investors and transfer wealth to auditors is unjustified. The cost of audit should be balanced against the benefits induced by the increased trading and mutually beneficial exchanges made possible by the signalling institution.

Benston (1969) reports that as of 1926, 82 percent of the firms listed on the New York Stock Exchange were audited by a CPA. All firms published a balance sheet, 55 percent disclosed sales, 45 percent disclosed cost of goods sold, 71 percent disclosed depreciation, and 100 percent disclosed net income. These disclosures and the hiring of auditors were made voluntarily prior to government mandated requirements. These facts are consistent with the need for some managers (1) to signal messages attested to by auditors, and (2) to provide a means for monitoring contractual bonding and monitoring agreements.[1] Benston (1976) also observes that the penalties imposed on auditors for not fulfilling their duty satisfactorily take different forms in different countries. In the UK there is, as a result of the traditional English heritage, greater peer pressure toward conformity to accepted behavior. Censure by peers and professional societies apparently are effective in deterring negligent conduct. In the US the penalties assume a more formal dimension. The auditor in the US is exposed to a large potential of legal action. The greater liability for legal suits in the US stems from (1) the 1933 and 1934 US Securities Acts, and (2) the SEC's preference for enforcement to be effected through private actions.

Watts (1977) reports numerous examples of monitoring and bonding activities consistent with the hypothesis that managers seek reduced agency costs of both debt and equity. Examples include (1) the covenant that restricts the payment of dividends (Black and Scholes (1973), Black et al. (1974), and Myers (1976) discuss the implications for debt valuation); (2) management compensation plans that tie management remuneration to shareholder wealth directly via stock options or via bonus plans that depend on net income; and (3) covenants restricting the payment of dividends to amount of profits remaining after deducting a reserve fund for maintenance repair, depreciation and renewals.[2]

Watts notes that the theory of agency costs makes possible the formulation of testable hypotheses regarding the voluntary production and dissemination of financial statements as a means for monitoring covenant agreements. Clearly, if covenants existed, one would expect financial statements to be provided that include all the information necessary for the enforcement and monitoring of the covenants. A less trivial empirical observation would be one that associates the voluntary writing of covenants with company economic characteristics that indicate the incidence of high agency costs. Such characteristics include the manager's relative share of the corporation's equity and the amount of the corporation's risky debt.

---

[1] I shall argue that such activities are consistent not only with the enforcement of monitoring and bonding agreements, but also with the purpose of informing existing and potential stockholders of attributes of states of the world known to managers so as to affect stock value. In fact, as the agency cost analysis suggests, there would be no motivation for managers to reduce agency costs, unless such reduction increases the value of the stock and facilitates monitoring through the provision of information.

[2] As examples, Watts (1977) discusses articles of some UK corporations in the nineteenth century, such as the 104th article of London Tramways Co. as reported in the action Davidson vs. Gillies (1879).

2.7. Is regulation necessary?

Does the existence of restricting covenants and the voluntary production and dissemination of information consistent with these covenants imply that in the absence of government regulation (or private regulation under the oversight of the government, as is the case of the FASB's establishment of accounting principles under the oversight of the SEC[3]), financial statements will be produced and be attested to in a manner that minimizes agency costs? In light of the above discussion, the answer must be: not necessarily. As we have seen, if we rely on the market mechanism and the incentives it provides for management to contract with auditors to attest to information about their intended and actual consumption of nonpecuniary benefits, and to information that allows the monitoring of covenants we could observe an equilibrium consistent with a lessened amount of trading and mutually beneficial exchanges.

Because of the adverse selection problem, we would expect private institutions to come into being to minimize these costs. These private institutions include the licensing of auditors, the establishment of accounting standards that limit the manager's ability to convey ambiguous signals, the establishment of auditing standards that reduce the audit costs by limiting the range of possible audit procedures to a well-defined set, and finally the establishment of a system of penalties imposed on managers and auditors in the case of negligent or deliberate dissemination of misleading information. The penalties are required, as indicated above, to eliminate or reduce the agency costs that might be given rise to by a possible collaboration of the auditors with bad quality management.

In order to ensure the efficient operation of these private institutions that deal with the reduction of agency costs, enforcement procedures are necessary. The particular set of enforcement procedures to be set in motion clearly depends on the setting and the consequent relative costs and benefits. It is conceivable that the optimal enforcement procedures will differ from country to country, depending on economic, cultural and other characteristics of the societies involved. Professional peer pressure may suffice in England; but governmental regulation *may* be necessary in the US. In the absence of a careful cost–benefit analysis government regulation cannot be ruled out as socially wasteful.

Some – notably Benston (1976) and Watts and Zimmerman (1977) – would have us believe that accounting standards, the theory underlying such standards, and the procedures to implement the standards, develop primarily as "excuses" to satisfy the demand of vested interest groups affected by political institutions given rise to by government regulation. They argue that accounting theories (and thus standards consistent with the theories) are demanded primarily as useful justifications of the political lobbying for accounting changes. They claim

---

[3]See Horngren (1973) for the role of the SEC in the oversight of accounting standard setting.

that the justification demand for accounting theories increases with governmental regulation and intervention, that each group likely to be affected by an accounting change will demand a theory that satisfies its own self-interest; but at the same time, the theory has to have a "public interest" orientation since a "self-interest" motivation for a theory will not be palatable politically. There must be some element of truth in these allegations. Watts and Zimmerman (1977) claim that their hypothesis is supported by observing how accounting theories responded to the passage of regulatory legislation. In particular they examined the acts to regulate railroads (1840–1880), the corporate income tax laws (1909–1913) and the securities acts of 1933 and 1934.

One would naturally expect an impending regulatory act to generate a public discussion and to stir debate, speculation, theorizing and prescriptions. We are witnesses every day to debates in the Press, in the professional and the academic journals focusing on issues debated in Congress and other political organizations. But can we infer from the mere observation that these phenomena are associated that government regulation causes the public debate? More likely, what is being observed is a two-way process: academics and others motivated by the desire to achieve intellectual excellence in their pursuit of "scientific truth" and thus prominence and recognition among peers, advocate and publicize different accounting theories. As Watts and Zimmerman (1977) claim, some interest groups will "discover" convenient "excuses" in some of these theories that bear the legitimizing stamp of "public interest" and "social welfare" and peddle the theories to promote their own good. At the same time, however, in a democracy such as ours, public interest will be aroused, debate will be set in motion thereby giving rise to an onset of political processes that transcend and go beyond the narrow self-interests. Once the political process gains momentum, more theorizing and speculation will be generated in response to the political decision-making. Arguing merely that governmental regulation is the cause and that the supply of accounting theories and standards serving as "excuses" is the effect, leaves us without an explanation as to how the political process comes into being. No analysis is provided – no positive theory that allows us to predict regulatory activities.

The fallacy lies in the analogy that Watts and Zimmerman draw between the market for goods and the market for ideas. I fervently believe in the veracity of Stigler's (1976, p. 347) proposition: "...consumers generally determine what will be produced, and producers make profits by discovering more precisely what consumers want and producing it more cheaply," (as quoted by Watts and Zimmerman, p. 22). However, I do entertain a tinge of doubt about Stigler's implied proposition: "...it is useful to say that consumers direct production – and therefore, do they not direct the production of words and ideas of intellectuals, rather than, as in the first, vice versa?" (p. 345 as quoted by Watts and Zimmerman, p. 22). The market for ideas differs by at least one essential respect from the market for goods. Theories and ideas are "collective goods".[4] As a result, both the producer of the theory and the consumer whose "self-interest" position is supported by the theory, capture only a fraction of the social benefit (or cost in the case of a bad theory!). In particular, other consumers could use the same theory (or standard) to attack the first consumer's position on a different issue that the theory does not support or is not consistent with. Given, as in fact Watts and Zimmerman argue, that "vested interest groups use different theories (excuses) for different issues" (p. 46), the likelihood that any interest group would find a given theory consistent with some of its positions and inconsistent with others is quite large. Thus, given the nature of theories and ideas as collective goods, the political process imposes penalties on the would-be demander for "excuses". This will tend to lessen the demand for excuses. On the other hand, widespread consumption by different interest groups of a given theory will tend to increase the demand for theories that are not necessarily supportive of any particular position. The intellectuals will gain some non-pecuniary benefits from the popularity accorded by the usage of theories by different interest groups, but they will also gain the recognition by peer groups of intellectually superior ideas. All this militates against the hypothesis of a unidirectional flow of theories from intellectuals to consumers. Intellectuals thus could well be engaging in the production of theories that lie beyond the narrow domain of any particular social or political group.

3. The informativeness role

The agency cost reduction role of accounting is merely the modern counterpart of what is more traditionally known as the stewardship function. But while the old stewardship function was not derived from a descriptive theory of accounting, the agency cost approach is more concerned with economic incentives than with concepts such as "fairness" and "right to know". A second, relatively more recent role for accounting is informativeness. This role is launched in terms of social benefit arguments. Its most recent expression is contained in the FASB's Conceptual Framework Discussion Memorandum (1976):

> "Financial statements of business enterprises should provide information within the limits of financial accounting, that is useful to present and potential investors and creditors in making rational investment and credit decisions" (p.10).

---

[4]These were defined by Demsetz (1969) as goods from the consumption of which nonpurchasers *cannot* be excluded. Compare this with Demsetz's definition of "public goods", which can be enjoyed by additional persons at no additional cost.

And then,

> ...confidence in financial information is vital, not only to insure that individ-
> ual decisions result in an equitable allocation of capital, but to insure
> continuing public support of the free enterprise system as a whole" (p. 3).

We have seen in the analysis of agency costs that the monitoring mechanisms
will require information to be provided to equity-holders and bondholders in
order to enforce monitoring and bonding contracts. These monitoring requirements and the need for social arrangements that assure reliability of the
accounting signals, so as to combat the adverse selection problem caused by
information asymmetry, come very close to being reflected – though only implicitly – in the above objective.

3.1. The social welfare objective

Underlying the above FASB statement are the objectives agreed upon by the
Trueblood Committee (1973): An expression of the social welfare argument is
reflected in the following:

> ...accounting should serve the goals of both the private and public sectors of
> the economy. By fulfilling the information needs of those in the private sector
> who make economic decisions, accounting assists in a more efficient alloca-
> tion of resources, thus contributing to the attainment of broad social goals
> (p. 61).

The motivation for this statement comes from the decision that accounting
information should serve ultimately to enhance social welfare (Ronen (1974)):

> Although individual users of accounting information have a multitude of
> goals and types of decisions, the broad objective of the economy as a whole is
> defined to be the efficient allocation of resources (p. 82).

> When this objective is pursued within a private enterprise system in which it is
> assumed that individuals seek to maximize their wealth, the accounting
> objectives must be formulated so that the use of accounting information by
> individuals to maximize their wealth causes resources to be allocated most
> efficiently in the economy (p. 83).

The reduction of agency costs was included in this objective. In a footnote to the
above quote, relating to the efficient resource allocation, it was stated:

> This includes the efficient allocation of resources within the firm as one part
> of the economy, and it thus implies the provision of information to control
> and motivate actions within the firm, to insure efficient allocation of the
> firm's resources (p. 83).

The social welfare role of accounting information was also recognized in *A Statement of Basic Accounting Theory* (American Accounting Association (1966)). Among the objectives:

> ...to facilitate the operations of an organized society for the welfare of all (p. 5).

Reference to the social good as an objective of accounting was not made in the earlier literature. Definitions of accounting primarily related to describing the mechanical process of recording. For example, Paton (1924) describes accounting as the mechanism through which

> The financial data of the particular concern are recorded, classified, and periodically presented and interpreted, with a view, thereby, to the rational administration of the enterprise (p. 1).

Similarly, Leake (1912) and Sanders et al. (1938) emphasized the needs of the enterprise management in discussing the functions of accounting.

Why did the social welfare argument emerge recently? I would hypothesize that with the rising complexity of the business environment in the developed countries, and especially in the United States, and with the rise in the extent of interdependencies among corporations in the US, individuals and groups in society have become more affected than ever by accounting policies. With the increase in the number of owners of equity and with the increased diffusion of ownership, the agency costs have begun to affect a greater number of individuals in the economy, but furthermore, with the increase in diversification by equity-holders in the stock of numerous firms, accounting changes in one firm now affect not only its stockholders but also investment consumption decisions by others. In addition, the increase in externalities, or side effects, as an inevitable product of advances in technology and communication has heightened the awareness of the social impact of corporations and the demand for information on social impacts. Thus, the social welfare argument is more likely rooted in business environmental changes than in incentives to satisfy the demand for "excuses". Indeed, as Beaver and Demski (1974) recognized, financial information may affect the choice of productive alternatives and therefore aggregate supply in the economy. As a result, financial information will affect resource allocation.[5] It therefore seems quite reasonable to expect an increasing emphasis on the effect of information on resource allocation.

The objective of resource allocative efficiency in the economy can serve as an overall guideline for examining the desirability of accounting alternatives. It seems to be a natural outgrowth of the increasing interdependencies and externalities in a way that makes a choice of an accounting alternative affect not only users of the statements of the corporations that made the change, but also

---

[5]Some, like Benston (1976) argue that financial statements do not affect investor's decisions and resource allocation. This issue is addressed in a later section.

others. And in fact, the injection of the resource allocative efficiency objective is merely *an extension* of the agency cost reduction role of accounting information. The latter role requires signalling and accountability to the immediate bond-holders and equity holders of the corporation. The economy-wide resource allocative efficiency objective requires providing information to these same groups but in addition to the public at large. Providing information for the purpose of monitoring agency costs is aimed at countering a decline in the company's value. But this requires that the information becomes known to all potential investors as well. If we also ask that information used by investors and lenders in assessing companies' value be such that it would eliminate externalities, the objective of resource allocative efficiency follows immediately.[6] In regimes based on anarchy, externalities may be eliminated by war or physical retaliation. In democracies, externalities are reduced by governmental intervention, hopefully in an efficient and orderly manner. Once it is recognized that information causes divergences between social net benefits and private net benefits, the promotion of resource allocative efficiency becomes a natural candidate for political consensus.

The extension of the accountability objective to the social welfare role of accounting has been succinctly stated by Cyert and Ijiri (1974):

> The American economy is based on a network of accountability relationships. The separation of ownership and management of economic resources has created a basic need for accountability. But in our modern economy, account-ability is not limited to the relationship between management and owners. Within the management hierarchy, a subordinate is considered to be account-able to his supervisor for the management of resources entrusted to him. Externally, the firm is accountable not only to its shareholders, but also to its creditors and governments at all levels. The recent emphasis on the quality of the environment (clean air, water) has added the public to the list of parties to whom a firm is accountable (pp. 30–31).

3.2. The informativeness of accounting information

The informativeness role of accounting has both descriptive and normative implications. Descriptively, is accounting information being used under the present market institutional environment? Normatively, *should* the informational effects of accounting on market transactors' decisions be considered in selecting among different accounting technologies or alternative principles? A descriptive finding that accounting information is used in decision-making by market transactors is a necessary, but not sufficient, condition for the argument that the

---

[6]Externalities in the dissemination of accounting information exist in that accounting information constitutes a collective good for which the social value differs from the private value.

consequences of market agents' decisions based on accounting information should be used as a criterion in selecting among accounting alternatives. The necessity follows from the simple proposition that if accounting information is not used it will have no consequences on market agents' decisions and therefore nothing remains to be considered in the process of choice among accounting alternatives. The insufficiency follows from the need to ascertain whether the equilibrium produced, as the information is assimilated in the market, is in fact optimal, or whether the equilibrium could be improved through the regulatory specification of what principles ought to be followed in the generation of information.

3.3. Is accounting information used?

Benston (1976) argued:

> ...the statistical evidence on annual reports, then, are generally consistent with the conclusion that the information content of financial statements is essentially "known" by the time that statements are available to the public (p. 132).

Watts (1977) argued in a similar vein:

> The evidence suggests that corporate financial statements convey relatively little information which causes the capital markets to change the value of the corporation's securities (p. 22).

Watts further argues that descriptively, managers of corporations are not likely to have incentives to supply information in corporate financial statements, since even when they do possess inside information (information about the corporations' future cash flows obtained before outsiders discover it), they will maintain exclusive access to the information until the publication of financial statements since they can trade on the information and increase their wealth.

Unfortunately, the argument that inside information will be reflected in security prices ignores two important aspects: (1) some inside information may not be reflected, especially if it is a negative foreknowledge, in view of the penalties expected by insiders from legal action that could be brought against them in case they trade on the basis of the information or sell it,[7] and (2) even if

---

[7]For an elaborate discussion of the effects of insider trading rules on the generation and disclosure of information by corporations, see Ronen (1977). Ronen concluded that the net effect of insider trading rules is most likely the inhibition of the generation, processing and communication of inside information. And to the extent that insider information has allocative effects, the net effect of insider trading rules will be the deterrence of the production and dissemination of information that improves the allocation of resources. Foreknowledge is defined as facts that will become known, whether or not information about them is generated (see Hirschleifer, 1971).

there were no insider trading rules, the fact that the manager will not be motivated to disclosure insider information sheds little light on the *desirability* of imposing a requirement that he do so. Note in particular that the process through which insider information will be reflected even in the absence of insider trading rules, may in itself be inefficient and undesirable. As Ronen (1974) indicated, insiders may not have a comparative advantage in selling information or in offering portfolio management services; if information were to be made immediately available, there would be a greater likelihood that individuals with sufficient capital and individuals who possess comparative advantages in selling information would be included among the recipients of the information. Also, the likelihood of a single individual or a small knowledgeable group being able to interpret the inside information properly is less than the likelihood of the same information being ably interpreted if it were available to many persons in many groups, i.e. publicly available. And, finally, insider trading or selling of information would produce wealth transfers that may be undesirable from a social welfare viewpoint.

As to the claim that accounting information has no effect on prices, it simply does not seem to be borne out. Gonedes and Dopuch (1974) for example, concluded that studies that attempted to assess the information content of newly announced accounting numbers do suggest that accounting income reflect events pertinent to valuing a firm (p. 84). Indeed, it would have been surprising to observe otherwise. It is true that accounting operates in a competitive context where alternative sources of information provide signals pertinent to the valuation of the company. But this need not imply that accounting numbers do not have an incremental information content. Accounting numbers do include information that reflects economy-wide events and industry-wide events that can also be obtained from other indicators such as industrial reports, and national income reports. But the likelihood of alternative sources of information existing with respect to the firm's specific events is minimal. While it is possible that alternative sources with regard to firm's specific events do exist, since such events typically constitute transactions involving other entities which potentially could provide the information, the cost of reconstructing a firm's specific events from numerous and possibly scattered sources is probably prohibitive. As a result, the reconstruction of events may not be undertaken by investors since the cost can exceed the perceived benefits. Indeed, an equilibrium in which market agents do not seek information because of the high cost of search, even when such information exists, is consistent with whatever evidence there exists with respect to the efficient market hypothesis.[8] And when

---

[8]Grossman and Stiglitz (1975) analyze an equilibrium where only some transactors decide to become informed by seeking information and others do not when information is costly. When information is costly, arbitrage is impossible and prices never fully reflect all the information on a company's value.

accounting information is provided about firms' specific events, for which alternative sources of information are too costly to seek out, transactors are justified in relying on the accounting information. Additionally, there is one special subset of firms' specific events with respect to which there clearly do not exist alternative sources of information: this consists of inside information that management can be motivated to signal to outsiders so as to maximize its expected utility. In a signalling equilibrium context, the accounting system could be viewed as a vehicle for management to communicate expectations about the firm's cash flows, while investors view accounting information as a useful signal that they utilize wherever the perceived benefits of the signals exceed the costs.

It is true that firms' specific events could be anticipated as a result of announcements by firms' managements through releases issued by market newsletter services and reports by the companies to the SEC, and so on. But these announcements come from the company itself and could well be viewed as part of the accounting disclosure system, formal or informal. Has accounting numbers not been provided and anticipated, market reactions might have been different, since the information contained in the accounting numbers might have been too costly to obtain elsewhere. Below, the major findings regarding usage of accounting information are briefly reviewed.

3.4. Evidence on usage of accounting information

Most studies of the impact of accounting information on stock prices utilize some version or another of the two-parameter capital asset pricing model. The two parameter capital asset pricing model[9] implies that the equilibrium expected on a period rate of return on the ith asset for period t is given by[10]

$$E(\tilde{R}_{it}) = E(\tilde{R}_{zt}) + \left[E(\tilde{R}_{mt}) - E(\tilde{R}_{zt}) \right] \beta_{it}.$$

Given the above model, the effect of new information on asset i for period t is

$$\tilde{\varepsilon}_{it} = \tilde{R}_{it} - E(\tilde{R}_{it} | E(\tilde{R}_{zt}), E(\tilde{R}_{mt}), \beta_{it}).$$

[9]Based on the work of Tobin (1958), Markowitz (1959), Sharpe (1964), Lintner (1965), Mossin (1966), Fama (1968) and Black (1972), among others.

[10]A discussion of this model and its application to empirical assessments of effects of accounting numbers and changes is provided in Gonedes and Dopuch (1974). Sufficient conditions for this relationship to hold are:
(1) market agents behave as price takers in a frictionless market;
(2) market agents are risk-averse;
(3) there exists unrestricted short selling of every asset;
(4) at each time t, agents behave as if the x vector of rate of return on all assets has a multivaried normal distribution; and
(5) investors agree on the multivariate distribution of returns at each t.

If the capital market is efficient, $\tilde{\varepsilon}_{it}$ should be expected to behave as a fair game random variable; that is $E(\tilde{\varepsilon}_{it})=0$ and, for all $s>0$, $E(\tilde{\varepsilon}_{i,t+s}|\tilde{\varepsilon}_{i,t+s-1}, \tilde{\varepsilon}_{i,t+s-2,...}, \tilde{\varepsilon}_{i0})=0$ (see Gonedes and Dopuch (1974, p. 82)). And given the assumptions in the footnote, the marginal distribution function, $F(\varepsilon_{it})$ is a normal distribution.

The empirical model used to assess the effects of accounting changes is derived from the above relationship as reflected in the following:

$$E(R_{it}|R_{zt},R_{mt})=\gamma_{it}+\delta_{it}R_{zt}+\beta_{it}R_{mt},$$

where

$$\beta_{it}=\mathrm{cov}(\tilde{R}_{it},\tilde{R}_{mt})/\mathrm{var}(\tilde{R}_{mt}).$$

The two-parameter capital asset pricing model implies that $\gamma_{it}=0$ and $\delta_{it}=1-\beta_{it}$. This is a market model on the basis of which, conditional on R_{zt} and R_{mt}, the effect of new information is given by

$$\tilde{e}_{it}=\tilde{R}_{it}-E(\tilde{R}_{it}|R_{zt},R_{mt}).$$

The test for an effect of accounting changes makes use of the assumption under the null hypothesis of market efficiency that

$$E(\tilde{e}_{it}|\tilde{\theta}_{it})=E(\tilde{e}_{it})=0,$$

where θ_{it} denotes information about the firm.

Whenever any realization of θ_{it} is such that $F(\tilde{e}_{it}|\theta_{it})\neq F(\tilde{e}_{it})$ then the realization can be said to have information content in that it induces equilibrating price adjustments.

In one of the earliest tests of the information content of annual earnings numbers of companies, Ball and Brown (1968) assumed market efficiency (in the sense that security prices incorporate all publicly available information) to detect whether the earnings number are included in the set of relevant information that affects market prices. Specifically, they tested whether foreknowledge on the annual earnings numbers could allow investors to earn abnormal returns. To estimate what constituted "news" in the announced earnings numbers, i.e. the unexpected portion of the earnings number, they first estimated the expected portion of earnings numbers by using their previous finding that a substantial part of the firm's earnings variability is associated with the variability of the aggregate earnings of all firms (Ball and Brown (1967)). Ball and Brown's measure of market expectations was a conditional prediction of the firm's earnings based on aggregate earnings and the past relationship between the earnings of a specific firm and those of all other firms. Actual earnings were compared to the expectation measure. The difference was defined as "news".[11] Two portfolios were formed: first, firms with a positive prediction error, i.e. where actual earnings exceeded "expected" earnings and, secondly, firms with a negative prediction error. These portfolios were formed 12 months prior to the actual release of the income number to test whether the foreknowledge of the number would enable an investor to earn abnormal returns. Ball and Brown (1967) hypothesized that if the released income number contained new information not already reflected in prices, then good news (positive prediction error) would cause a firm's stock price to increase, whereas bad news (negative prediction error) would cause a firm's stock price to decrease. No news (no prediction error) was hypothesized to have no effect on the price, since the market's expectation was already reflected in the price and merely confirmed by the released income number.[12] The extent of the association between the income prediction errors and stock price changes was used to indicate the extent to which information contained in the income numbers was *used* by transactors in the marketplace.[13] The association was observed relative to residual price changes derived from a market model, as explained above.

Ball and Brown observed an accounting information effect on prices. Stocks with positive prediction errors tended to out-perform the market and those with negative prediction errors tended to do worse than the market. But Ball and Brown found that much of the price change occurred well in advance of the actual release of the income number: 50 percent or more of all the information about the individual firm that became available during the year had been captured in that year's income number. But most of the information was anticipated by the market before the income figure was announced; only about 10–15 percent of the price adjustment took place in the month of the announcement period. This suggested that a significant part of the released information reached the market before the release of the income number, possibly through other media such as interim reports and statements by company officials. Nonetheless, it seems that the release of the income figures provided the information that was used by investors in recomposing their security portfolios.

---

[11]The expected portion is not considered news since if exactly the expected number were released, there would be no information provided except for the confirmation of the expectation. But to a certain degree, the confirmation of expectation also constitutes "news". As long as the confirmation reduces the uncertainty surrounding the expectation, however little this uncertainty is, then it should theoretically have an effect on market prices even though the effect may be too minor to be captured through existing empirical methodologies.

[12]See, however, footnote 11. In fact, it could be argued that the "smooth" and the gradual climbing of the abnormal performance index used by Ball and Brown (1967) reflects the effect of successive confirmations of existing expectations.

[13]Some did and probably would infer from such association that the information is also relevant and useful. These inferences are incorrect, as elaborated below.

A replication of the Ball and Brown study using a variety of financial ratios as well as the earnings per share to generate measures of market expectations was reported by Gonedes (1974). He found that the earnings per share captured most of whatever information was available from the accounting numbers he tested.

The sensitivity of the effects of income on market prices to the procedure used to generate measures of market expectations was indirectly tested by Patell (1975), who replicated the Ball and Brown test by substituting management's estimate of earnings for their procedures for deriving a measure of market expectations. He did find that the management's forecast was more accurate in predicting actual earnings for the year but a trading strategy based on management's forecast assuming foreknowledge of actual earnings proved to be only slightly better than that utilizing Ball and Brown's prediction model.

Beaver (1974) used the magnitude as well as the sign of the prediction error to form portfolios. He found that portfolios that contained the largest positive and negative prediction errors out-performed portfolios consisting of firms whose prediction errors were moderate in magnitude. When portfolios were formed from stocks that were weighted in proportion to the magnitude of prediction errors, they out-performed unweighted portfolios, as reported by Patell (1975).

Additional studies reinforced the importance of both the sign and the magnitude of the earning numbers. Niederhoffer and Regan (1972) found that analysts consistently underestimated earnings of the best performing 50 firms and over-estimated the earnings for the worst performing 50 firms. Evidence of the importance of the decomposition of earnings by segments was provided by Collins (1975). He found that the trading strategy developed from segment-based earnings, not generally available prior to 1970, was profitable. Forecasts from segment-based earnings were compared to forecasts prepared from con-solidated statements to derive a measure of unexpected earnings changes. The trading strategy was profitable for firms which had not publicly reported segment numbers, whereas there was no significant profit from the trading strategy for firms which had voluntarily disclosed this information.

Beaver et al. (1970) observed a high degree of contemporaneous association between the accounting and market risk measures, specifically, a strategy of selecting and ranking portfolios according to accounting risk measures was found essentially equivalent to a strategy of ranking those same portfolios according to the market determined risk measures. The authors found this to be consistent with the joint hypothesis that accounting data do reflect the underly-ing events that determine differential riskiness among securities and that such events are also reflected in the market prices of securities.

The above evidence has no clear implication for how accounting data should be processed; how accounting numbers should be aggregated and presented; how frequently should the information be disclosed; how labels should be attached to numbers; how these labels are to be classified; precisely what information set should the auditor attest to; and what should be the scope and coverage of his attestation. Can it be inferred that presenting additional data, finer partitions of the data, and subjective forecasts of management, would be useful or desirable? It seems useful at this point briefly to summarize the main implications drawn from the "efficient market type" research in accounting for accounting disclosure and, indirectly, for the auditor's involvement with accounting reporting. Subsequent to this summary, I point out some of the pitfalls of interpreting existing findings of the "efficient market type" accounting research, and of drawing unduly strong implications based on these findings for the accountant's role.

3.5. Summary of implications drawn from accounting "efficient market" research

The main implications of accounting "efficient market" research for accounting policy and disclosure (see, for example, Beaver (1972), Ball (1972), Gonedes (1972), Gonedes and Dopuch (1974), Dyckman et al. (1975), Ronen (1974), and Lev (1974)) are the following:

(1) Capital market efficiency, taken by itself, does not provide sufficient justification for using prices of firm's ownership shares in assessing the desirability of alternative accounting techniques or regulations (Gonedes and Dopuch (1974), Ronen (1974)).

(2) Accounting reports are only one of the sources of information for capital market agents and they should only report information which is more costly (or infeasible) to obtain elsewhere and whose social benefits exceed the social costs incurred (Beaver (1973), and Gonedes and Dopuch (1974)).[14]

(3) The role of accounting information is to convey openly what otherwise constitutes inside information so as to prevent abnormal returns from accruing to individuals by trading upon or otherwise selling inside information (Beaver (1973) and Ronen (1974)).

(4) Publicly available accounting data cannot be used to detect overvalued or undervalued securities[15] (Beaver (1973)).

---

[14]Beaver mentions three types of costs: (1) the cost of abnormal returns earned by insiders who have monopolistic access to information; (2) the excessive information costs (which include the costs of failure to report an item that is more expensive to obtain elsewhere, or the cost to report an item that has less value than the cost, or that could have been reported through less expensive sources; and (3) unnecessary transaction costs incurred by investors erroneously believing that they can "beat the Market".

[15]Given existing knowledge about the equilibrium between risk and return, any information regarding the risk would also be helpful in estimating the return. And to the extent that inside information is revealed, thus improving the assessment of both the return and the risk, some individuals in the marketplace must be detecting deviations from the underlying value of the securities so that their acting upon this knowledge would bring the security price back into equilibrium. It seems that Beaver only means that "naive" or "ignorant" investors will not be able to detect such undervalued or overvalued securities.

(5) There should be no attempt to reduce a complex financial description to a low level of understanding compatible with the needs of an ignorant investor.

(6) The investor is concerned with assessing the risk as well as the expected returns. And in this context the role of financial statement data is to help assess the risk of the security (Beaver (1973)).

Gonedes and Dopuch (1974) attempted to draw the additional implication that capital market efficiency provides sufficient justification for using the prices of a firm's ownership shares in assessing the effects of alternative accounting procedures or regulations. However, there seem to exist problems with respect to assessing the "effects" of accounting information as well as the desirability of accounting alternatives by merely observing the association between accounting numbers and security price changes. This issue is addressed next.

3.6. Pitfalls in the interpretation of "efficient market" findings in accounting research with respect to both desirability (usefulness) of the accounting information and its effect

Ownership security would reflect the net benefits of accounting information if such information were sold at a competitive market price. But accounting information does not constitute a "private" good in the sense that it is exchanged in the marketplace. It cannot be sold to consumers (users of accounting information) because of the difficulty of guaranteeing exclusive access to the information if it were sold. As a result, since security prices do not reflect the net benefits of accounting information, they cannot be used to assess the net benefits of different accounting alternatives.

Even if accounting information could be sold, observation of security prices would not necessarily help assess the desirability of accounting information and of the audit function; such desirability can only be assessed in the context of explicitly stated objectives of accounting. If, for example, the objectives include the economy-wide efficiency of resource allocation as well as particular wealth distributions, then the mere observation that the information was used as manifested in security price changes would not be an indication that these objectives were achieved. Indeed, the kind of market equilibrium consistent with presently available accounting information may not be the equilibrium consistent with the prespecified objectives. Equilibrium is a descriptive phenomenon and not in itself an indication that some normative criterion has been satisfied. The present equilibrium prices cannot be used as a normative criterion for choosing accounting alternatives that best satisfy the objectives. The satisfaction of the objectives might well require and produce a different equilibrium associated with different prices.

Pitfalls exist not only in inferring desirability but also in assessing the "effects" of accounting and auditing methods. Indeed, it can be argued that the observation of an effect (i.e. the observation that the announcement of an accounting number or of an accounting change in method or regulation is associated with a corresponding movement of stock prices) cannot be necessarily attributed to the accounting manifestation. Let us consider the two cases: (1) when an effect is observed, and (2) when no effect is observed.

(1) The observation that an "effect" is observed is consistent with one or more of the following possibilities.

(a) The accounting manifestation associated with the price movement is in itself systematically associated with another nonaccounting event which would have produced the price movement at the same point in time and in the absence of the accounting manifestation.[16]

(b) The accounting manifestation was not associated with any other events that affect the firm's real cash flows, but it nonetheless had an effect because it was accepted as a genuine reflection of management's expectations about the future prospects of the firm. Such expectations could be perceived as valuable information because of the management's comparative advantage in forecasting future consequences contingent on management's own actions.[17]

(2) Market transactors use the accounting information because they perceive the cost of seeking other sources as being higher than using financial statements. In the absence of the accounting manifestation, they might have sought the next least expensive source for that information.

(3) The same as (2) above except that the next least expensive source would still be perceived as too costly to search, so that a different equilibrium of security prices would have emerged in the absence of the accounting manifestation. Under this situation transactors could react and induce stock price movements conditioned on accounting information even when the latter is devoid of implications for the firm's distribution of returns.

Thus, the observation of an "effect" does not imply that in the absence of the accounting manifestations securities' price would or would not have been different. In short, the observance of "effects" does not supply conclusive evidence with respect to the behavior of stock prices in the absence of the accounting manifestation.[18]

The observation of "no effect" is also not very useful for drawing implications for accounting disclosure and auditing. First, even if there is no observed effect on market prices, the accounting manifestation may have an effect on wealth

---

[16]This aspect is briefly discussed by Sunder (1973).

[17]Revisions and expectations regarding future flows could be conveyed by management within the prescriptions of Generally Accepted Accounting Principles through selecting the accounting alternative that best allows users to infer the revision. An example is the selection of depreciation methods (Brief and Owen (1970, 1973)).

[18]These comments are of course conditional on efficient capital markets that assume costless access to information and homogeneous expectations. But the fact that an observation of an "effect" is consistent with all of the above possibilities also holds under efficient markets with costly information and heterogeneous expectations.

transfers among individuals — clearly a relevant factor if wealth distribution is considered important. Indeed, very short-term price changes coincident with the appearance of the information are generally construed as consistent with "no effect" but can reflect transactions among individuals acting erroneously.

We should be alert to the fallacy of composition: the efficient market hypothesis only involves the market *in the aggregate* and *on the average* and does not apply to individuals; findings confirming the efficient market hypothesis are consistent with temporary adjustments that cause individual transfers.

Secondly, the effect of an accounting manifestation may become visible subsequent to the issue of the accounting report. To clarify this, consider the following scenario.

The cash flows of a firm are consequences both of events not controllable by a firm's management and of actions that management takes. Suppose that management takes action A conditional on expectations of an event X occurring. Also assume that the only two actions available to management are A and B. Of course, the alternative to nonaction is also available. Also assume that the consequences of A and B and nonaction are identical if X occurs. Should event Y rather than X occur, the outcomes, however, will differ from one another. Now, given an expectation by the market of the occurrence of event X, then the disclosure that management took action A or B has no implication for the distribution of returns on the security because the expected cash flows of the firm would be invariant under both actions and therefore we would expect no impact on market prices. But assume that at some later period it is now thought that event Y is more likely to occur than event X or that event Y has indeed occurred.

The implication for the firm's returns would *now* differ depending on whether management had taken action A, taken action B or taken no action. Only then would we expect to observe the "effect" of the previous disclosure that management had taken action A, action B, or no action.

Clearly, we cannot argue that the "effect" observed on the security prices contingent on the disclosure of the information about the event's occurrence is solely attributable to the information on the event. The effect is a joint result of the occurrence of that particular event and the action taken by management which had previously been disclosed in the accounting reports. In other words, the observance of no effect at the time of disclosure of action A or B in the annual reports implies only that, at the time of the announcement, and given the set of expectations extant at that time, that there was no effect. However, the disclosure may have an "effect" that is conditional on additional information which becomes available only later. In this circumstance it is wrong to claim that the disclosure of the action in the annual report had no effect. Empirical research regarding effects of accounting items' disclosure on security prices to date has not yet been designed to detect these types of effect. Consequently, given the state of the art, the observation of no "effect" cannot be truly interpreted as such. In other words, the observation of security market prices cannot be used definitively to assess whether the accounting information has an effect on market equilibrium.

To sum up, other than the fact that the market is efficient and adjusts in an unbiased way that makes the dissemination of relevant information worthwhile because we know that such information will be used, existing evidence and research in the efficient market area gives us little guidance as to how to structure the accounting model, how to report, and how to formulate the objectives, scope and procedures of auditing. Indeed, it is precisely because the market is efficient that a formulation of the desirable scope and content of accounting becomes a useful exercise. The efficiency of the market indicates that accounting information and information on the accuracy of such information will quickly be utilized by transactors in the marketplace. Had this not been the case, the formulation of accounting objectives and scope would have become a useless exercise. A related set of accounting studies focused on examination of the impact of accounting changes on stock market price movement. These studies and their implications are reviewed briefly below.

3.7. Evidence on the impact of accounting changes

A number of studies examined stock price reactions around the announcement of annual earnings for a year in which a company switched from one accounting policy to another. If the market were to be misled by earning increases induced by accounting changes, a maximum impact would likely occur in the first year of the change.

Kaplan and Roll (1972) observed a set of companies that changed from the deferral to the flow-through method of accounting for investment credit and that switched from accelerated depreciation to straight line. The firms that made the change in depreciation procedure for external reports continued to use accelerated depreciation for tax purposes. This led Kaplan and Roll to assume that the switches to the straight line depreciation as well as to the flow-through method accounting for the investment credit had no implications for the distribution of the stock returns since they did not affect the tax report. To assess the effect of their selected changes in accounting technique, they observed the average cumulative $\tilde{e}_{it}$. Under the null hypothesis of "no effect" this expected value is zero. By observing the average cumulative $\tilde{e}_{it}$, they inferred that the effects of the changes investigated were positive, but temporary. The effects associated with the investment credit change appeared to be statistically significant, whereas the effect associated with the depreciation method change did not. Gonedes and Dopuch (1974) point out that almost all of the investment credit switches occurred in one year: 1964. They claim that this suggests that Kaplan and Roll's analysis may be heavily influenced by cross-sectional correlation among the estimated errors. They argue that the potential cross-sectional correlation would affect the measures of dispersion that Kaplan and Roll computed, and if such estimated errors were positively cross-sectionally correlated, then they would have induced understated observed estimates of dispersion and thus overstated the significance of the results. Gonedes and Dopuch (1974) thus conclude that Kaplan and Roll's results are even more consistent with the null hypothesis, i.e. that the changes investigated did not alter the changing firm's equilibrium values.

Ball (1972) attempted to assess the effect, on the average, of a large number of accounting changes of different types. Many of these changes were from one external reporting technique to another. Ball assumed that none of their changes caused the incurrence of costs, either internally within the firm, or externally by users. Ball found that the returns of firms that tended to make such changes were generally less than normal during the period prior to the year in which the switch was made. At the same time, no unusual price behavior was manifested during the year of the change itself. His maintained hypothesis was that accounting changes had no information content, and thus tested the hypothesis of capital market efficiency. But he observed that the relative risk of the firms in the sample appeared to be nonstationary. When he applied ad hoc procedure to correct for nonstationarity, his findings were generally consistent with capital market efficiency after abstracting from changes in firms' relative risk.

Sunder (1973) observed the stock price movements of firms that switched from FIFO to LIFO and from LIFO to FIFO. Specifically, he examined four distinct cases:

(1) firms adopting or extending the use of LIFO for reporting purposes only;
(2) switching to LIFO for both tax and reporting purposes;
(3) switching from LIFO which had been used for reporting purposes only; and
(4) switching from LIFO for both tax and reporting purposes.

Sunder hypothesized that the effect of the inventory method change in case 2 would be positive; he hypothesized zero effect for cases 1 and 3 and negative effect for case 4. In general, he hypothesized that the effect would be non-negative for firms in cases 1 and 2 and nonpositive for firms in cases 3 and 4. While his results seem in general to be consistent with his hypothesis, they were heavily influenced by particular industries and years (see Gonedes and Dopuch (1974)). Furthermore, some of the changes he examined could have induced changes in relative risk. Like Ball (1972), he attempted to adjust for these impacts on the parameters in the market model that he used. But these attempts were ad hoc, and not based on prior hypothesized relationships between the parameters and the changes (see Gonedes and Dopuch (1974)). Archibald (1972), like Kaplan and Roll (1972), observed the prices of 65 firms that switched from accelerated to straight line depreciation for external reporting purposes during the period 1 January 1955 to 31 December 1966. His results were ambiguous. He detected a slight tendency for the estimated conditional mean of the return residuals to fluctuate below zero for the months prior to and above zero for the months subsequent to the changed date. Gonedes and Dopuch (1974) discuss the statistical problems that may have caused this phenomenon.

Patz and Boatsman (1972) investigated the price performance of oil exploration companies around the issuance of a draft APB opinion which would have required companies that used full-cost accounting to switch to the successful efforts method, which induces a decrease in reported earnings. The results of the study indicated no adverse effect on the stock prices of these companies, but there were statistical problems similar to those of other studies that were pointed out by Gonedes and Dopuch (1974).

All the researchers reviewed above expected not to reject the null hypothesis. That is, they believed that accounting changes would have no effect on market prices and tended to interpret their results in that light. For example, Ball (1972) found that firms that changed their accounting techniques in a way that increased income, were generally firms that experienced bad news. The cumulative average residuals continued to decrease (see his fig. 2 on p. 14) until month zero, beginning in month -14, but then the cumulative average residual leveled off around approximately -0.32. From then on the changes in the cumulative average and residual were insignificant. Is it just possible that the change in the accounting method increasing income signaled other events or management actions designed to improve the company's performance? A similar phenomenon was observed by Kaplan and Roll (1972). This tends to reinforce the above interpretation as one that is consistent with their observations.

Sunder (1973) found that the average stock price of firms that switched to LIFO, experienced a steady abnormal increase over and above the expected covariation of these stocks with a market index during the year preceding the accounting change. Moreover, the increase was unlikely to have occurred by random noise in a sample of the size that Sunder used. During the 12 months following the accounting change, there was no distinguishable abnormal price change. Sunder offered three possible explanations for his finding: (1) the switch to LIFO had no effect whatever on the market price; (2) the anticipatory price increase could be attributable to the expected switch to LIFO associated with lower expected tax; and (3) that there was a selection bias in the sample of firms that changed to LIFO and that the accounting change could indicate an attempt to smooth income, to clean house, etc. In fact, Sunder (1973, p. 27) asserts

It is possible that the increase in stock prices during the first 12 months occurred because of good business prospects for these firms and an income smoothing motive led their managements to make a change to LIFO. Thus the association of stock price increase with accounting change may be spurious. The improved earnings of the firm caused a rise in stock prices on the one hand and caused the management to make the accounting change on the other.

To the extent that this third interpretation is correct, one could at least conclude that the change to LIFO was a signal that was effective in that it halted the continuous rise in stock price experienced 12 months prior to the month of change.

3.8. The objective of accounting informativeness viewed in a signalling context

The researchers reviewed above concluded from their empirical studies that accounting changes that are not associated with real changes but merely describe differently the firm's results for operations and/or its financial position, have no effect on stock prices. In particular, they concluded that management cannot, by increasing its income through a mere accounting change, cause its stock price to increase. In fact, some, e.g. Benston (1969), go as far as to contend that financial statements in general have no information content. This view ignores the incentives that might exist for management to convey its expectations of future cash flows via accounting numbers within the constraints of generally accepted accounting principles by changing its accounting treatments so as to convey a number that better reflects management's expectations. Similarly, management might engage in voluntary disclosure of various items such as segment information (Ronen and Livnat (1977)) or forecasts when it is in its benefit to do so. As in the case of disclosing voluntary forecasts or segment information and as in the case when management takes actual action to signal its inside information to outside investors (Ross (1977)), management may resort to making accounting changes to signal.

Accounting changes, as a means of signalling, may have an additional advantage over other voluntary disclosures (such as forecasts) in that the information is conveyed within the framework attested to by auditors, whereas voluntary forecasts are not. The attestation may add credibility and therefore enhanced reliance on the produced numbers in making investment consumption decisions by market agents. But for management to wish to signal, it must expect the signals to be *received* and *used* in making decisions whose consequences benefit the management. For this, two conditions are required: (1) market semistrong efficiency,[19] and (2) credibility of the signal. If the market is not semistrong efficient, the process of utilizing information contained in the signal

[19]For a review see Fama (1970).

will lag; and if the signal is not credible, the extent of the usage of and reliance on the information will decline. The condition of credibility highlights the importance of audit attestation which adds validity to the disseminated numbers. In the absence of attestation, information asymmetry, i.e. the assumption that management has superior information production opportunities, creates the same kind of adverse selection and moral hazard problems discussed by Akerlof (1970) and mentioned in reference to the agency costs above. These ideas are elaborated upon below.

The informativeness role of financial reports is to convey information to market transactors about events relevant for assessment of the distributions of returns on the company's securities. In the context of a semistrong efficient market, the role of the firm's accounting system – as that of any production system – is to generate and disseminate that information which other producers can only generate and disseminate at higher costs. An examination of the extent to which market transactors utilize accounting information as manifested in movements of stock prices, is important for understanding the possible motivations of managers to signal. Particularly, the benefit to management from signalling can only exist *if* market transactors *use* the information.

Unless management expects gain as a result of the information disseminated and being used by market investors, it is not likely to engage in the information dissemination activity. It seems safe to assume that the probability of assessment by management that information will be used is a monotonic nondecreasing function of the degree to which information is actually used. In other words, managers are assumed to be sensible in that they do not consistently assess a high probability of a particular signal being used by the market, when in fact that signal is not consistently used and, conversely, management will not assess a very low probability of a signal not being used by the market, when in fact it is consistently used. Once we accept management's sensibility in the above precise sense, we would have to explain why managers continue to implement accounting changes when empirical evidence shows that the market, on the average and in the aggregate, cannot be fooled by mere accounting changes not associated with actual economic events that induce revisions and assessments of return distributions.

So far, the implications drawn from these studies (see above) are that managers are acting foolishly in that they incur costs to implement accounting changes that have no impact on stock prices. This latter viewpoint assumes that the assessed probability of an information's impact by management is independent of the actual average impact in the marketplace. Fig. 20.2 illustrates the different viewpoints.

The implication of studies regarding the effect of accounting changes on market prices are that managers' behavior is of the type characterized by the southwest square, wherein investors are nonfools but managers are fools. It

	MANAGERS 'Fools'	MANAGERS 'Non fools'
INVESTORS 'Fools'	Inconsistent with the efficient market hypothesis An equilibrium situation if investors and managers are fools and do not learn	Wise managers attempt to fool the fools Assumes the market does not learn Inconsistent with the efficient market hypothesis
INVESTORS 'Non fools'	MANAGERS DO NOT LEARN	Accounting treatment conveys expectations — signalling Purpose of change is not to manipulate STABLE POSITION

Figure 20.2. Foolishness–wisdom matrix.

seems quite obvious that such an equilibrium is neither tenable nor consistent with individual rationality. It is, rather, far more appealing to resort to the southeast square to explain empirical observations. In this case both managers and investors are sensible. I would argue that the choice among accounting treatments within generally accepted accounting principles when devoid of implications for return distributions is a means of signalling to market transactors. Managers will signal whenever the anticipated effects of the signals are favorable to management. And since the more credible the signals, the greater the likelihood that they would be used (because of the adverse selection problem), management may prefer to convey signals that are attested to by auditors. This may mean that the choice of accounting treatments as a means of signalling would be preferred to unattested methods such as forecasts. Thus, accounting changes like forecasts, segment reports and others, could be explained as signalling phenomena. Assume that (1) managers follow the market value rule, and (2) signalling is costly, (3) the signalling costs differ among firms, (4) market agents hold homogeneous beliefs, and (5) in the absence of signals the market assesses for any given company the level of attribute α as equal to the assessed average of the attribute over all companies. We can then expect a signalling equilibrium whereby some companies signal and some do not. Let α_i be company i's management's assessment of attribute α. Furthermore, assume that the signal provided with respect to the attribute α can be mapped one to one with the attribute level α_i. For a particular company i,

$$\alpha_i - \bar{\alpha} > C_i(S_i),$$

where $\bar{\alpha}$ is the company's assessment of the mean of attribute α over all companies and C_i is the cost of signalling for company i, and where S_i denotes the amount of signalling. The company will not signal if

$$\alpha_i - \bar{\alpha} < C_i.$$

For the market as a whole, equilibrium is achieved when

$$\alpha_i' - \bar{\alpha} = C_i'.$$

That is to say, signalling will cease when for the marginal firm i' the benefit from signalling equals the cost. Thus, in equilibrium we can obtain companies that signal and companies that do not. Companies with high (desirable) levels of α will successfully signal until, for the marginal company i', the equality between the benefits and the costs of signalling holds.

Notice that whatever signalling equilibrium holds, it need not be socially optimal. In fact, in a world of pure exchange, wherein the information produced does not affect resource allocations, but only leads to wealth transfers (such as analyzed by Fama and Laffer (1971) and Hirschleifer (1971)), an equilibrium in which no company signals is preferred to any other equilibrium. Society would be worse off by the total cost of signalling under the pure exchange environment. However, when information production affects resource allocation, which is the case that probably better describes real life situations, the social optimality of the signalling equilibrium would depend on whether private benefits of the signalling companies equal social benefits. If private benefits are in excess of social benefits, too many resources would be allocated to signalling; more likely, however, the social benefits of signalling would exceed the private benefits so that too few resources would then be allocated to signalling. In that case regulations that produce an optimal amount of signalling (or informativeness) may be necessary.

One special case of signalling as an explanation for the observation that company managements engage in making changes in accounting techniques deserves special mention. That is when the signal (such as the income number) directly affects management's utility because of the prevailing compensation schemes on the basis of which management is rewarded. It can be shown that in the simple case where management bonuses are tied directly to the reported income number of the period, management would have an incentive (depending on the cost of switching from one accounting technique to another) to make switches so as to maximize its bonuses.

4. Concluding remarks

Accounting has a dual role: (1) *accountability*; i.e. the monitoring and bonding activities undertaken by management to reduce agency costs; and (2) *informativeness*: the supplying of information to market agents so as to promote the efficiency of resource allocation in the economy as a whole.

The first role, accountability, could be also construed to be designed to promote the efficiency of resource allocation – but within the firm itself. While in recent discussions in the accounting literature reviewed in this paper several claimed that the first objective, accountability, would be accomplished optimally within the free market mechanism without interference, I have argued that regulation might, and probably is, necessary as an efficient way of dealing with the problems of agency costs under conditions of information asymmetry.

It has also been claimed that the informativeness of financial statements, as an objective, is only a recent and unnecessary concept created only as an excuse to justify government regulation. Moreover, it has been alleged that financial statements have no information content and, furthermore, that corporation managers have no incentives to provide inside information, whether formally within the financial statements, or informally in news announcements or otherwise. These arguments ignore the incentives of management to signal both within and without the financial statements. The signalling concept was discussed in the context of accounting changes, income smoothing and other means such as forecasting. However, again because of the information asymmetry, management would have no incentive to provide information that has negative implications for the distribution of stock returns. This again could imply the necessity for regulation – the specification of accounting guidelines to attain the goal of efficient resource allocation.

References

Akerlof, George A. (1970) "The Market for 'Lemons': Qualitative Uncertainty in the Market Mechanism", *Quarterly Journal of Economics*, August.

American Accounting Association, Committee on Basic Accounting Theory (1966) *A Statement of Basic Accounting Theory* (American Accounting Association, Chicago).

American Institute of Certified Public Accountants (1973) *Objectives of Financial Statements*, Report to the Study Group on the Objectives of Financial Statements (AICPA, New York).

Archibald, R. T. (1972) "Stock Market Reaction to the Depreciation Switchback", *Accounting Review*; January, 22–30.

Ball, R. (1972) "Changes in Accounting Techniques and Stock Prices", *Empirical Research in Accounting: 1972, Supplement to Journal of Accounting Research* X, 1–38.

Ball, R. and P. Brown, (1967) "Some Preliminary Evidence on the Association Between the Earnings of a Firm, It's Industry, and the Economy", *Empirical Research in Accounting: Selected Studies, 1967, Supplement to Vol. 5, Journal of Accounting Research*, 55–77.

Ball, R. and P. Brown (1968) "The Empirical Evaluation of Accounting Income Numbers", *Journal of Accounting Research*, Autumn, 159–177.

Beaver, W. (1972) "The Behavior of Security Prices and Its Implications for Accounting Research (Methods)", Committee Reports, *Supplement to Accounting Review*, 407–437.

Beaver, W. (1973) "What Should Be the FASB's Objectives?" *Journal of Accountancy*, August, 49–56.

Beaver, W. (1974) "The Information Content of the Magnitude of Unexpected Earnings", Stanford University Working Paper, presented to 1974 Stanford Research Seminar. (1974).

Beaver, W. H., and J. S. Demski (1974) "Summary and Synthesis: The Nature of Financial Accounting Objectives", *Journal of Accounting Research*, An Empirical Conference, Winter. 1974.

Beaver, W., S. Kettler and M. Scholes (1970) "The Association Between Market Determination and Accounting Determined Risk Measures", *Accounting Review*, October.

Benston, G. A., (1969) "The Value of The SEC's Accounting Disclosure Requirements", *Accounting Review*, July, 515–532.

Benston, G. A. (1976) *Corporate Financial Disclosure in the U.K. and the U.S.A.* (Saxon House, West Mead, U.K.).

Black, F. M. (1972) "Capital Market Equilibrium With Restricted Borrowing", *Journal of Business*, July 444–454.

Black, F. M. and M. Scholes (1973) "The Pricing of Options and Corporate Liabilities", *Journal of Political Economy*, May–June, 637–654.

Black, F.M., H. Miller and R. Posner (1974) "An Approach to the Regulation of Bankholding Companies", unpublished paper, University of Chicago.

Brief, R. and J. Owen, (1970) "The Estimation Problem in Financial Accounting", *Journal of Accounting Research*, Autumn.

Brief, R. and J. Owen, (1973) "A Reformulation of the Estimation Problem", *Journal of Accounting Research*, Spring.

Bull, R.J. (1972) "Changes in Accounting Techniques in Stock Prices", *Empirical Research in Accounting: Selected Studies, 1972, Statements of Journal of Accounting Research* 10.

Collins, D.W. (1975) "SEC Product-Line Reporting and Market Efficiency", *Journal of Financial Economics* II, June, 125–164.

Cyert, R. M. and Y. Ijiri (1974) "A Framework for Developing Objectives of Financial Statements", in: *Objectives of Financial Statements*, Vol. 2 (AICPA, New York).

Demsetz, H. (1969) "Information and Deficiency: Another Viewpoint", *Journal of Law and Economics*, April, 1–22.

De Ste Croix (1956) "Greek and Roman Accounting", in: A.C. Littleton and V. K. Zimmerman, eds., *Studies in the History of Accounting* (Richard D. Irwin, Inc., Homewood, Illinois), pp. 14–74.

Dyckman, T., D. Downs and R. Magee (1975) *Efficient Capital Markets and Accounting: A Cultural Analysis* (Prentice-Hall, Englewood Cliffs).

Fama, E.F. (1968) "Risk Return on Equilibrium: Some Clarifying Comment", *Journal of Finance*, March, 29–40.

Fama, E.F. (1970) "Efficient Capital Markets: A Review of Theory and Empirical Work", *Journal of Finance*, May.

Fama, E.F. and A.B. Laffer (1971) "Information and Control Markets", *Journal of Business*, July, 28–98.

Financial Accounting Standards Board (1976) *An Analysis of Issues Related to Conceptual Framework for Financial Accounting and Reporting: Elements of Financial Statements and Their Measurement* (FASB, Stamford).

Gonedes, N. (1972) "Efficient Capital Markets and External Accounting", *The Accounting Review*, January, 11–21.

Gonedes, N. (1974) "Capital Market Equilibrium and Annual Accounting Numbers: Empirical Evidence", *Journal of Accounting Research*, XII, Spring, 26–62.

Gonedes, N. J. and N. Dopuch (1974) "Capital Market Equilibrium, Information Production and Selectivity Accounting Techniques: Framework and Review of Empirical Work", *Studies on Financial Accounting Objectives, Supplement to the Journal of Accounting Research*, 48–161.

Grady, P. (1965) "Accounting Research Study Number 7", in: *Inventory of Generally Accepted Accounting Principles for Business Enterprises*.

Grossman, S. and J. Stiglitz (1975) "On the Impossibility of Informationally Efficient Markets", Presented at the Econometric Society Meetings.

Hirschleifer, J. (1971) "The Private and Social Value of Information and the Reward to Inventive Activity", *American Economic Review*, September, 561–574.

Horngren, C. (1973) "Marketing of Accounting Standards", *Journal of Accounting*, October.

Jensen, M. C. and W. H. Meckling (1976) "Theory of the Firm: Managerial Behavior, Agency Costs and Ownership Structure", *Journal of Financial Economics*, October, 305–360.

Kaplan, R. S. and R. Roll (1972) "Investor Evaluation of Accounting Information: Some Empirical Evidence", *Journal of Business*, April, 225–257.

Larsen, M.T. (1976) *Old Assyrian Caravan Procedures* (Netherlands Historik-Archeological Institut in Het Nabije Oosten, Istanbul).

Leake, P.D., (1976) *Depreciation and Wasting Assets and Their Treatment in Assessing Annual Profit and Loss* (1912); reprinted by (Arno, New York).

Lev, B. (1974) *Financial Statements Analysis: A New Approach* (Prentice-Hall, Englewood Cliffs).

Lintner, J. (1965) "Security Prices and Maximal Gains from Diversification", *Journal of Finance*, December, 587–615.

Littleton, A.C. and V. K. Zimmerman (1963) *Accounting Theory: Continuity and Change* (Prentice-Hall, Englewood Cliffs).

Markowitz, H. (1959) *Portfolio Selection: Efficient Diversification of Investments* (John Wiley, New York).

Mossin, J. (1966) "Equilibrium in a Capital Asset Market", *Econometrica*, October, 768–783.

Myers, S. C. (1976) "Determinants of Corporate Borrowing", unpublished paper, Massachusetts Institute of Technology.

Niederhoffer, V. and P. Regan (1972) "Earnings Changes, Analysts' Forecasts, and Stock Prices", *Financial Analysts' Journal* XXVIII, May–June, 65–71.

Patell, J. (1975) "Corporate Earnings Forecasts: Empirical Tests and A Consumption-Investment Model", Ph. D. Dissertation, Carnegie-Mellon University.

Paton, W.A. (1924) *Accounting* (Macmillan, New York).

Patz, D.H. and J.R. Boatsman (1972) "Accounting Principle Formulation in an Efficient Markets Environment", *Journal of Accounting Research* 10, Autumn, 392–403.

Ronen, J. (1974a) "A User-Oriented Development of Accounting Requirements", in: J.J. Kramer and G. H. Sorter, eds., *Objectives of Financial Statements*, vol. 2, Selected Papers, (AICPA, New York), pp. 80–103.

Ronen, J. (1974b) "The Need for Accounting Objectives in an Efficient Market", in: J.J. Kramer and G.H. Sorter, eds., *Objectives of Financial Statements*, vol 2, Selected Papers, (AICPA, New York), pp. 36–52.

Ronen, J. (1977) "The Effect of Insider Trading Rules on Information, Generation and Disclosure by Corporations", *Accounting Review*, April, 438–449.

Ronen, J. and J. Livnat (1977) "Incentives for Segment Reporting", unpublished manuscript, The Vincent C. Ross Institute of Accounting Research, New York University.

Ross, S. (1977) "The Determination of Financial Structure: The Incentive Signalling Approach", *Bell Journal of Economics*, Spring, 23–40.

Sanders, T.H., H.H. Hatfield, U. Moore (1938) *Statement of Accounting Principles* (AICPA, New York).

Sharpe, W.F. (1964) "Capital Asset prices: The Theory of Market Equilibrium Under Conditions of Risk", *Journal of Finance*, September, 425–442.

Stigler, G.J. (1976) "Do Economists Matter?", *Southern Economic Journal*, January, 347–363.

Sunder, S. (1973) "Relationships Between Accounting Changes and Stock Prices: Problems of Measurements and Some Empirical Evidence", *Empirical Research in Accounting: Selected Studies, 1973, Supplement to the Journal of Accounting Research* 11.

Tobin, J. (1958) "Liquidity Preference as Behavior Towards Risk", *Review of Economic Studies*, February, 65–86.

Watts, R. (1977) "Corporate Financial Statements, A Product of the Market and Political Processes", *Australian Journal of Management*, April.

Watts, R.L. and J.L. Zimmerman (1977) "The Demand for and Supply of Accounting Theories, the Market for Excuses", unpublished working paper GPB 77-7, Graduate School of Management, The University of Rochester.

Yamey, B. S. (1962) "Some Topics in the History of Financial Accounting in England, 1500-1900", in: W.T. Baxter and S. Davidson, eds., *Studies in Accounting Theory* (Sweet and Maxwell, Ltd., London), pp. 14–43.